Television
Production
Handbook

WADSWORTH SERIES IN MASS COMMUNICATION

Rebecca Hayden/Senior Editor

General

The New Communications by Frederick Williams

Mediamerica: Form, Content, and Consequence of Mass Communication, 2nd, by Edward Jay Whetmore

The Interplay of Influence: Mass Media & Their Publics in News, Advertising, Politics by Kathleen Hall Jamieson and Karlyn Kohrs Campbell

Mass Communication and Everyday Life: A Perspective on Theory and Effects by Dennis K. Davis and Stanley J. Baran

Mass Media Research: An Introduction by Roger D. Wimmer and Joseph R. Dominick

The Internship Experience by Lynne Schafer Gross

Telecommunications

Stay Tuned: A Concise History of American Broadcasting by Christopher H. Sterling and John M. Kittross

Writing for Television and Radio, 4th, by Robert L. Hilliard

Broadcast Programming: Strategies for Winning Television and Radio Audiences by Susan Tyler Eastman, Sydney W. Head, and Lewis Klein

Advertising in the Broadcast and Cable Media, 2nd, by Elizabeth J. Heighton and Don R. Cunningham

Strategies in Broadcast and Cable Promotion by Susan Tyler Eastman and Robert A. Klein

Modern Radio Station Practices, 2nd, by Joseph S. Johnson and Kenneth K. Jones

The Magic Medium: An Introduction to Radio in America by Edward Jay Whetmore

Audio in Media by Stanley R. Alten

Television Production Handbook, 4th, by Herbert Zettl

Sight-Sound-Motion: Applied Media Aesthetics by Herbert Zettl

Journalism

Reporting Processes and Practices: Newswriting for Today's Readers by Everette E. Dennis and Arnold H. Ismach

Excellence in College Journalism by Wayne Overbeck and Thomas M. Pasqua

When Words Collide: A Journalist's Guide to Grammar and Style by Lauren Kessler and Duncan McDonald

News Editing in the '80s: Text and Exercises by William L. Rivers

Reporting Public Affairs: Problems and Solutions by Ronald P. Lovell

Free-Lancer and Staff Writer: Newspaper Features and Magazine Articles, 3rd, by William L. Rivers and Shelley Smolkin

Magazine Editing in the '80s: Text and Exercises by William L. Rivers

Newswriting for the Electronic Media: Principles, Examples, Applications by Daniel E. Garvey and William L. Rivers

This Is PR: The Realities of Public Relations, 2nd, by Doug Newsom and Alan Scott

Writing in Public Relations Practice: Form and Style by Doug Newsom and Tom Siegfried

Creative Strategy in Advertising by A. Jerome Jewler

FOURTH EDITION

Television Production Handbook

HERBERT ZETTL
San Francisco State University

Wadsworth Publishing Company
Belmont, California
A Division of Wadsworth, Inc.

The cover features an ENG/EFP camera photographed courtesy of Ampex. The inset shows KPIX news anchors Dave McElhatton and Wendy Tokuda momentarily off-camera during a videotape insert; photographed courtesy of KPIX, Channel 5, San Francisco. Cover photo: Dow, Clement and Simison

Senior Editor: Rebecca Hayden
Production Editor: Gary Mcdonald
Cover and interior design: Cynthia Bassett
Copy Editor: Jonas Weisel
Art Editor: Catherine Aydelott
Technical Illustrator: J & R Services
Composition: Graphic Typesetting Service

ISBN 0-534-01464-X

Printed in the United States of America

1 2 3 4 5 6 7 8 9 10--88 87 86 85 84

Library of Congress Cataloging in Publication Data
Zettl, Herbert.
   Television production handbook.

   Bibliography: p.
   Includes index.
   1. Television—Production and direction—Handbooks, manuals, etc.   I. Title
PN1992.75.Z4   791.45'0232   83-6850
ISBN 0-534-01464-X

Photo Credits

AKG Acoustics, Inc.: 8.6b, 8.38
American Optical Corporation: Color Plate II
Ampex Corporation: 1.15, 2.14a, 2.27, 9.13, 9.14, 9.20, 10.9, 10.10, 10.11, 10.12, 10.15, 10.16, 10.30, 11.10b, 12.13, 12.15, 13.22b, 13.24b,c, pp. 62, 63, 77, 237, 266, 268, 298, 306, 308, 330, 364, 365, 394
Angenieux, Inc.: 3.4, 3.15b
Beyer Dynamic, Inc.: 8.38
Bosch (Fernseh, Inc.): 10.14, p. 268
Broadcast Electronics, Inc.: 9.22
Commercial Electric, Inc.: 2.14c
CBS: 14.1
CEI/Panavision Electronics: 2.14c
Central Dynamics Corporation: 1.24, 11.8, 12.8
CMX Orrox: 11.10c,d
Comprehensive Video Supply Corporation: 4.9
Crown International, Inc.: 8.38
EECO: 9.25, 11.5
Electro-Voice, Inc.: 8.10, 8.38
Fujinon, Inc.: 3.2, 3.12
General Electric: 6.47
Gotham Audio Corporation, NYC: 8.38
The Grass Valley Group: 12.11, 12.14, 13.17, 13.25, pp. 344, 345, 358, 366
Hitachi Denshi America, Ltd.: 2.10, 2.19
HM Electronics, Inc.: 8.21
Ikegami Electronics (USA), Inc.: 18.2, pp. 30, 32, 55, 63

Innovative Television Equipment: 4.4b, 4.6b, 4.7, 4.12, 4.13

Interand Corporation, Chicago, IL.: 14.31b,c

JVC Company of America: 1.12, 10.20, 10.24, 10.32

Stuart Lefkowitz: 5.1, 5.2a-d, 5.3c, 5.4b, 5.5a, 5.11, 9.26, 11.17, 11.18, 11.26, 13.41, 14.18, 14.41, 14.42, 14.43, 14.59b

Listec Television Equipment Corporation: 4.3, 4.17, 4.18, 4.19, pp. 86, 88, 99

Lowel-Light Manufacturing, Inc.: 6.23, 6.24b, 6.25, 6.26, 6.34, 6.35

Mathews Studio Equipment: 6.38

Mole-Richardson Co., Hollywood, CA., USA: 6.8, 6.12, 6.13, 6.14, 6.16, 6.17, 6.21, 6.22, 6.29, 8.19

Nagra/Kudelski: 9.21

Philips Audio Video Systems Corp.: 2.21b, 6.1

Q-TV: 15.4, 15.7

RCA Corp.: 1.11, 2.4, 2.13, 2.14b, 2.17b, 2.20b, 2.20c, 2.26, 4.6a, 4.11, 4.14, 8.38, 10.13, 10.34, 10.43, 10.44, 10.46b, pp. 32, 55

R.D. Systems of Canada, Limited, Toronto, Ontario: 8.37

Steve Renick: 1.7, 1.8, 3.5a, 3.6a, 3.11, 3.13, 3.14, 3.16, 3.19, 3.20, 3.22, 4.1, 4.2, 4.4a, 4.15, 5.7, 5.12a, 5.13a, 5.16, 5.20, 5.25, 6.5, 6.7, 6.15, 6.18, 6.19, 6.24a, 6.27, 6.28, 6.30, 6.31, 6.32, 6.33, 6.36, 6.37, 6.41a, 6.42, 6.43, 7.9, 7.19a, 9.4, 9.7, 9.8, 13.12, 13.13, 13.14, 13.16, 13.18, 13.25, 14.3, 14.4, 14.5, 14.13, 14.16, 14.25, 14.30, 15.2, 15.3, 15.5, 17.1

Selco Products Company: 9.10

Sennheiser Electronic Corp.: 8.15, 8.38

Shure Brothers, Inc.: 8.7, 8.38

Sony Corporation of America: 2.17a, 2.18, 2.20a, 2.21a, 2.31, 2.32, 8.38, 10.21, 10.22, 10.23, 10.31, 10.33, 10.38

William Storm: 8.1, 8.5, 9.12, 9.23

Studio Five: 4.19

Swintek Enterprises, Inc.: 8.22

Telex Communications, Inc.: 8.11, 8.13, 8.23

Walter Trepashko: 1.6, 1.18, 2.7a, 2.34, 2.35, 3.5a, 3.15, 8.35, 11.19a,b, 11.22, 11.23, 11.24, 11.25, 17.10, 17.12, 17.13, 17.14, 14.33, 14.40, 2, 102, 104, 123, 168, 345, 444, 446, 461, 466, 467, 492, 500, 501, 530

Uni-Set Corp.®: 14.34

Videotex America: 14.31a

Vital Industries: 1.14, 13.20, 13.45, p. 358

Herbert Zettl: 1.3, 1.4, 1.5, 1.13, 1.16, 1.19, 1.20, 1.21, 1.22, 1.25, 2.7b, 2.11, 2.12, 2.15, 2.16, 3.9, 3.10, 3.17, 3.18, 3.19, 3.20, 3.21, 3.22, 3.23, 3.24, 3.25, 3.26, 3.27, 3.28, 3.29, 3.30, 3.31, 4.8, 5.2, 5.3b, 5.4, 5.5b, 5.6, 5.8, 5.9, 5.10, 5.14a, 5.15, 5.16, 5.17, 5.18, 5.19, 5.20, 5.21, 5.22, 5.23, 5.26, 6.3, 6.4, 6.9, 6.10, 6.11, 6.20, 6.34b, 6.39, 6.40, 6.41a, 6.44, 6.48, 6.49, 6.50a,b, 7.2, 7.3a, 7.4a, 7.5a, 7.6a, 7.7a, 7.8, 7.11b, 7.15a, 7.16a, 7.21b, 7.30, 7.31, 8.6a, 8.8, 8.9, 8.12, 8.14, 8.16, 8.17, 8.18, 8.20, 8.24, 8.25, 8.26, 8.36, 8.39, 9.1, 9.2, 9.5, 9.6, 9.9, 9.24, 9.27, 10.17, 10.18, 10.25, 10.26, 10.27, 10.28, 10.29, 10.35, 10.42, 10.45, 11.6, 11.7b, 11.9, 11.14b, 11.16, 11.19b 11.20, 11.21, 12.12, 12.16, 13.7, 13.8, 13.9, 13.10, 13.15, 13.37, 13.46, 13.48, 14.6, 14.7, 14.12, 14.26, 14.38, 14.39, 14.46, 14.47, 14.48, 14.52, 14.54, 14.55a, 14.56, 14.57, 14.61, 17.1, 17.6, 17.16, 18.1, 18.3, 18.9, pp. 1, 2, 20, 77, 104, 123, 126, 128, 159, 166, 168, 186, 200, 202, 232, 236, 237, 258, 298, 308, 330, 400, 401, 429, 446, 461, 492, 501, 530, 556, 557, 581

To Erika

C O N T E N T S

The fourth edition of the *Television Production Handbook* is, once again, a new book. The constant and rapid development of television equipment and subsequent production techniques does not allow simple revisions. While the basic objective of the *Handbook*—to help readers understand the tools and processes of television production—remains unchanged, the fourth edition differs considerably in approach and organization from the previous editions. Here are some of the main features:

SYSTEMS APPROACH

The entire production process is considered a system, in which many elements interact in an essential way. When seen as a system, the many individual pieces of equipment and operational procedures become less arbitrary and their functions and interconnections more readily visible to the learner.

THE BASIC TELEVISION SYSTEM

As in any other system, every single piece of equipment in the television system depends on the proper functioning and interaction of all the others. This complexity makes learning and teaching television production so difficult. For example, to explain properly the potentials and limitations of an ENG camera, we must go into the workings of lenses, the electronic characteristics of the camera pickup tube, lighting requirements, power supplies, and VTR connections. To provide such an overview, the first chapter of this book presents a basic television system that shows the interrelatedness of the principal television production equipment.

BASIC PRINCIPLES

Major emphasis is put on equipment *categories* and production *principles* rather than on specific brand names or equipment codes used by manufacturers. Nevertheless, because much production terminology derives from specific equipment names, certain items have been identified by manufacturer and equipment number.

INCLUSION OF ENG/EFP

Whenever appropriate, ENG and EFP equipment and techniques are *integrated* into the chapters with the discussion of studio techniques. Modern television requires us to move freely and easily among all three production modes. A single chapter dealing with ENG/EFP no longer suffices.

AESTHETICS

Although microcomputers render the electronics of television equipment more and more complex, the operation of the equipment requires less and less engineering knowledge. The aesthetic elements of television production are, therefore, stressed throughout the book.

BASIC AND ADVANCED SECTIONS

To keep the information manageable for the reader without sacrificing important aspects of television production, each chapter is divided into two sections. Section One of each chapter contains the basic information about a specific topic. Section Two presents more advanced or more detailed aspects about certain pieces of equipment and production procedures. Because Sections One and Two have no essential connections, they can be read together or separately.

ILLUSTRATIONS

Almost all of the 900 or so illustrations are new. Photos are used to illustrate television facilities and aesthetic principles. Diagrams are designed to illustrate systems and production processes. The script samples reflect new production approaches.

KEY TERMS

As in the previous edition, the key terms used in a given chapter appear at the beginning of each chapter. These terms are then repeated as part of the glossary at the end of the book. Also, all terms in boldface within the text appear again in the glossary.

These devices are intended to help the reader learn the new terminology as quickly and painlessly as possible.

SUMMARIES

To give the reader an idea of what to expect in a given chapter, each chapter begins with a brief pre-summary of the major topics. A more extensive main points summary appears after each chapter section.

INDEX

The many page references to a single item, such as the television camera or director, can prove quite frustrating when looking for the major discussion of the topic. To facilitate such a search, the page (or pages) with the major discussion of a listed item is printed in boldface in the index.

As in the previous edition, I enjoin the reader once again to realize that the dos and don'ts of television production techniques as expressed in this book are intended as a guide, not as a credo. But we need to know the conventional approach before we can go beyond it, or abandon it judiciously at the appropriate moment.

ACKNOWLEDGMENTS

I am greatly indebted to a number of people from whom I learned a great deal about television production and who willingly and repeatedly extended their expert help in the preparation of this book. Peter Dart, University of Kansas; Frank Messere, SUNY at Oswego; Glenn Nosse, KPIX; and Donald Wiley, San Diego State University, painstakingly reviewed the whole manuscript and, in the process, made many helpful suggestions for improvement; and Nikos Metallinos, Concordia University in Montreal, and H. Wayne Schuth, University of New Orleans, were among those who offered early suggestions that challenged me to think long and hard about the scope and organization of this edition. Ed Cosci,

KTVU; Jerry Higgins, Jim LeFever, and David Wiseman, all from the Broadcast Communication Arts (BCA) Department, San Francisco State University, contributed their vast technical knowledge on many occasions. Hamid Abdullakhani and Walter Trepashko coordinated the photo-taking sessions. As usual, Wadsworth Publishing Company proved to be an understanding, cooperative, and demanding partner in the making of this book. Rebecca Hayden, Mary Arbogast, Catherine Aydelott, Cynthia Bassett, Sharon Dew, Gary Mcdonald, Tracy Sims, and Jonas Weisel deserve special credit.

These people and organizations assisted me kindly with specific information and materials: ABC Television Network; AKG Acoustics; Ampex Corporation; Paul Berliner and Robert Brilliant, Ampex Corporation; Angenieux, Inc., Arbitron Television; John Barsotti, Stuart Hyde, Paul Courtland Smith, and Vince Waskell, BCA Department, San Francisco State University; the students of the BCA Department, San Francisco State University, who appear in many of the photographs; Beyer Dynamic, Inc.; Bogen Photo Corporation; Bosch-Fernseh, Inc.; Canon U.S.A., Inc.; CBS Television Network; Central Dynamic Corporation; CETEC Vega; Chyron Corporation; Cinema Products Corporation; Clear-Com Intercom Equipment; CMX/Orrox; Colortran, Inc.; Comprehensive Video Supply Corporation; Convergence Corporation; Digital Video Systems Corporation; EECO, Inc.; Electro-Voice, Inc.; Fujion, Inc.; Grass Valley Group; Gotham Audio Corporation; Hitachi Denshi America, Ltd.; Ikegami Electronics (U.S.A.), Inc.; Innovative Television Equipment; Interand Corporation; Telestrator Division, Interand Corporation; L. Jenner, Travel Channel; JVC Company of America; Houshang Moaddeli, KDOC: Kliegl Brothers; KPIX; Bruno Cohen, Dave McElhatton, Doug Murphy, Bob Rice, Wendy Tokuda, and Ruth Whitmore, KPIX; KRON; Darryl Compton, KRON; Charlie Rose (formerly KPIX), KRON; KTVU Cox Communications; Ray Swenson and Ian Zellick, KTVU; Listec Television Equipment Corporation; Lowell-Light Mfg., Inc.; L.T.M. Corporation of America; McCann-Erickson, Inc.; MCI/Quantel; Skip Long, Mobiltape, Inc.; Mole-Richardson Company; Nagra Magnetic Recorders, Inc.; NBC Television Network; Panasonic Industrial Company; Philips Television Systems, Inc.; Q-TV/Telesync; Quick-Set, Inc.; RCA Commercial Communication Systems Division; Rosco Labs; Frank Moakley, San Francisco State University; Sennheiser Electronic Corporation; Shure Brothers, Inc.; SONY Corporation of America; Studer Revox America, Inc.; Swintek Enterprises, Inc.; Tele-Cine Corporation; Telescript, Inc.; Telidon Infomart; Uni-Set Corporation; Vital Industries, Inc.; Ward-Beck Systems, Ltd. Victor Webb (formerly with KNXT); and Alex Zettl, University of California at Berkeley.

Many special thanks to my wife, Erika, who provided much needed support throughout this vast project, and to Renee and Alex who, by simply inquiring how the book was coming, gave me the energy to go on.

Television
Production
Handbook

The Television Production Process

This chapter presents an overview of the television production system and the key production personnel. You will find that it is easier to learn the individual elements of production when they are seen as part of the total production system and its interactions.

In Section One, we will discuss these major points:

1. The basic television system.

2. The expanded television system.

3. The major production elements: the camera, lighting, audio, videotape recording and film, switching, postproduction editing, special effects, and design.

4. The key production personnel.

The presentation of these major points generally follows the order of subsequent chapters.

Section Two focuses on the three major production centers of the television studio:

1. The studio itself—its physical layout and major installations.

2. The control center, which includes the studio control room and master control.

3. The studio support areas.

To learn television production is not an easy task. The major problem is that you should know everything at once, because the various production elements and activities interact and depend on one another. Since nobody can learn everything at once, we begin with a broad overview of the television production system. This overview introduces (1) the basic television system, (2) the expanded system, (3) production elements, and (4) production personnel.

vision set into visible screen images, the television pictures. The microphone converts whatever it "hears" (the actual sounds) into electrical signals that are reconverted into sounds by the loudspeaker. The picture signals are called *video signals* (from the Latin "I see"), and the sound signals, *audio signals* (from the Latin "I hear"). In general the television system transduces one state of energy (optical image, actual sound) to another (electrical energy). (See 1.1.)

BASIC TELEVISION SYSTEM

A system is a collection of elements that work together to achieve a specific purpose. None of the individual elements of a system can do the job alone.

The **television system** consists of equipment and people who operate this equipment for the production of specific programs. Whether the productions are simple or elaborate, they work on the same basic systems principle. The television camera converts whatever it "sees" (the optical image) into electrical signals that can be reconverted by the tele-

THE EXPANDED SYSTEM

The effectiveness of a system depends on two additional features: control, and the possibility for expansion without rendering the basic system elements obsolete. An expanded television system (see 1.2) needs equipment and procedures that allow for the selection of various picture and sound sources, for the control of picture quality and sound, and for the integration of additional equipment for more complicated procedures.

The expanded video system consists of (1) one

Television is not just a pipeline through which the software is pushed by the hardware people; rather it is a creative process in which people and machines interact to provide the viewer with significant experiences. Television production therefore requires an intimate knowledge of the creative process—of how machines and people interact.

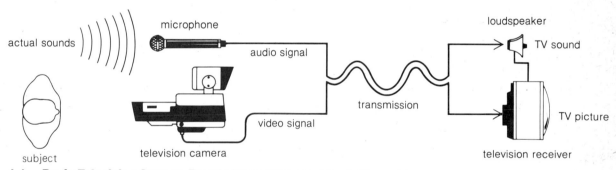

1.1 Basic Television System The television camera converts what it sees into electrical signals that are usually transmitted (wireless or by cable) and reconverted by the television receiver into visible screen images. The microphone converts actual sounds into electrical signals that are transmitted and reconverted into audible sounds by the loudspeaker.

or more cameras, (2) a camera control unit or units, (3) preview monitors, (4) a switcher, (5) a line monitor, (6) a videotape recorder, and (7) a transmitter.

The audio portion of the expanded system consists of (1) a microphone or microphones, (2) an audio console, (3) an audio monitor (speaker), and (4) the "line-out" that transports the sound signal either to the videotape recorder or to the transmitter.

Let us put the system to work. Camera 1 and

camera 2 are focused on two people talking to each other. Person A wears microphone 1 and person B microphone 2. Mic (short for microphone) 1 carries the signals of person A's voice to the audio console, and mic 2 does the same for person B. Similarly, camera 1 feeds the picture of person A and camera 2 the picture of person B to the switcher.

The *audio console* lets you select which microphone or other audio source (audiotape or record)

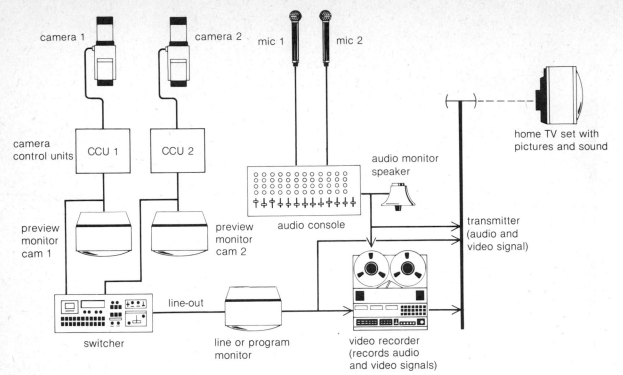

1.2 **Expanded Television System** The expanded television system contains quality controls (CCU and audio console), selection controls (switcher, audio console), and monitors so that the selected pictures and sound can be previewed and preheard before they are put on videotape or transmitted to the home receivers.

will be heard and lets you mix various audio sources. Larger audio consoles afford control of both *selection* and sound *quality*. You can make the sound louder or softer and more brilliant or more reverberating. You can switch from a person's voice to music or combine them so that we can hear both at the same time.

The *video signals* from cameras 1 and 2 are quality controlled by their respective *camera control units (CCUs)*. If person A is standing in a shadow area and person B in bright sunlight, the CCU of camera 1 can make picture A lighter and the camera 2 CCU can make picture B slightly darker. The colors, too, can be adjusted to look the same from camera to camera.

The preview monitors let us see the pictures from cameras 1 and 2 before we select one for the viewer. This selection process happens at the *switcher*.

Pressing the button for camera 1 or camera 2 puts that camera's picture on the line monitor. Whatever appears on the line monitor will then be sent to the videotape recorder and/or the transmitter. The audio signal is simultaneously fed to the videotape recorder or transmitter.

With this overall television system in mind, let's take a look at the major production tools one by one to see how they work. When learning about the camera, lighting, audio, video recording and film, the switcher and editing, special effects, and design, always try to see these production elements and the people who use and coordinate these elements as part of an overall system. This should make each piece of equipment and each part (or subsystem) of the basic television system easier to understand and the production functions of each subsystem more self-evident.

camera light

shotgun microphone

zoom lens

ENG camera

SONY

camera cable to portable VTR

1.3 **ENG Camera** The ENG camera is light enough so that it can be carried rather easily by the camera operator. Usually, the camera operator also carries the videotape recorder, which records the video (picture) and audio (sound) signals.

PRODUCTION ELEMENTS

The Camera

The most obvious production element, the camera, comes in all sizes and configurations. Some cameras can be easily carried and operated by one person, whereas others are so large and heavy that it takes two people to lift them on a special camera mount. The camera mount enables the camera operator to move the camera about with relative ease. Portable cameras (see 1.3) are often used for news gathering and for more extensive production in the field. Hence, they are called ENG (electronic news gathering) or EFP (electronic field production) cameras. The heavier cameras are primarily used in the studio (see 1.4).

All important television productions are done with color cameras. Monochrome (black-and-white) cameras are still used for inexpensive home videotaping, training, surveillance, and a variety of industrial applications.

Parts of the Camera The television camera has *three major parts:* (1) the lens, (2) the camera itself, and (3) the viewfinder.

The Lens In all photography (meaning "writing with light"), the lens selects part of the visible environment and produces a small optical image of it. In still and film cameras the image is then projected onto a film; in television cameras it is projected on the *camera pickup tube,* which converts the light from the optical image into an electrical signal.

All color cameras have zoom lenses with which

1.4 Studio Cameras with Pneumatic Studio Pedestal
High-quality studio cameras are usually quite heavy and are put on a special studio pedestal for easy maneuverability.

you can move continually from a long shot (showing a wide vista) to a close-up view without moving the camera or the object you are photographing. With the lens you can also control the amount of light going through it.

The Camera Itself   The camera itself contains many devices that convert the optical image as projected by the lens into an electrical signal, called the *video signal*. The major conversion element is the *camera pickup tube*. The pickup tube responds to light in a manner that resembles a light meter. When the pickup tube receives a large amount of light, it produces a strong video signal (just as the light meter goes up); when it receives little light, it produces a weak video signal (just as the light meter goes down).

Other electronic components enable the camera to reproduce the colors and the light variations of the actual scene as faithfully as possible, and to amplify the relatively weak video signal so that it can be sent to the camera control unit without getting lost on the way.

The Viewfinder   The **viewfinder** is a small television set mounted on the camera that shows you what pictures the camera is "seeing." All camera viewfinders are monochrome. That means that even when operating a color camera, you will see only black-and-white pictures in the viewfinder.

Mounting Equipment   Portable cameras are usually built so that they rest comfortably on your shoulder,

a   b

1.5   Noseroom (or Leadroom*) and Balance
*A term coined by Thomas D. Burrows and Donald N. Wood in *Television Production,*
Dubuque, Iowa: Wm. C. Brown Company Publishers, 1982.

and they have attachments that help you carry and work the camera without getting too fatigued.

The heavy studio cameras, however, need special mounts. These range from simple tripods to rather heavy camera cranes. The most common camera mount is the studio pedestal (see 1.4), which enables you to move the camera smoothly about the studio floor and to raise and lower the camera while it is "**hot**" (on the air). A special mounting head lets you pan (turning the camera horizontally) and tilt the camera (pointing it up or down).

Picture Composition   All visual presentations can be more or less effective, depending on how you arrange the objects within the frame of the television screen. Just as in painting, the picture composition on the television screen can either enhance or diminish the visual communication effect.

Which of the two pictures in 1.5 and 1.6 would you select for having the better composition?

You probably chose 1.5b and 1.6a. Good. The woman's nose in 1.5b no longer collides with the screen edge; in 1.6a, she is properly centered, and her head appears no longer glued to the top edge.

Once you are thoroughly familiar with the technical production aspects of the camera, you will be able to put your effort into composing maximally effective pictures.

Lighting

Like the human eye, the camera cannot see without a certain amount of light. Because it is not objects we actually see but the light reflected off them, manipulating the light falling on the object influences the way we finally perceive the object on the screen. Such manipulation is called *lighting.*

Lighting has three broad purposes: (1) to provide the television camera with adequate *illumination* for technically acceptable pictures, (2) to provide us with *information*—that is, to tell us *what* the objects shown on the screen actually look like, *where* they are in relation to one another and to their immediate environment, and *when* the event is taking place in respect to time of day or season— and (3) to establish the general *mood* of the event.

Types of Illumination   In all television lighting you work basically with two types of illumination: directional and diffused. Directional light has a sharp beam and produces harsh shadows. You can aim the light beam to illuminate a precise area. A flashlight or car headlights, for example, produce directional light. Diffused light has a wide, indistinct beam that illuminates a relatively large area and produces soft, translucent shadows. The fluorescent lamps in a department store produce diffused lighting.

a   b

1.6   Headroom and Balance

1.7   Lighting Setup Studio lighting is generally accomplished by a variety of spotlights (which emit a directional beam of light) or floodlights (which emit diffused light). They are usually suspended from battens.

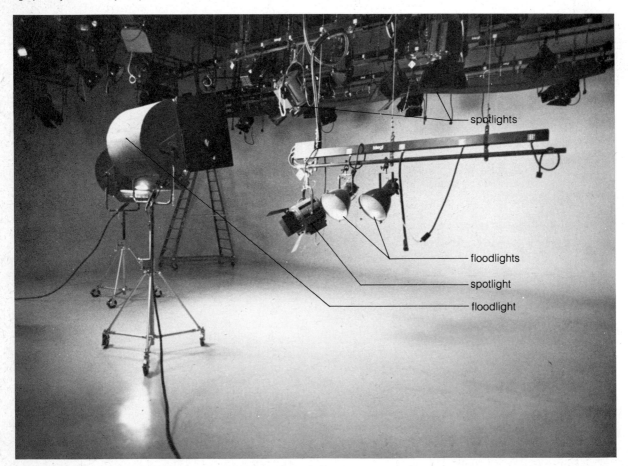

spotlights

floodlights

spotlight

floodlight

Lighting Instruments The lighting instruments that produce directional light are called *spotlights,* and the ones that produce diffused light are called *floodlights.* In the television studio the various types of spotlights and floodlights are usually suspended from the studio ceiling (see 1.7).

The studio lights are much too heavy and bulky to be used outside the studio, especially when you are engaged in ENG or EFP operations. In electronic news gathering, when you are concerned more with seeing well than with aesthetic effect, a single portable light is generally used. This small yet efficient lighting instrument is either mounted on the portable camera or held by the camera operator or some other member of the news crew.

Most electronic field productions (EFP) use portable lighting packages that consist of several small, highly efficient instruments and collapsible floorstands and clips. Generally, these instruments can be adjusted so that they can serve either as spotlights or floodlights (see 1.8).

Lighting Techniques All television lighting is based on a simple principle: using some instruments (usually spotlights) to illuminate specific areas, and other instruments (usually floodlights) to control the shadows and to bring the overall light on a scene to an acceptable level (see 1.9). In general, television lighting has less contrast between light and shadow areas than film or theater lighting.

Audio

Although the term *television* does not include audio, the sound portion of a television show is nevertheless one of its most important elements. Television audio not only communicates precise information, but also contributes greatly to the mood and atmosphere of the scene. To realize the information function of sound, simply turn off the audio during a newscast. Even the best actor would have a hard

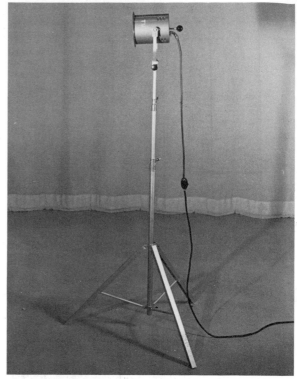

1.8   Portable Lights Portable lights can be put on stands or hand-held. They are primarily used to illuminate scenes outside the studio.

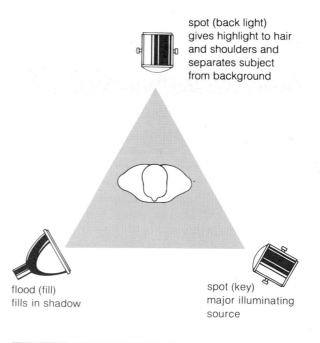

spot (back light) gives highlight to hair and shoulders and separates subject from background

flood (fill) fills in shadow

spot (key) major illuminating source

1.9   Basic Triangle Lighting The basic triangle lighting has a principal light source (key light), a fill light that softens the shadows (fill light), and a light that separates the object from the background (back light).

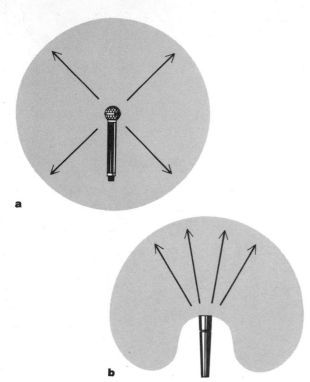

a

b

1.10 Microphone Pickup Patterns Some microphones "hear" sounds from all directions almost equally well; others can "hear" better in one direction. The pickup pattern is a graphic representation of the directions from which the microphone can pick up sounds. Microphone (a) can hear rather well in all directions; microphone (b) can pick up sounds better from one direction (front) than from others (sides and back).

time communicating news stories through facial expression, graphics, and videotape alone.

The aesthetic function of sound (to make us perceive, or feel, an event in a particular way) becomes obvious when you listen to the background sounds during a police story, for example. The tire-squealing sounds during a high-speed chase are real enough, but the rhythmically fast, exciting background music that accompanies the scene is definitely artificial. After all, the police car and the getaway car are hardly ever followed in real life by a third vehicle playing background music. But we have grown so accustomed to such devices that we probably would perceive the scene as less exciting if the music were missing.

The various audio production elements are (1) microphones, (2) sound recording and playback devices, and (3) sound control equipment.

Microphones All microphones convert sound waves into electrical energy. This electrical energy is amplified and sent to the loudspeaker, which converts it back into audible sound. There is a great variety of microphones designed to take care of different tasks. To pick up a newscaster's voice, to capture the sounds of a tennis match, and to record a rock concert may all require different microphones or sets of microphones. Some mics, or mikes (both are short for microphones), are designed to pick up sounds from all directions, whereas others "hear" better when the sounds come from the direction in which they are pointed. Likewise, some mics are used primarily for the pickup of music; others are more efficient for voice pickup (see 1.10).

Sound Recording and Playback Devices In live television the sound of a scene is always produced simultaneously with the pictures. But even when a scene is recorded on videotape, its sound is usually recorded simultaneously with the picture. If the program is shot in the studio, background music and sound effects are often added simultaneously to the live pickup of the actors' voices. In large productions, however, the audio requirements are so extensive that certain sound elements, such as the background music or police sirens, are added to the dialogue in later postproduction sessions.

Television sound is normally recorded on one of the sound tracks of the videotape. Besides the sound pickup through microphones, audiotape cartridges, called "carts," or cassettes are often used. They allow almost instant starts and stops by simply pressing the correct button on the cart machine. Sometimes regular records and reel-to-reel audiotapes are used as well.

Sound Control The *audio console* is used to control the sounds of a program. At the audio console you can (1) select a specific microphone to deliver the sound signal, (2) amplify the weak signals that come from that microphone for further processing, (3) control the volume (loudness) and the quality of the sound, and (4) mix (combine) two or more incoming sound sources. For example, one sound input may be the voice of the newscaster reading over a videotaped event whose sounds we also hear (second sound input). The third input is some background music for all of this. The audio console permits you to mix all three sounds together while controlling the volume and quality of each sound independently (see 9.5).

Videotape Recording and Film

Most shows you see on television have been prerecorded on videotape. Even during live football games you will see recorded material. The instant replays have all been recorded on videotape for fast ("instant") replay at the appropriate time. Even film commercials are usually transferred to videotape for easier playback. Feature films and filmed documentaries are generally mailed to the local stations as 16mm films (referring to the film width) and projected directly into special television cameras for transmission.

Although the unique feature of television is its aliveness—its ability to capture and distribute an event while it is actually taking place—the control that videotape provides over production (the building of a show) and programming (when and over which channel the show is telecast) has made it an indispensable production element.

With videotape you can (1) record entire programs for immediate playback or playback at a later time without noticeable quality loss, (2) assemble a coherent show from parts that have been recorded at different times and/or locations, (3) duplicate programs, and (4) preserve programs for later reference. The sophisticated, yet easy to operate, electronic editing devices make videotape as flexible as, or often more flexible than, film in postproduction activities. *Postproduction* generally refers to editing—putting the various video and audio segments into a continuous sequence—and to the adding of various video and audio elements during the editing process.

Videotape Recorders All videotape recorders (VTRs) work on the same principle. They record video and audio signals on a single tape, the videotape, and convert them back into television pictures and sound during playback. But there are many different models of professional-quality videotape recorders, using tape formats ranging from 2 inches to $\frac{1}{4}$-inch in width. This means that the old and so convenient division of videotape recorders into the professional 2-inch videotape recorders and the nonprofessional "small-format" recorders (using tape narrower than 2 inches) is no longer feasible. We will, therefore, classify the various videotape recorders as reel-to-reel machines and cassette recorders.

In reel-to-reel recorders the videotape is fed from a supply reel past the video and audio erase and recording heads to a separate takeup reel. Reel-to-reel recorders come in the 2-inch and 1-inch format (referring to tape width). The high-quality 1-inch machines have all but replaced the bulkier 2-inch ones as the industry standard. Half-inch reel-to-reel machines were once popular in nonbroadcast video production. They have been replaced by the much more efficient Beta or VHS videotape recorders (see 1.11).

Video cassette recorders (VCRs) work on the same operational principle as audio cassettes. Although video cassette recorders are more complex electronically and mechanically than audiotape recorders, they are not more difficult in their operation. The ease of handling VCRs and their portability make them the preferred recorder for ENG and EFP.

The most popular VCRs use the $\frac{3}{4}$-inch tape format. When combined with special image-enhancing devices, the $\frac{3}{4}$-inch machines can deliver pictures acceptable for broadcast (see 1.12). Some of the $\frac{1}{2}$-inch cassette machines, originally marketed for home recording devices, are now used successfully for television production projects. Some ENG cameras have a small $\frac{1}{2}$-inch cassette recorder attached to them, so that the operator no longer has to carry a separate tape recorder. As you can see, the trend is toward extremely small, portable, high-quality videotape recording equipment.

Video Discs For home use, video discs are for playback only. You can buy video discs on which whole movies have been recorded. Some video disc recorders can record in digital (computerlike) form a single picture, such as a slide or single video frame for quick retrieval.

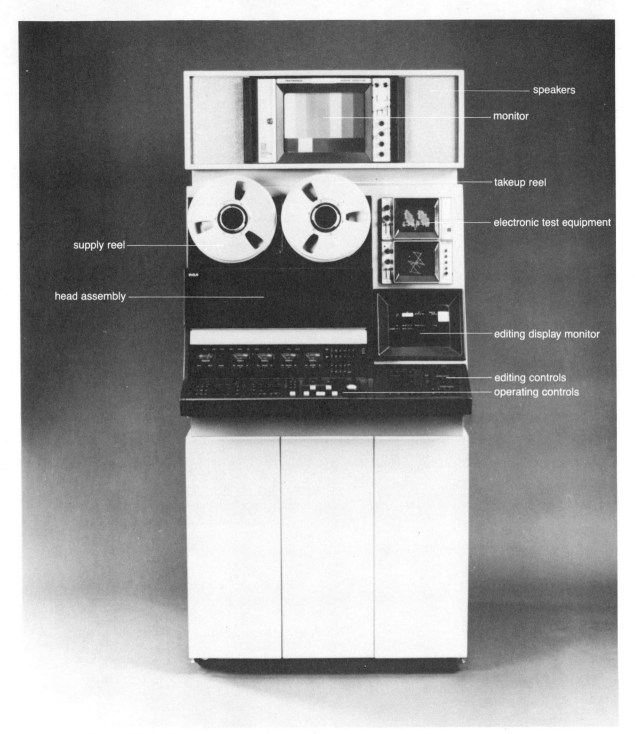

speakers

monitor

takeup reel

electronic test equipment

supply reel

editing display monitor

head assembly

editing controls
operating controls

1.11   Reel-to-Reel Videotape Recorder All reel-to-reel videotape recorders move the tape from the supply reel past a head assembly (where video and audio signals are recorded and/or erased) to the takeup reel. They also have editing facilities and show pictures while playing faster or slower than normal speed.

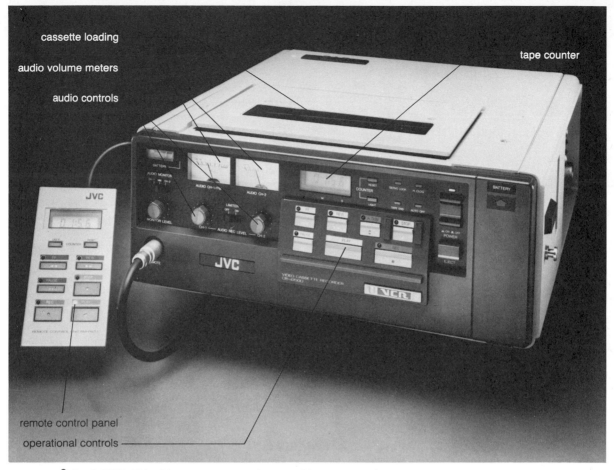

cassette loading

audio volume meters

audio controls

tape counter

JVC

remote control panel

operational controls

1.12   A ¾-inch VCR This video cassette recorder uses video cassettes for recording and playback. The cassette makes the operation of this video recorder relatively simple.

Film   Film is used in television primarily to show motion picture features and film documentaries. Commercials that are produced on film and the occasional news film supplied by an outside source to the station are generally transferred to videotape before they are telecast.

The major pieces of equipment needed to show film are combined in the *film chain,* or *film island.* The film chain consists of at least one film projector, a slide projector, a mirror system called a *multiplexer,* and a telecine camera. The multiplexer directs film or slide images into the *telecine camera,* a stationary color television camera. The room that houses the film islands is usually called the *telecine room,* or *telecine* for short (see 1.13).

Switching

The switcher permits instantaneous editing. This means that you can combine pictures from a variety of video sources while the show or show segment is in progress. You can also assemble pictures that come into the switcher from two or three videotape recorders. This latter technique is often used in postproduction editing.

Before learning about the switcher, recall for a

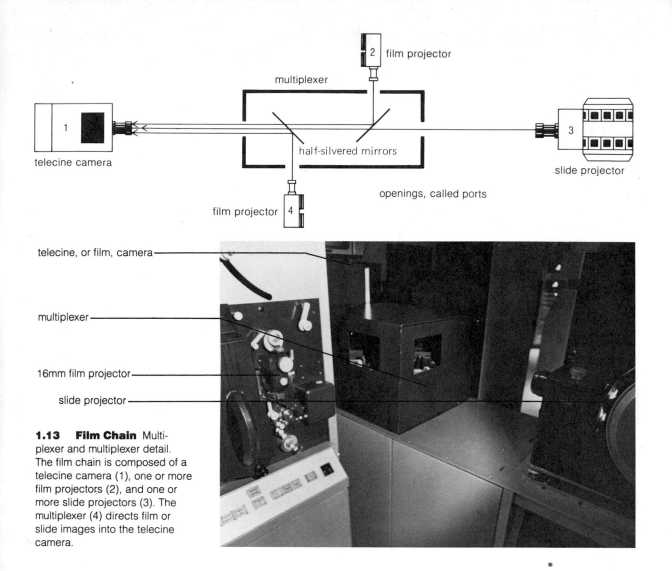

2 film projector

multiplexer

half-silvered mirrors

1

telecine camera

3

slide projector

openings, called ports

film projector 4

telecine, or film, camera

multiplexer

16mm film projector

slide projector

1.13　Film Chain Multiplexer and multiplexer detail. The film chain is composed of a telecine camera (1), one or more film projectors (2), and one or more slide projectors (3). The multiplexer (4) directs film or slide images into the telecine camera.

moment the expanded television system diagram (see 1.2). Cameras 1 and 2 deliver their pictures first to the camera control and then to the preview monitors. Preview monitor 1 shows all the pictures camera 1 is taking, and preview monitor 2 carries the pictures of camera 2. These video signals are fed into the switcher. Each camera has its own switcher input. Pressing the camera 1 button puts camera 1's pictures on the line monitor. Pressing the camera 2 button shows camera 2's pictures on the line monitor. This switcher "output" is what goes on the air or is put on videotape.

Any switcher, whether simple or complex, can perform three basic functions: (1) select an appropriate video source from several inputs, (2) perform basic transitions between two video sources, and (3) create or retrieve special effects. Most switchers have further provisions for remote start and stop of videotape recorders, and for film and slide projectors.

Each video input on a switcher has its corresponding button, just as each letter on a typewriter has its corresponding key. This is why even relatively simple switchers have several rows of buttons and levers. To produce a simple "mix," such as a dissolve from camera 1 to camera 2 (whereby the two images briefly overlap), you need identical inputs

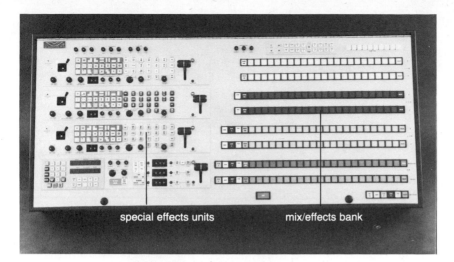

special effects units   mix/effects bank

1.14 Production Switcher The production switcher has several rows of buttons, usually two or more fader bars, and dials and other controls. Each button can put an incoming video source to the line-out. With the fader bars you can bring in or take out a picture gradually, or show two or more pictures simultaneously. The various buttons and dials are special effects controls.

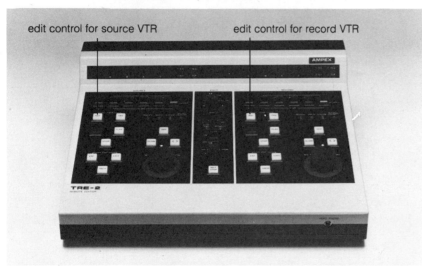

edit control for source VTR   edit control for record VTR

1.15 Editing Control Unit With the editing control unit you can select certain videotaped material from one videotape recorder and transfer it to another in a specific order.

repeated in an additional row of buttons and a lever that can activate either one or the other row (called *bus*), or both at the same time. More complicated effects need even more buses and levers (called *fader bars*), and other special effects buttons (see 1.14).

Postproduction Editing

If you are working with prerecorded material, you can achieve the proper picture sequence and desired effects through *postproduction editing*. Most videotape recorders have an *electronic editor* built in,

which allows you to assemble the desired picture and sound sequence without having to cut the videotape physically. In effect, you play back the master tape, which contains all the good and bad *takes* (the various scenes and parts of scenes) in no sensible order of continuity, and select and then record the good takes in a desirable order. So for postproduction editing, you need at least two videotape recorders: one to play back the selected takes from the original videotape recording, and another to record this material in the proper sequence.

An *editing control unit* can speed up your editing and make it more precise (see 1.15). The editing control unit helps you to find a particular scene quickly and accurately, even if it is buried in the middle of the tape. It starts and stops the machines and activates the electronic editor to perform the edit at the precise point you have designated. The more elaborate postproduction systems are computer-assisted. This means that a computer will remember your editing decisions and then tell the editing control unit what to do and when to do it.

Large postproduction projects use picture enhancement devices, which can not only help to preserve the quality of the original video but may even improve some of it. For example, you can shade the colors of two scenes so that they match, increase the contrast, or add sharper outlines to the picture elements. However, such postproduction is time-consuming and expensive. The better your original material is, the easier and more efficient your postproduction activities will be. Postproduction should be an *extension* of your creative process, not a salvage operation.

Special Effects

Special effects can be as simple as adding a show title to a background scene, or as elaborate as the gradual change of a dancer into a series of intensely colored, mosaiclike screen patterns.

Basically, you can generate special effects electronically, optically, or mechanically. Most of the effects you now see on television are produced *electronically*. With modern switching equipment and effects-generating accessories, electronic effects are readily available. You can see them frequently on television news. Most of the lettering and the graphs and many of the "window" inserts that appear over the newscaster's shoulder are electronically generated. *Optical effects* are generally produced by distortion of the image through mirrors or special lens manipulations or attachments. *Mechanical effects* include the simulation of rain, smoke, wind, snow, or other events that usually occur outside the studio. They are used only in elaborate studio productions, such as soap operas, musicals, and comedy or drama specials.

Design

Design is not part of the basic television system, but it is an important element for the enhancement of production. Design often determines the specific style of a show or even the whole "look" of a station or network. The most basic aspects of design are *graphics* and *scenery*.

Graphics Television graphics include anything from a simple title that identifies the name of the show to a flashy animated station or network logo. One important criterion for good television graphics is that they be *readable* on the relatively small and low-definition television screen. They must also fit the horizontally oriented *aspect ratio* of the television screen, which is three units high and four units wide.

A simple and inexpensive way of preparing titles for television is to use rub-on letters and transfer them from their plastic backing onto a studio card. You can also use simple printing devices that produce strips of letters. These strips can then be pasted onto the studio card. Maps and charts are either electronically produced or redrawn for clarity and to fit the aspect ratio. Most television operations use a *character generator,* a small computer that electronically generates a great variety of styles and sizes of letters. The more elaborate machines, called *graphics generators,* go way beyond producing simple letters. They can make the letters dance, expand, glow, or zoom in and out, and they can draw graphs, flash in different colors, and so forth. They are all part of the DVE family, *digital video effects* equipment.

Scenery Television scenery consists of the three-dimensional elements used in the studio to create a specific environment for the show or show segment. The most common scenic element is the *flat,* a wooden frame covered with soft material (muslin or canvas), or hard boards (plywood or various types of fiberboard). The flat is generally used to simulate walls. Other scenic elements include columns, pedestals, platforms, doors, windows, and steps.

Furniture, curtains, pictures that hang on the wall, lamps, books, desks, and telephones are considered the *properties* and *set dressings*. The properties we use to make the set functional, such as

1.16 Television Scenery A set provides a specific environment in which the performers or actors move about. Some sets simulate a real environment; others provide suitable working space or backgrounds.

tables and chairs, are the *set properties*. Items handled by the performers, such as the telephone, are called *hand properties*. Pictures, indoor plants, sculptures—everything that is used to dress up the set a little—constitute the *set dressings*.

Depending on the type of show, your set will have to simulate a real environment, such as a living room or dining room, or simply provide an efficient and attractive working environment, as a news set, for example (see 1.16). Whatever the purpose of the set may be, it must allow for (1) optimum camera angles and camera and microphone boom movement, (2) good lighting, and (3) smooth and logical action of the performers.

PRODUCTION PERSONNEL

Television production is *teamwork*. Even if you happen to be alone when covering a news story with ENG equipment, you still need the rest of the news department to get your story on the air. You may soon discover that the major task of television production is working not so much with equipment as with *people*. The most sophisticated television production equipment cannot make ethical and aes-

thetic judgments for you; it cannot tell you exactly what part of the event to select and how to present it for optimal communication. *You* have to make such decisions within the context of the general communication intent and through communication with the other members of your production team—the people in front of the camera (talent) and those behind (production staff and engineering crews, and other station personnel).

The television system needs people to operate it competently and creatively. The progressive automation of television equipment will not make people obsolete. On the contrary, easy-to-operate equipment frees production people to concentrate on the creative aspects of production. But this is possible only if the technical and nontechnical production specialists work together for a common goal: an effective production. The technical people are usually part of the *engineering* personnel of a station, and nontechnical people part of the *production* staff. In small stations, especially in college and university operations, the engineering and production functions often overlap considerably. More and more television equipment is *operator designed,* which means that you do not need specialized engineering knowledge to work it effectively. However,

Personnel	Function	Personnel	Function
Production Staff		Floor Manager	Sometimes called Stage Manager. In charge of all activities on studio floor. Directs talent on the floor, relays director's cues to talent, and supervises floor personnel. In small stations, responsible for setting up scenery and dressing the set.
Executive Producer	In charge of one or several program series. Manages budget and coordinates with station management, advertising agencies, financial supporters, and talent and writers' agents.		
Producer	In charge of an individual production. Is responsible for all personnel working on the production and for coordinating technical and nontechnical production elements. Often serves as writer and/or director.	Floorpersons	Also called grips, stagehands, or facilities persons. Set up and dress sets. Operate cue cards or other prompting devices, easel cards, and graphics. Sometimes operate microphone booms. Assist camera operators in moving camera dollies and pulling camera cables. In small stations, also act as wardrobe and makeup people.
Associate Producer	Assists producer in all production matters. Often does the actual coordinating jobs, such as telephoning talent and confirming schedules.		
Field Producer	Assists producer by taking charge of remote operations (away from the studio). In small stations may be part of producer's responsibilities.	**Engineering Staff**	
		Studio or Remote Supervisor	Also called engineering supervisor. Oversees all technical operations
Production Assistant (P.A.)	Assists producer and director during actual production. During rehearsal takes notes of producer's and/or director's suggestions for show improvement.	Technical Director (T.D.)	Does the switching and acts as engineering crew chief.
		Camera Operators	Operate the cameras; often do the lighting for simple shows.
Director	In charge of directing talent and technical facilities. Is finally responsible for transforming a script into effective video and audio messages. At small stations, may often be the producer as well.	Lighting Director (L.D.)	In charge of lighting; found only in large production centers or on large productions.
		Video Engineer or Video Operator	Adjusts camera controls for optimal camera pictures (shading). Sometimes takes on additional duties, especially during remote operations.
Associate Director (A.D.)	Assists director during the actual production. Often does timing for director. In complicated productions, helps to "ready" various operations (such as presetting specific camera shots or calling for a VTR to start).	Audio Engineer	In charge of all audio operations. Works audio board during the show.
		Videotape Engineer or Videotape Operator	Runs the videotape machine and does videotape editing. These operations are often done by nontechnical personnel.

labor union restrictions may prevent you from operating equipment that has been traditionally in the engineers' domain.

Table 1.17 lists the key production personnel (production staff and engineers) and their principal functions.

There are, of course, many more people involved in television operations, such as office workers, stage carpenters, graphic designers. However, we restricted the production personnel to the key people in the production system. We will describe the functions of the talent in Chapter 15.

1. The basic television system consists of equipment and people who operate this equipment for the production of specific programs. In its simplest form, the system consists of a television camera that converts what it sees into a video signal, a microphone that converts what it hears into an audio signal, and a television set and loudspeaker that reconvert the two signals into pictures and sound.

2. The expanded television system adds equipment and procedures to the basic system to make possible a wider choice and quality control of pictures and sound, and the recording and/or transmission of video and audio signals.

3. The major production elements are (1) the camera, (2) lighting, (3) audio, (4) video recording and film, (5) switching, (6) postproduction editing, (7) special effects, and (8) design.

4. All television cameras have three main parts: (1) the lens, (2) the camera itself with the camera pickup tube, which converts an optical image into an electrical signal, and (3) the viewfinder, which reconverts the signal into visible images.

5. Lighting is the manipulation of light falling on an object. The three broad purposes of lighting are (1) to provide the camera with enough light to function technically, (2) to enable viewers to see what the object looks like and where it is, and (3) to establish a mood.

6. The two types of illumination are (1) directional light, produced by spotlights, and (2) diffused light, produced by floodlights.

7. Audio, the sound portion of a television show, is necessary to give us specific information and to help set the mood of a scene.

8. Audio production elements include (1) microphones, (2) sound recording and playback devices, and (3) sound control equipment.

9. Most shows are prerecorded on videotape. With videotape, we can (1) assemble a coherent show from recorded program segments, (2) record entire shows for later replay, (3) duplicate programs, and (4) preserve programs for later reference. There are a variety of videotape recorders, which differ basically in size and portability, tape width, recording process, and quality.

10. Film is primarily used to play back motion picture features and documentaries.

11. The switcher enables us (1) to select a specific picture from several inputs, (2) to perform basic transitions between two video sources, and (3) to create or retrieve special effects.

12. Postproduction editing means the assembly of videotaped program segments in a specific order. With electronic editing and an editing control unit, we can select certain videotaped material from one videotape recorder and transfer it to another in a specific order without having to cut the videotape physically.

13. There are three types of special effects: (1) electronic, (2) optical, and (3) mechanical. Most special effects are produced electronically.

14. Television design includes (1) graphics, such as title cards or maps, and (2) scenery with properties and set dressings. Many of the graphics are generated electronically by character generators and the more elaborate graphics generators.

15. Television production requires teamwork from the talent—the performers and actors—and the production and engineering personnel.

Telecasts can originate anywhere, indoors or outdoors, as long as there is enough room for one camera and its associated equipment and enough light for the camera to see. With the development of highly portable, battery-powered cameras and recording facilities, and the mobile microwave transmitters, television is no longer confined to the studio. In tandem with satellite transmission, it has the whole world as its stage.

Television's important freedom from the studio does not render the studio obsolete, however. Television studios continue to exist primarily because, if properly designed, they can offer *maximum control* combined with *optimal use* of the television equipment. A television station has three major production centers: (1) the origination center, the television studio; (2) the control center, the studio control room and master control; and (3) studio support areas.

THE TELEVISION STUDIO

A well-designed studio provides for the proper environment and coordination of all major production elements—cameras, lighting, sound, scenery, and the action of performers. We will briefly look at the physical layout of a typical studio and the major studio installations.

Physical Layout

Most studios are rectangular with varying amounts of floor space. Although the zoom lens has drastically reduced the actual movement of the camera (the zoom lens can simulate movement toward or away from the scene), the size of the room still affects production complexity and flexibility to a great extent.

Size   The larger the studio, the more complex the productions can become, and the more flexible they will be. If all you do in the studio is news and an occasional interview, you may get by with amazingly little space. In fact, some news sets are placed right in the middle of the actual newsroom (see 1.18). Other news sets may take up a good portion of a large studio. Elaborate productions, such as music shows, dramas, dance, or audience participation shows, need large studios. It is always easier to produce a simple show in a large studio than a complex show in a small one.

A television studio and its production centers provide a setting for the most careful and polished works of television production. Here, unlike many field situations, the environment is controlled, the equipment is of the highest standard, and the personnel is precisely coordinated.

actual newsroom working area

performance area in newsroom

1.18   News Set in Newsroom This news set is part of a working newsroom. The producers feel that such an arrangement will increase in the viewer the feeling for the up-to-date character of the news.

Floor   The studio floor must be level and even so that cameras can travel on it smoothly and freely. Also, it should be hard enough to withstand the moving about of heavy equipment, scenery, and set properties. Most studios have concrete floors that are polished or covered with linoleum, tile, or hard plastic spray.

Ceiling Height   Adequate ceiling height—a minimum of 12 feet—is one of the most important design factors of a television studio. If the ceiling is too low, the lights are too close to the scene for good lighting control and there is not enough room above them for the heat to dissipate. Also, the low lights and the boom microphone will hang into the cameras' picture. Many large studios therefore have ceilings over 30 feet high.

Acoustic Treatment   All studio walls and the ceiling are usually treated with layers of rock wool, held in place by wire mesh. Such acoustic treatment prevents the sound from bouncing indiscriminately about the studio.

Air Conditioning   Because television studios have no windows (to keep out unwanted sounds and light), air conditioning is essential. The lights produce a large amount of heat, which has an adverse effect on delicate electronic equipment and on performers. Unfortunately, many air conditioning systems are too noisy for studio productions and must be turned off during the taping of a show—just when cool air is needed the most.

Doors   Studios need heavy, soundproof doors that are large enough to allow scenery, furniture, or even automobiles to be moved in and out. There is nothing more frustrating than trying to squeeze scenery and properties through undersized studio doors, or to have the doors transmit outside sounds, like a fire truck going by, right in the middle of the show.

Major Installations

Although any fairly large room with a high enough ceiling can serve as a studio in case of need, certain basic installations are essential for effective studio operations.

Intercommunication System   The intercommunication system, or "**intercom**," allows all production and engineering personnel actively engaged in the production of a show to be in constant voice contact with one another. For example, the director, who sits in the control room physically isolated from the studio, has to rely totally on the intercom system to communicate cues and instructions to every member of the production team during the show.

In most small stations the **P.L.** (private or phone line) system is used. Each member of the production team wears a small telephone headset with an earphone and a small microphone for talkback. Larger stations use a *wireless* intercom system. (For a more thorough discussion of intercom systems, see Section Two of Chapter 9.)

Studio Monitors   Television sets (**studio monitors**) that carry the same pictures as the line monitor are impor-

tant for the production crew working in the studio and the talent. The production crew can see the shots the director has selected and thus anticipate their future tasks. For example, if you see that the on-the-air camera is on a close-up rather than a long shot, you can work closer to the set without getting into camera range. Also, after seeing that one camera is on a close-up, the other camera operator can now go to a different shot to give the director a wider choice. The studio monitor is essential for the newscaster to see whether the various tape or live inserts are actually appearing as per script. In audience participation shows several studio monitors are usually provided so that the studio audience can see how the event looks on the screen.

In small studios you can suspend a single monitor from the lighting grid. If the bright studio lighting threatens to wash out the monitor picture, you can attach a simple cardboard hood to reduce the light spill on the screen (see 1.19).

Program Speakers   The **program speakers** fulfill a function for audio similar to what the studio monitors do for video. Whenever necessary, they can feed into the studio the program sound, or any other sound—dance music, telephone rings, or other sound effects—to be synchronized with the studio action.

Wall Outlets   As insignificant as they may seem at first, the number and position of wall outlets are important factors in studio production. The outlets for camera and microphone cables, intercoms, and regular household current should be distributed along the four studio walls for easy accessibility. If all the outlets are concentrated

---

Control Room   A room adjacent to the studio in which the director, the technical director, the audio engineer, and sometimes the lighting technician perform their various production functions.

Feed   Signal transmission from one program source to another, such as a network feed or a remote feed.

House Number   The in-house system of identification; each piece of recorded program must be identified by a certain code number. This is called the house number, since the numbers differ from station to station (house to house).

Intercom   Abbreviation for intercommunication system. The most widely used system has telephone headsets to facilitate voice communication on several wired or wireless channels among all production and engineering personnel involved in the production of a show.

Line Monitor   Also called master monitor. The monitor that shows only the line-out pictures, the pictures that go on the air or on videotape.

Line-out   The line that carries the final video or audio output.

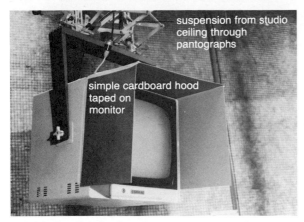

suspension from studio ceiling through pantographs

simple cardboard hood taped on monitor

1.19   Studio Monitor In case of excessive light spill in the studio, you can build a simple cardboard hood for the monitor that will shield the screen from the light and make the picture more visible.

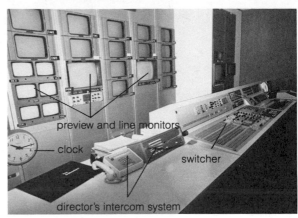

preview and line monitors

clock

switcher

director's intercom system

1.20   Studio Control Room All control rooms have distinct controlling areas: the program control, the switcher, the audio control, and sometimes the light control (the dimmer control board).

on one side of the studio, you will have to string long and cumbersome cables around the various sets to get equipment into the desired positions. Outlets must be clearly marked to avoid patching cables into the wrong outlets.

Lighting Patchboard   Most studios have a dimmer control board to regulate the relative intensity of the studio lights. The patchboard that connects the individual instruments to the dimmers is usually located in the studio. The dimmer board itself is either in a corner of the studio or in the control room (see 6.43).

THE STUDIO CONTROL ROOM

The **control room,** a separate room adjacent to the studio, is the place where all the production elements, such as camera, sound, videotape recording, and the talent and crews, are coordinated. Here the director, the assistant director, the technical director, and a variety of producers and production assistants make the decisions concerning maximally effective picture and sound sequences, which are to be videotaped or broadcast live (see 1.20).

Log   The major operational document. Issued daily, the log carries such information as program source or origin, scheduled program time, program duration, video and audio information, code identification (house number, for example), the title of the program, the program type, and additional special information.

Master Control   Nerve center for all telecasts. Controls the program input, storage, and retrieval for on-the-air telecasts. Also oversees technical quality of all program material.

Monitor   1. Audio: speaker that carries the program sound independent of the line-out. 2. Video: high-quality television receiver used in the television studio and control rooms. Cannot receive broadcast signals.

P.L.   Abbreviation for private line, or phone line. Major intercommunication device in television production.

Preview Monitor   1. Any monitor that shows a video source, except for the line (master) and off-the-air monitors. 2. A monitor that shows the director the picture he or she intends to use as the next shot.

Program Speaker   Also called audio monitor. A loudspeaker in the control room that carries the program sound. Its volume can be controlled without affecting the actual line-out program feed.

Studio Talkback   A public address, or P.A., loudspeaker system from the control room to the studio. Also called S.A. (studio address) system.

1.21 Control Room

Monitors The many monitors in the control room represent the video choices for the director. He or she cannot choose an image for on-the-air use that does not first appear on one of the monitors. The monitors show images as supplied by live studio cameras, telecine cameras, the various VTR machines, special effects and character generators, and remote inputs. Then there are the preview, line, and off-the-air monitors that show the on-the-air choices.

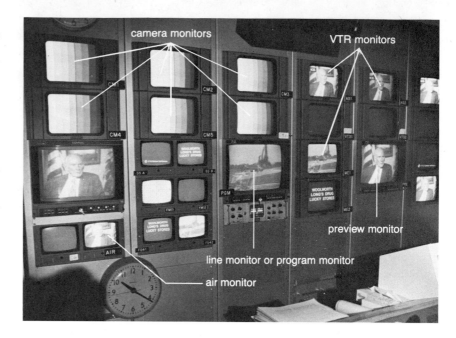

camera monitors

VTR monitors

preview monitor

line monitor or program monitor

air monitor

Program Control

The program control area is equipped with (1) video monitors, (2) monitor speakers for program sound, (3) intercom systems, and (4) clock and stopwatches.

Video Monitors Even a simple control room holds an amazingly large number of video monitors. There is a **preview monitor** for each of the studio cameras and separate preview monitors for film chains, videotape recorders, and character generators or other special effects devices. There is also a special color preview monitor that shows the director and technical director the upcoming picture before it is punched up (put on the air), and the color **line monitor** (also called master monitor or program monitor) that is fed by the video **line-out.** If you do a live remote or if you are connected with a network, you need at least two more monitors to preview the remote and network sources. Finally, there is the off-the-air monitor, a regular television set that receives off the air what you are telecasting. It is not uncommon to find thirty or more monitors in the control room of a medium-sized studio (see 1.21).

Speaker for Program Sound The production personnel in the control room, especially the director, must hear what audio is going on the air. The director has a volume control with which the volume of the monitor speaker can be adjusted without influencing the volume of the line-out audio.

Intercommunication Systems Besides the all-important P.L. (private line) intercom that connects the director with all other members of the production crew, there is an additional intercom system called the **P.A.** (public address system), or simply the director's **studio talkback.** The P.A. system allows the director to talk directly to the crew or talent in the studio when the show is not in progress. With the *I.F.B.* (interrupted feedback), or *program interrupt,* system the director and producers can talk directly to the talent while the show is on the air.

Clock and Stopwatches Time is an essential organizing element in television production. Programs are aired according to a second-by-second time schedule called the log.

The two timing tools for the director are the clock and the stopwatch. The clock indicates when a certain program should start or finish. All television clocks in the country are precisely synchronized with one another. The stopwatch is used for timing inserts, such as a 47-second videotape insert within a news program. Most control rooms have a regular clock (with hands), a digital clock (showing time in numbers), and digital stopwatches that can run forward and backward.

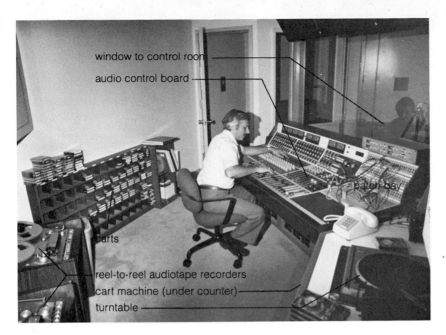

window to control room

audio control board

carts

reel-to-reel audiotape recorders

cart machine (under counter)

turntable

patch bay

1.22   Audio Control The audio control area contains the audio control board, through which the various sound inputs are selected, amplified, mixed, and distributed to the line-out, reel-to-reel tape machines, or at least the controls for them, tape cartridge machines, turntables, speakers and intercom controls, and patching facilities. In essence, the audio control area in the television control room represents a small radio station.

The Switcher

The **switcher** is located right next to the director's position. Although the director and the person doing the switching (usually the technical director, or T.D.) are connected by P.L. intercom, the director often resorts to pointing and finger snapping to speed up the cues to the T.D. In some stations the director does his or her own switching, but this arrangement has more disadvantages than advantages.

The Audio Control

The audio control booth can be considered a small radio station attached to the television control room. It usually houses the audio control board and a patchbay, audiotape recorders and cart or cassette machines, at least one turntable, cue and program speakers, a clock, and a line monitor (see 1.22). The audio engineer must be able to work undisturbed by the apparent confusion and inevitable noise in the control room. So the audio control booth has visual contact with the control room through a large window, but is otherwise self-contained. The audio engineer listens to the director's cues either through the P.L. intercom, or through a small intercom speaker.

The Lighting Control

Some stations prefer to have the lighting control board in the control room so that all the control functions are near one another. Like any other member of the production crew, the lighting control operator is connected with the director by P.L. intercom.

MASTER CONTROL

Master control is the nerve center of a television station. Every second of programming you see on your home screen has gone through the master control room of the station to which you are tuned. Master control acts as a clearinghouse for all program material. It receives program feeds from various sources and telecasts them at a specific time. The major responsibility of master control is to see that the *right program material* (including commercials and public service announcements) is put on the air at the *right time*. Master control is also responsible for the *technical quality* of the programs. This means that it has to check all program material being aired against technical standards set by the FCC (Federal Communications Commission).

PROGRAM LOG

DATE 06/05/

TIME OFF 0610P PDT   PAGE 53

LINE NUMBER	ON	OFF	SCHED TIME HR:MIN:SEC A/P	PROGRAM - ADVERTISER - PRODUCT	TIME ON	TIME OFF	VIDEO	AUDIO	ANN CODE	PROGRAM S TYPE	LENGTH	PROJECTION ROOM DATA AND SPECIAL INSTRUCTIONS	INT. #
E 23 R1462				NEWS CLOSE			V	V			0:15	*8631 SEE DIR.*	
E 23 R1295			10:57:40 P	STATION BREAK							2:20		
E 23 P 32				-----OUTLOOK (M.,F ONLY) -------			V	V		1 40	1:00	OUTLOOK *8502*	
C1473540015				FEDERAL EXPRESS 1 AIR FREIGHT			V	V	C		0:30	QFAS1326	663
C1314516175				DISCOVERY BAY 1 REAL ESTATE			V	V	C		0:30	DISCOVERY BAY 19822404	2404
C1560543948				SCHEFFLIN 1 BLUE NUN			V	V	C		0:10	IEBN1021	3043
S 54 R 267			10:59:50 P	RET. FR THE ASHES/LEGAL CB046			V	CT/O ID		0:10	SID *8046*	
				************									
E 23 R1286				************							0:00		
E 101 P 219			11:00:00 P	-----BENNY HILL			V	V		3 20		#58	
E 101 R1615				SEGMENT 1			V	V			1:11		
E 101 R1445				CUT A WAY #1 -------							2:00		
C 565532034				NISSAN MOTORS 1 DATSUN AUTOS			V	V	C		0:30	NOPP2453	1623
C 431532042				GENERAL FOODS 1 GOOD SEASONS			V	V	C		0:30	GFGS1162	1651
C 705531621NA				FURNITURE USA 1 FURNITURE			V	V	C		0:30	0430DFUSA64-1	2205
C138545193				PROMOTION L BARNEY MOVES #1			V	V	PR		0:30	BARNEY MOVES #1	4357

1.23 Program Log As you can see, the log shows (1) the program origin, or source, (2) the scheduled event time, (3) the duration of the program, (4) specific video information, (5) specific audio information, (6) identification codes, (7) the title of the program, (8) the type of the program, or class, and (9) any pertinent special information. The log, issued daily, is the most important production and programming document; its actual format and arrangement vary from station to station. The major criteria for log format are easy readability and consistency.

The specific activities of master control consist of program input, program storage, and program retrieval.

Program Input

Program material may come into master control directly from its own studios, from remote lines (network, remote origination by own station, or someone else), or by mail in the form of videotape and film. Some of the programs (station-originated live shows or network **feeds**) are routed immediately to the transmitter for broadcast, but the bulk of the program material (videotaped shows and film) must be stored before being broadcast.

Master control also puts together the various station breaks. A **station break** is the cluster of commercials, brief announcements of upcoming programs, public service announcements, and station identifications that appears between major programs.

Program Storage

All recorded program material (videotape, film, and slides) is stored in master control itself or in a special storage room. Each program is given a station code, or a **house number**, for fast identification and retrieval. Although computer retrieval has introduced some commonality in terms, many stations have their own procedures and codes (see 1.23).

Program Retrieval

Program retrieval means the *selection, ordering,* and *airing* of all program material. The program retrieval is masterminded by the program **log,** a second-by-second listing of every type of program aired on a particular day (see 1.23). In general, the log identifies (1) scheduled time, (2) length of program, (3) program title, (4) video and audio origin (videotape, network, film, live, or slide), and (5) house numbers and other special information. The program log is issued daily, usually one or two days in advance. It is normally distributed in a printed form that may cover sixty to seventy pages. Some larger stations display the log on the screens of computer terminals (see 1.24).

The *master control switching area* looks like the combined program control and switching area of the studio control room. Master control has preview monitors for all studio cameras, videotape and video cassette machines, special effects, film islands, network and other remote feeds, plus at least one off-the-air monitor (see 1.25).

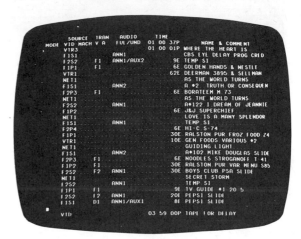

1.24 Computer Display of Log Information If you have the assistance of a computer, the log, besides being available in a hard-copy printout, can be displayed on any of the screens of the computer terminals at the push of a button. You can feed the computer last-minute log corrections and it will change, remember, and initiate the new roll cues for the various machines at the new times, and immediately produce an updated hard copy.

The switcher itself, which looks similar to the studio switcher, basically facilitates the switching *between various program sources,* such as VTR, studio, network, film, or remote. Most master control switchers are computer-assisted. This means that once preset and programmed, the switcher can activate, at the push of just one button, a whole sequence of events. For example, it can start a specific VTR and switch the picture and sound on the air at the exact log time, change to a slide and roll an audio cart with the pre-recorded announcer's voice, switch to another brief VCR insert, and then switch to the network program. If the house number of the actual program does not match the number as specified in the log, the computer will flash a warning in time to correct the possible mistake. Moreover, because even the computer does not entirely trust itself, there is an override button that can be pushed to return the whole system to manual operation in case of emergency.

STUDIO SUPPORT AREAS

The studio support areas include space for *property storage, scene storage* and possibly construction, and

on-air monitors

preset monitor

log

master control switcher
(computer controlled)

1.25 Master Control Switching Area Master control is the nerve center of a television station. It oversees program input, since every bit of incoming material is eventually routed to master control; it stores it if necessary (except for live telecasts), and retrieves the appropriate program material for every second of the station's telecasting day. Additionally, master control is responsible for the technical quality of all program material being aired.

makeup and dressing rooms. If you produce a large number of vastly different programs, from daily newscasts to complex television dramas, you need large prop and scenery storage areas. Otherwise, your support areas can be fairly simple.

The most important part of any storage area is its *retrieval efficiency.* If you must search for hours to find the props to decorate your office set, even the most extensive prop collection is worth very little. Clearly *label* all storage areas, and then put the props and scenery back *every time* in the designated areas.

But however well-equipped your studio and control and support areas may be, they are only as good as the people who use them. It is, finally, *you*—your technical production skills and aesthetic sensitivity—who determines the relative success of the show.

MAIN POINTS

1. Telecasts can originate almost anywhere, but the television studio affords maximum production control.

2. The studio has three major production centers: (1) the studio itself, (2) the studio control room and master control, and (3) the studio support areas.

3. Important aspects of the physical layout of the studio are (1) a smooth, level studio floor, (2) adequate ceiling height, (3) acoustic treatment and air conditioning, and (4) large, soundproof doors.

4. Major installations include intercom systems, studio video and audio monitors, various wall outlets, and the lighting patchboard.

5. The studio control room houses (1) the program control with the various preview monitors, clocks, and program speakers, (2) the switcher, (3) audio control with the audio control board, cart machines, turntables, and reel-to-reel recorders, and sometimes (4) the lighting control board through which the intensity of the studio lights is regulated.

6. Master control is the nerve center of a television station. It has facilities for (1) program input, (2) program storage, and (3) program retrieval. It also checks the technical quality of all programs that are broadcast.

7. The program retrieval is coordinated by the program log, a second-by-second listing of every type of program aired on a particular day.

8. The studio support areas include space for property and scenery storage, and makeup and dressing rooms.

FURTHER READING

Bensinger, Charles. *The Video Guide*. 3rd ed. Santa Fe, NM: Video-Info Publications, 1983.

Burrows, Thomas D., and Donald N. Wood. *Television Production: Disciplines and Techniques*. 2nd ed. Dubuque, IA: Wm. C. Brown Co., 1982.

Cheshire, David. *The Video Manual*. New York: Van Nostrand Reinhold Co., 1982.

Gross, Lynne Schafer. *Telecommunications: An Introduction to Radio, Television, and the Developing Media*. Dubuque, IA: Wm. C. Brown Co., 1983.

Millerson, Gerald. *Effective TV Production*. Rev. Edition. Woburn, MA: Focal Press, 1982.

The Camera

The camera is the single most important piece of production equipment. Other production equipment and techniques are influenced by the camera's technical and performance characteristics.

In Section One, we examine the following areas:

1. Parts of the camera: (a) the lens, (b) the camera itself with the camera pickup tube and the internal optical system, and (c) the viewfinder.

2. How the camera works—the conversion of an optical image into electrical signals.

3. Standard and digitally controlled camera chains.

4. Monochrome (black-and-white) camera principles.

5. Color camera principles.

6. Types of cameras and their operational features: (a) digitally controlled cameras, (b) nondigital cameras, (c) studio cameras, (d) ENG/EFP cameras, and (e) convertible cameras.

Section Two deals with some basic electronic processes of television and major color principles:

1. The basic scanning process.

2. The workings of the major imaging devices: (a) the vidicon principle and (b) the charge-coupled device.

3. The properties of color.

4. Internal optical systems and color separation devices.

5. ENG control features.

6. High-definition television (HDTV).

In Section One we will cover the following aspects of the television camera: (1) parts of the camera, (2) how the camera works, (3) the camera chain, (4) the monochrome camera compared to the color camera, (5) the inner mechanisms of a camera, (6) the two camera systems, and (7) the three types of cameras.

PARTS OF THE CAMERA

The standard television **camera** consists of three main parts (see 2.1):

1.   Lens, which selects a certain field of view and produces a small optical image of this view. The lens and certain attachments to it are sometimes called the **external optical system.**

2.   Camera itself with its camera pickup tube(s), or solid-state imaging device, and the **internal optical system,** which consists of a series of mirrors or prisms.

3.   Viewfinder.

The camera, which combines the lens, the pickup device and internal optical system, and the view-

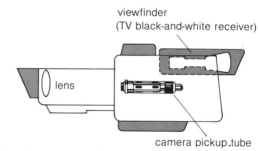

2.1   Parts of the Camera The main parts of a television camera are (1) the lens, (2) the camera itself with the camera pickup tube, and (3) the viewfinder.

finder, is called the **camera head** because it is at the head of a chain of other essential electronic camera equipment (see 2.3). The camera head itself has a series of attachments and controls that help you use the camera efficiently and creatively. Portable cameras, used for **ENG** (electronic news gathering) or **EFP** (electronic field production), are self-contained, which means that they contain all the electronic equipment necessary to produce and deliver to a portable videotape recorder high-quality color pictures.

In recent years, microprocessors, or small computers, have made new cameras simpler to operate under a variety of production conditions. However, cameras today are also far more sophisticated and electronically complex. In order to utilize the camera's potential and to understand how it affects the rest of the production, you need to know some of the basic principles of the instrument.

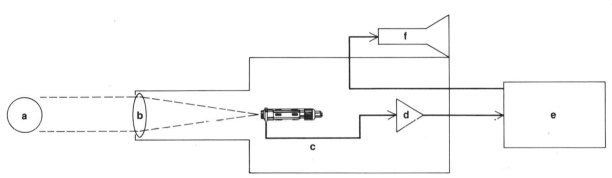

2.2   Basic Principle of a Television Camera The light, reflected off object (a) is gathered by the lens (b) and focused on the camera pickup tube (c). There, light is transformed into electrical energy, the video signal. It is amplified and processed (d, e) and converted back to visible screen images in the viewfinder (f).

HOW THE CAMERA WORKS

All television cameras, whether color or monochrome (black-and-white), big studio models or small portable ones, work on the same basic principle: *the conversion of an optical image into electrical signals that are reconverted by a television set into visible screen images* (see 2.2).

Specifically, the light that is reflected off an object (a) is gathered by the lens (b) and focused on the imaging device, in this case a camera pickup tube (c). The pickup tube is the principal camera element that transforms the light into electrical energy, called the video (picture) signal. This signal is amplified and processed so that it can be reconverted into visible screen images (see 2.2).

THE CAMERA CHAIN

As already mentioned in Chapter 1, the studio camera is only part of a system of electronic components, called the "camera chain," which controls the camera's picture.

The standard **camera chain** for nondigitally controlled cameras consists of (1) the camera head, (2) the camera control unit, (3) the synchronization source (sync generator), and (4) the power supply (see 2.3).

Each camera has its own **camera control unit**, or **CCU**. The CCU performs two functions: setup and control. During *setup,* or "chipping" (so called because one of the setup charts has chips of various grays), each camera must be aligned (so that a circle does not look egg-shaped) and adjusted for accurate registration (so that all three images from the three separate color channels inside the camera overlap perfectly), the trueness of color, and the contrast range between the brightest and darkest area of a scene.

During the show all cameras must be continuously adjusted to the various lighting conditions of the different scenes. The CCU provides this *control.* If the cameras are properly set up and have fair **stability** (which means they retain their setup values), the video operator usually need only control "master black," or **pedestal** (adjust the camera for the darkest scene area), and the "white level," or **iris** (adjust the camera's lens opening so that it will permit only the desired amount of light to go through

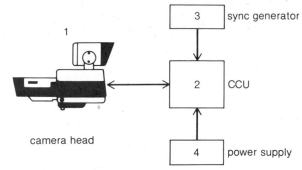

2.3 Standard Camera Chain The standard camera chain consists of the camera head (the actual camera), the camera control unit (CCU), the sync generator, and the power supply.

the camera lens). The video engineer can check on the **waveform monitor**, or **oscilloscope** (see 2.4), whether the master black-and-white levels have been set for optimal camera performance.

The **sync generator** produces electronic synchronization pulses that keep the scanning in the various television equipment (cameras, monitors, videotape recorders) in step. The *power supply* generates the electricity necessary to drive the television equipment.

Digitally controlled studio cameras also have a CCU. However, because the setup and control functions are in separate pieces of equipment they have been given different names. The equipment is also so new that the manufacturers have not yet agreed on what to call the various units. The microprocessor-assisted chain consists of three basic units: (1)

Base Station Also called camera processing unit or CPU. Equipment, separate from the camera head, that is used with digitally controlled cameras to process signals coming from and going to the camera.

Camera Chain The television camera (head) and associated electronic equipment. For conventional cameras, this equipment includes the camera control unit, sync generator, and the power supply. In digitally controlled cameras, the equipment consists of the base station, or camera processing unit, and the remote control unit.

Camera Control Unit Also called CCU. Equipment, separate from the camera head, which contains various video controls, including registration, color balance, contrast, and brightness. With the CCU the video operator adjusts the camera picture during the show.

Camera Head The actual television camera, which is at the head of a chain of essential electronic accessories. In some ENG/EFP cameras, the camera head contains all the elements of the camera chain.

CCU See Camera Control Unit.

Charge-Coupled Device Also called CCD or "chip." The imaging device used in some color cameras instead of a camera pickup tube. Within the device, image sensing elements translate the optical image into a video signal. It has the advantage of small size but does not produce pictures equal in quality to those produced with pickup tubes.

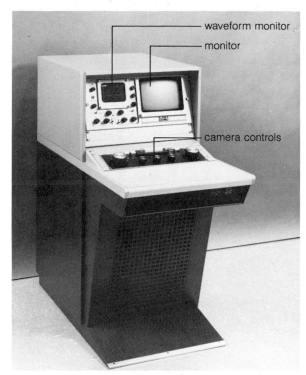

waveform monitor

monitor

camera controls

2.4   Camera Control Unit (CCU) The conventional CCU has control buttons and dials that adjust master black-and-white levels, as well as the three primary colors of a color camera (red, green, and blue). It also has a waveform monitor and a monitor.

the *camera head*, (2) the **base station**, which processes the various signals coming from and going to the camera (therefore also called *camera processing unit*, or *CPU*), and (3) the **remote control unit**

(**RCU**), which has a minimal amount of controls necessary for the continual adjustment of the camera during its operation. The big difference between a conventional and a digitally controlled chain is that for digitally controlled cameras there is only one setup panel that can adjust several cameras simultaneously. After the cameras have been set up, the setup panel or terminal is unplugged; it has no function during camera operation (see 2.5).

Although the color camera is used exclusively in all broadcast and nonbroadcast television production, you should still know about the major aspects of monochrome cameras. Monochrome cameras are still used in many college and university television operations, and the basic handling of the television camera is the same for color and monochrome cameras. We will, therefore, briefly discuss some of the major points of monochrome cameras.

MONOCHROME CAMERAS

The **monochrome camera** is color blind. Its single camera pickup tube reacts only to the various degrees of brightness, which are the light and dark areas and shades of gray of a scene as seen by the lens. Basically, the light areas in the scene produce a relatively strong video signal, the dark areas a weak one. When reproduced on a television monitor, the strong video signal shows up as bright spots on the screen, and the weak video signal as the dark areas (see 2.6). If two colors happen to be of the same

Chrominance Channel   The color (chroma) channels within the color camera. A separate chrominance channel is responsible for each of the three primary color signals.

Contrast   The difference between the brightest and the darkest spots in the picture (often measured by reflected light in foot-candles), expressed in a ratio. The maximum contrast ratio for color cameras is 30:1.

Dichroic Mirror   A mirrorlike color filter that singles out, of the white light, the red light (red dichroic filter) and the blue light (blue dichroic filter), with the green light left over.

Digitally Controlled Camera   A camera that uses microprocessors primarily to automate the alignment of the camera and ensure optimal performance under a variety of production conditions.

EFP   Electronic field production. Television production activity outside the studio usually shot for postproduction (not live).

ENG   Electronic news gathering. The use of portable cameras, videotape recorders, lights, and sound equipment for the production of daily news stories and short documentaries. ENG is usually done for immediate postproduction, but the pictures and sound can also be transmitted live from the field.

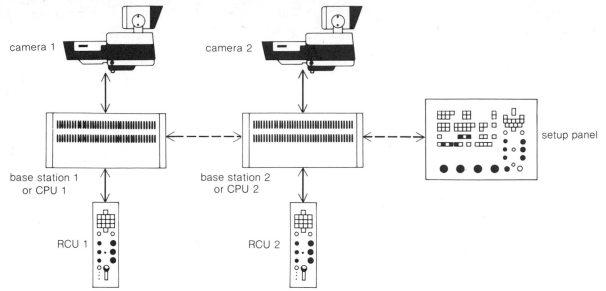

camera 1

camera 2

setup panel

base station 1
or CPU 1

base station 2
or CPU 2

RCU 1

RCU 2

2.5   Digitally Controlled Camera Chain The digitally controlled camera chain consists of the camera head (the actual camera), the base station (also called the camera processing unit), the RCU (the remote control unit), and the setup panel (can be used for more than one camera).

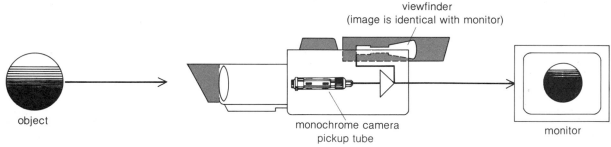

viewfinder
(image is identical with monitor)

object

monochrome camera
pickup tube

monitor

2.6   Monochrome Camera Principle The monochrome camera converts the reflected light (off the object) into video signals representing various shades of gray.

ENG/EFP Cameras   Electronic news gathering or electronic field production cameras. Replacing the film camera for news reporting, these television cameras are portable, self-contained, and largely automated.

Lag   Smear that follows a moving object or motion of the camera across a stationary object. It occurs especially with color and monochrome vidicon cameras under low light levels.

Luminance Channel   A separate channel within color cameras that deals with brightness variations and allows color cameras to produce a signal receivable on a black-and-white television set. The luminance signal may be taken out of the green channel or electronically combined from the three chrominance signals.

Microprocessors   Small digital computers used in color cameras to set up and maintain a camera's optimal performance under a variety of production conditions.

Pickup Tube, or Camera Tube   The main camera tube that converts light energy into electrical energy, the video signal.

Remote Control Unit   Also called RCU. Part of the camera chain with which the video operator achieves optimal pictures during the production.

brightness, a monochrome camera produces video signals of identical strengths, which, in turn, show up on the monitor as the same shade of gray (see Color Plate II).

The original high-quality monochrome cameras were quite heavy and served primarily as studio cameras. It was a major effort to take these heavy cameras outside for remote telecasts. When a small portable camera and videotape recorder were first developed, they did not meet broadcast-quality standards (as determined by the FCC, the Federal Communications Commission) and could not, therefore, be used for ENG or EFP. But this first small portable camera-recording unit, generally known as portapak and used primarily by nonbroadcast people, nevertheless demonstrated the production potential of such a portable unit. The modern ENG camera-recorder units still operate on the portapak principle, though they have become much more sophisticated electronically and more versatile in production (see 2.7).

THE COLOR CAMERA

The color camera works on the same fundamental principle as the monochrome camera: the conversion of light into electrical energy, and the reconversion of the electrical energy (video signal) into visible screen images. But the color camera is more complicated than its monochrome ancestor. In order for you to understand some of the dos and don'ts of color production, you need to know some of the basic workings of the color camera. We will, therefore, briefly discuss these points: (1) internal optical systems, (2) imaging devices, (3) electronic characteristics of color cameras, and (4) camera types and operational characteristics.

INTERNAL OPTICAL SYSTEMS

In the monochrome camera the lens catches the light and focuses it directly onto the front surface of a single camera pickup tube. The color camera, however, first splits the entering beam of light into the three primary light colors: red, green, and blue (see Color Plate IV). These three colors are then processed by separate channels, the so-called chrominance (color) channels. Thus, we have a red channel to process the red light into the red signal, the green channel for the green signal, and the blue channel for the blue signal.

Beam Splitters

The color separation device that splits the white light into the three primary colors (or, into some other colors for some ENG cameras) is called the **beam splitter.** There are three types of beam splitters: (1) the dichroic mirror system, (2) the prism block, and (3) the striped filter.

Dichroic Mirror System In the **dichroic mirror** system the light that comes through the lens is sep-

---

Resolution The characteristic of a camera that determines the sharpness of the picture received. The lower a camera's resolution, the less fine picture detail it can show. Resolution is influenced by the pickup tube, lens, internal optical system, and the television set. It may be improved by digital image enhancers.

Signal-to-Noise Ratio The relation of the strength of the desired signal to the accompanying electronic interference, the noise. A high signal-to-noise ratio is desirable (strong video or audio signal and weak noise).

Stability The degree to which a camera (or camera chain) maintains its initial electronic setup.

Studio Camera Heavy, high-quality camera that cannot be maneuvered properly without the aid of a pedestal or some other type of camera mount.

Sync Electronic pulses that synchronize the scanning in the origination source (live cameras, videotape) and the reproduction source (monitor or television receiver).

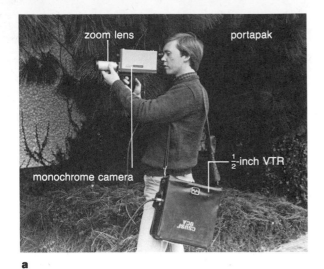

zoom lens

portapak

monochrome camera

$\frac{1}{2}$-inch VTR

a

zoom lens

shotgun mic

camera light

ENG camera

camera cable

$\frac{3}{4}$-inch VTR

b

2.7 (a) Portapak and (b) ENG Color Camera-Recorder Unit (Sony BVP-250) Modern ENG/EFP camera-videotape recorder units work on the same operational principle as the old black-and-white portapak units that were used extensively for nonbroadcast video productions.

arated by three dichroic (light-separating) mirrors into the three primary light colors (red, green, and blue) and directed by other mirrors and lenses into the three camera pickup tubes (see Color Plate IV).

The Prism Block Because the dichroic mirror system is so critical in its alignment and, therefore, quite vulnerable to physical shock, most cameras, especially the ENG/EFP cameras, use as their internal optical system the **prism block.** The incoming light is separated and directed to the pickup tubes by prisms and color filters. Since prism blocks soak up less light than dichroic mirrors, they are used in high-quality cameras (see 2.8 and Color Plate V).

The Striped Filter The third color separation device is a **striped filter** that makes up the front surface of the pickup tube of a single-gun (tube) camera. The incoming light is dissected into specific colors (usually the light primaries red, green, and blue) and translated into the video signal (see Color Plate VI).

Chrominance and Luminance Channels

Since the three channels process the primary light colors, red, green, and blue, they are called **chrominance channels** (from the Greek *chroma* = color). But as you may know from painting or color printing, the colors alone are usually not sufficient to give the picture the necessary crispness and depth. Besides the colors, a good picture needs to show variations in brightness (from white to various shades of gray to black—see the section on the grayscale in Chapter 14). Television pictures are no exception. We perceive monochrome television pictures by distinguishing among brightness variations. Color pictures get these necessary brightness variations through a separate signal, called the **luminance channel** (from the Latin *lumen* = light). Some of the first color cameras contained a separate pickup tube for the luminance channel. In the present cameras the luminance signal is usually derived from the green channel, because the green signal is strong enough to serve two purposes at once. Sometimes, all three chrominance signals are matrixed (elec-

2.8 Prism Block The prism block separates the incoming light into the primary light colors (red, green, and blue) and directs the colored light to the pickup tubes. See Color Plate V for more information.

2.9 Television Pickup Tubes (from top to bottom): $4\frac{1}{2}$-inch Image Orthicon; 3-inch Image Orthicon; 25mm Plumbicon; 1-inch vidicon; $\frac{2}{3}$-inch vidicon.

tronically combined) into a monochrome luminance signal (see Color Plate I).

IMAGING DEVICES

In a color camera the principal electronic component that converts light into electricity is called the *imaging device*. There are two major types: the camera pickup tube, and the charge-coupled device (CCD), or as it is commonly called, the chip. At the present state of development, most cameras use the various types of pickup tubes as an imaging device.

Types and Formats of Pickup Tubes

The **Image Orthicon**, or **I-O**, tube was the standard camera **pickup tube** in high-quality monochrome cameras and the first generation of color cameras. But because of its large size and electronic fickleness it was soon replaced by the smaller and more stable vidicon tube and its vastly improved descendants.

Today all pickup tubes are improved models of the original *vidicon tube*. The two most commonly

used tubes are the various versions of the *Plumbicon*™ and the *Saticon*™.* The *Diode Gun* pickup tube is an improved Plumbicon tube. You may hear of many more "cons," which all try to minimize the negative aspects of the camera pickup tube and maximize the positive ones in order to produce optimal pictures in a great variety of production conditions.

Camera pickup tubes come in four "formats," which actually refer to the diameter of the front surface of the tube. Thus, we have 30mm (1.2-inch) tubes, 25mm (1-inch) tubes, $\frac{2}{3}$-inch (18mm) tubes, and $\frac{1}{2}$-inch (13mm) tubes. The 18mm and 13mm tubes are almost always referred to as the $\frac{2}{3}$-inch and $\frac{1}{2}$-inch tubes (see 2.9).

The large studio cameras usually have 30mm or 25mm tubes. Most ENG/EFP cameras that use a pickup tube as imaging device use the small $\frac{2}{3}$-inch format. Some ENG cameras, especially the camera-VTR combinations (see 2.20), use $\frac{1}{2}$-inch tubes.

Why the various formats? All other things being equal, the larger format tubes (tubes with a larger front surface) produce higher quality pictures than the $\frac{2}{3}$-inch tubes. You may want to compare the various pickup tube formats to the size of a film negative. A 35mm film generally produces a sharper

*Plumbicon is a registered trademark of N. V. Philips.
Saticon is a registered trademark of Hitachi Denshi, Ltd.

picture than a 16mm film, which again is superior in quality to a super-8mm film. However, constant efforts are being made to manufacture **small-format** tubes that produce high-quality pictures.

The Charge-Coupled Device

The **charge-coupled device** (CCD) is radically different from the camera pickup tube. Whereas the pickup tube utilizes an electron beam that scans a light-sensitive photoconductive target to produce the video signal, the CCD has a great number of image-sensing elements that transfer an optical image into many spots carrying an electric charge. These charges are temporarily stored and then translated line by line into a video signal (voltage).

The major advantage of the CCD over the tube is the former's small size. Television cameras using the CCD as an image device are considerably smaller than even the smallest ENG cameras using a pickup tube. So far, the major disadvantage of the CCD camera is that it does not produce the high-quality pictures of cameras that use pickup tubes as an imaging device (see 2.10).

2.10   Charge-Coupled Device This charge-coupled device performs the same basic functions as the camera pickup tube.

ELECTRONIC CHARACTERISTICS

The *electronic characteristics* of a camera depend primarily on the performance of the imaging device used. However, the camera incorporates certain electronic equipment and controls that either boost the positive or minimize the negative aspects of the imaging device. Because the electronic characteristics of the camera influence many other production aspects, such as lighting, graphics, and what people should and should not wear, we will take a brief look at (1) color response, (2) resolution, (3) operating light level, and (4) contrast.

Color Response

Ideally the camera should respond to all colors alike. However, this is not the case. The Plumbicon tube, for example, has had a continuous battle with the color red. Red produces not only a weak video signal but also a fuzzier image than other colors.

Improved Plumbicon tubes, and especially the Saticon, are designed to treat all colors as equally as possible. In an inexpensive color camera you can use the same type of vidicon tube for all three chrominance channels. This is why the color response in less sophisticated cameras is not "true"—that is, certain colors do not reproduce exactly like the original color in the scene. High-quality color cameras not only use a special tube for each chrominance channel, but have special color-correction filters and electronic circuits as well.

Resolution

The camera pickup tube is the principal element in the camera that determines the crispness of the picture. Other elements that influence the **resolution** of a picture are the lens, the quality of the internal optical system, and, of course, the television set on which you see the picture reproduced. The power of resolution in a pickup tube is very much like printing. For instance, take a magnifying glass and look at a photo that is reproduced in a newspaper. Then look at one in a slick magazine. You will notice that the newspaper picture consists of rather coarse dots (see 2.11), whereas the individual dots are hardly discernible in the magazine picture (see 2.12). The newspaper picture has a lower resolution than the magazine picture.

COLOR PLATE I

Properties of Color

chroma or chrominance

hue (actual color)

saturation (color strength)

luminance

brightness (light reflectance— how light or dark a color shows up on the gray scale)

COLOR PLATE II

Brightness Attribute of Color Since the black-and-white camera responds primarily to the brightness attribute in color (and not to hue and saturation), the black-and-white camera is color blind. It cannot detect differences in hue when the brightness remains the same.

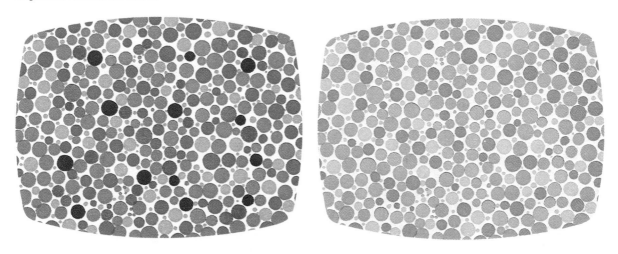

Although the hue is sufficiently different for this letter to show up on color television, it is barely readable on a black-and-white monitor. The brightness contrast is insufficient for good monochrome reproduction.

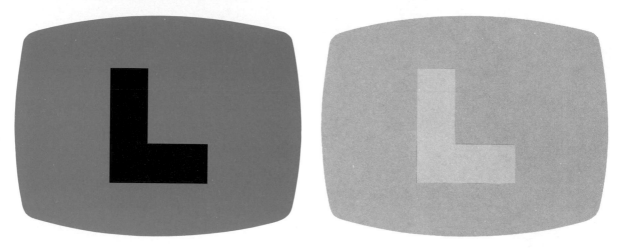

The lettering on this card has enough hue and brightness contrast to show up equally well on a color and black-and-white television receiver.

COLOR PLATE III

Additive Color Mixing   When mixing colored light, the additive primaries are red, green, and blue. All other colors can be achieved by mixing certain quantities of red, green, and blue light. For example, the additive mixture of red and green light produces yellow.

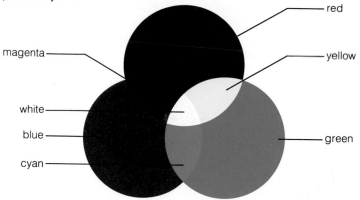

COLOR PLATE IV

Dichroic Mirror System   White light enters the camera through the lens and is split by dichroic mirrors into red, green, and blue light. These three light beams are directed through regular mirrors and relay lenses into three camera pickup tubes: one each for the red, green, and blue light. Special filters correct minor color distortions before the light beams enter the tubes.

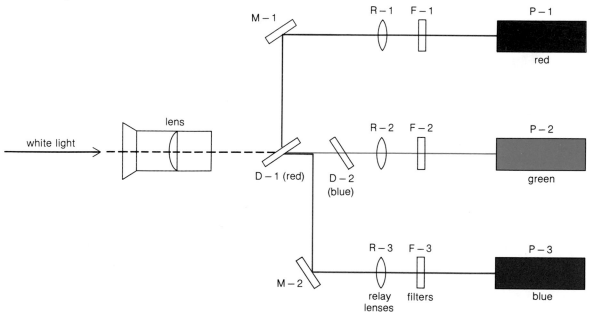

COLOR PLATE V

The Prism Block Most color cameras use a beam-split prism block instead of dichroic mirrors for their internal optical system. The incoming white light is split and relayed into the three pickup tubes through dichroic layers and color filters.

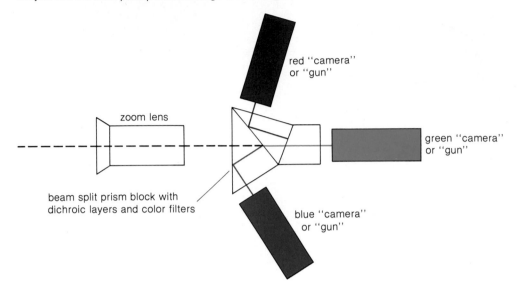

red "camera" or "gun"

zoom lens

green "camera" or "gun"

beam split prism block with dichroic layers and color filters

blue "camera" or "gun"

COLOR PLATE VI

Striped Filter The striped filter, located at the front surface of the camera pickup tube, divides the incoming light into the primary light colors (red, green, blue). Each of these colors is then treated as a separate video signal.

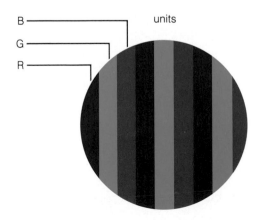

B

G

R

units

2.11 Low-Resolution Picture This picture is made up of relatively few dots. It has, therefore, a low resolution.

2.12 High-Resolution Picture This picture uses many more dots than 2.11. Because there is a higher resolution, there is sharper picture detail.

As pointed out earlier, manufacturers are trying to make a small camera pickup tube that produces a high-resolution image. For the present, however, the large-format tubes still have a better resolution than the $\frac{1}{2}$-inch and $\frac{2}{3}$-inch tubes and are, therefore, preferred for the high-quality studio cameras. So far, the CCDs have a considerably lower resolution than the quality camera pickup tubes.

The lower the resolution of the camera, the less fine picture detail it can show. Special electronic devices, called *image enhancers,* are generally used to sharpen the picture detail as delivered by the camera. However, although this device can *enhance* the image as delivered by the camera, it cannot invent detail the camera did not see in the first place. You should, therefore, be conscious of the limited resolution of the television picture, especially when dealing with television graphics and similar areas of production where fine picture detail predominates.

Operating Light Level

Because it is the job of the camera pickup tube to convert light into electricity, the camera needs some light to produce a video signal and requires a specific amount of light to produce an optimal image. Most color cameras need an **operating light level** from 100 to 250 foot-candles of illumination. You

will hear and read that certain cameras can produce pictures with "full video" (which means that the video signal has a certain prescribed intensity) with as little as 3 foot-candles of illumination. There are certain electronic devices that compensate for the lack of illumination, such as the *gain control,* which boosts the brightness of the picture, and the *bias light,* a small light that illuminates evenly the front surface of the camera pickup tube, providing a weak video signal even if no light comes through the lens. Neither of these devices can entirely prevent the various negative effects of minimal levels of illumination, such as video noise, lag, and color distortion.

Video Noise Under low light levels, even the best of cameras cannot avoid "noisy" pictures. A "noisy" picture has a great amount of **snow**, white vibrating spots in the picture that occur when the video signal as produced by the pickup tube is not strong enough to override the electronic interference that the system usually and unfortunately generates. Video **noise** works very much like audio noise. Even the best high-fidelity system has some inherent electronic noise. You can hear the speakers hiss a little as soon as you turn on the amplifier. Or, when the music is very low (which is equivalent to a weak audio signal), you may become aware of the rumble of the turntable. As soon as the music gets louder again (equivalent to a stronger audio signal), you are no longer aware of the noise. The relation of the strength of the picture signal to the accompanying interference, the noise, is generally expressed in a **signal-to-noise ratio**. A high signal-to-noise ratio is desirable. It means that the signal is high (strong) relative to the noise under normal operating conditions.

Lag and Comet-Tailing **Lag** is a following image that occurs under low lighting conditions, especially when a bright object moves against a dark background, or when the camera moves past some bright objects against a dark background. Lag occurs quite frequently during the televising of a concert. For example, when watching a concert on television, you may notice that the conductor's white cuffs and baton cause large colored streaks against the dark background of the unlit house. The same effect occurs when, during the televising of a football game, the players who run from a brightly lighted area of the field to a shadow area suddenly seem to emit streaks of red flames.

Comet-tailing is similar to lag, except that it occurs when the camera pickup tube is unable to process "video hits," extremely bright highlights that are reflected off highly polished surfaces. You may have observed the red flames that seem to trail shiny trumpets whenever they are moved in a brightly illuminated area. This effect is called comet-tailing because the red flames resemble the fiery tail of a comet.

Although such effects may, on occasion, be considered a welcome intensification of the televised event, they nevertheless represent bad video. The bias light, the diode-gun pickup tube, and special electronic circuits, called comet-tail compression, are all designed to minimize lag and comet-tailing.

Contrast

The **contrast** range of the camera pickup tube is limited to a 30:1 ratio. This means that the brightest spot in the picture can only be thirty times brighter than the darkest spot. If the scene exceeds this limit, special automated circuits in the camera (or the video operator) have to adjust the picture so that it does fall within the contrast tolerances of the pickup tube. This is usually done by reducing, or "pulling down," the brightest areas of the scene. Unfortunately, this pulling down of the whites renders the dark areas uniformly black. This is why you do not see much detail in the shadows of a high-contrast scene. Some high-quality cameras permit the reducing of the white level without affecting too much the subtle differentiations in the dark areas. This process is called *image compression*.

In the studio you should try to keep the scenery, clothing, and lighting within the 30:1 ratio. Some video engineers still prefer and work with a 20:1 ratio, which used to be the standard for monochrome television. This does not mean, however, that you must keep all colors of medium brightness, or that you should not build contrast into your lighting. You can, for example, use rather dark colors in one set area and rather bright ones in another. In fact, video operators like to have something white and something black in the set so that they can set the appropriate video levels. But try to avoid having the extremely bright and the dark color right next to each other. For example, it is very difficult for the camera to reproduce your true skin color if you wear a highly reflecting, starched white shirt or blouse and a light-absorbing, black jacket. If the camera adjusts for the white shirt by clipping the white level (bringing down the whites to acceptable limits), your face will go dark. If the camera tries to bring up the black level (making the black areas in the picture light enough to distinguish shadow detail), your face will wash out.

A few items that sparkle will not upset the 30:1 contrast ratio, however, especially when using high-quality color cameras. For example, a few rhinestones in a dress make the picture alive and give it sparkle.

When you are shooting outdoors in sunny weather, the contrast of the scene will certainly exceed the 30:1 ratio. There is little you can do, except adjust your camera to the brightest areas in the scene and use reflectors to lighten dense shadows (see Chapter 7). You will then have to use the **neutral density filters** (see 2.13). They act like sunglasses of varying density, reducing the amount of light that falls on the pickup tubes without distorting the actual colors of the scene. But even the darkest of the neutral density filters will not prevent major damage to the camera pickup tube if you point the camera into the sun.

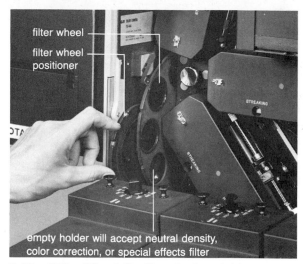

filter wheel

filter wheel positioner

empty holder will accept neutral density, color correction, or special effects filter

2.13 Filter Wheel The filter wheel can hold a variety of neutral density or color correction filters. In some cameras, the filter wheel can be turned by remote control.

TYPES OF CAMERAS

There is a bewildering array of cameras on the market. Their names and the way they are classified are equally confusing. The simplest way to keep them straight is to classify them, first, according to their basic electronic system and then according to their function—what they are supposed to do and how they are principally used.

Described by their basic electronic systems, cameras may be (1) digitally controlled cameras, and (2) conventional, nondigital cameras.

Classified according to their function, cameras may be (1) studio cameras, (2) ENG/EFP cameras, and (3) convertible cameras.

Digitally Controlled Cameras

Digitally controlled cameras make extensive use of various digital processing systems, which automate some of the electronic operations of the camera and make most of the electronic functions faster and more reliable than with conventional electronics. Most of the newer, high-quality cameras have **microprocessors** to help them get set up for optimal performance and maintain a high-level performance under a great variety of production conditions.

Some of the advantages of a digitally controlled camera are as follows:

1. The basic setup of the camera is very fast. Whereas a conventional camera needs at least a half hour for such setup procedures, the digitally controlled camera can accomplish the same thing within a few minutes.

2. With the digital setup terminal, several cameras can be set up simultaneously.

3. The camera continuously checks and corrects itself if it should drift from its original setup values.

4. The camera can remember setup values and go back to them if needed. For example, the camera can remember the standard lighting of your news set and go back to it at the push of a button, even if you have to use it between the morning news and the noon news for an outdoor production with totally different lighting conditions.

5. It generally uses a *triax* (*triaxial*) or *fiber optics* cable. These cables are much thinner and lighter than the multicore cables. Also, compared with conventional multicore cables, the camera can be almost twice the distance from the CCU.

However, digital cameras are quite complicated electronically and expensive to purchase and to maintain.

Nondigital Cameras

Most older, high-quality cameras and the less expensive modern cameras are nondigital. This does not necessarily mean they produce less satisfactory pictures; it does mean they need more attention by the video and camera operator before and during the production. The advantages of the conventional camera are that it is much less complex than the digitally controlled camera, cheaper, and, so far, easier to fix.

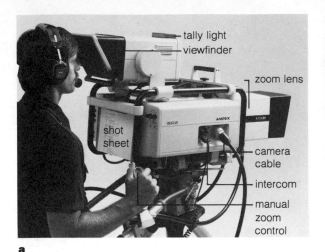

tally light
viewfinder
zoom lens
shot sheet
camera cable
intercom
manual zoom control

a

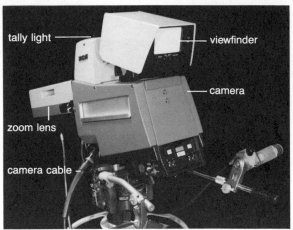

tally light
viewfinder
camera
zoom lens
camera cable

b

2.14   Studio Cameras: (a) Ampex BCC-21 Digi-cam Studio Camera, (b) RCA TK-47, (c) CEI Foton I Studio Camera High-quality studio cameras have three pickup tubes and microprocessor-controlled electronic systems. They also generally have large zoom lenses and viewfinders.

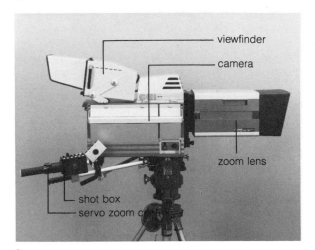

viewfinder
camera
zoom lens
shot box
servo zoom c

c

STUDIO CAMERAS

The name "**studio camera**" is somewhat misleading because the studio camera may also be used in the field during big remotes. However, the term is generally used to describe a high-quality camera that is so heavy that it cannot be maneuvered properly without the aid of a pedestal, or some other type of camera mount (see 2.14).

We will now briefly list some of the major operational features of the studio camera.

Operational Features

The major features of the studio camera are (1) imaging device, (2) viewfinder, (3) cable, (4) filter wheel, (5) intercom, and (6) general ruggedness of the camera.

Imaging Device   All studio cameras have three pickup tubes (usually 25mm or some still 30mm) and an internal optical system. Most cameras use the prism block as a beam splitter.

Viewfinder   The fairly large (5–7 inches) and high-resolution viewfinders are monochrome for all cameras. As a camera operator you are not able to see the pictures in color. This is somewhat unfortunate, especially if you are sensitive enough to use color as a compositional factor. The viewfinders can be tilted and rotated so that you can maintain a full view of the viewfinder screen, no matter how much you might have to raise or lower the camera, or pan it from a tight spot that prevents you from staying behind the camera. Inside the viewfinder hood most viewfinders contain a small **tally light** that indicates when the camera is "hot" (switched on the air). The

a   b

2.15   Star Filter Effect The star filter changes bright light sources (a) into four- or six-point starlike light beams (b).

pictures taken by another camera can be switched into the viewfinder of your camera so that you can match the shot of the other camera, or purposely avoid duplication of shots.

Cable   Most studio cameras still operate with the standard *multicore* cable, which can be used for up to 2,000 feet (about 600 meters). This is more than enough for all studio work and ample cable length for most standard remote telecasts. However, there are circumstances in which you need much longer cable runs (up to 1 mile or even longer) between the camera and the camera controls, as for example in covering ski racing or golf. Then the multicore cables have to be replaced with triax (triaxial) or fiber optics cables. With triax cable (one central wire surrounded by two concentric shields) or fiber optics cables (made up of a series of flexible glass fibers), the signals can be *multiplexed*, which means that several signals can be put through the same wire simultaneously. Most cameras need special adaptors before triax or fiber optics cables can be used.

Filter Wheel   The filter wheel is located inside the camera between the zoom lens and the beam splitter (see 2.13). The filter wheel usually holds two *neutral density* filters (ND-1 and ND-2), several *color correction* filters, and *special effects* filters.

The *neutral density* filters reduce the light before it is transmitted to the camera pickup tubes, without affecting the colors.

The *color correction* filters reduce the bluishness of fluorescent or outdoor light to color-correct the light for the established color standard of the camera pickup tube (see Chapter 6).

There are several *special effects* filters that can be attached to the lens. The most popular one is the four- or six-point star filter, which changes bright highlights into starlike configurations (see 2.15). There are also various diffusion filters, which create a fog effect (see 2.16).

Most filter wheels have a "cap" position that prevents any light from the lens from reaching the camera pickup tubes.

Intercom   All studio cameras have at least two channels for intercommunication—one for the production crew and the other for the engineers. Some cameras even have a third channel that carries program sound.

Ruggedness   In general, the intricate electronic components and the internal optical system make even large studio cameras quite vulnerable to physical shock. You must be especially careful with cameras that have a dichroic mirror system. All cameras

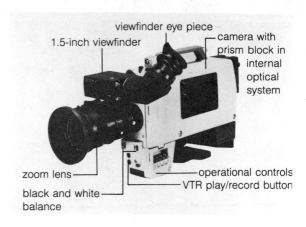

viewfinder eye piece
1.5-inch viewfinder
camera with prism block in internal optical system

zoom lens
black and white balance
operational controls
VTR play/record button

a

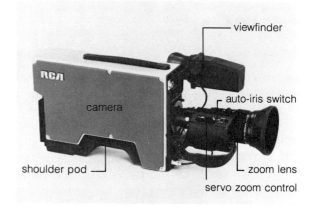

viewfinder
RCA
camera
auto-iris switch
shoulder pod
zoom lens
servo zoom control

b

2.16 **Diffusion Effect** The diffusion filter can create a fog effect for the entire picture, or parts of the scene (depending on the particular diffusion filter used).

2.17 **Three-Tube ENG Cameras: (a) Sony BVP 330, (b) RCA TK-86** The ENG/EFP camera is a self-contained unit that can be carried and operated by one person. It is usually battery powered.

are relatively sensitive to extreme temperatures and moisture. Try not to expose your camera to extreme heat or cold, and put a plastic sheet or an umbrella over it when working in rain.

ENG/EFP CAMERAS

The **ENG/EFP cameras** are *portable*, which means that they are usually carried by the camera operator rather than put on a camera mount. They are largely *self-contained* and can be operated without additional camera control equipment. In news gathering

the ENG camera has replaced the film camera. When using an ENG camera, you can either record your scene on the portable VTR (videotape recorder), or send your signals via microwave link to the station or directly to the transmitter for a live telecast. The VTR can be played back immediately; unlike film, it does not need to go to the lab for processing. In EFP situations the portable camera can be easily carried into locations that could accommodate larger cameras only with great difficulty.

The ENG/EFP cameras are *automated* as much as possible. When running after a news story, you do not have time to perform intricate camera setup

carrying handle

viewfinder

lens

camera

manual zoom control

focus ring

servo zoom
control

2.18 Single-Tube Camera (Sony BVP-110) The single-tube ENG/EFP camera is even smaller and lighter than the three-tube ENG/EFP camera. However, it produces lower quality pictures than the three-tube camera.

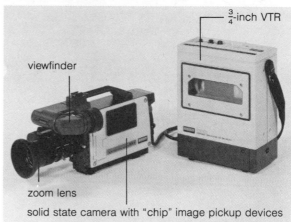

$\frac{3}{4}$-inch VTR

viewfinder

zoom lens

solid state camera with "chip" image pickup devices

2.19 Solid-State CCD Camera (Hitachi Mag Camera) The solid-state cameras use a change-coupled device (CCD) instead of the camera pickup tube. Because the CCD is much smaller than the pickup tube, the camera is even smaller than the single-tube ENG/EFP camera.

maneuvers. Nor do you have time to do much camera adjustment while shooting. Fortunately, most ENG/EFP cameras are fully operational within just a few seconds after switching them on, and you can make them adjust to extreme production situations just as quickly and easily.

Portable Camera Types

You will probably come across many types of portable cameras. The big difference among the various models of portable cameras is picture quality and degree of automation. There are currently four types of ENG cameras: (1) the three-tube (or three-gun) camera, (2) the single-tube (or one-gun) camera, (3) the CCD (charge-coupled device) camera, and (4) the camera-recorder unit. The two-tube camera is now largely obsolete.

The Three-Tube Camera The high-quality three-tube portable camera works on the same principle as the three-tube studio camera, except that it contains the smaller format $\frac{2}{3}$-inch or $\frac{1}{2}$-inch camera pickup tubes. Its internal optical system can either be the dichroic mirrors or the prism block. The latter is preferred, because it makes the camera more sensitive to light and less sensitive to physical shock (see 2.17).

The Single-Tube Camera The single-tube camera contains a single $\frac{1}{2}$-inch, $\frac{2}{3}$-inch, or 25mm (1-inch) tube with a striped filter as color separation device. It is usually smaller and lighter than the three-tube camera, but its pictures are of lesser quality (see 2.18).

The CCD Camera The smallest camera is the one using a CCD as the imaging device. Although such "solid-state" cameras have many advantages over the conventional cameras with pickup tubes as imaging device (small size, long life, no lag), the relatively low resolution of the chip has so far prevented the CCD camera from replacing the heavier and more sensitive pickup tube camera (see 2.19).

The Camera-Recorder Unit, or Combo Cameras The camera-recorder unit is a hybrid of an ENG camera and a minirecorder that attaches directly onto the back of the camera. This unit, which is just slightly heavier than a three-tube ENG camera, rests on your shoulder. There is no need for an additional VTR dangling from your shoulder or for cables to connect your camera with the VTR. This camera-recorder combination comes close to the traditional news film camera in weight and operation. They generally

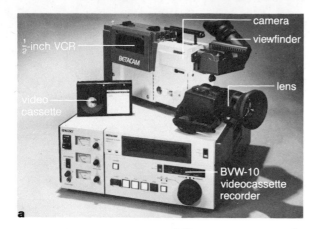

2.20   Camera-VTR Units: (a) Sony Betacam, (b,c) RCA Hawkeye The combo camera combines a camera and small VTR in one unit. The front half (the camera) and the back half (the VTR) can be used independently.

use a single $\frac{1}{2}$-inch Plumbicon or Saticon tube and have all the automated features of a three-tube ENG camera. The camera and the VTR can be separated and used independently. You can, for example, use another VTR to record off the "front half" of the unit. The "back half" of the unit, the VTR, uses $\frac{1}{2}$-inch tape cassettes, which are good for a 20-minute recording. With the use of advanced, solid-state electronics, this camera-VTR unit will become the standard ENG device (see 2.20).

The Two-Tube Camera   Very few two-tube cameras are in operation. The two-tube camera had one $\frac{2}{3}$-inch striped filter tube for a chrominance channel, and a second $\frac{2}{3}$-inch tube for a luminance channel. In effect, you had to have all the trimmings of a three-tube camera, but without the benefit of the three-tube picture quality. Its greater size and weight, compared to the simpler one-tube camera, added to its lack of popularity.

Let us now take a brief look at the operational features of the ENG/EFP camera, and the principal operational modes.

Operational Features

Most broadcast-type portable cameras have similar operational features, regardless of manufacturer or model (see 2.17). Like any other camera, the portable camera has basically three parts: (1) the zoom lens, (2) the camera itself with the imaging device (usually a camera pickup tube or tubes), and (3) the viewfinder. Unlike other cameras, the portable cameras have a special holder for the battery (their own power supply) and a clip for an external microphone.

Zoom Lens   The zoom lenses for ENG cameras are much smaller and lighter than their studio camera counterparts, and their zoom range is different from that of the studio lenses (see Chapter 3).

Viewfinder   The viewfinder is relatively small (about $1\frac{1}{2}$-inches) but produces a high-resolution image. It is shielded from outside reflections by a flexible rubber eyepiece that you can adjust to your eye.

The viewfinder contains a number of control lights or displays that indicate the status of certain camera or production functions. Most viewfinders display automatically some or all of this information: (1) VTR record, (2) end-of-tape warning, and (3) battery status (a warning light will go on or flash when the battery is low). When you are connected with a control unit by cable, some cameras have a special intercom signal light in the viewfinder that lights up when you are to communicate back to the base station.

Furthermore, most viewfinders display on command (1) color bars, (2) a zebra-striped pattern that indicates the correct exposure for an optimal video level, (3) a white balance light or horizontal line whenever the camera has adjusted itself to the color temperature of the prevailing light, (4) black balance (establishing TV black relative to the white), and (5) centering (**registration**, making the images of the three tubes overlap perfectly) (see 2.33). Most cameras permit the viewfinder to be used as a playback monitor from the VTR.

The advantage of having all these controls in the viewfinder is that you do not need any additional setup equipment, and once set up, you do not have to lose contact with the scene as displayed in the viewfinder when checking vital operational functions (see Section Two). Most professional-type ENG cameras have provision for a larger viewfinder if you need to use the camera in ambitious field productions or as a supplementary studio camera.

Cable   If you use the VTR's battery pack for a power source, you can run a 30-foot (10-meter) cable between the camera and the VTR. This is especially advantageous if you have a second person on the team who operates the VTR and holds the microphone. If you operate as the traditional "one-person band," which means you carry and operate the VTR as well as the camera, you obviously need much less cable from the camera to the VTR. If you hook up your camera to a camera control unit (see 2.24), you can use cable runs as long as 2,000 feet (approximately 600 meters). Some high-quality ENG/EFP cameras can operate with 2,000 feet of cable without a CCU.

Power Supply   All portable cameras run on 12 volts **DC** (direct current). This power can be supplied by a variety of sources: (1) a battery, which can be clipped on the camera; (2) the VTR battery, which can also power the camera at the same time; (3) a 30-volt battery belt (with adaptor); (4) a car battery (with adaptor); and (5) household **AC** current (with adaptor).

The *camera battery* can supply power for the camera to run up to two hours continuously, before having to be recharged. Some of the older types of battery will develop a "memory" if you recharge them before they have completely run down. This means that the battery will think that it is completely recharged, and its faulty memory will prematurely cut off the charging operation. To keep the battery from developing such a memory, run the battery until it has lost almost all of its power before recharging it, or discharge it purposely from time to time.

If you run the camera off the *VTR battery*, you will have less weight to carry but only enough power to run the camera for about 40 continuous minutes. A good rule of thumb is to replace your battery every time you have gone through two (20-minute) videotape cassettes. Some ENG camera operators replace it after every one and a half cassettes.

Make sure that you have the appropriate *adaptors* when running the camera off a 30-volt battery belt, the car battery, or household AC current (120 volts). Use the car battery only in emergencies. Car batteries are hazardous to the operator as well as to the camera.

Filter Wheel   Like the studio cameras, the portable cameras have various ND (neutral density) and color correction filters mounted on a filter wheel. In some models you can select the appropriate filter by turning a clearly marked thumb wheel; in others they can be put in place automatically. Most high-quality cameras have a "**cap**" position on the wheel. Although the primary function of the cap is to protect the camera pickup tube, it can also be used for the automatic adjustment of the black level, or when the camera is off or in a standby mode. The color correction filters are used to reduce the very high color

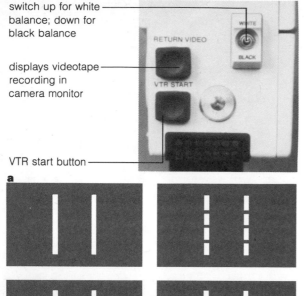

switch up for white balance; down for black balance

displays videotape recording in camera monitor

VTR start button

a

1. Select auto-white balance and display parallel vertical white lines. Televise reference white object between lines. Press auto-color balance button.
2. If white balance is achieved, vertical lines become broken.
3. If left-hand line only becomes broken, add color filter.
4. If right-hand line only becomes broken, remove color filter.

b

2.21   VTR Start and White and Black Balance: (a) Sony BVP-300A, (b) Philips LDK 14-S On most quality ENG/EFP cameras the white and black balance is rather easily accomplished by activating automatic circuits.

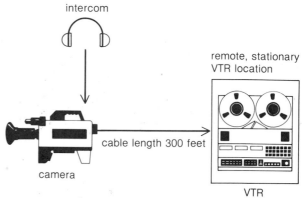

(cable length is 15 feet)

camera

VTR (carried by camera operator or second crew member)

2.22   Portable VTR Mode When using the ENG/EFP camera-VTR unit in the portable VTR mode, the operator (and, sometimes, a second crew member) carries the camera and the VTR unit near one another.

intercom

remote, stationary VTR location

cable length 300 feet

camera

VTR

2.23   Stationary Mode In the stationary VTR mode the VTR unit is not carried with the camera but put in a stationary position (production van, or protected spot on location). VTR operator and camera operator can be connected through headphone intercom.

temperature levels of sunlight and blue sky (extreme bluishness of colors), because the ENG camera is calibrated for indoor color temperature (3,200° K). (See Chapter 6.) Some filter wheels have color correction and ND filters combined.

VTR Start   One of the most important controls on your ENG camera is the VTR start button. After all, it is of little use to your news program if you see an event in your camera viewfinder but fail to record it so that it can be communicated to the audience during broadcast time. The VTR start button is usually right next to the zoom controls, or right below the lens. Thus, you do not need to take your eye off the viewfinder to find the right button (see 2.21a).

White and Black Balance   In the studio the adjustment of the colors to the prevailing color temperature (relative reddishness or bluishness of the light) and to the amount of light and contrast is generally done by the video operator. When you are in the field by yourself, however, you have to do your own adjustments. Fortunately, the camera does all these jobs for you automatically. All you have to do is activate the white and black balance switch before using your camera to cover a scene (see Chapter 5).

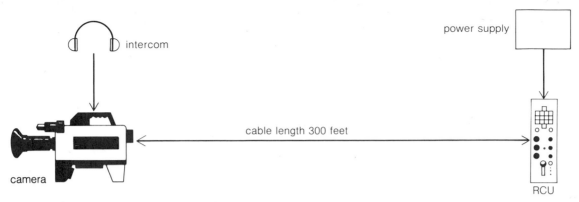

intercom

power supply

cable length 300 feet

camera

RCU

2.24   RCU Mode When used in the RCU mode, the ENG/EFP camera is controlled through a stationary camera control unit and powered by a separate power supply. There is a headset intercom connection between the camera operator and the RCU station. Through the RCU (remote control unit) the camera system permits greater flexibility than with the single camera unit for moving from light to dark areas.

A display or a light in the viewfinder tells you when the camera has adjusted itself to the lighting conditions of the particular scene (see 2.21).

Somewhere on the side of the camera you will find several more switches and connectors that help you to operate the camera at peak efficiency. We will discuss these controls in detail in Section Two.

Operational Modes

All quality ENG/EFP cameras can be used in four different operational modes: (1) portable VTR mode, (2) stationary VTR mode, (3) RCU (remote control unit) mode, and (4) EFP/studio mode.

Portable VTR Mode In the portable VTR mode the ENG camera is connected by a short cable (up to about 15 feet, or 5 meters) to the portable VTR, which you (the camera operator) or a second person carries. In the portable VTR mode the camera is usually powered by the VTR battery, battery belt, or battery pack attached to the camera (see 2.22).

The Stationary VTR (EFP) Mode If you intend to shoot longer scenes from a relatively fixed position, you can use a larger VTR that is located in a stationary position (usually in a station wagon when outdoors, and a specific room when indoors). Some ENG cameras accept cable lengths up to approxi-

mately 100 feet (30 meters) without special adaptors. Cable adaptors are needed for longer cable runs up to 300 feet (100 meters).

In the stationary VTR position headsets can be used for communication between the camera operator and the VTR operator who works the VTR and/or transmission equipment in the stationary outdoor (mobile unit) or indoor (room or hallway) location (see 2.23).

RCU Mode In the remote control unit (RCU) mode the ENG camera works, as in the stationary VTR mode, within a relatively restricted area and relays its pictures back to a stationary VTR. You use this mode if picture quality is paramount, and when scenes change fairly drastically as to lighting and color. For example, suppose you are using a single camera to shoot a commercial during which children first watch television in a rather dark room and then run outside across a sun-filled meadow into a fairly dark, wooded area with streaks of sunlight coming through the trees. You would need to have a skilled video operator control the video via the RCU. The power comes from the RCU, which is plugged into a normal household AC outlet, generator, or batteries. The usual cable runs for this mode go up to 300 feet (approximately 100 meters). Camera operator, video operator, and VTR operator are interconnected by headsets (see 2.24).

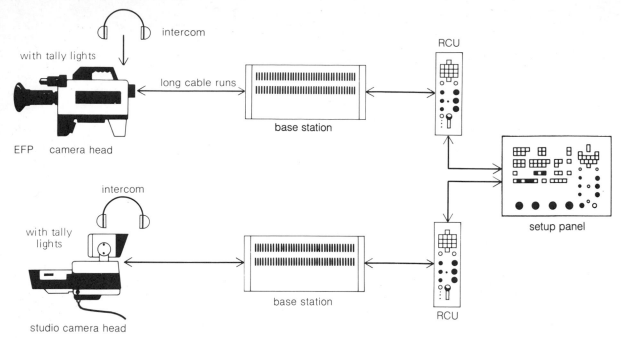

2.25 EFP/Studio Mode In the EFP/studio mode the ENG/EFP camera is used like another studio camera in a multicamera setup.

EFP/Studio Mode In the full-fledged EFP/studio mode the ENG camera is used like a studio camera during a remote. The ENG camera is used as a camera head in a regular camera chain, consisting of base station and RCU. Through the base station and RCU, full camera control is available. If the camera accepts or can be adapted for triax cable, for example, cable runs of one mile or longer can be achieved, just as with studio cameras. The base station and the camera are powered by the base station's power supply (usually through a field generator or AC power). Full intercom with program sound is available. This mode is generally used for larger EFP operations in which multiple cameras and a switcher are used (see 2.25).

CONVERTIBLE CAMERAS

Studio cameras that can be stripped down so that they become portable and ENG/EFP cameras that accept certain accessories are called **convertible cameras.** The items that make the camera convertible are usually (1) the lens, (2) the viewfinder, (3) the camera frame and mount, and (4) certain camera controls.

When changing the camera from studio to portable field configurations, you usually replace the large studio zoom lens with a smaller lens and change the large viewfinder to a small, eyepiece type. The whole camera head lifts out of the frame, and you can attach a shoulder brace so that the camera can be carried. Certain controls, such as zoom controls and VTR start, either come with the smaller lens or are added in a special control handle (see 2.26). Also, some cameras require some fairly simple technical changes that make the usually remotely controlled camera self-contained.

The convertible studio camera is generally used in its field configuration when you need especially great camera mobility combined with the quality of the other studio cameras. This may be either in the field when first-rate pictures are necessary (such as televising a concert on location) or in the studio when high camera mobility is desired.

Most high-quality ENG/EFP cameras accept a

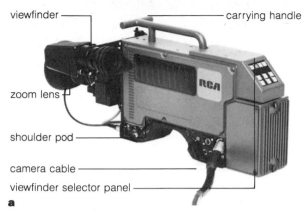

viewfinder ──────   carrying handle

zoom lens ──────

shoulder pod ──────

camera cable ──────

viewfinder selector panel ──────

a

2.26 Convertible Studio Camera (RCA TKP-47)
The convertible camera (b) is a high-quality studio camera
that can be "stripped" down to the field configuration (a). It
is often used as the most mobile camera in a multicamera
studio setup.

────── 5-inch viewfinder

b

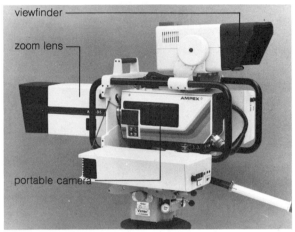

viewfinder ──────

zoom lens ──────

portable camera ──────

**2.27 Convertible ENG Camera (Ampex BCC
20/21)** Some of the ENG/EFP cameras accept a larger
viewfinder and zoom lens for studio use.

larger viewfinder and bigger lens for studio use.
You can also assign certain camera controls to remote
control (for example, white and black level controls,
as well as color controls). Some convertible ENG
cameras come with a special frame that holds the
camera and supports the larger lens and viewfinder.
The whole new camera assembly is then mounted
on a tripod. When using such a configuration, make
sure that the quality of the convertible camera
matches that of the other cameras used and that the
colors are properly matched among all cameras (see
2.27).

MAIN POINTS

1. The television camera is one of the most important production elements. Other production equipment and techniques are often influenced by what
the camera can and cannot do.

2. The major parts of the camera are (1) the lens
(sometimes called the external optical system because
it includes filters and other optical accessories),

(2) the camera itself with the major imaging device
(camera pickup tube or chip) and the internal optical system, and (3) the viewfinder.

3. All television cameras work on the same basic
principle: the conversion (transduction) of an optical image into electrical signals that are reconverted
by a television set into visible screen images.

4. The camera, as we know it, is only part of a
chain of electronic equipment necessary to produce
television pictures.

5. The standard camera chain (for nondigitally controlled studio cameras) consists of (1) the camera head (the actual camera), (2) the CCU (camera control unit), (3) the sync generator, and (4) the power supply. Digitally controlled cameras often have common setup panels (base stations) and remote control units (RCUs), which control the individual cameras while in operation. ENG/EFP cameras contain the whole chain in the camera head.

6. Few monochrome (black-and-white) cameras are still in use. Monochrome cameras have a single pickup tube for the conversion of an optical image into electronic signals.

7. The color camera needs an internal optical system to process color. This is done by splitting the entering light (white light) into specific light colors, usually the primary colors red, green, and blue.

8. The device that separates the entering white light into the primary colors is called the beam splitter. There are three types of beam splitters: (1) the dichroic mirror system, (2) the prism block, and (3) the striped filter.

9. Color cameras contain two channels: (1) the chrominance channel, which processes the primary light colors, and (2) the luminance channel, which processes the brightness variations.

10. The principal electronic component that converts the optical image as gathered by the lens into electricity (the video signal) is the imaging device. The two major imaging devices are (1) the camera pickup tube and (2) the charge-coupled device (CCD), usually called "chip."

11. The various types of pickup tubes are all based on the vidicon principle. The most common are the Plumbicon and the Saticon. The camera pickup tubes come in different formats: 30mm, 25mm, $\frac{2}{3}$-inch, and $\frac{1}{2}$-inch tubes.

12. The charge-coupled device (CCD) is a solid-state imaging device that allows for smaller cameras but produces lower quality pictures than the tube cameras.

13. The electronic characteristics of the camera are (1) color response (how faithfully a color is reproduced by the camera), (2) resolution (how much detail can be seen), (3) operating light level, (4) the problems of lag and comet tailing, and (5) contrast range (maximum of 30:1).

14. The types of cameras include (1) digitally controlled cameras, which use microprocessors (small computers) to aid and maintain setup values, and (2) nondigital (conventional) cameras, which need more attention by video operators before and during operation.

15. We have three camera types classified according to function: (1) studio cameras, (2) portable (ENG and EFP) cameras, including the camera-recorder unit, and (3) convertible cameras, which convert from studio cameras to ENG/EFP use, or from ENG/EFP cameras to studio cameras.

16. The ENG/EFP cameras can be used in four operational modes: (1) the portable VTR mode, whereby the self-contained camera is connected to a portable VTR; (2) the stationary VTR (EFP) mode, whereby the camera is connected to a high-quality stationary VTR; (3) the RCU mode, whereby the video quality is maintained through a remote control unit; and (4) the EFP/studio mode, whereby an EFP camera is integrated with high-quality studio cameras and used like a studio camera.

Although color television cameras are becoming increasingly sophisticated, they still rely on a number of fundamental principles about how light and color behave. Given the predominance of color in production today, it is important to understand these principles and learn how they apply to the latest cameras.

In this part of the chapter we will briefly discuss (1) the basic scanning process, (2) imaging devices, (3) properties of color, (4) the internal optical system and color separation, (5) ENG control features, and (6) high-definition television.

BASIC SCANNING PROCESS

The electron beam, which is emitted by the **electron gun**, scans the television screen (and the target area of the camera pickup tube) much as we read, from left to right and from top to bottom. Unlike a person reading, however, the beam skips every other line during its first scan, reading only the odd-numbered lines (see 2.28a). Then, the beam jumps back and scans all the even-numbered lines (see 2.28b). This procedure is called *interlaced scanning*.

The scanning of either the odd- or even-numbered lines constitutes a **field**. The scanning of two consecutive fields—that is, the one complete reading of both odd- and even-numbered lines—makes up a television **frame** (see 2.28c). The frame constitutes the smallest complete picture unit. A television frame in our system (U.S.) consists of 525 scanning lines ($262\frac{1}{2}$ odd-num-

bered and $262\frac{1}{2}$ even-numbered lines). The scanning process produces sixty fields, or *thirty frames, per second*.

HOW IMAGING DEVICES WORK

As pointed out in Section One, we generally use improved versions of the *vidicon tube* as a camera pickup device. Some cameras are experimenting with solid-state pickup devices such as the *charge-coupled device*.

Vidicon Tube Principle

We mentioned earlier in this chapter that the camera pickup tube converts light into electrical energy, the video signal. The image of a scene is gathered by the lens and focused on the front surface of the pickup tube. The photosensitive surface of the **target** conducts electricity when exposed to light. The different amounts of light striking the tube cause a pattern of electric charges to form on its target. An electron beam, produced by the electron gun in the back of the tube, scans the target from the back in a precise scanning pattern that is identical to the scanning pattern in a television receiver. As the electron beam scans the back of the target, electrons flow from it. This flow of electricity, which has a certain strength (voltage), constitutes the video signal (see 2.29).

The Charge-Coupled Device (CCD)

The charge-coupled device is a solid-state optical imaging device. The light-sensitive imaging area consists of a large number of individual silicon sensing devices, arranged much like many small tiles of a mosaic. In operation, the desired optical image is focused by the lens on the imaging area, where an image charge is created on each of the elements. These individual charges are called **pixels.** Each pixel can have a certain amount of luminance and chrominance. The charges are then "read" by a synchronized "clocking" signal applied in a line-by-line scanning sequence to each of the elements. The whole pattern is then temporarily stored in the storage area, which is similar in construction to the imaging area. From the storage area the information is then transferred, a line at a time, to an output register whose output signal is amplified into a workable video signal (see 2.30).

PROPERTIES OF COLOR

When you look at colors, you can easily distinguish the three basic color sensations, called *attributes*: (1) the **hue**, which is the color itself—red, green, blue, or yellow; (2) **saturation**, which describes the color's richness or strength; and (3) **brightness**, which indicates how dark or light a color appears on the monochrome television screen, or more technically, how much light the color reflects (see Color Plate I).

In a color camera the *chrominance channels* are dealing with hue and saturation. The *luminance channel* concerns itself with the brightness attribute. A monochrome camera responds basically to brightness only. It does not respond to hue and saturation. This is why a red and a green of the same brightness appear as the same gray on monochrome television, although they differ greatly in hue (see Color Plate II).

Ordinary white light, like sunlight or the light from a light bulb, can be separated into three basic, or primary colors: red, green, and blue. Obviously, when we mix the three primaries together again, we get white light. But we can also mix these three primary colored lights in various proportions, that is, various light intensities, and achieve almost all the colors we ordinarily perceive. For example, take three slide projectors and put a clear red slide (filter) in one, a clear green one in the second projector, and a clear blue one in the third projector. Then hook each of the slide projectors to a separate dimmer. When you have the dimmers up full (assuming equal light transmission by all three filters) and shine all three light beams together on the screen, you get white light, as we mentioned before. Full-strength red and full-strength green will give you yellow. But if you now dim the green projector a little, the yellow will turn orange. If you dim the red instead of the green projector, you will get a brownish color. The blue and red together will yield a reddish purple, called magenta.

This mixing process of colored light is called *additive color mixing*, and the three primary colors are called **additive primary colors**. When we mix paints of two colors together, however, they filter each other out and form a new color. They subtract each other's wavelength. This process is, therefore, called *subtractive*

Additive Primary Colors   Red, blue, and green. Ordinary white light (sunlight) can be separated into the three primary light colors. When these three colored lights are combined in various proportions, all colors can be produced.

Field   One-half a complete scanning cycle, two fields being necessary for one television picture frame. There are sixty fields per second, or thirty frames per second.

Frame   A complete scanning cycle, consisting of two fields. The frame represents a complete television picture. There are thirty frames per second.

High Definition Television (HDTV)
The use of special cameras and recording equipment for the production of high-quality pictures. The pictures have a higher resolution (show smaller detail more clearly) than the regular television pictures.

Pixel   Small silicon sensing devices arranged in a mosaiclike pattern for the light-sensitive imaging area of a CCD (charge-coupled device) holding an electric charge.

Target   Light-sensitive front surface of the camera pickup tube, which is scanned by an electron beam.

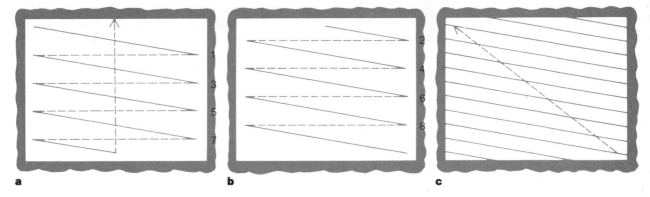

a   b   c

2.28   Television Scanning

(a) The electron beam first scans all odd-numbered lines, from left to right. When the beam jumps back to the left of the screen, it is so weak that it leaves no trace on the television screen (horizontal blanking).

When all odd-numbered lines have been scanned, this constitutes a field. Then the beam jumps back to the top of the screen (vertical blanking) to start scanning the even-numbered lines.

(b) When all even-numbered lines have been scanned, this constitutes a second field.

(c) The two fields (the scanning of all odd- and even-numbered lines) make up one complete television picture, called a frame.

At that point, the beam returns to the left-hand corner to start with another first field.

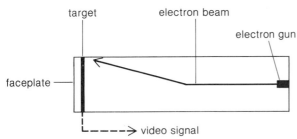

2.29   Vidicon Tube Principle In the vidicon tube, light striking the front surface of the tube causes a pattern of electric charges to form on its target. As an electron beam, generated by the electron gun in back of the tube, scans its target, electrons flow from the target. This flow of electrons, a voltage, is the video signal.

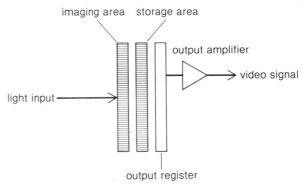

2.30   Charge-Coupled Device In a charge-coupled device (CCD) light strikes the light-sensitive imaging area. This imaging area consists of a large number of individual silicon sensing devices. When light strikes these individual spots, an image charge—a pixel—is created on each spot. The pattern, consisting of many pixels, is then stored in the storage area and transferred, line by line, to an output register. There the weak output signal is amplified into a workable video signal.

color mixing. The **subtractive primary colors** are magenta (a bluish red), cyan (a greenish blue), and yellow. Since it is light, not paint, that enters the camera, color television operates with the additive color-mixing process (see Color Plate III).

INTERNAL OPTICAL SYSTEM AND COLOR SEPARATION

As discussed in Section One, there are basically three different methods of color separation: (1) the dichroic mirror system, (2) the prism block, and (3) the striped filter. We will briefly diagram each of the three processes.

Dichroic Mirror System

The light gathered by the lens is separated by a series of dichroic (color-separating) mirrors into the three primaries of light (see Color Plate IV). The dichroic mirror D1 splits off the red color from the incoming white light, letting green and blue light pass. Dichroic mirror D2 splits off the blue color, letting the remaining green color pass. Regular high-quality mirrors (M1 and M2) reflect the separated colors into their respective pickup tubes.

The **relay lenses** (R1, R2, R3) help to transport the three separate colored light images to the pickup tubes. The lenses make sure that the images remain sharp and clear throughout their travel until they reach the pickup tubes.

The *filters* (F1, F2, F3) keep out all unwanted light that might interfere with the purity of each of the primary colors—red, green, and blue. The red, green, and blue images finally reach the surface of the pickup tubes, where they are transduced into video signals.

The Prism Block

The prism block separates the colors through special prisms that direct each of the primary colors into separate ports. Each of the prisms has a special dichroic layer and color correcting filters (see Color Plate V). Some prism blocks have built-in bias light.

The Striped Filter

The striped filter is either on the front surface of the camera pickup tube or integrated into the target assembly. There are several configurations of color-separating striped filters. Most filters have consecutive red-green-blue stripe units. However, some filters have cyan and white (clear) stripe combinations with diagonal overlays of yellow and white (clear) stripe combinations. The cyan (blue-green) and white combinations produce the red signal, the yellow and white combinations the blue signal. The green signal is then "matrixed" (produced electronically) out of the two chrominance signals (see Color Plate VI).

ENG CONTROL FEATURES

Somewhere on the camera (usually in the back or at the side), you will find several switches that help you operate the camera at peak efficiency. Although they vary from one camera model to another, they usually include (1) camera preheat and "on" switch, (2) VTR save and standby switch, (3) extended gain control, (4) output mode, (5) level indicator, (6) VTR return, (7) centering switch, (8) intercom and microphone jacks, and (9) paint pots (see 2.31 through 2.35).

Camera Preheat and "On" Switch

Very much like your car, your camera needs to warm up before being put to use. The camera preheat switch warms up the camera while drawing a minimum of power. When you are ready to shoot, you flip the switch from "preheat" to the "on" position and your camera will be fully operational in less than five seconds.

VTR Save and Standby Switch

The VTR save switch warms up some of the VTR circuits without actually activating the record head. You activate the record head when you flip the switch to the VTR standby position. In some cameras (like the Sony cameras), the camera and VTR preheat function and the camera "on" and VTR standby function are combined in a single switch (see 2.31).

Extended Gain Control

This two- or three-position switch allows you to gain more signal strength when working under very low light conditions (see 2.31). However, as pointed out in Section One, although the gain allows you to work in a low-light environment with relatively little effect on the colors of the scene, it causes the pictures to become pro-

2.31 ENG Control Switches All ENG/EFP camera control switches are conveniently located at the camera head.

2.32 VTR Return Switch The VTR controls and automatic color balance (white and black balance) can be activated by the camera operator with the camera on the shoulder in shooting position.

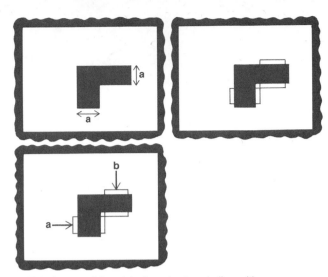

1. Televise special registration chart and align with indications on viewfinder screen.
2. Press momentary auto-centering button to display two centering windows. Left and above the center area.
3. When inverted 'L' is aligned with windows as shown auto-centering takes place with 'a' aligning vertically and 'b' aligning horizontals

2.33 Auto Centering The auto centering device helps to overlap the pictures of the three camera pickup tubes so that they are perfectly registered (form one image).

gressively "noisy" and "soft" because of the wide-open lens aperture.

Output Mode

The output switch shows you in your viewfinder either what the lens sees or the color bars the camera can generate (see 2.31).

Level Indicator

This switch generates a zebralike pattern in the viewfinder by which you can judge whether or not your lens is set correctly. By watching the pattern, you can adjust the lens aperture (iris) manually for proper exposure.

Centering

Some ENG cameras have an "auto center" switch that takes care of the registration automatically without the need of a special registration chart. Modern cameras put this information in their memory and retain it for some time even after the camera has been turned off (see 2.33).

Intercom and Microphone Jacks

All high-quality ENG/EFP cameras have intercom jacks (see 2.34). If in EFP you are connected to an RCU or the base station, you can communicate through standard P.L. headsets. In ENG all communication is wire-

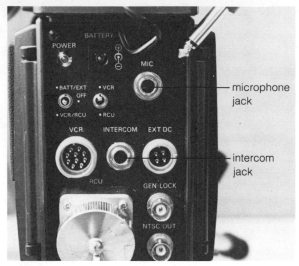

2.34 Intercom and Mic Jacks (Panasonic 3900)
The intercom and microphone jacks are also located on the ENG/EFP camera.

2.35 Paint Pots (Panasonic 3900) The paint pots allow you to adjust the various colors manually, so that you can maintain the proper color temperature under various lighting conditions.

less. Most portable cameras also have an input for an external microphone and an output (line-out) audio monitor jack that allows you to monitor the audio while running the camera.

Paint Pots

Semiautomated cameras have "paint pots," which are color controls needed to set the white balance (see 2.35).

HIGH-DEFINITION TELEVISION (HDTV)

HDTV (High-Definition Television) is a specially developed camera system that produces television pictures many times sharper than the best of the ordinary studio systems can presently deliver. The high resolution is achieved through working with more than twice the number of scanning lines (which comprise the television picture) of our present American television standard, and complex signal-processing methods. Primarily developed to replace the film camera in motion picture production, the system duplicates not only the high-quality pictures of 70mm film, but also its aspect ratio. Instead of the 3 × 4 aspect ratio of television (each screen is three units high and four units

wide), HDTV operates with a 3 × 5 aspect ratio, which approximates the horizontally stretched CinemaScope format. We speak of an HDTV *system,* because the camera alone is not the only element necessary to produce high-definition television. Key elements in the system are also the videotape recorders, which must process more information, and especially the television sets, which must be able to reproduce such high-definition pictures. Several major technical obstacles may prevent us from using such a system for broadcasting, at least in the next few years. However, there are many fields of nonbroadcast applications, such as electronic film production, cable, medical research, or postal services, where HDTV offers exciting possibilities.

MAIN POINTS

1. In the basic scanning process, the electron beam reads all odd-numbered lines first (comprising one field) and the even-numbered lines second (comprising another field). The two fields constitute a single television frame. There are sixty fields, or thirty frames, per second.

2. In the vidicon tube (the generic type of tube imaging device), the optical image is focused on the front surface of the tube, the target, causing a pattern of

electric charges. An electron beam, generated by the electron gun, scans the back of the target, producing a flow of electrons that varies according to the target pattern. This flow is amplified and constitutes the video signal.

3.   The charge-coupled device (CCD) consists of many silicon sensing elements upon which the light image is focused. Through the light, an image charge—a pixel—is created at each element. The pixels are then stored, read out line by line, and amplified into the video signal.

4.   The properties, or attributes, of color are (1) hue, (2) saturation, and (3) brightness. In the color camera, the chrominance channel processes hue, and the luminance channel processes brightness.

5.   Color television works with the additive color-mixing process, in which the three additive (light) primary colors—red, green, and blue—are combined in various intensities to produce a full range of colors.

6.   There are three types of beam splitters that separate the white light into the three additive primary colors: (1) the dichroic mirror system, (2) the prism block, and (3) the striped filter.

7.   ENG (electronic news gathering) cameras have these control features: (1) camera preheat and "on" switch, (2) VTR save and standby switch, (3) extended gain control, (4) various video level and color adjustment controls, and (5) VTR and lens operating buttons. They also have intercom and microphone jacks.

8.   High-definition television (HDTV) is a television system (camera, VTR, and monitor) that produces exceptionally high-quality (high-resolution) pictures.

FURTHER READING

Millerson, Gerald. *The Technique of Television Production.* 10th ed. Woburn, MA: Focal Press, 1981.

Paulson, C. Robert. *BM/E's ENG/EFP/EPP Handbook.* New York: Broadband Information Services, Inc., 1981.

Lenses

In chapter 2 we talked about the television camera. An important production element of the camera is its lens. The lens produces the light image that the imaging device of the camera converts into video signals and greatly affects how we perceive an environment shown on the television screen.

Section One of this chapter describes:

1. Optical characteristics of lenses, including (a) focal length, (b) focus and presetting the zoom lens (c) lens aperture, and (d) depth of field.

2. Operational controls of lenses, including (a) manual and servo zoom controls and (b) focus controls

Section Two is devoted to the performance characteristics of wide-angle, normal, and narrow-angle lenses. The major performance characteristics discussed are (a) field of view, (b) object and distance distortion, (c) response to movement, and (d) depth of field.

One type of lens can give you a wide vista, although you may be relatively close to the scene; another type may give you a close view of an object that is quite far from the camera. Different types of lenses also determine the basic visual perspective—whether you see an object distorted or whether you perceive more or less distance between objects than there really is. Because the lens determines what the camera can see, you need to know (1) the basic optical characteristics of lenses, and (2) the chief operational controls.

OPTICAL CHARACTERISTICS OF LENSES

All broadcast-type color cameras are equipped with zoom lenses, or, as they are called in technical language, **variable-focal-length lenses.** Some of the older monochrome (black-and-white) cameras use individual, fixed-focal-length lenses, which are mounted on a **lens turret** so that the camera operator can quickly flip to one of four different lenses. Each one of the four lenses performs its specific function. Although you will not find any turrets on

modern cameras, we will nevertheless refer to fixed-focal-length lenses (like the one on your still camera) because the basic optical and performance characteristics are more readily explained and understood this way.

We will now discuss these optical characteristics: (1) focal length, (2) focus, (3) lens aperture, and (4) depth of field.

Focal Length

The **focal length** of a lens determines how wide or narrow a vista a particular camera has, and how much and in what ways objects appear magnified. Consequently, we identify lenses by their focal lengths: (1) wide-angle, or short-focal-length, lenses; (2) normal, or medium-focal-length, lenses; (3) narrow-angle, or long-focal-length, lenses, often called telephoto lenses, and (4) zoom, or variable-focal-length, lenses.

The wide angle or narrow angle refers to the **field of view**, the relative vista of the lens. The "short" and "long" refer to the actual focal length, the distance from the optical center of the lens (often the midpoint between the front and back lens ele-

Lenses are used in all fields of photographic art. Their primary function is to produce a small, clear image of the viewed scene on the film, or in the case of television, on the camera pickup tube.

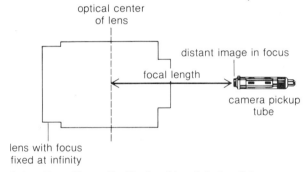

3.1 Focal Length The focal length is the distance from the optical center of the lens to the front surface of the camera pickup tube, with the lens set at infinity.

ments) to the point where the distant image as seen by the lens is in focus (see 3.1).

With a **wide-angle lens**, or short lens, you can see more; you have a wider vista. Objects very close to the lens appear quite magnified, but the ones just a little farther back look rather small. With a **narrow-angle lens**, or long lens, you have a narrower vista. But what you see, even the distant objects, is greatly magnified. A short lens creates an effect similar to looking through binoculars the wrong way.

A long lens is similar to binoculars used correctly. The **normal lens** gives you approximately the view of normal human vision.

Contrary to the fixed-focal-length lenses, the **zoom lens** can assume all focal lengths from the wide-angle position to the narrow-angle position. This is why it is called a *variable-focal-length* lens. You can change from a wide-angle to a narrow-angle position in one continuous operation, without changing lenses or moving the camera. To *zoom in* means to change the vista gradually from a wide-angle (faraway) view to a narrow-angle (close) view. On the television screen a zoom-in appears as though the object is gradually coming toward you. Actually, all the many moving elements within the zoom lens gradually magnify the object while keeping it in focus. When the lens zooms out, the object becomes smaller and seems to move away from you. But the camera remains stationary during both operations.

Zoom Range If your zoom lens gives you an overview of the whole tennis court and part of the bleachers when zoomed all the way out, and (without having to move the camera closer to the court) a tight close-up of a player's tense expression when zoomed all the way in, you have a lens with a good zoom range. A good zoom range also allows you to zoom from a large wide-angle view of the whole news set to a tight close-up view of the newscaster's small lavaliere microphone.

The **zoom range** is the degree to which you can change the focal length of the lens (and thereby the angle of view, or vista) during the zoom. The zoom range of a lens is often stated as a ratio. A 10:1 zoom means that you can increase the focal length ten times, a 15:1, fifteen times, and so forth. Other designations simply say 10× (ten times), or 15× (fifteen times). These ratios refer to the degree of magnification, or the increase in focal length in a continuous zoom. Still another specification gives information about the zoom range and the shortest focal length of the lens, how wide the view will be at the start of the zooming in. A 15 × 12.5 (fifteen by twelve-point-five) means that the focal length can be increased by fifteen times (it has a 15:1 zoom ratio), and that the widest focal length position is 12.5mm. (Focal lengths are usually stated in millimeters, or mm.) What, then, is the focal length of the zoom in the extreme telephoto position (all the way zoomed in)? Simply 15 × 12.5mm, which is approximately 188mm. In this example the zoom lens goes from a wide-angle 12.5mm focal length to a telephoto position of 188mm.

Types of Zoom Lenses
We classify zoom lenses by the way they are used. If you use your zoom lens

lens housing, including lens elements and servo zoom and focus mechanisms

3.2   Studio Zoom The studio and field zoom lenses are covered by a protective housing. Inside are the actual lens, the servo zoom controls, and the focus controls.

mostly for studio work, you need a *studio zoom*. This lens has a zoom range that, within the space of a normal-sized studio, allows a fairly wide vista and a rather tight close-up from one camera position. If your primary production requirement is fieldwork, such as sports remotes, a studio zoom lens would probably not allow you to get tight enough to the action. For this you need to use a *field zoom*. The field zoom cannot zoom out quite as wide as a studio zoom, but it has a much more powerful telephoto position when zoomed all the way in. This is important because in the field you are usually much

Aperture   Diaphragm opening of a lens; usually measured in *f*-stops.

Depth of Field   The area in which all objects, located at different distances from the camera, appear in focus. Depth of field is dependent upon focal length of the lens, *f*-stop, and distance between object and camera.

Diaphragm   Adjustable lens-opening mechanism that controls the amount of light passing through a lens.

Fast Lens   A lens that permits a relatively great amount of light to pass through (low *f*-stop number). Can be used in low lighting conditions.

Field of View   The extent of a scene that is visible through a particular lens; its vista.

Focal Length   The distance from the optical center of the lens to the front surface of the camera pickup tube with the lens set at infinity. Focal lengths are measured in millimeters or inches. Short-focal-length lenses have a wide angle of view (wide vista); long-focal-length (telephoto) lenses have a narrow angle of view (close-up). In a variable-focal-length lens (zoom lens) the focal length can be changed continuously from wide angle to narrow angle and vice versa. A fixed-focal-length lens has a single designated focal length only.

Lens Format	Use	Zoom Ratio	Range—Focal Length (mm)	With Extender
$1\frac{1}{4}$-inch (30mm) Pickup Tubes	Studio Studio Field	11× 15× 25×	18–200 16–240 wide-angle 27–675	× 1.5: 40.5 mm–1012.5mm × 2 : 54mm–1350 mm
1-inch (25mm) Pickup Tubes	Studio Studio Field Field	11× 15× 25× 30×	14–150 12.5–190 wide-angle 20–500 26–800	× 1.5: 30mm–750mm × 2 : 40mm–1000mm
$\frac{2}{3}$-inch (18mm) Pickup Tubes	ENG/EFP ENG/EFP ENG/EFP	10× 15× 20×	11–110 8.5–125 12–240	× 2: 17mm–250mm

farther away from the action than in the studio. A third category of zoom lens is designed specifically for ENG/EFP cameras. The *ENG zoom lenses*, which are much smaller than the studio zooms, have a different zoom range. The important difference is that you can adjust the focus with the focus ring, which is at the lens itself, and you can also adjust the lens opening with the aperture, or iris ring (see 3.4).

Thus, we have (1) studio zooms, (2) field zooms, and (3) ENG/EFP zoom lenses. There are also combination lenses, called *studio–field zoom* lenses, that have a very wide zoom range so that you can use the lens either in the studio or in the field. (See 3.2 through 3.4.)

3.4 ENG/EFP Zoom Lens Although the ENG/EFP zoom lens is considerably smaller and lighter than the studio zooms, it has many of the studio zoom's features, such as servo zoom control, manual zoom control, and range extender switch. It can also be used in the servo iris mode.

Focus A picture is in focus when it appears sharp and clear on the screen (technically, the point where the light rays refracted by the lens converge).

f-stop The calibration on the lens indicating the aperture, or diaphragm opening (and therefore the amount of light transmitted through the lens). The larger the f-stop number, the smaller the aperture; the smaller the f-stop number, the larger the aperture.

Macro Position Position on zoom lens that allows it to be focused at very close distances from the object. Used for close-ups of small objects.

Normal Lens A lens with a focal length that will approximate the spatial relationships of normal vision when used with a particular film or pickup tube format.

Range Extender An optical attachment to the zoom lens that will extend its narrow-angle focal length.

Slow Lens A lens that permits a relatively small amount of light to pass through (high f-stop number). Can be used only in well-lighted areas.

Telephoto Lens Same as long-focal-length lens. Gives a close-up view of an event relatively far away from the camera.

Wide-Angle Lens Same as short-focal-length lens. Gives a broad vista of a scene.

Zoom Lens Variable-focal-length lens. It can change from a wide shot to a close-up in one continuous move.

Pickup Tube Format   As you remember, some studio cameras have a $1\frac{1}{4}$-inch pickup tube, some have a 1-inch pickup tube, and most ENG/EFP cameras have $\frac{2}{3}$-inch pickup tubes. There are some ENG/EFP cameras that have a $\frac{1}{2}$-inch pickup tube. If, for example, you were to mount a 15 × 12.5 zoom lens first on the camera with the largest pickup tube format, then on the 1-inch tube camera, then on the ENG camera, you would not get the same field of view when testing your zoom range. With your large-tube camera you would get a much wider shot when zoomed all the way out than with your ENG camera. When zoomed all the way in, your large-tube camera would not get as close a shot as your ENG camera. Fortunately, the manufacturers match the tube format with the corresponding **lens format.**

Range Extenders   If your zoom lens does not get you close enough to a scene, you can use an additional lens element called a **range extender**, or simply *extender*. This does not actually extend the *range* of a zoom, but rather shifts the *magnification*, the telephoto power, of the lens toward the narrow-angle end of the zoom range. With a range extender you can zoom in to a closer shot, but you cannot zoom back to as wide a shot as you could without the extender. Other disadvantages of the range extenders are (1) because of the additional glass, they cut down considerably the light entering the camera, which is a problem especially when you have to do a remote pickup under low light conditions; and (2) the picture is usually not as crisp as without the extender.

Macro Mode   Many zoom lenses on ENG/EFP cameras have a **macro position**, which allows you to move the camera very close to an object without getting out of focus. Once in the macro position, the zoom lens becomes a fixed-focal-length lens. We will refer again to the macro position in the discussion of minimum object distance later in this chapter.

Focus

A picture is "in focus" when the projected image is sharp and clear. The **focus** depends on the distance from lens to film (as in a still or movie camera) or from lens to camera pickup tube (as in a television camera). Simply changing the distance from lens to film, or pickup tube, brings a picture into focus or takes it out of focus.

In television the pickup tube takes the place of the film. To get into and keep in focus, you must adjust the distance between the lens and the camera pickup tube (for single-tube color cameras) or tubes (for multitube color cameras). This adjustment is accomplished by moving certain lens elements inside the zoom lens relative to each other through the zoom focus control. In monochrome cameras the single camera pickup tube, rather than the lens, is moved.

Focusing the Color Camera   A zoom lens has several lenses that move in relation to one another when you zoom as well as when you focus. One set of these sliding elements, normally located at the front part of the lens, takes care of the focusing. The focus controls come in various configurations. Studio cameras have them attached to the panning handle. Portable cameras have a focus ring that you must turn by hand on the lens (see 3.7). If properly preset, a zoom lens keeps in focus during the entire range, assuming that neither the camera nor the object moves very much. Because you carry, walk, or even run with ENG/EFP cameras, you cannot always prefocus the zoom. In fact, most of the time you have to "follow focus" while zooming. This means that you have to work the focus mechanism at the same time as you are zooming in or out.

Presetting (Calibrating) the Zoom   The following procedure should be used to preset, or calibrate, the zoom so that the camera remains in focus throughout the zoom. Zoom all the way in on the farthest object in the zoom range that you need to cover during the production, such as the map behind the newscaster. Focus on this object (the map) by turning the zoom focus control. When zooming back to a long shot, you will notice that now everything remains in focus. The same is true when you zoom in again. You should now be able to maintain focus over the entire zoom range.

If, however, you move the camera, or if the object moves after you preset the zoom lens on it, you need to preset the zoom once again. For example, if you have preset the zoom on the news set and the director instructs you to move the camera closer to the set and a little to the left so that the newscaster can read the copy better off the teleprompter, you will not be able to maintain focus without presetting the zoom from your new position. If the camera, the object, or both are in motion during a zoom, you must "follow" focus, which means you must try to adjust the focus control and the zoom control at the same time—not an easy task even for an experienced camera operator. We will mention the calibrating of zoom lenses for monochrome lenses in Section Two of this chapter.

Minimum Object Distance   No matter what type of camera you use, there is a limit to how close you can get to the object to be photographed and still be able to focus on the object. The point where the camera is about as close as it can get and still focus on the object is called the **minimum object distance** of the lens. The minimum object distance of most zoom lenses is usually 2–3 feet, unless you have a special provision for a macro lens attachment or for a macro position of the zoom lens. Macrophotography means that the camera can get so close to the object that you can enlarge the image on the screen several times the object's actual size. When the lens is in the macro position, you can almost touch the object with the lens and still retain focus; however, you can no longer zoom. When in the macro position, the zoom lens has become a fixed-focal-length lens. But you will have no trouble getting a screen-filling close-up of rather small objects, such as postage stamps, which is virtually impossible within your regular zoom range.

Lens Aperture

Like the pupil in the human eye, all lenses have a mechanism that controls how much light is admitted through them. This mechanism is called the **diaphragm** or **iris**. The iris consists of a series of thin metal blades that form a fairly round hole, the **aperture** or lens opening, of variable size (see 3.5a). If you "open up" the lens as wide as it will go, or more technically, if you set the lens to its *maximum aperture,* it admits a maximum amount of light. If you now "close" the lens somewhat, the metal rings of the diaphragm form a smaller hole, the aperture is

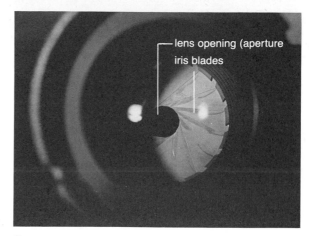

a

lens opening (aperture
iris blades

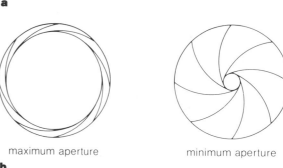

maximum aperture   minimum aperture

b

3.5   Lens Iris   The lens iris, or diaphragm, consists of a series of thin metal blades that form, through partial overlapping, a lens opening of variable size.

somewhat smaller, and less light goes through the lens. If you now close the lens all the way—that is, if you set your lens to its *minimum aperture*—very little light goes through (see 3.5b). Some diaphragms can be closed entirely, which means that no light at all goes through the lens.

f-stop   The standard scale that indicates how much light goes through a lens, regardless of whether it is a wide-angle or telephoto lens, or any type of zoom lens, is the **f-stop** (see 3.6). If, for example, you have two cameras—an ENG camera with a 20 × zoom lens and a 35mm still camera with a 50mm lens—and both lenses are set at *f*/5.6, the pickup tube in your ENG camera and the film in your still camera will receive identical amounts of light.

f-stops are expressed in a series of numbers,

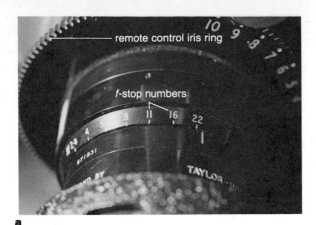

remote control iris ring

f-stop numbers

TAYLOR

a

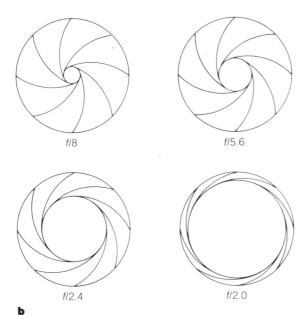

f/8

f/5.6

f/2.4

f/2.0

b

3.6 *f-stop and Lens Aperture* (a) The *f*-stop is a calibration that indicates how large or small the iris, or lens opening, is. (b) The larger the iris opening, the smaller the *f*-stop number.

ings and *high* f-*stop numbers* relatively *small iris openings*, rather than the other way around, is that the *f*-stop numbers actually express a ratio. In this sense *f*/2 is actually *f*/$\frac{1}{2}$ (read: *f* one-half). (See 3.6.)

The *quality* of a lens is measured not by how little light it allows to enter the camera, but by *how much* light it lets in. A lens that allows a great deal of light to enter is called a **fast lens**. A **slow lens** is one through which relatively little light can pass. Most good studio zoom lenses open up to *f*/1.8, which is fast enough to make the camera work properly even in low light conditions.

In general, lenses that have an extreme tele-photo position (narrow-angle view) are not as fast (cannot open as wide) as lenses with a normal zoom range. Hence, field zoom lenses are generally slower than studio lenses. The same is true for fixed-focal-length lenses. Short-focal-length (wide-angle) lens-es are generally faster (with a wider maximum aper-ture) than long-focal-length (narrow-angle) lenses.

Remote Iris Control Because the amount of light that strikes the camera pickup tube is so important for the quality of the picture, the continual adjust-ment of the iris (aperture) is an important aspect of video control. Studio cameras today have a *remote iris control,* which means that the aperture can be continually adjusted by the video operator from the CCU (camera control unit). If the set is properly lighted and the camera properly set up (electroni-cally adjusted to the light-dark extremes of the scene), all the video operator has to do to maintain good pictures is work the remote iris control (open the iris in low light conditions and close it down when there is more light than needed).

Automatic Iris Control Most cameras, especially ENG/EFP cameras, can be switched over to the *auto-iris* mode. The camera then senses the light entering the lens and automatically adjusts the lens opening for optimal pickup tube performance. Although this procedure seems ideal for ENG/EFP work, it does not always work to your advantage. In its desire to please the camera pickup tube with fairly even illu-mination, and unable to exercise aesthetic judg-ment, the auto iris closes down when it sees an extremely bright area in your scene, or opens up

such as *f*/1.2, *f*/1.8, *f*/5.6, *f*/8, *f*/22. The *lower* f-*stop numbers* indicate a relatively *large aperture* (lens is relatively wide open). The *higher* f-*stop numbers* indicate a relatively *small aperture* (lens is closed down considerably). A lens that is set at *f*/2 has a much larger iris opening and, therefore, admits much more light than one that is set at *f*/16. The reason why the *low* f-*stop numbers* indicate *large iris open-*

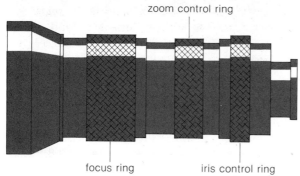

zoom control ring

focus ring   iris control ring

3.7 ENG/EFP Lens Iris Control Ring On most
ENG/EFP zoom lenses the focus ring is closest to the front
of the lens, the zoom control ring is in the middle, and the
iris control ring is toward the back of the lens.

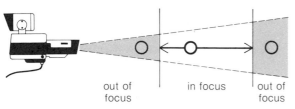

out of focus   in focus   out of focus

3.8 Depth of Field The depth of field is the area in
which all objects, although located at different distances
from the camera, are in focus.

when sensing a rather dark set area. The automatic
iris control responds to whatever light it receives,
regardless of the light's origin. For example, if you
took a shot of a woman wearing a bright white hat,
the automatic iris would adjust to the white hat, not
to the darker (shadowed) face under the hat. Therefore, the auto-iris control would give you a perfectly
exposed hat, but an underexposed face. In this case
you should switch to manual iris control, zoom in
on the face so as to eliminate most of the white hat,
and adjust the iris to the light reflecting off the face
rather than the hat. This is why most ENG/EFP camera operators prefer to run their cameras with manual iris control (see 3.7).

Depth of Field

If you place objects at different distances from the
camera, some of them will be in focus and some of
them out of focus. The area in which the objects are

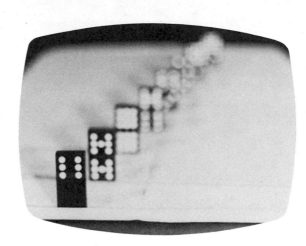

3.9 Shallow Depth of Field In a shallow depth of
field, blurring begins at relatively short distances from the
focused object.

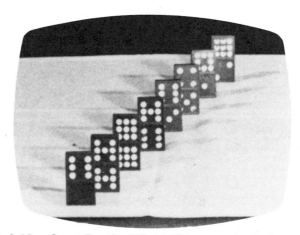

3.10 Great Depth of Field With a great depth of
field, almost everything in the camera's field of view
appears in focus.

seen in focus is called **depth of field**. The depth
of field can be shallow or great. If you have a shallow
depth of field and you focus on an object in the
middleground, the foreground and background
objects will be out of focus. If the depth of field is
great, all objects (foreground, middleground, and
background) will be in focus, even though you focus
on the middleground object only. (See 3.8–3.10.)

If you have a great depth of field, there is a large sharp zone in which people or objects can move without getting out of focus, or without any need for adjusting the camera focus to keep them sharp and clear. However, if they move in a shallow depth of field, they quickly move out of the depth of field and get out of focus, unless you adjust the camera focus. A similar thing happens when you move the camera. A great depth of field makes it relatively easy to **dolly**, or move the camera toward or away from the object, because you do not have to work any controls to keep the picture in focus. If you dolly in a shallow depth of field, however, you have to adjust the focus continuously if you want your target object to remain sharp and clear.

The depth of field depends on the coordination of three factors: (1) the focal length of the lens, (2) the aperture (lens opening), and (3) the distance of camera to object.

Focal Length

Given a fixed camera-to-object distance, short-focal-length lenses or wide-angle zoom positions have a great depth of field. Long (telephoto) lenses or narrow-angle zoom positions have a shallow depth of field.

Aperture

Large lens openings (small f-stop numbers, such as $f/1.8$ or $f/2$) cause a shallow depth of field. Small lens openings (large f-stop numbers, such as $f/16$ or $f/22$) provide a great depth of field. Here is an example of how everything in television production seems to influence everything else. If you have to work in low light conditions, you need to open up the lens (increase the aperture) in order to get enough light for the camera. But this reduces the depth of field. Thus, if you are to cover a news story when it is getting dark and you have no time or opportunity to use artificial lighting, the focus becomes critical; you are working in a rather shallow depth of field. On the other hand, in bright sunlight you can stop down (decrease the aperture), thereby achieving a large depth of field. Now you can run with the camera or cover people who are moving toward or away from you without too much worry about keeping in focus—provided that the zoom lens is in a wide-angle position.

Camera-to-Object Distance

The closer the camera is to the object, the shallower the depth of field. The farther the camera is from the object, the greater the depth of field. The camera-to-object distance also influences the focal-length effect on depth of field. For example, if you have a wide-angle lens (or a zoom lens in a wide-angle position), the depth of field is great. But as soon as you move the camera close to the object, the depth of field becomes quite shallow. The same is true in reverse. If you work with a long lens (or with the zoom in a narrow-angle position), you have a rather shallow depth of field. But if the camera is sufficiently far away from the object (such as a field camera located high in the stands to cover an automobile race), you work in a fairly great depth of field and do not have to worry too much about adjusting focus, unless you zoom in to a close-up.

In general, we can say that *close-ups have a shallow depth of field* and *long shots have a great depth of field.*

Let's test this rule. Assuming a moderate lens opening ($f/5.6$), what depth of field do you have when you are zoomed in all the way on an object in the middleground? A shallow depth of field. Suppose you now zoom all the way out but move the camera so close to the object that you more or less duplicate the previous close-up? You still have a shallow depth of field. If you now dolly back to the original spot (with the zoom lens still in the wide-angle position) to get a fairly wide shot of the whole scene, the depth of field is fairly great, and you may well find that not only the middleground object is in focus, but the foreground and background objects as well.

OPERATIONAL CONTROLS

You need two basic controls to operate a zoom lens: (1) the **zoom control unit**, which activates the variable focal length of the lens (the zooming mechanism), and (2) the **focus control unit**, which activates the intricate focus mechanism in a zoom lens. Both controls can be operated either *manually* or *automatically* by a *servo control.*

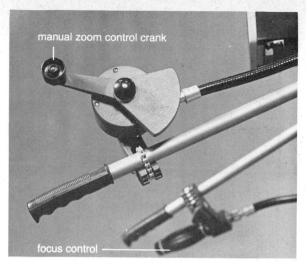

manual zoom control crank

focus control

3.11 Manual Zoom Control on Studio Camera With most zoom controls, you turn the handle clockwise to zoom in and counterclockwise to zoom out. The faster you turn the handle, the faster the zoom.

servo zoom control — macro position switch

— manual focus ring

hand strap

3.12 Manual Zoom Control—ENG/EFP Camera By moving the zoom lever up or down, you can zoom in or out.

Zoom Control Unit

Manual Zoom Control Unit In studio cameras the *manual zoom control* usually consists of a small crank mounted on the right panning handle or on a small extender at the right side of the camera. A small lever next to the crank enables you to select at least two turning ratios, slow or fast. The slow ratio is for normal zooming, the fast for exceptionally fast zooms.

When you turn the crank of the zoom control, a special zoom drive cable mechanically activates the zoom mechanism in the lens. Regardless of what zooming ratio you have selected, the faster you turn the crank, the faster the zoom will be. (See 3.11.)

All portable cameras have the manual zoom control directly on the lens. To zoom in or out, you turn a ring on the lens barrel either clockwise or counterclockwise. Some of the rings have a small lever attached to make zooming somewhat easier. (See 3.12.)

Whatever the device may be, it takes some skill and practice to accomplish smooth zooms with such on-the-lens zoom controls.

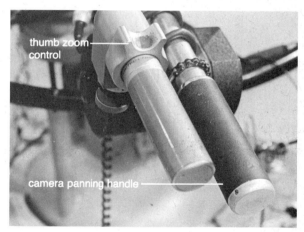

thumb zoom control

camera panning handle

3.13 Servo Zoom Control This zoom control is simply mounted next to the camera panning handle.

Servo Zoom Control Unit The **servo zoom control** unit does not activate the lens mechanism directly; rather, it signals a complex motor system that in turn drives the zoom mechanism in the lens. In actual operation the servo control unit is quite similar to the mechanical zoom controls. It is nor-

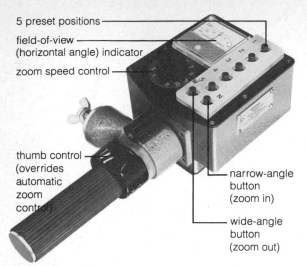

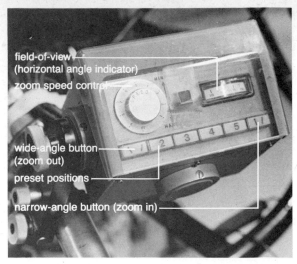

5 preset positions

field-of-view
(horizontal angle) indicator

zoom speed control

thumb control
(overrides
automatic
zoom
control)

narrow-angle
button
(zoom in)

wide-angle
button
(zoom out)

field-of-view
(horizontal angle indicator)

zoom speed control

wide-angle button
(zoom out)

preset positions

narrow-angle button (zoom in)

3.14   Shot Box The shot box comes in a variety of configurations, but with similar components, such as the field-of-view meter, zoom speed control, wide-angle and narrow-angle zoom buttons, and buttons for preset positions.

mally mounted on the right panning handle, and you zoom in and out by moving the thumb lever either right or left. The farther you move the lever from its original central position, the faster the zoom will be. A two-speed switch permits you to select a zoom speed four times as fast as the normal zoom rate. With the servo system the zoom speed is automatically reduced as the zoom approaches either of the extreme zoom positions. This reduction prevents jerks and abrupt stops when you reach the end of the zoom range. (See 3.13.)

To make the zoom even more precise, a zoom preset system, called a **shot box**, has been developed. Generally mounted on the right panning handle, it allows you to preset any of a number of zoom speeds (up to twelve in some models) and several (four or five) zoom positions. By activating wide- and narrow-angle buttons or switches, you make the lens zoom either out or in. A special meter indicates the angle of view of the lens. The shot box is usually combined with a servo zoom control unit that lets you override the shot box at any time. (See 3.14.)

Most of the more sophisticated ENG cameras have a servo zoom control to ensure smooth zooming. A lever control is usually mounted right on the

servo box that surrounds the lens. (See 3.15 a and b.)

There are several advantages to the servo system. Zooms are steady and smooth, especially during slow zooms. The zoom control is easy to operate and allows you to concentrate more on picture composition and focusing. The servo zoom frees your left hand to operate the manual focus and aperture controls.

Focus Control Unit

For studio cameras the *manual focus control* ordinarily consists of a twist grip that is very similar to a motorcycle handle. It is generally mounted on the left panning handle. Two or three turns are sufficient to achieve focus over the full zoom range. As with the zoom, the focus operations are transferred by the drive cable from the panning handle control to the lens (see 3.16).

The *servo focus control units* are not widely used. Once the zoom lens has been preset, it should stay in focus during the entire zoom range. The only time you need to work the focus during a zoom is when the camera or the object is in motion at the

servo zoom control

VTR switch
(activates
VTR)

servo zoom
control
in pistol grip;
pistol grip
is detachable

a   b

3.15   ENG/EFP Servo Zoom Control On some camera units (a) the zoom control is activated by the right index finger. On pistol-grip servo zoom controls (b) zooming is done with the thumb.

same time. Then, however, even the smartest servo focus control does not quite know how fast the camera or the object is moving. Therefore, most camera operators prefer to put the servo focus control in the manual mode, thus defeating its automatic function.

Some cameras come equipped with an *auto-focus device* that works on a simple radar principle. The camera sends out an infrared beam that is bounced back to the camera by the object to be photographed. The camera then computes the distance and adjusts the focus accordingly. Obvious problems occur when you want to focus not on the object that lies next to the camera, but on the one farther away.

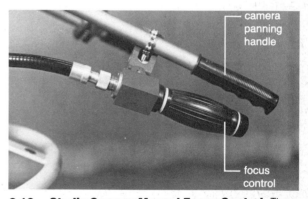

camera
panning
handle

focus
control

3.16   Studio Camera Manual Focus Control The twist grip of the manual focus control turns clockwise and counterclockwise for focusing.

MAIN POINTS

1.   The primary function of the lens is to produce a small, clear optical image on the front surface of the camera pickup tube or other imaging device.

2.   All color television cameras are equipped with zoom (variable-focal-length) lenses.

3.   The major optical characteristics of lenses are (1) focal length, (2) focus, (3) lens aperture, and (4) depth of field.

4.   The focal length of a lens determines how wide or narrow a vista the camera has and how much or how little objects appear magnified. When classified by focal length, lenses may be (1) wide-angle, (2) normal, (3) narrow-angle (or telephoto), or (4) zoom (variable-focal-length).

5. A wide-angle lens gives a wide vista. A narrow-angle lens gives a narrow vista but magnifies the object so that it appears closer to the camera than it really is. A normal lens approximates the angle of human vision.

6. A zoom lens can assume all focal lengths within its zoom range—from a given wide-angle position to the most narrow-angle position the lens can assume.

7. A range extender (additional lens element) extends the telephoto power of the zoom lens (permits a closer shot) but reduces the range at the wide-angle end.

8. There are three major types of zoom lenses: (1) studio zoom lenses, (2) field zoom lenses, and (3) ENG/EFP zoom lenses.

9. A picture is in focus when the projected image is sharp and clear. Before it is zoomed in or out, the zoom lens needs to be preset (calibrated) so that focus is maintained over the zoom range.

10. The lens diaphragm, or iris, controls the amount of light going through the lens. It consists of a series of thin metal plates that form a hole known as the aperture, or lens opening.

11. The f-stop is a standard scale indicating how much light goes through the lens. Low f-stop numbers indicate large iris openings; high f-stop numbers indicate small openings.

12. Studio cameras have a remote iris control, which is operated from the CCU. ENG/EFP cameras can be switched from manual to auto-iris mode, whereby the lens adjusts itself for optimal exposure (amount of light reaching the imaging device).

13. The area in which objects at different distances from the camera are seen in focus is called depth of field. The depth of field depends on (1) focal length of the lens, (2) aperture (f-stop), (3) distance from camera to object, and (4) the interaction of all these three.

14. The two basic operational controls for the zoom lens are the zoom control and the focus control. Both can be operated either manually or automatically by servo control.

The performance characteristics of a lens refer to what it can and cannot do, and how it generally behaves in common production practice. Because the camera processes only information the lens can see, a knowledge of the performance characteristics will aid you greatly in composing effective shots and in many other production tasks.

In this section, we will briefly describe (1) performance characteristics of lenses and (2) the presetting (calibrating) of zoom lenses for monochrome cameras. Although monochrome cameras are a thing of the past, you will find a surprising number of them alive and well in the training centers of colleges and universities.

PERFORMANCE CHARACTERISTICS

Three topics especially pertinent to the discussion of performance characteristics of television lenses are (1) field of view, including focal length and zoom range, (2) relationship of focal length to performance, and (3) relationship of depth of field to performance. As pointed out earlier in this chapter, we will use fixed-focal-length lenses for the explanation of performance characteristics. We will then transfer their characteristics to the zoom lens whenever appropriate.

In order to discuss the relationship of the focal lengths of the lenses to performance characteristics, we will group the lenses into (1) wide-angle (short-focal-length) lenses, or wide zoom-lens positions; (2) normal lenses, or midrange zoom-lens positions; and (3) narrow-angle (long-focal-length or telephoto) lenses, or telephoto zoom-lens positions.

The Wide-Angle Lens (Wide Zoom Position)

Field of View   The wide-angle lens affords a *wide vista*. You can have a relatively wide field of view with the camera rather close to the scene. When you need a wide vista (long shot) or, for example, when you need to see all five people on a panel and your studio is relatively small, a wide-angle lens, or rather a wide-angle zoom position, is mandatory. When you use a wide-angle lens, objects relatively close to the camera look large and objects only a short distance away look quite small. (See 3.17 and 3.18.)

Object and Distance Distortion   When you are using a wide-angle lens, objects look distorted and proportions exaggerated. However, this **distortion**—large foreground objects, small middleground, and even smaller background objects—helps to increase the *illusion of depth*. Because parallel lines seem to converge faster with this lens than we ordinarily perceive, we now have a forced perspective that aids the illusion of exaggerated distance and depth. With a wide-angle lens you can make a small room appear rather spacious, or a hallway much longer than it really is. (See 3.18 through 3.22.)

In order to get such object distortions, you need

3.17 Wide-Angle Long Shot The wide-angle lens (or wide-angle zoom position) affords a wide vista. Although the camera is relatively close to the news set, we can see the entire area.

3.19 Wide-Angle Distortion: Ship Here, the dock building appears to be much longer than it is. Note that the mooring line is larger in the foreground than the entire ship.

3.18 Long Shot in Small Studio The wide-angle lens (or wide-angle zoom position) can make a small room appear rather spacious. This news set is actually crammed into a very small studio.

3.20 Wide-Angle Distortion: Automobile Even a small car, like a VW, can be made to look like a rather powerful racer.

Back Focus The distance between zoom lens and camera pickup tube at which the picture is in focus at the extreme wide-angle zoom position. In monochrome cameras, the back focus can be adjusted by moving the pickup tube through the camera focus control.

Front Focus The proper relationship of the front elements of the zoom lens to ensure focus during the entire zoom range. Front focus is set at the extreme close-up position with the zoom focus control. Color cameras have a front-focus adjustment only because the pickup tubes cannot be moved.

3.21 **Wide-Angle Distortion: Depth Articulation** Shooting through a prominent foreground piece with the wide-angle lens creates a spatially articulated, forceful picture.

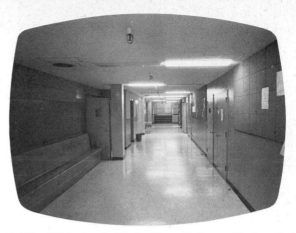

3.22 **Wide-Angle Distortion: Hallway** The length of this hallway is greatly exaggerated by the wide-angle lens.

to bring the camera quite close. Be careful not to hit the object with the lens.

Such distortions can also work against you. If you take a close-up of a face with a wide-angle lens, the nose, which is closest to the lens, looks unusually large compared to the other parts of the face (see 3.23).

With an extreme wide-angle lens you may notice that the vertical lines on the left and right sides of the picture appear to be somewhat curved. This is called **barrel distortion**.

Looking down on an object can also create undesirable distortions. For example, a close-up of a washing machine with a wide-angle lens looks especially distorted when the camera looks at it from above (see 3.24a). You can reduce such distortions by lowering the camera (or raising the object closer to lens height), or by using a slightly longer lens or zoom-lens position (see 3.24b).

3.23 **Distorted Face** Wide-angle lens distortion of a face is generally undesirable, unless you want to imply in the shot some psychological distortion.

Movement The wide-angle lens is also a good *dolly lens*. Its wide field of view deemphasizes camera wobbles and bumps during dollies and trucks. However, the zoom lens makes it so easy to move from a long shot to a close-up or vice versa that dollying with a zoom lens has almost become a lost art. Most of the time, a zoom will be perfectly acceptable as a means to change the field of view. However, you should be aware that there is a *significant aesthetic* difference

between a zoom and a dolly. Whereas the zoom seems to bring the scene to the viewer, a dolly seems to take the viewer into the scene.[1] Because the camera does not move during the zoom, the spatial relationship between objects remains constant. The objects appear to be glued into positions; they simply get bigger (zoom in) or smaller (zoom out). In a dolly, however, the rela-

[1]Zettl, *Sight-Sound-Motion*, pp. 194–197, 288.

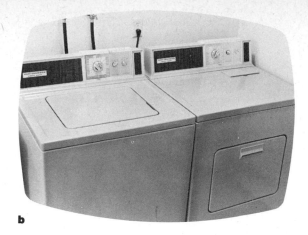

a

b

3.24   Reducing Wide-Angle Distortion
(a) The wide-angle lens distortion in this shot makes the washing machine appear much too dynamic and unstable. (b) When the machine is shot more from eye level (either by lowering the camera or by placing the object closer to lens height), or by using a longer lens, the undesirable effect of distortion is greatly reduced.

tionships between objects change constantly. You seem to move past them when dollying in or out. Be sure to reset (recalibrate) the zoom when you have reached the end of the dolly so that you can zoom in and out from the new position without losing focus.

The wider the lens or the zoom position, the more rapidly the objects increase or decrease in size during a dolly, and the more exaggerated the dolly speed appears. Similarly, when people or objects move toward or away from the camera, their speed appears greatly accelerated by the wide-angle lens. The wide-angle zoom position is often used in dance programs in order to emphasize the speed and distance of the dancers' leaps toward and away from the camera.

Depth of Field   Assuming a small aperture (f/16, for example), the wide-angle lens has a great depth of field (see 3.25). But when you move the camera in to get a close-up of the object with the wide-angle lens, the depth of field is shallow (see 3.26).

The Normal Lens (Midrange Zoom Position)

Field of View   The normal lens offers a field of view that approximates that of normal vision. It covers about as much area (horizontal angle of view) as you would see without turning your head (see 3.27).

Object and Distance Distortion   Whereas the wide-angle lens makes objects seem farther apart and makes rooms seem larger than they actually are, the normal lens or the midrange zoom positions make objects and their spatial relationships appear closer to our normal vision (see 3.27).

When shooting graphics, especially title cards, you should use the normal lens or put the zoom in the midrange position. These are the main advantages: (1) You can quickly correct the framing on the card by zooming in or out slightly, or by dollying in or out without undue focus change. (2) You are far enough away from the easel to avoid camera shadows, yet close enough so that the danger of someone's walking in front of the camera is minimal. (3) By placing the easel at a standard distance from the camera, the floorperson can help you frame and focus on the easel card with a minimum of effort and time.

The most common mistake is to zoom in on an easel card from a fairly great distance. There are four problems with this method: (1) Your focus at the telephoto position of the zoom lens is quite critical. (2) With the zoom lens in the telephoto position even the slightest camera vibration makes the letters on the studio card appear to be moving. (3) If the director requires a closer shot after you have zoomed in most of the way, you have to move the whole camera closer to the easel and preset the focus again—a maneuver that can be quite time and energy consuming. Even if you are still

**3.25   Great Depth of Field with Wide-Angle
Lens** When taking a medium shot with a wide-angle lens,
you have a great depth of field. The objects closer to the
camera, as well as the background objects, are in focus.

3.26   Shallow Depth of Field during Close-up If
you take a close-up with a wide-angle lens (or wide-angle
zoom position), the depth of field is quite shallow.

**3.27   Normal Lens Perspective and Field of
View** The normal lens offers a field of view that approximates normal vision.

able to zoom in, a smooth zoom is quite difficult to
achieve at the telephoto zoom range. (4) As already
mentioned, if you are too far from the easel, studio
personnel who are unaware that you are focused on
the easel card may walk right in front of the camera.

Movement The normal lens or the midrange zoom
positions let you dolly the camera while on the air. However, it is much harder to keep the camera in focus

than when using a wide-angle lens, and the camera
wobbles become a little more noticeable.

Because the distance and object proportions
approximate our normal vision, the dolly speed and
the speed of objects moving toward or away from the
camera also appear normal.

Depth of Field The normal lens has a shallower depth
of field than the wide-angle lens under similar conditions (same *f*/stop and object-to-camera distance). You
might think that a very great depth of field would be
the most desirable condition in studio operations
because it shows everything in focus. But a medium
depth of field is often preferred because the in-focus
objects are set off against a slightly out-of-focus background. Thus, the objects are emphasized, and busy
background designs or the inevitable smudges on the
television scenery receive little attention. The unlit top
portion of the set blends quite naturally into the dark
studio space, suggesting a ceiling. Most importantly,
foreground, middleground, and background are better
defined.[2]

Of course, a large depth of field is necessary when
there is considerable movement of camera and/or subjects. Also, when two objects are located at widely different distances from the camera, a great depth of field
enables you to keep both in focus simultaneously. Most

[2]Zettl, *Sight-Sound-Motion,* pp. 188–191.

3.28 Narrow-Angle Lens The narrow-angle (tele-photo) lens seems to shrink space.

3.29 Telephoto Lens Distortion: Traffic When you use a telephoto lens, the background is greatly enlarged compared to the foreground. The distance between the cars seems, therefore, reduced and the impression of a traffic jam is heightened.

outdoor telecasts, such as sports remotes, require a large depth of field, the principal objective being to help the viewer see as much and as well as possible. Fortunately, when you shoot outdoors during the day, there is enough light for you to stop down the lens (make the lens opening smaller)—an arrangement that, as you remember, helps to increase the depth of field. When shooting indoors, you usually have to open up your lens considerably to get enough light for proper camera operation. As a result, the depth of field is quite shallow. If you need a larger depth of field, additional lighting becomes mandatory.

The Narrow-Angle Lens (Telephoto Zoom Position)

Field of View   The narrow-angle, or long, lens has a narrow field of view. The same is true for the zoom lens when in the telephoto position (zoomed all the way in). The narrow-angle lens not only reduces the field of view, but also magnifies the objects in the lens's field of view. Quite contrary to the wide-angle lens, which makes objects only a short distance away look relatively small, the long lens makes objects located even at a fairly large distance from the camera look quite large compared to similar objects close to the camera (see 3.28).

Object and Distance Distortion   Because the enlarged background objects look rather big in comparison to the foreground objects, an illusion is created that the distance between foreground, middleground, and background has decreased. The long lens seems to shrink the space between the objects, in direct contrast to the effect created by the wide-angle lens, which exaggerates object proportions and therefore seems to increase relative distance between objects. A narrow-angle lens, or a zoom lens in its telephoto position, crowds objects on the screen.

This crowding effect, called *compression,* can be positive or negative. If you want to show how crowded the freeways are during rush hour, for example, use a long lens, or use your zoom lens in the telephoto position. The long focal length will reduce the distance between the cars and make them appear to be driving bumper to bumper (see 3.28).

But such depth distortions by the narrow-angle lens also work to disadvantage. You are certainly familiar with the deceptive closeness of the pitcher to home plate on your television screen. This depth distortion occurs because the zoom lens is used in a fairly extreme telephoto position, since the camera is placed far to the rear of the pitcher in center field. Because television cameras must remain at a considerable distance from the action in most sports events, the zoom lenses usually operate at their extreme telephoto positions or with powerful range extenders. The resulting compression effect of shrinking space makes it difficult for the

3.30   Telephoto Lens Distortion: Baseball This shot was taken with a zoom lens in an extremely long focal length position. Note how the runner, the pitcher, the batter, the catcher, and the umpire all seem to stand only a few feet apart from one another. The actual distance between the pitcher and the batter is 60½ feet.

viewer to judge actual distances and to tell with accuracy who is ahead of whom (see 3.29).

Another important performance characteristic of the long lens, or the zoom lens in a telephoto position, is the illusion of reduced speed of an object moving toward or away from the camera. Since the narrow-angle lens changes the size of an object moving toward or away from the camera much more gradually than the wide-angle lens, the object seems to move more slowly than it actually does; in fact, an extreme narrow-angle lens virtually eliminates such movement. The object does not seem to change its size perceptibly even when it is traveling a considerably large distance relative to the camera. Such a slowdown is especially effective if you want to emphasize the frustration of someone running but not getting anywhere.

Depth of Field   Long lenses have a shallow depth of field. Like the crowding effect, this shallow depth of field can have advantages and disadvantages. Let us assume that you are about to take a quick close-up of a medium-sized object, such as a can of dog food. You do not have to bother to put up a special background for it. All you need do is move your camera back and zoom in on the display (or use a narrow-angle lens). Your zoom lens is now in a telephoto (narrow-angle) position, decreasing the depth of field to a large extent. Your background is now sufficiently out of focus to pre-

3.31   Selective Focus (a) In this shot the camera (foreground object) is out of focus, drawing attention to the woman (middleground); (b) here, the focus is shifted from the woman (middleground) to the camera (foreground).

vent undesirable distractions. This technique is called **selective focus,** meaning that you can focus either on the foreground, with the middleground and background out of focus; or on the middleground, with the foreground and background out of focus; or on the background, with the foreground and middleground out of focus.

You can also shift emphasis from one object to another quite easily with the help of selective focus. For example, you can zoom in on a foreground camera, thus reducing the depth of field, and focus (with your zoom lens at the telephoto position) on it. Then, by simply "racking focus"—that is, by refocusing—on the person behind it, you can quickly shift the emphasis from the camera (foreground) to the person about to take a picture (middleground). (See 3.30.)

The advantage of a shallow depth of field also applies to unwanted foreground objects. In a baseball pickup, for example, the camera behind home plate may have to shoot through the fence wire. But because your camera is most likely zoomed in on the pitcher, or other players performing at a considerable distance from the camera, you work with a relatively short depth of field. Consequently, everything fairly close to the camera, such as the fence wire, is so much out of focus that for all practical purposes it becomes invisible. The same principle works for shooting through bird cages, prison bars, or similar foreground objects.

You *cannot dolly* with a *long lens,* or with a zoom lens in its telephoto range. Its magnifying power makes any movement of the camera impossible. If you work outdoors, even wind can become a problem. A stiff breeze may shake the camera to such a degree that the greatly magnified vibrations become clearly visible on the television screen.

In the studio the telephoto position of the zoom lens may present another problem for you. The director may have you zoom in on part of an event, such as the lead guitar in a band concert, and then, after you have zoomed in, ask you to truck (move the camera sideways) past the other members of the band. But this movement is extremely difficult to do in the telephoto zoom position. Instead, you should *dolly* in with a *wide-angle zoom position* and then truck, with the lens still in the wide-angle position.

When you have to walk or perhaps even run with the portable camera for a news story or another type of electronic field production, make sure that your zoom lens is in the wide-angle position. If you are zoomed in to the telephoto position, your pictures will be rendered useless by the camera wobbles and focus problems.

PRESETTING THE ZOOM LENS FOR MONOCHROME CAMERAS

Monochrome cameras require a different presetting (calibrating) procedure from color camera zoom lenses. Just in case you have to preset the zoom on a monochrome studio camera, here are the steps to follow:

1. Zoom all the way out to a long shot (widest angle setting on your zoom lens). Focus on the scene with the camera focus control. You are now adjusting the distance of the camera pickup tube relative to the zoom lens. This is called **back focus.**

2. Once the camera is in focus, zoom all the way in on the object that is farthest from the camera and that needs to be included in the zoom. This object is now most likely out of focus. Do not correct the focus with the camera control. Use the zoom control to bring this close-up into focus. Make sure that you are zoomed in all the way to your narrowest angle lens setting. You have now adjusted the lens elements within the zoom lens. This is called **front focus.**

3. Now zoom back again slowly, without touching any focus control. You should remain in focus through the entire zoom range. Sometimes, when you are zoomed out all the way again, you may have to touch up your focus just a little with the camera focus control. But now, you should maintain good focus throughout the zoom, as long as camera and object remain in the same position.

MAIN POINTS

1. The composing of effective shots and the general use of a television camera presuppose a knowledge of the performance characteristics of lenses.

2. The performance characteristics of wide-angle, normal, and narrow-angle lenses (or a zoom lens adjusted to these focal lengths) include (1) field of view, (2) relationship of focal length to performance, and (3) relationship of depth of field to performance.

3. A wide-angle lens (or a zoom lens zoomed out to the wide-angle position) offers a wide vista. It gives a wide field of view with the camera relatively close to the scene.

4. A wide-angle lens distorts objects close to the lens and exaggerates proportions. Objects relatively close to the lens look large, and those only a short distance farther away look quite small. Hence, it makes objects look farther apart and makes rooms look larger than they really are.

5. A wide-angle lens is a good dolly lens. The camera can be moved without the wobbles of the camera being emphasized. Since the wide-angle lens has a relatively large depth of field, it is easy to keep the picture in focus during the camera movement.

6. The normal lens gives a field of view that approximates that of normal vision. The normal lens (or mid-

range zoom position) does not distort objects or the perception of distance. It is used when a normal perspective is desired.

7.   When a camera is moved with the lens in the mid-range (normal lens) zoom position, the camera wobbles are emphasized more than with a wide-angle lens. The shallower depth of field makes it harder to keep the picture in focus.

8.   A narrow-angle lens (or a zoom lens in the telephoto position) has a narrow field of view, and it enlarges the objects in the background. Exactly opposite to the wide-angle lens, which increases the distance between objects, the narrow-angle lens seems to shrink the space between objects that lie at different distances from the camera.

9.   The magnifying power of a narrow-angle lens prevents any camera movement while on the air. Long lenses have a shallow depth of field, which makes keeping in focus more difficult but allows for selective focus.

FURTHER READING

Bensinger, Charles. *The Video Guide.* 3rd ed. Santa Fe, NM: Video-Info Publications, 1983.

Davis, Phil. *Photography.* 4th ed. Dubuque, IA: Wm. C. Brown Co., Publishers, 1982.

Editors of Time-Life Books. *The Camera.* New York: Time-Life Books (Life Library of Photography), 1970.

Langford, Michael. *The Step-by-step Guide to Photography.* New York: Alfred A. Knopf, 1978.

Mounting Equipment

In order to assure ease and fluidity of camera movement, a variety of camera mounts have been developed for studio cameras as well as for ENG/EFP cameras. In Section One of this chapter we will discuss:

1. The four most common camera mounts: (a) tripod dolly, (b) studio pedestal, (c) low-angle dollies, and (d) body mounts.

2. The various camera mounting heads: (a) cam head, (b) fluid head, and (c) cradle head.

3. The ten standard camera movements facilitated by these camera mounts.

  In Section Two we will briefly mention the studio crane, which is used only for special productions in large studios.

CAMERA MOUNTS

Five basic types of camera mounts ensure ease and fluidity of camera movement in the studio and the field: (1) the tripod dolly, (2) the studio pedestal, (3) the low-angle dolly, (4) the body mount, and (5) the studio crane. The studio crane, which is too large and heavy to be found in most small studios, is discussed in Section Two.

The Tripod Dolly

The tripod **dolly** consists of a metal **tripod** usually fastened to a three-caster dolly base. The three casters can be used either in a freewheeling position, which ensures quick and easy repositioning of the camera in all directions, or locked into one position for straight-line dollying. If you do not want the dolly to move, you can lock each caster into a different direction so that each one works against the others. In effect, you have "put the brakes" on your tripod dolly. (See 4.1.)

Various cable guards in front of the casters help to prevent their rolling over or hitting the camera

4.1 Locking Positions of Tripod Dolly With all three wheels locked into different directions, the dolly has to stay put and the tripod is locked into position.

cable. Make sure that you screw the cable guards close to the studio floor, especially when using a small-diameter minicable on your camera.

That the tripod and the dolly base are collapsible makes them the ideal camera mount for most remote operations. The tripod can also be adjusted to the height of the camera operator, but this manipulation takes time and energy. Quick and easy ele-

Although high-quality cameras are becoming smaller and lighter from year to year, they still need a variety of camera mounts for smooth and efficient operation.

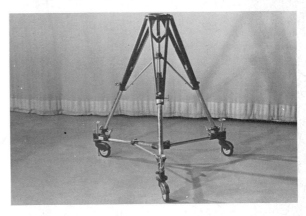

4.2   Tripod Dolly Collapsed and Assembled   The tripod and the dolly can be used separately or as a unit.

vation of the camera is, therefore, not possible. (See 4.2.)

Some stations use wooden tripods for ENG/EFP cameras. These tripods are very popular supports for 16mm film cameras. When putting them under the heavier ENG/EFP camera, however, you must put the tripod on a dolly or a base support, called a *spreader*, to keep the tripod from collapsing.

The Studio Pedestal

With the studio **pedestal** you can dolly very smoothly, and elevate and lower the camera easily while on the air. The more portable field-studio pedestals still allow easy up-and-down movement, but not when the camera is on the air. This up-and-down movement adds an important dimension to the art of television photography. Not only can you adjust the camera to comfortable working height, but you can also look up at an event or down on it. We have known for centuries that looking up at a thing or an event makes it appear more powerful; looking down on it makes it less powerful than it would appear from eye level. With the studio pedestal you can, at least to some degree, bring about these points of view.

Of the great variety of available studio pedestals, we will consider only the most commonly used: (1) the lightweight field-studio pedestal, (2) the counterweighted studio pedestal, and (3) the pneumatic studio pedestal.

The Lightweight Field-Studio Pedestal The lighter cameras made the use of lightweight pedestals more and more common. The lightweight field-studio pedestal is a cross between a tripod and a studio pedestal. Each of the tripod legs can be independently adjusted so that the camera is level on uneven ground. The tripod can be put on a dolly with oversized casters. Most field-studio pedestals have adjustable cable guards.

The pedestal itself can be raised and lowered, either by a hand crank or pneumatically through compressed air (see 4.3). Neither method is smooth

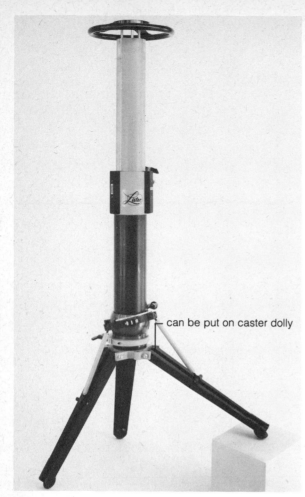

— can be put on caster dolly

4.3 Listec Porta-Ped Pedestal This portable ENG/EFP pedestal can be lowered to about 27 inches (0.70 meters) and raised to about 55 inches (1.4 meters). It has adjustable legs for both height and direction to fit uneven terrain. The camera cannot be raised or lowered on the air.

Arc To move the camera in a slightly curved dolly or truck.

Cam Head A special camera mounting head that permits extremely smooth tilts and pans.

Crab Sideways motion of the camera crane dolly base.

Cradle Head Cradle-shaped camera mounting head. Permits smooth up-and-down tilts and horizontal pans.

Crane 1. Camera dolly that resembles an actual crane in both appearance and operation. The crane can lift the camera from close to the studio floor to over ten feet above it. 2. To move the boom of the camera crane up or down. Also called boom.

Dolly 1. Camera support that enables the camera to move in all directions. 2. To move the camera toward (dolly in) or away from (dolly out or back) the object.

Fluid Head Most popular head for lightweight ENG/EFP camera. Because its moving parts operate in a heavy fluid, it allows very smooth pans and tilts.

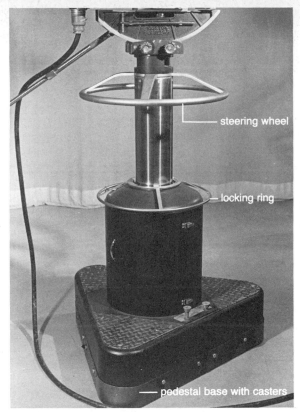

steering wheel

locking ring

pedestal base with casters

4.4   Counterweight Studio Pedestal With the counterweight studio pedestal the camera can be raised and lowered while on the air.

enough to allow the camera to be raised or lowered while on the air.

Whenever you use a tripod dolly or a field-studio pedestal on a remote, be especially careful with the assembly and operation of the camera mount. Because everybody is in a hurry during remote operations, the usual safety precautions are unfortunately not always upheld.

The Counterweighted Studio Pedestal This pedestal (see 4.4) has proved to be one of the most reliable and workable pieces of studio production

---

Pan   Horizontal turning of the camera.

Pedestal   1. Heavy camera dolly that permits a raising and lowering of the camera while on the air. 2. To move the camera up and down via a studio pedestal.

Tilt   To point the camera up and down.

Tongue   To move the boom with the camera from left to right or from right to left.

Tracking   Another name for truck (lateral camera movement).

Truck   To move the camera laterally by means of a mobile camera mount.

Zoom   To change the lens gradually to a narrow-angle position ("zoom-in") or to a wide-angle position ("zoom-out") while the camera remains stationary.

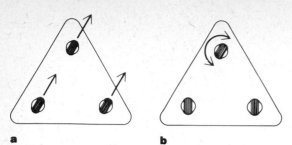

4.5 **Parallel and Tricycle Steering** (a) parallel; (b) tricycle.

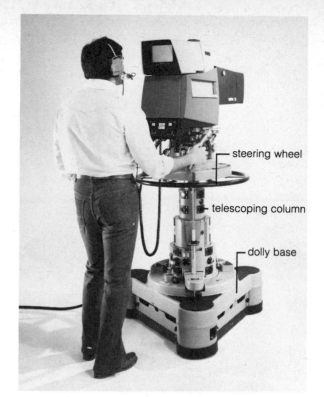

steering wheel

telescoping column

dolly base

equipment. You can lower and raise the camera while on the air, and you can steer the pedestal smoothly in any direction with one control, the large steering wheel. The pedestal column, which raises and lowers the camera, can be locked at any vertical position by a special device, usually a locking ring at the top of the counterweight base. Generally, you work the pedestal in the parallel synchronized, or crab, steering position. This means that all three casters point in the same direction. If, however, you want to rotate the pedestal itself in order to get the whole piece of equipment closer to the easel, you must switch to the tricycle steering position in which only one wheel is steerable (see 4.5).

The counterweight dolly is, however, not without disadvantages. It is very heavy to move about, especially when loaded down with a color camera, big zoom lens, and perhaps a **teleprompter** (a mechanical prompting device). Moreover, the heavier the equipment the pedestal is to support, the more counterweights you need. Because it is so heavy, it cannot be taken readily on remote location. Although the camera can be elevated to about $6\frac{1}{2}$ feet (approximately 2 meters) above the studio floor, it can be lowered to only about 4 feet (approximately 1.20 meters). This is low enough for most normal productions, but it can become a serious handicap if you want to use the camera creatively—in a drama, for example. From this height, you cannot tilt up the camera enough to look at somebody who is standing on the studio floor.

The Pneumatic Studio Pedestal

The pneumatic studio pedestal is the most efficient pedestal. It operates quite similarly to the counterweighted pedestal, except that the camera is balanced by a column of

4.6 **Pneumatic Studio Pedestal** The pneumatic studio pedestal permits the camera to be lowered considerably more than with the counterweight pedestal. Also, the pneumatic pedestal is much lighter.

compressed air. The major advantage of the pneumatic pedestal is that you can lower the camera to about 2 feet (a little over .5 meters) and raise it to about 6 feet (1.80 meters), which is just about as high as the counterweight pedestal will go. This important height range is achieved through telescoping columns. Most pneumatic pedestals are much lighter than the counterweight models, which means that you can move them about the studio floor much more easily. The disadvantage is that you need an air compressor to replenish the air that inevitably escapes over some period of time, even if you do not operate the dolly for some time. But the ease and smoothness of operation have made the pneumatic pedestal one of the most widely used types of mounting equipment for studio cameras in network and big-city studios. (See 4.6.)

The Low-Angle Dolly

One of the problems of using a studio pedestal is that you cannot get the camera low enough for certain dramatic shots. If such low-angle shots are imperative, you need to use a specially constructed **high hat** and a **low-angle dolly**, or as it is often called, a **camera sled.**

The high hat is a cylinder-shaped device that accepts the usual camera mounting heads. It can be bolted either onto part of the scenery or, more commonly, on a tripod dolly (see 4.7). When mounted on a tripod dolly, it is generally called a camera sled (see 4.19).

The Body Mount

Portable cameras for ENG/EFP use are usually carried on the operator's shoulder. This way, you can quickly and easily point the camera into practically any direction, walk with it, and even run with it. The shoulder pod keeps the camera balanced on your shoulder, but it does not make it any lighter. Special **body mounts** are sometimes used to distribute the camera's weight to the operator's waist. However, the body mount picks up the breathing motion of the operator; the lens, especially when in a telephoto position, magnifies these breathing motions into intolerable picture wiggles. This is why most ENG/EFP camera operators prefer to work with the camera's shoulder pod (see 4.8 and 4.9).

4.7   High Hat The high hat is a camera mount that can be bolted to bleachers, the boards of a platform, or to any homemade dolly. It permits the camera to work low to the ground or on the edge of a balcony.

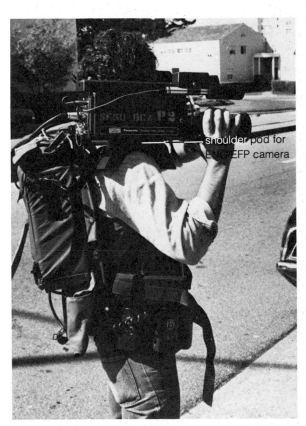

shoulder pod for ENG/EFP camera

4.8   ENG Camera Shoulder Pod Almost all ENG cameras come equipped with a shoulder pod that helps the camera to rest balanced on the shoulder of the operator. It also serves as a stand when the camera is set down.

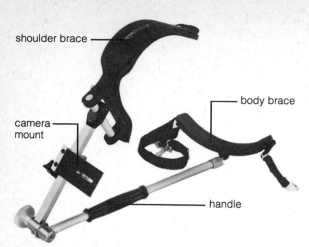

4.9 **ENG Body Mount** The ENG/EFP camera body mount helps to balance cameras without a shoulder pod or those cameras that need additional support.

body brace

electronic viewfinder

counter-balancing spring

ENG/EFP camera

4.10 **Steadicam** With the Steadicam mount the camera operator can move at will while the camera remains steady. The camera operator views the camera pictures in a small electronic viewfinder mounted halfway between the camera and the operator.

Special body mounts, like the **Steadicam,** have built-in **servo stabilizers** that absorb the wobbles and jitters caused by someone carrying the camera. When an operator is walking or running with the Steadicam mount, the movement of the camera resembles that of an extremely smooth dolly or truck. However, the Steadicam mount is very heavy, and only experienced operators can wear it and the camera for an extended period of time (see 4.10).

CAMERA MOUNTING HEADS

The camera mounting heads connect the camera to the tripod or camera pedestal. The mounting head allows the camera to tilt (pointing the camera up and down) and pan (turning it horizontally). Three types of mounting heads have proved useful for most operations: (1) the cam head, (2) the fluid head, and (3) the cradle head.

The Cam Head

Although cameras are getting lighter, the zoom lenses for studio cameras have yet to shrink in size. Studio cameras are often saddled with a heavy prompting device so that the total weight resting on the camera head is fairly heavy. A good camera mounting head should be able to counterbalance easily and quickly whatever weight the camera and accessories have in order to make the panning and tilting easy and smooth for the operator. The **cam head** is generally used for heavy studio cameras and accessories. All types of mounting heads have separate controls to control the degree of friction, called **drag,** during the panning and tilting. There are also pan and tilt lock devices that prevent the camera from moving when left unattended (see 4.11).

For lighter ENG/EFP cameras, there is a lightweight camera mounting head, which can be adjusted to various camera and lens loads by a simple adjusting screw. Though not a cam head, the lightweight mounting head nevertheless works operationally very much like the cam head (see 4.12).

The Fluid Head

When you are using a lightweight ENG/EFP camera, even the most carefully balanced cam heads make

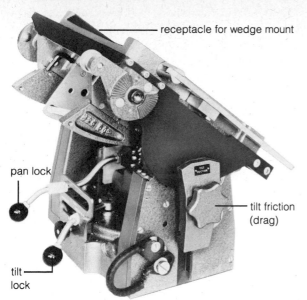

receptacle for wedge mount

pan lock

tilt friction (drag)

tilt lock

4.11   Cam Head The cam head counterbalances even the heaviest of studio cameras to permit smooth tilts and pans.

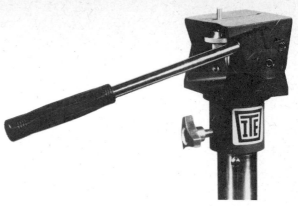

4.12   Lightweight Mounting Head The lighter ENG/EFP cameras are often mounted on simple (often spring-loaded) lightweight heads, especially if the camera is used in the field.

it rather difficult for you to pan and tilt the camera smoothly. **Fluid heads** are, therefore, preferred. They achieve the counterbalancing by having their moving parts operate in a rather heavy fluid. You can adjust the desired balance, or drag, by turning a selector ring (see 4.13).

The Cradle Head

Some of the heavier cameras may be mounted on a **cradle head**, which balances the camera by distributing more or less evenly the center of gravity of the camera-lens system. The problem with the cradle head is that it is difficult to get just the right pan and tilt drag for smooth operation. Like all the other camera mounting heads, the cradle head has a horizontal and vertical lock and drag mechanism (see 4.14).

All cam heads and some fluid and cradle heads use a **wedge mount** to attach the camera to the mounting head. A plate with the male wedge is attached to the underside of the camera and then slid into the female wedge plate, which is bolted

4.13   Fluid Head The most popular heads for lightweight cameras are fluid heads. They allow extremely smooth pans and tilts. Most fluid heads have a bubble for leveling the tripod.

onto the mounting head. Once you have adjusted the wedge for proper camera balance, all you have to do is slide it into the female plate of the mounting head and the camera will arrive at the proper balanced position (see 4.15).

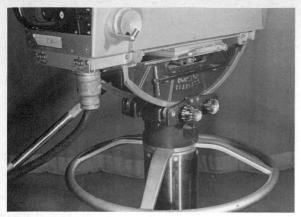

4.14 Cradle Head The cradle head is still used for some of the heavier studio cameras. It operates on a gravity-balance principle but is difficult to adjust for smooth panning and tilting.

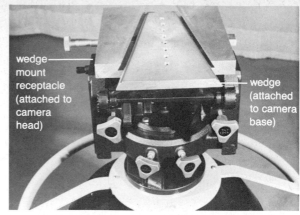

wedge mount receptacle (attached to camera head)

wedge (attached to camera base)

4.15 Wedge Mount The female part of the wedge mount is attached to the mounting head; the male part is attached to the camera. With the wedge mount the camera can be easily and accurately mounted on the pedestal and removed very quickly.

Lighter cameras are sometimes attached to the mounting head by a screw similar to those used to mount a 35mm camera on a tripod. There are also some quick-release assemblies, which allow for rapid attachment and removal of the camera from the camera mounting head by rotating a spring-loaded lever.

Many lightweight tripods have a ball adjustment that allows the operator to level the camera.

CAMERA MOVEMENTS

Before learning to operate a camera, you should become familiar with the most common camera movements. "Left" and "right" always refer to the camera's point of view.

The camera mounting equipment has been designed solely to help you move the camera smoothly and efficiently in various ways. The major camera movements are (1) pan, (2) tilt, (3) pedestal, (4) tongue, (5) crane or boom, (6) dolly, (7) truck or track, (8) crab, (9) arc, and (10) zoom. (See 4.16.)

■ **Pan:** Turning the camera horizontally, from left to right or from right to left. To "pan right," which

means that you swivel the camera to the right (clockwise), you must push the panning handles to the left. To "pan left," which means to swivel the camera to the left (counterclockwise), you push the panning handles to the right.

■ **Tilt:** Making the camera point down or up. A "tilt up" means that the camera is made to point up gradually. A "tilt down" means that the camera is made to point down gradually.

■ **Pedestal:** Elevating or lowering the camera on a studio pedestal. To "pedestal up," you raise the pedestal; to "pedestal down," you lower the pedestal.

■ **Tongue:** Moving the whole camera from left to right or from right to left with the boom of a camera crane. When you tongue left or right, the camera usually points into the same general direction, with only the boom moving left (counterclockwise) or right (clockwise).

■ **Crane** or **Boom:** Moving the whole camera up or down on a camera crane. The effect is somewhat similar to pedestaling up or down, except that the camera swoops over a much greater vertical distance. You either "crane, or boom, up" or "crane, or boom, down."

■ **Dolly:** Moving the camera toward or away from an object in more or less a straight line by means of a mobile camera mount. When you "dolly in," you move the camera closer to the object; when you "dolly out, or dolly back," you move the camera farther away from the object.

■ **Truck** or **Track:** Moving the camera laterally by means of a mobile camera mount. To "truck left" means to move the camera mount to the left with the camera pointing at a right angle to the direction of the travel. To "truck right" means to move the camera mount to the right with the camera pointing at a right angle to the direction of the travel.

■ **Crab:** Any sideways motion of the crane dolly base or its smaller cousin, the crab dolly. A crab is similar to a truck, except that the camera mount does not have to stay lateral to the action all the time; it can move toward or away from the action at the same time. "Crabbing" is used more in film than in television.

■ **Arc:** Moving the camera in a slightly curved dolly or truck movement with a mobile camera mount. To "arc left" means to dolly in or out in a camera-left curve or to truck left in a curve around the object; to "arc right" means to dolly in or out in a camera-right curve or to truck right in a curve around the object.

■ **Zoom:** Changing the focal length of the lens through the use of a zoom control while the camera remains stationary. To "zoom in" means to change the lens gradually to a narrow-angle position, thereby making the scene appear to move closer to the viewer; to "zoom out" means to change the lens gradually to a wide-angle lens position, thereby making the scene appear to move farther away from the viewer.

MAIN POINTS

1. The four major camera mounts are (1) tripod dolly, (2) studio pedestal, (3) low-angle dolly, and (4) body mounts.

2. A tripod dolly consists of a tripod fastened to a three-caster dolly base. The tripod can be used separately from the dolly base. Because both units are collapsible and relatively light, the tripod dolly is often used in field productions.

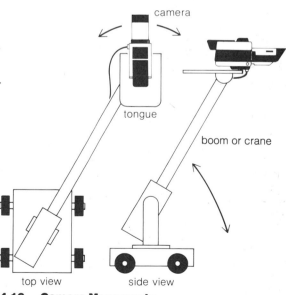

4.16 Camera Movements

3. The studio pedestals can support heavy studio cameras and permit extremely smooth camera movements, such as dollies, trucks, and arcs. Also, with most studio pedestals, the camera can be raised and lowered while on the air.

4. There are three types of commonly used studio pedestals: (1) the lightweight field-studio pedestal, (2) the counterweighted studio pedestal, and (3) the pneumatic studio pedestal.

5. The lightweight field-studio pedestal, which is a cross between the tripod dolly and a studio pedestal, can be raised or lowered by a crank or pneumatically. However, the camera cannot be pedestaled up or down while hot (on the air).

6. The counterweighted studio pedestal balances the weight of the camera through weights in the pedestal. This added weight makes the pedestal-camera unit quite heavy to operate.

7. The pneumatic studio pedestal counterweights the camera through a column of compressed air. It is lighter than the counterweighted pedestals and has a telescoping column that permits a greater range of vertical camera movement.

8. Low-angle dollies use a special mount, called high hat, or a sledlike dolly, called camera sled, to get the camera as close to the studio floor as possible for low-angle shots.

9. Portable cameras for ENG/EFP use are usually carried on the operator's shoulder. A shoulder pod, which is either part of the camera construction or mounted onto the ENG/EFP camera, makes it easier to balance the camera on the shoulder.

10. Special body mounts distribute the camera's weight to the waist of the operator. A special body mount, the Steadicam, keeps the camera steady through servo-stabilization devices, even when the operator walks or runs with the camera.

11. There are three types of mounting heads: (1) cam heads, (2) fluid heads, and (3) cradle heads. These camera mounting heads connect the camera to the pedestal or tripod and allow the camera to be smoothly tilted up and down and panned horizontally.

12. The most common camera movements are (1) pan, turning the camera horizontally, (2) tilt, pointing the camera up and down, (3) pedestal, lowering or elevating the camera on a studio pedestal, (4) tongue, moving the whole camera from left to right or from right to left with the boom of a camera crane, (5) crane or boom, moving the whole camera up or down on a camera crane, (6) dolly, moving the camera toward or away from the object, (7) truck, moving the camera laterally, (8) crab, moving the whole base of a camera crane sideways, similar to a truck, (9) arc, moving the camera in a slightly curved dolly or truck movement, and (10) zoom, changing the focal length of the lens while the camera is stationary. Although not a camera movement, the zoom effect looks similar to that of a moving camera and is, therefore, classified as such.

A crane can make the camera move about in ways not possible with other mounting devices. The importance of a crane is that it permits fast and especially fluid changes in camera positions.

In this section, we will briefly mention (1) the studio crane, (2) the dolphin crane arm, and (3) the camera sled.

THE STUDIO CRANE

Although a crane is desirable for creative camera work, it is used in very few studios. In most cases, the limited floor space and ceiling height prohibit the use of the crane. Also, a studio crane needs at least one dolly-and-boom operator, in addition to the camera operator; when the crane is motor-driven, still another person is needed to drive the crane about the studio floor.

Nevertheless, in some production situations a crane may be necessary. With a crane, you can get the camera close to the studio floor (about 1 foot high) and about 10 feet (3 meters) above it, and you can go from one height to the other swiftly and smoothly. The crane boom can be panned a full 360 degrees, still allowing the camera a panning radius of 180 degrees. All movements can be carried out simultaneously, allowing excellent opportunities for creative camera work. (See 4.17.)

When a studio crane is used, it is desirable to install a monitor directly on the crane for the dolly operator to watch. The coordination of camera operator and dolly

4.17   Studio Crane   The crane can raise and lower the camera more than any other camera mount. However, it takes up much studio space and requires several operators. It is, therefore, used only for major productions in big studios.

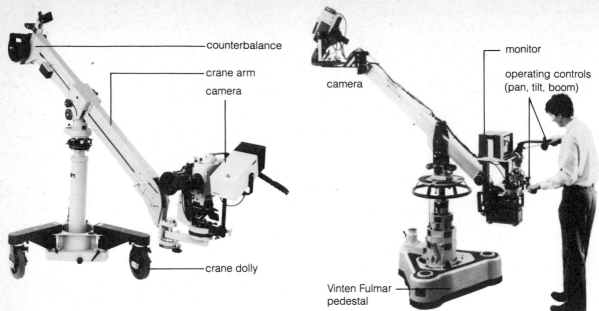

counterbalance

crane arm

camera

monitor

camera

operating controls (pan, tilt, boom)

crane dolly

Vinten Fulmar pedestal

4.18 **Dolphin Crane Arm** With the dolphin crane arm, a single camera operator can move the camera from very close to the floor to over 7 feet above the studio floor in one smooth motion, while tonguing the arm and panning and tilting the camera at the same time.

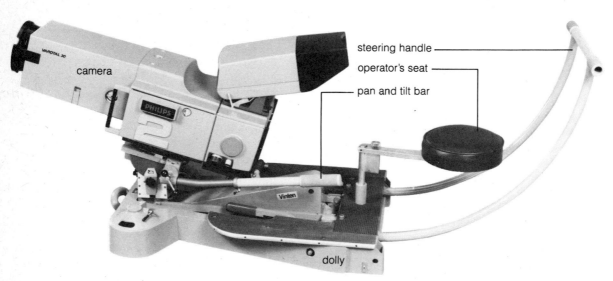

camera

steering handle

operator's seat

pan and tilt bar

dolly

4.19 **Camera Sled** The camera sled is a cranelike low-angle dolly that permits extreme low-angle shots.

operator is essential for smooth and effective camera handling. The dolly operator is also greatly aided if, in addition to listening to the director's signals, he or she can actually see the pictures the camera is taking.

THE DOLPHIN CRANE ARM

This cranelike device lets you lower the camera almost to the studio floor and then raise it to as high as you can reach while operating the camera. At the same time you can tongue the boom or pan and tilt the camera. The advantages of the dolphin crane arm are that it is comparatively light and that it needs no other people than the camera operator. However, it takes considerable practice to get this crane arm—and with it, the camera—to move smoothly and fluidly. The somewhat more limited, but more easily operated, studio pedestal is, therefore, preferred in most operations. (See 4.18.)

THE CAMERA SLED

Some commercially made camera sleds look like a small crane. The rather short crane arm, which can be hydraulically operated, lowers the camera smoothly from about 2 feet above ground (60 centimeters) to less than 4 inches high (approximately 10 centimeters). Unless you do a great amount of television drama or special effects video, such elaborate camera sleds are not a sound investment for most television operations. (See 4.19.)

MAIN POINTS

1. The studio crane permits the camera to be elevated almost twice as much as with a studio pedestal and lowered as close to the studio floor as with a camera sled. With a crane, the camera can also be swung left and right while panning and tilting. All camera motions can be performed at the same time in one smooth motion.

2. Most cranes need additional operators to help the camera operator execute the various crane movements.

3. In many cases, the limited floor space and ceiling height of studios make the use of the crane impractical or impossible.

FURTHER READING

Millerson, Gerald. *The Technique of Television Production.* 10th ed. Woburn, MA: Focal Press, 1981.

Wurtzel, Alan. *Television Production.* 2nd ed. New York: McGraw-Hill Book Co., 1983.

Camera Operation and Picture Composition

Now that you have learned the major aspects of television cameras and their lenses, you need to know how to operate a camera and how to compose effective pictures.

In Section One of this chapter we will take up:

1. How to work a studio camera, including the basic steps before, during, and after the show.
2. How to work a portable camera, including camera setup, the actual camera operation, and camera care.
3. The major factors of picture composition. We will concentrate on field of view, organizing screen area, organizing screen depth, and organizing motion.

Because some of the old turret cameras are still used in several production learning centers, the operation of the turret camera will be briefly mentioned in Section Two.

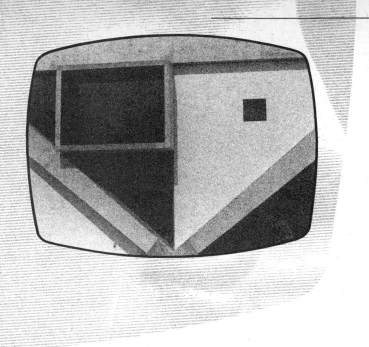

HOW TO WORK A CAMERA

We will first concentrate on some of the basic steps of how to work a studio camera and a portable camera.

Working a Studio Camera

When operating a camera, you must go through some basic steps *before, during,* and *after* the show or the rehearsal.

Before

1. Put on your headset and check whether the intercommunication system is functioning.

2. Unlock the pan and tilt mechanism on the camera mounting head and adjust the drag, if necessary. Check whether the camera is balanced on the mounting head. Unlock the pedestal, and pedestal up and down. Check whether the pedestal is correctly counterweighted. A properly balanced camera remains put in any given vertical position. If it drops down or moves up by itself, the pedestal is not properly counterweighted.

3. See how much camera cable you have, and whether it is tightly plugged in at the wall outlet and the camera head. Is the cable coiled so that it will uncoil easily when you move the camera? If not, recoil it.

4. If the camera is already warmed up and correctly set up by the video engineer, ask to have the camera uncapped, or whether you can uncap it. You will now see in the viewfinder the pictures the camera actually takes. Is the viewfinder properly adjusted?

5. Check the zoom lens. Zoom in and out. Does the zoom lens "stick," that is, does it have problems moving smoothly throughout the zoom range? What exactly is your range? Get a feel for how close you can get to the set from a certain position. Does the shot box work? Preset for a few zoom positions and see whether the zoom lens actually moves to the preset position. Is the lens clean? If it is unusually dusty, use a fine camel's hair brush and carefully clean off the larger dust particles. With a small rubber syringe or a can of compressed air, blow off the finer dust. Do not just blow on it with your mouth. You will fog up the lens and get it dirtier than it was.

Like bicycling, working a camera is something you learn by doing. There is no substitute for practice. The guidelines in this chapter are intended only to facilitate the learning process.

In this section we will discuss two main points: (1) how to work the camera, and (2) some principles of effective picture composition.

6. **Rack through focus**—that is, move the focus control from one extreme position to the other. Can you move easily and smoothly into and out of focus?

7. Preset the zoom lens. Just to remind you how it is done: Zoom all the way in on the farthest object in the zoom range, like the map behind the newscaster, or the door on the far wall of the living room set. Focus on this "far" object. Now zoom all the way back to the widest angle setting. You should now remain in focus throughout the zoom, provided that neither object nor camera moves.

8. If you have a shot sheet (a list of your upcoming shot sequence—see Chapter 10), this is a good time to practice the more complicated zoom shots.

9. If you have a teleprompter attached to the camera, check all the connections. Since this mechanism is usually operated by a member of the floor crew, ask him or her to check it out.

10. Lock the camera again (pedestal, and panning and tilt mechanism) before leaving it. Do not ever leave a camera unlocked even if it is for only a short while.

11. Cap the camera if you leave it for any prolonged period of time.

During

1. Put on earphones and establish contact with the director, technical director, and video control. Unlock the camera and recheck tilt and pan drag, and the pedestal movement.

2. Preset the zoom at each new camera position. Make sure that you can stay in focus over the entire zoom range.

3. Preset the zoom positions if operating with a shot box. Do not move the camera after you have preset the lens; if you must move, preset the zoom positions again.

4. When checking the focus between shots, rack through focus a few times so that you can determine at which position the picture is the sharpest. When you are focusing on a person, the hairline usually gives you enough detail to determine the sharpest focus.

5. If you anticipate a dolly with the zoom lens, make sure that the lens is set at a wide-angle position. When dollying with a zoom lens, preset the focus approximately at the midpoint of the dolly distance. With the zoom lens at the wide-angle posi-

tion, the depth of field should be large enough so that you need to adjust focus only when you get close to the object or event. When using a tripod dolly, make sure that you have the wheels swiveled in the direction you are about to move.

6.   You will find that a heavy camera pedestal allows you to dolly extremely smoothly. However, you may have some difficulty getting it to move, or stopping it without jerking the camera. Start slowly to overcome the inertia, and try to slow down just before the end of the dolly or truck. If you have a difficult truck or arc to perform, have a floorperson help you steer the camera. You can then concentrate on the camera operation. In a straight dolly, you can keep both hands on the panning handles. If you have to steer the camera, steer with your right hand. Keep your left hand on the focus device.

7.   If you pedestal up or down, make sure that you brake the camera before it hits the stops at the extreme pedestal positions. Generally keep your shots at the talent's eye level unless the director instructs you to shoot either from a high or low angle.

8.   When you operate a freewheel dolly, always have the wheels preset in the direction of the intended camera movement. This will prevent the camera dolly from starting off in the wrong direction. Make sure that the cable guards are down far enough so that you do not hit the camera cable with the casters.

9.   Be sure you know the approximate reach of the camera cable. Know how much you have before you start a dolly in or a truck. Cable drag on the camera can be irritating when it prevents you from achieving a smooth dolly. Although the minicables (such as the triaxial cables) have reduced drag to a minimum, you may still find that in a long dolly the cable tugs annoyingly at the camera. Do not try to pull the cable along with your hand. To ease the tension, you may want to carry it over your shoulder, or tie it to the pedestal base, leaving enough slack so that you can freely pan, tilt, and pedestal. On complicated camera movements, have a floorperson help you with the cable; otherwise, the dragging sound may be picked up quite clearly by the microphone. If your cable gets twisted during a dolly, do not just drag the whole mess along. Have a floorperson untangle it for you.

10.   At all times during the show, be aware of all other activities around you. Where are the other cameras? The microphone boom? The floor monitor? It is your responsibility to keep out of the view of the other cameras, and not to hit anything (including floor personnel or talent) during your moves. Watch especially for obstacles in your dolly path, such as scenery, properties, floor lights. Floor rugs are a constant hazard to camera movement. When you dolly into a set that uses a floor rug, watch the floor so that you do not dolly up on the rug all of a sudden. Better yet, have a floorperson warn you when you come close to the rug. Be particularly careful when dollying back. A good floor manager will help to clear the way and will also tap you on the shoulder to prevent you from backing into something.

11.   In general, keep your eyes on the viewfinder. If the format allows, you can look around for something interesting to shoot between shots. Your director will appreciate good visuals in an **ad lib** show (in which the shots have not been previously rehearsed). But do not try to outdirect the director from your position. He or she is the only one who knows at any given point what the other cameras are doing.

Bust Shot   Framing of a person from the upper torso to the top of the head.

Close-up   Object or any part of it seen at close range and framed tightly. The close-up can be extreme (extreme or big close-up) or rather loose (medium close-up).

Closure   Short for psychological closure. Mentally filling in spaces of an incomplete picture.

Follow Focus   Controlling the focus of the lens so that the image of an object is continuously kept sharp and clear, regardless of whether camera and/or object move.

Headroom   The space left between the top of the head and the upper screen edge.

12. Watch for the tally light to go out before moving the camera into a new shooting position or presetting the zoom.

13. During rehearsal, inform the floor manager or the director of unusual production problems. If you simply cannot prevent a camera shadow, the lighting must be changed. The camera may be too close to the object to keep it in focus. Or the director may not give you enough time to preset the zoom again after you move into a new shooting position. Alert him or her if your zoom is in a narrow-angle position (zoomed in fairly close) and he or she has you move the camera while on the air. Sometimes it is hard for the director to tell from the preview monitor at exactly what zoom position the lens is.

14. If you work without shot sheets, which give you the exact sequence of shots for your camera, try to remember the type and sequence of shots during the rehearsal. A good camera operator has the next shot lined up before the director calls for it. If you work from a shot sheet, go to the next shot immediately after your previous one. Do not wait until the last minute. The director may have to come to your camera ("punch it up" on the air) much sooner than you remember from rehearsal. Do not zoom in or out needlessly during shots unless you are presetting the zoom lens.

15. Mark the critical camera positions on the studio floor with some masking tape. If you do not have a shot sheet, make one up on your own. Mark particularly the camera movements (dollies, trucks) so that you can set your zoom in a wide-angle position. Be sure to line up exactly on these marks during the actual show.

16. Try to avoid unnecessary chatter on the intercom. Use the talkback system only in emergencies.

17. Listen carefully to what the director tells all the camera operators, not just you. This way, you will be able to coordinate your shots with the shots of the other cameras. Also, you can avoid wasteful duplication of shots by knowing approximately what the other cameras are doing.

After

1. At the end of the show, wait for the "all clear" signal before you lock the camera.

2. Ask the video engineer whether the camera may be capped.

3. Now lock the camera mounting head and the pedestal and push the camera into a safe place in the studio. Do not leave it in the middle of the studio; a camera can be easily damaged by a piece of scenery being moved or by other kinds of studio traffic.

4. Coil the cable again as neatly as possible in the customary figure-eight loops.

Working a Portable Camera

When working a portable camera in an ENG situation, you are usually alone, or at best, you have a second person take care of the VTR unit and the microphone. In any case, you do not have a video engineer to look after you and your camera to make sure that both yield peak performances. Therefore, you have to know something about *camera setup, camera operation,* and *camera care.* Again, we will discuss these items within the operational steps before, during, and after the news coverage. Many

---

Knee Shot Framing of a person from the knees up.

Long Shot Object seen from far away or framed very loosely. The extreme long shot shows the object from a great distance.

Medium Shot Object seen from a medium distance. Covers any framing between long shot and close-up.

Noseroom The space left in front of a person looking toward the edge of the screen. Also called leadroom.

Over-the-Shoulder Shot Camera looks over a person's shoulder (shoulder and back of head included in shot) at another person.

Two-Shot Framing of two people.

of these steps also apply to the more elaborate electronic field productions, except that during EFP, you have more crew members available to take care of many of the technical steps.

Even if you are in a tremendous rush to get a breaking news story covered, handle all electronic equipment (camera, VTR, microphone, batteries, lights) with *extreme care*. The ENG cameras and VTRs are amazingly rugged; but they can tolerate only so much mishandling. We will, therefore, familiarize you with a few warnings before listing some of the operating steps.

1. Do not leave the camera or VTR *unprotected* in the hot sun, or worse, exposed in your car during a hot day. When you need to work the camera and VTR in extremely cold weather or in rain, protect them with a "raincoat" or at least some plastic sheet. Some zoom lenses stick in extremely wet or cold weather. Check out the lens before using it on location.

2. *Never,* really *never,* point the camera into the sun, regardless of whether the camera is turned on or not. Even the best of camera pickup tubes cannot cope with bright sunlight and will get damaged or burn out altogether. The sun is sometimes fully reflected by store windows, car windows and chrome parts, or still water. Realize that shooting such reflections is like shooting the sun itself. Always cap the lens in two ways: by putting the aperture ring in the "c" position and by turning the filter wheel to the "cap" position. If the lens has an actual cap that fits over the lens (like on a regular 35mm camera), put this one on too, for added protection.

3. Do not store the camera or hold it for a prolonged period of time with the lens *pointing down.* Some of the particles that are inevitably present inside the camera pickup tube will fall on and adhere to the target, causing specks to appear on the television picture. When putting the camera down, always put it upright on the shoulder pod. If you lay the camera on its side, you run the risk of damaging either the viewfinder, or the clipped-on microphone on the other side.

4. *Do not drop* the batteries, or expose them to the sun for a prolonged period of time. Although a battery may look quite rugged from the outside, it is nevertheless quite sensitive to heat and shock.

5. Do not yank or step on the connecting cable between the camera and the VTR.

After these important warnings, here are some of the steps you must follow before operating the camera and VTR units. At this point we are still assuming that you are a one-person team, which means that you are carrying and operating the camera and the VTR.

Before

1. Make sure all batteries are fully charged and working, including the spare batteries. Also check the nonpower supply batteries in your system, such as the small battery in the VTR that drives the counter, the small battery in the camera that helps the camera remember the white balance even if the camera is off the main power, and the one in the shotgun mic. Some batteries develop a "memory" and indicate that they are fully charged when actually they are not. The way to keep the battery from building up this memory is not to recharge it until it has run almost all the way down, or to discharge it deliberately from time to time.

2. Check the connecting cable between the camera and the VTR. Most ENG camera operators leave the camera and VTR connected at all times. This will not only save time, but also keep the white balance in the camera's memory.

3. Check whether the external microphone (usually a hand mic) and mic that is attached to the camera are working properly. Most shotgun microphones need to be switched on before they become operational. Do you have enough cable so that the reporter can work far enough away from the camera? Again, keeping the external mic plugged in saves time and minimizes costly mistakes. You can coil the mic cable and bow-tie it with a shoelace. One tug, and the cable is uncoiled.

4. Does the portable camera light work? Do not just look at the bulb. Turn it on for a few seconds with the battery belt as power source. If you have additional lights, are they all operational? Do you have enough AC extension cords and simple three-prong to two-prong adaptors to fit older household outlets?

5. Make sure the VTR unit is in good working order. (See Chapter 10 for more detail on VTR operation.) Do not forget to put a cassette in the VTR, and to take some spare cassettes along. Whenever handling a cassette, develop a routine of taking up the tape slack by turning back the supply wheel with your finger and turn the cassette over to see whether the safety tab (usually red) is on the cassette. If it has been removed, you cannot record on this tape (see Chapter 10).

6. Clean the heads on the VTR, but only if you have learned how to do it properly. Otherwise, let an experienced engineer do it for you. Double-check on the VTR battery, which usually drives the camera, too.

7. Check whether the VTR is in the power-on mode and push the VTR button on the camera. The viewfinder should indicate the record mode. If there is trouble (warning light blinking in the viewfinder and audio beeps in the earphone), check the status lights on the VTR (see Chapter 10).

8. Make sure you carry a spare fuse. Some ENG/EFP cameras have a spare fuse right next to the active one. The first thing you do if the camera is not working is to check the fuse. Also, it is a good idea for you to check periodically whether these items are part of your production emergency kit: several video cassettes, an audio cassette recorder and several audio cassettes, an additional microphone and a small microphone stand, one or more portable lights and stands, additional lamps for all lights, AC cords, spares for all types of batteries, VTR head cleaning fluid and cotton swabs, various clips or clothespins and gaffer tape, a small reflector, a roll of aluminum foil, a small white card for white balance, light diffusing material, various effects filters, a can of compressed air for cleaning lenses, camera raincoat, a normal flashlight, and such personal survival items as an umbrella and some spare clothes. Once you have worked in the field a few times, you will know how to put together your own camera kit.

During

You will probably develop your own method of carrying and operating all the ENG equipment, but there are some basic steps that are well established.

1. The camera rests on your right shoulder. Your right hand slips through the loop at the lens and supports the camera. You also activate the servo zoom with your right hand (usually the index finger of your right hand), and the VTR start and stop (on some models with your thumb, pressing a button on the bottom of the lens).

2. Assuming you operate a camera that does not have the VTR attached to it, the VTR dangles from your left shoulder. Your left hand works the lens focus and iris (aperture) ring on the lens (unless you are in the auto-iris mode). You also switch the camera light on and off with your left hand, and perform additional balancing acts such as holding a reflector, or yourself when shooting in precarious situations.

3. There are some ENG cameras that have a small earphone attached to the side of the camera. In this case, you listen to the audio with your right ear resting against the earphone-speaker. Usually, camera operators hear the audio through a molded ear piece that fits the left ear.

4. When using the portable camera light, you also need to carry the 30-volt battery belt, either slung over your left shoulder or tied around your waist.

5. Turn on the VTR and the camera. Do not forget to turn on the shotgun mic attached to the camera.

6. Do the white and black balance. If you do not have a white card, focus the camera on anything white such as a coffee cup, somebody's shirt, or a poster. Repeat the white balance each time you encounter new lighting conditions. When balancing for black, cap the camera. Usually the camera goes automatically into the cap position when doing the black balance. Switch back and do the white balance again. Now you are ready to record.

7. Try to keep the camera as steady as possible and zoom as smoothly as possible. The viewer should not be conscious of your camera movements or your zooms. If you walk with the camera while recording or on the air, keep the camera as steady as possible. Aim the camera with your whole upper body; have your legs absorb all the wiggles and bumps. Walk with the zoom lens only in the wide-angle position. Do not panic if you lose the subject temporarily in the viewfinder. Keep the camera steady, see where

the subject is, and aim the camera smoothly in the new direction. Or, simply zoom out to a wide shot until you have reoriented yourself to the new situation. With the zoom lens in the wide-angle position, you are often closer to the object than the viewfinder image indicates. Watch, therefore, that you do not bump into something or somebody with the camera, especially if you walk the camera into a crowd or other tightly spaced group of people. Whenever possible, walk backward with the camera so that you can keep the event in front of you. Moving backwards also forces you to walk on the balls of your feet, which are better shock absorbers than your heels.

8. If there is time, preset the zoom lens. More often than not, you will find that you do not have time for such routine studio procedures and that you need to **follow focus** as well as you can. It is easier to keep in focus when you start with a closeup and then zoom back than the other way around. In effect, what you are doing is presetting the zoom while on the air. When you shoot under low light conditions, you will need to pay more attention to the focus than when shooting in bright daylight. The low light necessitates a wide lens opening, which in turn reduces the depth of field. Try to avoid any fast camera movements. Under low light conditions, even the best of the camera tubes are not entirely free of lag. You may get comet-tailing in bright sunlight, especially if there is great contrast between the highlights and the shadow areas.

9. Most camera operators prefer not to have the camera in the auto-iris mode, but to work the lens opening manually (with the left hand). This is especially important if you shoot a high-contrast scene (see Chapter 7).

10. Whenever you have the camera going, record sound, whether somebody is talking or not. This sound is important to achieve continuity in post-production editing. When working in relatively quiet surroundings, record in the AGC (automatic gain control) mode. Otherwise, you need to switch to manual gain control, take a level, and record (see Chapters 8 and 9 for more ENG sound information). When the reporter is holding the external mic, do not start running away from him or her in order to get a better shot of the event. Either you run together, or you must stay put.

11. Heed the warning signals in the viewfinder and on the VTR. It is usually the equipment, not the warning light, that is malfunctioning.

12. If you are lucky enough to have a two-person ENG team, make sure that all the preceding functions are properly assigned. The best way to guarantee success in ENG is to assign each team member separate functions. For example, you might run the camera, and your team member could carry the VTR and take care of all VTR functions, the audio, and the lighting. But if you decide to carry the VTR on some occasions and not on others, you are inviting trouble. When you are working as a member of a multicamera team, rules similar to those in the operation of studio cameras apply.

13. Above all, use common sense. Always be mindful of your and other people's safety. Use sound judgment in determining whether the risk is worth the story. In ENG, reliability and consistency are more important than sporadic feats, however spectacular. Do not risk your neck and the equipment to get a shot that would simply embellish a story already on tape. Leave this type of shooting to the gifted amateurs.

After

1. Unless you have just shot a really hot story that needs to get on the air immediately, even unedited, take care of the equipment first before delivering the tape. If you are properly organized, this should take but a few minutes.

2. Take the cassette out of the VTR and immediately replace it with a new one.

3. Make sure all the switches are in the "off " position, unless you are heading for another assignment. In this case, put the camera into the standby position. Do not forget to switch off the shotgun mic attached to the camera.

4. Cap the camera with the iris cap position and the filter wheel cap position. If you have a regular cap for the front of the lens, put this one on, too.

5. Roll up the mic cable and bow-tie it again with the shoelace.

6. Put everything back into the designated boxes or bags right away. Do not wait until tomorrow because you may find yourself having to cover an important news story on your way home.

7. If the camera battery is low, or if you have a no-memory battery, recharge it as soon as you get back to the station.

8. If the camera and/or VTR got wet, make sure everything is dry before putting it away. Moisture is one of the most serious threats to the ENG equipment.

9. If you have time, check all the lights so they will work for the next assignment. Coil all the AC extensions. You will not have time to untangle them when trying to cover your next breaking news story.

PICTURE COMPOSITION

Your basic purpose in framing a shot is to show things as clearly as possible, and present them so that they convey meaning and thought. What you do essentially is to clarify and intensify the event before you. When engaged in ENG, you are the only one who sees the television pictures before they are videotaped. Therefore, you cannot rely on a director to tell you how to frame every picture for maximal effectiveness. The more you know about picture composition, the more effective your clarification and intensification of the event will be. But even if you are working as a camera operator during a multicamera studio show or large remote, where the director can preview all camera pictures, you need to know how to compose effective shots. The director might have enough time to correct some of your shots, but he or she will certainly not have enough time to teach you the fundamentals of good composition each time you frame a shot.

Like any other pictures, television pictures are subject to the conventional aesthetic rules of picture composition. First, however, you should be aware of a few factors peculiar to the television medium that influence the framing process to some extent: (1) screen size, (2) screen area, (3) depth, and (4) motion.

1. *Screen Size.* The size of the television screen is small. To show things clearly, you must show them relatively large within the frame of the screen. In other words, you have to operate more with **close-ups** (CU) and **medium shots** (MS) than with **long shots** (LS) and **extreme long shots** (XLS). Since the home viewer cannot see the whole event in its overall context, you must try to pick those details that tell at least an important part of the story. Shots that do not obviously relate to the event context are usually meaningless to the viewer.

2. *Screen Area.* You must always work within a fixed frame, the television aspect ratio of 3:4. Some new screens have a 3:5 ratio, which is more like the modern movie screen. If you want to show something extremely tall, you cannot change the aspect ratio into a vertical framing. About 10 percent of the picture area gets lost through the television transmission and reception process (see discussion on essential area in Chapter 14). You must compensate for this loss by framing somewhat more loosely than what you have visualized. Some camera operators draw black lines on their monitors to indicate the essential framing area.

3. *Screen Depth.* The pictures on the television screen are two-dimensional. You must create the impression of a third dimension through various techniques.

4. *Motion.* The objects in front of the camera (which is a substitute for the viewer's eyes) as well as the camera generally move about. This means that you must consider motion as well as static arrangement of objects within the frame.

Most likely you are already familiar with the basic principles of picture composition. You can probably tell, for example, whether a color photograph is well or badly composed, whether it is properly balanced, whether it contains aesthetic tension, or whether it is dull.

In the following discussion of television framing, no attempt is made to give you an exhaustive treatment of media aesthetics;[1] nevertheless, understanding the few compositional principles and conventions should aid you in framing effective shots with sureness and ease.

[1] For such a treatment, see Herbert Zettl, *Sight-Sound-Motion* (Belmont, Calif.: Wadsworth Publishing Co., 1973).

Framing	Step	Symbol	Framing	Step	Symbol
	Extreme Long Shot	XLS or ELS		Bust Shot	Bust Shot
	Long Shot	LS		Knee Shot	Knee Shot
	Medium Shot	MS		Two-Shot (two persons in frame)	2-Shot
	Close-up	CU		Three-Shot (three persons in frame)	3-Shot
	Extreme Close-up	XCU or ECU		Over-the-Shoulder Shot	O-S

5.1   Field-of-View Steps Note that these shot designations are relative and that several steps lie between each designation. If you start with a rather tight medium shot, which may be similar to our close-up framing, your extreme close-up may end up considerably tighter than the one shown here.

5.2   Other Shot Designations

These principles include (1) field of view, (2) organizing the screen area, (3) organizing screen depth, and (4) organizing screen motion.

Field of View

The field of view of the camera is basically organized into five steps (see 5.1): (1) extreme long shot (XLS or ELS), (2) long shot (LS), (3) medium shot (MS), (4) close-up (CU), and (5) extreme close-up (XCU or ECU).

Six other usual shot designations (five of which are in 5.2) are (1) **bust shot,** (2) **knee shot,** (3) **two-shot,** with two people or objects in the frame, (4) **three-shot,** which frames three, (5) **over-the-shoulder shot** (O-S), and (6) **cross-shot** (XS).

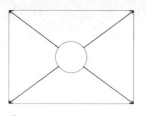  

a   b   c

5.3   Screen-Center Framing The most stable picture area is screen-center (a). If you want to convey stability, or show or emphasize a single object as directly as possible, put the object into screen-center (b). In this position the screen area is symmetrically balanced. Put a speaker who is talking directly into the camera into screen-center (c).

Organizing the Screen Area

When framing objects or people that do not move, you organize the screen area very much in the tradition of painting or still photography. Here are some of the conventions of picture composition that are accepted throughout the world:

Object Centering   The most stable, as well as most prominent, picture area is screen-center. If you want to convey stability, or show or emphasize a single object as directly as possible, put the object into screen-center (see 5.3).

In object centering the screen area is symmetrically *balanced.* For example, if the newscaster is talking directly to you (the camera), put him or her in screen-center. Placing the newscaster slightly off-center does not make the person or the message any more interesting; it merely distracts from what he or she has to say. But if you have a visual that appears over the newscaster's shoulder, the off-screen placement of the newscaster is not only justified but necessary to maintain the balance (see 5.4).

Nonsymmetrical Division   However, when you frame landscapes or other large vistas with distinct vertical objects—people, trees, buildings—you can make the shot more interesting by putting the distinct vertical objects off to one or the other side, rather than in the center. This principle, known as **nonsymmetrical division,** is also true for horizon lines. The picture looks more dynamic if the horizon cuts the picture at the one-third or two-thirds mark rather than exactly in the middle (see 5.5a and b).

a   b

5.4   Newscaster Placement If the newscaster is alone in the shot, place her in a screen-center position (a). Moving the newscaster somewhat off-center makes little sense and would merely impair the directness of the communication. However, if you have additional visual elements, such as a key insert, in the picture, you need to put the newscaster somewhat to the side in order to maintain pictorial balance (b).

a   b

5.5   Nonsymmetrical Framing When framing landscapes or other large vistas with distinct vertical objects—people, trees, telephone poles, spires—you will find that by letting the prominent horizontal and vertical lines divide the picture nonsymmetrically (or asymmetrically), your picture will look more interesting than with a symmetrical arrangement (a, b).

Division ratios of roughly $\frac{2}{5}$ to $\frac{3}{5}$ or $\frac{1}{3}$ to $\frac{2}{3}$ are the most common asymmetrical states of balance.

5.6 Level Horizontal Plane Make sure that the horizon line is level (a), unless you plan on special effects. This is especially important when your major concern in a shot is with the foreground rather than the background.

5.7 Tilted Horizontal Plane Any camera angle that is drastically different from our ordinary visual experience renders an otherwise balanced picture unstable and provides heightened energy. For instance, tilting the usually level horizon line creates this effect.

Horizontal Plane Under normal circumstances we expect people and other vertical things, such as houses, poles, or towers, to stand upright on level ground. Try, therefore, to keep the **horizontal plane** in your pictures as level as possible. In the excitement of getting a good story, it is easy to forget to *look behind* the object of primary attention. For example, when you are shooting outdoors, the depth of field is usually great enough for the camera to see not only the person you may be focused on in the foreground, but the background as well. If you intend to keep the picture (and with it the reporting) as stable as possible, watch for the background to be as level as possible (see 5.6).

There are times, however, when you may want to upset our ordinary visual experience and tilt the horizontal plane on purpose. Such camera angles create a highly dynamic and unstable picture com-

a b

5.8   Headroom Because we usually have space above us, indoors as well as out, and because the borders of the screen seem to exert some magnetic pull on the objects within the screen, you should leave space above people's heads in normal close-up, medium, and long shots (b). Do not have the top of the person's head glued to the top edge of the screen. You must counteract this pull by leaving some headroom. Notice that the subject's eyes mark approximately the upper third of the frame.

position. A tilted horizon line generates heightened energy (see 5.7).

Headroom   Because we usually have space above us, indoors as well as out, you should leave some space above people's heads in normal close-up, medium, and long shots. Do not have the top of a person's head glued to the upper edge of the screen. The lack of **headroom** is emphasized by the graphic magnetism of the frame, which seems to pull everything toward the screen edge that comes close to it. (See 5.8.)

Noseroom or Leadroom   When someone looks or points in a particular direction other than straight into the camera, you must leave some space in the direction of the looking or pointing. For some reason we seem to need space for the "pointing force" to play out (see 5.9 and 5.10). Because we usually must leave some space in front of somebody's nose, we call this space **"noseroom"** or "leadroom."

Even if you keep the person centered while he or she is looking at the right or left side of the screen, your picture will look annoyingly out of balance.

Closure   Psychological **closure** means that our mind fills in spaces that we cannot actually see on

5.9   Noseroom or Leadroom When someone looks in a particular direction (other than straight into the camera), you must compensate for the new graphic force by placing the person somewhat off-center. The more profile the performer turns, the more space you must leave in front of him or her in order to maintain proper balance. This space is generally called noseroom or leadroom.

the screen or otherwise. Take a look around you. You actually see only parts of the objects that lie in the field of your vision. There is no way you can ever see an object in its entirety unless the object moves around you or you around the object. Through experience we have learned to supply the missing

5.10 Lack of Noseroom If you do not compensate for the new graphic force while the performer is looking to one side, your picture becomes annoyingly unbalanced.

5.11 Facilitating Closure Beyond Frame In this shot we certainly perceive the whole figure of a person, although we actually *see* only a relatively small part of him. But the shot is framed in such a way that we can easily apply closure, that is, fill in the missing parts with our imagination.

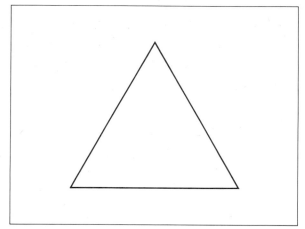

5.12 Triangle Arrangement We tend to see similar things together and to put them into simple geometrical shapes. You can use this organizing tendency to group similar objects into easily recognizable patterns. This group of cups forms an easily perceivable pattern: a triangle.

parts mentally. Because the television screen is relatively small, we often show objects and people in closeups, leaving many parts of the scene to the imagination of the viewer. When framing a shot, you should always be conscious of giving the viewers enough clues so that they can easily extend the figure and make it a sensible whole (see 5.11).

This tendency for closure also helps us in arranging many similar elements in such a way that they are perceived as a unit by the audience. It is usually best to arrange the objects so that they form simple geometrical patterns, such as a triangle (see 5.12) or a semicircle (see 5.13).

However, this facility for closure can also *work against* good composition. Here are some of the more common examples.

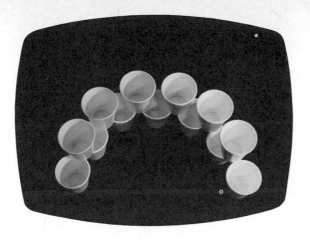

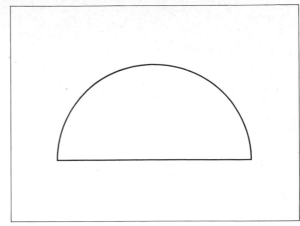

5.13 **Semicircle Arrangement** These objects organize the screen space into a prominent semicircle.

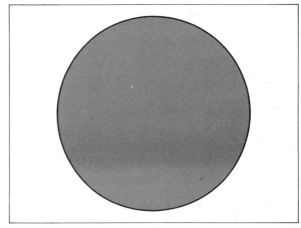

5.14 **Undesirable Closure** This shot is badly framed because we can apply closure within the frame—that is, perceive the detail as a complete picture. We can see a complete thing within the frame, and this prevents us from continuing the figure beyond the frame.

When framing an extreme close-up (ECU) of a person's head, make sure that there are enough clues to make us *project beyond* the screen edges. If this is not done, we will apply closure within the frame and perceive a strangely disembodied head (see 5.14).

You must also be careful not to have the **natural cutoff lines** of persons (the imaginary lines formed by the eyes, mouth, chin, waist, hemline,

and knees) coincide with the screen edge. Try to have these cutoff lines fall within or without the screen so that we can project beyond these imaginary lines (see 5.16).

Our desire to see screen space organized into simple patterns is so strong that it often works against reason. You should be especially careful not to frame a shot in such a way that the background objects are

5.15 Projection Beyond Frame This tight close-up is properly framed. We can easily extend the parts of the head beyond the screen. Notice that even in an extreme close-up the eyes of the subject remain in the upper third of the frame.

eyes, nose, mouth line

chin

bust

waist

hands

hemline

5.16 Undesirable Cutoff Points In general, try not to have natural cutoff lines, such as eyes, mouth, chin, hands, hemline, or knees, coincide with the screen edge. Rather, try to have these cutoff lines fall within or without the screen.

perceived to be joined to the people standing in front of them. The popular rubber plant in the studio can easily be perceived as growing out of people's heads (see 5.17). But there are other items in the studio that may contribute to amusing juxtapositions if you are careless with framing (see 5.18).

Organizing Screen Depth

Because the television screen is a flat, two-dimensional piece of glass upon which the image appears, we must create the *illusion* of a *third dimension*. Fortunately, the principles for creating the illusion of depth on a two-dimensional surface have been amply explored and established by painters and photographers over a long period of time. For **depth staging** you need to consider the choice of lens (wide-angle lenses seem to exaggerate depth, narrow-angle lenses seem to reduce the illusion of a third dimension), the positioning of objects relative to the camera (along the line representing an extension of the lens rather than sideways), depth of field (a shallow depth of field is usually more effective than a large depth of field), and lighting and color (brightly lighted objects with strong colors seem closer than the ones that have low-saturation, or washed out, colors and are dimly lighted). In any case, you should always try to establish a picture

5.17   Closure Working Against Good Composition The tendency for closure into simple patterns is not always positive. Avoid odd juxtapositions of performers with background objects, such as giving the appearance of plants growing out of people's heads.

5.18   Odd Juxtaposition through Closure How about this for a balancing act? A good camera operator would have avoided such a distracting juxtaposition simply by trucking a slight distance to one side or the other, by dollying in or out, or by pedestaling up or down.

a

b

5.19   Screen Depth If you include a prominent foreground piece in your shot, you immediately distinguish more clearly between foreground and middle- and backgrounds than without the foreground piece (a, b). Another foreground piece close to the camera gives an even clearer indication of the third dimension—foreground, middleground, and background (c).

division into clear foreground, middleground, and background areas (see 5.19a, b, c).

Organizing Screen Motion

Contrary to the painter or still photographer, who deals with the organization of static images within

c

a

b

5.20   Leadroom in Lateral Motion When following lateral movement, lead the moving subject or object with the camera (a); do not trail it (b).

the picture frame, the television camera operator must almost always cope with framing *images in motion* on the television screen. Composing moving images requires your quick reaction and your full attention throughout the telecast. Although the study of the moving image is an important part of learning the fine art of television and film production, we will at this point merely point out some of its most basic principles.[2]

Movements *toward or away from the camera* (downstage or upstage) are *stronger* than any type

[2]For further information on the aesthetics of the moving image, see Zettl, *Sight-Sound-Motion,* pp. 243–326.

5.21   Person Leaving Frame If you have a two-shot and one of the persons moves out of the frame, stay with just *one* of them. By zooming back in order to catch them both, you may overshoot the set, or reveal the boom microphone.

a   b

5.22 Correcting Over-the-Shoulder Shot If two persons block each other in a two-shot (a), correct the situation through a slight arc or truck to the right or the left (b).

of lateral motion. Fortunately, they are the easiest to frame. You simply keep the camera as steady as possible and watch so that the moving object does not go out of focus as it approaches the camera. Remember that a wide-angle zoom lens position (or a wide-angle lens) gives the impression of accelerated motion toward or away from the camera, whereas the narrow-angle zoom lens position (or the narrow-angle lens) slows the motion for the viewer.

If you frame lateral movement—that is, motion to screen left or screen right—you should *lead* the person or the moving object with the camera. The viewer wants to know where the object is going, not where it has been. Also, the forces of an object moving toward the screen edge must be absorbed by leaving some space ahead of the moving object (see 5.20).

If you are on a closeup and the person moves back and forth, do not try to follow each minor wiggle. You might run the risk of making viewers seasick; at least they will not be able to concentrate on this sort of motion for very long. Keep the camera pointed at the major action area, or zoom out (or pull back) to a slightly wider shot.

When you have a two-shot and one of the persons moves out of the frame, stay with just *one* of them. Do not try to keep both of them in the frame (see 5.21).

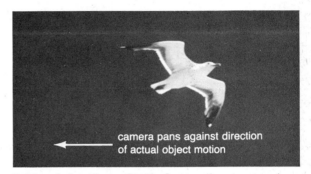

camera pans against direction of actual object motion

5.23 Animating a Static Scene If you are to animate a static scene through camera movement, such as a photo of a seagull in flight, pan *against* the direction in which the object is expected to move (and was actually moving when the photo was taken). Otherwise, the object seems to travel backward.

Even after extensive rehearsals you may find that in an over-the-shoulder shot the person closer to you (the camera) often blocks the other person who is farther away from the camera. In this case, you need to solve the problem by arcing or trucking to the right or left (see 5.22).

Sometimes you are asked to animate a still picture of an object in motion through camera movement. You must then pan against the direction in which the object is expected to move. Otherwise, the object seems to be traveling backward (see 5.23).

Whatever you do to organize screen motion, do it *smoothly*. Try to move your camera as little as possible, unless you need to follow a moving object, or dramatize a shot through motion. Because the ENG/EFP camera can be moved so easily, it may be tempting for you to "animate" a basically static scene to get more life into it. Don't do it. One of the distinct marks of an amateur camera operator is excessive camera motion.

MAIN POINTS

1. There are certain procedures to follow for studio cameras before, during, and after the show or rehearsal.

2. Before the show, check your headset, your camera mount (tripod dolly, pedestal, crane), your zoom and focus mechanisms.

3. During the show, pay particular attention to presetting your zoom, smooth camera movements, and focus.

4. After the show, lock your camera mounting head and put the camera in a safe place in the studio. Cap your camera.

5. When working a portable camera, be sure to handle the camera with extreme care. Do not leave it unprotected in the hot sun or especially in rain.

6. Do not point the camera into the sun or at objects that reflect the sun, regardless of whether the camera is turned on or not.

7. Before using the portable camera, make sure that the batteries are fully charged and that you have enough videotape for your assignment. Also, check the VTR and the microphones.

8. During the operation of the portable camera, pay particular attention to black and white balance, presetting your zoom, recording ambient sound at all times, and responding immediately to the warning signals in your viewfinder and the VTR.

9. After the show, put everything back carefully so that your camera/VTR unit is ready for the next assignment.

10. Some major points of picture composition are field of view, from XLS to XCU, organizing the screen area, organizing screen depth, and organizing screen motion.

11. In organizing the screen area, the major points are: (1) object placement within the frame, (2) keeping the horizon line level or tilting it, (3) headroom and leadroom or noseroom, and (4) closure, whereby we mentally fill in things we cannot see.

12. In organizing screen depth, we should try to create the illusion of a third dimension by establishing a foreground, middleground, and background.

13. In organizing screen motion, movements toward and away from the camera are stronger than lateral movements (from one side of the screen to the other).

14. When following lateral movement, the moving subject should have space in front of it throughout the motion.

Although large monochrome studio cameras have not been manufactured for quite some time, they are still used in university and college broadcast departments for training purposes. The following operating steps for a turret camera differ from those for a color camera.

HOW TO WORK THE TURRET CAMERA

1.   The normal **turret** holds four 35mm lenses, ranging from a wide-angle lens to a narrow-angle lens. On I-O (image-orthicon) cameras they are 50mm (wide-angle), 75mm or 90mm (normal), and 135mm and $8\frac{1}{2}$-inch (narrow-angle) lenses. (See 5.24.)

Only one of these lenses is in the "taking" or "on-the-air" position at one time. This means that the **taking lens** is positioned in front of the camera pickup tube. In order to change the field of view, you need to change lenses.

2.   You *change turret lenses* by rotating the turret with the turret control handle on the back of the camera (see 5.25). By squeezing the turret handle, you release the turret so that it can be rotated either clockwise or counterclockwise. Once the desired lens is in the "taking" position, which is usually marked by a white dot on the camera, you should release the grip gently until it engages in a catch, thereby locking the turret solidly in its new position. Because the turret control is spring loaded, be sure to depress and engage the turret handle slowly and gently; otherwise, the loud clicks of the engaging springs will be picked up quite noticeably by the microphone.

3.   The *focus control* for turret cameras is a large

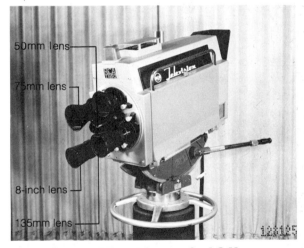

5.24   Standard Turret Lenses for I-O Monochrome Camera The normal turret holds a 50mm lens, a 75mm or 90mm lens, a 135mm lens, and an $8\frac{1}{2}$-inch lens.

knob on the right side of the camera. In effect, the knob moves the camera pickup tube closer to, or away from, the stationary turret lens. The number of turns necessary to keep the picture in focus depends on the speed of the camera or object, the focal length of the lens used, and the iris opening of the lens. Some focusing

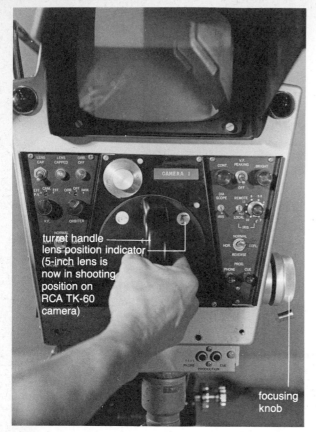

turret handle
lens position indicator
(5-inch lens is
now in shooting
position on
RCA TK-60
camera)

focusing knob

5.25   Turret Handle and Focusing Knob on Mono-chrome Studio Camera The specific turret lens can be rotated into shooting position with the turret handle.

knobs have an additional little crank that permits fast focusing (see 5.26). You usually turn the knob toward you (counterclockwise) when dollying in, and away from you (clockwise) when you dolly back.

4.   When *dollying,* keep your left hand on the panning handle and steer the camera with your right hand on the large steering wheel of the pedestal. When the focus gets critical (when the camera begins to get close to the object), put your right hand on the focus knob and move the camera with the panning handle.

5.   Make sure that your tally light is out before *changing lenses.* You should have the lenses clearly marked on the turret handle plate so that you can rack to the required lens without having to go through the whole rotation. If there are long lenses on the turret, you must be especially careful with your **racking** because the heavy lenses can easily damage the turret mechanism.

6.   Presetting the zoom lens on monochrome cameras is quite different from color cameras (see Chapter 3). Here are the steps for monochrome cameras: (1) Zoom all the way out to a long shot (widest angle lens setting). Focus up on the scene with the *camera focus control* on the side of the camera. (2) Zoom all the way in on the object farthest away from the camera that needs to be included in the shot. This object most likely is out of focus. Do not correct with the camera focus control. Use the *zoom control* to get the object into focus. When zooming back to the long shot, you should remain in focus through the entire zoom range. You may have to touch up both controls just a little by zooming in and out once again.

5.26   Camera Focus and Zoom Focus Controls on Monochrome Studio Camera

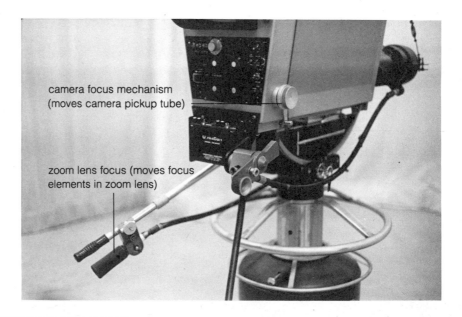

camera focus mechanism (moves camera pickup tube)

zoom lens focus (moves focus elements in zoom lens)

MAIN POINTS

1. The normal turret holds four lenses. For I-O cameras, they are: 50 mm (wide-angle), 75 mm or 90 mm (normal), 135 mm and $8\frac{1}{2}$-inch (narrow-angle).

2. The focus control for turret cameras is a knob on the side of the camera, which moves the camera pickup tube toward or away from the lens.

FURTHER READING

Millerson, Gerald. *The Technique of Television Production*. 10th ed. Woburn, MA: Focal Press, 1981.

Stroebel, Leslie, Hollis Todd, and Richard Zakia. *Visual Concepts for Photographers*. Woburn, MA: Focal Press, 1982.

Zettl, Herbert. *Sight-Sound-Motion: Applied Media Aesthetics*. Belmont, CA: Wadsworth Publishing Co., 1976.

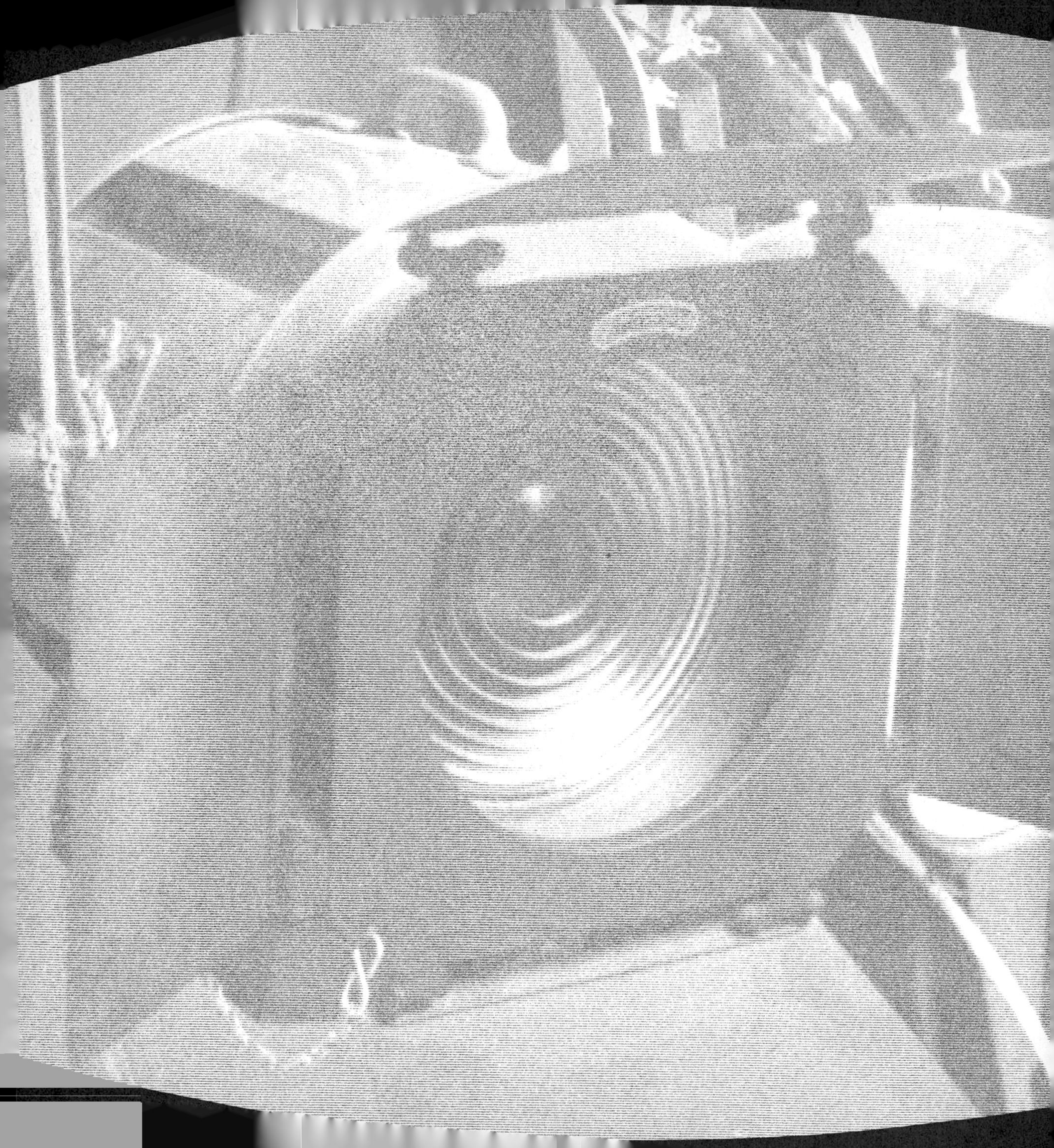

Lighting

We have two broad purposes for lighting: (1) to provide the television camera with adequate illumination so that it can see well—that is, produce technically acceptable pictures, and (2) to convey to the viewer the space, time, and mood of the event. Lighting helps to tell us what the objects shown on the screen actually look like, where they are in relation to one another and to their immediate environment, and when the event is taking place—time of day, season, or weather conditions.

In Section One of this chapter we will therefore consider:

1. Types of light and illumination: directional and diffused, indoor and outdoor.
2. Color temperature, the relative reddishness or bluishness of light.
3. The technical lighting objectives, which include baselight levels and techniques, contrast ratios, color temperature and white balance, and measuring incident and reflected light.
4. The tools with which we can accomplish our objectives—the lighting instruments and control equipment.

In Section Two we will discuss:

1. Color temperature.
2. The inverse square law.
3. The nontechnical lighting objectives—to indicate form and dimension, to create an illusion of reality and nonreality, and to indicate mood.

Like the human eye, the television camera needs light in order to see and function properly. Unlike the human eye, the television camera is much more demanding as to the amount of light, the color of the light, and its relative harshness and direction.

For example, although we may see quite well with only a flashlight as the illuminating source or under extremely bright sunlight, the camera may be allergic to both these types of light. The flashlight may not radiate enough light for the pickup tube to give off sufficient electricity. The resulting television picture lacks signal strength and consequently suffers from an excess of video noise, often called picture snow. Bright sunlight, on the other hand, may be too much for the camera to handle. At best, the picture looks washed out; at worst, the superabundance of light can destroy the camera pickup tube.

A lamp, which appears to the eye to give off a perfectly white light, may look so red to the camera that the resulting picture has a reddish tint on the color monitor. Another lamp may produce light that looks to the camera quite bluish, although our eyes again perceive it as normal white light.

A harsh light, or a light coming from an unusual direction, may produce shadows that conceal rather than reveal the actual shape of an object.

Controlling illumination for the television camera is, therefore, crucial. To explain how we control lighting, this section covers the following areas: (1) types of illumination, (2) color temperature, (3) technical lighting objectives, (4) measuring illumination, (5) studio lighting instruments, (6) portable lighting instruments, and (7) lighting control equipment.

TYPES OF ILLUMINATION

As in all photographic arts, in television you encounter two basic types of light and illumination. The two types of light are (1) directional and (2) diffused. The two types of illumination are (1) outdoor and (2) indoor.

The television camera demands that we control carefully the illumination of an object or a scene. This control of illumination we achieve through lighting.

Directional and Diffused Light

Directional light illuminates only a relatively small area with a distinct light beam. It produces well-defined shadows and causes fast **falloff,** which means that the light area changes rather abruptly into a dense shadow area. To achieve directional light, we use **spotlights.**

Diffused light illuminates a relatively large area with a wide, indistinct light beam. It produces soft, rather undefined shadows and causes *slow falloff,* which means that the light changes gradually into soft, rather transparent shadow areas. The lighting instruments that emit diffused light are called **floodlights.**

The various spotlights and floodlights are sometimes classified by the bulb they use (called luminants). Thus we have (1) **incandescent** lights, which have ordinary tungsten light bulbs such as you use at home; (2) **quartz** lights, which are also incandescent lights, but whose lamps are small quartz bulbs or tubes that contain a **tungsten-halogen** filament; (3) **HMI (Halogen-Metal-Iodide) lights,** which use special kinds of arc lamps; and (4) **fluorescent** lights, which use the familiar fluorescent tubes. We will discuss the production advantages and disadvantages of the first three types of lamps in Section Two. Fluorescent lights are seldom used in television lighting, except when they happen to be one of the major light sources already in place during location shooting.

Outdoor and Indoor Illumination

Outdoor illumination is accomplished by one of the most reliable sources we have—that is, the sun. But as you know, the light the sun emits is not always the same. On a cloudless day, the sun acts like a spotlight and emits highly directional light with harsh, dense shadows. This type of illumination is definitely *fast falloff.* On an overcast day, however, the clouds or fog act like a filter and change the directional light of the sun into a highly diffused light. The falloff is extremely slow, and the shadows transparent, if noticeable at all. Although we use special lights and reflectors to articulate the lighting as much as possible when outdoors, we generally have *little control* over outdoor illumination.

Indoor illumination almost always requires the use of lighting instruments, even if the room is partially illuminated by *available light* (outdoor light coming through windows). Whereas on the average ENG assignment, we simply boost the available light with a single hand-held light, or perhaps two additional high-intensity lights on stands, in EFP and especially in the studio we can exercise *precise control* over lighting.

We can also distinguish the various types of illumination by color temperature. Outdoor illumination has a much higher color temperature than indoor illumination, except perhaps during a late afternoon sun.

COLOR TEMPERATURE

Color temperature is a standard by which we measure the relative reddishness or bluishness of white light. You have certainly noticed that a fluorescent tube gives off a "colder" light than a candle. The fluorescent light actually emits a bluish light; the candle a reddish light. This difference can be precisely measured and expressed in degrees of **color temperature,** or degrees of **Kelvin.** (See Section Two for a more detailed explanation of color temperature.) The standard color temperature for television illumination is 3,200°K, which is a fairly white light with just a little reddish (warm) tinge. All studio lighting instruments are rated at 3,200°K, assuming they receive full voltage. Lighting instruments that are used to augment or simulate outdoor lighting have bulbs that emit a 5,600°K light. We will discuss these instruments later in the chapter when we deal with specific lighting instruments.

When you dim a lamp that is rated at 3,200°K, the light takes on more and more of a red tinge, similar to sunlight at sunset. Although under normal circumstances we are quite unaware of the different color temperatures in various types of illumination, the color camera is not. It not only faithfully reflects but seems to exaggerate the red in a lower color temperature or the blue in higher color temperatures. You can test this sensitivity of the color cam-

Barn Doors Metal flaps in front of lighting instruments that control the spread of the light beam.

Baselight Even, nondirectional (diffused) light necessary for the camera to operate optimally. Customary baselight levels for studio cameras are: for standard three-tube Plumbicon cameras, 150–250 ft-c (foot-candles); for one-tube color cameras, 75–200 ft-c; for vidicon tube cameras, 150–300 ft-c; for monochrome I-O cameras, 75–100 ft-c.

Bias Light A small light that illuminates the front surface of the pickup tube to boost the video signal without undue increase in noise. Especially useful when the camera operates in low light levels.

Broad A floodlight with a broadside, panlike reflector.

Clip Lights Small internal reflector bulbs that are clipped to pieces of scenery or furniture via a gator clip.

Color Temperature Relative reddishness or bluishness of light, as measured in degrees Kelvin. The norm for indoor TV lighting is 3,200°K, for outdoors 5,600°K.

Cookie (A short form of *cucalorus*, Greek for breaking up light, also spelled *kukaloris*.) Any cutout pattern that, when placed in front of a spotlight, produces a shadow pattern. The cookie, usually made from a thin, cutout metal sheet, is inserted into a pattern projector.

Diffused Light Light that illuminates a relatively large area with an indistinct light beam. Diffused light, created by floodlights, produces soft shadows.

Dimmer A device that controls the intensity of the light by throttling the electric current flowing to the lamp.

Directional Light Light that illuminates a relatively small area with a distinct light beam. Directional light, produced by spotlights, creates harsh, clearly defined shadows.

Ellipsoidal Spotlight Spotlight producing a very defined beam, which can be shaped further by metal shutters.

Flag A thin, rectangular sheet of metal used to block light from falling on specific areas.

Floodlight Lighting instrument that produces diffused light.

Foot-Candle The unit of measurement of illumination, or the amount of light that falls on an object.

era to color temperature quite readily. Put a large white card on an easel and illuminate it with a spotlight hooked up to a dimmer. Watch the color of the card when you dim the light. You will probably notice how the card takes on a slight orange tinge that gets more reddish the more you dim the light. Now focus a color camera on the white card and watch the same experiment on a color monitor. You will have little trouble seeing the card actually *change color.*

Some lighting experts warn, therefore, against any dimming of lights that illuminate performers or performing areas. The skin tones are, after all, the only real standard the viewers have by which to judge the "correctness" of the television color scheme. If the skin colors are greatly distorted, how can we trust the other colors to be "true"? So goes the argument. However, practice has shown that you can dim a light by 10 percent (about 320°K) from its normal 3,200°K without having the color change become too noticeable on the color monitor. Dimming the lights by about 10 percent not only reduces your power consumption, but just about doubles the life of the bulbs.

How to influence and control color temperature is covered in the following discussion of lighting objectives.

TECHNICAL LIGHTING OBJECTIVES

The technical lighting objectives are to provide enough light so that the camera can see well, to limit the contrast between highlight and shadow areas, and to produce light that will not distort colors.

Hence, we will take a closer look at (1) operating light level: baselight; (2) contrast; and (3) color temperature control.

Operating Light Level: Baselight

To make the camera "see well" so that the pictures are relatively free of video noise and lag, you must establish a minimum operating **light level,** called **baselight** or **base.** Baselight is the general, overall light level on a set or another event area.

Fresnel Spotlight   One of the most common spotlights, named after the inventor of its lens, which has steplike concentric rings.

Gel   Generic name for color filter put in front of spotlights or floodlights to give the light beam a specific hue. "Gel" comes from "gelatin," the filter material used before the invention of much more heat- and moisture-resistant plastics.

HMI Light   HMI stands for Halogen-Metal-Iodide lamp. An extremely efficient, high-intensity light that burns at 5,600°K—the outdoor illumination norm. It needs an additional piece of equipment, a ballast, to operate properly.

Incandescent Light   The light produced by the hot tungsten filament of ordinary glass-globe light bulbs (in contrast to fluorescent light).

Incident Light   Light that strikes the object directly from its source. Incident light reading is the measure of light (in foot-candles) from the object to the light source. The foot-candle meter is pointed directly into the light source or toward the camera.

Patchboard   Also called patchbay. A device that connects various inputs with specific outputs.

Pattern Projector   An ellipsoidal spotlight with a cookie (cucalorus) insert, which projects the cookie's pattern as shadow.

Preset Board   A program device in which several lighting setups (scenes) can be stored, and from which they can be retrieved when needed.

Quartz Light   A high-intensity light whose lamp consists of a quartz or silica housing (instead of the customary glass) and a tungsten-halogen filament. Produces a very bright light of stable color temperature (3,200°K).

Reflected Light   Light that is bounced off the illuminated object. Reflected-light reading is done with a light meter (most of them are calibrated for reflected light) that is held close to the illuminated object.

Scoop   A scooplike television floodlight.

Scrim   A spun-glass material that is put in front of a lighting instrument as an additional light diffuser.

Softlight   A television floodlight that produces extremely diffused light. It has a panlike reflector and a light-diffusing material over its opening.

Spotlight   A light instrument that produces directional, relatively undiffused light.

Baselight Levels   Many an argument has been raised concerning adequate minimum baselight levels for various cameras. The problem is that baselight levels do not represent absolute values but are dependent on other production factors, such as the make and age of camera and pickup tubes used, lighting contrast, general reflectance of the scenery, and desired mood. When shooting outdoors on an ENG assignment, you do not have much say about baselight levels; you must accept whatever light there is. There, you often run into the problem of too much light, which, as far as the camera is concerned, can be just as troublesome as too little.

As you may remember from Chapter 2, the ND filters on the camera filter wheel are usually sufficient to reduce excessively high baselight to optimal levels; however, they pull down the entire light scale, rendering dark shadow areas even denser. Although **bias lighting** and the gain control permit the camera to work in light levels ordinarily too low for the camera pickup tube, they cannot prevent a marked increase of lag, comet-tailing, and especially video noise. The best thing to do, therefore, is to establish proper baselight levels, assuming that you have this option.

But what are "proper" baselight levels? Through experience we have established general baselight levels that prove satisfactory for most ordinary television productions. These are:

For the standard three-tube (Plumbicon or Saticon) camera:	150–250 ft-c (foot-candles), with 200 ft-c the norm
For the one-tube color camera:	75–200 ft-c, with 100 ft-c the norm
For the vidicon-tube camera (color or monochrome):	150–300 ft-c, with 250 ft-c the norm
For the monochrome I-O camera:	75–100 ft-c

Generally, the video engineer has less trouble producing high-quality, crisp pictures when the baselight level is fairly high and the contrast somewhat limited than under a very low baselight level with high-contrast lighting.

Also, if the baselight levels are too low, the lens iris must be wide open in order to allow as much light as possible to strike the camera pickup tubes. But, because the depth of field decreases as the lens opening increases, a lens whose iris is set at its maximum opening gives you a fairly shallow depth of field. Consequently, focusing becomes a noticeable problem when baselight levels are low.

If you need a large depth of field, high baselight levels are prerequisite.

A set whose colors and texture absorb a great amount of light obviously needs more illumination (higher baselight level) than one whose brightly painted surface reflects a moderate amount of light.

Baselight Techniques   You can achieve a sufficient baselight level in two quite different ways. First, you can establish a basic, highly diffused illumination through floodlights, upon which you then superimpose the spotlights for the specific lighting of people and set areas.

Second, and this is by far the preferred method, you light the people and specific set areas as carefully as you can with spotlights, and then add fill light to reduce harsh shadows, without worrying about the baselight as such. Once you have completed your lighting, take a general incident light reading of your set (see p. 136), and see whether your set averages the desired **foot-candles** (measurement of intensity) of illumination. Most often, the lighting instruments aimed at the designated areas, and the spill and reflection off the scenery and studio floor should provide the baselight level. If not, you can always add some floodlights in specific areas in order to raise the operating light level. Unfortunately, this technique, which creates plastic and expressive lighting effects, demands a little more skill and especially more time than the first method. On remote locations, where time and lighting facilities are limited, establishing the baselight first is still the more practical and efficient method.

Contrast

In Chapter 2 you learned that the color camera can tolerate only a limited contrast between the lightest and darkest spots in a scene if it is to show subtle brightness differences in the dark picture areas, the middle ranges, and the light picture areas. Contrast does not depend so much on how much light comes from the lighting instruments as on how much light is reflected by the colors and various surfaces that are illuminated. For example, a white refrigerator, a yellow raincoat, or a polished brass plate reflects much more light than a dark-blue velvet cloth, even if they are illuminated by the very same source. If you now put the brass plate on the velvet cloth, you may already have too much contrast for the television camera to handle properly—and you have not even begun with the lighting.

The same contrast problem may occur if you put your talent in front of a very light or very dark background. If the camera adjusts to the white background, the face goes dark. In front of a black background, the face looks quite overexposed. What you have to consider in dealing with contrast is a constant *relationship* among various factors, such as how much light falls on the subject or object, how much light is reflected, and how much difference there is between the lightest and darkest spot in the same picture. Because we deal with relationships rather than absolute values, we express the camera's contrast limit in a *contrast ratio*.

Contrast Ratio   For most color cameras, this *contrast ratio* is 30:1. This means that the brightest spot can be only thirty times lighter than the darkest picture area. If this brightness spread is greater than 30:1, the camera ignores the subtle brightness differentiations in the light as well as the dark picture areas.

The video operator, who usually has to wrestle with contrast (more appropriately called **"shading"**), can now try to "pull down" the excessively bright values to make them match the established "white level" (which represents a 100 percent video signal strength). But then, because the darkest value cannot get any blacker and move down with the bright areas, the darker picture areas are "crushed" together into a uniformly muddy, noisy dark color. If you insist on seeing detail in the dark picture areas, the video operator can "stretch the blacks" toward the white end. But this causes the bright areas to lose their differentiation and take on a uni-

formly white and strangely flat and washed-out color. In effect, the pictures look either as though the contrast control in your television receiver is set much too high, with the brightness set much too low, or the contrast too low with the brightness turned up much too high.

A camera with *auto-iris* fares no better. The auto-iris faithfully responds to the brightest picture area—no matter how bright—and reduces it to the peak signal level (100 percent signal strength), moving the rest of the brightness values down toward the black end of the scale. The farther the brightest spot has to be pulled down to meet the white level, the more the dark colors are crushed into "the mud." The electronic *contrast compression* devices, which we mentioned in Chapter 2, help the camera maintain the value differentiation in the dark areas (stretching the blacks) without overexposing the whites too much. Still, the best assurance for quality pictures is to try to limit the contrast to the 30:1 ratio.

Limiting Contrast   To keep the contrast ratio within the 30:1 limits, follow these three guidelines:

1.   Be aware of the *general reflectance* of the objects. A highly reflecting object obviously needs less illumination than a highly light-absorbing one.

2.   Try to avoid *extreme brightness contrasts* in the same shot. For example, if you need to show the highly reflecting brass plate, put it not on the velvet but on a more light-reflecting cloth. This way you can limit the amount of light hitting the plate without making the tablecloth appear too dark and muddy.

3.   *Lighten the shadow areas* through a generous amount of fill light. This will help to show some of the detail otherwise hidden in the shadow, and at the same time reduce contrast.

All three contrast-limiting devices are especially important when you light people. If, for example, you have a performer do a commercial in a light-colored, highly reflecting kitchen set, you need to limit the amount of illumination on the reflecting background rather than pouring an excessive amount of light on the face to make it appear less dark in relation to the bright background.

Even the best lighting person will have trouble maintaining your skin color if you wear a starched white shirt or blouse and a black suit or dress. If the video operator (or the auto-iris camera) adjusts for the extreme bright areas, your face will go dark, and the black suit or dress will look anything but neatly black. But when the video operator now wants to try to shade for the dark areas so that we can see some detail in the dark suit or dress, your face will take on the washed-out look of an overexposed picture. Therefore, even if the cameras have contrast compression circuits built in, you should still wear something less contrasting with your skin tones.

Whenever you light for closeups or medium shots of people, as in a news program for example, you need to make the shadows on the face translucent through a generous amount of fill light. After all, we do want to see the whole face, not just half of it. Be careful, however, not to eliminate the shadows altogether; otherwise, you may end up with a face that looks flat and without character.

Color Temperature Control

One of the important technical objectives is to have the colors appear as "true" as they are in the actual scene. The common reference point is to make white look white under a variety of lights. We accomplish this by controlling the color temperature. There are basically three ways to do this: (1) electronic white balance, (2) filters, and (3) lights.

Electronic White Balance   In studio cameras the electronic white balance is done by the video engineer. Once the lighting is completed, the video engineer adjusts the camera color controls, called "paint pots," until a white object appears as white on the monitor. Most ENG/EFP cameras have automatic white balance controls. Each time you walk into a new light environment with the camera, you must reset the white balance, even if the lighting looks the same to your eye. Simply press the white balance button and watch for the particular viewfinder display (usually a light) to tell you when the white balance is accomplished (see 6.1). Although

any white area in your new environment will do, it is usually better to use a small white card by which to set up your white balance.

Some less expensive cameras are not automated and require slightly more work to set the white balance. Again, you need a white reference (like the white card) for setting up the camera. But rather than just pressing a button for white balance, you need to adjust the red and blue color controls (rotating gain control knobs on the back or the side of the camera) until the viewfinder display indicates that you have achieved the optimal white balance setting (see 6.2).

Filters   In order to achieve a good white balance, you may need to use one of the built-in filters on your camera filter wheel. The filters usually reduce the high color temperatures of fluorescent indoor lighting (4,500°K to 6,500°K) or outdoor light (4,500°K to 7,500°K) to the 3,200°K norm. Obviously, if you have to move from a bright outdoor scene, for which you needed a 6,000°K filter, to an indoor scene that is lighted with incandescent lamps, you need to remove the filter before you can achieve a proper white balance again. On the other hand, if you move from the outdoor location to a department store with daylight fluorescent lamps, you may just have to keep the 6,000°K filter in place for the new white balance.

In elaborate studio or field productions you may see large filterlike plastic sheets glued on the windows to match either indoor or outdoor color temperatures. You can also get ND filters of various densities in the form of large sheets that can be glued on windows. These devices are especially handy if you have to videotape somebody who insists on having a large window in the background. The ND filter reduces the brightness of the background (light coming through the window) sufficiently so that the person in the foreground can be lighted without an undue amount of illumination. Some special ND filters can function as light diffusers as well.

If you do not have a large plastic color filter to "gel" the windows (cover them with the plastic material), but you intend to match the indoor lighting with the relatively high color temperature of the

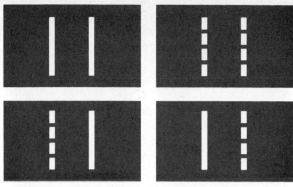

1. Select auto-white balance and display parallel vertical white lines. Televise reference white object between lines. Press auto-color balance button.
2. If white balance is achieved, vertical lines become broken.
3. If left-hand line only becomes broken, add color filter.
4. If right-hand line only becomes broken, remove color filter.

6.1   Auto-White Balance Viewfinder Display (Philips CDK-14S ENG/EFP Camera)

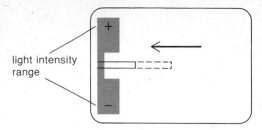

light intensity range

white balance indicator line—the minimum horizontal indicator line means the best white balance is achieved

6.2   White Balance Viewfinder Display for Manual White Balance (Panasonic WV–3900 ENG Camera)

daylight coming through the window, you can use *dichroic filters* on the portable lighting instruments. These filters boost the normal 3,200°K of the lamps to approximately 5,600°K, the standard for daylight illumination. The disadvantage of these filters is that they absorb a great amount of light.

Because it is rather easy to balance ENG/EFP cameras, many production people do not hesitate to mix various color temperatures, such as fluorescent and incandescent lights. The argument goes that the 3,200°K lights on the persons will usually wash out most of the bluishness of the higher temperature fluorescent baselight.

Lights   Various types of lights burn with different color temperatures. As we mentioned already, studio lights burn at 3,200°K. Fluorescent lights burn at a much higher color temperature (though at a much cooler thermal temperature), from about 4,500°K to 6,500°K. There are also some special lights that burn at 5,600°K, which is the established daylight standard. We will cover these instruments in our discussion of portable lights.

MEASURING ILLUMINATION

In order to establish the proper baselight levels and control brightness contrast, you can no longer trust your eyes, as good as they may be. You need to measure the various amounts of light falling on the subject or various set areas, and the light reflected from the subject or pieces of scenery.

Hence, we have two ways of measuring illumination: (1) the **incident light** measure, and (2) the **reflected light** measure. The incident light reading gives you a general idea about the baselight levels. The reflected light reading tells you more about brightness contrast.

Measuring Incident Light

The incident light reading gives you some idea of the *baselight levels* in a specific set area. You are actually measuring the amount of light that falls on a subject or on a specific set area.

To measure incident light, you must stand in the lighted area or next to the subject and point a foot-candle meter *toward the camera lens*. This gives you a quick reading of the baselight level in this particular set area. If you want a more specific reading of the amount of light coming from the particular instruments, you should point the foot-candle

6.3 Incident Light Reading The light meter is pointed into the lights or at the camera while the measurer is standing next to the lighted subject.

meter *into the lights* (see 6.3). This way, you can get a pretty good idea of the intensity with which each lighting instrument burns. Such a record may come in quite handy, especially when you are to duplicate the illumination for a scene or scenes shot in the same set over a period of several days. For some reason, lighting instruments are temperamental and do not always produce the same light intensity, even if you faithfully duplicate the dimmer settings of the previous day. An incident light check, however, guarantees identical intensities.

If you want to discover possible "holes" in your lighting (unlighted or underlighted areas), walk around the set with your light meter generally pointed at the major camera positions. Watch your light meter. Whenever the needle dips way down, you have a "hole."

Measuring Reflected Light

The reflected light reading gives you an idea of how much light is bounced off the various objects. It is primarily used to *measure contrast.*

In order to measure *reflected light,* you must use a reflected light meter (most common photographic light meters measure reflected light) and point it close to the lighted object, such as the performer's face or white blouse or the dark blue background flat, from the direction of the camera (the back of the meter should face the principal camera position) (see 6.4). Make sure that you are not standing between the light source and the subject when taking this reading. Otherwise you will measure only your shadow, instead of the light actually reflecting off the subject. The brightest spot (the area reflecting the greatest amount of light) is the *reference white* and determines the white level. The area reflecting the least amount of light is the *reference black.* The reference white should not reflect more than thirty times the light of the reference black. If your light meter indicates a greater difference between light and dark, you have exceeded the 30:1 contrast ratio the camera can handle, and you must make every effort to reduce the contrast in order to obtain good pictures.

Keep in mind that the contrast is determined not necessarily by the amount of light generated by the lamps but by how much light the objects reflect back into the camera lens.

Do not be too much of a slave to all these measurements and ratios. Usually, a quick check of the baselight is all that is needed for most lighting situations. In especially critical situations you may want to check the reflectance of faces or especially bright objects. Some people get so involved in reading light meters that they forget to look into the monitor to see whether or not the lighting looks the way it was intended. If you combine your knowledge of how the camera works with artistic sensitivity and especially common sense, you will not have the light meter tell you how to light; rather you will use it as a guide to make your job more efficient.

STUDIO LIGHTING INSTRUMENTS

All studio lighting is accomplished with a variety of *spotlights* and *floodlights.* These instruments (sometimes called luminaires) are designed to operate from the studio ceiling or from floorstands. Most

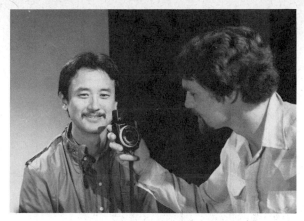

6.4 Reflected Light Reading The light meter is pointed close to the lighted object, thereby measuring the light reflected by the object.

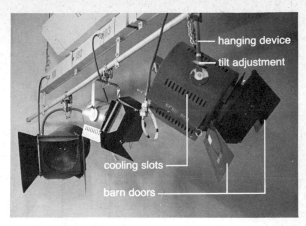

6.5 Fresnel Spotlight

studio lights have *quartz* (tungsten-halogen) lamps, but many instruments still use the ordinary incandescent (tungsten) bulb. So, if you hear lighting people refer to the "incandescent" spot or the "quartz" spot, they are referring to the difference in what bulbs (luminants) the instruments have; there is no difference, however, in the production application of the two instruments.

Spotlights

Most studio lighting can be accomplished with two basic types of spotlights: (1) the Fresnel spotlight and (2) the ellipsoidal spotlight.

The Fresnel Spotlight Named for Augustin Fresnel, who invented the lens used in it, the **Fresnel spotlight** is the most widely used in television studio production (see 6.5). The Fresnel spotlight is relatively light and flexible. It has a high light output, and its light beam can be made narrow or wide by a spot-focusing device. The spotlight can be adjusted to a "flood" beam position, which then gives off a rather wide, spread beam; or it can be "spotted" or "pinned" to a sharp, clearly defined light beam. There are several ways of *flooding* (adjust to a wide, flooded beam), or *spotting,* or *focusing* (adjust to a narrow, clearly defined beam) a Fresnel spotlight.

The most common method is to push or pull

the bulb-reflector unit inside the light instrument toward or away from the lens. To *flood* a spotlight beam, turn the focusing spindle or focusing loop in such a way that the bulb-reflector unit *moves toward* the lens. To *spot* or *focus,* the beam, turn the spindle or focusing loop so that the bulb-reflector unit *moves away from* the lens. (See 6.6.)

Whenever you adjust the beam, do it gently. You cannot very well adjust a light beam with the instrument turned off. But when the bulb is turned on, it is highly sensitive to shock. In order to protect the hot lamp as much as possible from any damaging jolt, two further focusing devices have been developed.

On the back of some smaller quartz fixtures, you will find a lever that can be moved horizontally—or, in other models, turned clockwise or counterclockwise—for quick flooding or spotting of the beam. This device is called a *sweep focus* (see 6.7).

In order that the hot lamp does not have to be moved, some lighting instruments focus by having the *lens* move toward or away from the fixed (and spring-mounted) lamp. In this way, called the "ring-focus" method, you can adjust the drag of the focus ring so that you can focus the instrument with a lighting pole from the studio floor, even after the lamp has been on for several hours. (See 6.8.)

Fresnel spotlights come in different sizes,

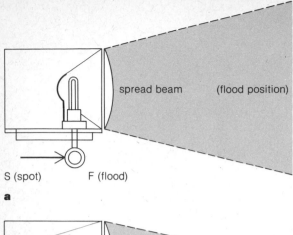

spread beam   (flood position)

S (spot)   F (flood)

a

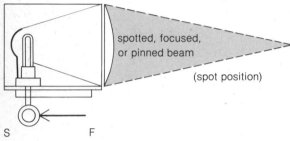

spotted, focused,
or pinned beam

(spot position)

S   F

b

6.6   Beam Control of Fresnel Spotlight (a) In
order to flood or spread the beam, turn the focus spindle or
focusing loop so that the bulb-reflector unit moves toward
the lens. If the lighting instrument has an outside indicator,
the indicator should move toward *F* (for "flood" position).
(b) In order to spot, or focus, the beam, turn the focus spindle or focusing loop so that the bulb-reflector unit moves
away from the lens. The focus indicator should move toward
S (for "spot" position).

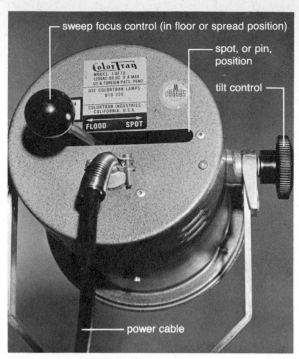

sweep focus control (in floor or spread position)

spot, or pin, position

tilt control

power cable

6.7   Sweep Focus on External Reflector Light
The beam can be spread or spotted by moving the sweep
knob horizontally to the flood or spot positions.

depending on how much light they are to produce.
Obviously, the larger instruments produce more light
than the smaller ones. The size of Fresnel spotlights
is given in the wattage of the lamp, or, occasionally,
the diameter of the lens.

What size of lighting instruments you should
use depends on several factors: (1) the type of camera and the sensitivity of the pickup tubes, (2) the
distance of the lighting instruments from the objects
or scene to be illuminated, and (3) the reflectance
of the scenery, objects, clothing, and studio floor.

Color cameras generally need 150–250 ft-c for
optimal performance. The lower the lights are rel-

ative to the set or action areas, the less light you
need. (See Section Two.) Highly reflecting objects,
scenery, clothing, and studio floors need less light
than if they were dark and light absorbent.

In most television studios, the largest Fresnel
spotlights rarely exceed 5,000 watts. The most commonly used Fresnels are of the 1,000-watt and 2,000-
watt variety. For maximum lighting control, most
lighting technicians prefer to operate with as few as
possible, yet adequately powerful, lighting instruments.

The Ellipsoidal Spotlight   This kind of spotlight can
produce an intense, sharply defined light beam. For
example, if you want to create pools of light reflecting off the studio floor, the **ellipsoidal spot** is the
instrument to use. Even in their pinned, or focused,
position, the Fresnels would not give you that sharp
an outline.

As with the Fresnel, you can spot and spread
the light beam of the ellipsoidal. Similar to the ring-

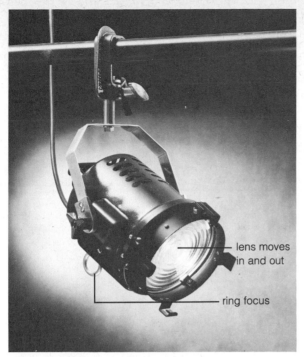

6.8 Ring Focus Fresnel Spotlight When the ring is turned (often with a light pole from the studio floor), the lens rather than the lamp assembly moves for flooding or spotting (focusing) the light beam.

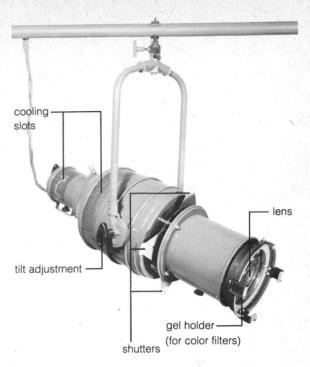

6.9 Ellipsoidal Spotlight The beam of the ellipsoidal spotlight can be shaped by the shutters. It produces the most directional light of all spotlights.

focus Fresnel, you push or pull the lens away from the lamp, rather than moving the lamp. Because of the peculiarity of the ellipsoidal reflector (which has two focal points), you can even shape the light beam into a triangle or a rectangle, for example, by adjusting four metal **shutters** that stick out of the instrument (see 6.9).

Some ellipsoidal spotlights can also be used as **pattern projectors.** In this case, the lighting instrument has a special slot right next to the beamshaping shutters, which can hold a metal pattern called a cucalorus or, for short, **cookie.** The ellipsoidal spot projects the cookie as a clear shadow pattern on any surface. Most often, it is used to break up flat surfaces, such as the **cyclorama** or the studio floor. (See 6.10.)

Ellipsoidal spotlights come in sizes from 500 watts to 2,000 watts, but the most common is the 750-watt. The ellipsoidal spot is generally used, not for the standard television lighting, but only when specific, precise lighting tasks have to be performed.

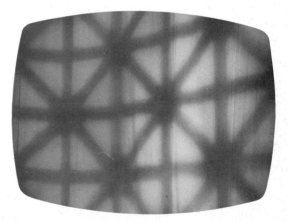

6.10 "Cookie" Pattern on Cyclorama. The cookie pattern is projected by a special ellipsoidal spotlight (pattern projector). Because the spotlight can be focused, the pattern can be projected in sharp or soft focus.

shutters

handle for aiming light

6.11 Follow Spot The follow spot has controls through which you can simultaneously pan and tilt the instrument, spread or spot, and shape the light beam, all while following the action. Some follow spots can also project a variety of patterns.

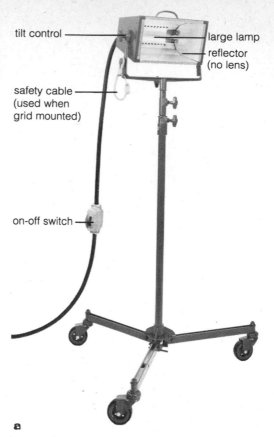

tilt control

large lamp

reflector (no lens)

safety cable (used when grid mounted)

on-off switch

a

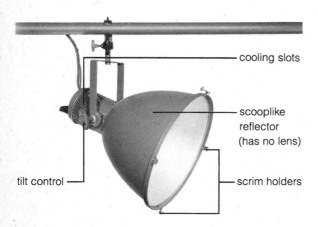

cooling slots

scooplike reflector (has no lens)

tilt control

scrim holders

6.12 Scoop

b

6.13 Small and Large Broad (a) Small broad. (b) Large broad.

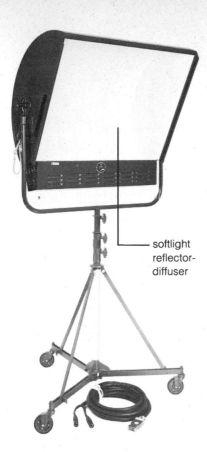

softlight
reflector-
diffuser

There are four basic types of floodlights: (1) the scoop, (2) the broad and softlight, (3) the floodlight bank, and (4) the strip, or cyc, light.

The Scoop   Named for its peculiar scooplike reflector, this floodlight is one of the most versatile and popular. Like most other floodlights, the **scoop** has *no lens.*

There are *fixed-focus* and *adjustable-focus* scoops. The fixed-focus scoop permits no simple adjustment of its light beam. Focusing the beam is not possible at all. You can, however, increase the diffusion of the light beam by attaching a *scrim* in front of the scoop. A scrim is a spun-glass material held in a metal frame. Although the light output is considerably reduced through their use, some lighting people put scrims on all scoops, not only to produce highly diffused light but to protect the studio personnel in case the hot lamp inside the scoop shatters.

Some of the quartz scoops have adjustable beams, from medium-spread positions to full flood. The adjustable scoops are especially handy for filling in shadows in precisely defined areas.

Most scoops range from 1,000 watts to 2,000 watts, with the 1,000-watt and 1,500-watt sizes being the more popular ones. (See 6.12.)

The Follow Spot   Sometimes you may find that a television show requires the use of a **follow spot,** a powerful special effects spotlight that is used primarily to simulate theater stage effects. The follow spot generally follows action, such as dancers, ice skaters, or single performers moving about in front of a stage curtain. (See 6.11.)

Floodlights

Floodlights are designed to produce a great amount of highly diffused light. They are principally used to slow down falloff (reduce contrast between light and shadow areas) and to provide baselight.

Because even in floodlights the spread of the beam should be somewhat controllable so that undue spill into other set areas can be minimized, some floodlights, like spotlights, have adjustable beams.

The Broad and the Softlight   The **broad** (from broadside) and **softlight** instruments are used to provide extremely diffused, even lighting.

Broads act like a series of scoops. They illuminate evenly a rather large area with diffused light, with some provision for beam control. (See 6.13.)

Some broads have barn doors, or movable metal flaps, to block gross light spill into other set areas; others have even an adjustable beam, similar to the adjustable scoops. They are sometimes called "multiple broads."

Softlights, on the other hand, are used for extremely diffused, even lighting. If, for example, you want to increase the baselight level without in the least affecting your specific lighting (highlights and shadow areas carefully controlled), you can turn on a few softlights. They act like fluorescent tubes, except that they burn with a lower (3,200°K) color temperature. (See 6.14.)

The Floodlight Bank   This consists of a series of high-intensity internal reflector bulbs arranged in banks of six, nine, twelve, or more spots. The floodlight bank is mostly used on remotes, either to illuminate fairly large areas over a considerable distance, or to act as a *daylight booster,* usually to make the harsh shadows created by the sun more translucent for the camera. Because they are large and awkward to handle, you will not often find them in studios. For studio lighting, the softlight outperforms the floodlight bank, at least in operational ease. (See 6.15.)

The Strip, or Cyc, Light   This is commonly used to achieve even illumination of large set areas, such as the **cyc** (cyclorama) or some other uninterrupted background area. Very similar to the border or cyc lights of the theater, television **strip lights** consist of rows of from three to twelve incandescent or quartz lamps mounted in long, boxlike reflectors. The more sophisticated strip lights have, like theater border lights, glass color frames for each of the reflector units, so that the cyc can be illuminated in different colors. (See 6.16.)

You can use strip lights also as general floodlights by suspending them from the studio ceiling, or you can place them on the studio floor to separate ground rows from the cyclorama, or pillar and other set pieces from the lighted background. Strip lights are sometimes used for silhouette lighting (where the background must be evenly illuminated, with the foreground pieces remaining unlit).

PORTABLE LIGHTING INSTRUMENTS

Obviously, you can use studio lighting instruments on remote location. However, you may find that they are too bulky to move around easily, that their large three-pronged plugs or twist-lock plugs do not fit the household receptacles, and that, once in place and operating, they do not provide the amount or type of illumination you need for good remote lighting. Besides, most studio lights are suspended on the overhead lighting grid. To take them down each time you have to light a remote telecast not only

wastes valuable production time, but more important, robs the studio of the lighting instruments.

Special *portable lighting packages* have, therefore, been developed to fulfill the basic lighting requirements for simple productions away from the studio. You will find that the basic requirements for remote lighting are (1) a great amount of illumination with as few instruments as possible; (2) compact instruments that take up very little room, and that can be set up and struck (taken down) with minimal time and effort; (3) instruments that can be operated with household current without danger of overloading circuits; and (4) lightweight, but durable, instruments.

Even in studio lighting, such portable units can prove extremely helpful, especially if your studio is rather small or if your studio ceiling is too low for overhead suspension of lighting instruments—as in a converted classroom, for example. As with the studio lighting package, the portable lights are grouped into (1) spotlights and (2) floodlights.

Spotlights

Portable spotlights are designed to be light, rugged, efficient (which means that the light output is great relative to the size of the instrument), easy to set up and transport, and small enough so that they can be hidden rather effectively even in cramped interiors.

The three most frequently used are (1) the HMI Fresnel spot, (2) the external reflector spotlight, and (3) the internal reflector spotlight.

The HMI Light   The HMI (Halogen-Metal-Iodide) light is a Fresnel spotlight that has proved highly successful in EFP. It has an arc lamp that delivers from three to five times the illumination of a quartz instrument of the same wattage, uses less power to do so, and develops less heat. The HMI lights are designed for location shooting and burn not with the customary 3,200°K, but with the photographic daylight standard of 5,600°K, and range from 200 watts to 4,000 watts. Some manufacturers provide even larger instruments, which are used for big productions. For the normal EFP work, you usually use the 200-watt, 575-watt, and 1,200-watt instruments.

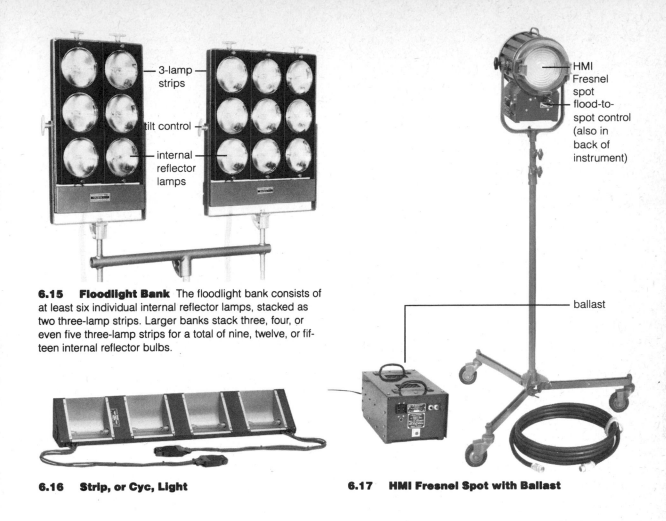

3-lamp strips

tilt control

internal reflector lamps

HMI Fresnel spot

flood-to-spot control (also in back of instrument)

ballast

6.15   Floodlight Bank The floodlight bank consists of at least six individual internal reflector lamps, stacked as two three-lamp strips. Larger banks stack three, four, or even five three-lamp strips for a total of nine, twelve, or fifteen internal reflector bulbs.

6.16   Strip, or Cyc, Light

6.17   HMI Fresnel Spot with Ballast

These do fine to fill in shadows when shooting outdoors or to light interiors that are partially illuminated by available daylight, without the problem of mixing color temperatures. The HMI light has a Fresnel lens, and its beam can be focused.

One of the advantages of the super-efficient HMI lights is that you can plug even the larger instruments (like the 1,200-watt light) into an ordinary household outlet. A single plug is sufficient to power five 200-watt instruments without danger of overloading the household circuit, assuming that nothing else is plugged into the same circuit. Because you plug most of the lights into household outlets, you can light most interiors with a minimum of effort

and time. All you actually need is plenty of extension cords and spider boxes (boxes with multiple outlets).

Unfortunately, the HMI light is not without drawbacks. One is that each instrument needs a special box that contains a starter-ballast unit similar to fluorescent lights. They get quite warm when turned on and occasionally hum. This rather awkward accessory makes the HMI light impractical for ENG. Also, most HMI lights take about a minute or so to build up full illumination power from the time they are switched on. Obviously, this is not a good feature for ENG, because you often have to light and shoot on the run. (See 6.17.) All HMI lights are quite expensive, and the high-powered HMI lights (2,500

tilt control

reflector (no lens)

quartz bulb

a

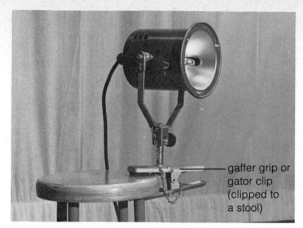

gaffer grip or gator clip (clipped to a stool)

6.19 External Reflector Spot with Gaffer Grip

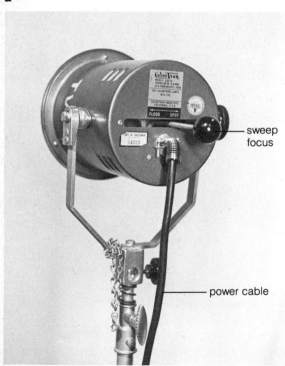

sweep focus

power cable

b

6.18 External Reflector Spot on Stand

and 4,000 watts) are large and heavy. They are, therefore, used only in elaborate electronic field productions or films.

The External Reflector Spotlight Mainly because of weight consideration and light efficiency, this spotlight has no lens. We use the term "external reflector" so as to distinguish it from the small Fresnel studio spot (which, of course, can also be used on remote location) and the internal reflector spotlight, which we will discuss in a moment.

The lack of a good lens makes the beam of the external reflector spot less precise than that of the Fresnel spot. But in most remote lighting tasks, a highly defined beam would offer no particular advantage. Because you usually have to work with a minimum of lighting instruments on remote location, a fairly flat, yet *even,* illumination is often better than a dramatic, yet extremely spotty, one. Still, even on remote location, you should try to light as precisely as possible without sacrificing a sufficient operating light level.

The external reflector spot makes fairly precise lighting possible. You can spot or spread the beam of the high-efficiency quartz lamp through a sweep-focus control lever or knob in the back of the instrument. (See 6.18.)

Unfortunately, the focused beam is not always even. When you have to place the lighting instru-

6.20 Clip Light The clip light consists of a regular internal reflector bulb (such as a PAR 38) and a socket with a simple clip that can be attached to any number of objects.

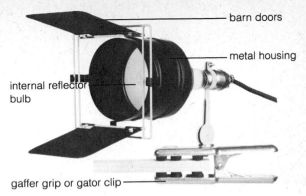

barn doors

metal housing

internal reflector bulb

gaffer grip or gator clip

6.21 Clip Light with Metal Housing and Barn Doors

ment rather close to the object, you may notice (and the camera will surely notice) that the rim of the beam is quite intense and "hot," while the center of the beam has a hole, a low-intensity dark spot. In extreme cases, especially when lighting a face, this uneven beam may look as though you had forgotten to turn on one of the instruments. By spreading the beam a little, however, you can correct this problem rather easily.

All external reflector spotlights have a special bracket for floor mounting on a lightweight stand (see 6.18) or on a heavy clip, called a **gaffer grip,** or **gator clip** (see 6.19).

Most external reflector spotlights can be plugged into a regular household receptacle. Be careful, however, not to overload the circuit; that is, do not exceed the circuit's rated amperage by plugging in more than one instrument per outlet.

The Internal Reflector Spotlight This spotlight looks like an overgrown, slightly squashed household bulb. You have probably used it already in your still photography. The reflector for the bulb is inside the lamp. All you need for using this kind of spot is a light socket and a clamp with which to fasten the bulb onto a chair, a door, a windowsill, or a small pole. Because internal reflector spotlights are usually clipped onto things, they are often called **clip lights.**

You can use clip lights to light small areas easily and also to fill in areas that cannot be illuminated with the other portable instruments. The clip light is an excellent device to provide additional highlights and accents in areas whose lighting looks too flat. (See 6.20.)

Internal reflector spots come in a *variety of beam spreads,* from a soft, diffused beam to a hard, rather precisely shaped beam. For even better beam control, as well as for the protection of the internal reflector bulb, the lamp can be used in a metal housing with barn doors attached (see 6.21).

Floodlights

If you need to light large interiors, the HMI lights prove again to be the most efficient instruments (see 6.22). A few 1,200-watt or even 575-watt instruments in the "flood" position are all you need to light the local gymnasium for the basketball game. Make sure, however, that the cameras are adjusted to the daylight color temperature of the HMI lights (5,600°K). In the absence of HMI lights, you can always use the broads and softlights to illuminate interior scenes for elaborate electronic field productions. Most often, however, you will find that the portable softlights (see 6.23) and even external reflector spots operate as efficient floodlights when put in the "flood" posi-

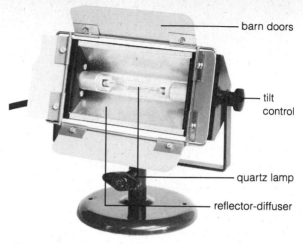

barn doors

tilt control

quartz lamp

reflector-diffuser

a

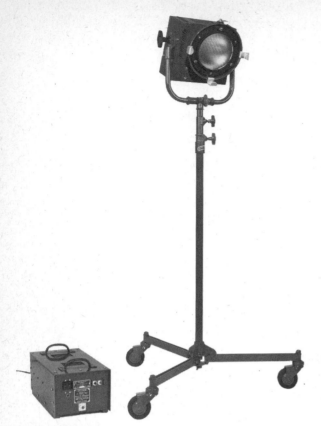

6.22   HMI Mole Solar Arc (575-watt)

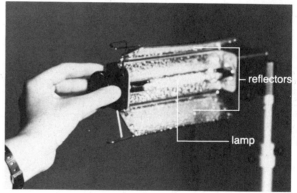

reflectors

lamp

b

6.24   Small Floodlights (a) Nooklight. (b) Lowel Totalight.

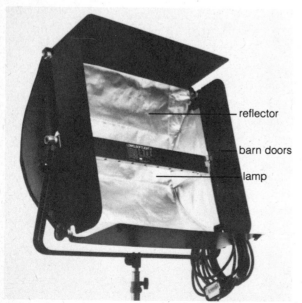

reflector

barn doors

lamp

6.23   Portable Softlight (Lowel Softlight 2)

tion, and, if possible, bounced off light-colored walls and ceilings.

There are a variety of very small floodlights available that you can clamp on practically anything and hide rather easily from camera view (see 6.24). You can put several of these small instruments on a single stand to get a more powerful single light source. Or you can achieve very even illumination by diffusing the light through the traditional light-reflecting umbrella (see 6.26).

Most of the small floodlights can be powered

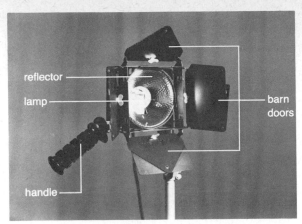

reflector

lamp

barn doors

handle

6.25   Omni-Light (Lowel) Lightweight, highly efficient lights that can be carried by the ENG camera operator or clipped on the ENG camera are extremely important for the mobility of ENG. The Omni-Light is a popular ENG light.

6.26   Omni-Light with Umbrella The Omni-Light can also be fastened to a stand or other objects, and changed into a softlight through the umbrella.

radiation of the quartz instruments makes working in cramped quarters especially uncomfortable); and (3) you will conserve energy.

Hand-Held Lights

ENG requires yet another type of light, which can be held by the camera operator or assistant, and powered by battery. These lights must be small and lightweight, yet capable of producing a generous amount of light. One of the more popular hand-held lights is the *Omni-Light*. It has a number of handy features that make it a good ENG light. For instance, you can (1) run it off a 30-volt battery belt (giving off uninterrupted illumination for over 1 hour), or household current; (2) change the beam continuously from spot to flood; (3) attach barn doors for further beam control (see p. 151); (4) put in various reflectors and color correction and diffusion filters; (5) either hold it or clip it on the camera or any other convenient object (such as a door, chair, and so forth); and (6) use it with a light-diffusing umbrella (see 6.25 and 6.26).

On occasion, you may still see the *sun gun,* the veteran instrument in this category. However, compared to the more modern portable lights, the sun gun is heavier and much less flexible.

Whatever light you use, be sure to have the right lamp for the right current (30 volt DC, or 110 volt AC), and to keep count of how long you have run the lamps, because they have a rather short life of around 12 to 20 hours.

by ordinary 120-volt household current, or by a 30-volt battery, provided that you have the appropriate lamp for each current. The extension cables of most of the portable lights have an on-off switch close to the instrument, making it unnecessary to unplug the instrument every time you want to turn it off. You should keep portable lighting instruments turned off as much as possible, because (1) you will prolong the rather limited life of the lamp (often not more than 20 hours); (2) you will keep the performance area as cool as possible (the excessive heat

LIGHTING CONTROL EQUIPMENT

Television operation necessitates flexible lighting equipment for several reasons:

1.   In the studio, moving cameras and microphone booms make any permanent lighting setup on the studio floor impractical.

2.   When a limited number of lighting instruments are available, the instruments must be flexible enough to provide adequate light throughout the entire studio.

6.27 Pipe Grids The *pipe grid* consists of rather heavy pipe strung either crosswise or parallel and mounted from 12 to 18 feet above the studio floor. The height of the grid is, of course, determined by the studio ceiling height, but even in rooms with low ceilings, the pipe should be mounted approximately 2 feet below the ceiling so that the lighting instruments or the hanging devices can be easily mounted onto the pipe.

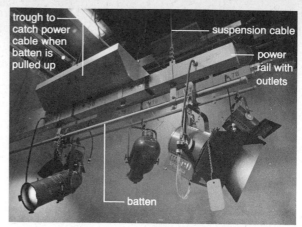

6.28 Counterweight Battens The *counterweight battens* can be lowered and raised to any desired position and locked firmly into place. The battens and the instruments are counterweighted by heavy steel weights and moved by means of a rope-and-pulley system or individual motors. The advantage of counterweight battens over the pipe grid system is that the instruments can be hung, maintained, and adjusted to a rough operating position directly from the studio floor. However, even this arrangement does not altogether eliminate the use of a ladder. Especially in small studios, the studio floor is rarely sufficiently clear of cameras, microphone booms, or scenery for the battens to be lowered all the way to comfortable working height. You will find that after having adjusted the lighting instruments as to direction and beam focus, you will still need a ladder or the lighting pole for the accurate final trimming once the battens have been raised to the proper position.

3. There is rarely enough time and personnel available to design and follow a careful lighting plan for each television production.

In order to understand lighting control, you need to become familiar with these four major points: (1) mounting devices, (2) directional controls, (3) intensity controls, and (4) color controls.

Mounting Devices

Studio Mounts Studio lights are hung from either fixed *pipe grids* or counterweight **battens,** which can be lowered and raised to a specific vertical position. (See 6.27 and 6.28.) The lighting instruments are either directly attached to the light batten by a **C-clamp,** or hung from the batten by hanging devices that enable you to *vary* the *vertical position* of the instrument without raising or lowering the battens (see 6.29). If you have a fixed pipe grid rather than the movable counterweight system, these hanging devices are extremely important. The most com-

mon are the **pantograph** and the **telescope hanger.** (See 6.30 and 6.31.)

Not all studio lights are mounted on the lighting grid or battens. Some are mounted on vertical roller-caster floorstands (see 6.32) that can be rolled around the studio and vertically extended. Such stands can hold any type of lighting instrument: scoops, broads, spots, and even strip lights. The stands usually have a switch attached with which you can turn the lighting instrument on and off.

Portable Mounts Because you will usually find no battens or lighting grids conveniently installed when you do on-location shooting, you need to carry the lighting supports with you. A great variety of light-

6.29 C-clamp Most C-clamps have a small extension hanger attached, which makes the turning of the lighting instruments a little easier than with the standard C-clamp.

pantograph

6.30 Pantograph This spring-counterbalanced hanger can be adjusted quickly and easily from the studio floor to any height within its more than sufficient 12-foot range. Depending on the lighting instrument attached to it, you need one or two sets of springs for counterbalancing. Heavier springs permit the mounting and counterbalancing of other equipment, such as a studio monitor. In most studios, where the grid height rarely exceeds 18 feet, you can pull the lighting instrument down to almost floor level, make the necessary lighting adjustment, and push the instrument back into the desired position, all in a matter of seconds.

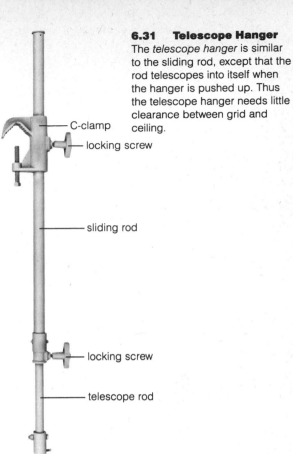

6.31 Telescope Hanger The *telescope hanger* is similar to the sliding rod, except that the rod telescopes into itself when the hanger is pushed up. Thus the telescope hanger needs little clearance between grid and ceiling.

C-clamp

locking screw

sliding rod

locking screw

telescope rod

6.32 Floorstand The floorstand can support any type of lighting instrument and can even be adapted for an easel stand.

6.33 Portable Light Stand Portable lights do not require as heavy a floorstand as studio lights. For all portable lighting instruments, special collapsible stands have been developed that telescope from a 2-foot minimum to an over 8-foot maximum height.

6.34 Extendable Pole

Most lighting poles can be extended and wedged between floor and ceiling. Some models are spring-loaded. You can also use this pole as a cross brace and hang lights from it as from a lighting batten. Some small poles can be attached to furniture, or even to an open door or window, to support a small light instrument. Such a device comes in handy when working in cramped quarters.

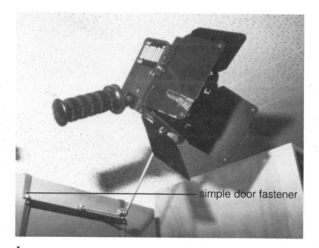

a

b

weight and durable mounting devices are available, and all of them consist basically of collapsible stands and extendable poles (see 6.33 and 6.34). You can attach to the stands and poles a great variety of portable lighting instruments and other lighting devices, such as reflectors, scrims, and flags (see p. 152).

In elaborate productions you may find that small booms are used. These allow you to dangle the light over the scene, out of camera view (see 6.35).

However, if you engage in such large electronic field productions, you can always use one of your small microphone booms, or simply build a light support with lumber (such as 1 × 3 boards).

Directional Controls

We have already discussed the spot and flood beam control on spotlights. Several other devices can help you control the direction of the beam.

Barn Doors This admittedly crude beam control method is extremely effective if you want to block certain set areas partially or totally from illumination. For example, if you want to keep the upper part of some scenery dark, without sacrificing illumination of the lower part, you simply "barn-door" off the upper part of the beam. Or, if you want to

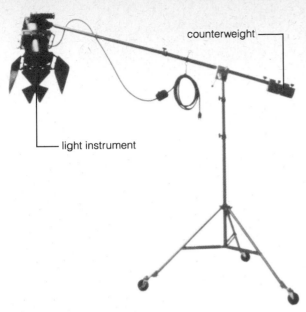

counterweight

light instrument

6.35   Portable Boom (Lowel) When you are working in rather spacious environments, a small light boom, or even a small microphone boom, can be used for suspending lights. The advantage of such a boom is that it permits easy and quick relocation of the lighting instrument.

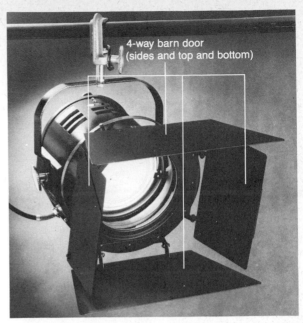

4-way barn door
(sides and top and bottom)

6.36   Two-Way Barn Door The two-way barn door has two movable metal flaps. They can be attached to the lighting instrument so that they block either the top and bottom part of the light beam or its right and left spread.

eliminate a boom shadow, you may be able to do so by partially closing a barn door. (See 6.36 and 6.37.) **Barn doors** are also important for blocking the back light from shining into the camera lens, causing lens flare.

Because the barn doors slide into their holders rather easily, they have a tendency to slide out of them just as readily. Make sure, therefore, that they are chained to the instrument so that they cannot drop on you, especially when you are adjusting them from the studio floor with a light pole. Also, barn doors get very hot. Wear protective gloves if you handle them while the instrument is turned on.

Flags   These are rectangular metal frames with heat-resistant cloth, or thin metal sheets of various sizes that act very much like barn doors, except that you do not place them directly on the lighting instrument. Rather, **flags** are put anywhere on the set where they can block the light from falling on a specific area without being discovered by the cam-

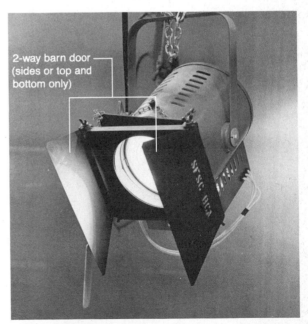

2-way barn door
(sides or top and
bottom only)

6.37   Four-Way Barn Door With the four-way barn door, all four sides—top and bottom, and left and right sides—of the beam spread can be blocked simultaneously.

era during the "take" (shooting the scene). Obviously, flags can only be used if the camera and people movements have been carefully blocked and rehearsed (see 6.38).

Reflectors   Reflectors are usually highly reflecting metal sheets that bounce back a strong light source (usually the sun) onto an object or a scene to slow down falloff (make the shadows more translucent). In fact, you do not need commercially available reflectors. Any white cardboard sheet will do in most cases. You can also make an effective reflector very easily by first crumpling up some aluminum foil to get an uneven surface (for a more diffused reflection) and then taping it on a piece of cardboard (see 6.39).

By the way, you should always carry a roll of aluminum foil and several rolls of gaffer's tape on any remote. With the foil, you can extend or make barn doors, or you can use it as flags or as efficient reflectors. You can also use it as a heat shield if you have to mount your lighting instruments close to wood paneling, curtains, or other combustible material.

Scrims   These are spun-glass diffusers that you can put in front of floodlights or external reflector spots in order to achieve maximum diffusion of the light beam. The problem with using **scrims** is that they absorb a great amount of light—something you can rarely afford in EFP lighting. In the studio, however, they are frequently used to produce soft light, especially if you need to light a large area evenly or if you want to raise the overall baselight level (see 6.40).

Intensity Controls—Dimmers

The simplest way of controlling light intensity is obviously to turn on only a certain number of instruments of a specific size (wattage). Other techniques are to use scrims not only for light diffusion, but for reducing the light intensity as well. There are also thin wire-mesh screens that are put in front of the lighting instruments in order to reduce the light output without influencing the color temperature of the light. The problem with such devices, however, is that the heat of the quartz light tends to

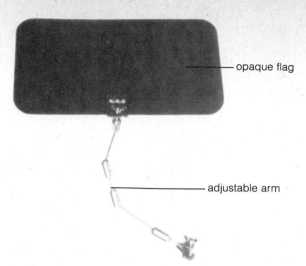

opaque flag

adjustable arm

6.38   Flag Flags are rectangular sheets of opaque material that are used to prevent the light from hitting specific areas.

"burn up" these scrims within a relatively short time, which means that they become brittle and eventually disintegrate.

The most flexible light control is the **dimmer.** With a dimmer, you can easily manipulate each light, or a group of lights, to burn at a given intensity, from zero ("off" position) to full strength.

Although dimmers are technically quite complex, their basic operational principle is quite simple: *By allowing more or less current to flow to the lamp, the lamp burns with a higher or lower intensity.* If you want the lighting instrument to burn at full intensity, the dimmer lets all the current flow to the lamp. If you want it to burn at a lesser intensity, the dimmer reduces somewhat the voltage that flows to the lamp. If you want to dim the light completely, called a *blackout,* the dimmer permits no current—or at least an inadequate current—to reach the lamp.

You may argue that dimmers are not always useful because we cannot dim any given instrument by more than 10 percent without running the risk of lowering the color temperature so much that the scene will turn red. This is true. But dimmers perform a variety of functions, all of which are vital to

6.39 Aluminum Foil Reflector You can make a simple, yet effective reflector by taping aluminum foil on a piece of cardboard or simply by holding up a white card. On the right the ENG camera operator uses a simple reflector to illuminate the reporter's face.

good television lighting. They are: (1) intensity control, (2) illumination change, (3) color change, and (4) special effects lighting.

1. *Intensity Control.* Lowering the intensity of a light is helpful not only to preserve the life of the lamp, but also to control contrast. In most lighting situations, you will find that merely turning off some lights and turning on others will not give you the control you need to achieve subtle differences between light and shadow, or to make shadow areas properly translucent. With dimmers you can control falloff quite readily, without having to dim any one of the instruments so drastically that the change in color temperature begins to show. The 10 percent in the upper range of the light intensity is often enough to make the bright areas less "hot" (intense), or to adjust the relative density of a shadow area.

2. *Illumination Change.* Dimmers enable you to change quickly and easily from one type of lighting in a particular area to another. Also, with the aid of a dimmer, you can light several studio areas at once, store the lighting setup in the dimmer's storage device, and activate part or all of the stored lighting information whenever necessary.

6.40 Scoop with Scrim The scrim is made of heat-resistant spun-glass material that is clamped onto the scrim holder and put in front of the scoop.

6.41 Dimmer Controls (a) Manual dimmer control console. (b) Computer-assisted dimmer control.

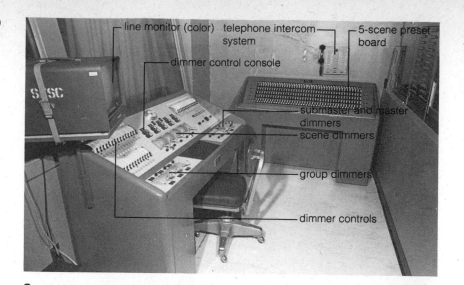

line monitor (color)   telephone intercom system   5-scene preset board

dimmer control console

submaster and master dimmers

scene dimmers

group dimmers

dimmer controls

a

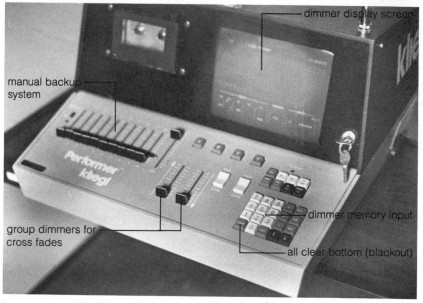

dimmer display screen

manual backup system

Performer kliegl

dimmer memory input

group dimmers for cross fades

all clear bottom (blackout)

b

3. *Color Change.* Some special shows may require you to go from one type of color background to another. With the dimmer you can simply "bring up" (activate) all instruments that, for example, throw red light onto the background, and then bring up the blue lights, while fading down the red ones at the same time.

4. *Special Effects Lighting.* With the help of the dimmer, you can achieve a variety of special effects lighting, such as silhouette, series of pools of light, color, day and night, without affecting the standard lighting setup in any way.

There are many types of dimmers on the market, ranging from a simple rheostat to a sophisticated computer-assisted model. Regardless of the electronics involved, the dimmer systems used in television studios have these features: (1) a series of

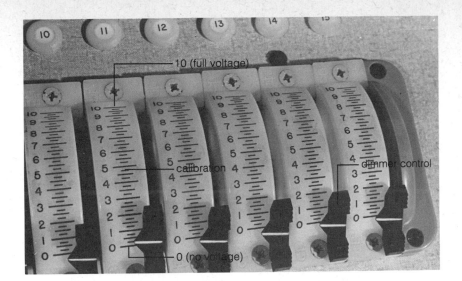

individual dimmers, (2) a patchboard and other grouping devices, and (3) storage and retrieval device (see 6.41).

Individual dimmers A useful dimmer system should have a fair number of individual dimmers (20 or more), each of which has an *intensity calibration.* The usual calibration is in steps of 10, with 0 preventing any current from reaching the instrument (the light is off), and with 10 allowing the full current to flow to the lamp (the lamp burns at full intensity) (see 6.42).

In manual dimmers you push the control lever to the desired setting. In computer-assisted dimmers you simply enter the desired dimmer setting on the keyboard (see 6.41b). Such calibrations are necessary not only to set the initial light intensity, but also to record the exact intensity settings so that they can be repeated with a minimum of effort.

Patchboard and Grouping Devices The **patchboard,** sometimes called *patchbay,* is a device that connects lighting instruments to the dimmer control. Regardless of make and design, all patchboards work on the same principle: *to connect widely scattered instruments to a specific dimmer,* or separate

dimmers, on the dimmer control board. Most of the important lighting instruments in the studio terminate at the patchboard.

Let's assume that you have fifty overhead lighting instruments in your studio. Let's further assume that each one of these has its corresponding patch. Each of the fifty outlets on the light battens is numbered, and the patchcords for each light have corresponding numbers. (Do not number the instrument itself, because, if you were to shift the instrument into a different position, your patchcord number would no longer correspond with the lighting instrument.)

Now, for example, if you want to patch instrument no. 5 (a spotlight plugged into the no. 5 batten outlet) and instrument no. 27 (a scoop plugged into the no. 27 batten outlet at the other end of the studio) into dimmer no. 1, you simply take the patchcords no. 5 and no. 27 and plug them into the receptacles for dimmer no. 1. Depending on the rated power of the dimmer, you may plug several lighting instruments into a single dimmer. If you now bring up dimmer no. 1 at your dimmer board, both instruments, spotlight no. 5 and scoop no. 27, will light up simultaneously (see 6.43).

The patchboard thus allows many combinations of specific lighting instruments from different stu-

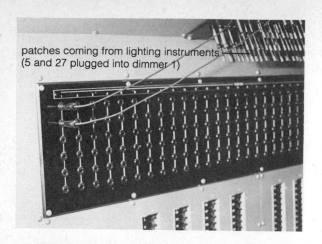

patches coming from lighting instruments
(5 and 27 plugged into dimmer 1)

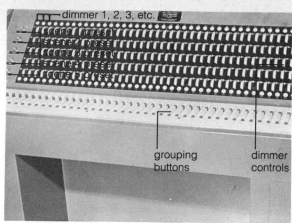

dimmer 1, 2, 3, etc.

grouping buttons

dimmer controls

6.44   Five-Scene Preset Board Each row of dimmers represents the preset for a scene. Row 1 dimmers are the presets for Scene 1, row 2 for Scene 2, and so forth. Each individual thumb wheel can be adjusted from intensity 0 to 10 (full power). The grouping buttons in front permit the various lighting instruments to be grouped together to a single dimmer control.

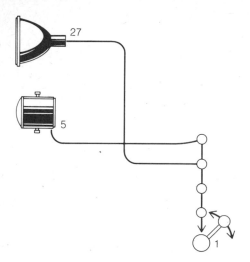

6.43   Patching As you can see, the patches for the lighting instruments no. 5 (spot) and no. 27 (scoop) are both patched into dimmer no. 1. Consequently, both lighting instruments respond identically to any no. 1 dimmer setting.

dio areas so that they can be controlled individually or in groups as to their intensity.

There are additional *grouping devices* that make it possible for you to combine various lighting instruments so that you can dim them, or turn them "on" or "off" simultaneously with a single dimmer control. If, for example, you want change from normal studio lighting to silhouette effect, you can group together all the floodlights that illuminate the background, while at the same time dimming the other lights all the way down. By moving a single control lever, the normal lighting will then change into the silhouette lighting. Computer-assisted dimmers can accomplish a whole series of such groupings by simply entering the desired grouping into the computer and then activating the desired grouping sequence by the push of a button.

Storage and Retrieval A good dimmer control must allow for easy storage and retrieval of various lighting setups. Older type dimmers have a **preset board,** which is usually separate from the actual dimmer control board. It consists of several rows of dimmers, with each row duplicating the dimmers as they appear on the actual dimmer control board (see 6.44). The rows constitute the various "scene presets." With this preset board, you can, for example, use one instrument, such as our spotlight no. 5, and preset it so that it will operate at full intensity in Scene 1, at three-quarter intensity in Scene 2, at full intensity again in Scene 3, and at half intensity for the special effects Scene 4. All this can be done without repatching. The preset board stores the different settings of dimmer no. 1 (full, three-quarter, full, half) and relates this information to the dimmer control board whenever Scene 1, 2, 3, or 4 is activated.

The computer-assisted dimmer control boards do not need a special preset board. Presetting different intensities for various scenes is part of its software (program). Depending on the capacity of the microprocessor (small computer) used with the dimmer control and the software (programming the number and relative complexity of preset programs), you can store and retrieve a greater number of preset combinations with much less effort than with the older manual preset board.

Color Controls

You can control color in lighting in two basic ways: (1) through a manipulation of color temperature, and (2) through color media (filters) that produce colored light.

Color Temperature Control We have already discussed how different lamps may burn at various color temperatures, and how dimming affects color temperature. You have learned that the two most common methods of controlling color temperature are as follows:

1. You can use lamps with a specific and uniform Kelvin rating, such as 3,200°K (studio lights) and 5,600°K (remote lights with daylight rating). Dimming the lights about 10 percent of their full intensity does not affect color temperature to any appreciable extent. But any further dimming does result in an increasing reddishness of the light. Therefore you should try not to dim lights that are used for principal performance areas. The skin tones are in effect the only reliable indicator of the trueness of

the color scheme televised. If you now dim extensively the lights that fall on performers, their skin tones will take on an unnatural red glow, and the television viewer will have no reference as to the color scheme.

2. You can use color correction filters on the light source (lighting instruments or windows), and/or inside the camera. For example, you can lower a high color temperature by a slightly orange filter (so that outdoor light matches the lower temperature indoor light), and boost a low-color temperature by a bluish filter (by making the reddish indoor light match the more bluish outdoor light).

Colored Light Control You can produce a great variety of colored light simply by putting different *color media,* or *color gels,* in front of the lighting instrument. Color media are sheets of highly heat-resistant plastic that act as color filters. You can cut these sheets, which come in a great variety of colors, so that they will fit into the frame of the "gel" holders of the various lighting instruments. (**"Gel"** is a short form of gelatin, which was the color medium before the more durable plastic was developed.) Again, do not use colored light in performance areas unless you desire a special effect, like in a rock-and-roll show, where distorted skin colors help, rather than hinder, the intended effect.

As you learned from our discussion of how the camera works, *colored lights mix additively,* which means that they do not mix like paints (which mix subtractively). In a colored light mixture, red and green give off a rich yellow, not a muddy brown as paint would produce.

MAIN POINTS

1. The two types of light are directional, which causes fast falloff, and diffused, which causes slow falloff.

2. The two types of illumination are outdoor and indoor.

3. Color temperature is the standard by which we measure the relative reddishness or bluishness of white light. It is measured in degrees Kelvin.

4. The technical lighting objectives are (1) proper baselight levels, which means the overall light level necessary for the camera to operate properly, (2) contrast, which refers to a basic limit between highlight and shadow areas, or light and dark colors, and (3) white balance, which is necessary to make the colors appear as true as possible under a variety of lights.

5. Baselight levels and proper contrast ratios require the measurement of illumination. Incident light readings measure primarily baselight levels. Reflected light readings measure primarily contrast levels.

6. All studio lighting is accomplished by a variety of spotlights and floodlights. The most prevalent studio lighting instruments are: (1) the Fresnel spot, (2) the ellipsoidal spot, and among the floodlights, (1) the scoop, (2) the broad or softlight, (3) the floodlight bank, and (4) the strip, or cyc, light. Portable lights include (1) the external reflector spots, (2) the clip light, (3) portable softlights, and (4) very small versatile lights that can be hand-held.

7. Most television lighting instruments have quartz (tungsten-halogen) lamps. Other lamps used are the normal incandescent lamps and the HMI lamps, which burn with an outdoor color temperature.

8. Lighting control equipment includes (1) mounting devices for studio and portable lights, (2) directional controls, such as barn doors and various focus devices, (3) intensity controls, such as scrims and dimmers, and (4) color controls, such as filters and color media.

Television lighting should fulfill technical as well as aesthetic requirements. The television camera requires a certain number and type of lights to "see" properly, and the objects should be lighted in a certain way so that we can make out their true form and dimensions on the television screen. Lighting also contributes to how we feel about an event.

In this section of Chapter 6, we will discuss some more technical lighting details and the major nontechnical lighting objectives. The technical lighting section will give information on (1) how various lamps compare with one another, (2) how color temperature is measured, (3) how light intensity is calculated, and (4) how single and multiple patching are accomplished. We will then take up some of the major nontechnical lighting objectives: (1) to indicate form and dimension, (2) to create an illusion of reality and nonreality, and (3) to indicate a specific mood.

COMPARISON OF LAMPS

As you saw in the first part of this chapter, lighting instruments are sometimes classified by the lamps they use. The table on page 160 shows a comparison of the three principal types of lamps used in television lighting: (1) incandescent (tungsten), (2) quartz (tungsten-halogen), and (3) HMI (gas arc in a quartz enclosure) (see 6.45).

COLOR TEMPERATURE

Color temperature is measured in Kelvin degrees. Lord Kelvin devised this scale by heating up a carbon filament, which he considered to be totally light-absorbing and therefore a "black body," from absolute zero to various degrees centigrade. He observed that the hotter the black body got, the more bluish the radiated light became. The more the temperature dropped, the more reddish the light became. When the black body was heated to 3,200°K (3,200 degrees centigrade from absolute zero), it emitted a fairly white light. Thus, we consider 3,200°K the standard for "white" indoor light. Outdoor illumination is bluer than indoor light; its "white light" standard has, therefore, a higher color temperature (5,600°K).

Some of the small, high-efficiency lights (like the photo floods or portable ENG lights) are "overrun" in order to achieve the 3,200°K or higher color temperatures. This means that their filaments receive a higher voltage than that for which they are actually rated. Although this is an easy method of boosting light output and color temperature, it contributes to a relatively short lamp life. HMI arc lamps, on the other hand, are

Factor	Type		
	Incandescent (Tungsten)	Quartz (Tungsten-Halogen)	HMI (Halogen-Metal-Iodide)
filament	regular tungsten filament	tungsten filament in halogen gas, all within a quartz or silica tube	mercury arc in argon gas within a quartz tube, similar to tungsten-halogen type
size	rather large, needs large instrument	quite small; needs much smaller instrument than incandescent of equal wattage	quite small, though somewhat larger than T-H lights
efficiency	not very efficient; much energy lost in heat	produces twice the illumination of incandescent instrument of same wattage	extremely efficient; produces at least three times the illumination of T-H light with same wattage, and more than six times that of an incandescent instrument
heat	gets quite hot; develops much heat in studio, especially when large and/or many instruments are used	develops more heat than incandescent instrument, but uses lower powered and fewer instruments to do the same job; however, the heat is so intense that color media, scrims, and even barn doors burn up within a relatively short time	develops much less heat than T-H lamp; rooms remain fairly cool even when several large instruments are used
lamp life	relatively long (up to 1,000 hours)	relatively short; only half of regular tungsten lamps; life can be doubled by dimming T-H lights by about 10 percent	longer than T-H lamps, but not as long as regular tungsten lamps (750 hours)
color temperature	3,200°K; reduces with age due to "blackening"	3,200°K; remains constant throughout life of lamp	5,600°K; remains constant throughout life of lamp
accessories	none	none	needs starter-ballast unit similar to fluorescent lamps

designed to produce a high color temperature (5,600°K) without being "overrun." This is also one of the reasons why they radiate less heat and have a longer life than their quartz or photo-flood counterparts.

LIGHT INTENSITY

You may have heard about the **inverse square law** when dealing with illumination. This law states that if you have a light source that radiates *uniformly in all directions,* such as a candle or single light bulb burning in the middle of a room, the light intensity falls off as $\frac{1}{d^2}$, where d is the distance from the source. For example, if the intensity of a light source if 1 foot-candle at a distance of 1 foot from the source, its intensity at a distance of 2 feet is $\frac{1}{4}$ foot-candle (see 6.46).

However, as you just learned, television lighting instruments do not radiate light uniformly in all directions. In fact, spotlights are specifically designed to focus, or *columnate,* the light to a certain extent. Even floodlights radiate their light more in the direction of the reflector opening than its back.

The *more columnated* the light—that is, the more focused the light beam—the *less quickly* its intensity decreases with distance. The light beams of car headlights, a flashlight, and a Fresnel or ellipsoidal spot are all columnated and, therefore, do not obey the inverse square law. An example of an extremely well-columnated light is a laser beam, which, as you know, maintains its intensity over great distances. This is why we "spot," or focus, a spotlight when we want more light on an object and "flood" its beam when we want less light to fall on the object without changing the distance between lighting instrument and object. Although the light intensity of focused spot lights does not fall off according to the inverse square law, it still decreases with distance. Therefore, you can lower the intensity of a focused spotlight without the use of a dimmer by simply increasing the distance between lighting instrument and object. Because soft fill lights are the least columnated, they behave more according to the inverse square law than spotlights.

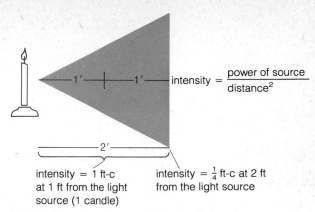

$$intensity = \frac{power\ of\ source}{distance^2}$$

intensity = 1 ft-c
at 1 ft from the light
source (1 candle)

intensity = $\frac{1}{4}$ ft-c at 2 ft
from the light source

6.46   Inverse Square Law Note that the inverse square law applies *only* to light sources that radiate the light isotropically (uniformly in all directions).

PATCHING

It is rather important for you to understand the principle of patching and grouping various lights to specific dimmers. We will, therefore, do a little exercise.

Let's assume that you have to patch some instruments so that you can effect a simple lighting change for a specific studio area. First, you light the designated studio area A with three spotlights. These happen to be plugged into the batten outlets nos. 5, 12, and 18. Since all the spotlights should turn on and off at the same time and burn at the same intensity, you can patch them into the same dimmer, dimmer no. 1. Now, let's assume that you want to change from this rather harsh spotlighting to a softer floodlighting of the same area. You will now pick three scoops that will illuminate area A from the direction of the spotlights. These scoops happen to be plugged into the batten outlets nos. 6, 13, and 19. You look for the patchcords nos. 6, 13, and 19 at the patchboard and plug all three patches into the dimmer no. 2 receptacles.

If you bring up dimmer no. 1, area A is illuminated with three spotlights. If you now want to change to the diffused lighting of the scoops, you simply bring down dimmer no. 1 (which turns off the spotlights) and bring up dimmer no. 2 (which turns on the scoops). If you bring up dimmer no. 2 while bringing down dimmer no. 1, your light change will be very gradual, very much like a picture dissolve.

If you want to control each light separately so that you can balance the intensity of each of the six lighting instruments (the three spots and the three scoops), you will have to assign a separate dimmer to each instrument. Therefore, spot no. 5 will be patched into dimmer no. 1; spot no. 12 into dimmer no. 2; spot no. 18 into dimmer no. 3; scoop no. 6 into dimmer no. 4; scoop

no. 13 into dimmer no. 5; and scoop no. 19 into dimmer no. 6. (See 6.47a.) Unless you have further sophisticated grouping or preset facilities, you will now have to work all six dimmers simultaneously to effect the simple lighting change in area A. As you can see, without a preset board, it is often more practical to patch several lighting instruments into a single dimmer than to use a separate dimmer for each one. (See 6.47b.)

NONTECHNICAL LIGHTING OBJECTIVES

The nontechnical, or aesthetic, lighting objectives are (1) to indicate form and dimension, (2) to create an illusion of reality or nonreality, and (3) to indicate mood.

Form and Dimension

Because the television screen has only two dimensions, height and width, the third dimension, depth, must be created by illusion. A proper control of light and shadow is essential for the clear revelation of the actual shape and form of three-dimensional objects, their position in space and time, and their relation to one another and to their environment. In fact, it is often the *shadows that indicate the form and dimension* of an object rather than the light. You will find, therefore, that the purpose of lighting is more frequently the control of the placement and the relative density of the shadow than the creation of bright picture areas. (See 6.48 and 6.49.)

a

b

6.47 Single and Multiple Patching (a) Single patching. (b) Multiple patching.

a

6.48 Shadow Defining Object Shape (a) It is often the shadow that reveals the true shape of the object. In this picture it is difficult to tell whether the object is a flat figure or a cube. (b) Darkening of the shadow area makes it immediately apparent that the object is a cube.

The emphasis or deemphasis of shadows on a surface of an object also helps to sharpen, or reduce, the textural characteristics of the object. Lighting that emphasizes shadows can make a relatively smooth surface look richly textured; lighting that deemphasizes shadows smooths a relatively rough surface.

Reality and Nonreality

Lighting helps to achieve an illusion of reality or nonreality. It aids in setting a *specific* time and place. For example, long shadows suggest late afternoon or early morning; harsh, bright light helps to establish a sun-flooded outdoor scene. The periodically flashing light as seen through the closed venetian blinds from the inside of a motel room gives us a quick clue as to the kind of establishment, if not the whole neighborhood. A windowless interior rather brightly lighted can give the impression that it is still daylight outside. But the same interior with rather low-key lighting (high-contrast and low overall light level) suggests nighttime.

Special lighting techniques can also help to create

a

a

b

b

6.49 Shadows and Light Defining Spatial Position and Texture (a) In this photo, it is difficult to see exactly where the woman's hair ends and the background begins; nor can we see any texture in the background. (b) With a special light separating the shadows, and another light giving some definition to the background, we have now a clearer idea as to her spatial position and the texture of the background.

6.50 Mood Change through Shadow Reversal (a) Lighting from above, whereby the shadows fall in the customary below-the-object position, gives the scene a normal appearance. (b) Lighting from below creates an unreal, mysterious mood. We perceive the shadows in what seems to be an unnatural position.

the illusion of a specific source of illumination. For example, many lighting instruments may be needed to give the impression that a scene is lit by a single candle.

Illogical or special effects lighting can create the *illusion of nonreality.* For example, an extremely low-contrast scene that is purposely washed out may provide us with an environment as unreal as one in which the contrast is purposely pushed beyond the customary limits.

Mood

Next to sound, lighting is one of the chief means of creating a desired mood. Various psychological effects, such as gaiety, mystery, or gloom, can be achieved through lighting techniques (see 6.50).

The long shadows looming in the deserted street suggest danger; the reflection of water and the shadows of leaves dancing on a face or a wall suggest happiness and calm. Intense lighting from the back tends to glamorize the fashion model.

Lighting from below eye level can create a mysterious mood. Because under normal conditions we experience the principal illumination as coming from above, we expect the shadows to fall below the object. A reversal of the shadows immediately suggests something unusual. If all the other production elements—set design, color, sound, actions—are in harmony with the special lighting effect, the mysterious mood is firmly established.

Note that one production technique, such as lighting, is usually not strong enough alone to establish a feeling of nonreality or mystery, for example. We usually need to have *all other production elements work in unison* to achieve the desired effect.

MAIN POINTS

1. In comparing the lamps used in lighting instruments, we need to consider the type of filament, size, efficiency (light output per wattage), heat, lamp life, and color temperature.

2. The color temperature standard for white indoor light is 3,200° K, and for outdoor light, 5,600° K.

3. The inverse square law in illumination applies only if the light source radiates uniformly in all directions, such as a bare light bulb or a candle. But even with columnated light, such as a spotlight, the general principle still holds true that the farther away the object is from the light source, the less light will fall on it.

4. The nontechnical lighting objectives are (1) to indicate form and dimension, (2) to create the illusion of reality and nonreality, (3) to indicate mood. These three objectives require the careful control of shadows.

FURTHER READING

GTE Sylvania. *Lighting Handbook.* 6th ed. Danvers, MA: GTE Sylvania, Inc. Lighting Center, 1977.

Millerson, Gerald. *The Technique of Lighting for Television and Motion Pictures.* 2nd ed. Woburn, MA: Focal Press, 1982.

Techniques of Television Lighting

The techniques of television lighting tell you what instrument to use in a particular position and adjustment to achieve a desired lighting effect.

In Section One of this chapter, we will acquaint you with the five areas that are especially important for mastering the techniques of television lighting: (1) operation of lights, (2) definition of lighting terms, (3) the photographic or triangle lighting principle, (4) additional light sources, and (5) the light plot.

Section Two will be devoted to (1) remote lighting techniques, and (2) special lighting tehniques, such as cameo, silhouette, and color background lighting.

There are usually many solutions to one problem; therefore, a universal lighting recipe that works for every possible lighting situation cannot and should not be given here. An attempt is made, however, to list some basic lighting principles that you can then adapt to your specific requirements. But do not start with the anticipated limitations. Start with how you would like the lighting to look and then adapt to the existing technical facilities.

Section One deals with (1) operation of lights, (2) definition of lighting terms, (3) the photographic, or triangle, lighting principle, (4) additional light sources, and (5) the light plot.

OPERATION OF LIGHTS

When initially hanging the lights, divide the studio into major performance areas and hang the appropriate instruments (spotlights and floodlights) in the triangular arrangements of the basic photographic principle, which is described in detail later in this chapter. Try to position the instruments so that they can serve *multiple functions*. This procedure will help you to illuminate all major performance areas adequately with the least number of instruments and effort.

In the actual operation of lighting instruments and the associated control equipment, you should heed the rule for all production activities: *safety first*. Secure the lighting instruments to the battens by *safety chains* or *cables*. If you have pantographs, make sure that they are securely fastened to the battens, and the light instruments safety-chained to the pantographs. Chain all barn doors to the instruments. If you have diffusers in front of the scoops, make sure that they are securely fastened in place. Check all C-clamps periodically, especially the bolts that connect the lighting instruments to the hanging device.

When the lights are on, be very careful when moving the instrument. Because the *hot lamps* are especially vulnerable to physical shock, try not to jolt the lighting instrument. Move it gently.

Whenever you adjust the beam, such as the focus device or the barn doors, without the use of a light pole, make sure that you *wear gloves*. The quartz lights especially get extremely hot.

In small stations, and especially in many ENG/EFP situations, available space, time, and people influence lighting techniques and usually limit lighting possibilities to a considerable extent. These limitations, however, do not mean that good and creative television lighting is impossible; they simply call for greater ingenuity on the part of the lighting technician.

When moving ladders for fine trimming (fine beam adjustment), watch for obstacles below and above. Do not take any chances by leaning way out to reach an instrument. Move the ladder.

When adjusting a light, try *not* to *look directly* into it. Rather, look at the object to be lighted and see how the beam strikes it. If you have to look into the light, wear dark glasses.

When patching lights at the patchboard, have all dimmers in the "off" position. Do *not* "hot-patch"; otherwise, the patches themselves will become so pitted that they no longer make the proper connection.

Try to "warm up" large instruments through reduced power. You will not only prolong the lamp life but also prevent the Fresnel lenses from cracking.

Do not overload a circuit. It may hold during rehearsal but then go out just at the wrong time during the actual show.

Do not waste energy. Try to bring the lights down as close to the object or scene to be illuminated as possible. The light intensity drops off enormously the farther the light moves away from the object. Bring the lights up full only when necessary. Dry runs (without cameras) can be done just as effi-ciently when illuminated by work lights as with full studio lighting.

When replacing lamps, wait until the instrument has cooled down somewhat. Make sure that the power is turned off before reaching into the instrument to get at the burned-out lamp. As a double protection, unplug the light at the batten. *Do not touch* the new quartz lamp *with your fingers.* Our skin inevitably secretes some acid that affects the quartz housing of the tungsten-halogen, or arc, lamp. Wear gloves, or if you have nothing else, use your handkerchief when handling the lamp.

If you intend to use a (well-adjusted) color monitor as a guide for lighting, you must be ready for some compromise. As we have said before, the lighting is correct if the studio monitor shows what you want the viewer to perceive. In order to get to this point, you should use the monitor as a guide to lighting, rather than the less direct light meter. But you may run into difficulties. The video engineer may tell you that he cannot align the cameras before you have finished the lighting. And your argument may be that you cannot finish the lighting without checking it on the monitor.

Let's approach this argument with a readiness

for compromise, because both parties have a valid point.

You can do the basic lighting without the camera. A foot-candle meter can help you in detecting gross inadequacies, such as insufficient baselight levels, or extremely uneven illumination. With some experience, you will also be able to tell whether or not a shadow is too dense for adequate reproduction of color and detail. But then, for the fine trimming, you need at least one camera. Ask the video engineer to work *with* you. After all, it is his or her responsibility, too, to deliver technically acceptable pictures. This single camera can be roughly aligned to the existing illumination and pointed into the set. With the direct feedback of the picture on the studio monitor, you can now proceed to correct glaring discrepancies, or simply touch up some of the lighting as to beam direction and intensity.

After this fine trimming, *all* cameras can then be aligned and balanced for optimal performance.

DEFINITION OF LIGHTING TERMS

You can apply the techniques of television lighting only if you are, first of all, thoroughly familiar with the basic terminology. In lighting for television (as well as for film and still photography) the instruments are labeled according to *function,* that is, their particular role in the lighting process.

Baselight is an extremely diffused, overall illumination in the studio, coming from no one particular source. A certain amount of baselight is necessary for the technical acceptability of a television picture.

Key light is the apparent principal source of directional illumination falling upon a subject or an area.

Back light is directional illumination coming substantially from behind the subject.

Fill light is a generally diffused light to reduce shadow or contrast range. It can be directional if the area to be "filled in" is rather limited.

Background light or **set light** is an illumination of the background or set separate from the lights provided for the performers or performing areas.

Side light is a directional light that illuminates the front side of a subject, usually on the opposite side of the camera from the key light.

Kicker light is a directional illumination from the back, off to one side of the subject, usually from a low angle usually opposite the key light.

Camera light, or **eye light,** is a small spotlight mounted on top of the television camera. It is used

Background Light Also called set light. Illumination of the set, set pieces, and backdrops.

Back Light Illumination from behind the subject and opposite the camera.

Camera Light Small spotlight, also called eye light or inky-dinky, mounted on the front of the camera; used as an additional fill light. (Frequently confused with Tally Light.)

Fill Light Additional light on the opposite side of the camera from the key light to illuminate shadow areas and thereby reduce falloff. Usually accomplished by floodlights.

Key 1. Key light: principal source of illumination. 2. Lighting: high- or low-key lighting. High-key lighting: light background and ample light on the scene. Low-key lighting: dark background and few selective light sources on the scene.

Kicker Kicker light, usually directional light coming from the side and back of the subject.

Light Ratio The relative intensities of key, back, and fill. A 1:1 ratio between key and back lights means that both light sources burn with equal intensities. A 1:$\frac{1}{2}$ ratio between key and fill lights means that the fill light burns with half the intensity of the key light. Because light ratios depend on many other production variables, they cannot be fixed. A key:back:fill ratio of 1:1:$\frac{1}{2}$ is often used for normal triangle lighting.

Photographic Lighting Principle The triangular arrangement of key, back, and fill lights, with the back light opposite the camera and directly behind the object, and the key and fill lights on opposite sides of the camera and to the front and side of the object. Also called triangle lighting.

Side Light Usually directional light coming from the side of the object. Acts as additional fill light and provides contour.

for additional fill or eye sparkle, as principal light source for objects located in dark corners of the studio, or to provide illumination when another instrument causes the camera to cast an unwanted shadow.

There are several variations for these terms; however, most television operations use this terminology as their standard.

THE PHOTOGRAPHIC PRINCIPLE, OR BASIC TRIANGLE LIGHTING

As one of the photographic arts, television is subject to photographic lighting principles.

The most basic photographic lighting principle—or, as it is frequently called, basic **triangle lighting**—consists of three main light sources: (1) key light, (2) back light, and (3) fill light.

Each of the three main instruments is positioned in such a way that it can optimally fulfill its assigned function. This arrangement is the **lighting triangle** (see 7.1). But what exactly are the functions each instrument is to fulfill? Let's find out.

Functions of Main Light Sources

Each of the three main light sources, key, back, and fill, has to fulfill a very specific function so that the major objective can be reached: the revelation of form and dimension—or, in lighting terms, the manipulation of light and shadow in order to produce the impression of a three-dimensional object on the two-dimensional television screen.

Key Light   As the principal source of illumination, the major function of the key light is to reveal the *basic shape* of the object (see 7.2). In order to reveal the basic shape, the key light must produce some shadows. Fresnel spotlights, medium spread, are normally used for key illumination. But you can use a scoop, or even a softlight, for a key as well, as long as your aim is simply even illumination. If, however, you want to establish a specific direction from which the principal illumination is coming, the spotlights do a better job for you.

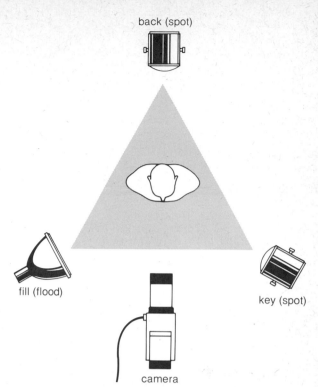

7.1   Basic Photographic Principle As you can readily see, the three principal lights, key (spot), back (spot), and fill (flood), form a triangle, with the back light as its apex, opposite the camera.

Because we usually expect the principal light source to come from above, the key light is placed above and to the right or left front side of the object, from the camera's point of view.

If you look at 7.2, which shows the cube illuminated with the key light only, you notice that the falloff is very fast and that the shadows of the cube blend in with the background, making its true dimension rather ambiguous. To help make the object appear more distinct, we obviously need light sources other than the single key light.

Back Light   The back light has several important functions. As you see in 7.3, it helps to distinguish between the shadow of the cube and the dark background; it emphasizes the outline, the *contour* of the object, separating it from its background. We

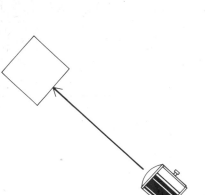

7.2 Key Light The key light reveals the basic shape of the object.

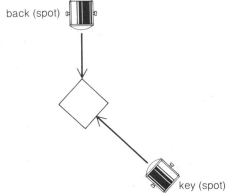

7.3 Back Light The back light helps to separate the object from its background and to reveal more of the object's true form and dimension.

have now established a clear figure-ground relationship, which means that we can perceive quite easily a figure in front of a background. The back light adds a new spatial dimension and gives sparkle to the scene (see 7.3).

Generally, try to position the back light as directly behind the object (opposite the camera) as possible; there is no inherent virtue in placing it somewhat to one side or the other. A more critical problem is controlling the angle at which the back light strikes the object. If it is positioned directly above the object, or somewhat in that neighborhood, the back light becomes an undesirable top light. On the other hand,

if hung too low, the back light may shine into the camera lens, causing **flare** or **halo**—that is, dark or colored flashes produced by signal overload. Instead of revealing the contour of the object so that it stands out from the background, the light simply brightens its top.

In order to get good back lighting in a set, make sure that the *performance areas* (the areas in which performers move) are *not too close* to the scenery. Furniture used by the performers, such as chairs, tables, sofas, or beds, should always be moved away from the walls as far into the center of the set as possible. Otherwise you have to place the back lights

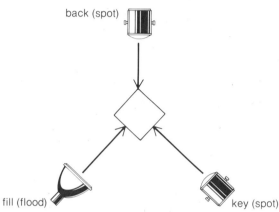

back (spot)

fill (flood)

key (spot)

**7.4 Key Light, Back Light, and Fill Light
Illumination** The fill light is placed on the opposite side
of the camera from the key light to make the shadow areas
more translucent (slow down falloff) and to reveal more
detail in the shadow areas.

at so steep an angle that undesirable top light results.
From a purely technical standpoint, it is better not
to tilt the lighting instrument down too steeply,
because in some instruments an extreme down-
ward position prevents the heat from ventilating
properly and may cause the lamp to explode. In
general, **lighting angles** of 45 degrees are considered ideal for normal lighting situations.

Fill Light   Now take another look at 7.2 and 7.3.
The falloff from light to dark is extremely fast, and
the shadow side of the cube is so dense that the
camera sees no object detail. If the cube were ren-

dered in color, the color would be either lost entirely
in the dense shadow area or, at best, distorted. We
must now try to slow down this falloff and lighten
up the dark side of the cube without erasing the
shadow effect altogether, which would eliminate the
modeling effect of the key light.

You can *fill in* some of the shadows by placing
a floodlight, generally a scoop, in front and a little
to the side of the cube, *on the opposite side of the
camera from the key light.* If you have a dimmer,
put the fill light on a dimmer and see how you
can render the shadow progressively translucent
by supplying an increasing amount of fill light.
(See 7.4)

Some stations still light rather **"flat,"** which means
that the fill light has almost the intensity of the key
light, eliminating most of the shadows. This practice
was somewhat justified in the earlier days of color
television, when the color cameras worked best
within a highly limited contrast ratio. The newscasters liked it, too, because it seemed to eliminate
their wrinkles better than makeup. But the elimination of shadows also eliminated the three-
dimensionality of the person and rendered the image
two-dimensionally "flat." This is why, with better
cameras, lighting has reverted back to the basic photographic principle, whereby we have a definite
"light" side (key light) and a "shadow" side (made
translucent by the fill light).

Because you simply want to lighten up a shadow
area rather than produce new, harsh shadows on
the other side of the cube, the fill light should be
reasonably diffused. Also, watch out for color temperature changes if you intend to do some drastic
fill light dimming.

Sometimes you may find that the fill light spills
into other set areas. If the scoops have a focus control, focus the beam to its narrowest spread. Or, if
you want even more beam control, you can use a
Fresnel spotlight as fill light by spreading the beam
as much as possible. With barn doors, you can then
prevent part of the spread beam from hitting the
other set areas.

For very soft fill, use softlights or broads with a
light-diffusing scrim attached to them.

With the three main light sources in the triangle
position, you have now established the basic pho-

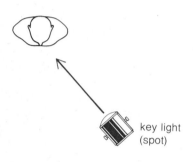

7.5 Key Light on Person The key light represents the principal light source and reveals the basic shape of the object or person. Note that we cannot see much of the left side of the face.

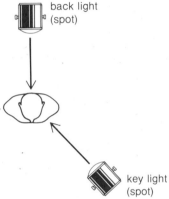

7.6 Key Light and Back Light Here you can see that the back light not only reveals the true dimension of the object, in this case the shape of the man's hair and jacket, but also clearly separates the figure from the ground (background).

tographic principle of television lighting. But you are not through just yet. You should now take a good hard look at the lighted object or, if possible, the studio monitor, to see whether or not the scene (in our case, the cube) needs some further adjustment for optimal lighting. Are there any undesirable shadows, or shadows that distort, rather than reveal, the object? How is the light balance? Does the fill light wash out all the necessary shadows? Or are the

shadows still too dense? Is the key-fill combination too strong for the back light?

We are obviously still concerned with the finer points of directional and intensity controls.

Let's now replace the cube with a person and see how the principle works out when applied to a real situation. Try to see how each light contributes to the revelation of the basic shape and the separation of figure and ground (see 7.5 through 7.7).

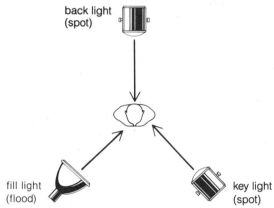

back light
(spot)

fill light
(flood)

key light
(spot)

7.7 Key Light, Back Light, and Fill Light Notice that with the fill light, we can also see the left side of the face and make out detail without losing the shadows altogether. The jacket, too, has received enough light so that we can see the detail on the shadow side (which, in a high-intensity fill situation, looks not much different from the key side).

Directional Adjustments

Assuming that you have hung all three light instruments—the key, the back, and the fill lights—into approximately the right triangular position and that you have pointed them reasonably well toward the subject, there are usually two major areas that need further attention: (1) vertical key light position and eye shadows, and (2) boom shadows.

Key Light and Eye Shadows A fairly *high* key-light *position,* which means that the key light strikes the object from a *steep angle,* causes large dark shadows under any protrusion or in any indentation, such as in the eye sockets, under the nose, and under the chin. If the subject wears glasses, you may find that the shadow of the upper rim of the glasses falls right across her or his eyes, thus preventing the camera (and the viewer) from seeing them clearly (see 7.8a).

There are several ways of reducing these undesirable shadows. First, try to widen the angle of the key light by either lowering the light itself or using a key light farther away from the subject (see 7.8b).

If you lower it (with a movable batten or a pantograph), you notice that the eye shadows seem to move farther up on the face, or at least get smaller, the lower the key light moves and the nearer it approaches the subject's eye level. When the key light reaches eye level, the eye shadows have disappeared altogether. If you move it *below the eye level* of the subject, however, the shadows now reverse themselves, producing a *ghostly* and *mysterious effect.* You have seen these "lighting from below" effects many times in mystery movies (see 6.50).

Unfortunately, in television, where the cameras must move freely about the studio floor, lighting instruments that hang low are a definite production hazard. Not only do they create a serious traffic problem, but they also make it almost impossible for the other cameras to get a clear view of the scene, or for the boom to move about.

But because the vertical positioning of the key light is so important to lighting aesthetics (illusion of reality and nonreality, and mood), you should nevertheless try to make the Fresnel spots, which are used mostly for key lighting, as vertically flexible as possible. Perhaps you might try to suspend them on telescope rods or pantographs, although such practice has not found much acceptance so far.

If you cannot move the key light down closer to the eye level of the subject, try to use a Fresnel spot that is farther away. The light beam coming from a greater distance will necessarily strike the subject from a flatter angle and cause less prominent eye shadows.

The second method is to use a *fill light* that

a   b

7.8   Shadow Caused by Glasses (a) The angle of the key light causes the
upper rim of this woman's glasses to fall right across her eyes. (b) By lowering the key
light instrument somewhat, you can eliminate the shadows.

strikes the subject from a lower angle. This is the preferred method of filling in eye shadows, because the fill lights at the same time produce the necessary illumination for the baselight. Most scoops are, therefore, mounted on pantographs, or telescope poles, so that they can be pulled down into the desired low-angle fill position. Some lighting experts prefer to point some of the scoops toward the light-reflecting studio floor. This reflected, highly diffused, light strikes the subject from below eye level, filling in shadows without causing the ghostly from-below key light effect.

The third solution is to use a *camera light,* sometimes called inky-dinky, which is a small 150-watt baby spotlight mounted on the camera (see 7.9). This can be controlled by the camera operator through a small dimmer. Be careful not to dim the camera light too severely, especially on a closeup, or you will lower the color temperature of the lamp so much that the reddish light will cause color distortion.

Boom Shadows   Now if we move a boom microphone in front of the lighted scene—in this case a single person—and move the boom around a little, you may notice boom shadows whenever the microphone or the boom passes through a spotlight beam.

(You can easily substitute a broomstick or the lighting pole for the boom.) The more diffused light of the scoop casts a soft, less-defined shadow. One obvious solution to this problem is to light everything with diffused light, so that the shadows are barely noticeable. Or, you may want to "wash out" the boom shadow with additional fill light. Both of these methods are less than ideal, because they also cause the elimination of *needed* shadows, making the lighting too flat or upsetting the contrast ratio.

What we must do instead is to light in such a way that the boom shadows are cast into places where the camera does not see them. Whenever a boom is used, try to position the boom or the key light in such a way that the boom does *not* have to *travel through the key light.* Some lighting directors use the key lights and fill lights close to the side light positions, with the boom running down the middle "corridor." Or, you may have to light *steeper* than usual (use a spotlight that hangs overhead, yet fairly close to the subject, so that it has to be pointed down at a steep angle) in order to throw the boom shadows onto floor areas that are hidden from the camera's view, rather than on the scenery behind.

Barn-dooring off part of the key light is another useful method of avoiding some of the boom shadows.

500 watt spotlight

7.9 Camera, or Eye, Light A small spotlight is sometimes mounted on the camera to provide additional fill light, highlights (to add sparkle to eyes, for example), or general illumination for easel cards.

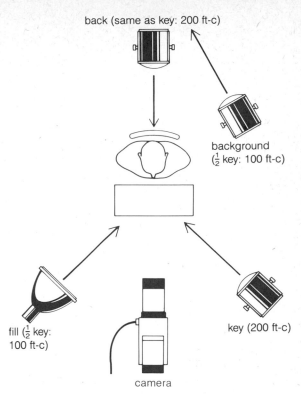

back (same as key: 200 ft-c)

background ($\frac{1}{2}$ key: 100 ft-c)

fill ($\frac{1}{2}$ key: 100 ft-c)

key (200 ft-c)

camera

7.10 Lighting Ratios

The easy way out, of course, is not to use the boom microphone but to rely on hand, desk, or lavaliere microphones (see Chapter 8). The nature of the show, however, may make their use not always possible or desirable.

Intensity Adjustments

Even if you have carefully adjusted the position and beam of the key, back, and fill lights, you still need to *balance* their relative *intensities*. In fact, it is not only the direction of the lights that orients the viewer in time, for example, but also their relative intensities. A strong key and back, and a low-intensity fill light can create the illusion of sunlight, whereas a strong back light, extremely low key, and medium-intensity fill can suggest moonlight.[1]

There is some argument about whether to balance the key and back lights first, or the key and fill lights. Actually, it matters little what you do first, as long as the end effect is a well-balanced picture.

We will, therefore, briefly talk about *relative intensities,* rather than priority. These relative intensities are expressed as a **light ratio.** Again, you

[1] Herbert Zettl, *Sight-Sound-Motion* (Belmont, Calif.: Wadsworth Publishing Co., 1973), pp. 44–45.

should realize that the proper balance depends on so many other production factors, such as contrast requirements of the camera, or the relative reflection of the illuminated object, that it is impossible to give universally valid ratios. All we can do here is give you some basic clues.

Key-to-Back-Light Ratio Generally, in normal conditions, back lights have approximately the same intensity as key lights. An unusually intense back light tends to glamorize the subject; a back light with an intensity much lower than that of the key tends to get lost on the monitor. A television performer with blond hair and a light dress or suit will need less back light than a dark-haired performer in a dark dress or suit. Also, bald men need little backlight.

The 1:1 key-to-back-light ratio (key and back lights have equal intensities) can go as high as 1:1$\frac{1}{2}$ (the back light has 1$\frac{1}{2}$ times the intensity of the key) if you need a fair amount of sparkle. (See 7.10.)

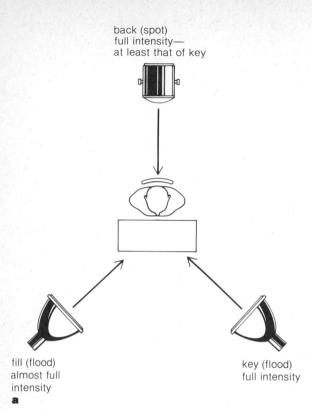

back (spot)
full intensity—
at least that of key

fill (flood)
almost full
intensity

key (flood)
full intensity

a

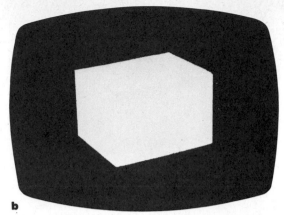

b

7.11   Photographic Principle for Low-Contrast Scene (a) When lighting for low-contrast (extremely slow falloff) scenes, you may want to use a floodlight (such as a scoop, broad, or softlight) for a key and keep the fill at almost the same intensity. But the back light needs to be a spot light to have its concentrated light beam provide the necessary sparkle. (b) You will inevitably lose some spatial dimensions.

Key-to-Fill-Light Ratio   The fill-light intensity depends on how dense the shadows are that need to be filled and on the desired speed of falloff. If you want *fast falloff, little fill* is needed. If you want very *slow falloff, higher-intensity fill* is needed. It is, therefore, futile to state a standard key-to-fill-light ratio. Just for starters, you may want to try a fill-light intensity that is one-half that of the key light, and go from there. Just remember that the more fill light you use, the less modeling the key light is doing, because the form-revealing shadows are all but eliminated. If you use almost no fill light, the dense shadows reveal no picture detail, and you run the risk of serious color distortion in the shadow areas. If, for example, the detective refers to the small scar on the left side of a woman's face, and your closeup of her face shows nothing but a dense shadow where the scar should be, your key-to-fill-light ratio is obviously wrong.

If you are asked to light for a high-baselight, low-contrast scene (called "high-key" lighting), you may want to use floodlights for both the key and the fill, with the fill burning at a slightly lower intensity

than the key. The back light, however, needs to be a spot so that its beam can compete with the high overall light level and supply the necessary outline and sparkle. In this case, the back light should probably burn with a higher intensity than the key or the fill light (see 7.11).

Again, as helpful as light meters are to establish rough lighting ratios, do not rely solely on them. *Your final criterion is how the picture looks on the monitor.*

Now that you are aware of the range of lighting ratios, try to light a person with the following intensities: key light, 200 ft-c; back light, 200 ft-c or slightly more; fill light, 100 ft-c, and background illumination of approximately 100 ft-c.

The ratios in this setup are: key to back 1:1, and key to fill $1:\frac{1}{2}$. The combination of these light intensities should give you a baselight illumination of approximately 200 ft-c to 230 ft-c. If this level is too high for you, simply dim the whole setup down a little. Be careful not to dim too heavily; otherwise the color-temperature change becomes noticeable on the monitor.

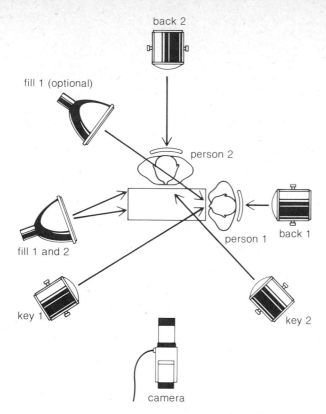

back 2

fill 1 (optional)

person 2

fill 1 and 2

person 1

back 1

key 1

key 2

camera

7.12 Multiple Application of Photographic Principle (Lighting Triangle) In the multiple application of the basic photographic principle, separate key and back lights are used for each person (performance area). Note, however, that the same fill light is used for both people. However, you may find that the fill is much stronger on person no. 2 than on person no. 1 because person no. 1 is farther away from the light and, therefore, receives considerably less illumination. If the difference is too great, you may need an additional fill light after all. Make sure that if person no. 1 is keyed from his or her left, person no. 2 is keyed from the left also. A key-light reversal (person no. 1 from left, person no. 2 from right) and the resulting shadow reversal would be very confusing to the viewer, especially when persons no. 1 and no. 2 are separated by closeups.

The Photographic Principle and Continuous Action

One added problem in television lighting is movement—movement of the performer or performers, and movement of the camera or cameras. Fortunately, the basic photographic principle of key, back, and fill lights can be multiplied and used for each performing or set area. Even if you have only two people sitting at a table (see 7.12), you have to use a multiple application of the photographic principle.

In order to compensate for the movement of the performers, you should illuminate all adjacent performance areas in such a way that the basic triangle-lighted *areas overlap*. The basic purpose of overlapping is to give the performer continuous lighting as he or she moves from one area to another. It is all too easy to concentrate only on the major performance areas and to neglect the small, seemingly insignificant, areas in between. You may not even notice the unevenness of such lighting until the performer moves across the set. All of a sudden he or she seems to be playing a "now you see me,

now you don't" game, popping alternately from a well-lighted area into dense shadow. This is the time when a light meter might come in handy.

When lighting several set areas at once for continuous action, you may find that you do not have enough instruments to apply the overlapping triangle lighting. You may then have to place the lighting instruments in such a way that each one can serve two or even more *different functions*.

In reverse-angle shooting, for instance, the key light for one performer may become the back light for another, and vice versa (see 7.13). Or, you may have to use a key light to serve as directional fill in another area. Because of their diffused light beam, fill lights are often used to serve more than one area simultaneously.

Of course, the application of lighting instruments for multiple functions requires *exact position* of set pieces, such as tables and chairs, and *clearly defined* performing areas and blocking (movements of performers). Directors who decide to change blocking or move set pieces after the set has been lighted are not very popular with the lighting crew.

Accurate lighting is always done with a basic *camera position* and viewpoint in mind. It helps greatly, therefore, if the lighting technician knows at least the basic parameters of the camera movement. For example, an object that appears perfectly well lighted from a six o'clock camera position may look woefully unlit from a ten o'clock camera position. Sometimes, as in variety shows, for example, "unlighted" shots from shooting angles that lie outside the lighted parameters may look quite dramatic; in most other shows of less flexible lighting formats—news shows, interviews—these shots simply look bad.

For lighting a large area, such as an audience area or an orchestra, the basic photographic principle still holds. All you do is partially overlap one triangle over another, until you have adequately covered the entire area. However, instead of key-lighting just from one side of the camera and fill lighting from the other, you key-light from both sides of the camera. This method is generally called **cross-keying** (see 7.14). The key lights from one side act as fill for the key lights from the other side. The back lights are strung out in a row or a semicircle opposite the main camera position. The fill lights, if necessary, come directly from the front. If the cameras move to the side, some of the key lights also function as back lights.

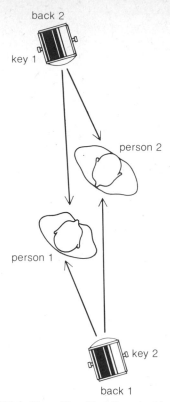

ADDITIONAL LIGHT SOURCES

Several additional light sources are often used in connection with the basic photographic lighting setup. They include (1) the background or set light, (2) the side light, (3) the kicker light, and (4) the camera light (described on page 176).

The basic functions of the additional light sources are to sharpen the viewer's orientation in space and time, to add sparkle and snap to the picture, and to help establish a general mood. In short, they help in clarifying and intensifying the screen event for the viewer.

The Background or Set Light

The most important additional light source is the background light or, as it is frequently called, the set light. Its function is to *illuminate the background* (walls, cyclorama) of the set, or portions of the set that are not a direct part of the principal performing areas.

Make sure that the background lights strike the background from the same side as the key strikes the subject. Otherwise we may assume that there

7.13   Multiple Function Lighting In this multiple-function lighting, key light no. 1 also functions as back light no. 2, and key light no. 2 as back light no. 1.

are two separate light sources illuminating the scene or, worse, that there are two suns in our solar system. (See 7.15.)

This light frequently goes beyond its mere supporting role to become a major production element. Besides accentuating an otherwise dull, monotonous background with a slice of light or an interesting cookie, the background light can be a *major indicator* of the show's *locale, time of day,* and *mood.* For example, a cookie projection of prison bars on the cyc, in connection with the clanging sounds of cell doors closing, immediately sets the scene of a prison. Simply by replacing the prison bar cookie with that of a cathedral window or silhouette of a cross, and the clanging sounds with organ music, we have transferred the prisoner instantaneously into a different environment, without ever touching the lighting on the actor (see 7.16).

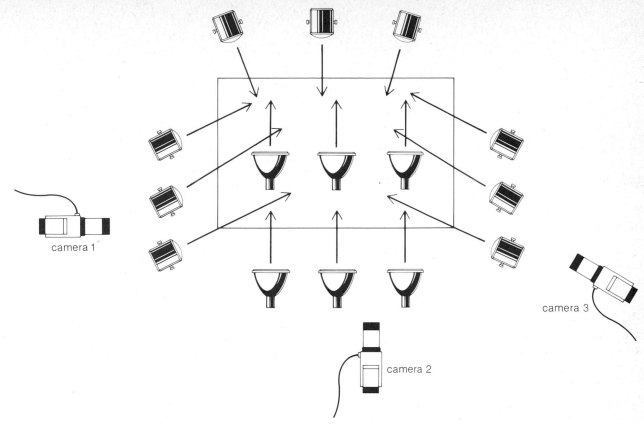

7.14 Large Area Lighting and Cross-Keying Large area lighting usually employs cross-keying, whereby the Fresnel spotlights assume multiple functions. From one side they serve as key lights; from the other, as directional fill; and from a side camera position, they may even act as back lights. The regular back lights are strung out behind the main action area, opposite the major camera positions. If any fill is necessary, it usually comes directly from the front. In effect, we have simply partially overlapped the triangles of the basic photographic principle.

A long slice of light, or long shadows, falling across the back wall of an interior set suggests, in connection with other congruent production clues, late afternoon or evening. Dark backgrounds and distinct shadows generally suggest a low-key scene with a dramatic or mysterious mood. Light backgrounds and a generally high baselight level are usually regarded as a high-key scene with an upbeat, happy mood. This is why comedies are much more brightly lighted (higher baselight level and less contrast) than mystery dramas (lower baselight level, high-contrast lighting). But do not now confuse "high-key" and "low-key" with high and low vertical hanging positions of the key light, or even the intensity with which it burns. The term *key* means here the general level of illumination. **High-key lighting** usually means that the background is light and the general illumination is bright. **Low-key lighting** means that the background is generally dark and the illumination has a high contrast between lighted areas and shadow areas.

In normal background lighting of an interior setting, try to keep the *upper portions* of the set rather *dark,* with only the middle and lower portions (such as the walls) illuminated. The reasons for this common lighting practice are quite appar-

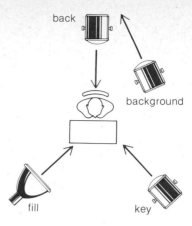

7.15 Direction of Background Light When using a background light, make sure that the background light and the key light come from the same direction. Otherwise, the viewer experiences a shadow reversal in the same shot.

7.16 Background Lighting: Indication of Locale Through a change in background lighting, you can easily effect a change in locale, with no rearrangement of the actual lighting of the performance area. As you can see here, we can transform a scene from a prison to a church by a mere change of cookies (background projection). Together with appropriate music, such a change is entirely convincing to the viewer.

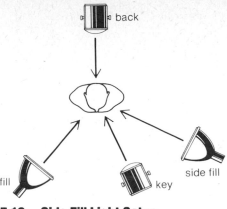

7.18   Side Fill Light Setup

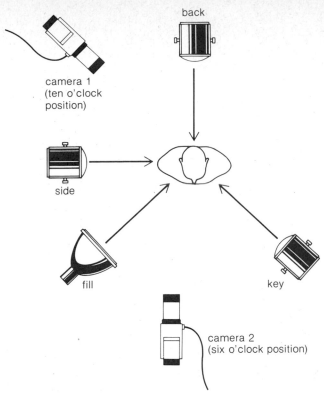

7.17   Multiple Functions of Side Light The side light, striking the subject from the side, acts as additional fill light and provides contour accents. It can also act as a key light for extreme camera position. The side light becomes a key light for camera 1, and the key light becomes the back light for camera 1. We assume that camera 2 is in the normal position.

ent: First, most indoor lighting is designed to illuminate low working areas rather than the upper portions of the walls. Second, the performer's head is more pleasingly contrasted against a slightly darker background. Too much light at that height might cause a silhouette effect, rendering the face unusually dark. On the other hand, furniture and medium- and dark-colored clothing are nicely set off from the lighter lower portions of the set. Third, the dark upper portions hide the lack of a ceiling and help to eliminate undesirable boom shadows.

You can darken the upper portions of the set rather easily by barn-dooring off any spotlight (including the background lights) that would hit those areas.

The Side Light

Generally placed directly to the *side of the subject,* the side light is used in place of or, more frequently, in addition to the fill light. It helps to reduce dense shadows that are not reached by the front fill light, and accentuates the contour of the subject. It becomes an essential light source if the camera's shooting parameter is exceptionally wide. If, for instance, the camera arcs around the subject from a six o'clock position to a ten o'clock position, the side light takes on the function of the key light and provides essential modeling (lighting for three-dimensional effect). (See 7.17.)

Fresnel spotlights, with a wide beam, are generally used for side lighting.

For brilliant high-key lighting, you may find it helpful to support the key light with side fill light. This gives the "key" side of the subject basic illumination, with the key light providing the necessary sparkle and accent. For such side lighting you use, of course, a floodlight rather than a spotlight. (See 7.18.)

The Kicker Light

The kicker light, generally a sharply pinned Fresnel spot, strikes the subject *from behind and off to one side.* Its main purpose is to *highlight the contour* of the subject at a place where key-light falloff is the densest, where the dense shadow of the subject

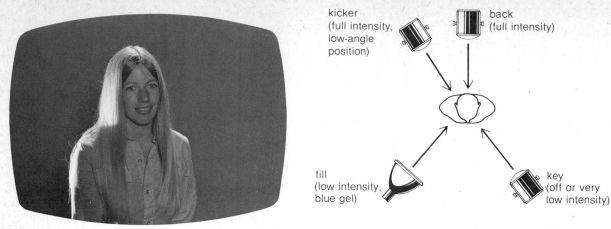

7.19 **Kicker Light** The kicker light rims the object opposite the key and thus emphasizes contour. Like the back light, the kicker helps to separate the object from the background.

opposite the key-lighted side tends to merge with the dark background. The function of the kicker is quite similar to that of the back light, except that the kicker light "rims" the subject not at the top-back, but at the lower side-back. It usually strikes the subject from below eye level. (See 7.19.)

Kicker lights are especially useful for creating the illusion of moonlight.

THE LIGHT PLOT

The **light plot** shows (1) the *location* of the lighting instrument relative to the set and illuminated objects and areas, (2) the principal *direction* of the light beam, and (3) the *type* and *size* of the instruments used (see 7.20).

In order to draw a successful light plot, you need to have an accurate floor plan, which shows the scenery and the stage props, the principal talent positions and moves, and the principal camera positions and shooting angles. Because all this information is generally not available for routine shows,

they are lighted without the use of a light plot. However, if you have to light a special show, such as a television play, a light plot makes your lighting less arbitrary and saves considerable time and energy for the crew.

MAIN POINTS

1. Exercise caution during all lighting operations. Don't look directly into the lights when lighting, and wear gloves when handling the hot instruments.

2. In most television lighting setups the basic photographic or triangle lighting principle of key, back, and fill light is used.

3. The key light is the principal source of illumination, which reveals the basic shape of the object. The back light distinguishes the shadow of the object from the background and emphasizes the object's outline. It gives the object sparkle. The fill light makes the shadows less dense.

4. In lighting for continuous action, we can use

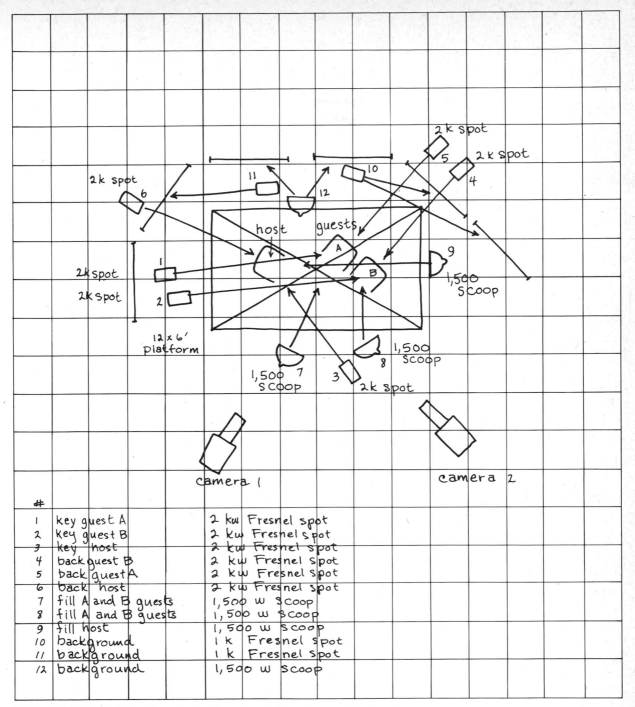

#		
1	key guest A	2 kw Fresnel spot
2	key guest B	2 kw Fresnel spot
3	key host	2 kw Fresnel spot
4	back guest B	2 kw Fresnel spot
5	back guest A	2 kw Fresnel spot
6	back host	2 kw Fresnel spot
7	fill A and B guests	1,500 w Scoop
8	fill A and B guests	1,500 w Scoop
9	fill host	1,500 w Scoop
10	background	1 k Fresnel spot
11	background	1 k Fresnel spot
12	background	1,500 w Scoop

7.20   Light Plot: Interview Ordinarily, such a simple setup would not require a light plot for lighting. This setup was used to keep the light plot example from getting too complex. Note that the lighting instruments and cameras are not in scale.

multiple, overlapping lighting triangles, each one consisting of key, back, and fill.

5.   Additional light sources are often used in connection with the basic photographic lighting setup. These are (1) the background or set light, which illuminates the background of the scene and the set; (2) the side light, which acts as additional fill; and (3) the kicker light, which is used to outline the contour of an object that would otherwise blend in with the background.

6.   The light plot indicates the location of the lighting instrument, the principal direction of the light beam, and the type and size of the instruments used.

When lighting remote productions, you should realize that you are not working in the studio, where all the lighting equipment is in place and ready to go. Every piece of equipment, however large or small, must be hauled to the remote location and set up in places that always seem either too small or too large for good television lighting. Also, you never get enough time to experiment with various lighting setups in order to find the most effective one. You must, therefore, get the job done with a *maximum of planning* and a *minimum of equipment*. Whatever the remote lighting task, you need to be especially efficient in the choice of instruments and their use.

This section explains the particular demands of remote lighting and describes a number of special lighting techniques not covered in Section One.

We will divide the discussion of remote lighting into (1) ENG lighting and (2) EFP lighting. There is no clear-cut division between the two lighting techniques. When lighting for ENG, you generally face less elaborate lighting tasks than in EFP, but you also have less time and equipment to do the lighting.

ENG LIGHTING

When engaged in ENG, you will find yourself confronted with *outdoor* and *indoor* lighting problems. Most of the time you have to work with *available light,* the illumination already present at the scene. But there are also many occasions when you have to supplement available light and some occasions when you have to provide the entire light for the scene. In any case, you have to work quickly and efficiently in order to obtain not only adequate lighting, but the best lighting possible under the circumstances.

Outdoor Light

The ideal light for outdoor shooting is an overcast day. The clouds or fog act as diffusers for the hard sunlight, providing an even illumination, similar to that of soft-lights. Do not be surprised if you have to use an ND and/or color correction filter when white-balancing the camera on an overcast day. The light of a cloudy day is often surprisingly bright and has a high color temperature. Because the diffused light of an overcast day creates rather soft shadows, and therefore low-contrast lighting, you can put the camera on auto-iris. But even in diffused lighting, try not to position a person in front of a white or otherwise light background. The auto-iris will read and adjust to the light background rather than the person, who now will be underexposed. If you have to shoot against a light background, switch to manual iris control, zoom in on the person (thereby avoiding as much of the bright background as possible), and adjust the iris to meet the light requirements of the person rather than the background.

Most lighting problems occur when you shoot in bright sunlight. Here are some hints:

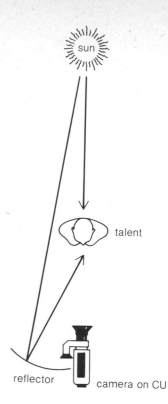

reflector
lightening up
face of newscaster

sun

talent

reflector   camera on CU

7.21 Use of Reflector When Shooting Against Sun When shooting against the sun, go to an extreme close-up (ECU) and reflect sunlight back to talent with a simple reflector.

1.   Do not use your camera in the auto-iris mode when shooting in bright sunlight, unless you have no time to do anything but aim and shoot.

2.   Whenever possible, shoot *with* the sun, not into it. If you shoot against the sun, you have to adjust the iris to the sunlight in the background rather than the objects and people in the foreground. This underexposes the foreground figures, rendering them almost as silhouettes. An added danger is that you may inadvertently shoot into the sun, which may damage or burn out the camera pickup tubes. If you cannot avoid placing someone so that you have to shoot against the sun, try to get as close a shot as possible and use a reflector or the camera light with a dichroic filter to bounce as much light on the person as possible (see 7.21).

3.   In sunlight the problem of bright backgrounds is much more severe than in the diffused light of an overcast day. Again, try to avoid shooting against a bright, sunlit background. Even if you are on manual iris control and adjust for the foreground figure, the bright background pushes the contrast way beyond the 30:1 limit. Just as in low-lighting conditions, the extreme contrast causes background overexposure. If you can-

not avoid the bright background, try to get such a tight shot of the person or foreground object that you eliminate the background.

    Here is a typical contrast problem you may encounter in ENG or EFP: You are to cover a brief interview with the winner of a women's golf tournament. During the interview the dark-haired woman insists on wearing a white sun-visor that has become a good-luck piece for her. What can you do?

    One of the quickest solutions is to cut out the visor by zooming in to an extreme close-up (ECU) of her face and setting the iris according to the light on her face. The use of a reflector would help little because its reflected light would spill beyond the face to the visor, making matters worse. Or you can remain on a medium or long shot, in which case the white visor will be small enough in the pictures not to dominate the total exposure (iris opening).

4.   Bright sunlight inevitably produces dense shadows. Watch where the shadows are, and consider them when composing shots. There is little you can do about shadows when you rush after a breaking news story. But if you set up an on-location interview, and if you are

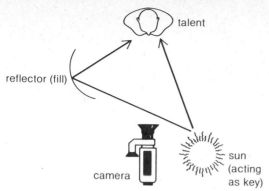

7.22 Use of Reflector to Lighten Shadows When you are shooting in bright sunlight, the hard shadows can be lightened through the use of a reflector.

lucky enough to have an assistant, you may want to lighten the shadows (slow down the falloff) somewhat by asking the assistant to hold a white card or a simple reflector so that it bounces back some of the sunlight and renders the dense shadows more translucent (see 7.22).

5.   When shooting in inadequate outdoor illumination, try to keep the camera as steady as possible in order to minimize lag or comet-tailing. If you have to shoot against a busy street, where the moving car headlights inevitably cause some comet-tailing, you may once again try to zoom in to a close-up of the object or subject, eliminating as much background as possible. Note that the lens is wide open when shooting under low light conditions, shrinking the depth of field and making the focus more critical than when shooting in bright sunlight.

Shooting at Night

When covering a night event, you sometimes have enough illumination from car headlights, a blazing fire, or the lights of an emergency vehicle to get pictures that at least reflect the atmosphere and excitement of the event. Most often, however, you need to get a shot of the police chief or fire marshal, or the reporter describing the event. Here again are some points to consider:

1.   Assuming you do not have an assistant and only one camera light, powered by a battery belt, clip the light on top of the camera and aim it straight at the field reporter. The closer the reporter is to the camera (which is also the light source), the stronger the illumination.

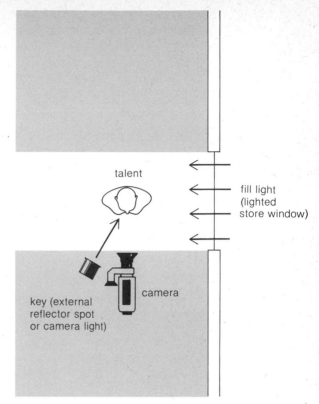

7.23 Using Available Light as Fill Light When you are shooting at night, any available light source may serve as a much needed fill light. In this case, a lighted store window acts as fill.

You can change the light intensity by moving just one or two steps toward or away from the reporter.

2.   If you have an assistant, he or she can hold the light somewhat above camera level (to avoid shining the light directly into the eyes of the reporter) and a little to the side of the camera so that the single camera light acts more like a key light. Try to use any additional light sources, such as lighted store windows or street lamps, as fill light (see 7.23).

3.   Once again, avoid shooting against a brightly lighted background. If moving traffic is part of the story, the unavoidable comet-tailing of the car headlights might add to the visual excitement of the story. Otherwise try to avoid moving light sources.

4.   If you are to cover a brief feature report outside the county hospital, for example, and if you are not under great time pressure, use two portable external

reflector lamps on stands. Use one as key, the other as fill (see 7.24). If possible, plug the lights into regular household outlets to save the batteries.

5.   If the reporter needs a remote teleprompter, make sure that the light in the teleprompter is working or that you can illuminate the copy with an external light.

6.   Whenever you go on night assignment, carry a flashlight. It helps to locate equipment in the car, exchange batteries and videotape on location, and perhaps even help you and the reporter find your way back to the news car.

Indoor Light

When shooting indoors, you encounter various amounts and kinds of light. Some interiors are illuminated by the daylight that comes through large windows, others with fluorescent banks that make up a light ceiling. Still others have desk and floor lamps augmenting the little daylight that manages to penetrate the draped windows. The major problem here is not so much how to supply additional light, but how to match the various color temperatures.

Working with Daylight   The typical problem is having to shoot against a large window. Often a company official wants to make his or her brief statement from behind a desk, and the desk may be located right in front of a large view window. The lighting problem is identical with that of having a person stand in front of a bright background. If you set the iris according to the background brightness, the person in front tends to turn into a silhouette. If you adjust the iris for the person in front, the background is overexposed. Here are some possible solutions:

1.   Draw the drapes or the blinds and light with portable instruments. Or go to a tight close-up and cut out as much of the background as possible. Unfortunately, many of the windows do not have drapes or blinds, and not all company officials look good on an ECU.

2.   Move the camera to the side of the desk and have the person turn so that she or he faces the camera. You can now shoot parallel with the window (see 7.25). This way, you can use the light from the window as key, and fill with one additional light on a stand. If you use

an HMI, you do not need to worry about mixing different color temperatures. As you remember, the HMI lights burn at the daylight standard of 5,600°K. But if you use an external reflector spot for fill light, you need to boost the color temperature by inserting either a dichroic daylight filter or a light blue gel. Put the instrument into the flood position to avoid harsh shadows. To make the picture really look professional, place another HMI spot or external reflector spot (with the dichroic filter and in the spot position) behind the person to add back light.

3.   If you do not have any additional lights, you can use a reflector as a substitute fill light (see 7.25).

4.   If the person insists on having the window in the background, you must cover the window with large plastic sheets that come as ND filters of varying densities and/or color temperature filters. In case of emergency, you can cover the windows neatly with ordinary tracing paper, which has an ND filter effect. But these procedures take up a great amount of time and are generally left to EFP.

Working with Fluorescents   The basic problem of working with fluorescent lights is their color temperature. It is always higher than the 3,200°K standard of incandescent lights. So, if you turn on the camera light for additional illumination, you are confronted with two color temperatures. Some lighting people advise turning the fluorescent off altogether when working with quartz lights (3,200°K). But this is unrealistic. If you need to get a fast-breaking story and you shoot in a hallway that is illuminated by fluorescent lights, you certainly do not have time, first, to locate and persuade the building manager to turn off the lights, and then to relight the scene before starting to shoot.

If the fluorescent lights give you enough illumination, simply use the appropriate color temperature filter (to bring down the high color temperature of the fluorescents) and white-balance the camera with the available light. If you have to use a camera light for additional illumination, either boost the color temperature of the camera light (by inserting a dichroic filter), or white-balance the camera with the illumination provided by the camera light (3,200°K). Generally, the camera light is strong enough to wash out the fluorescent baselight. Even if you could turn off the fluorescent lamps, you might want to leave them on to have enough baselight. A higher baselight level allows you to work with smaller lens openings, which increases the depth of field and makes it easier for you to focus.

If you turn on the camera light, try not to shine it

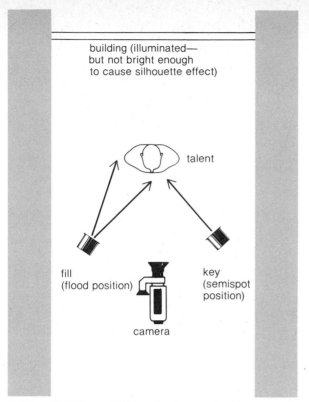

7.24 **Lighting with Two Instruments** One external reflector spot can function as the key light (in a semispot position), the other as fill (in full flood position). A background building that is not too brightly illuminated adds dimension to the picture.

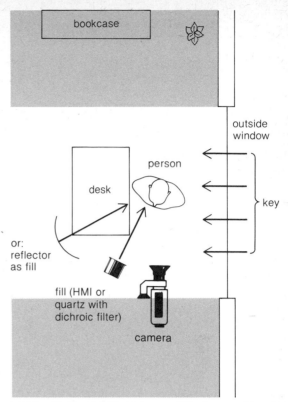

7.25 **Using Daylight from a Window as Key** If the desk is located in front of a window, the daylight coming through the window can be used as key light, with a reflector or an additional light serving as fill. In this case, the camera shoots parallel to the window, not toward it.

directly on the scene. Point the camera light toward the ceiling first and then tilt it down gradually. This maneuver is difficult to do if you are alone; but if you have an assistant who takes care of the light (and the VTR and sound), this procedure should become routine. The reason for this gradual illumination is that it is often annoying to a person to have a high-powered light pop into his or her eyes without at least a little warning. Also, in case the lamp explodes when turned on (which happens on very rare occasions), the hot glass will pop up rather than hit the people in front of the camera.

Working with Baselight Sometimes you have to deal with groups of people who are gathered in locations with inadequate illumination. Typical examples are convention meetings in small rooms, gatherings in hotel lobbies, or hallways. Most of the time, a camera light provides enough illumination to cover the speaker and individual audience members. However, if you are to do a rather extensive live feature from such a location, you need additional illumination. The quickest and most efficient way to light such a location is to establish a general, nondirectional baselight level. Simply use two or three external reflector spots in the flood position, and bounce them off the ceiling or walls. If this is not possible, direct the lights on the group, but diffuse the light beam with scrims. The most efficient method is to use two or three small, high-intensity lights (such as Tota-lights) and diffuse their beam with umbrellas (see 7.26).

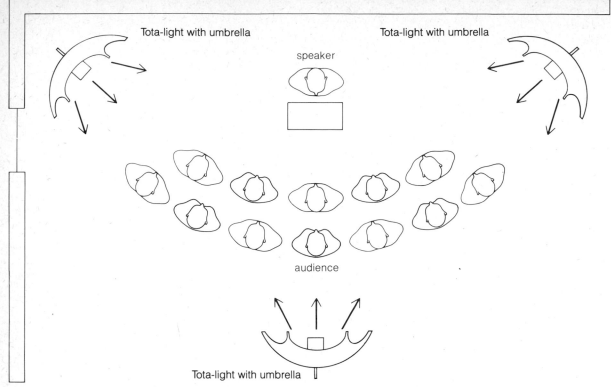

7.26   Establishing Nondirectional Baselight To establish an adequate baselight level, you need highly diffused, nondirectional light. Here, three Tota-lights and umbrellas provide maximally diffused baselight. If the room is small, you may want to use portable quartz lights with diffusion scrims.

EFP LIGHTING

Lighting for EFP can range from a simple interview in someone's office to complex scenes shot on location. One of the advantages of lighting for EFP is that you generally have more planning and setup time than in ENG. But you will soon find out that in EFP, as in ENG, time is at a premium. You must, therefore, do your planning within the realistic context of available time and equipment. Be prepared to compromise, and strive for optimal lighting *relative to the other production requirements.*

Here are some points to consider: (1) safety, (2) power supply, (3) location survey, and (4) lighting setup.

Safety

As in all types of television production, you must be safety conscious at all times. No production, however exciting or difficult, should excuse you from abandoning safety for expediency or effect. Be especially careful with electrical power when on location. A charge of 110 volts can be deadly. Secure cables so that people do not trip over them. String them above doorways, tape them to the floor, and cover them with a rubber mat at points of heavy foot traffic. A loose cable can not only trip somebody, but topple a lighting instrument and start a fire. See that all lighting stands are secured. You may have to weigh some down with sandbags, or tie them to walls or furniture with gaffer's tape. The lighting instruments should also be far enough away from combustible material, such as curtains, drapes, books, tablecloths, wooden ceilings, and walls. It pays to double check.

Power Supply

In EFP you have to work with three types of power for lighting instruments: (1) household current (usually 110–120 volts), (2) generator, and (3) 30-volt battery belt.

The most frequently used power supply is *household current*. When using the regular wall outlets, you need to be aware of the *power rating* of the circuits, which is usually *15 amps* (amperes) per *circuit*. This means that you can plug in a 1,500-watt instrument, or any combination of lights that does not total more than 1,500 watts without overloading the circuit, provided nothing else is on the same circuit. If you need to power more lights than a single circuit can handle, you need to plug them into different circuits. A simple way of figuring the total wattage per circuit is to multiply the number of amps of the circuit by 100 (assuming the household current rates between 110 and 120 volts). This gives you a conservative and safe limit (15 amps × 100 volts = 1,500 total allowable wattage).

Sometimes, several of the double wall outlets are connected to the same circuit. You can determine which outlets are on the same circuit by plugging one low-powered lamp into a particular outlet. Find the specific circuit breaker or fuse that turns off the lamp. Now, plug the light into the next convenient outlet and switch off the same circuit breaker or fuse. If the light goes out, the plugs are on the same circuit. If the light stays on, you are on a different circuit.

Obviously, you need enough extension cords to get from the outlets to the light. You can minimize cable runs by using spider boxes (multiple outlet boxes), especially if you use low-wattage lights. Have enough and various kinds of adaptors available so that lights can be plugged into the existing household outlets.

Whenever there is doubt about the availability or reliability of power, you need to use a *generator*. In this case, the engineering crew is responsible for setting up the generator. The circuit ratings and allowable combined wattage of the lights per circuit still apply.

For relatively simple on-location productions, you may power the lights with *batteries*. In this case, make sure that the batteries are properly charged and that you have enough spares to last for the entire production.

Location Survey

One of the most important aspects of lighting for EFP is a thorough **location survey** of the remote site. The survey checklists in 7.27, as with all the other discussions of lighting for EFP, are intended for relatively simple productions. The lighting for large and complex electronic field productions is more closely related to motion picture techniques and is not included here.

Lighting Setup

As mentioned earlier, you should try to achieve good lighting with as few instruments as possible. It is, therefore, important for you to acquaint yourself as much as possible with the planned production. Find out from the director what type of shooting he or she intends to do (short scenes with time to relight for each new camera position or shot, or long, uninterrupted scenes that stress the continuity of action). If possible, ask the director for the principal camera positions and shots (extreme angles, camera movement, field of view). As in ENG, the lighting setup also depends on how much time you have for the preparation and actual setup. Still, you will find that many situations repeat themselves, and you will learn to do a good lighting job in a minimum amount of time. Here are some typical EFP situations:

1. *Baselight illumination.* If you are pressed for time, and if the action within the room is not specified, you can use floodlights to produce a general illumination (see 7.26). Although this ENG lighting is anything but imaginative, it gets the job done and is certainly better than highly specific lighting that happens to be in the wrong places.

2. *Available light.* In general, compared to studio shows, scenes that are shot in available light look strangely lifeless. The main reason is that they lack *back light*. So, if you are really pressed for time, or if you have only one instrument in addition to adequate available light, use the additional light source as back light.

3. *The office interview.* You can light the typical office interview with two or three lights (see 7.28). Two external reflector spots, placed opposite each other, serve the multiple functions of key and back lights. You can use the third instrument as background light or, if needed, as fill on the guest. The lighting can be set up for an interview in a hotel room, hallway, living room, or

Survey Item	Key Questions	
	Indoors	*Outdoors*
Available Light	Is the available light sufficient? If not, what additional lights do you need? What type of available light do you have? Incandescent? Fluorescent? Daylight coming through windows?	Do you need any additional lights? Where is the sun in relation to the planned action? Is there enough room to place the necessary reflectors?
Principal Background	Is there any action planned against a white wall? Do you have windows in the background? If there are windows, do they have curtains, drapes, or venetian blinds that can be drawn? If you want to use the daylight coming from the window, do you have lights that match the color temperature of the daylight (5,600°K)? If the window is too bright, or if you have to reduce the color temperature coming through the window, do you have the appropriate ND or color filters to attach to the window? Note that you will certainly need some reflectors or other type of fill-light illumination.	How bright is the background? Even if the sun is not hitting the background at the time of the survey, will it be there when the actual production is taking place? When shooting at the beach, does the director plan to have people perform with the ocean as background? You will need reflectors and/or additional lights (HMI's) to prevent the people from turning into silhouettes, unless the director plans on ECU's most of the time.
Contrast	If there are dense shadows or if the action moves through high-contrast areas (light-dark), you need extra fill light to reduce the contrast.	Does the production take place in bright sunlight? You must then provide for a generous amount of fill light (reflectors and/or HMI spotlights) in order to render the shadows translucent. Are people moving from the sunlight into dense shadow areas, and back into sunlight again? You must make provisions to reduce the contrast (reflectors that light the people in the shadow areas), or shoot the scenes in the bright areas separately from the ones in the shadow areas.
Light Positions	Can you place the lights so that they are out of camera range? What light supports do you need (gaffer grip, clamps, stands)? Do you need special pole cats (extendable metal poles that can be locked between floor and ceiling) and/or battens to place the light in the correct position? Are the lighting instruments far enough away from combustible materials? Are the lights positioned in such a way that they do not interfere with the event to be covered? People who are not used to television complain mostly about the brightness of the lights.	If you need reflectors or additional lights on stands, is the ground level enough so that the stands can be securely placed? Will you need to take extra precautions because of wind? (Take plenty of sandbags along, or even some tent pegs and rope so that you can secure the light stands in case of wind.)
Power Requirement	Do you know exactly where the outlets are, what the rating of the circuits is, and which outlets are on the same circuit? Make a rough sketch of all outlets and indicate the distance to the corresponding light or lights. What adaptors do you need to plug lights into the available outlets? If the electrical circuits on location are protected by fuses, are there appropriate spare fuses? Do you have the necessary cables, extension cords, and spider boxes so that you can get by with a minimum of cable runs? In the projected cable runs, have you applied all possible safety precautions?	You will find that you do not need to use lighting instruments very often when shooting outdoors, unless you shoot at night or need to fill in particularly dense shadows that cannot be reached with a simple reflector. Your main concern will be power and how to get it to the lighting instruments. Do you have the necessary power available nearby? Do you need a generator? If you can tap available power, make sure you can tell the engineer in charge the approximate power requirement for all lights. (Simply add up the wattage of all the lights you plan to use, plus another 10 percent just to make sure you get enough power.) Do you have the necessary extension cables to reach all the lighting instruments?

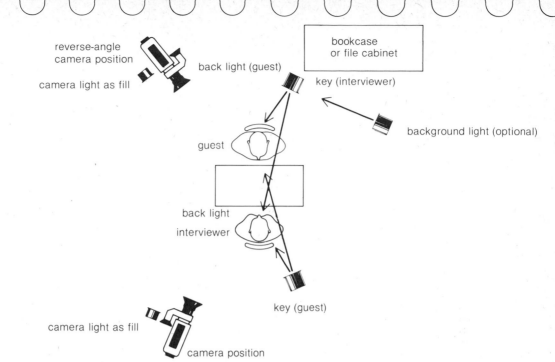

7.28 Interview Lighting with Two or Three Instruments The two lights serve multiple functions: key and back lights for the interviewer and key and back lights for the guest. If a third light is available, it can be used as background light. You can use the camera light with a scrim as fill light for the shadow side of the interviewer and guest.

any other such location. We have already talked about how to deal with office windows (see p. 190).

4. *The company official's announcement.* This happens with the official standing next to a chart or sitting behind the desk, on the desk, or in a comfortable chair. In all these cases you can apply the basic photographic principle of key, fill, and back lights. If you have a fourth light, you can use it as a background light or to light the chart. If you do not have enough baselight, diffuse the fill light as much as possible so that it spills throughout the area (see 7.29). If you are working with only three lights, substitute a reflector for the fill light and use the third light as background light, or to light the object the official may want to demonstrate. Make sure that the lights are high enough so that they do not throw distracting shadows on the desk or behind the official. The more diffused the light, the less the per-

son's wrinkles will show, but the flatter the picture will look. Always keep the back light in the spot position. If the office is ordinarily illuminated by fluorescent lights, leave them on to provide the necessary baselight. The quartz lights on the official will dictate the proper color temperature.

5. *Large interiors and large groups.* To illuminate large interiors, you can either cross-key (see p. 181), or simply use a few floodlights to provide as much even light as possible. Again, if you have some idea of shooting angles and the action, try to set up a few back lights to give the scene the necessary sparkle. It is usually safer to provide an adequate amount of even light than to light selectively, especially if the action is not specifically staged. Again, use all the available light for the necessary baselight unless the light sources actually interfere with the lighting.

7.29 Photographic Principle in EFP When you apply the photographic principle in EFP, you use the key light in a spot or semi-flood position, the back in a spot position, and the fill light in full flood position. If a background light is available, it is also in spot position. If only three lights are available, and a background light is needed, a reflector can serve the fill light function. Note that the background light comes from the same side as the key for consistent direction in shadow fall.

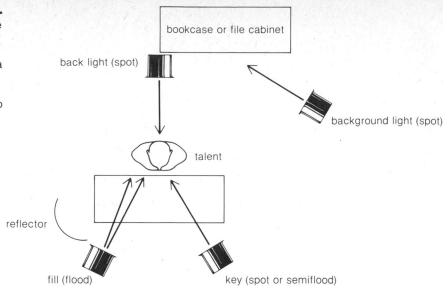

bookcase or file cabinet

back light (spot)

background light (spot)

talent

reflector

fill (flood)

key (spot or semiflood)

camera

SPECIAL LIGHTING TECHNIQUES

Four special lighting techniques deserve further attention: (1) cameo, (2) silhouette, (3) color background, and (4) chroma key area lighting.

Cameo Lighting

Certain television shows, especially those of a dramatic nature, are staged in the middle of an empty studio against an unlighted background. This technique, where only the performers are highlighted against a dark background, is commonly known as **cameo lighting** (from the cameo stone in which a light relief figure is set against a darker background stone). (See 7.30.)

All cameo lighting is **highly directional** and is achieved entirely with spotlights. In small studios, the background areas are carefully shielded with black, light-absorbing draperies from any kind of distracting spill light.

Although cameo lighting was a highly effective technique in monochrome television, it is rather difficult to handle in color. The major problems are the high contrast, dense shadows, and the low baselight levels, all adverse factors to good color lighting. However, in certain circumstances, cameo lighting can, even in color, be highly effective.

Silhouette Lighting

The lighting for a silhouette effect is exactly opposite to cameo lighting. In silhouette lighting, you light the *background* but leave the *figures* in front *unlighted*. Silhouette lighting shows only the contour of objects and people, but no volume and texture. Obviously, you light only those scenes in silhouette that gain by emphasizing the contour of things (see 7.31).

You can also use silhouette lighting for concealing the identity of a person appearing on camera.

In silhouette lighting, you use highly diffused light (usually from scoops with scrims or softlights) to get the background evenly illuminated.

7.30 Cameo Lighting To achieve the cameo lighting effect, you leave the background unlighted and illuminate the people with highly directional spotlights.

7.31 Silhouette Lighting Silhouette lighting is the exact opposite of cameo lighting. In silhouette lighting, the background is lighted, while figures in front remain unlighted. Silhouette lighting emphasizes the outline of people and things.

Color Background Lighting

To change the colors of the set background, you can use various color media (filters) to gel the background lights. If, for example, you want a background of an even red color, you gel all the background scoops with a red color medium. If you wish to have a few dark blue color wedges break up your neutrally colored background, you gel a few background spotlights with the appropriate blue color medium.

By using several sets of background lights (several instruments grouped together), with different color gels for each set, you can easily change background colors by dissolving from one set (on group dimmer 1) to another (on group dimmer 2). Of course, if you operate in a key mode, you can generate the various background colors through a special effects switcher.

Chroma Key Area Lighting

The chroma key set area consists of a blue background and the foreground area, such as a newscaster's desk or interview chairs and table. The blue background is used for chroma key matting (see p. 370).

The most important aspect of lighting the chroma key set area is *even background illumination.* In order to achieve an optimally effective chroma key matte, the blue background must be lighted with highly diffused instruments, such as softlights or scoops with scrim attachments. If there are **hot spots** (undesirable concentrations of light in one spot) on the blue background, or unusually dark areas, the *matte* (electronically supplied background image) looks discolored, or, worse, has a tendency to break up. When lighting the foreground set, make sure that there are no spotlight beams hitting the background area so that you can preserve the evenness of the chroma key background illumination.

Sometimes you may have noticed that the outline of the newscaster vibrates with a variety of colors, or that the contour is not sharp during a chroma key matte. One of the major reasons for such moiré effects (vibrating color patterns) is that especially dark colors or shadows at the contour line take on a blue tinge, similar to the blue of the background. During the chroma key process, these blue spots become transparent and let the background picture show through. In order to counteract the bluishness of the shadows, you might try putting yellow gels (color media) in all of the back lights or kicker lights. Thus, the back lights not only separate the foreground subject from the background picture through contour illumination, but also neutralize the blue shadows through the complementary yellow color. Be careful, however, not to let any of the yellow light hit the face, arms, or hands of the newscaster.

MAIN POINTS

1. Remote lighting requires the control of outdoor and standard indoor lighting. Most of the time, the camera has to be adjusted to available light.

2. On-location light varies greatly in intensity and color temperature. Outdoor light and fluorescent lights have a higher color temperature than the customary incandescent indoor lights.

3. Reflectors are a good way to fill in the shadows during outdoor shooting.

4. The capacity of the household outlets must be carefully checked before the remote lighting instruments are plugged in.

5. Special lighting techniques include: (1) cameo lighting, (2) silhouette lighting, (3) color background lighting, and (4) chroma key area lighting.

FURTHER READING

Millerson, Gerald. *The Technique of Lighting for Television and Motion Pictures.* 2nd ed. Woburn, MA: Focal Press, 1982.

Ritsko, Alan J. *Lighting for Location Motion Pictures.* New York: Van Nostrand Reinhold Company, 1979.

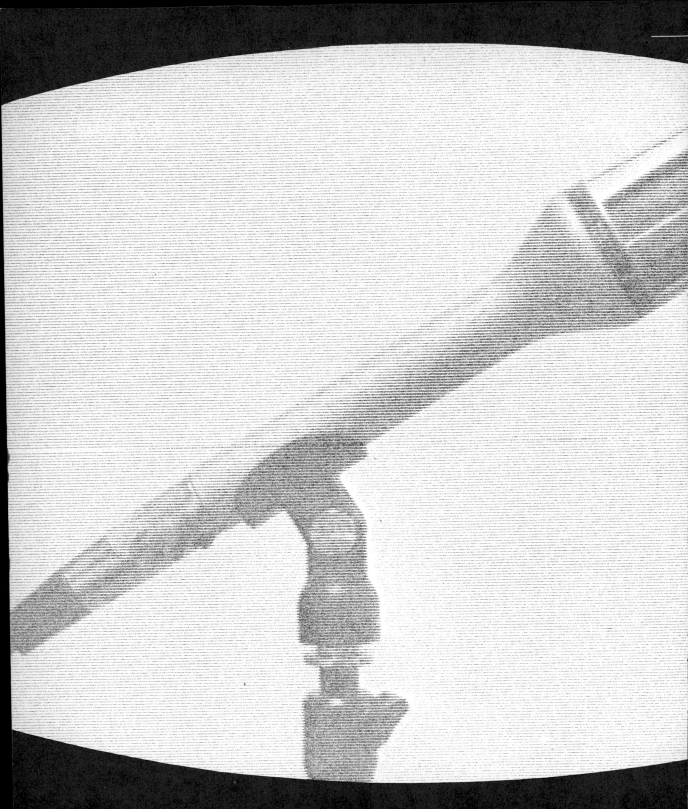

CHAPTER 8

Audio: Sound Pickup

In the preceding chapters we have been concerned primarily with the video, or picture portion of television. In the following two chapters we will discuss another essential part of television production—audio, the sound portion of television.

In Section One of this chapter we will concentrate on sound pickup—that is, the types, characteristics and use of various microphones. Specifically, we will take up these main points:

1. The electronic characteristics of microphones, including the types of microphones as distinguished by the sound-generating element, pickup patterns, and special features.
2. The operational characteristics of mobile and stationary microphones.
3. The uses of various microphones for maximum effect.

Section Two examines the technical aspects of sound-generating elements in more detail and offers a number of specific guidelines for using microphones in ENG.

You should realize that audio is an important production field in its own right, and that it requires specific and unique skills and knowledge. If you are especially interested in television audio, you should make a concerted effort to learn as much as possible about sound recording and radio techniques, and the finer points of television and film audio production.

In television the audio portion performs a number of functions. Frequently, for instance, it is the sound that gives us more precise *information* than the pictures. At one time or another, you have surely experienced a temporary interruption of the picture transmission right in the middle of a fascinating program. As long as you could hear the audio portion, you were probably still able to follow the story more or less accurately. But have you noticed how difficult it is to keep up when the sound portion fails? Besides giving information, audio can help to establish a specific *locale,* such as a downtown location through traffic noises, or a specific *time,* through typical day or night sounds. Sound is essential for the establishing of *mood,* or for the *intensification* of action. There is hardly a good chase sequence that does not have a whole barrage of sounds, some part of the actual scene, and many (such as music) that are added to the natural sounds. Sound also helps us to *connect* the visual pieces and fragments of the relatively small, low-definition television image into a meaningful whole.

If sound is, indeed, such an important production element, why do we fail to have better sound on television? Even when you produce a short little scene as an exercise in your studio, you will probably notice that, although the pictures may look acceptable, the sound portion certainly could stand some improvement.

It is frequently assumed that by sticking a microphone into the scene at the last minute we have taken care of the audio requirements, but good television audio needs at least as much preparation and attention as the video portion. Also, television audio, like any other production element, should not be "added"; it should be *integrated* into the production planning from the very beginning.

The **pickup** of live sounds is done through a variety of **microphones.** How good or bad a particular microphone is depends not only on how it

Audio (from the Latin verb *audire,* to hear) stands for the sound portion of television and its production. Although the term *television* (far-seeing) ignores audio entirely, the sound part of television plays a vital part in the television communication process.

is built, but especially on how it is used. We will, therefore, talk briefly about the basic electronic characteristics of microphones, and then concentrate on their use, or operational characteristics.

ELECTRONIC CHARACTERISTICS

In order for you to choose the most appropriate microphone and to operate it for optimal sound pickup, you should know these basic electronic characteristics: (1) sound-generating element, (2) pickup pattern, and (3) special features.

Sound-Generating Element

All microphones transduce (convert) *sound waves* into *electrical energy,* which is amplified and reconverted into sound waves by the loudspeaker. This initial conversion is accomplished by the **generat-**

ing element of the microphone. Because there are three major types of sound-converting systems, we classify microphones according to these three types: (1) dynamic, (2) condenser, and (3) ribbon.

Generally, **dynamic mics** are the most *rugged.* They can tolerate reasonably well the rough handling television microphones frequently (though unintentionally) receive. They can be worked close to the sound source and can withstand extremely high sound levels without damage to the microphone or even excessive distortion of the incoming sound (input overload). They can also withstand fairly extreme temperatures. **Condenser** and **ribbon microphones** are much more sensitive to physical shock, temperature changes, and input overload than dynamic mics, but they usually produce higher quality sound when used at greater distances from the sound source.

Contrary to the dynamic and ribbon mics, the condenser microphones (or, called more precisely, the electret condenser) need a small battery to power their built-in preamplifier. Although these batteries last for 1,000 hours, you should always have some spare batteries on hand, especially if you are using condenser mics for ENG or EFP (see 8.1).

Pickup Pattern

Like our ears, any type of microphone can hear sounds from all directions as long as the sounds are within its hearing range. But whereas some microphones hear sounds from all directions equally well, others hear better in a specific direction. The territory within which a microphone can hear well is called its **pickup pattern.** Its two-dimensional representation is called the **polar pattern** (see 8.2 through 8.4).

In television production, there are *omnidirectional* and *unidirectional* microphones. The **omnidirectional microphone** hears sounds from *all* (*omnis* in Latin) *directions* equally well. The **unidirectional microphone** hears better in *one* (*unus* in Latin) *direction,* the front of the microphone, than from its sides or back. Because the polar patterns on unidirectional microphones are roughly heart-shaped, they are called **cardioid** (see 8.3). The *supercardioid, hypercardioid,* and *ultracardioid* microphones have progressively narrower pickup

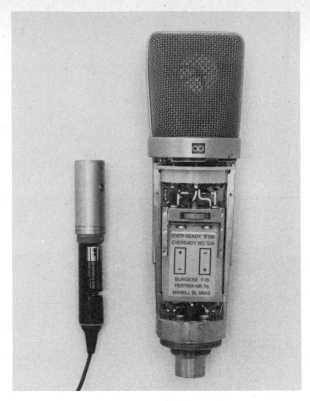

8.1   Power Supply Battery for Condenser Microphone Make sure that the battery is inserted correctly with the + and − poles as indicated in the power supply housing.

Audio The sound portion of television and its production. Technically, the electronic reproduction of audible sound.

Condenser Microphone A microphone whose diaphragm consists of a condenser plate that vibrates with the sound pressure against another fixed condenser plate, called the backplate.

Dual Redundancy The use of two identical microphones for the pickup of a sound source, whereby only one of them is turned on at any given time. A safety device that permits switching over to the second microphone in case the active one becomes defective.

Dynamic Microphone A microphone whose sound-pickup device consists of a diaphragm that is attached to a movable coil. As the diaphragm vibrates with the air pressure from the sound, the coil moves within a magnetic field, generating an electric current.

Gain Level of signal amplification for video and audio signals. "Riding gain" is used in audio, meaning to keep the sound volume at a proper level.

Lavaliere An extremely small microphone that can be clipped onto the lapel of a jacket, a tie, a blouse, or other piece of clothing. A larger variety is suspended from a neck cord and worn in front of the chest. Also called neck or chest mic.

Microphone Also called mic. A small, portable assembly for the pickup and conversion of sound into electrical energy.

Noise Audio: unwanted sounds that interfere with the intentional sounds; or unwanted hisses or hums inevitably generated by the electronics of the audio equipment.

8.2 Omnidirectional Pickup Pattern You can think of the omnidirectional pickup pattern as a large rubber ball with the mic in its center. All sounds that originate within the confines of the rubber ball (the pickup pattern) are picked up by the microphone without any marked quality difference.

The two-dimensional representation of its pickup pattern is called the *polar pattern,* which for an omnidirectional mic is roughly circular.

8.3 Cardioid Pickup Pattern The most common unidirectional pickup pattern is called *cardioid,* heart-shaped. If you think of an apple with the mic sticking into it where the stem should be, you will have an idea of the three-dimensional pickup pattern of most unidirectional television microphones.[1]

As you can see, the pickup at the side of the microphone is considerably reduced with the cardioid microphone, and almost eliminated at its rear. The polar pattern of the cardioid microphone clearly shows the heart-shaped pickup area.

[1] Electro-Voice, *Microphone Primer* (Buchanan, Mich.: Electro-Voice, Inc., n.d.).

Omnidirectional A type of pickup pattern in which the microphone can pick up sounds equally well from all directions.

Pickup Sound reception by a microphone.

Pickup Pattern The territory around the microphone within which the microphone can "hear well," that is, has optimal sound pickup.

Polar Pattern The two-dimensional representation of a microphone pickup pattern.

Pop Filter A bulblike attachment (either permanent or detachable) to the front of the microphone that filters out sudden air blasts, such as plosive consonants (*p*'s, *t*'s, *k*'s) delivered directly into the mic.

Radio Frequency Usually called RF; broadcast frequency, which is divided into various channels. In an RF distribution, the video and audio signals are superimposed on the radio frequency carrier wave.

Ribbon Microphone A microphone whose sound-pickup device consists of a ribbon that vibrates with the sound pressures within a magnetic field. Also called velocity mic.

Unidirectional A type of pickup pattern in which the microphone can pick up sounds better from one direction, the front, than from the sides or back.

Wind Screen Similar to Pop Filter. A rubberlike material that is put over the front end of the microphone to cut down undesirable low-frequency wind noises in outdoor use.

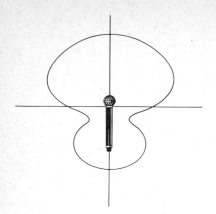

8.4 Hypercardioid Pickup Pattern The supercardioid, hypercardioid, and ultracardioid pickup patterns narrow the angle of sound pickup in front (by eliminating most of the sounds coming from the side) but become more sensitive to sounds at the back of the microphone. They seem to have a long "reach," which means that they produce sounds that seem to come from close by, although the mic may be a good distance away from the source.

patterns, which means that their hearing is more and more concentrated to what is happening in front rather than to the side.

Which type you use depends primarily on the production situation and the sound quality required. If you are doing a stand-up report (standing in front of the actual scene) on the conditions of the local zoo, you would want a rugged, omnidirectional mic that favors your speech but also includes some of the animal sounds for authenticity. If, on the other hand, you are in a studio trying to pick up the low-key, intimate conversation of two people, you need a unidirectional mic. For example, a supercardioid mic, or **shotgun mic,** would give you a good pickup of their conversation, even if the mic has to be relatively far away from the people so as to be out of the picture. Unlike the omnidirectional mic, the shotgun mic ignores most of the other sounds present, such as the inevitable noises of an active studio (people and cameras moving about, humming of lights, or rumble of air conditioning).

Special Features

Microphones that are held close to the mouth have a built-in **pop filter,** which eliminates the sudden breath pops that might occur when someone is speaking directly into the mic (see 8.5). When used outside, all types of microphones are susceptible to wind, which they reproduce as low rumbling noises. To reduce wind noise, you should put a **wind-** **screen** made of acoustic foam rubber over the microphone (see 8.6).

To eliminate the need for several microphones with various pickup patterns, a **system micro-phone** has been developed. This microphone consists of a base upon which several "heads" can be attached. These heads change the pickup pattern from omnidirectional to hypercardioid.

OPERATIONAL CHARACTERISTICS

When classifying microphones according to their actual operation, we have those that are used primarily for picking up moving sound sources, and others for stationary sound sources. The former we call *mobile microphones,* the latter *stationary microphones.* Of course, any of the mobile mics can be used in a stationary position and the stationary mics can be moved about if the production situation so requires.

MOBILE MICROPHONES

The *mobile* microphones include (1) lavaliere microphones, (2) hand microphones, (3) boom microphones, (4) wireless, or RF, microphones, and (5) headset microphones.

8.5 Pop Filter The built-in pop filter eliminates breath pops that could occur when someone is speaking into the mic at close distance. It also reduces distortion when the mic is held close to a very loud sound source.

a

b

8.6 Windscreen (a) The windscreen, which is made of acoustic foam rubber, is put on the microphone in order to eliminate, or at least reduce, the low rumble of wind noise. (b) When used outside, shotgun mics are entirely covered by acoustic foam or a windscreen.

Lavaliere Microphones

The **lavaliere microphone** is probably the type you use most often in small studio operations. The extremely small, high-quality microphone has helped to improve television audio considerably, while at the same time simplifying production procedures.

The larger lavaliere microphones (about as big as your little finger) are hung on a neck cord close to the chest of the performer; the small ones (about the size of a small thimble) are clipped to the dress or the tie. (See 8.7 through 8.9.)

The omnidirectional lavaliere microphone, with a dynamic or condenser generating element, is designed primarily for voice pickup. The *quality* of even the smallest one is amazingly *good*. It reproduces equally well the high-frequency overtones that give each voice its distinct character, and the deep bass resonance that some voices possess. The small lavaliere is relatively immune to physical shock.

Once the lavaliere microphone is properly attached to the performer (approximately six inches below the chin, *on top* of the clothes, and away from anything that could rub or bang against it), he or she no longer needs to worry about the sound pickup.

8.7 Lavaliere Microphone with Neck Cord This type of lavaliere microphone can be worn with a neck cord, or even used as a small hand mic (without the cord clip).

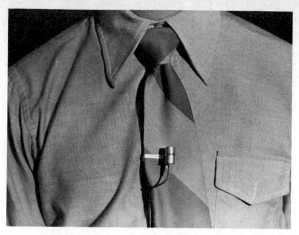

8.8 Small, Clip-on Lavaliere Microphone This lavaliere mic is properly attached for maximum sound pickup. It is securely fastened *on top* of the clothing, minimizing the danger of causing highly distracting rubbing noises. The mic cord is concealed. In spite of its small size and its distance from the sound source, the quality of sound pickup in this small microphone is excellent.

The audio engineer, too, has less difficulty "riding the **gain**" (adjusting the volume) of the lavaliere than the boom or hand mic. Because the distance between the mic and the sound source does not change during the performance, an even sound level can be achieved more easily than with other mobile microphones.

The use of lavaliere microphones frees the lighting people from "lighting around the boom" in order to avoid shadows; they can now concentrate more on the aesthetic subtleties of lighting as required by the scene.

Although the action radius of the performer is still limited by the lavaliere microphone cable, the cable nevertheless is so light and flexible that he or she can move quickly and quite unrestrictedly in a limited studio area without having to hold a microphone, or worry about being properly followed by the boom mic. The attached mic permits the performer to work even in cramped quarters without the need for special operators or special booms or stands.

The high quality of the lavaliere microphone has extended its production use considerably. Here are some examples:

Panel shows: Rather than using desk mics, which are apt to pick up the unavoidable banging on the table, you can achieve excellent audio by using individual lavaliere microphones.

Interview: As long as the interview takes place in one location, the wearing of lavaliere microphones by the interviewer and each of the guests ensures excellent audio.

News: The lavaliere mic is the most efficacious sound pickup device for all types of news shows.

Instructional Shows (with a principal performer, or television teacher): The lavaliere works beautifully as long as the instructor moves within a limited performance area (from desk to blackboard, for example).

Music: The lavaliere mic has been successfully used on singers (even when accompanying themselves with a guitar, for example) and for the pickup of certain instruments, such as a string bass, where it is taped below the fingering board. In this area, there is still room for experimentation. Do not be too awed by convention. If the lavaliere sounds as good as or better than a larger, more expensive mic, stick to the lavaliere.

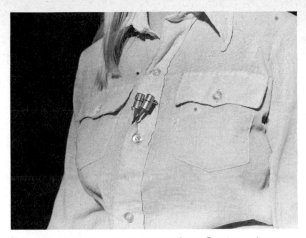

8.9 Dual-Redundancy Lavaliere System A special clip permits the use of two lavalieres for dual-redundancy pickup. In case one microphone goes out, the audio engineer simply switches over to the other without losing audio. Two single clips will work in an emergency.

Again, there are some disadvantages to the lavaliere microphone: (1) The wearer cannot move the mic any closer to his or her mouth; consequently, if there is extraneous noise, it is easily picked up by this omnidirectional mic. (2) The lavaliere can be used for only one sound source at a time, that of the particular wearer. Even for a simple interview, the interviewer and the guest each has to wear his or her own microphone. For a small discussion group you need several. (3) Although the lavaliere mic allows considerable mobility, it limits the performer's activity to some extent. When two or more performers are "wired" in this fashion, their movements are even more restricted. (4) Because it is attached to clothing, the lavaliere mic tends to pick up occasional rubbing noises, especially if the performer is moving about a great deal. This is emphasized when the microphone is concealed underneath a blouse or jacket. (5) If the performer's clothes generate static electricity, this discharge may be picked up by the mic as loud, sharp pops. (6) If two lavaliere mics are at a certain distance from each other, they may cancel out some frequencies and make the voices sound strangely "thin" (see pp. 221–222).

How to Use Lavaliere Microphones Lavaliere microphones are easy to use, but there are some points you need to consider.

1.   Make sure to put it on. You would not be the first performer to be discovered sitting on, rather than wearing, the microphone by air time.

2.   To put on the microphone, bring it up underneath the blouse or jacket and then attach it on the outside. Clip it firmly to the piece of clothing so that it does not rub against anything. Do not wear jewelry in proximity to the mic. If you get rubbing noises, put a piece of foam rubber between the mic and the clothing.

3.   Fasten the microphone cable to your belt or clothing so that it cannot pull the microphone sideways.

4.   If you need to conceal the mic, try not to bury it under layers of clothing.

5.   When using the lavaliere outdoors, attach the little windscreen.

6.   If you encounter electrostatic pops, try to treat the clothes with antistatic laundry spray, available in any supermarket. Some experts claim that by putting an actual knot in the mic cable you can eliminate most of the rubbing and popping noises.[2] Put this knot as close to the mic as possible.

7.   If you use the **dual-redundancy** microphone system (which uses two microphones for each sound source in case one of the mics becomes inoperative), have both mics fastened securely so that they do not touch each other. There is a special clip that holds two lavaliere microphones. (See 8.9.)

8.   Avoid hitting the microphone with any object you may be demonstrating on camera.

9.   If the lavaliere is a condenser mic, make sure that the battery is in good condition and installed correctly (see 8.1).

10.   After the show, do not get up and try to leave the set without removing the microphone. Unclip it, take it off, and *put it down gently.*

[2] See C. Robert Paulson, *BM/E's ENG/EFP/EPP Handbook,* New York: Broadband Information Services, Inc., 1981, p. 311.

8.10 Dynamic Hand Microphone for Outdoor Use One of the most reliable hand microphones for outdoor use is the Electro-Voice RE-50. It has a built-in windscreen and is cushioned to prevent rubbing sounds from the talent's hands. Otherwise, it is identical to the proven E-V 635 mic.

8.11 Ribbon Hand Microphone for Quality Sound Pickup The Beyer M-500 is a high-quality ribbon microphone with a cardioid pickup pattern and excellent frequency response. It is a favorite microphone with professional singers.

Hand Microphones

As the name implies, the *hand microphone* is handled by the performer. It is used in all production situations in which it is most practical, if not imperative, for the performer to exercise some control over the sound pickup. Hand microphones are, therefore, extensively used in ENG, where the reporter often works in the midst of much surrounding commotion and noise. In the studio or on stage, hand mics are used by singers and by performers who do audience participation shows. With the hand mic, the performer can walk up and talk at random to anyone in the audience. For singers, the hand mic is part of the act. They switch the mic from one hand to the other to support visually a transition in the song, or they caress and cuddle it during an especially tender passage.

Most importantly, however, the hand mic enables singers to exercise sound control. First, they can choose a hand mic that suits their voice quality and style of singing. Second, they can "work" the mic during a song, holding it close to the mouth to increase the feeling of intimacy during a soft passage, or farther away during louder, more external ones. Third, the hand mic gives them freedom of

movement, especially if it is a wireless hand mic (see p. 212).

The wide variety of usage makes heavy demands on the performance characteristics of a hand mic. Because it is handled so much, it must be rugged and rather insensitive to physical shock. Because it is often used extremely close to the sound source, it must be insensitive to plosive breath pops and input overload distortion (see Section Two). Because it is often used outdoors on remote locations, it must be able to withstand rain, snow, humidity, summer heat, and extreme temperature changes. And yet, it must be sensitive enough to pick up the full range and subtle tone qualities of a singer's voice. Finally, it must be small and slim enough to look unobtrusive and to be handled comfortably by the performer.

Of course, no single hand mic can fulfill all these requirements equally. *Dynamic* hand mics, which are the most rugged, are excellent for ENG and other fieldwork. Their built-in pop filter and sometimes even built-in windscreen (see 8.10) make them good outdoor mics. However, they do not meet the quality standard demanded by studio performers, such as singers. On the other hand, the high-quality *condenser* and *ribbon* hand microphones (see 8.11) used

8.12   Correct Hand-Microphone Position (a) When you are in a fairly quiet environment, the hand mic should be held chest high, parallel to the body. (b) In a noisy environment, the mic must be held closer to the mouth. In both cases, you speak across, rather than into, the mic.

by singers would not stand up too well to the demands of ENG.

The major *disadvantage* of the hand microphone is what we just listed as one of its advantages: the sound control by the performer. If somebody is inexperienced in using a hand mic, he or she might produce more pops and bangs than intelligible sounds, or give the camera operator an awkward shot that has the mic blocking the mouth of the performer.

Another disadvantage of most hand mics is that their cables might restrict your movements somewhat, especially in ENG, when you are tied to the camera person or the one who operates the VTR.

How to Use Hand Microphones   Working the hand microphone requires dexterity and foresight. Here are some hints:

1.   Although the hand mic is fairly rugged, treat it gently. If you need both hands during your performance, do not just drop the mic; put it down gently, or wedge it under your arm.

If you want to impress on the performer the sensitivity of a microphone, especially that of the hand mic, turn it on to a high volume level and feed the clanks and bangs back out into the studio for the performer to hear. Even a gentle handling of the microphone produces awesome noises.

2.   Before the telecast, check your action radius and see whether the mic cable is long enough for your actions and laid out for maximum mic mobility. This is especially important in ENG, where you are rather closely tied to the camera/VTR unit.

3.   Check out the microphone before the show or news report by speaking into the mic, or scratching lightly its pop filter and/or windscreen. Do not blow into it.

4.   When doing a stand-up news report in the field under normal conditions (no excessively loud environment, no strong wind), hold the microphone at chest level. Speak toward the camera, across the microphone rather than into it. If the background noise is high, raise the mic closer to your mouth while still speaking across it (see 8.12a and b).

5.   When using a directional hand mic, you must hold it close to your mouth at approximately a 45-degree angle in order to achieve optimal sound pickup. Unlike the reporter, who speaks across the omnidirectional hand mic, the singer sings *into* the mic (see 8.13).

6. Do not remain standing when interviewing a child. Stoop down so that you are on a level with the child. This way, you are able to keep the microphone close to the child in a natural way. You become the psychological equal to the child, and also help the camera operator frame an acceptable picture (see 8.14a and b).

7. When interviewing someone, hold the microphone to your mouth whenever you are speaking and to the guest's whenever he or she is answering. This obvious procedure has been unfortunately reversed by many a beginning performer.

8. If you happen to run out of mic cable, do not yank on it. Stop and try to get the attention of the floor manager.

9. When walking a considerable distance, do not pull the cable with the mic. Tug the cable gently with one hand, while holding the microphone with the other.

10. Always coil the mic cables immediately after use to protect the cables and have them ready for the next project.

8.13 Position of Directional Hand Microphone During Song For optimal sound pickup, the singer holds the microphone close to her mouth, at approximately a 45-degree angle.

Boom Microphones

When a scene, such as a dramatic scene, requires that you keep the microphone out of camera range, you need a microphone that can pick up sound over a fairly great distance while making the sound seem to come from close up (called "presence"), and one that keeps out most of the extraneous noises surrounding the scene. The *shotgun* microphone fills that bill. It is highly directional (supercardioid or hypercardioid) and has a far reach with little or no loss of presence (see 8.15). Because it is usually suspended from some kind of boom or hand-held, whereby your arms act as a "boom," we call it a *boom microphone*.

We will now describe these boom operations: (1) the hand-held shotgun and fishpole boom, (2) the big, or perambulator, boom, and (3) the giraffe, or tripod boom.

The Hand-held Shotgun and Fishpole Boom The most common ways of using the shotgun mic in EFP or small studio productions are to hold it by hand or to suspend it from a **fishpole** boom. Both methods work fairly well for short scenes, where the microphone is to be kept out of camera range. The advantages of holding it or suspending it from a fishpole boom are (1) the microphone is extremely flexible; you can carry it into the scene and aim it in any direction without any extraneous equipment; (2) by holding the shotgun, or by working the fishpole, you take up very little production space; (3) you can easily work around the existing lighting and see that the mic shadow falls outside the camera picture.

The disadvantages are (1) you can cover only relatively short scenes without getting tired; (2) you have to be close to the scene in order to get good sound pickup, which is often difficult, especially if the set is crowded; (3) if the scene is shot with multiple cameras (as in a studio production), you are often in danger of getting in the wide-shot camera's view; and (4) when you are holding it, the microphone may inevitably pick up some handling noises, even if you carry it by the shock mount.

a b

8.14 Correct Use of Hand Mic When Interviewing a Child (a) Most children are intimidated by having to talk to a microphone rather than a person. Also, the great difference in height between the interviewer and the child makes it difficult to achieve good composition. (b) When the interviewer stoops down, the child is aware more of the interviewer than the microphone. Also, the camera is now able to frame a better shot. Of course, the child can also be put on a riser or step to compensate for the differences in height.

How to Use the Hand-held Shotgun Mic and Fishpole Boom When *holding the shotgun mic* during a production, you should pay particular attention to these points:

1. Always carry the shotgun mic by the shock mount. Do not carry it directly; otherwise, you end up with more handling noises than actor's dialogue.

2. Do not cover the **ports** (openings) at the sides of the shotgun with anything but the windscreen. These ports must be able to receive sounds in order to keep the pickup pattern directional. Holding the mic by the shock mount minimizes this danger.

3. Watch that you do not hit anything with the mic and that you do not drop it.

4. Aim it as much as possible toward whoever is doing the speaking, especially if you are quite close to the sound source (see 8.16).

5. Always wear earphones so that you can hear what the mic is actually picking up in one of the

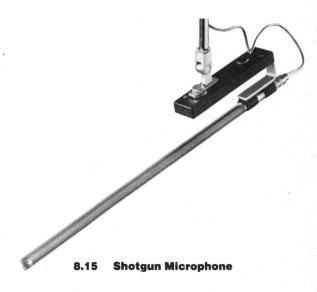

8.15 Shotgun Microphone

earphones, and the director's or audio engineer's instructions in the other. This is especially important in order for you to stay out of camera range.

6.   Watch for mic shadows.

When using the fishpole, many of the preceding points apply. Here are some more:

1.   Make sure that the microphone is properly shock-mounted so that it does not touch the pole.

2.   Fasten the mic cable properly to the pole. Some of the commercially available poles run the cable through the inside rather than the outside.

3.   Hold the boom from either above or below the sound source (see 8.17a and b). If you are picking up the sound of two people talking to each other, point the mic at whoever is speaking.

4.   If the actors speak while walking, walk with them at exactly the same speed, holding the mic in front of them during the entire take (from start to stop of the show segment being videotaped).

5.   Watch for obstacles that may block your walk, such as cables, lights, cameras, pieces of scenery, or tree stumps. Because you usually walk backward while watching the actors, rehearse your walk a few times.

6.   Make sure you have enough mic cable for the entire walk.

7.   If you have a long fishpole, anchor it in your belt and lower it into the scene as though you were "fishing" for the appropriate sound (see 8.18).

The Big, or Perambulator, Boom   The **perambulator boom** facilitates rapid and smooth movement of the microphone above and in front of the sound sources from one spot to another anywhere in the studio within its extended range. In order to keep the microphone out of the picture while following a moving sound source, you can extend or retract the microphone with the boom, simultaneously pan the boom horizontally, move it up and down vertically, and rotate the mic at the end of it to allow for directional sound pickup. During all these operations, you can have the whole boom assembly moved

8.16   Hand-held Shotgun Microphone   When holding a shotgun microphone, make sure that you hold it by its shock mount and that you do not cover the ports along the microphone.

to various locations, in case it cannot reach them when fully extended. (See 8.19.)

But there are some major disadvantages in using the "big boom" in a small studio or in small station operations: (1) For proper manipulation it needs two operators: the boom operator, who works the microphone boom, and the boom dolly operator, who helps to reposition the whole assembly whenever necessary. (2) The floor space that the boom takes up may, in a small studio, cut down the maneuverability of the cameras considerably. (3) The boom requires special lighting so that its shadow falls outside camera range. Even in larger studios, the lighting problems often preclude the use of a boom, available manpower and space notwithstanding.

The Giraffe, or Tripod Boom   The smaller boom, called a **giraffe** or *tripod boom,* is often preferred in small studios. It can do almost anything the big boom can do with the exception of extension and retraction of the boom itself. Because the giraffe is on casters, the boom operator alone can move the whole boom assembly quite easily toward or away from the sound source. There are some more advantages of the giraffe over the big boom: (1) It

a

b

8.17 **Handling the Short Fishpole Microphone** (a) A short pole is usually held as high as possible and then dipped into the scene as needed or (b) held low so that the mic is aimed at the sound source without getting into camera range.

8.18 **Fishpole Boom** The long fishpole can be anchored in the belt and raised and lowered similar to an actual fishpole. If the pole gets too heavy, you can support it with a unipod at the midpoint of the pole.

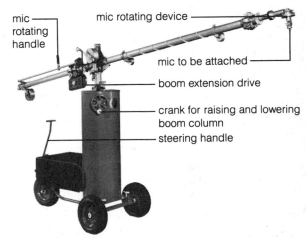

mic rotating handle

mic rotating device

mic to be attached

boom extension drive

crank for raising and lowering boom column

steering handle

8.19 **Big Studio, or Perambulator, Boom** The big microphone boom is mounted on a special dolly, called a perambulator, that permits rapid relocation anywhere in the studio. The operator's platform can be cranked up or down to the necessary operating height. Usually, a line monitor is mounted on the boom for the operator. The counter-weighted boom can be extended, tilted up and down, and the microphone itself can be rotated by about 300 degrees. Some booms have a round platform that permits a 360-degree pan of the whole boom, and they often have a small seat for the operator.

8.20 Giraffe, or Tripod Boom The giraffe boom moves on a simple tripod dolly and can be easily repositioned by the boom operator. The boom itself can be tilted up and down, and rotated (with the dolly) but not easily extended. The microphone can also be rotated.

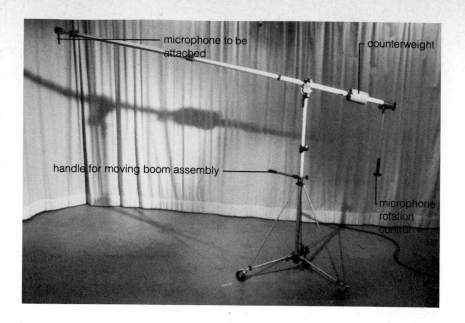

microphone to be attached

counterweight

handle for moving boom assembly

microphone rotation control

takes up much less studio space; (2) because of its low height and narrow wheelbase, it can be easily moved from one studio to another through narrow doorways or hallways; and (3) it can be disassembled quickly and taken to remote locations if necessary (see 8.20).

Unfortunately, even the giraffe is not without serious operational disadvantages: (1) The lighting is at least as critical for the giraffe as for the big boom and, in fact, becomes more of a problem because the giraffe usually works at a lower height and closer to the sound source. (2) Because of the considerable weight of a good cardioid boom microphone, the extension of the relatively light giraffe boom is limited. This requires the boom operator to stand closer to the sound source, a position that not only tends to increase the general noise level but may also prevent the camera from getting wide cover shots of the scene. (3) Even with vertical extensions for the rotating device and the mic suspension, the boom has to remain relatively low, which presents another danger of getting the microphone into the picture or causing unwanted mic shadows. (4) Because of its lightness, the boom is subject to shock and vibrations. Therefore, the microphone attached to the giraffe is more exposed to physical shock than that on the smoothly operating big boom.

How to Use Boom Microphones Here are some operating techniques for boom microphones:

1.   Try to keep the microphone as *low* as possible without getting it into the picture, and *in front* of the sound source. Do not ride the mic directly above the performer's head; after all, he or she speaks with the mouth, not with the top of the head.

2.   If you have a line monitor (which shows the picture that goes on the air or is videotaped) on the boom dolly, try to ascertain during rehearsal how far you can dip the microphone toward the sound source without getting the mic or the boom into the picture. The closer you are with the mic, the better the sound. (In boom-mic operation, you never get close enough to violate the minimum distance required of cardioid mics in order to avoid breath pops or similar sound distortions.) The optimum distance for boom mics is when the talent can just about touch the mic by reaching up at about a 45-degree angle.

3.   If the boom gets into the picture, it is better for you to *retract* it than to raise it. By retracting, you pull the microphone out of the camera's view and at the same time keep the mic in front of rather than on top of the sound source.

4. Watch shadows. Even the best lighting engineer cannot avoid shadows but can only redirect them into areas that are hopefully not picked up by the camera. If the boom positions are known before the show, work with the lighting engineer so he or she can light around the major moves of the boom. Sometimes you may have to sacrifice audio quality in order to avoid boom shadows.

If you discover a boom shadow when the camera is already on the air, do not try to move the microphone too quickly. Everybody will then be sure to see the shadow travel across the screen. Rather, try to sneak it out of the picture very slowly, or, better, just keep the mic and the shadow *as steady as possible* until a relief shot permits you to move the mic into a more advantageous position.

5. Anticipate the movements of performers so that you can *lead* them, rather than frantically follow them, with the microphone. Unless the show is very well rehearsed, do not lock the pan and tilt devices on the boom. If the performers rise unexpectedly, they may bump their heads on the locked microphone. Not even dynamic mics are that shockproof.

6. Watch for good audio balance. If you have to cover two people who are fairly close together and rather stationary, you may achieve good audio balance by simply placing the mic between the two and keeping it there until someone moves. Favor the weaker voice by pointing the mic more toward it. More often, however, you will find that you must rotate the unidirectional mic toward whoever is talking. In fully scripted shows, such as soap operas, the audio engineer in the booth follows the scripted dialogue and signals the boom operator each time the mic needs to be rotated from one actor to the other.

A slight movement of the performer can mean a complicated boom operation. Even though the performer merely turns his or her head from left to right while talking, for instance, you have to pan the boom horizontally several feet and rotate the microphone in order to keep it in front of the sound source. If the performer simply stoops down while talking, a great vertical drop of the boom is required. Vertical movements are usually difficult to manipulate quickly, especially when the boom is racked out as far as it will go.

7. When moving the perambulator, make sure that you warn the boom operator of this move, and that you do it extremely smoothly. Watch for cables on the floor and especially for low lighting instruments.

Wireless Microphones

In production situations, where complete and unrestricted mobility of the sound source is required, **wireless microphones** are used. If, for example, you are recording a group of singers who jump around as much as they sing, or if you are asked to pick up a skier's comments, groans, and breathing, and the clatter of the skis as he or she tests a new downhill course, the wireless mic is the obvious choice.

Wireless mics actually *broadcast* their signals. They are, therefore, also called **RF (radio frequency)** mics or radio mics.

Wireless microphones come as either hand or lavaliere mics. The *wireless hand mics* have the transmitter built into the microphone itself. Some models have a short antenna sticking out from the bottom of the mic (see 8.21); others have the antenna incorporated into the microphone housing (see 8.22).

The *wireless lavaliere mics* are connected to a small battery-powered transmitter that is either worn in the hip pocket or taped to the body. The antenna is strung along the pants, skirt, or shirt sleeves or around the waist (see 8.23).

The other important part of the wireless microphone system is the *receiving station*. The receiving station tunes into the frequency of the wireless transmitter and can receive the signals from as far as 1,000 feet (approximately 330 meters) under favorable conditions. When the conditions are more adverse, the range may shrink to about 100 feet (about 33 meters).

The wireless microphone works best in the controlled environment of a studio or stage. There you can determine the precise range of the performer's movements and find the optimal position for the receiving antenna. When in the studio, you can also control spurious signals that might interfere with the transmission of the wireless mic. More and more singers prefer working with the wireless hand mic, because it affords them unrestricted

8.21 Wireless Microphone with External Antenna This wireless hand mic has a small transmitting antenna at the bottom of the mic. The transmitter is inside the microphone.

8.22 Wireless Hand Microphone with Internal Antenna This microphone has the antenna incorporated in the housing. No external antenna is needed for signal transmission.

person) and the receiver, you may encounter fades and even occasional dropouts. Some receiving stations, therefore, use two or more antennas that are tuned to the same frequency, so that one can take over when the signal from the other gets weak. This is called "diversity reception." (2) The perspiration of the person wearing the transmitter can reduce signal strength, as does, of course, the increasing distance from transmitter to receiver. (3) Large metal objects, high voltage lines and transformers, x-ray machines, and microwave transmission can all interfere with the proper reception of the signals from the wireless mics. (4) Although most modern wireless equipment operates in a frequency that is higher than police, fire, taxi, or CB transmissions, there is still some danger of picking up extraneous signals, especially if the receiver is not accurately tuned, or if it operates in the proximity of other strong radio signals. (5) The receiving stations and the personnel to operate them are quite expensive.

How to Use Wireless Microphones
The basic operational techniques of wireless microphones are identical with those of the wired lavaliere or hand microphones. But here are some additional points to watch:

1. Make sure that all batteries are fully charged and operational.

2. The lavaliere transmitter antenna must always be fully extended.

3. If you have to tape the transmitter to the body, try not to attach the tape directly to the skin, unless

movement. It is also quite useful in audience participation shows, where the performer walks into the audience and picks random people for brief interviews. The wireless lavaliere microphones have been used successfully for musicals and dramatic shows, and, of course, in many ENG/EFP situations.

Despite the obvious advantage of the performer not being tied to a cable when using the microphone, the use of wireless mics has been restricted to highly specific production tasks. The major problems of using wireless mics are: (1) The signal pickup can be quite uneven, especially if the sound source moves over a fairly great distance and through hilly terrain, as, for example, our ski racer. If you do not have line of sight between the transmitter (on the

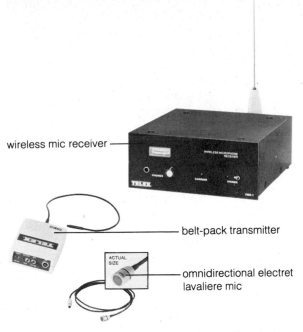

wireless mic receiver

belt-pack transmitter

ACTUAL
SIZE

omnidirectional electret
lavaliere mic

8.23   Wireless Lavaliere Microphone The wireless microphone has as its sound-pickup device a small lavaliere mic that is attached to a transmitter. A special receiving station receives the signal and sends it to the audio control console.

headset mic

8.24   Headset Microphone The headset microphone is almost identical to a regular telephone headset, except that it has a better microphone and a split audio feed (one earphone carries program sound, the other the P.L. line information, such as the director's cues).

you use an "ouch-less" tape. You can also use an elastic bandage to keep the transmitter in place.

4.   Be sure that the receivers are in the optimal positions so that there are no blind spots (ideally in line of sight with the transmitter at all times).

5.   Always test the sound pickup over the entire range of the sound source. Watch for possible interfering signals or objects. In the case of our downhill skier, you need to set up several receiving stations to maintain a continuous signal.

Headset Microphones

Headset microphones are used in special production situations, such as sports reporting, or ENG from a helicopter or convention floor. The headset mic isolates you sufficiently from the outside world so that you can concentrate on your specific reporting job in the midst of much noise and commotion, while keeping your hands free to shuffle statistics, grab people for an interview, pilot a helicopter, or even run a camera at the same time.

The headset microphone consists of a small omnidirectional or unidirectional microphone attached to earphones. One of the earphones carries the program sound (whatever sounds the headset mic picks up or is fed from the station), and the other the cues and instructions of the director or producer (see 8.24). Some of the headset microphones can be used as wireless mics.

There are no special ways of using it. You simply put it on and talk into it.

STATIONARY MICROPHONES

The *stationary* microphones include (1) desk, (2) stand, (3) hanging, (4) hidden, and (5) long-distance microphones. Once put into place and properly aimed at the sound source, they are not moved during the show or show segment.

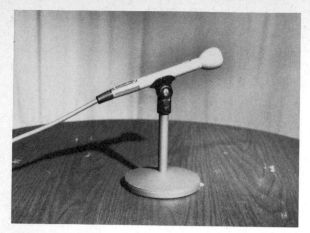

8.25 Desk Microphone on Stand In television the desk microphones are usually hand mics clipped onto a desk stand.

8.26 Pressure Zone Microphone (PZM) The PZM is mounted on a reflecting surface to build up the "pressure zone" at which all sound waves reach the microphone at the same time.

Desk Microphones

As the name implies, desk microphones are usually put on tables or desks. They are widely used in panel shows, public hearings, speeches, press conferences, and all other programs where the performer is working from behind a desk, table, or lectern. These microphones are used for *voice pickup* only. Because the performer behind the desk is usually doing something—shuffling papers, putting things on the desk, accidentally bumping the desk with feet or knees—desk microphones must be rugged and quite insensitive to physical shock. *Dynamic, omnidirectional* microphones are generally used. However, if a high separation of sound sources is desired, unidirectional mics are used as well. Generally, most hand mics double as desk mics. All you do is put them into a desk stand or mount them on a gooseneck floorstand (see 8.25) and position them for optimal sound pickup.

One of the special types of desk microphones is the **PZM**[3] **(pressure zone microphone)**, which looks quite different and operates on a different principle from ordinary microphones (see 8.26).

The PZM stops the sound waves (through a plate, the table, or the floor), building up a "pressure zone"

[3]PZM is a trademark of Crown, International, Inc.

at which the sound waves are reflected into the microphone all at the same time. (Ordinary mics hear the direct sound waves, but also the reflected ones at a slightly later time.) PZMs have a wide, hemispheric pickup pattern and are, therefore, ideal mics for the pickup of large group discussions and audience reactions. You can, for example, simply lay the PZM on a table and achieve a remarkably good pickup of the people sitting around it (see 8.27). Unfortunately, when used as a table mic, the PZM also picks up paper rustling, finger tapping, and the thumps of people knocking against the table.

As with the hand mic, no attempt is made to conceal the desk mike from the viewer. Nevertheless, when placing it on the desk, table, or lectern, you should consider the camera picture as well as optimal sound pickup. The performers certainly appreciate it if the camera shows more of them than the microphone. If the camera shoots from straight on, place the desk mic somewhat to the side of the performer and point it to his or her collarbone rather than mouth. This gives you a reasonably good sound pickup while giving the camera a clear shot of the performer (see 8.28).

How to Use Desk Microphones When using desk microphones, experienced as well as inexperienced television performers may feel compelled to grab

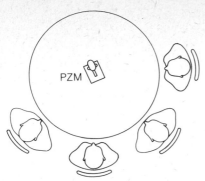

8.27 PZM Used as Table Microphone When the PZM is used as a table mic, the table acts as a reflecting surface. The sound pickup is entirely equal for people sitting around the table in a semicircle.

8.28 Desk Microphone Placement for Single Performer When using a desk mic, put it to the side of the performer (if he or she uses a floor monitor, put it to the monitor side, because a person is more apt to speak toward the monitor than the opposite side) so as to maximize the camera view, and pointed up toward his or her collarbone so that he or she speaks across the mic rather than directly into it.

the desk mic and pull it toward them, no matter how carefully you might have positioned the mic. Requests not to touch the mics do not always prevent this movement. Therefore, it might be a good idea to tape the mic stand to the table, if possible, or at least to tape the microphone cables securely and unobtrusively.

Having taken care of the most common problem, we can turn to a few more tips on using the desk mic:

1.   If you use two desk mics for the same speaker as a dual-redundancy precaution, use identical mics and put them as close together as possible. Do not activate them at the same time, unless you are feeding separate audio channels. If you have both mics on at the same time, you may experience **multiple-microphone interference.** When two mics are close to each other, but far enough away that they pick up the identical sound source at slightly different times, they sometimes cancel out certain sound frequencies, giving the sound a strangely thin quality. If you have to activate both of them at the same time, put them as close to each other as possible so that they receive the sound at the very same time (see 8.29).

2.   When using desk mics for a panel discussion, do not give each member a separate mic unless they sit far apart from each other. Using one mic for each

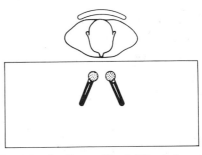

8.29 Dual-Redundancy Desk Microphones When using two desk mics as a dual-redundancy system, or for possible stereo pickup, place them as close together as possible to avoid microphone interference.

two panel members not only saves you microphones and setup time, but also minimizes multiple-microphone interference. Just make sure that they are at least *three times as far apart as any microphone is from its user* (see 8.30).

3.   Place the microphones in such a way that you achieve optimal sound pickup from all members *actively engaged in the discussion.* Finalize the position of the mics only after having seen the total panel setup and the interaction of the panel members.

4.   Remind the panel members or anyone working with a desk mic *not to reposition the mic once it is set,* and to avoid as much as possible banging on the

table or kicking the lectern, even if the discussion happens to get lively.

5. When two people are sitting opposite each other, give each one a mic.

6. Try to conceal the mic cables as much as possible. Do not just drop them in front of the desk, but string them as neatly as possible along the side of the desk before routing them to the microphone jacks. Use masking tape to cover the cables on the floor if they are in camera range. Special panel desks have holes through which the cables can be dropped and concealed from the cameras.

7. When on an ENG assignment, always carry a small desk stand along. This way, you can use the hand mic, or even the shotgun mic, usually clipped on the camera, as a desk mic. A clamp-on mic holder with a gooseneck is very handy to add your mic to the cluster of other mics you find on the speaker's lectern during a news conference.

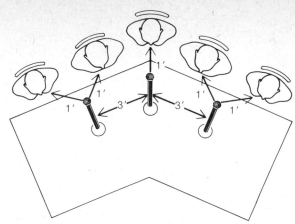

8.30   Multiple Desk Microphone Setup When using a multiple-microphone setup, you should keep the individual microphones at least three times as far apart as any microphone is away from its user.

Stand Microphones

Stand microphones are used whenever the sound source is fixed and the type of programming permits them to be seen. For example, there is no need to conceal the microphones in a rock group. On the contrary, they are an important show element.

The quality of stand mics ranges from dynamic hand mics clipped onto a stand to highly sensitive condenser mics used exclusively for music recording sessions.

How to Use Stand Microphones   The sound pickup of an *instrumental group,* such as a rock group, is normally accomplished with *several* stand microphones. These are placed in front of each speaker that emits the amplified sound of a particular instrument, or in front of the unamplified sound source, such as the drums. The use of multiple microphones is essential when multiple-track recordings are made (each microphone, or group of microphones, is recorded on a separate tape track), and extremely helpful even in single-track recordings for maximum audio control during the sound mixing.

The type of microphone used depends on such a variety of factors that specific suggestions would probably be more confusing than helpful at this stage.

For example, studio acoustics, the type and combination of instruments used, and the aesthetic quality of the "sound" finally desired all play an important part in the choice and placement of microphones. Quite generally, rugged, dynamic, omnidirectional or cardioid mics are used for high-volume sound sources, such as drums, electric guitar speakers, and some singers, whereas ribbon or condenser mics are used for the "more gentle" sound sources, such as strings and acoustical guitars.

Although there are many factors that influence the type of microphone used and its placement, 8.31 through 8.33 may give you some idea of how three different, yet typical, musical numbers may be set up with mics.

Hanging Microphones

Hanging microphones are used whenever any other concealed-microphone method (boom or fishpole) is impractical.

You can hang the microphones (high-quality cardioid) by their cables over any fairly stationary sound source. Most often, hanging mics are used in dramatic presentations, where the action is fully blocked so that the actors are in a precise location for each delivery of lines. The actor has to make

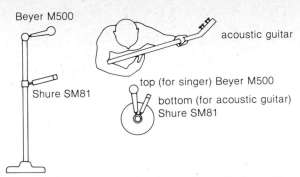

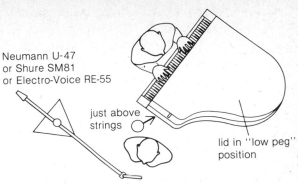

Sennheiser MKH-415 on boom

8.31 Microphone Setup for Singer and Acoustic Guitar The customary way to set up mics for a singer who is accompanying himself or herself on an acoustic guitar is to have two microphones on a single mic stand, such as a Beyer M500 for the singer (pointing just below the singer's mouth), and a Shure SM81, pointing at the guitar.

8.32 Microphone Setup for Singer and Piano A singer who is accompanied by a piano might have a Sennheiser MKH-415 (or even an 815) suspended from a boom. There could be a Neumann U-47 (or a Shure SM81, or an Electro-Voice RE-55) for the piano, placed just above the strings on the high-string side, with the lid in the low-peg position (half open). The formality of the recital probably forbids the use of a hand microphone.

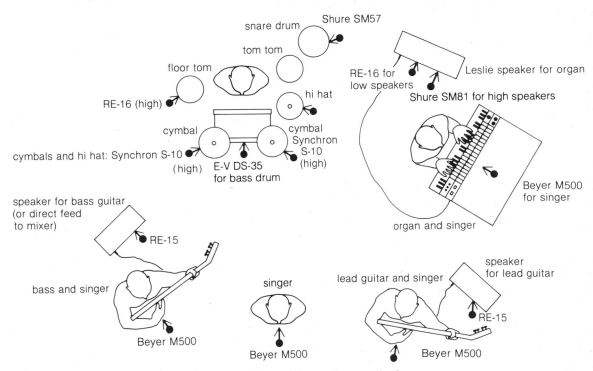

8.33 Microphone Setup for a Small Rock Group When setting up mics for a rock group, you need microphones for the singers, drums, and other direct sound-emitting instruments, such as flutes and pianos, as well as for the speakers that carry the sound of the amplified instruments, such as electric guitars and organs. The microphones must be placed so that they do not cause audio feedback or multiple-audio interference. The type of mic depends on the instrument to be picked up *and* on the acoustics of the room.

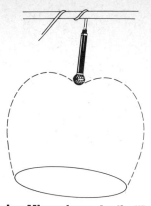

8.34 Hanging Microphone Audio "Pool" A high-quality microphone is suspended from the lighting grid to the lowest position that the camera's view can tolerate over the designated performance area. The maximum audio pickup limits are within the "audio pool," a pickup configuration very much like a wide pool of light. Be sure to separate the microphone cables from the AC cables of the lighting instruments; otherwise you may experience electronic interference.

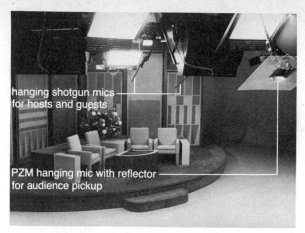

hanging shotgun mics for hosts and guests

PZM hanging mic with reflector for audience pickup

8.35 PZM Used as Hanging Mic When using a PZM as hanging microphone, you need to mount it on an additional sound-reflecting board and angle it toward the sound source for optimal sound pickup.

sure to speak only within the "audio pool" of the hanging microphone. Similar to the spotlight pool, where the actor is visible only as long as he or she moves within the limited area of the light, the actor is heard only when he or she speaks within the limited range of the audio pool. (See 8.34.)

Although high-quality cardioid mics are generally suspended from the lighting grid, the pickup quality is not necessarily the best. The sound source is always relatively far away from the microphone, and if the person is not exactly within the sound pool (the pickup pattern) of the mic, his or her voice appears off-mic. Hanging mics have the annoying tendency of picking up the shuffling of feet almost as well as voices. A further disadvantage of hanging microphones is that the light cables may cause a hum in the audio pickup.

Nevertheless, hanging mics are quite popular in studio productions, dramatic shows, and audience participation shows. When the mics are suspended from the light grid, they are out of camera range without having to use booms. Even if you do not like the pickup quality of ordinary hanging mics, the PZM may change your mind. This microphone works from above as well as when used as a table

mic. All you need to do is mount it on a sound-reflecting board (such as a 3 × 4-foot Plexiglas or plywood sheet), suspend it above and in front of the general sound-generating area (such as an audience area), and angle the reflecting board for optimal pickup. Regardless of whether the sound source is close to the PZM or farther away, the sounds have equally good presence. This positive aspect turns negative in dramatic productions, where sound perspective (close-ups sound closer and long shots farther away) is an important factor. This is why in complex productions the boom is still preferred to the PZM (see 8.35).

How to Use Hanging Microphones

1. Hang them as low as possible, to get reasonably good presence.

2. If necessary, mark the studio floor for the actor at the spot of the best sound pickup.

3. Be sure to secure the mic cable sufficiently so that the mic does not come crashing down.

4. Separate the mic cables as much as possible from the light cables. If this is not possible, cross

lavaliere mic taped to rear view mirror ⌐

8.36   Use of Lavaliere as Hidden Mic in Car
Excellent audio has been achieved by simply taping a small lavaliere microphone to the rearview mirror inside an automobile. This is workable for stationary scenes only.

the mic and light cables at right angles to minimize electronic interference.

5.   Be especially careful when striking (taking down) the hanging microphones. Do not drop the mic or the cable connectors.

6.   Do not hit hanging mics inadvertently with ladders, lighting poles, or lighting instruments.

Hidden Microphones

Sometimes you may find that you need to hide a small lavaliere microphone in a tuft of flowers, behind a table decoration, or in a car to pick up a conversation during certain studio productions or EFP where microphones should be out of camera range (see 8.36). Whenever you use hidden mics, realize that it is quite time consuming to place a hidden mic so that it yields a satisfactory pickup. Often you get a marvelous pickup of various noises caused by people hitting the table or moving their chairs, but only a rather poor pickup of their conversation. Worse, if hidden mics are too close to hardwall scenery, the set may act as echo chamber and produce considerable sound distortion.

Again, the PZM can serve as an excellent "hidden" mic, especially because it does not look like an ordinary mic at all. You may get away with not hiding it at all, but simply placing it on a table among other exotic table decorations.

How to Use Hidden Microphones

1.   Try to shock-mount the lavaliere so that it does not transfer unintentional banging noises. Use the lavaliere clip or put some foam rubber between the mic and the object to which it is attached.

2.   Do not try to conceal the mic completely, unless there is an ECU of the object to which it is attached.

3.   Make sure that you hide not only the microphone, but the cable as well.

4.   Secure the microphone and cable with tape so that they do not come loose. Your setup must withstand the rigors of the rehearsals and the videotaping sessions.

5.   If cables are a problem, you can use a wireless lavaliere and hide the transmitter in some appropriate place, such as a book whose pages have been partially cut out.

Long-Distance Microphones

You may hear of *long-distance microphones,* especially in the field of sports coverage. We have finally come to realize that it is often the sound more than the pictures that carry and communicate the *energy* of a sports event. The simplest way to pick up the sound in sports events, such as tennis or ice hockey, is to place long-distance mics at strategic positions.

The long-distance microphones are nothing but hypercardioid or ultracardioid shotgun mics aimed at the main action. A single tennis game may have six or more microphones to pick up the sounds of the players, the judges, and the crowd.

An old but successful method used to pick up sounds over fairly long distances is to use a parabolic reflector mic. The parabolic reflector mic consists of a small parabolic dish (similar to a small microwave dish) that has an omnidirectional microphone facing inward right at its focal point. Thus, all incoming sounds are concentrated at the mic (see 8.37).

8.37 Parabolic Reflector Microphone The parabolic reflector microphone is primarily used for voice pickup over long distances, such as the quarterback's signals during a football game. The parabolic mic uses an omnidirectional mic in the focal point of a small parabolic reflector.

The parabolic reflector mic is often used to pick up voices over long distances, such as the signals of the quarterback during a football game. The problem with the parabolic reflector mic is that the low frequencies are lost during the pickup, which gives the voices a slight "telephone" quality.

MAIN POINTS

1. Audio is the sound portion of a television show. Audio transmits specific information (such as a news story), helps to establish the specific locale and time of the action, contributes to the mood, and provides continuity for the various picture portions.

2. The pickup of live sound is done through a variety of microphones.

3. The three major types of microphones are dynamic, condenser, and ribbon. Each type has a different sound-generating element that converts sound waves into electrical energy.

4. Some microphones can hear sounds equally well from all directions; others hear better in a specific direction. The polar pattern is a two-dimensional representation of the microphone's directional sensitivity. Microphones are either omnidirectional, hearing well from all directions, or unidirectional, hearing better from one direction.

5. Microphones are classified according to their operation and are either mobile or stationary. The mobile types include lavaliere, hand, boom, wireless, and headset microphones. The stationary types are desk, stand, hanging, hidden, and long-distance microphones.

6. The lavaliere microphone is the most commonly used in small studio operations. It is usually clipped to clothing. Although it is extremely small, it provides quality sound reproduction.

7. Hand microphones are used in situations in which the performer needs to exercise some control over the sound pickup.

8. When the microphone must be kept out of camera range, it is usually mounted on and operated from a microphone boom. The three types of booms are (1) the fishpole boom, (2) the big or perambulator boom, and (3) the giraffe or tripod boom. The hand-held shotgun mic belongs to the boom mic category.

9. When unrestricted mobility of the sound source is required, a wireless, or RF (radio frequency) microphone is used.

10. Headset microphones are practical for sports reporting or ENG from a helicopter or convention floor.

11. Desk microphones are simply hand mics clipped to a desk stand. They are often used for panel discussions.

12. Stand microphones are employed whenever the sound source is fixed and the type of programming permits them to be seen by the camera.

13. Hanging microphones are popular in some studio productions because the mics are kept out of camera range without using booms.

14. Hidden microphones are small lavaliere mics concealed behind or within set decorations.

Type		Pickup Pattern	Characteristics	Use
Sennheiser 816		Hypercardioid, extremely directional	New version of 815; condenser, sensitive, excellent presence over long distance	Boom, fishpole, hand-held; for long-distance pickup
Sennheiser 416		Supercardioid, very directional	New version of proven 415; condenser, sensitive, excellent presence	Boom, fishpole; excellent for all kinds of remote audio pickups
AKG 900E		Hypercardioid, very directional	Dynamic; excellent presence	Boom, fishpole; good for all kinds of remote audio pickups
Electro-Voice DL-42		Hypercardioid, very directional	Dynamic, fairly rugged, especially with acoustic foam mic cover	Boom, fishpole, hand-held; good for all long-distance pickups
PZM (Pressure Zone Microphone)		Hemispheric (roughly 180 degrees)	Modified condenser (responds to pressure zone), sensitive; needs reflecting board; excellent presence	Can be used in place of boom mic, hanging mic, and desk mic for area pickup

(continued)

Type	Pickup Pattern	Characteristics	Use
Electro-Voice 635A	Omnidirectional	Dynamic, very rugged	Excellent all-purpose mic—desk, stand, or hand; very good for outdoor use
Electro-Voice RE-50	Omnidirectional	Dynamic, very rugged	Same as E-V 635A, except that it has built-in pop filter; standard ENG on-location mic
Shure SM61	Omnidirectional	Dynamic, rugged, good blast filter	Fine hand mic; also good on stand for singers and music pickup
Shure SM81	Cardioid	Condenser	Good utility mic; good for vocal and general music pickup
Shure SM58	Cardioid, directional	Dynamic, fairly rugged	Good hand, stand, or desk mic; good for close audio, such as singers

Type	Pickup Pattern	Characteristics	Use
Beyer M160	Hypercardioid, extremely directional	Ribbon; fairly sensitive, but not subject to input overload	Good as hand and stand mic; very good for music (bass, strings, or brass); excellent vocal mic
Beyer M500	Hypercardioid, extremely directional	Ribbon, fairly rugged, very good quality	Hand and stand mic; excellent for vocal recording, good for music, especially brass instruments
AKG 224E	Cardioid, directional	Dynamic, quite rugged, very good quality	Hand, desk, stand, hanging; good for voice, singers, and music recording
Electro-Voice CS-15	Cardioid, directional	Condenser with blast filter; quite rugged	Excellent for voice pickup; very good for on-location work; hand, desk, hanging mic; even good on boom, if mics are set up tightly
Electro-Voice RE-15	Supercardioid, very directional	Dynamic, good quality, fairly sensitive to popping	Desk, hanging, stand; good for music recording

Type	Pickup Pattern	Characteristics	Use
Electro-Voice RE-16	Supercardioid, very directional	Similar to RE-15, but with pop filter; somewhat more rugged than the RE-15	Very good for desk, stand, hanging; good for vocals and music recordings (drums, guitar)
Neumann U-87	Multiple pattern: from omni to cardioid	Condenser, fairly sensitive; very good quality	Good for studio recording use
AKG 414B	Multiple patterns: from omni to hypercardioid	Condenser, very good quality	Good for studio recording use, especially for vocals and music
Neumann U-89	Multiple patterns: from omni to hypercardioid	Similar in quality to the U-87, yet more rugged; can take high input overload	For all critical studio recordings; though relatively large, can be used on camera for music recordings

Type		Pickup Pattern	Characteristics	Use
RCA 77-DX		Bidirectional (live on two sides)	Ribbon, quite large, excellent quality; very sensitive to input overload	Classic mic, used for voice and music recording, especially strings; not good for tight mic setups
Sony ECM-50/ Sony ECM-250		Omnidirectional	(Shown: ECM-50) Condenser, fairly rugged, yet excellent quality; very small and lightweight; ECM-250 is improved version of ECM-50	Excellent, widely used lavaliere; also good for music pickup; ECM-250 is excellent lavaliere
Beyer MCE5		Omnidirectional	Electret condenser	Very small lavaliere of excellent quality
Shure SM11		Omnidirectional	Dynamic; one of the smallest lavaliere mics available; very good quality	Often used as hidden lavaliere

In this section we will take a closer look at (1) the various sound-generating elements and how they work, and (2) the special microphone use in ENG.

SOUND-GENERATING ELEMENTS

All microphones have (1) a **diaphragm,** which vibrates with the sound pressures, and (2) a *generating element,* which changes the physical vibrations of the diaphragm into electrical energy.

In the *dynamic* microphone, the diaphragm is attached to a coil, the voice coil. When somebody speaks into the mic, the diaphragm vibrates with the air pressure from the sound and makes the voice coil move back and forth within a magnetic field. This produces a fluctuating electric current, which, when amplified, transmits these vibrations to the cone of a speaker, making the sound audible again.

Because the diaphragm-voice coil element is physically quite rugged, the microphone can withstand and accurately translate high sound levels or other air blasts close to the microphone.

In the *ribbon* or *velocity* mic, a very thin metal ribbon vibrates within a magnetic field, serving the function of the diaphragm and the voice coil. The ribbon is

so fragile, however, that even moderate physical shocks to the microphone, or sharp air blasts close to it, can damage and even destroy the instrument. When it is used outdoors, even the wind moves the ribbon and thus introduces a great amount of noise. You should not use this kind of microphone outdoors, therefore, or in production situations that require its frequent movement. A good ribbon mic, such as the classic RCA 77-DX, is nevertheless an excellent recording mic, even in television productions. Although it has a low tolerance to high sound levels, the delicate ribbon responds well to a wide frequency range and reproduces with great fidelity the subtle nuances of tone color, especially in the bass range.

In the *condenser* microphone, the diaphragm constitutes one of the two plates necessary for a condenser to function. The other, called the backplate, is fixed. Because the diaphragm moves with the air vibrations against the fixed backplate, the capacitance of this condenser is continuously changed, thus modulating the electrical current. The major advantage of the condenser microphone over the other types is its extremely wide frequency response and pickup sensitivity. But this sensitivity is also one of its disadvantages. If placed close to high-intensity sound sources, such as the high-output speakers of a rock band, it overloads and distorts the incoming sound—a condi-

Simply speaking, microphones convert one type of energy to another—sound waves to electrical energy. But the particular process each mic uses to accomplish this conversion determines that mic's quality and use.

tion known as **input overload distortion.** However, if properly placed, the condenser mic is a superior recording mic, especially when used under highly controlled conditions of studio recording.

SPECIAL MICROPHONE USE IN ENG

In general, you will find that the microphone techniques discussed in Section One will get you through most ENG or even EFP situations. However, there are a few more items worth considering:

1.   When working with semiprofessional equipment, you have to watch that the impedance of the microphone and the recorder matches. **Impedance** is a type of resistance to the signal flow. You can have high-impedance (sometimes abbreviated **high-Z**) and low-impedance (low-Z) microphones. A high-impedance mic (usually the less expensive and lower-quality microphones) works only with a relatively short cable (a longer cable has too much resistance), whereas a low-impedance mic (all high-quality professional mics) can take up to several hundred feet of cable. If you need to feed a low-impedance recorder with a high-

impedance mic, or vice versa, you need a special **impedance transformer.**

2.   Semiprofessional mics do not have as wide a **frequency response** as high-quality microphones. This means that high-quality mics can hear higher and lower sounds than the less expensive mics. Also, many high-quality mics are built to hear equally well over the entire frequency range, called **flat response.** However, do not be misled by specifications or professional and semiprofessional labels. Use whatever microphone gives you the sound you want.

3.   All professional microphones and mic cables have three-pronged connectors, called **XLR connectors** (see 8.39). But when you work with semiprofessional equipment, you may run across three more types of audio connectors: (1) the phone plug, (2) the RCA, or phono, plug, and (3) the miniplug (see 8.40). Make sure to have the necessary adaptors with you, especially when on ENG or EFP assignments.

4.   When on an ENG assignment, *always* have a microphone open to catch the ambient sounds, even if you shoot "silent" footage. In fact, when you use the hand mic for a stand-up report (with the reporter telling about a news event while standing in particular location), you should also turn on your shotgun mic, which

8.39   XLR Connector

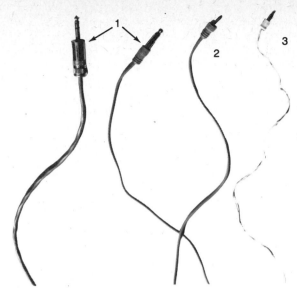

8.40   Various Types of Audio Plugs (1) phone plug; (2) RCA, or phono, plug; (3) miniplug.

is clipped onto your camera, for the ambient sounds. Feed each mic into a separate VTR audio track. Such ambient sounds are essential for sound continuity in postproduction.

5.   If you have only one microphone with you and must use it for voice pickup, record the ambient sounds on a small portable audio cassette recorder. Again, the editor appreciates it very much if he or she has some authentic sounds with which to bridge the edits. Time and circumstances permitting, many ENG camera operators like to record an interview simultaneously on the audio track of the videotape and on the audio cassette. This gives the reporter or camera operator a chance to "pre-listen" to the interview while driving back to the station—not otherwise possible with the no-playback portable VTR.

6.   When covering a panel discussion that is already set up with table microphones, try to tie into the ampli-

fication system. If you cannot do that, you need an assistant who holds and aims the shotgun mic at whoever is speaking. When interviewing a person in his or her office, clip a hand mic to a desk stand, or use a lavaliere.

7.   Make sure you carry windscreens for all mics that do not have one built in.

MAIN POINTS

1.   All microphones have a diaphragm, which vibrates with sound pressures, and a generating element, which changes the physical vibrations of the diaphragm into electrical energy.

2.   In the dynamic mic, the diaphragm is attached to the voice coil. The air pressure makes the voice coil move back and forth within a magnetic field. This type of generating element is quite rugged.

3.   In the ribbon or velocity mic, a thin metal ribbon vibrates within a magnetic field. Because the ribbon is quite fragile, the mics are generally used indoors under controlled conditions.

4.   The condenser mic has a condenserlike generating element. The diaphragm constitutes one of the two condenser plates. The varying air pressure of the

Flat Response   Measure of a microphone's ability to hear equally well over the entire frequency range.

Frequency Response   Measure of the range of frequencies a microphone can "hear" and reproduce.

incoming sounds moves the plate against a fixed back-plate, thus continuously changing the capacitance of the condenser and modulating the current of the audio signal. Condenser mics have a wide frequency response.

5.　Ribbon and condenser mics are subject to input overload. Especially loud incoming sounds have a tendency to overload the microphone system and distort the sound.

6.　Impedance, usually expressed as high or low Z, is a type of resistance to the signal flow. The impedance of the microphone and recorder must be matched.

7.　High-quality microphones pick up sounds equally well over a wide frequency response. They can hear higher and lower sounds without distortion than low-quality mics.

8.　Microphones and mic cables may have a variety of connectors, such as XLR, phone plug, RCA plug, or miniplug.

9.　Ambient sound should always be recorded, preferably on a separate audio track. These sounds are essential for continuity in postproduction.

FURTHER READING

Clifford, Martin. *Microphones*. 2nd ed. Blue Ridge Summit, PA: TAB Books, 1982.

Nisbett, Alec. *The Use of Microphones*. 2nd ed. Woburn, MA: Focal Press, 1983.

Audio: Sound Control

In the previous chapter we were mostly concerned with sound pickup—the proper choice and use of microphones. In Section One of this chapter we will discuss the various aspects of sound control:

1. The audio control area in the television control room.
2. Basic audio equipment, including the patch panel, audio console, turntable, audio-tape recorder, cartridge and cassette machines, and audio synchronizer.
3. Operational factors, including volume control, sequence control, mixing and sound quality control.

Section Two pays attention to these additional areas of television audio:

1. Analog and digital recording processes.
2. Time compression and expansion.
3. Various intercommunication systems.
4. Aesthetic factors, such as environment, figure-ground, perspective, continuity, and energy.

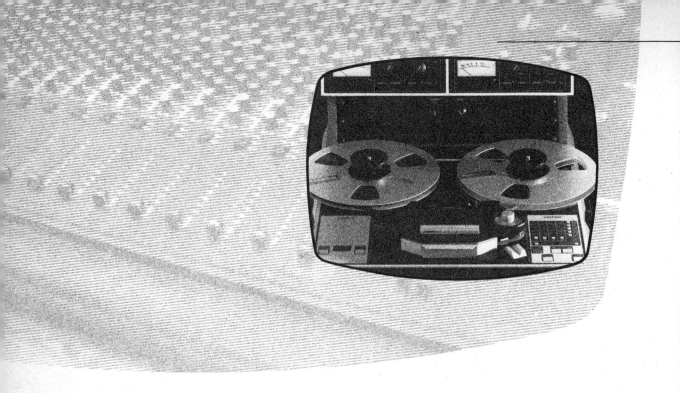

AUDIO AREA

As you learned in Chapter 1, the audio control facilities are isolated, though in proximity to the program control section of the studio control room. The *audio control booth* houses the audio, or mixing, console; several cart (audio cartridge) and/or cassette machines; a reel-to-reel audiotape recorder; one or two turntables; a patch panel; one or two cue and program speakers; P. L. intercom; studio talkback system; a clock; and a line monitor (see 9.1). One audio engineer takes care of all audio control operations during a show.

Because of the many and various audio production demands in postproduction, larger stations and all network operations have a separate *audio production room* or facility. This room, which resembles a small control room of a recording studio, is not used for the sound control of the daily telecasts that originate in the studio. Rather, it serves the various audio postproduction demands, such as adding certain sound effects to the audio track of a play, inserting parts of the laugh track from the rehearsal audience into the final version of the sit-

uation comedy, and assembling on various audio carts (cartridges) the various music bridges and announcements for the next day's programming. The production room usually contains: (1) a fairly elaborate audio console; (2) two or more multitrack audiotape recorders (ATRs); (3) two turntables; (4) cart and cassette machines; (5) a production switcher that can activate and mix synchronously the audio and video; (6) patch panels; (7) a time code synchronizer that provides the time code address for the audiotapes, drives synchronously the audiotape and videotape machines, and activates on command other related equipment; and (8) high-fidelity monitor speakers (see 9.2).

AUDIO EQUIPMENT

We will now take a closer look at the following major components of audio equipment: (1) patch panel or patchbay, (2) audio console, (3) turntable, (4) audiotape recorder, (5) cartridge and cassette machines, and (6) audio synchronizer.

Sound, as picked up by a microphone, must be carefully controlled before it can be broadcast. Involved here are sophisticated equipment, intricate processes, and personal judgment.

Patch Panel

The primary function of the patch panel is the connecting and routing of various pieces of equipment. Let us assume that you want to have two microphones, a remote feed from a field reporter, and a cartridge machine operating during a newscast. Mics nos. 1 and 2 are the newscasters' lavaliere mics. The remote feed comes from the field reporter who reports a live insert. The cart machine contains the news theme music. Just as the individual lighting instruments can be patched into any one of the dimmers, you can patch any one of these audio "inputs" to individual volume controls (pots) in any order desirable. For instance, suppose you want to operate the volume controls in the following order, from left to right: cart machine, lavaliere 1, remote feed, and lavaliere 2. You can easily patch these inputs to the audio console in that order. If you want the inputs in a different order, you do not need to unplug the equipment. All you do is pull the patches and repatch the inputs in the new order (see 9.3 and 9.4).

All patch panels contain rows of holes, called **jacks,** which represent the various outputs (from microphones, cartridges, turntables, or tape recorders) and inputs (to different pots or channels at the audio console). The connection between output and input is made through the *patch cord*. Patch panels are usually wired so that the various input jacks are directly below the output jacks (see 9.4). Certain frequent connections between outputs (a specific mic or a cart machine) and inputs (specific volume controls) that are normally used are directly wired, or *normaled,* to one another. This means that the output and input of a circuit are connected without a patch cord. By inserting a patch cord into one of the jacks of a normal circuit, you *break,* rather than establish, the normal connection.

Audio Console

Regardless of individual designs, all audio consoles, or audio control boards, are built to perform five major functions: (1) *input:* to preamplify and control the volume of the various incoming signals; (2) *mix:* to combine and balance two or more incoming signals; (3) *quality control:* to manipulate the sound characteristics; (4) *output:* to route the

9.1 Audio Control

Booth The audio control booth contains the audio control board, through which the various sound inputs are selected, amplified, mixed, and distributed to the line-out, reel-to-reel tape machines, or at least the controls for them, tape cartridge machines, one or two turntables, one or two speakers and intercom controls, and patching facilities. In essence, the audio control booth in the television control room represents a small radio station.

9.2 Audio Production

Room The audio production room usually contains a multichannel audio console; two turntables; two reel-to-reel tape recorders, one of which is usually a multitrack recorder; cart machines; cassette machines; audio synchronizer; and a line monitor. Sometimes, it also contains a production switcher and videotape recorders.

monitors

turntable

audiotape recorders

AGC Automatic Gain Control. Regulates the audio or video level automatically.

Balance Audio: a proper mixing of various sounds.

Bus (or Buss) Audio: a common central circuit that receives from several sources or feeds to several separate destinations; a "mix bus" collects the output signals from several inputs and feeds them into the line-out.

Cartridge, or Tape Cartridge Also called "cart" for short. An audiotape recording or playback device that uses tape cartridges. A cartridge is a plastic case containing an endless tape loop that rewinds as it is played back.

Cassette A video- or audiotape recording or playback device that uses tape cassettes. A cassette is a plastic case containing two reels, a supply reel and a takeup reel.

Distortion Audio: unnatural alteration or deterioration of sound.

Dub The duplication of an electronic recording. Dubs can be made from tape to tape, or from record to tape. The dub is always one generation away from the previous recording.

Equalization Audio: controlling the audio signal by emphasizing certain frequencies and eliminating others. Equalization can be accomplished manually or automatically through an equalizer.

Feedback Audio: piercing squeal from the loudspeaker, caused by the accidental reentry of the loudspeaker sound into the microphone and subsequent overamplification of sound.

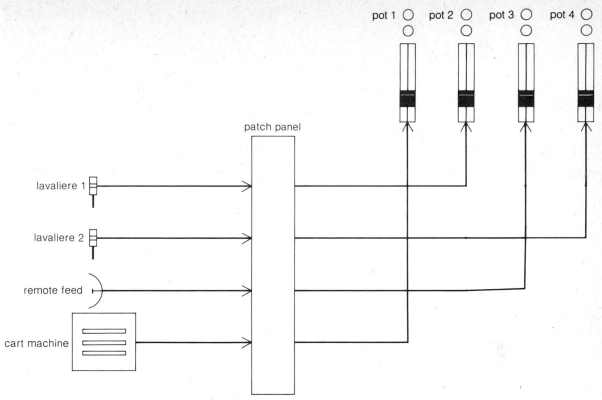

pot 1 ○   pot 2 ○   pot 3 ○   pot 4 ○

patch panel

lavaliere 1

lavaliere 2

remote feed

cart machine

9.3   Patching Through patching, we can route various sound sources to specific audio console inputs. Here, the cart machine is patched into pot 1, the lavaliere mic 1 into pot 2, the remote feed into pot 3, and the lavaliere mic 2 into pot 4.

Head Assembly   Audio head assembly: a small electromagnet that (a) erases the signal from the tape (erase head); (b) puts the signals on the audiotape (recording head); and (c) reads (induces) them off the tape (playback head).

Ips   An abbreviation for inches-per-second, indicating tape speed.

Jack   A socket or phone-plug receptacle (female).

Lip-sync   Synchronization of sound and lip movement.

Mix-down   Final combination of sounds on a single or stereo track of an audio- or videotape.

Mixing   Audio: the combining of two or more sounds in specific proportions (volume variations) as determined by the event (show) context.

Peak Program Meter   Also called PPM. Meter in audio console to measure loudness. Especially sensitive to volume "peaks," it indicates overmodulation.

Reverberation   Audio echo; adding echo to sound via an acoustical echo chamber or electronic sound delay; generally used to liven sounds recorded in an acoustically dull studio.

Volume   The relative intensity of the sound; its relative loudness.

VU Meter   A volume-unit meter; measures volume units, the relative loudness of amplified sound.

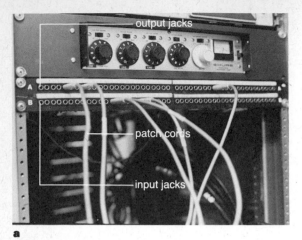
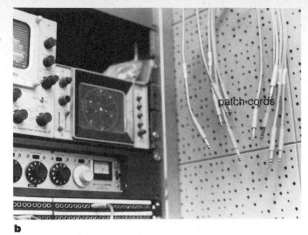

9.4   Patch Panel The patch panel connects specific audio sources (microphones, cart machines, or turntables) to specific audio console control functions (pots, channels). The holes are called *jacks* and the connecting cables *patch cords*. The upper rows of jacks are the outputs (which carry the signals that originated from the mics, turntables, and so forth); the row of jacks immediately below the output jacks is made up of input jacks, which are connected to the console controls.

combined signals to a specific output; and (5) *monitor:* to listen to the sounds before their signals are actually recorded or broadcast. (See 9.5.)

Input   In the recent example we used for patching, you had to work with four sound sources: two lavaliere mics, a remote line, and a cart machine. If you want to control any one or all of these four sound sources—or, more precisely, sound signals—at the same time, you need four *inputs* at the console. Many of the portable ENG/EFP "mixers" (as small consoles are called) may have only four, or at best, eight such inputs. Of course, if you have only one or two mics, you can use the audio inputs on your VTR for sound control. No mixer is necessary.

Most studio consoles, on the other hand, have as many as sixteen or even more inputs. Although that many inputs are rarely used in the average broadcast day, they need to be there for the special program you may have to do from time to time. If you come up against a show with especially complex audio requirements, you should contract with one of the professional audio services. This will be much less expensive than buying and trying to operate a bigger audio console.

Let us now take a closer look at the input section of an audio console.

Each of the inputs that can receive the signal from a sound source (such as a microphone, a remote line, a record, or tape) has a **preamp** (preamplifier) that boosts incoming, low-level signals, and a *volume control.* The larger consoles also have a variety of *quality controls, switches* (mute or solo switch) that *silence* all the other inputs when you want to listen to a specific one, and *assignment switches* that will route the signal to certain mix buses and signal outputs (see 9.6).

Volume Control   All sounds fluctuate in loudness (**volume**). Some sounds are relatively weak, so that you have to increase their volume in order to make them perceivable on the television speaker; others are coming in so loud that they overload the audio system and become **distorted,** or outweigh the weaker ones so much that you no longer have the proper **balance** between the two. The control that helps you to adjust the incoming sound signals to their proper **level** is usually called **pot** (short for potentiometer), or **fader.** Other names for it are attenuator and gain control.

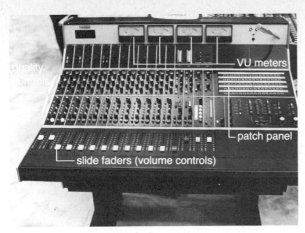

9.5 TV Audio Console

9.6 Input Module Each input module has a volume control (slide fader), various quality controls, and assignment buttons.

The pots are either rotary knobs (see 9.7) or slide faders (also called vertical faders) (see 9.8). To increase the volume, which makes the sound louder, turn the knob clockwise, or push the fader up, away from you. To decrease the volume, which makes the sound softer, turn the knob counterclockwise, or pull the fader down, toward you.

Small portable mixers have mostly rotary pots, but almost all large consoles have slide faders. The advantages of slide faders over rotary pots are as follows: (1) You can work several faders simultaneously more easily than the equal number of knobs. For example, you can rather deftly work four or five faders at the same time, whereas with rotary pots this action would constitute quite a feat. (2) You can readily *see* a volume *pattern* with faders, whereas such a visual impression of the whole pattern is not possible with rotary pots. (3) Slide faders take up less room.

Mix If you want to combine the signals from the two lavaliere mics, the remote line, and the cart, you need to feed all four inputs to a **mix bus,** or mixing channel. The mix bus combines the various sounds, that is, the signals, from the four sound sources.

Without the **mixing** capability of the board, you could record or broadcast only one input at a time.

A mix bus is like a large intersection at which the cars (signals) from several streets (inputs) come together (are mixed) and then move out again as a unit (mixed sound signal) along a wide, single street (output, or line-out).

9.7   Rotary Pot When the pot is turned counterclockwise, the volume is decreased. Turning it clockwise increases the volume.

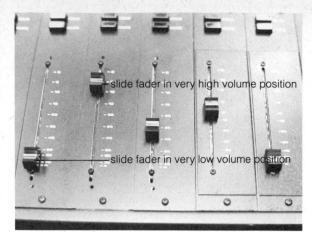

slide fader in very high volume position

slide fader in very low volume position

9.8   Slide Faders Pushing the slide faders up increases the volume; pulling them down decreases the volume.

Quality Control   Most of the small portable mixers you might use in ENG and small electronic field productions have no sound quality controls. They mix and deliver the sounds at the output the way they came in—that is, possibly with hisses and hums. Large consoles, however, have various controls that can shape the character of a sound (see 9.9). Among the most important are **equalization** and **reverberation** (reverb) controls. The *equalizer* works very much like the tone control on your home receiver. It can boost or reduce selected frequencies and thereby influence the character of the sound. For example, you can make a sound more brilliant by boosting the high frequencies, or more solid by boosting the lows, or eliminate a low-frequency hum from a lighting instrument, or the high-frequency hiss that often sneaks in during critical recording sessions. The *reverb* controls can add an increasing amount of reverberation to each of the selected inputs.

Output   The mixed signal is routed from the mix bus to the output, sometimes called "line-out." Just to make sure that the mixed signals stay within the acceptable volume limits, they are regulated by a final volume control, the *master pot,* and metered by a volume indicator.

The most common volume meter is the **VU (volume unit) meter.** As the volume varies, the needle of the VU meter oscillates back and forth along a calibrated scale (see 9.10). If the volume is so low that the needle barely moves from the extreme left, you are riding the gain (or volume) "in the mud." If the needle oscillates around the middle of the scale and peaks at, or occasionally over, the red line on the right, you are riding correct gain. If the needle swings almost exclusively in the red on the right side of the scale, and even occasionally hits the right edge of the meter, the volume is too high; you are "bending the needle," or "spilling over."

The VU meters in some audio consoles consist of light-emitting diodes (LEDs), which show up as thin colored light columns that fluctuate up and down a scale. When you ride the gain too high, the column shoots up on the scale and even changes its color (see 9.11).

Some audio consoles have additional **peak program meters** (PPMs), which measure loudness. They react more quickly to the volume "peaks" than the needle of the VU meter and show quite clearly when you are overmodulating (riding the gain too high).

Output Channels   We often classify audio consoles by the number of output channels. All of the older type television consoles had several inputs, but only one output channel, because television sound was *monophonic.* However, today even the small tele-

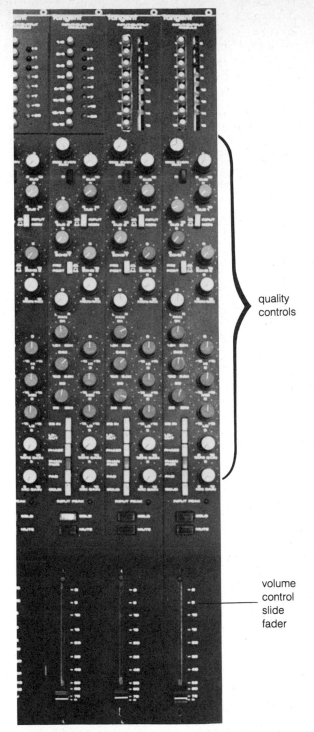

quality
controls

volume
control
slide
fader

9.9   Quality Control on Input Module The various quality controls (echo, equalization, and others) are located in rows above the slide faders.

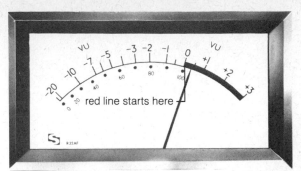

red line starts here

9.10   Analog VU Meter The VU (volume unit) meter indicates the relative sound volume, the loudness of sound that has been picked up by a microphone and amplified. The upper figures ranging from −20 to +3 are the volume units (decibels). The lower figures represent a percentage scale, ranging from 0 to 100. If the needle swings within the left section (thin line—it is black on the VU meter) from 0 to 100, the sound volume is kept within tolerable limits. If the needle "peaks" primarily in the red line section (the thick black line in this figure on the right side of the meter), the sound is amplified too much; it is too loud and subject to distortion.

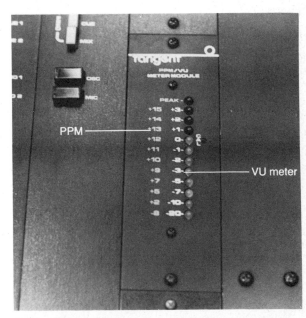

PPM

VU meter

9.11   LED VU Meter The LED VU meter indicates overmodulation (too high a volume) by lighting up in a different color.

vision boards have at least two output channels to handle *stereophonic sound,* or to be able to feed two sources (such as the transmitter and an audio-tape recorder) simultaneously with two independent mixes.

The increasing demand for quality audio has led to the increased use of *multichannel* consoles in television. Most larger television audio consoles have eight or more output channels (with eight master pots and eight VU meters), each of which can carry a separate sound signal or mix. The advantage of multiple outputs is that you can feed individual signals onto a multitrack tape recorder for post-production mixing. If, for example, you have twenty-four inputs, but only two outputs, you need to mix the various input signals down to two, which you can then feed to the left and right channels of a stereo recorder, for example. But if you want to keep the various sounds separated in order to exercise more control in the final postproduction mix, you need more outputs and, of course, a tape recorder that has an equal number of recording tracks. With eight outputs, for example, you can feed an eight-track audiotape recorder with eight individual signals or mixes, or you can take care of various different, simultaneous operations. When covering a simple rock concert, for example, you may have to provide one mix for the musicians, a separate one for the audience, and still another one for the audiotape recorder. You will be surprised how fast you run out of available inputs and outputs on even a rather big console.

Because television sound is usually monophonic, or at best stereophonic, the multichannel consoles need to be able to mix down the various signals in the proper proportions to a monophonic or stereo audio track. This is why television consoles still need one or two more final mix buses and outputs. A 24 × 12 × 2 console, for example, has twenty-four inputs, twelve mix buses (and outputs), and two additional outputs for a final stereo signal.

Some of the more elaborate consoles have *I/O circuits,* which means that each input has its own output. If, for example, you have twenty-four inputs and each one receives a different sound signal, you can send them directly to a twenty-four-track recorder

without having them go through any of the mix buses. This way, you use the console to control the volume and quality of each input, but the console does not function as a mixing device.

Monitor   Another output, which is independent of the line-out, feeds the *audio monitor* speaker. This audio monitor system allows you to listen to and adjust the sound mix before switching it to the lineout. A separate *audition* or *cue* system lets you hear a particular sound source without routing it to the mix bus. This is especially important when you want to cue up a record or an upcoming tape while on the air with the rest of the sound sources.

Computer-Assisted Consoles   Many newer consoles contain a microprocessor through which you can preset and recall some of the audio control functions. For example, you can try out a particular mix, store it in the computer's memory, try something else, and then recall the old setup within seconds.

Turntable

Professional turntables are very much like the one you probably use at home, except that the drive mechanism and the cartridge and needle are probably of somewhat higher quality than the home models. Most modern turntables have provisions to play two speeds, $33\frac{1}{3}$ rpm (revolutions per minute) and 45 rpm, as well as all record sizes. You may need a special attachment to play the wide-hole 45 rpm records. Most professional turntables can accommodate 45s without any turntable modification. The old 78 rpm records are no longer played in television stations. However, many stations keep one of their old 78 rpm turntables in working condition, just in case they need to dub off a 78 record for some special occasion. Most cartridges and needles are capable of reproducing stereo sound (see 9.12).

One of the disadvantages of using a turntable in television audio is that it needs constant attention while in operation. For example, in order to play a record, you need to cue it up, start the turntable, watch the elapsed time or the position of the tone arm, and listen to the record to make sure you catch the out-cue. With a cart, the playback of the same material requires considerably less attention. Once inserted and started, it does everything else automatically. Records are especially inconvenient if your playback sequence is computerized. This is why more and more records are duplicated, or **dubbed,** onto carts for television playback.

Audiotape Recorder (ATR)

The **reel-to-reel** audiotape recorder is generally used for recording and playing back longer pieces of audio material. For example, the background music and the sound effects, such as traffic noise, are generally premixed (prerecorded) on audiotape and then played back and mixed again with the dialogue during the actual production of a play. The audiotape recorder is also used to record material for archival purposes.

Although there are a great variety of audiotape recorders used in television production, they all operate on similar principles, and with similar controls. All professional audiotape recorders have five control buttons that regulate the tape motion, besides the switch for the various recording speeds. These buttons are (1) *play,* which moves the tape at the designated recording speed; (2) *fast forward,* which advances the tape at high speed (it deactivates the heads); (3) *stop,* which brakes the reels to a stop; (4) *reverse,* which rewinds the tape at high speed; and (5) *record,* which activates both the erase and record heads.

Many use $\frac{1}{4}$-inch magnetic **tape,** and record and play back at various speeds. The most popular recording speeds are $3\frac{3}{4}$ **ips** (inches of tape travel per second), $7\frac{1}{2}$ ips, and 15 ips. The higher the speed, the better the fidelity of the recorded material. The most *common speed* used in television operation is $7\frac{1}{2}$ ips. Some of the professional audiotape recorders do not play at $3\frac{3}{4}$ ips. If someone hands you a tape recording to play on the air, make sure that your tape recorder can play back the tape at the speed it

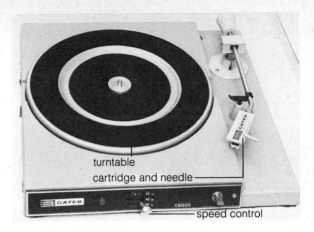

9.12 Turntable

was recorded. Except for critical music programs, the 15 ips speed is rarely used. (See 9.13.)

The tape moves from a **supply reel** to a **take-up reel** over at least three "heads": (1) the erase head, (2) the record head, and (3) the playback head. (See 9.14.) This **head assembly** arrangement is standard for all tape recorders. When the audiotape recorder is being used for recording, the *erase head* clears the portions of the tape that receive the recording (tracks) of all audio material that might have been left on the tape from a previous recording; the *record head* then puts the new audio material on the tape. When you are playing back, the *playback head* reproduces the audio material previously recorded on the tape. The erase and recording heads are not activated during playback.

When threading the tape, make sure that the magnetic (usually dull) side of the tape moves over the heads. The base (usually shiny) side does not carry any sound.

Usually, the $\frac{1}{4}$-inch tape is divided into various *tracks,* each of which can receive separate audio information. Some machines use up half of the tape for a single track; other machines use up only a quarter of the tape for a single track. (See 9.15 through 9.18.) Hence, we have **full-track, half-track,** and **quarter-track** machines. Although the quarter-track machine can play tapes that are recorded on a half-

9.13 Reel-to-Reel Tape Recorder All reel-to-reel tape recorders have five basic operational controls: (1) record, (2) play, (3) fast forward, (4) reverse, and (5) stop.

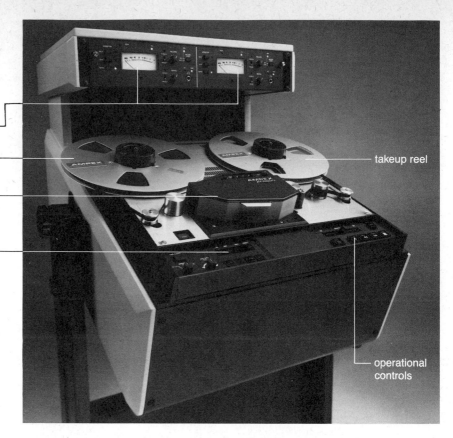

VU meters for stereo recording

supply reel

head assembly: erase, record, and playback heads

tape timer

takeup reel

operational controls

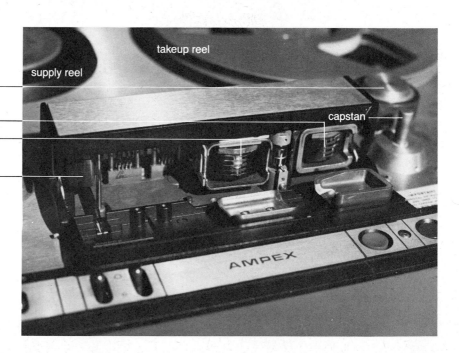

takeup reel

supply reel

pinch roller

4-track playback head

4-track record head ($\frac{1}{2}$-inch audiotape)

erase head

capstan

AMPEX

9.14 Head Assembly of Reel-to-Reel Recorder The head assembly consists of an erase head, a record head, and a playback head.

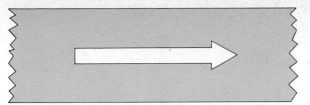

9.15 Full-Track Monophonic System In a full-track monophonic system, the recording head puts the audio signal on the full width of the tape.

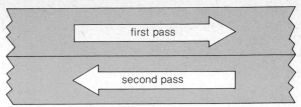

9.16 Half-Track Monophonic, or Monaural, System In monophonic, or monaural (one-channel), recording, the recording head puts audio information on half the tape. When the tape is reversed—that is, if after the first complete pass of the tape you use the full takeup reel as supply reel and thread the tape again for another pass—the other half of the tape receives new audio information.

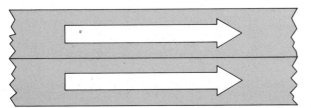

9.17 Half-Track Stereo System In a tape recorder equipped for stereophonic recording, both tracks receive audio information on the first pass. One half carries the audio information of the first channel (left), the other half carries the audio information of the second channel (right). Because both halves of the tape are already taken up, the tape cannot be reversed for a second pass. Otherwise, you erase the first recording.

9.18 Quarter-Track Stereo System Most stereophonic audiotape recorders record and play back on quarter-tracks, or four-tracks. Two tracks (1 and 3) are used for the two channels on one pass, and two further tracks (2 and 4) on the reverse pass.

track machine, quarter-track tapes with separate audio information on all four tracks cannot be reproduced on a half-track machine.

Do not confuse quarter-track machines with four-track machines. On a quarter-track machine, you can play only two tracks at a time in one direction. In order to play the other two tracks, you need to rewind the tape and use the other side of the reel. With a four-track machine, however, you can play all four tracks simultaneously (see 9.19).

Some of the audio production rooms in large stations use multitrack recorders that use wider tape formats ($\frac{1}{2}$-inch, 1-inch, and 2-inch) to accommodate the multiple tracks (up to thirty-two tracks). (See 9.20.) High-quality four-track machines use $\frac{1}{2}$-inch tape; eight-track machines use 1-inch tape. The 2-inch tape is used for sixteen or more tracks. Some

digital recorders can put thirty-two tracks on a 1-inch tape without danger of "*crosstalk*"—one track bleeding into the other. Such multitrack machines make sense only if you regularly produce complex audio tracks, such as music or a dramatic series. Otherwise, the $\frac{1}{4}$-inch machines suffice.

For EFP, high-quality audiotape recorders are available (see 9.21). You may use them to record continuous background sounds, or you may even record the dialogue on separate tracks, provided you have a synchronizer for accurate **lip-sync** in postproduction (see p. 252).

When you play back audiotape, quickly check the following items: (1) Tape speed. What was the recording speed? Can you play back at the recording speed (some home recorders may record at speeds that are too slow for your machine)? (2) Tracks. Is

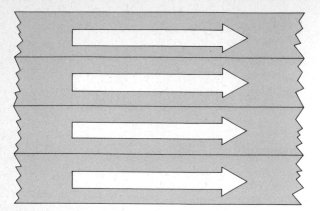

9.19　Four-Track System In a four-track system all four tracks are used in one pass. Each of the tracks represents a separate channel.

9.21　Nagra 4.2 Portable Audiotape Recorder The Nagra tape recorder is battery powered and extremely compact. It uses a full-track monophonic recording system with $\frac{1}{4}$-inch tape.

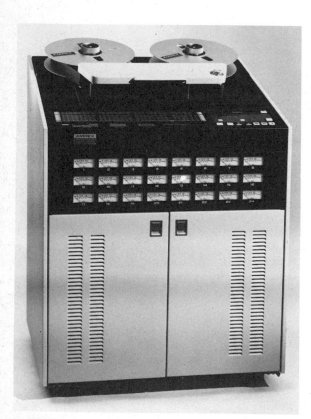

9.20　Multitrack Audiotape Recorder A multitrack tape recorder is many tape recorders in one. Each track has its own erase, recording, and playback head as well as its own VU meter. This multitrack recorder puts twenty-four tracks on 2-inch audiotape.

it a half-track or quarter-track recording? Is it mono or stereo? Do all tracks contain audio information? (3) Length of recording. For example, is the recording of sound effects long enough for the scene?

Cartridge and Cassette Machines

A great proportion of audio playback consists of short announcements, musical bridges, news inserts, and other types of brief informational material that accompanies slides or brief videotape inserts. The most efficient method for playing such short audio material is the **tape cartridge** system. Tape cartridge playback units can hold and play back several (often ten or more) cartridges, or **carts,** individually or simultaneously. All you do is plug in a cartridge (which contains an endless tape loop that rewinds itself as it is played back) and press the button of the cartridge you want to play back. The cartridge, which cues itself automatically through a cue tone on the audiotape, plays back the tape immediately without annoying *wows* (initial sound distortion before the record or tape is up to speed) or pauses. By removing the auto cue, you have an endless loop that you can use for sound effects. (See 9.22 and 9.23.)

There are special audio recorders that record the audio information directly onto cartridges. You

9.22 Three-Unit Cartridge Machine The cartridge machine allows instantaneous start and cues the next program segment automatically.

9.23 Audio Cartridge Audio cartridges use $\frac{1}{4}$-inch magnetic tape (like that used for reel-to-reel recorders). The tape forms a continuous loop.

can, of course, transfer information onto cartridges from any other audio recording.

Audio cartridge systems are extremely reliable and easy to operate. The only thing to watch in using an audio cartridge is to let it recue itself before you punch the button again for a possible replay or before ejecting it from the playback machine.

Cartridges come in different lengths, from 10 seconds to somewhat over 10 minutes. Make sure that you have a large enough cartridge to accommodate all your material. On the other hand, if you need only a 5-second **signature** (theme music) for a station break, do not waste a 10-minute cartridge on it.

The **cassette tape** system works on a different principle. Whereas a cartridge has only one reel, with the tape forming an endless loop, a tape cassette has *two* small *reels,* one of which acts as the supply reel, the other as the takeup reel (see 9.24). The advantages of the cassette over the cartridge are that (1) the cassette can hold more information (standard cassettes play up to 90 minutes, with special cassettes up to 180 minutes) and (2) the cassette produces higher quality sound, especially if it is of the newer metal-particle coated variety. Cassettes are, therefore, becoming more and more popular in television operations that concentrate on music or other high-quality audio productions.

9.24 Audio Cassette The tape cassette has two small reels—a supply reel and a takeup reel—and uses $\frac{1}{8}$-inch audiotape. The cassette can hold much more information than the cartridge. A cassette's playtime is usually up to 90 minutes.

Many cartridge and some cassette systems are interfaced (coupled) with a microprocessor through which the operation can be largely automated. For example, you can program a whole sequence of short announcements for several station breaks and have the computer cue, start, put on the air, and recue each cartridge in a programmed sequence. However, you should realize that the computer does

9.25 Audio Synchronizer The audio synchronizer uses one of the audio tracks (such as the second track of a stereo recorder) for the SMPTE time code. This code marks every thirtieth of a second, which enables the audiotape to be synchronized with the frames of the videotape.

of the audiotape. For example, you can use the left channel of a stereo recorder for the sound portion, and the right channel for the time code. By reading the time code on the audiotapes and/or videotapes, the synchronizer can keep all machines running at exactly the same speed, locate specific "addresses," and respond to the programmed commands (such as start, stop, edit) at these points.

OPERATIONAL FACTORS

We will now discuss some of the more important operational control factors. They include (1) volume control, (2) sequence control, and (3) mixing and sound quality control.

Volume Control

Earlier in this chapter we described the VU meter and its functions. Assuming that you now have some idea of riding gain, we will mention a few more practical aspects of volume control, such as taking a level, using a control tone, preventing overmodulation, and using the automatic gain control (AGC).

Taking a Level Except when literally running after a story during an ENG assignment, you should take a level before starting your videotape recording. Ask the talent to talk long enough so that you can adjust the volume to fluctuate within the accepted limits (not riding in the mud and not bending the needle). An experienced performer will then stay within this volume range even in subsequent takes. Unfortunately, when asked to give a level, most performers consider this an intrusion on their concentration and simply count rapidly to three or four. Then, when they are on the air, their voice rises to the occasion—and also in volume. Therefore, be prepared for this sudden volume change. Really experienced performers give a few of the opening sentences, in about as loud a voice as they will use when on the air. If you are in the field and do not have a chance to ride gain during the videotaping, turn down the pot just a bit from where you had it while

not program itself. You still have to put the information on the carts, put the carts in the right slots, and then give the computer the necessary instructions as to what to roll at which time. Such programming is time consuming, but once in place, even a complicated sequence of short announcements gets on the air at exactly the right time.

Audio Synchronizer

The **audio synchronizer** can (1) run two or more audiotape recorders or an audiotape recorder and a videotape recorder in sync, (2) mark and transfer automatically certain program segments from one audiotape to another, (3) transfer some sound portions from audiotape to videotape at a specific programmed spot, and (4) interact with the video switcher for some special audio-video effects (see 9.25).

To perform all these miracles, the audio synchronizer uses the *SMPTE time code* (see p. 314), which divides the audiotape into imaginary "frames." These frames correspond with those of the videotape and provide a mutual "time address" as specified by hours, minutes, seconds, and frames (30 frames make up 1 second). The time code is usually taken from the videotape, or supplied by a time code generator and put on one of the unused tracks

taking a level. This way you can be pretty sure not to overmodulate once on the air.

Using a Control Tone   Most audio control boards, including the small portable mixers, can generate a control tone. By watching the VU meter, you can adjust the pot so that the tone has exactly the maximum allowable volume, with the needle sitting rather steadily at the beginning of the red line (zero VU on the upper scale, and 100 on the lower). Record this test tone for a minimum of 10 seconds at the beginning of the tape, preferably with the color bars.

Preventing Overmodulation   You may have noticed that during music recordings, the audio engineer lets the needle jump occasionally into the red zone. This is not bad, because brief volume peaks do not lead to sound distortion. However, when recording speech, you should try to keep the needle from peaking into the red zone. When overmodulating speech (riding the gain consistently at too high a level), you end up not with a recording that is slightly too loud, but with *distorted* sound. Although it is relatively easy to boost sound that was recorded at a low level (even at the risk of amplifying some of the noise with the low-level sounds), it is very difficult and often impossible to fix distorted sound in postproduction. Be especially conscious of this problem when on ENG or EFP assignments during which you may have little time to watch the sound levels. Just to play it safe, turn down the pot somewhat after having taken a level.

However, when combining speech with music, such as in the opening of a newscast, you need to ride the music *at a lower level* than the voice (usually at 80 percent maximum, or −2 on the lower scale). The reason for this mix is that we perceive *sustained* sounds, such as music, as louder than unsustained sounds, such as speech. Also, one audio portion may sound louder than another simply because it is *structured* differently, not because it shows a higher volume on the VU meter. For example, a commercial during which the announcer speaks fast and with great urgency may *feel* louder than the preceding program material, which progressed in a much quieter rhythm, though at the same volume as the commercial. Such psychological loudness does

not show up on the VU meter. You need to *listen* in order to decide the appropriate volume level. We will talk more about mixing various sounds later in this chapter.

Using the Automatic Gain Control   If you are on an ENG assignment and cannot watch the VU meter on the VTR, switch on the **AGC** *(automatic gain control)*. The AGC boosts low sounds and reduces high-volume sounds so that they conform to the tolerable volume range. However, in trying to please, the AGC does not discriminate between wanted and unwanted sounds. It faithfully boosts the noise of the faraway truck or overhead jet, the coughing of a crew member, or even the noise of the "silences" when the field reporter is pausing to think of something clever to say—as much as the important, but faint utterings of a tired eyewitness. Whenever possible, therefore—but especially when in noisy surroundings—switch off the AGC, take a level, and hope for the best.

Sequence Control

Sequence control simply means *when to do what*. In the day-to-day studio operation, you are mostly concerned with the proper *playback sequence* of recorded material. The beginning of a simple newscast requires you to take care of the live teaser (the announcing of all the gruesome stories yet to come), the sound of the commercials and recorded announcements, the newscast theme, and the first anchorperson—all within less than a minute. Later in the newscast, you need to pay close attention to the alternating audio of the two newscasters, the videotape inserts, the commercials, the remote feeds, and the *bumpers*. (Bumpers are the brief material separating—or absorbing the shock of—news stories and commercials or other non-news material.) Your sequencing skills are most severely challenged during the opening of the newscast, the various breaks, and the closing. There you may have to switch from a live mic to a cart, to another cart, to still another cart, to the sound on videotape, to another videotape sound track, to still another cart over a slide, and back to one of the newscasters in the studio.

The log alone may not be enough information for you to follow the exact audio sequence. If it is not provided by the news department, you should make a list of the *sequence of the various audio sources.* Such a list is actually more helpful than a whole news script, because you can more easily follow the audio operations required.

When using computer-assisted audio playback devices (such as a programmed cart sequence), make sure that you have the various audio sources (carts and videotapes) in the right order. If you use more cassettes than you can load at one time, stack them so that the next to be used is on top of the pile.

Mixing and Sound Quality Control

Mixing means combining sounds. In mixing, you are concerned not so much with the sequence of the various sounds, but with how to *balance* the various simultaneous sounds. Although the basic principles of sound mixing are the same regardless of where you do it and what equipment you have available, there are some important differences between mixing in the *field* and in the *studio,* and between *simultaneous* and *postproduction* mixing.

Field Mixing   When doing ENG, you usually do not need a special mixer. As discussed before, you have the external mic plugged into one of the VTR audio inputs, and the camera shotgun mic plugged into the other audio input. However, there are always assignments where you have to control more audio sources than the two microphones. Even a simple tennis game may require the control of seven inputs: one desk mic for the commentator, one omnidirectional mic for the spectators, two shotgun mics at each end pointing toward the net, two additional shotgun mics close to the net pointing toward the players, and a directional stand mic for the judge. In this case, you need a portable mixer.

The mixing itself is fairly simple. Once you have set the levels for each input, you probably need to ride gain only for the announcer's mic and the mic of the audience during the game. Some announcers get very loud when excited, or speak with an unreasonably low voice during especially tense moments.

Also, you may want to bring up (increase the gain of) the audience mic to emphasize an especially fine play.

Although in an emergency you could probably pick up most of the sounds of the tennis by pointing a shotgun mic to the various areas, the multiple mic setup and the portable mixer afford you the necessary *control.*

Here are a few guidelines for basic ENG/EFP mixing:

1.   Even if you have only a few inputs, label each one with what it controls, such as announcer's mic, audience mic, and so forth.

2.   Double-check all inputs from wireless microphone systems. For some reason, they have a habit of malfunctioning just before the start of the event.

3.   Always put a test tone at zero VU (100 percent) on the videotape.

4.   Try to separate the inputs as much as possible. If you record for postproduction, try to put distinctly different sound sources on separate audio tracks—such as the announcer's voice on one of the tracks of the videotape, the environmental sounds (audience, players hitting the balls) on the other. This way, it will be easier for you in the sweetening session to balance the announcer's voice with the background sounds.

5.   It is usually simpler to do complicated and subtle mixing in the studio rather than in the field. This does not mean that you should not try to filter out as much unwanted sound as possible during the on-location pickup. But save the more subtle mixing and quality control until you are back in the audio production room.

6.   If you do a complicated mix in the field, protect yourself by feeding it not only to the VTR machine, but to a separate audiotape recorder as well for probable remixing in postproduction.

Studio Mixing   When in the studio, you are confronted with several types of mixing. You may, for example, have to do a *"live" mix* during the recording of a soap opera. This means that you mix the dialogue and all sound effects and record them on videotape simultaneously with the picture portion.

Let's take a simple scene from a television drama. Two people, a man and a woman, are sitting on the porch of their small country home. It is late evening. The telephone rings just as a car drives up. Because this scene happens in the studio, many of the actions are suggested by sound effects only. Assuming that you have not premixed any of the necessary sound effects, you will be quite busy mixing and balancing the various sounds so that, in combination with the video, the sound helps to convey the intended message.

What audio inputs do you need? First, the two people on the porch. Because it is a realistic scene, the microphones must be out of camera range. For the porch, we use a boom mic. Second, for the woman answering the phone off camera inside, we can use a stand mic or a small boom. We use the same mic for the mechanical ring. We do not want to use a sound effect for the ring, because you as the audio console operator cannot see just when she is picking up the phone. Third, we need sound effects to help (with the lighting, of course) establish the time, late evening, and the locale (country). Most likely you will use cricket sounds (night and country), and an occasional dog barking in the distance. Perhaps you can think of more original sound effects for the establishing of time and place, but do not be afraid to use the conventional. After all, these sounds do exist and they are easily recognized by the viewer. They have become conventional because they work.

Then you need the sound effect of a car driving up. Because the driveway of the old country home is probably not paved, the sound of the car approaching should include some tires-on-gravel effects.

So you have two microphone inputs, the boom and the stand mic near the off-camera telephone. The crickets chirp throughout the outdoor part of the scene, which means that you need reel-to-reel or cassette tape machines for the playback of this sound effect. Because the dogs bark only occasionally, you can put the bark on a cartridge. If possible at all, you should prerecord the continuous background sounds of the crickets and the occasional

dog barks on a single quarter-inch tape or a cassette. Because the car driving up is a relatively short affair, you can put this sound effect on a second tape cartridge. Remember we should hear the car off in the distance for some time before it gets to the driveway. We tend to hear better at night than in daytime, mainly because of the absence of the usual ambient daytime noises. So, record on your cartridge not just the sounds of the car driving into the driveway, but also the sounds of a gradually approaching car.

For dramatic emphasis, the director wants background music throughout the scene up to the ring of the telephone. The music can also go on a reel-to-reel or cassette recorder for continuous playback.

If you have premixed the two background sounds, you have to control simultaneously two microphones (boom and stand mics), the audiotape with the cricket and dog-barking sounds, the cartridge with the car approaching, and the tape or cassette with the background music. If you have not premixed the dogs barking—so that you can make the barking louder when the car approaches the house—you need another, separate cartridge channel for the bark.

A mere look at the single VU meter no longer suffices to indicate proper volume for this complex mixing job. What you now need most of all is *good ears*. The VU meter may indicate a perfectly acceptable overall level, but it does *not tell* you anything about *how well you balanced* the various sound sources. Another important point should become quite apparent. You need to know very intimately the total play, the director's concept of it, its development, climaxes, dramatic structure, and progression. You are now no longer a "board operator"; you have become an *artist*.

Besides studio mixing, there are the following additional audio control activities: (1) multiple feeds, (2) foldback, (3) mix-minus, (4) lip-sync, and (5) postproduction mixing.

Multiple Feeds Sometimes, a complex audio assignment, such as a special one-hour show with a famous rock-and-roll group, may require *multiple feeds*. For example, when doing audio for a rock concert, you may have to feed simultaneously a stereo mix for the musicians, another stereo mix for the local FM station, and a third, monophonic mix for the videotape recorder. Obviously, you provide such multiple mixes only if you have a multichannel board.

Foldback   This is the routing of sound to headphones so that the musicians or singers can hear themselves on headsets. The foldback most often required is playing back the singer's voice on the singer's headset channel.

Mix-minus   In another type of multiple feed, you send into the studio a complete mix (usually the band or orchestra), minus, however, the sound generated in the studio. This type of foldback is sometimes called **mix-minus.** For example, in order to simplify production and to save money, singers are often asked to sing with a prerecorded orchestra rather than doing it all live. In this case, the orchestra mix is sent into the studio or onto the stage and mixed again with the live voice of the singer for the final, line-out audio. Again, you need an audio console with at least two output channels: one for the mix-minus feed, the other for the complete mix that goes on the air or on videotape.

Lip-sync   Lip-sync is a technique similar to mix-minus, except that the singer *pretends* to sing, but does not actually do so. He or she simply synchronizes lip movement with the sound of the complete recording. Just make sure that the singer can hear the playback. If there are slight synchronization problems for some reason, stay away from close-ups.

Postproduction Mixing   The most complex mixing takes place in the postproduction and sweetening sessions. This is where the big audio consoles and multitrack tape recorders, the synchronizers, and other computer-controlled equipment come into play. Obviously, complex postproduction mixing should be left to the audio expert. But you should at least familiarize yourself with some of the possibilities and problems in audio postproduction.

The more the various sounds were isolated and put on separate tracks during the recording, the easier it is now to manipulate them in the final **mix-down** to the single or stereo track on the videotape. You could, for example, try various ways of mixing them without influencing the original recording. If you do not like one mix, simply try another. Some of the computer-assisted consoles even remember the mixes for you.

The *audio synchronizer* makes it possible to record and play back pictures on the videotape and sound on a separate audiotape as though pictures and sound were on a single videotape. This type of **double system** recording (a term borrowed from film) adds to the flexibility of television sound production. For example, you can use a high-quality multitrack audiotape recorder and run it in sync with the videotape, without having first to dub the sound onto the videotape. Or you can run two or more audiotape recorders in sync with the videotape, using the audiotapes like live inputs for a postproduction mix of sound effects, for example.

With a computer-assisted audio console and the audio synchronizer, you can do some of the sweetening with a minimum of time and effort. Let's assume that you want to improve the audio perspective of a scene by providing all close-ups with more sound presence. All you need to do is identify the time code address for the beginning and end of each close-up, preset the quality controls on the audio board for the desired level of sound presence, and enter this information into the console computer. The computer then automatically finds each close-up, "sweetens" the sound for the given length of each close-up, and advances to the next. However, do not be misled into believing that the computer and the audio synchronizer can do everything for you. The key to good television audio still lies in an optimal original sound pickup.

Here are some operational routines that may help you with relatively simple mixing assignments:

1.   Check out all pots and see whether they really control intended sources. Check all your patching. Put a piece of masking tape along the bottom of the console and label each sound source, such as announcer, cart 1, cart 2, VTR 4, and so forth. If there are several mics in proximity to one another, have the floor manager gently scratch the surface of the mics. The scratch is then picked up by the "on-mic" only. In any case, do not blow into the mics. Do not

put the mics on the floor. They do not like being stepped on and their magnetic elements attract dust. If you have remote inputs, double- and triple-check each input and your patching. Make sure you actually receive a signal from the remote line before switching to the remote for the actual pickup.

2.   Check all input levels and the monitor level. Put a zero VU test tone on the VTR and/or the audiotape.

3.   Make sure that the assignment switches route the various sound inputs to the desired mix buses. The VU meter tells you which source is going where.

4.   Do a test recording to see whether the outputs feed the intended recorders (VTR and audiotape recorders).

5.   Listen for hisses and hums that may have crept somehow into the system. One of the most common causes of hums is the studio lighting. A mic cable running parallel with a light power cable can cause a lot of audio interference.

6.   Check the studio speaker system for the proper level and be aware of possible **feedback** (the studio speaker feeding the sound back into the live studio mics, causing a high squeal).

7.   When you do a "live" mix, as in the example of the play, watch the script and the line monitor. Anticipate the director's cues. Do not panic if you hear some accidental noise, such as a door slamming shut. Although this may sound to you like irreparable damage, most people at home will not even be aware of it. This is not an invitation to sloppy sound control, but an appeal to common sense.

Controlling Sound Quality   This aspect of audio control is probably the most difficult. Not only do you need to be thoroughly familiar with the various types of signal processing equipment (such as equalizers, echo controls, filters), but you also need a trained ear.

As with the volume control in mixing, you need to be careful how you use these quality controls. If there is an obvious hum or hiss that you can filter out, do so by all means. But do not try to adjust the quality of each input before you have done at least a preliminary mix. For example, you may listen to

the sound effect of a police siren and decide that it sounds much too thin. When mixed with the traffic sounds, the thin and piercing siren may just turn out to be the perfect vehicle for communicating mounting tension.

Before making any final quality judgments, listen to the audiotrack in *relation to the video*. An audio mix that by itself sounds warm and rich may well lose these qualities when juxtaposed with a cool, tense video scene.

As in all other aspects of television production, the communication goal and your aesthetic sensitivity, not the availability and production capacity of the equipment, ought to determine what you want the audience to hear.

MAIN POINTS

1.   The audio area of a television station includes the basic audio control booth, which is used for the sound control of daily broadcasts, and, in some larger stations, the audio production room, which is used for audio control in postproduction.

2.   The major items of audio equipment are (1) patch panel or patchbay, (2) audio console, (3) turntable, (4) audiotape recorder (ATR), and (5) cartridge and cassette machines.

3.   A patch panel connects and routes various pieces of audio equipment and their audio signals. Just as individual lighting instruments can be patched into any one of the dimmers, audio inputs can be patched to individual volume controls on the audio console in any order.

4.   Audio consoles perform five major functions: (1) input—select, preamplify, and control the volume of the various incoming signals; (2) mix—combine and balance two or more incoming signals; (3) quality control—manipulate the sound characteristics; (4) output—route the combined signal to a specific output; and (5) monitor—route the output to a speaker so that the sounds can be heard independent of the line-out signal.

5.   Turntables are used to play records. Most television operations dub records onto carts or cassettes for more convenient playback.

6.   Reel-to-reel audiotape recorders are generally used for recording or playing back longer pieces of audio material. For most productions, $\frac{1}{4}$-inch magnetic tape is used. The most common ATRs use full-track and half-track monophonic, and half-track and quarter-track stereo systems. Multitrack recorders are used for more complicated postproduction work.

7.   An audio cartridge system facilitates the playback of brief program material. It allows instantaneous start and cues up the next program segment automatically. The audio cartridge uses $\frac{1}{4}$-inch magnetic tape, which forms a continuous loop.

8.   The audio cassette system can record and play back longer program material. The tape cassette contains a small supply and takeup reel for the $\frac{1}{8}$-inch tape.

9.   An audio synchronizer can run two or more audiotape recorders, or an audio and videotape recorder in sync; mark and automatically transfer certain program segments from one audiotape to another; transfer sound portions from audiotape to videotape at a specific spot; and interact with the video switcher for special audio-video effects.

10.   The operational factors include (1) volume control, (2) sequence control, and (3) mixing and quality control. Volume control means riding gain at an optimum level. Sequence refers to the proper playback sequence of recorded material. Mixing and quality control means how to combine sounds and how to manipulate the sound characteristics (piercing, rich sounds, and so on).

New computer developments in audio control allow us to produce a less distorted sound. However, such increased technical control does not diminish the need for a "good ear" and a strong sense of aesthetic judgment.

Four more areas in the field of audio need some attention. They are (1) analog and digital sound recording and control, (2) time compression and expansion, (3) intercommunication systems, and (4) aesthetic factors.

ANALOG AND DIGITAL SOUND RECORDING AND CONTROL

When involved in audio recording, even for television, you will undoubtedly hear much discussion about the advantages and disadvantages of analog versus digital recording. Although this subject deserves the attention it commands, we can only touch upon some of the major aspects in this context.

Analog System

As you remember from earlier chapters, an *analog signal* fluctuates exactly like the original stimulus (in our case, variations in sound) over its entire range. The electrical sound signal is *analogous* to the actual sound. The problem with **analog sound recording** systems is that their electronic circuits produce noise and then add it to every **generation.** When sounds are passed through the circuits time after time, as in successive dubbings during a mix-down, the original noise is not only dragged along, but added to the new noise the system inevitably generates. This process is similar to making Xerox copies: Each successive copy distorts the previous distortion. Equipment is available to keep these distortions to a minimum (for example, the well-known Dolby circuits and low-noise amplifiers), but even they cannot eliminate the additive noise process.

Digital System

In a **digital sound recording** system the original stimulus is translated into many computer-type, on-off pulses (binary digits), which are represented by zeros and ones. Hence, we deal no longer with varying voltages of a signal, but with numbers.

When you are using the digital system in recording, the digital codes—the bits—as represented by numbers can be amplified, modified, and re-recorded over and over again *without adding* the noise inevitably generated by the electronic circuits to the original signal (the original sound recording). Because the original signal has a specific code, which is numerically different from all others, it passes through the circuits as if they were transparent, regardless of how many times you re-record the original signal. This is why experts talk about the *transparency* of digital equipment. Occasionally, some of the bits representing the signal are lost, but they can be replaced by the system. The same principle applies to digital video recording (see Chapter 10).

Another big advantage of digital systems in audio production is the *control* they afford in the manipulation of the equipment and the sound itself, and their ability to interface (interconnect) with various other digital equipment in the television system.

TIME COMPRESSION AND EXPANSION

Time compression and expansion means that you can replay recorded video faster or slower without altering the original pitch of the audio. You undoubtedly have heard how normal speech sounds become chipmunk-like gibberish when a tape runs too fast, or slow and forced grunts when the tape runs too slow. Such pitch distortions can be easily corrected with a **time compressor.** The time compressor is extensively used in adjusting films and videotape to existing log time slots, without editing. If, for example, you have a commercial that runs for 31 seconds, and the log shows that you have only 28 seconds available to play it, you can pro gram the time compressor so that it plays the commercial at a slightly accelerated speed to make it fit the shorter time slot. There is no need now to edit out a few seconds of the already tightly structured commercial. Because the time compressor maintains the original pitch while making the commercial run faster, we are generally unaware of the speedup or slowdown

(in case the commercial is somewhat short) of the video portion.

One of the recurring problems in television operations is to make movies fit the allotted time slots. Even after editing for television, they always seem two or three minutes too long. With the time compressor, you can now speed up the movie just enough to make it fit the log time without the need for additional cutting.

INTERCOMMUNICATION SYSTEMS

The intercommunication system is the lifeline in television operation. It provides voice communication among all production and engineering personnel involved in a production. With a functioning intercom, the director, for example, can give cues to many members of the production team, triggering a variety of actions. With the increased ENG/EFP activities, the communication among the team working at a remote location and between them and the studio has put increased demands on the intercom system. We will, therefore, discuss (1) the studio intercom systems and (2) the field intercom systems.

Studio Intercom Systems

Most studios have a variety of intercom systems, each serving a specific communication task. The most common are (1) the P.L. system, (2) the I.F.B. system, and (3) the S.A. system.

The P.L. System   In most small stations, the *telephone intercommunication,* or *P.L. (private or phone line),* system is used. All production and engineering personnel

---

Analog Sound Recording   Audio recording system in which the electrical sound signal fluctuates exactly like the original sound stimulus over its entire range.

Digital Sound Recording   Audio recording system that translates original sound stimuli into many computer-type, on-off pulses. Compared to analog sound recording, this system has a better signal-to-noise ratio.

Double-Muff Headset   Special earphones used when working close to a high-volume sound source, such as a rock band, to keep out most of the environmental sounds.

Generation   The number of dubs away from the master tape. A first-generation dub is struck directly from the master tape.

Perspective   Sound perspective: far sound must go with far picture, close sound with close picture.

S.A.   Studio Address system. *See* Studio Talkback.

Studio Talkback   A public address loudspeaker system from the control room to the studio. Also called S.A. (studio address) or P.A. (public address) system.

Time Compressor   Instrument that allows a recorded videotape to be replayed faster or slower without altering the original pitch of the audio.

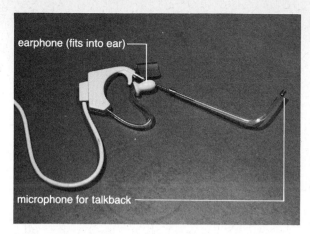

earphone (fits into ear)

microphone for talkback

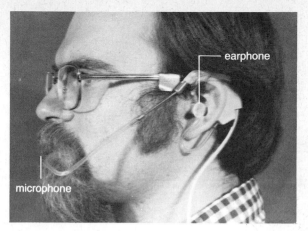

earphone

microphone

9.26   P.L. Headset The most vital link in television production is the intercommunication system. All production and engineering personnel who need to be in voice contact wear telephone headsets with a small earphone and a microphone for talkback.

who need to be in voice contact with one another wear standard telephone headsets with one small earphone and a small microphone for talkback. (See 9.26.) Each major production area has one or several intercom outlets for plugging in the headsets. For example, each camera generally has two intercom outlets: one for the camera operator, and the other for the floor manager or another member of the floor crew. If possible, though, the members of the floor crew should avoid connecting their headsets to the camera; it not only limits their operation radius but also interferes with the camera's flexibility. Usually, the floor personnel connect their headsets to separate intercom wall outlets through long, flexible, lightweight cables. But difficulties can arise with this arrangement, too, if the cable gets in the way of moving cameras and microphone booms or becomes tangled up in one of the many pieces of scenery on the studio floor.

Larger studios, therefore, employ a *wireless intercom system* for the floor personnel. They wear a small earplug, instead of the cumbersome headset, and carry a small pocket receiver that picks up signals sent into the studio by a transmitter. Unfortunately, the floor personnel cannot talk back to the control room with this system. At least the floor manager, who definitely needs two-way communication, should wear a talkback telephone headset.

Sometimes it is necessary to supply program sound and control-room signals simultaneously to such production personnel as the microphone boom operator

or studio musicians (usually the band or orchestra leader) who have to gear their actions to both the program sound and the director's cues. In this case, you can use a **double headset** in which one of the two earphones carries the intercommunication signals and the other the program sound. Although you may not need this split-intercom system very often, it should nevertheless be available to you.

Sometimes, when you work close to a high-volume sound source, such as a rock band, you may need a **double-muff headset,** which keeps out most of the environmental sounds. Also, the mic in such headsets does not transmit the surrounding noise. (See 9.27.)

In most television operations, production and engineering crews use the same intercommunication channel, which means that everybody can be heard by everybody else. Most intercom systems, however, have provisions for separating the lines for different functions. For example, while the technical director confers with the video engineer on one intercom channel, the director may, at the same time, give instructions to the floor crew. More often, the separate channels are used to switch into or out of the intercom systems of other studios or remote production centers.

The I.F.B. System   In shows with highly flexible formats or where important program changes are likely to occur, such as in newscasts or special events telecasts, a special intercommunication system is used to connect the control room (director, producer) directly with the

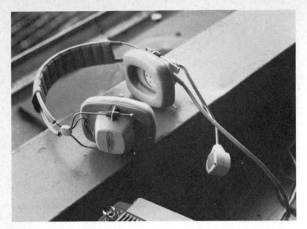

9.27 Double-Muff Headset The double-muff headset is used in an especially noisy environment. Sportscasters in the field always wear a double-muff headset.

stages of a rehearsal, needs to talk to everybody in the studio at once. Also, if most of the personnel happen to be off the intercom system, as is frequently the case during a short break, the director can use the talkback system to call them back to work.

Considering the importance of the intercommunication system, you should include it in routine program facilities checks. If you discover faulty headsets or an imperfect intercom line, report it to the maintenance crew and have it fixed. A faulty intercom can be more detrimental to a production than a defective camera.

Field Intercom Systems

Of the great variety of available intercom systems, these six fulfill most field communication requirements: (1) wireless paging system, (2) program sound receiver, (3) walkie-talkie, (4) wireless intercom system, (5) P.L. system, and (6) telephone.

Wireless Paging System Long used by doctors who need to be contacted when away from a telephone, the wireless paging system is a relatively simple and efficient means to contact reporters and ENG crew members in the field. The system consists of a centrally located transmitter and small receivers of the size of a pocket calculator, which can be clipped to the belt, hip pocket, or any other piece of clothing. You can dial any number of the small receivers within a radius of about 50 miles and cause them to beep, or to give short messages. The "beep" signals the person in the field to look for the nearest phone and call in. The more elaborate pager tells you whom to call and/or why.

Program Sound Receiver When in the field, you often need to hear the audio portions of your station's telecast, in order to pick up important cues. The program sound receiver, which looks like a pager, lets you hear the sound portion of the telecast in progress. Some stations even transmit I.F.B. cues with the program audio. Thus, the field reporter can hear the director's countdown for a videotape insert, or "stretch" or "wrap" (wrap up—finish—the commentary) cues. Of course, the television home receivers do not "read" such I.F.B. information.

Walkie-Talkie Hand-held two-way radios, called walkie-talkies, are one of the most flexible devices for communication among production crews working in the field. Walkie-talkies provide good two-way voice communication. The advantage is that they can be interfaced with other communication systems, such as

performers. This system is called the **I.F.B., interrupted feedback system.** Here the performer wears a small earpiece that carries the program sound unless the director, or any other member of the production team connected with the system, interrupts the program sound with special instructions. For example, the field reporter in Washington who is describing on camera the details of the arrival of foreign dignitaries hears himself or herself until the director cuts in and says to "throw it back to New York"—that is, tell the viewers that the program is returning to the origination center in New York. But while the director is giving these instructions, the viewer still hears the field reporter's description of the event. Relaying such messages through an off-camera floor manager would be much too slow and inaccurate in as tight a show as a live special events telecast. Needless to say, such a system works only with a highly experienced announcer and director. There are numerous occasions when the interrupted feedback system has unfortunately acted also as a performer interrupt device because the inexperienced performer could no longer maintain his or her commentary while listening to the director's instructions.

The S.A. System The **studio address (S.A.)** or **studio talkback** system is used by the control-room personnel, principally the director, to give special instructions to people in the studio not connected with the telephone intercom system. The talkback system is a great aid to the director, who, especially in the beginning

regular two-way radios, thus extending the inter-communication potential. Walkie-talkies operate on at least two separate channels. You can switch from the "common channel" (which connects the whole production team) to a second channel for talking with specific crew members only. For example, while you are using the common channel to give the field reporter some instructions, the T.D. may use this opportunity to give technical instructions to the camera operators.

The only real problem with using walkie-talkies during a production is that you have no control over when they start "talking." People who work close to a hot mic should, therefore, use extension earphones rather than the built-in loudspeaker. Some walkie-talkies accept a full headset (with earphones and mic), so that you can use the walkie-talkie like a regular P.L. system.

Wireless Intercom System   Although the paging systems and walkie-talkies are wireless systems, *wireless intercom* usually refers to more elaborate setups, including two-way radios and wireless headsets. The headsets have a small built-in transmitter that operates on several channels and is effective up to a half mile away.

P.L. System   If you use independent ENG cameras for a multiple-camera production in the field, you do not have camera cables through which to send your communications. A special P.L. system must, therefore, be set up. Most such systems are battery-powered, can feed up to thirty headsets on at least two channels, and can operate effectively over several miles of cable. The advantage of such wired systems is that, unlike the wireless, they are not affected by bad weather, large buildings, or nearby radio transmissions. Also, you can interconnect them readily with the regular camera P.L. systems, or with the wireless system. For sports remotes, these systems usually combine an I.F.B. channel with two or more P.L. lines, so that the announcer can receive information and cues from various sources.

The disadvantages of the P. L. system are that it takes time and effort to set up, and that you are always tied to a wire.

Telephone   Finally, there is the good, old telephone. You will find that when you are far away from the station, the telephone is still one of the most reliable intercom systems. Just make sure that you keep a line open to your station, especially when covering an important story. Many stations use the telephone to feed a field reporter program sound and I.F.B. information, espe-cially if the reporter is beyond the station's transmitting range. The telephone is also used as a backup audio channel for remotes. In case the signal gets lost during the microwave or satellite transmission, you can always continue feeding the audio through the regular telephone line.

AESTHETIC FACTORS

All the bewildering array of audio equipment is of little use, however, if you cannot exercise some aesthetic judgment—make some decisions about how to work with television sound artistically rather than technically. Five major factors are especially important to the aesthetic treatment of television sound: (1) environment, (2) figure-ground, (3) perspective, (4) continuity, and (5) energy.

Environment

Whereas in most sound recordings we try to eliminate as much of the ambient sound as possible, in television such sounds, when heard in the background of the main sound source, are often important indicators of where the event takes place or even how it feels. Such sounds help establish the general environment of the event. For example, if you cover a major downtown fire, the fire sirens, the crackling of the fire, the noise of the fire engines and the pumps, and the tense voices of the fire fighters and onlookers are important factors in communicating some of the excitement and tension of the event to the television viewers. Or think of the re-cording of a small orchestra, for example. If you do a studio recording, the coughing of one of the crew members or musicians would, during an especially soft passage, certainly prompt a retake. Not so in a live concert. We have learned to identify the occasional coughing and other such environmental sounds as important indicators of the aliveness of the event.

The environmental, or ambient, sounds are espe-cially important in ENG. As pointed out previously, you should, therefore, try to use one mic and audio track for the recording of the main sound source, such as the reporter or the guest, and the other mic (usually the one attached to the camera) and the second audio track of your videotape for the recording of the envi-ronmental sounds. Separating the sounds on different tracks makes it easier for the editor to mix the two sounds in the proper proportions in postproduction.

Figure-Ground

One of the important perceptual factors is the "figure-ground" principle. This means that we tend to organize our environment into a relatively mobile figure (a person, a car) and a relatively stable background (wall, houses, mountains). If we now expand this principle a little, we can say that we can single out an event that is important to us and make it into the foreground, while relegating all other events to the background, or as we just called it, the "environment." For example, if you are looking for somebody and finally discover him or her in a crowd of people, that person immediately becomes the focus of your attention—the foreground—while the rest of the people become the background. The same happens in the field of sound. We have the ability to perceive, within limits, the sounds we want or need to hear (the "figure"), while ignoring to a large extent all other sounds (the "ground"), even if they are relatively louder. When re-creating such a figure-ground relationship with sound, we usually make the "figure" somewhat louder and, more importantly, give it a distinct quality in relation to the background sounds. Sometimes, however, the background sounds become so dominant that they drown out the principal sounds (figure), regardless of how selective we want to be with our listening. Again, this can be done quite easily by making the background sounds louder than the principal sound, and giving them the "foreground" quality.

You can now see quite clearly why it is so important to separate sounds as much as possible during the recording. If you had recorded background and foreground all on one track, you would have to live with whatever the mic picked up. To manipulate the individual sounds would be very difficult, if possible at all. With the "figure" sounds on one track and the background sounds on the other, the manipulation is rather easy.

Perspective

Sound **perspective** means that close-up pictures are matched with relatively "close" sounds, and long shots with sounds that seem to come from farther away. Close sounds have more *presence* than far sounds—a sound quality that makes us feel as though we were in the proximity of the sound source. The easiest way to achieve this presence is to hold the mic close to the sound source, such as the person speaking. But the presence can also be influenced by adding or subtracting certain frequencies and reverberations. Also,

near sounds are generally slightly louder than far sounds, although the quality manipulation is far more important than the volume control in affecting presence.

Another important aspect of sound perspective is the amount of ambience you hear. Once again, you can compare our perception of sound to visual perception. If, for example, you take a long shot of two people standing at the corner of a busy intersection, you get an *overview* of the whole scene: the two people talking, the traffic, other people rushing by, the shop windows, and traffic lights. Under normal circumstances, we also expect an "overview" of sound: the voices of the two talking mixed together with a good amount of traffic noise and other "busy street corner" environmental sounds. But as soon as we take a close-up of the two, the picture changes. We now have established a definite figure-ground relationship: the two people as the prominent foreground, and the rest of the picture (traffic, people rushing by) as less distinct, usually out-of-focus background. The audio must follow suit. We should now be able to hear the conversation of the two people from close-up, while being only peripherally aware of the street-corner traffic. You need to increase the presence of the conversation, while reducing the traffic noise to background sound or *ambience*.

Sound perspective, or rather the lack of it, used to be a major problem for a popular soap opera because their sound pickup consisted of wireless lavaliere mics. Since the distance between the mic and the mouth of each actor remained the same for a tight close-up and extreme long shot, there was no corresponding sound perspective. All actors seemed to talk from identical spatial positions, although the pictures told us otherwise. As soon as the audio people went back to boom mics for sound pickup, the sound perspective improved dramatically. The mic could now be moved quite close to an actor during a close-up and somewhat farther away during a long shot—a simple solution to a big problem. If you have to compromise, it is usually better to keep a close-mic presence on close-ups as well as long shots than an off-mic presence for close-ups.

Continuity

Sound continuity is especially important in postproduction. You may have noticed the sound quality of a reporter's voice change depending on whether he or she was speaking on- or off-camera. When on-camera the reporter used one type of microphone and was reporting from a particular outdoor location. Then, the reporter narrated the off-camera segments of the videotaped story in the acoustically treated studio, using a high-quality mic. This change in microphones and locations gave the speech a distinctly different quality. Although this difference may not be too noticeable when you are doing the actual recording, it becomes amazingly apparent when edited together in the final show. The average viewers are probably not able to identify the specific sound problem. But they certainly notice that the reporter just does not sound "quite right."

What should you do to avoid such continuity problems? First, use identical mics for the on- and off-camera narration. Second, if you have time for a sweetening session, try to match the on-camera sound quality through equalization and echo manipulation. Third, if you have recorded some of the ambience of the on-camera location, mix this sound with the off-camera narration. When producing this mix, feed the ambient sounds to the reporter through earphones while he or she is doing the voice-over narration. This will help the reporter to re-create the on-site energy.

Sometimes, you may hear the ambience punctured by brief silences at each edit point. The effect is as startling as when the engines of an airplane change their pitch unexpectedly. The easiest way to restore the background continuity in this case is to cover up these silences with prerecorded ambience. Always record a few minutes' worth of "silence" (room ambience or background sound) before and after videotaping, or whenever the ambience changes decisively (such as a concert hall with and without an audience present).

Sound is also one of the chief elements to help establish visual continuity. A rhythmically precise piece of music can help a series of pictures, which otherwise do not cut together very well, achieve continuity. Music and sound are often the important connecting link between abruptly changing shots and scenes.

Energy

Unless you want to achieve a special effect through contradiction, you should match the general energy of the pictures with a similar energy of sound. Energy refers to all the factors in a scene that communicate a certain degree of force and power. Obviously, high-energy scenes, such as a series of close-ups of a rock band in action, can stand higher energy sounds than a more tranquil scene. Good television audio depends a great deal on your ability to sense the general energy of the pictures or picture sequences and to adjust the volume of the sound accordingly. No volume meter in the world can substitute for aesthetic judgment.

MAIN POINTS

1. In an analog system, the signal fluctuates exactly like the original stimulus over its entire range. In a digital system, the original sound stimulus is translated into many computerlike on-off pulses (bits). The digital system is more noise-free than the analog one, and allows for better control of equipment and sound.

2. A time compressor allows a recorded videotape to be replayed faster or slower without altering the original pitch of the sound track.

3. The most common intercommunication, or intercom, studio systems are: (1) the P.L. (phone or private line) system that allows all production and engineering personnel to be in voice contact; (2) the I.F.B. (interrupted feedback) system, which carries program sound to the performer via a small earpiece—this program sound can be interrupted by producer or director for special instructions; and (3) the S.A. (studio address) system, which allows the control room personnel to address the studio through studio speakers.

4. The field intercom systems add walkie-talkies, wireless systems (such as two-way radio), and telephones.

5. The five major aesthetic factors in sound control are: (1) environment—sharpening an event through ambient sounds; (2) figure-ground—the emphasis of the most important sound source over the general background sounds; (3) perspective—matching closeup pictures with "close" sounds and long shots with faraway sounds; (4) continuity—maintaining the quality of sound (such as a reporter's voice) when combining various takes; and (5) energy—matching the force and power of the pictures with a similar degree of sound.

FURTHER READING

Alten, Stanley. *Audio in Media*. Belmont, CA: Wadsworth Publishing Co., 1981.

Nisbett, Alec. *The Technique of the Sound Studio*. Woburn, MA: Focal Press, 1979.

Oringel, Robert S. *Audio Control Handbook*. 5th ed. New York: Hastings House, 1983.

Videotape and Film

Television production relies heavily on the use of videotape. The use of film is mostly restricted to the playback of feature films and the occasional production and playback of major documentaries.

Section One of this chapter deals with the production requirements and potential of videotape and with the various pieces of videotape equipment. Specifically, we will discuss:

1. Videotape in television production—including the building of a show, time delay, program distribution, and records for reference and study.

2. The six principal videotape recording modes.

3. The principal video recording systems: (1) quad (quadruplex); (2) helical, or slant-track; and (3) video disc.

4. Types of videotape recorders, including studio and portable reel-to-reel and video cassette recorders with different tape formats (widths).

5. Major videotape preproduction and production factors.

Section Two describes special recording systems (digital, LVR, and MBM), and examines the use of film in television: film format, film sound, the elements of the film chain, and the operation of film (projection, cuing, and timing).

The processes of switching and post-production editing will be covered in Chapters 11 and 12.

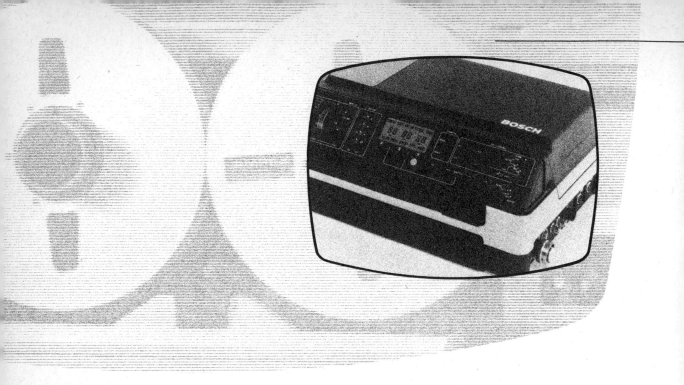

VIDEOTAPE IN TELEVISION PRODUCTION

Videotape is used principally for (1) the building of a whole show by assembling parts that have been recorded at different times and/or locations, (2) time delay, (3) duplication and distribution of programs, and (4) records for reference and study.

Building of a Show

Videotape is used to build a show from various pre-recorded tape segments. Similar to film production, the various scenes of a television play, for example, are videotaped at different times and often at different locations for later assembly through editing. Thus, the use of videotape permits more complex and especially more polished productions than live television. Major and minor production errors can be corrected by reshooting a particular scene. Contrary to film, which has to be processed before it can be viewed, the videotape recording of a scene can be replayed immediately after each take for close scrutiny.

The portable camera and **videotape recorder (VTR)** facilitated a whole new concept in television production: ENG and EFP. The advantage of videotape over film in news gathering is that videotape is a much faster and more flexible production device. Videotape does not have to be developed in a processing lab, and it can be edited much more quickly than sound film.

Time Delay

Through videotape, an event can be recorded and played back immediately or hours, days, or even years after its occurrence. In sports, where it is known as **"instant replay,"** the playback of a brief scene happens almost immediately after recording it.

The immediate **playback** capability of videotape has several benefits. Instant replay, for example, can give the viewer another look at an important play right after it has happened. Or the playback of a videotape can give the athlete, or any other performer, the opportunity to see himself or herself in action right after the performance and correct possible mistakes. In television production, the immediate playback is an important learning device.

Videotape and film are the two major television program sources. Most of the programs you see on television have been prerecorded on one or the other.

Although film is produced by its traditional film techniques and simply played back on television, videotape constitutes a major production element of television itself. Indeed, videotape has influenced television production techniques to a great extent.

As talent, you can observe yourself right after the performance, while your delivery and the problems connected with it are still fresh in your mind. As director, you probably lacked the time and the state of mind during the show to absorb the feel and relative quality of the total performance. You may remember one camera not framing correctly, the dissolve being too slow, or another camera's shaky zoom. But you may not even have been aware of the announcer giving the wrong address and telephone number over the last slide for his commercial tag. A playback immediately after your directing exercise, when you are more relaxed, makes it possible for you to perceive the camera handling, the general blocking, the cutting rhythm, and the announcer's delivery all together.

Program Distribution

Videotape can be easily duplicated and distributed to a variety of television outlets. Many production centers have syndicated their videotaped shows for distribution in major and minor markets. Because of the improved quality and ease of operation, videotape has all but replaced film for duplication and distribution of such program material as commercials and public service announcements (PSAs). However, 16mm film is still used for the distribution of movies, occasional commercial spots, and some documentaries.

Records for Reference and Study

Videotape is an excellent device for preserving a television event for reference or study, especially one-time happenings—sports, political gatherings, a difficult operation in a medical center, examples of supreme human achievement and failure. Such videotaped records can be stored, retrieved, and distributed via television with relative ease. The events are thus available for careful study by scholars all over the world. For extremely important projects, the recorded event can be translated into a television signal and transmitted via satellite to the new destination. Usually, though, videotape records are dubbed onto a videotape cassette and mailed to the interested party.

Technically, the quality of the playback of a broadcast-type videotape is superior to the playback of the best film (even the 35mm format). On a home

10.1 Single Camera–Single VTR Single-camera–single-VTR recording is used in news, and in dramatic productions recorded "film-style." In the ENG approach, the event is recorded in bits and pieces, but generally in the natural sequence of the event. When videotaping film-style, each change of field of view and camera angle is shot separately. The sequence is determined solely by production efficiency, not event sequence.

receiver, it is practically impossible to tell whether the program originates live or as a videotape playback, assuming that the videotape recording reflects the quality of the live event.

VIDEOTAPE RECORDING MODES

There are six principal approaches to videotape recordings: (1) ENG style: single camera–single VTR; (2) film style: single camera–single VTR; (3) live-on-tape style: multiple cameras–single VTR; (4) segment style: multiple cameras–single VTR; (5) isolated camera; and (6) multiple cameras–multiple VTRs.

ENG Style: Single Camera–Single VTR

In this approach, the video recording is done in bits and pieces, but mostly in the *natural sequence* of the event. For example, if you are to cover a downtown fire, you must start videotaping with whatever is going on when you arrive—most likely the fire in progress. If you missed the actual fire, you cannot go back and shoot it after the mop-up operation. Even the most obliging fire department will not start the fire again for you simply because you were late getting to the scene. Many EFP projects are videotaped the same way, except that the event is predictable and often rehearsed (see 10.1).

Film Style: Single Camera–Single VTR

Film style means that the production approach is quite similar to film making, except that the camera and recording methods are electronic. Each change of field of view (from long shots to close-ups) and each camera angle is shot separately. For example, in film-style shooting of a conversation at the breakfast table, you may cover some long shots first from a variety of angles, with lighting and setup changes for each angle; then you shoot several close-ups of the people talking; then you take some more close-ups of reaction shots. For good measure, you may take some close-ups of the eating action—coffee

Audio Track The area of the videotape that is used for recording audio information.

Color Bars A color standard used by the television industry for the alignment of cameras and videotape recordings.

Control Track The area of the videotape used for recording the synchronization information (sync spikes), which is essential for videotape editing.

Cue Track The area of the videotape used for such audio information as in-house identification or the SMPTE address code. Can also be used for a second audio track.

Freeze Frame Arrested motion, which is perceived as a still shot.

Head Assembly Video head: a small electromagnet that puts electric signals on the videotape or reads (induces) the signals off the tape. Video heads are usually in motion.

Helical Scan, or Helical VTR A videotape recording of one- and two-head videotape recorders, in which the video signal is put on tape in a slanted, diagonal way (contrary to transverse scanning, which goes across the tape). Since the tape wraps around the head drum in a spirallike configuration, it is called "helical" (from helix, spiral). Also called slant-track.

Jogging Frame-by-frame advancement of videotape with a VTR.

Preroll To start a videotape and let it roll for a few seconds before it is put in the playback or record mode in order to give the electronic system time to stabilize.

Quad Abbreviation for quadruplex videotape recorders.

Quadruplex A scanning system of videotape recorders that uses four rotating heads for recording and playing back of video information. All quadruplex, or quad, recorders use 2-inch-wide videotape.

being stirred, salt sprinkled over the eggs, and so forth. The necessary continuity will then be established in postproduction editing (see 10.1).

Live-On-Tape: Multiple Cameras–Single VTR

Live-on-tape means that the production is run as though it were a live show, but, mainly for purposes of time delay, the telecast is videotaped rather than transmitted live. In live-on-tape, multiple cameras are generally used, and the editing is done instantaneously with the switcher. There are no stop-downs of the VTR machines, except perhaps at places where commercials are to be put at a later time. Many interview shows, game shows, special events, and some soap operas are videotaped this way (see 10.2).

Segment Style: Multiple Cameras–Single VTR

The basic approach is similar to the live-on-tape coverage (multiple cameras feeding into a switcher, with the output recorded on a single VTR), except that the event is videotaped not straight through but in segments. Thereby, the segments can occur in the natural sequence of the event, or not. Many soap operas are taped in the segment style, whereby all scenes in one set area are taped first (usually in uninterrupted takes), then all scenes in the next set area, and so forth. In postproduction, the different segments and the commercials are lined up in the right sequence and edited together. However, there are different degrees of this production mode. Sometimes, the segments are so short and so unrelated to each other that the videotaping approaches the film-style technique.

Isolated (Iso) Camera

When using an **isolated**, or **iso, camera,** the general videotaping approach is very much like live-on-tape (multiple cameras, switcher, and single VTR), except that an isolated camera feeds its output not only into the switcher, but also into a second, separate VTR. Thus, the output of the iso camera can be used as part of the live-on-tape setup, but also for instant replays or important material for possible postproduction. This approach is used in sports, plays (dramas and comedies), and music programs. For example, if you do a live-on-tape coverage of the local band, and then discover that the cameras showed the clarinets when they were supposed to be on the tubas, you can easily fix this problem by cutting back to the conductor—provided that you had an iso camera on the conductor during the original videotaping (see 10.3).

Skew A distortion of videotape caused by variations in tape tension which affect the length of the video tracks. Shows up as a hooklike curve at the top of the screen or a curve swinging back and forth. It can be corrected by adjusting the skew control.

Slant Track Same as Helical Scan.

Slow Motion A scene in which the objects appear to be moving more slowly than normal. In film, slow motion is achieved through high-speed photography and normal playback. In television, slow motion is achieved by a multiple scanning of each television frame.

SOT Sound on tape. The videotape is played back with pictures and sound.

Stop-Motion A slow-motion effect in which one frame jumps to the next, showing the object in a different position.

Time Base Corrector (TBC) An electronic accessory to a videotape recorder that helps to make playbacks or transfers electronically stable. A time base corrector helps to maintain picture quality even in dubbing-up operations.

Video Cassette A plastic container in which a videotape moves from supply to takeup reel, recording and playing back short program segments through a video cassette recorder. Similar in construction and function to the audio cassette recorder.

Video Track The area of the videotape used for recording the video information.

VTR Videotape recorder or recording.

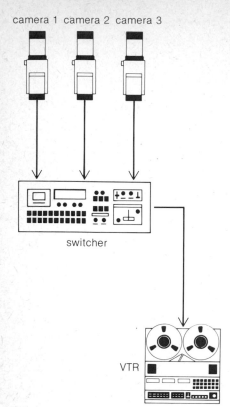

10.2   Multiple Cameras—Single VTR This mode is used for live-on-tape recording, where a show, produced as if it were live, is videotaped principally for time delay. The editing is done with the switcher simultaneously with the camera feed.

In the segment mode, the same equipment setup is used except that the show is videotaped in sequential or nonsequential segments.

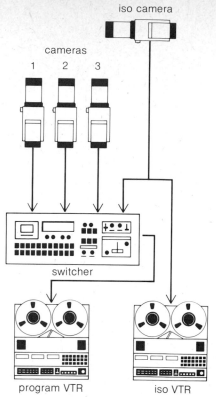

10.3   Isolated Camera The isolated camera, or iso camera, is used in addition to the regular multiple-camera–single-VTR setup. However, the iso camera feeds its output not only into the switcher (as do all the other cameras), but also into a second, separate VTR.

Multiple Cameras—Multiple VTRs

In this case, each camera feeds its output to its own separate VTR. If, for example, you cover a rock band with four cameras, you need four VTRs—one for each camera. In effect, you are working with four separate iso setups. Because all single tapes have a common reference, the SMPTE time code (see p. 314), the tapes are later combined into a single master tape through postproduction. If you have the facilities to run the various VTRs in sync during the videotaping and postproduction, you can treat the videotaped material as though it were supplied by live cameras. Consequently, you can feed the videotapes into the switcher and try various editing combinations until you are satisfied with the end product (see 10.4).

Of course, you will find that these modes are not exclusive of one another, but are frequently intermixed. For example, some situation comedies are videotaped with three or four iso cameras, each feeding its own VTR. However, these cameras are also routed into the switcher for instantaneous editing while the show is in progress. This technique gives the editor a rough "workprint" of how the various shots are to be assembled.

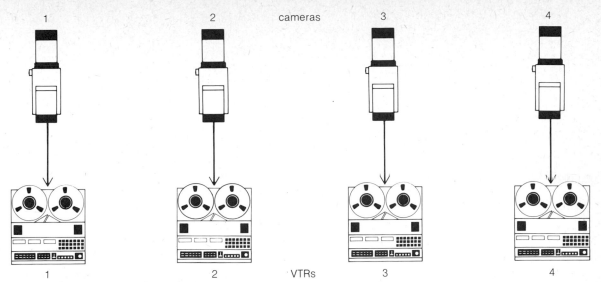

1   2   cameras   3   4

1   2   VTRs   3   4

10.4   Multiple Cameras—Multiple VTRs In the multiple-cameras—multiple-VTRs setup, each camera acts as an iso camera. This means that each camera feeds directly its own VTR. The mixing of the images is done in postproduction.

VIDEOTAPE RECORDING SYSTEMS

Videotaping is quite similar to the audiotape recording process. The electronic impulses of television pictures (the video signal) and sound (audio signal) are recorded on the plastic videotape through magnetizing its iron oxide coating. During playback, the recorded video and audio signals are converted again into television pictures and sounds.

There are three basic systems of video recording: (1) the quadruplex (quad), or transverse, scanning system; (2) the helical, or slant-track, recording system; and (3) the video disc. We will discuss the more special recording systems in Section Two.

The Quadruplex (Quad) System

In the **transverse,** or **quadruplex,** scanning process, four tiny rotating (14,400 rpm) recording heads put the video signal on a 2-inch-wide tape that moves past the rotating recording heads at speeds of $7\frac{1}{2}$ inches per second (ips) or 15 ips. In this process, 15 ips is the speed normally used for high-quality broadcast recordings.

The quadruplex videotape recorder (VTR) normally puts four different tracks on the 2-inch videotape: (1) the **video track** (the signal representing the television picture information), (2) the **audio track** (the signal representing the television sound), (3) the cue or address track, and (4) the control track (see 10.5). Some quadruplex recorders put on an additional sound track (five tracks total).

The **cue or address track** is in effect a second audio track. You can use it, for example, to record the director's P.L. (phone, or private, line) for future reference, or in-house information, such as the identification number of the tape, or special product number. Most often, the cue track is used for the time code, an electronic "address" system that enables you to find quickly any spot (address) in the videotape for editing purposes, or for synchronizing the videotape with audiotape recorders, for example. We will take up the function of the time code more thoroughly in Chapter 11. You can also put regular audio information on the cue track, such as the second channel of a stereo pickup, or special sound effects. However, when recorded on the cue track, the sound is of slightly lower quality than if put on the main audio track.

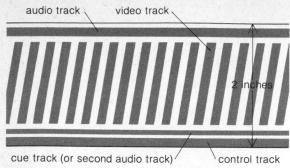

audio track   video track

2 inches

cue track (or second audio track)   control track

10.5   Quad Videotape Tracks The 2-inch videotape
for quadruplex videotape recorders normally has four
tracks: the video track (television pictures), the audio track
(television sound), the cue track (various code information
or a second audio track), and the control track (essential for
synchronization).

The **control track** consists of evenly spaced
blips or spikes, called the sync pulse, which mark
each frame. These pulses synchronize the tape speed
and the rotation speed of the recording heads so
that any tape made on a similar machine can be
played back without major picture breakups. In effect,
the sync pulses act like electronic sprocket holes.
The sync pulses also synchronize the scanning and
mark the spots where edits can be made.

The audio track can be recorded simultaneously with the video track, or separately. You can
have parts or all of the video or audio tracks erased
independently from each other. Sometimes you may
find that it is easier to record the video information
first and the audio track later. This technique is
especially advantageous if the audio track does not
have to be tightly synchronized with the video, as
in a running commentary over the video event, for
example. When, in the playback of a videotape segment, the audio information is played with the video,
we speak of **SOT,** sound on tape.

The Helical, or Slant-Track, System

In the **helical,** or **slant-track,** recording system,
one or two rotating heads that are mounted on a
large rotating drum, called "head drum," put the
video information on the tape in a *slanted* diagonal,
rather than transverse (up and down), manner.

In order to get the slant into the track, the tape
is wound around the head drum in a spirallike configuration. Because the Greek work for spiral is *helix,*
we call the tape wrap (and the whole recording
system) *helical* (see 10.6).

The other important features of the slant-track
system are: (1) tape format, (2) track arrangement,
(3) system standards, and (4) tape speeds.

Tape Format   This refers to the width of the videotape. Whereas all quad machines use 2-inch tape,
helical videotape recorders use four different tape
formats: 1-inch tape, $\frac{3}{4}$-inch tape, $\frac{1}{2}$-inch tape, and $\frac{1}{4}$-
inch tape. The 1-inch tape is generally used for high-
quality production VTRs. The $\frac{3}{4}$-inch tape is the format for the standard video cassette recorders. There
are no $\frac{3}{4}$-inch reel-to-reel machines. The $\frac{1}{2}$-inch format is used in cassettes (for the Beta and VHS home
recorders and some broadcast field recorders).

One manufacturer (IVC) produced a high-
quality 2-inch helical scan videotape recorder.
Although you will still find some of them in operation, they are slowly being replaced by the more
efficient 1-inch VTRs. Also, there are $\frac{1}{4}$-inch and $\frac{1}{2}$-
inch cassettes used for ENG; however, the majority
of the systems still use the $\frac{3}{4}$-inch format.

For almost two decades after the development
of the first helical scan recorders, you could easily
distinguish between broadcast-quality and nonbroadcast videotape recorders. Only the 2-inch quad
VTRs were considered broadcast quality. Helical scan
VTRs, which used smaller format tapes (1-inch, $\frac{3}{4}$-
inch, $\frac{1}{2}$-inch, and $\frac{1}{4}$-inch), were not. "Small-format"
became synonymous with more or less portable,
low-quality, nonbroadcast equipment. Today the 1-
inch VTR has all but replaced the 2-inch models as
the industry standard, and the $\frac{3}{4}$-inch format is the
accepted ENG/EFP standard. Some ENG operations
even use $\frac{1}{2}$-inch tape, which with high-speed tape
recorders produces broadcast-quality pictures. The
old formula, "the wider the tape the better the picture quality," does not hold true any longer. Although
some of the quad recorders still produce better pictures than a standard $\frac{3}{4}$-inch video cassette recorder,
we can no longer distinguish between broadcast-
quality and nonbroadcast VTRs simply by looking at
tape width.

Track Arrangement   Because of the great variety of helical VTRs with different tape formats, you will no longer find a standard arrangement of audio, control, and video tracks. Each format has its own arrangement, and despite efforts to standardize as much as possible, there are various track arrangements even within certain tape formats. We will indicate the specific track arrangements when we discuss the various types of videotape recorders.

System Standards   With all the various tape formats and recording systems, the interchangeability of helical recordings has always been a major problem. However, certain system standards have been developed to facilitate at least some interchangeability among each of the major tape formats. Organizations developing the standards include the Electronics Industry Association of Japan **(EIAJ)**, Society of Motion Picture and Television Engineers **(SMPTE)**, and European Broadcasting Union **(EBU)**.

In order to know which tapes you can play on your equipment, you need to know something about these *system standards:*

1.   *Tape Format.* Obviously, you cannot use a $\frac{3}{4}$-inch cassette and play it on a 1-inch VTR or a $\frac{1}{2}$-inch cassette recorder. If you have to play the $\frac{3}{4}$-inch cassette recording on a 1-inch machine, you need to "bump up" (or **"dub up"**) the tape, which means that you must dub the smaller format tape onto the larger format tape—in our case from the $\frac{3}{4}$-inch format cassette to the 1-inch reel-to-reel tape. If you want the $\frac{3}{4}$-inch cassette played back on a $\frac{1}{2}$-inch cassette recorder, you need to **"dub down"** the tape before the recording can be played on the smaller format cassette recorder. But then you may find to your dismay that not all 1-inch or $\frac{1}{2}$-inch formats are interchangeable.

2.   *One-inch Standards.* In the 1-inch format, the SMPTE agreed on *two* distinct recording systems, the Type C and Type B standards. Although the recordings made on a variety of Type C VTRs are interchangeable, as are the ones made on Type B VTRs, you *cannot* play back a recording made on a Type C machine on machines of the Type B standard.

The *Type C standard,* which is the more popular recording system, is used by all VTR manufacturers

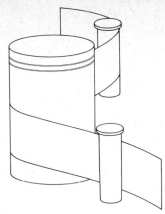

slanted video track

10.6   Helical, or Slant-track, Scanning System   In the helical, or slant-track, scanning system, the tape moves past the head drum at an angle. Because the scanning occurs diagonally, the tracks cover a much longer area of the tape than its width.

but one. Each track is *nonsegmented,* which means it represents a complete, uninterrupted field (two fields make up one frame—a complete picture). The advantages are that you can rather easily achieve different speeds of accelerated motion, slow motion, and **jogging** (frame-by-frame advancement) simply by varying the tape speed. By temporarily stopping the tape, you can get a **freeze-frame** effect. During fast and slow shuttle speeds (when in a fast-forward or rewind mode) you can see an image, rather than the usual video snow, which is of great advantage when editing (see 10.7).

The *Type B standard (or BCN system)* is the less popular system. It uses the *segmented* format, which means that each video track represents not a whole field, but only part of it. You need several tracks to make up a field. Operationally, this means that you cannot achieve accelerated or slow motion by simply increasing or reducing playback speed. Also, you cannot see an image during tape shuttle. In order

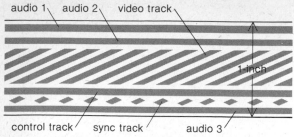

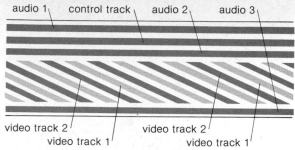

10.7 One-inch Type C Standard The 1-inch Type C standard videotape has three high-quality audio tracks and a control track. The audio 3 track and the control track are separated by a special sync track. Each video scanning track represents a complete field (with two fields making up one frame—a complete picture).

10.8 One-inch Type B Standard The 1-inch Type B standard videotape has three high-quality audio tracks and a control track. It needs five scanning tracks for one field (and ten for a complete frame). Two video heads alternate in writing the segmented track.

to obtain these features, you need to hook the Type B VTR to another piece of equipment, the frame store synchronizer. This amazing piece of equipment will be discussed in Chapter 13. Why, then, use Type B machines at all? Here are some of the advantages: (1) it records and reproduces extremely stable pictures; (2) you can use small, portable VTRs with 1-inch cassettes for high-quality EFP; (3) any cassette can be played back and edited on a reel-to-reel machine; (4) the cassettes can be programmed and played back by a computer-assisted automation system (see 10.8).

At this point you may wonder what happened to the Type A standard. It was a system that was soon replaced by the more practical Type C standard. Most of the Type A machines have been adapted to the Type C format.

3. *Three-quarter–inch Standard.* Fortunately, the *U-Matic* system is the single standard for all of the more popular $\frac{3}{4}$-inch video cassette recorders. Sometimes, the system is simply called the "U-system." (See 10.17 and 10.18.)

4. *One-half–inch Standard.* We are not so lucky with the $\frac{1}{2}$-inch video cassette recorders. There are two basic systems that permit interchangeability among, but not between, them. They are the *Beta-max* system and the *VHS* (Video Home System).

You may still find in operation some of the old $\frac{1}{2}$-inch reel-to-reel VTRs whose recordings are supposedly interchangeable. However, even when they were brand-new machines they did not always

comply with the specifications. More often than not, a $\frac{1}{2}$-inch VTR would refuse to play a tape that it did not record.

Tape Speeds These vary greatly among the various systems. In general, they are slower than the 15 ips of the quad recorders. Most $\frac{3}{4}$-inch cassettes record with a tape speed of $3\frac{3}{4}$ ips and play back from frame-by-frame jogging to ten times the recording speed while producing recognizable images. Rewind speeds can reach up to forty times the recording speed. A freeze-frame effect can be obtained by stopping the tape momentarily. Do not keep the recorder too long in this zero-tape-speed mode because it wears away the magnetic coating on the tape quite quickly.

The Video Disc System

The **video disc** is actually not a video*tape* recorder, because it uses a recording disc instead of a tape. Some of the commercially available discs serve only as playback of recorded material; you cannot use them to record video and audio material. Although they are very convenient for program analysis, such as the study of editing techniques used in a particular motion picture, they are of little use in television production.

The disc system still widely used in television production is the *magnetic disc*. It is used for the recording and instant replay of very short event sequences (up to 60 seconds). The most important

record/play head assembly

video disc

operational controls

variable speed control

10.9 Ampex Video Disc The video disc facilitates the recording and instant replay of short (up to 35–60 seconds) show segments. It can search out any part of the recorded action within seconds and play it back at real time (normal speed), or any variety of slow-motion speeds down to a freeze frame.

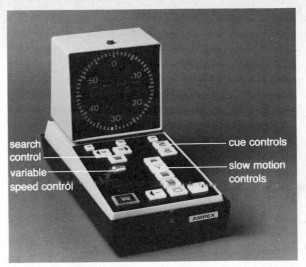

search control

variable speed control

cue controls

slow motion controls

10.10 Ampex Slow-Motion Controller The slow-motion controller makes the 1-inch helical VTRs as flexible for instant replay as the video disc. You can enter a cue during the actual recording of the event, then access this scene again within seconds through the search mode. The scene can then be replayed in variable slow-motion speeds, with the option of producing jitter-freeze frames at any time.

feature of this system is that it can search out up to twenty different parts of the recorded segment within seconds (a maximum of 5 seconds). This fast access time makes it the ideal device for *instant replay.* Each segment can be played back in real time, **slow-motion,** stop-motion (like frame-by-frame jogging), and in any number of freeze frames. If you feel like it, you can even play the whole scene backward. (See 10.9.)

However, when coupled with a slow-motion controller, the 1-inch helical videotape is almost as fast as the disc in retrieving scenes, and it can duplicate the various slow-motion and freeze-frame modes of the disc (see 10.10). The rather bulky disc system is, therefore, slowly being replaced by the more flexible helical VTRs.

TYPES OF VIDEOTAPE RECORDERS

There are two basic types of videotape recorders: (1) reel-to-reel recorders, and (2) video cassette machines. Within those two categories, you will encounter a variety of models that differ considerably in quality and sophistication. Some are designed exclusively for broadcast use. Others have become indispensable in broadcast operations, although they had originally been designed for nonbroadcast use. Still others were meant exclusively for home use, but found their way into broadcasting when coupled with additional image-enhancing equipment.

Reel-to-Reel Videotape Recorders

As you remember from Chapter 1, all reel-to-reel videotape recorders use a supply reel, from which the videotape is fed past the **head assembly** (containing a variety of erase and recording heads) to a separate takeup reel. There are two types of reel-to-

10.11 Ampex AVR-2

frequency range that permits higher resolution pictures with less noise than **low-band** color recorders (which operate in a lower frequency range)

2. Produce high-quality master recordings and many subsequent dubs with a minimum of quality loss

3. Do on-line editing (editing a final on-air production that will serve as master tape)

4. Record and erase the video and audio tracks together or independently

5. Operate reliably for hours on end.

However, quad machines *cannot:*

1. Produce slow-motion or freeze-frame effects without special accessory equipment

2. Permit fast shuttle speeds and therefore fast retrieval of taped material

3. Produce a recognizable image during tape shuttle

4. Be easily moved around for ENG or EFP.

Further drawbacks of the quad machines are that they take up a relatively large area and that the tapes are expensive, bulky, and difficult to ship and store. Also, quad machines may cause occasional **"banding,"** which shows up as wide, differently colored bands dividing the picture horizontally.

reel recorders: (1) the older 2-inch quad (quadruplex) VTR, and (2) the 1-inch VTR.

The Quad, or 2-inch, Videotape Recorder The quad recorder—the granddaddy of all videotape recorders—is still very much alive and active in many television stations. The main reasons for its longevity are (1) it is a reliable machine that reproduces high-quality pictures, (2) a great amount of material is still recorded and available on 2-inch tape, and (3) the 1-inch replacement machines of equal or better quality are very expensive (see 10.11).

Still, the more flexible 1-inch machines have become the top-of-the-line production standard, and the 2-inch machines are gradually being retired.

Here is what the quad recorder *can* do:

1. Record and play back high-quality pictures, and very good sound. All surviving quad machines are **high-band,** which means that they operate in a high-

The 1-inch Videotape Recorder The 1-inch top-of-the-line production models are no longer simple videotape recorders. They have become versatile production systems that can perform a number of intricate tasks, besides the recording and playback of high-band, high-quality video and audio signals (see 10.12 and 10.13).

The fully equipped 1-inch (Type C standard) production VTR *can:*

1. Record or play back 90 minutes of continuous program

2. Reproduce high-quality pictures that are very close in quality to that of a live camera picture

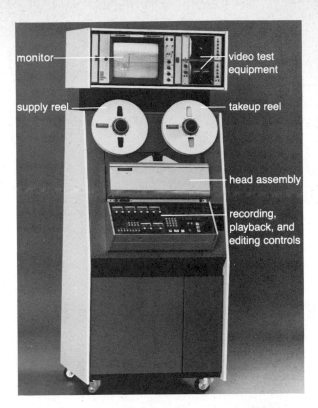

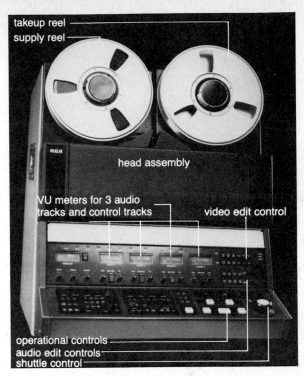

10.13 RCA TR-800 Videotape Recorder

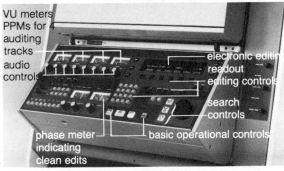

10.12 Ampex VPR-3 1-inch Type C Videotape Recorder and Operating Controls

3.   Record and reproduce high-fidelity sound on any one of its three sound tracks

4.   Produce high-quality master recordings from which several subsequent dubs can be made with a minimum of quality loss

5.   Record and erase the video and three audio tracks together or independently

6.   Play back in several modes: slow-motion, jog or **stop-motion** (frame-by-frame advance), and freeze-frame without additional equipment. With a slow-motion controller, it is as flexible as the video disc and used extensively for instant replay.

7.   Display a recognizable image during variable shuttle speeds

8.   Search automatically for the selected preroll point for edits

9.   Perform frame-accurate edits (see Chapter 11 for more detail on editing)

10.   Add continuous time code to the previous time-code frame during assemble editing (some models only)

11.   Interface with other equipment (such as additional VTRs or audiotape recorders, computer-controlled editing systems, and switchers) for expanded production systems.

10.14 BCN 50 Type B Standard VTR

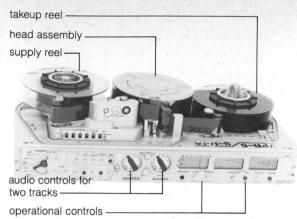

takeup reel
head assembly
supply reel

audio controls for two tracks

operational controls

10.15 Ampex Nagra VPR-5 Type C Portable VTR This is one of the lightest, high-quality 1-inch VTRs available.

The Type C 1-inch VTR *cannot:*

1. Play recordings made with a Type B (BCN) VTR
2. Play 1-inch cassettes.

The Type B 1-inch VTR can perform all the operations of the Type C models, *except* play recordings made with a Type C machine.

Type B reel-to-reel VTRs can play back Type B 1-inch cassettes without any adjustment to the drive mechanism. Also, their pictures are slightly more stable and jitter-free than those of the Type C machines (see 10.14).

The great advantage of the 1-inch VTR over quad VTRs is that without special attachments they can play at slow-motion speeds, do freeze frames, and display a recognizable image while in fast forward and reverse modes. Of course, the smaller size of the 1-inch machines and the videotape itself is an added bonus (see 10.15 and 10.16).

Video Cassette Recorders (VCRs)

The great advantage of **video cassette** recorders over reel-to-reel VTRs is *ease of operation*. There is no need for you to thread the tape from the supply reel past the head assembly to the takeup reel in a more or less complicated path; all you do with the cassette is put it in the slot and press a button. The machine takes over from there, threading and cuing up the tape and awaiting your further command (*play, fast forward, search*).

Because the tape is never handled and remains enclosed in a plastic case until inserted in the machine, the cassette affords more *protection* for the tape than ever possible with the reel-to-reel (or "open" reel) process (see 10.17). When you turn the cassette around, you notice a red button in the corner (see 10.18). This button must be in place if you intend to use this cassette for recording. By removing this button, you protect the cassette from being erased accidentally, and it will refuse any subsequent recordings. If you change your mind and want to use the cassette for recording after all, simply plug the red button back in again. Always take a quick look to see whether the red button is in place before using the cassette for recording. In an emergency a piece of gaffer's tape can replace the red button.

10.17 Video Cassette The standard video cassette houses the supply and takeup reels. The $\frac{3}{4}$-inch tape moves past an opening, through which the tape is automatically threaded by the VCR. The standard cassette can hold up to 60 minutes of programming.

10.16 Ampex VPR-20B 1-inch Portable VTR

10.18 Video Cassette Erase Protection The presence of the plastic button on the back of the cassette indicates that the tape can be used for recording. Any recording already on the tape is automatically erased. If you remove the button, the cassette cannot be used for further recordings, unless the button is replaced.

A great variety of VCRs are available to perform specific functions. Some of the better quality machines are used for the recording, editing, and playback of EFP/ENG material; others are solely for the recording of short event segments during ENG. Then there are special high-band quad machines that use 2-inch cassettes for handling the back-to-back play of very short program material.

To make some sense out of the great variety of VCRs, we will divide them into (1) standard $\frac{3}{4}$-inch VCRs, (2) portable VCRs, and (3) special VCRs.

Standard $\frac{3}{4}$-inch VCRs There is no television production unit—broadcast or not—that does not use several $\frac{3}{4}$-inch video cassette recorders. Do not be surprised if you count as many as forty in a medium-sized television station. The $\frac{3}{4}$-inch U-Matic format is the firmly established industry standard.

Cassettes recorded on $\frac{3}{4}$-inch U-Matic VCRs are all interchangeable. Besides the video track, the cassettes have two audio channels, one address code track (which can be used as a third audio channel), and a control track (see 10.19).

Like most other television equipment, the various VCR models differ in quality and sophistication. Some of them perform simple recording, playback,

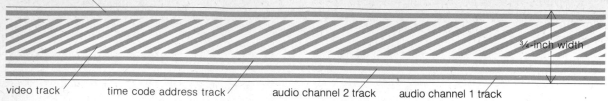

control track

¾-inch width

video track   time code address track   audio channel 2 track   audio channel 1 track

10.19 Track Arrangement of ¾-inch Videotape The ¾-inch U-Matic video-tape has the control track on top, a time code address track, and two audio channels (with the channel 1 audio track running parallel to the bottom edge of the tape).

and editing functions. Others are built specifically for more demanding broadcast use (see 10.20 and 10.21).

Most VCRs are low-band color recorders, which means that their signals must be further processed by accessory equipment, such as a time base corrector (TBC), before they can be broadcast. We will talk more about such signal-processing equipment in Chapter 13. But even with such allies as TBCs and picture-enhancing equipment, the standard ¾-inch VCRs produce lower quality pictures than the quad or 1-inch VTRs. However, there is no inevitable reason for this. Sooner or later, the standard will shift to the smaller-format tapes, without sacrificing and perhaps even improving the quality of the present larger format VTRs.

The biggest drawback of the older VCRs is that they are quite *slow* in their operation. Every time you go to a different operational mode, you have to press *stop* and wait for the cassette to unthread itself and then thread itself again. The shuttle speeds (*fast forward* and *rewind*) move at a snail's pace.

With the newer broadcast VCRs, these problems have been minimized or eliminated entirely. In some models, the shuttle speeds are as fast as those of a reel-to-reel VTR, and the built-in microprocessors execute a variety of instructions quickly and efficiently. Because the tape remains threaded during all but the eject operation (removing the cassette), you do not have to wait for the cumbersome load-unload cycle each time you go into a different operational mode. This seems like a small thing, but if you are pressed for time during an editing job, for

example, a slow rewind can really raise your blood pressure.

With some VCRs you may encounter two additional problems: *tracking* and *skew*.

Tracking refers to the video heads tracing exactly the video tracks on the tape. If the recording was made by another recorder, the playback machine sometimes has some difficulty with the perfect alignment of video heads to the video tracks of the recording. The picture shows a horizontal band of video noise that stays in one position, or slowly moves up and down the screen. Such tracking errors are usually eliminated by putting the tracking control in the automatic mode. Sometimes, however, you may need to turn the tracking control knob until the playback looks stable and relatively noise-free.

Skew is caused by variations in tape tension, which affect the length of the video tracks. If the pictures have a hooklike curve at the top of the screen, or if the curve swings back and forth (called "flag waving"), you need to adjust the skew control. If this does not eliminate the problem, the tape may have been stretched, which usually ruins the recording.

In order to give the recordings made on ¾-inch, or smaller format equipment, the picture stability necessary for broadcast, digital time base correctors (TBCs) or the more versatile frame store synchronizers are used. A **time base corrector** is a clocking device that keeps the scanning in step and fills in whenever the recorder misses a step. It eliminates picture jitter but does not improve picture quality. The **frame store synchronizer** does the

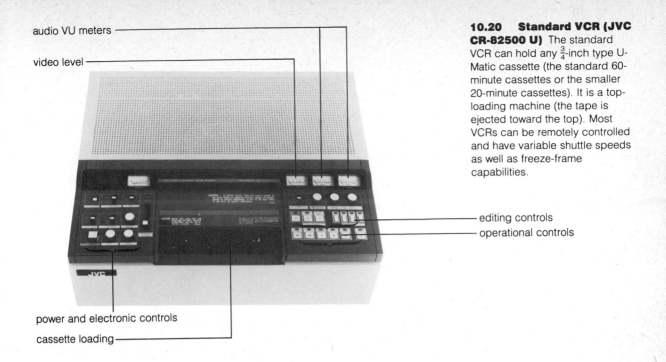

audio VU meters

video level

editing controls
operational controls

power and electronic controls

cassette loading

10.20 Standard VCR (JVC CR-82500 U) The standard VCR can hold any $\frac{3}{4}$-inch type U-Matic cassette (the standard 60-minute cassettes or the smaller 20-minute cassettes). It is a top-loading machine (the tape is ejected toward the top). Most VCRs can be remotely controlled and have variable shuttle speeds as well as freeze-frame capabilities.

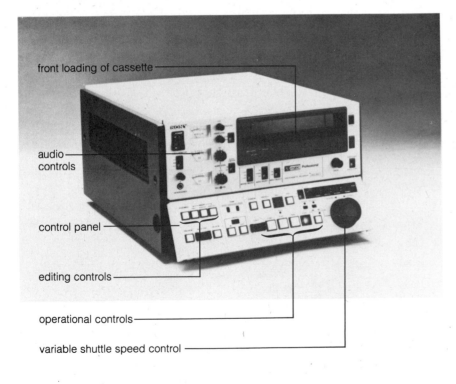

front loading of cassette

audio controls

control panel

editing controls

operational controls

variable shuttle speed control

10.21 Broadcast VCR (Sony BVU 800) Compared with regular VCRs, the broadcast VCRs have increased picture stability, faster tape shuttle speeds, and more convenient operational features. The Sony BVU 800 is a front-loading machine, which makes it possible to have it rack-mounted. Also, the control panel can be locked into various positions, or removed for remote control.

same thing, but more efficiently. We will talk more about the frame store synchronizer in Chapter 13.

Here is what a fully-equipped, broadcast VCR *can* do:

1. Accept cassettes up to 60 minutes maximum

2. Fast-forward a 60-minute cassette in less than 4 minutes and rewind it even faster

3. Switch from the *play* mode to *rewind* without having to go through *stop*

4. Record and erase selectively either of the two audio tracks or the video track

5. Record separate sound signals on tracks 1 and 2. Some machines even mix them for recording on either track 1 or 2

6. Go through continuously changing or preset shuttle speeds without losing the pictures during the shuttle

7. Let you preview edits before executing them (see Chapter 11 for more information)

8. Search automatically for certain precued program segments

9. Accept time code from an external time code generator for editing and integration with other equipment

10. Interface with computer-assisted equipment, such as other VTRs and editing systems

11. Offer remote control of all operational functions.

Most video cassette recorders *cannot:*

1. Produce high-quality pictures without the aid of picture stabilization and enhancing equipment

2. Maintain reasonable picture quality on subsequent dubs.

As you can see, there is not much the VCR cannot do. It is primarily a matter of quality that prevents the VCR from rendering the higher-format VTRs obsolete. With respect to operational ease and production versatility, the VCR remains, so far, unchallenged.

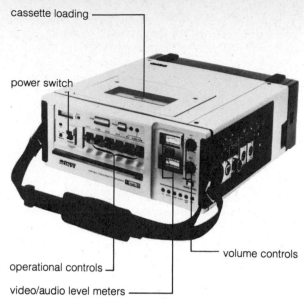

cassette loading

power switch

volume controls

operational controls

video/audio level meters

10.22 Sony BVU 110 Video Cassette Recorder This type of portable video cassette recorder has a 4-hour battery operation and records on 20-minute cassettes. It displays a viewable image even during fast tape shuttle. The BVU 110 is the more sophisticated version of the classic BVU 50 (which cannot play back tapes).

Here are some of the typical ways the more expensive VCRs are used in television production:

1. *Playback.* There are many unscheduled playback demands in any television operation. They include: auditions by prospective talent, samples of new programs or program series, productions from independent companies, previews of ENG and EFP assignments, and programs that are especially sensitive or up for awards. In production classes at colleges and universities, the VCRs permit careful analysis and study of all kinds of program material.

2. *Record.* All news stories that are relayed directly from the field to the station (by microwave link) are recorded on VCRs. Large productions, which are taped on high-quality quad or 1-inch machines, are often simultaneously put on cassettes. This way, you can preview the material without having to touch the master tapes. Newscasts, and many other locally produced shows, are generally recorded on cassettes for archival or review purposes.

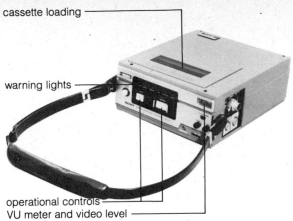

cassette loading

warning lights

operational controls

VU meter and video level

10.23. Sony BVU 50 Portable $\frac{3}{4}$-inch Cassette Recorder

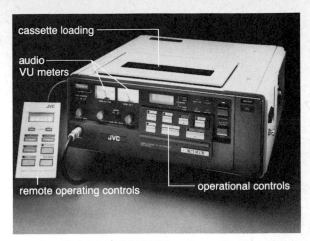

cassette loading

audio VU meters

remote operating controls

operational controls

10.24 JVC CR 4700 U Video Cassette Recorder

3. *Edit.* The high-quality VCR's editing capability was mainly responsible for the shift from "live-tape" recording (where a complete show is videotaped for distribution or time delay) or cosmetic editing (where only the mistakes are eliminated through editing) to postproduction editing. Postproduction means the building of a show by assembling video and audio program segments previously recorded. Large quad and 1-inch production VTRs would be much too expensive to use for all the postproduction editing requirements (see Chapter 11 for more detail).

4. *ENG.* News operations depend almost entirely on the VCR for news gathering (see the following section) and editing. Even a moderately sized news operation may have as many as fifteen VCRs in constant use. Some are designated for the recording and on-the-air playback of news stories, others for previewing material and editing.

Portable VCRs

Even the large video cassette recorders are small enough so that one person can carry them, if need be. However, portable VCRs are designed specifically for ENG work. This implies that they must be lightweight, rugged, easy to carry and operate, and reliable. This is no small order, but there are some

models that fulfill all of these operational requirements (see 10.22 through 10.24).

The following list gives you some idea of the operational characteristics of portable VCRs.

1. *Weight.* The small $\frac{3}{4}$-inch VCRs are still relatively heavy. Although a 25-pound recorder may not seem all that heavy when you start out in the morning, you may feel differently after a day of ENG. Do not be misled by the manufacturer's weight specifications. They usually do not include the weight of the battery, the cables, the carrying case, and the cassette. But, as in backpacking, those "little" items add up.

2. *Power Supply and Operating Time.* With a single 12-volt battery, you can run the recorder continuously for about 4 hours. However, if you also supply the power for the camera with the same battery, the total operating time shrinks to about $1\frac{1}{2}$ hours. You can, of course, run the camera-VCR unit off any household outlet, provided you have the appropriate AC/DC converter. In this case, there is no limit to the operating time, but you are always tied to an AC cord.

3. *Cassettes.* The maximum is 20 minutes. The 20-minute cassettes for portable recorders are somewhat smaller than the standard 60-minute cassettes.

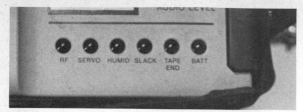

10.25 Portable VCR Warning Lights (Sony BVU 110) These are the problems when the warning lights go on:

RF—no video is being recorded, or video interference

Servo—video is out of sync

Humid—too much humidity in the machine; the recorder will turn itself off.

Slack—too much tape slack in the cassette

Tape end—the cassette tape has run out

Batt.—new battery needed (lights up with several minutes of power still left in the battery).

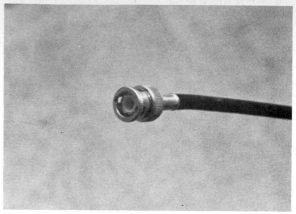

10.26 BNC Connector The BNC connector is the standard connector for the video signal.

The latter do not fit into portable VCRs. Some large cassettes contain only a 20-minute tape, but they still do not fit the portable recorder. On the other hand, the smaller cassettes play on any of the $\frac{3}{4}$-inch VCRs. Note that the smaller cassette does not mean a reduction in tape width; rather, it refers to a smaller housing.

4. *Operational Controls.* On the models with record and playback functions (such as the BVU 110), standard controls include the power on-off switch, and the *play, record, rewind, fast forward, stop,* and *eject* buttons. Each of the two audio channels has a VU meter and volume control. There is a switch with which you can select the AGC (automatic gain control) mode. Some of the more elaborate models have controls for *pause* (tape is stopped, delivering a freeze-framelike image) and an audio-dub control with which you can record additional audio without affecting the video portion of the recording. The play-record mode can be activated by the VTR switch on the camera.

The *record-only models* (such as the BVU 50) have a *minimum of controls:* power on-off button, *record* button, and an *eject* lever. You can assign either pot and the video output to the single VU meter through the select switch. The single VU meter can be switched to read the inputs of either channel 1 or channel 2 audio, or the video level.

5. *Warning Lights.* As you remember, the ENG/EFP cameras have control lights in the viewfinder that indicate certain camera functions and malfunctions, such as white balance, VTR mode, and low battery condition. Because you have little chance to read meters when operating the portable VCR (often in addition to the camera), a number of warning lights tell you certain operational conditions at a glance (see 10.25).

6. *Connectors.* All portable VCRs designed for professional use have 3-pin XLR audio connectors and standard BNC video connectors (see 10.26). Hence, you can connect various types of portable cameras to the portable VCRs without special cables or adaptors. There is a special connector for an attachable time code generator. Standard connectors are especially important if you rent or borrow equipment to supplement yours for more elaborate productions. It is still a good idea to double-check and see whether all plugs are, indeed, compatible.

7. *Time Counter.* There is a time counter that displays either the SMPTE/EBU time code, or the time recorded in minutes and seconds.

8. *Carrying Devices.* This may seem like an unimportant item, until you have to carry and operate the VCR. Most ENG/EFP people carry the recorder by a shoulder strap that is attached to the machine. Others put the recorder into a specially made bag that has

10.27   VCR Carried on Shoulder Strap The most practical method of carrying a portable VCR during ENG is by shoulder strap. This way, the camera operator can operate and observe the VTR while carrying the ENG camera.

VCR in backpack

10.28   VCR Backpack The most comfortable method of carrying a portable VCR is with a specially designed backpack. The disadvantage of the backpack method is that the camera operator cannot operate or observe the VCR when working the camera.

some protective padding and pockets for microphones, cables, spare batteries and cassettes, and other accessories. For EFP you may want to carry the VCR in a backpack or, to take the load off your shoulders, place the VCR in a small two-wheel cart (see 10.27 through 10.29).

Special VCRs

The special video cassette recorders include (1) the 2-inch cart recorder, (2) the $\frac{1}{2}$-inch VCR, and (3) the in-camera VCR.

The 2-inch Cart Recorder   The 2-inch "cart" recorder uses 2-inch video *cassettes* and the quadruplex recording system. Because they resemble the audio

cart machines in use and appearance, they were called **video "cart" (cartridge)** machines when they first appeared on the market, and the name has stuck ever since.

As pointed out before, the 2-inch cart recorders are used primarily for short program material during station breaks, such as commercials, station promotions, and public service announcements. You can program a sequence of such spots with the help of a microprocessor, and activate the sequence by remote control. A single cart machine can play continually up to twenty-three cassettes in the preprogrammed sequence. The computer also displays the house number (identification) of each cassette and checks it against the computer log entry. It flashes any discrepancy between the house number in the log and the number of the cassette about to be played.

The **lockup time** (time for the picture and sound to stabilize once the tape has been started) is so short that there needs to be no **preroll** (to start the tape and let it roll for some time before it is put in the playback or record mode). The 2-inch cassette has a maximum playing time of about 6 minutes—more than enough for station-break material. What would be an impossible feat for regular videotape recorders (loading, threading the tape, and starting the tape with the necessary preroll for every 10-second, back-to-back spot) can be done by the 2-inch cart machine with ease and reliability.

The disadvantage of the 2-inch cart machine is that it is quite large and bulky, as are the cassettes. Also, it is very expensive and, therefore, found only in larger stations. (See 10.30.)

The $\frac{1}{2}$-inch VCR   You might very well use a $\frac{1}{2}$-inch VCR in a television operation, although these machines were primarily designed for home use. For example, you do not really need a $\frac{3}{4}$-inch cassette or even a larger format VCR to screen tape segments for initial editing decisions, to preview programs or program segments for content, or to tape shows for archival purposes. Also, the top $\frac{1}{2}$-inch VCRs deliver pictures and sound that are often quite satisfactory for many nonbroadcast production tasks. The major criterion for using a particular VCR should not be tape format, but whether or not it meets the production requirements.

The two most popular models are the *Betamax* (usually called the "Beta" system) and the *VHS (Video Home System)* cassette recorders. Realizing the increased demand for inexpensive, good-quality recorders in all facets of television production, manufacturers upgraded some of the $\frac{1}{2}$-inch VCRs and equipped them with many of the $\frac{3}{4}$-inch VCR features (see 10.31 and 10.32).

For example, JVC has on the market a professional VHS unit that consists of a separate recorder and player. With these units, you can:

1.   Record and play a 2-hour program with a single cassette

2.   Shuttle the tape at ten times normal speed while maintaining a recognizable image

10.29   VCR Cart Some ENG and especially EFP teams prefer to have the portable VCR on a special cart. Like an airplane baggage cart, the VCR cart is very light, collapsible, and highly maneuverable.

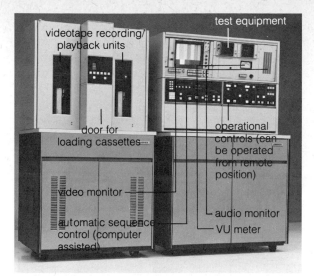

videotape recording/
playback units

test equipment

door for
loading cassettes

operational
controls (can
be operated
from remote
position)

video monitor

audio monitor

automatic sequence
control (computer
assisted)

VU meter

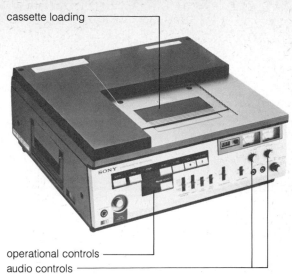

cassette loading

operational controls
audio controls

10.30   Two-inch "Cart" Recorder (Ampex ACR-25) The 2-inch videotape cassette allows the back-to-back use of short videotaped program material, such as a series of consecutive 10-second spots. The cassette recorder selects the tape cassette, threads the tape, and cues it, within seconds. (The *start* button starts the tape roll and puts the picture "on the air" in one operation. No preroll is necessary for the cassette.) The cassette recorder can record off any VTR, or another of its cassettes.

10.31   Sony SLO 323 MD Betamax $\frac{1}{2}$-inch Video Cassette Recorder The $\frac{1}{2}$-inch VCRs are of amazingly good quality and find more and more use in professional television operation. They have many of the $\frac{3}{4}$-inch VCR features, such as ten times normal speed for shuttle and automatic search, playback from still to five times normal speed in both directions with a visible image, two-channel audio, and interface capabilities with $\frac{3}{4}$-inch VCRs.

3. Jog the tape in both directions and stop it for freeze-frame effects

4. Use any of the two audio channels independently or together for stereo. There are two pots and VU meters for volume control

5. Interface the VHS recorder with identical models or $\frac{3}{4}$-inch VCRs and with editing control units for computer-assisted editing

6. Attach remote control units and random access units for quick retrieval of recorded material.

There are also stripped-down portable versions that look and function similar to their -inch $\frac{3}{4}$ relatives.

The In-Camera VCR   In Chapter 2, we talked about the camera part of the ENG camera/VTR combination. Now we will take a closer look at the VTR part.

The in-camera VTR of such "combi" cameras is actually a $\frac{1}{2}$-*inch video cassette recorder* that can be

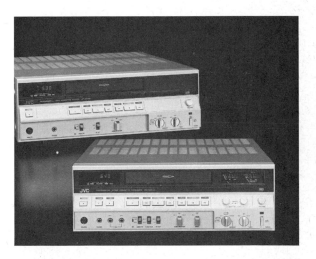

10.32   Half-inch VHS Recorder and Player Unit (JVC BR 6400 U and BP 5300 U) The operational features of the VHS $\frac{1}{2}$-inch VCRs are quite similar to those of the Beta format. Note that the two systems are not compatible, however. A Beta-format tape cannot be played on a VHS player, and vice versa.

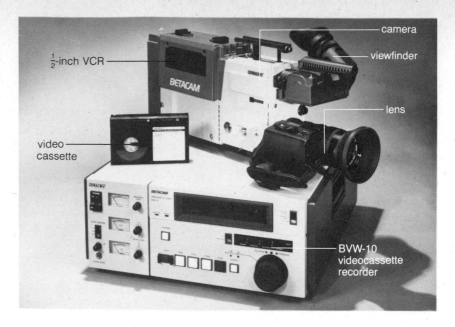

10.33 Sony Betacam System The Sony Betacam system consists of the Betacam camera; the Beta-format $\frac{1}{2}$-inch VCR, which can be attached to the camera or used independently as a portable VCR; and a cassette player.

$\frac{1}{2}$-inch VCR

video cassette

camera

viewfinder

lens

BVW-10 videocassette recorder

attached directly to the camera or used independently with any other type of ENG/EFP camera (see 10.33 and 10.34). Or you can use the camera part with any other type of videotape recorder.

The in-camera VCR is operationally quite similar to the record-only portable $\frac{3}{4}$-inch VCRs. It can:

1. Record up to 20 minutes on a single cassette

2. Operate continuously for 1 hour with a single battery

3. Record on two audio channels

4. Use the built-in time code generator to record time code on a third track

5. Use various warning lights to signal specific troubles, such as RF (video), servo (sync), humidity, slack, tape end, and battery.

For playback and postproduction, there is a larger cassette player that can perform all the usual VCR tasks, such as fast and slow shuttle, jog functions with viewable pictures, and auto-search. It interfaces

with other equipment, such as videotape recorders, editing controls, image stabilizing and enhancing equipment, switchers, and special effects units.

The various equipment manufacturers are constantly striving to reduce the size and weight of ENG equipment while maintaining or improving picture and sound quality. The $\frac{1}{2}$-inch cassette will probably be considered the "large" tape format in the not too distant future.

PRODUCTION FACTORS

There are certain operational steps in videotape recording that are especially important for preproduction, production, and postproduction activities. Since we will discuss postproduction extensively in Chapter 11, we will limit ourselves here to the major preproduction and production factors of videotape recording.

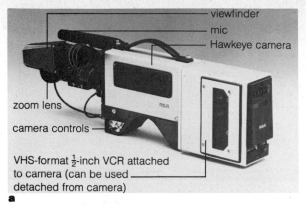

viewfinder
mic
Hawkeye camera
zoom lens
camera controls
VHS-format ½-inch VCR attached to camera (can be used detached from camera)

a

10.34   RCA Hawkeye System (a) The Hawkeye system by RCA has a ½-inch VHS-format VCR attached to the camera. It can record up to 20 minutes on a single cassette. The VCR can record on two audio tracks and can generate time code. The recordings are not compatible with the Betacam recordings or with regular VHS players.

(b) The VCR can be used separately from the camera, very much like the portable ¾-inch VCRs. The Hawkeye system has an additional studio recorder that can be interfaced with edit controllers for postproduction.

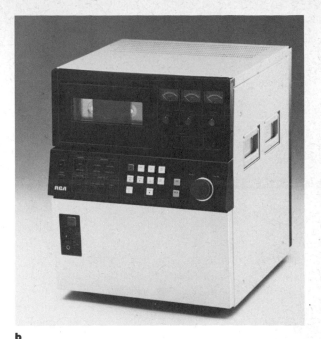

b

Preproduction

Production efficiency is determined to a large extent by the amount and precision of production preparation. In the area of videotape recording, you need to consider scheduling and certain factors for videotape playback, recording, and editing.

Schedule   The VTR schedule requires some information about VTR mode, type, and videotaping time. *Mode* refers to *how* you are going to use the videotape recorders—for playback, recording, dubbing, or editing. *Type* means what kind of VTR you are requesting. Obviously, the *type* must match the specific task. If you have to play back a quad recording, you need a 2-inch quad recorder to do the job. On the other hand, if the material is on 1-inch C-format tape, you need to schedule the 1-inch VTR. In case the recorder available does not fit your tape format, you have to dub the tape up or down before it can be played back. Try to keep the large production VTRs as free as possible for the on-the-air jobs.

Once you know the type of machine you need and what it is to do, you can *schedule* the most appropriate time for its use. In your time request, be sensitive to the other demands made on the machine and its operator. Except for the on-the-air playback or the recording of scheduled shows, there are always some time slots that fall outside the VTR rush hours. If you have a large-format tape (1-inch or 2-inch) that needs to be screened repeatedly, have it dubbed onto a smaller format tape (¾-inch or ½-inch cassette). This way, you keep the production recorders free for some of the more important on-the-air jobs.

Playback   Make sure the recording is *compatible* with your playback machine. Pay particular attention to the 1-inch format. You cannot play the B-format on your C-format machines. The same problem exists for the ½-inch cassettes: the Beta and VHS formats are not compatible, and Betacam and Hawkeye tapes must be played back on special equipment.

Pull all the playback tapes ahead of time and

check whether the various boxes contain the correct tapes. Do not rely solely on the label of the box, but check especially the label on the tape. If possible, preview just a minute or so of each tape to see whether its content matches the label. You may consider such procedures redundant and a waste of time. They are not. By making triple-checking routine, you will not only prevent costly production errors, but save time, energy, and ultimately nerves.

Record   Make sure that you have *enough tape* on hand. This is especially important if you have to record a live event in its entirety for playback at a later time, or if you do a "live on tape" production. This means that a show is shot, usually with multiple cameras, uninterrupted from beginning to end and put on videotape rather than on the air. If the largest reel does not hold enough tape for the entire event, you need to schedule two machines or you will lose a few minutes during the reel change. When using more than one type of VTR during a production, procure enough tape for each VTR type.

Although you may rightly assume that getting sufficient power for the equipment during an elaborate ENG or EFP assignment is the province of the engineering department, you should still double-check on what power is available and whether it is suitable for your VTRs. For example, if you use household AC as power supply, do you have the converter along to drive your ENG VCRs? Make certain that the batteries are fully charged before going to the remote location. Also, if the remote vehicle does not have its own generator, see whether it carries the necessary AC extension cords and adaptors to fit ordinary household outlets.

Edit   Editing is actually a postproduction activity. But if you intend to insert some more program material directly in the master tape (the one you are using for the original videotaping) at a later time, you need to lay a control track before using the tape even for the original recording (see the discussion of insert editing in Chapter 11). The easiest way to put a control track on tape is to record black. Realize, however, that laying a 60-minute control track takes 60 minutes. So, if you anticipate using several reels with prerecorded control tracks, you had better schedule several hours of VTR recording time before the actual videotaping.

Production

When playing back a properly recorded "air" master videotape recording, you will notice some "front matter" at the head of the tape: color bars, a steady tone, an identification slate, perhaps some numbers flashing by, with accompanying audio beeps for each number. These items, collectively called **video leader,** give important technical information and aid in the playback and editing process. Let's look at them one by one.

Color bars help the videotape operator match the technical aspects of the playback with that of the recording. It is, therefore, important that you record the color bars (fed by color bar generators located in master control or built into ENG/EFP cameras) for a minimum of 10 seconds each time you start a new taping session or exchange videotape equipment.

As already mentioned in Chapter 9, most audio consoles can generate a **test tone** that you can use to indicate a zero VU volume level. This zero VU test tone is recorded along with the color bars. The test tone and the color bars should be recorded with the equipment that you use for the subsequent videotaping. Otherwise, the playback will be referenced to the test signals (color bars and test tone), but not to the videotaped material. The director refers to these test signals as "bars and tone." You will hear the director call for "bars and tone" when calling for a videotape roll.

The **slate** gives important production information, along with some technical information. This small whiteboard is in the customary 3 × 4 aspect ratio (3 units high and 4 units wide) and has a surface that can be easily cleaned. It usually contains the following information: (1) show title, (2) name of series (if any), (3) scene number (matches the scene number in the script), (4) take number (how often you record the same thing), and (5) the recording date. Some slates also list the director, the location (especially important for EFP), the possible playback date, and additional in-house information, such as reel numbers, editing instructions, name of producer, and so forth (see 10.35). Studios with a character generator (see p. 418) often use the electronic character display as a slate.

Leader numbers and **beepers** are used for the accurate *cuing* of the videotape during playback. The leader numbers flash at 1-second intervals from 10 to 3 and are synchronized with short audio "beeps." The last two seconds are kept in black and silent so that they do not appear accidentally on the air if the videotape is punched up somewhat early. The recorded program material appears (or should appear) at the zero countdown. When cuing a videotape for playback, you can stop the tape at a particular leader number, say "5." This means that you must preroll the tape exactly 5 seconds before the program material is to appear on the air.

Sometimes only the beepers are used. They help not only with the initial tape cuing, but especially in locating separate programs or program segments on the tape. Provided that all program segments on the tape were preceded by the beeper series, you can now listen for them when in the shuttle mode. As soon as you hear the fast series of high-pitched tones, stop the tape. You are now in the vicinity of one of the recorded segments.

Some time ago, the SMPTE tried to standardize the video leaders, as they did with similar film leaders (see 10.36).

Aside from the color bars, test tone, and slate information, the video leader is not all that helpful. First, most modern VTRs have tape counters that display real time. This time readout is usually more accurate than the video leader numbers. Second, the newer VTRs stabilize so quickly that long prerolls are not done any more. Third, many of the video inserts are so short (such as news stories) that the leader would almost be as long as the insert itself.

Preroll   Although most VTRs gain operating speed and display a stable image within a second or so, most videotape operators like to preroll the tape anywhere from 2 to 5 seconds. Exactly how long the preroll should be depends on the responsiveness of the VTR, but also upon the habit of the videotape operators and directors. If, for example, the videotape operator is used to the 10-second countdown

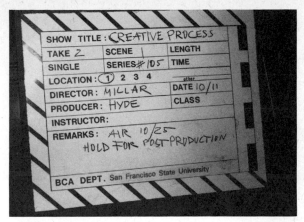

10.35   Slate The slate, which is recorded at the beginning of each take, shows vital production information, such as the title of the show, the scene and take numbers, the playback, and so forth.

that was necessary to get the old monochrome quad recorders up to speed, he or she will regard the customary 5-second preroll as frivolously short. Many directors, too, prefer some kind of countdown. They argue that it gives them some cushion and flexibility (albeit psychological) in the control of videotape sequences. Often, however, no preroll is used in VTR playback. What you do is park the helical VTR so that it displays a freeze frame of the beginning of your playback segment, and then start the playback by switching the VTR to the play mode. Sometimes, frame store synchronizers are used for the freeze-frame display. We will talk more about frame store equipment in Chapter 13.

If a certain preroll system has been established, make sure that you do not try to record the first scene before the machine has reached operational speed and is put in the record mode. As a director, you must wait for the videotape operator to give you the "in record" or "speed" cue before you can record the slate and the program material that follows.

Address   When you record several program segments on a single tape, you should have some means of identifying the location, or "address," of each segment and even each frame within the recording. With this identification you can locate any spot in the tape with speed and accuracy. Such an address

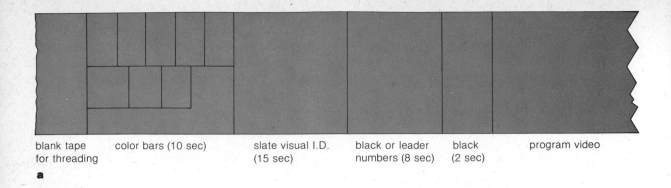

| blank tape for threading | color bars (10 sec) | slate visual I.D. (15 sec) | black or leader numbers (8 sec) | black (2 sec) | program video |

a

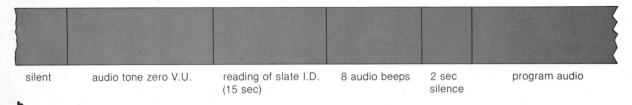

| silent | audio tone zero V.U. | reading of slate I.D. (15 sec) | 8 audio beeps | 2 sec silence | program audio |

b

10.36   SMPTE Video Leader (a) video; (b) audio.

system consists of the slate and beepers, and an address code. As pointed out earlier, the slate and the beeper assist you in giving some information about *where* the various segments are located, and *what* the segments are all about. The address code makes it possible to identify each frame.

Because the slate identifies the scenes as well as each take, you must use it every time you record a new take, regardless of how short or how complete the take may be. Let's assume you have just recorded about 30 seconds of the first take in your first scene when the performer stumbles over the name of the product he or she is advertising. You stop the tape, keep calm, roll the tape again, and wait for the "in-record" confirmation. Before coming up on the performer, you need to record the slate again. It reads: Scene 1, Take 1. But we are now starting with Take 2. Should you go on, or stop the tape again to correct the slate? Stop the tape again. The floor manager must change the take number from 1 to 2, unless you decide to start from the very beginning and erase the first take. Some directors opt for "tail-slating," which means that you tag the slate onto the end of the take. If you tail-slate a take,

make sure that you say so on the slate and the audio track.

It is the attention you pay to such seemingly minor production detail, not just your occasional creative leaps, that makes you a respected professional.

Whereas the slate guides you to a particular street or block, so to speak, the address code identifies each individual house on the block. You will read more about the address code systems in Chapter 11.

Record Keeping   Keeping accurate records of what you videotape and the proper labeling of the videotapes may seem insignificant while you are in the middle of the production activities, but they are of major importance once the tape is back at the station. You will be surprised how quickly you can forget the "unforgettable" production and especially the number and sequence of takes. Keeping accurate records *during* the production can save you hours of frustrating work in postproduction.

In order to record essential information, you need to use the **shot sheet** (also called take sheet or cue sheet). It usually contains: (1) production title,

(2) production job number, (3) taping date, (4) VTR reel number, (5) code use, (6) scene number, (7) take or shot number, (8) length of take, (9) in (entrance) and out (exit) code address, (10) acceptability of take, and (11) remarks (see 10.37). The remarks column can contain any type of information, such as the name of the scene, special problems you encountered, or important audio cues.

As soon as you are done with the videotape recording, label the tape container *and the tape itself* with the customary identification (usually show title, date of recording, and VTR number). The VTR reel number in the shot sheet and on the tape itself obviously must correspond. Put one copy of the shot sheet *with the tape* and another copy in your *production folder* (which contains the script, facilities requests, release forms, and so forth).

Additional Points   Here is a list of some additional points to consider when videotaping:

1.   Always do a brief initial test recording to see whether the whole system works properly. You can use these tests to record some of the ambient audio.

2.   Be sure to reset the tape counter on the VTR before starting with the actual program recording. If you use time code or if the counter writes and reads real time, you can easily record the actual lengths of the takes. Otherwise, you need to time the various takes with a stopwatch.

3.   Wait until the VTR has reached operating speed and has stabilized before starting to record. This lockup time may take anywhere from 2 to 7 seconds.

4.   Watch the audio and video levels during the recording. If you do not have a special audio setup, but feed the mic directly into the VTR, pay special attention to the audio portion. You will find that a director may become so captivated by the beautiful camera shots that he or she does not even hear the airplane noise interrupting the medieval scene shot on location, or the slate dropping with a loud bang during an especially tender moment of a song.

5.   When recording for postproduction, be sure to record enough of each segment so that the action overlaps with the preceding and following scenes. Such cushions or pads greatly facilitate editing. If you have enough tape, videotape the camera rehearsals. Sometimes you will get a better performance during rehearsal than during the actual take. But be sure to slate and/or note in your shot sheet every take you have on tape, rehearsal or not. At the end of each take, record a few seconds of black before stopping the tape. This **"run-out" signal** again acts as a pad during editing, or, if you do a live-on-tape recording, as a safety cushion during playback.

6.   Do not waste time between takes. If you are properly prepared, you can keep the intervals between taping to a minimum. Although the playback of each take may occasionally improve the subsequent performance by cast and crew, it usually does not justify the time it takes away from the actual production. If you pay close attention to what is going on during the videotaping, you do not need to review each take. Long interruptions not only waste time, but lower the energy level of the production team and talent. On the other hand, do not rush through taping sessions at a frantic pace. If you feel another take is necessary, do another one right then and there. It is far less expensive to repeat a take than to have to re-create a whole scene later, simply because one of your single takes turned out to be unusable. As one wise production expert says: "There is never enough time to do it right, but always enough time to do it over."

7.   Review only those takes that you felt were acceptable during the videotaping.

MAIN POINTS

1.   Videotape and film are the two major program sources.

2.   Videotape is used principally for (1) building of a whole show by assembling parts that have been recorded at different times and/or locations; (2) time delay; (3) duplication and distribution of programs; and (4) records for reference and study.

3.   There are six principal videotape recording modes: (1) ENG style: single camera–single VTR, whereby the event is recorded in bits and pieces, but generally in its natural sequence; (2) film style:

Production Title: _____

Producer/Director: _____

Taping Date: _____ VTR Reel Number: _____ Code: SMPTE/EBU: _____ Other: _____

Scene	Take	In				Out				Length	OK	Remarks													
		hr	min	sec	fr	hr	min	sec	fr																

10.37 VTR Shot Sheet

single camera–single VTR, whereby the event is recorded in bits and pieces, but not in its natural sequence and with takes repeated for different camera points of view; (3) live-on-tape style, whereby a production is run as though it were live, with its line-out signal going to a VTR instead of the transmitter; (4) segment style, whereby a show is recorded in longer program segments in or out of sequence for later assembly in postproduction; (5) isolated or iso camera, whereby the production is run very much like live-on-tape, except that an isolated camera feeds a second, separate, VTR; and (6) multiple cameras–multiple VTRs, in which each camera feeds its own VTR. Each camera acts as an iso camera.

4. The three basic video recording systems are: (1) the quad (quadruplex), or transverse, scanning system; (2) the helical or slant-track system; and (3) the video disc.

5. The quad VTR uses a 2-inch-wide tape. The helical VTRs use videotape of various widths: $\frac{1}{4}$-inch, $\frac{1}{2}$-inch, $\frac{3}{4}$-inch, and 1 inch. The different tape widths are called tape format.

6. There are different system standards. The 1-inch VTRs come in Type B, and the more popular Type C standards. They are not compatible. The U-matic system is the only one for the $\frac{3}{4}$-inch video cassette

recorders. The $\frac{1}{2}$-inch video cassette recorders belong either to the Betamax system or the VHS (Video Home Service) system. These two systems are not compatible.

7. The two basic types of videotape recorders are reel-to-reel and cassette recorders. Most reel-to-reel machines are the quad (2-inch) or 1-inch VTRs. These VTRs produce high-quality pictures and sound. The 1-inch VTRs can play back at several slow motion speeds and can produce a jitter-free freeze frame.

8. Video cassette recorders include the standard $\frac{3}{4}$-inch VCR, the portable $\frac{3}{4}$-inch VCR, and the $\frac{1}{2}$-inch VCR. Special VCRs include the 2-inch quad cart machine, and the $\frac{1}{2}$-inch and $\frac{1}{4}$-inch in-camera VCRs and playback units.

9. The preproduction factors for videotaping include the scheduling of VTRs for recording and playback, the acquisition of sufficient videotape, and the laying of control track, if the tape is used for postproduction (see Chapter 11).

10. The major production factors when using videotape are the video leader (color bars and test tone), slate information, beepers, and accurate record keeping of the various videotape segments. The record keeping is greatly aided by a shot sheet.

SPECIAL RECORDING SYSTEMS

The special recording systems include (1) the *digital VTR*, (2) the *LVR* (longitudinal video recording) system, and (3) the *MBM* (magnetic bubble memory). Undoubtedly, the increasing application of digital technology will give birth to many new recording devices. However, do not jump every time you read or hear about some development in this field. First, a new piece of equipment does not necessarily render the old one obsolete, unless the new development expands or changes your production capacity significantly. Second, unless equipment has been standardized, it limits your production to your own operation. Third, the first generation of new equipment is always more expensive than the subsequent ones. There is no need to abandon your old equipment right away, as long as it performs the production tasks with the expected quality, reliability, and efficiency.

The Digital VTR

The **digital VTRs** look similar to the present reel-to-reel machines, except that the tape receives digital rather than analog information. As with the digital audio,

the video information no longer consists of analog signals, but of a great number of zeros and ones. As numbers, the video and audio signals can then be manipulated for video and audio enhancement and for special effects. Best of all, digital video provides transparent copying, which means that no matter how many times a program is copied, it retains pretty much the quality of the original without adding more systems noise to each subsequent dub (see Chapter 9). But the problem of standards for interchangeability will have to be solved before such recorders can be used on a large scale.

The LVR System

The **longitudinal video recording (LVR) system** works in principle like a multitrack audiotape recorder, except that the parallel tracks that run (longitudinally) along the tape contain not audio, but video information. You may recall that a 24-track audiotape recorder, for example, has twenty-four recording heads stacked on top of each other, each one recording its audio information on the 2-inch tape. In the LVR system, more than two hundred video heads stacked on top of each other put their video tracks onto a $\frac{1}{4}$-inch tape. If properly developed, the LVR system would permit even smaller VTRs than the $\frac{1}{2}$-inch units now in use.

SECTION TWO

Because videotape recorder manufacturers
are constantly introducing more sophisticated recording systems and because news
stations often retain older equipment, you
need to be familiar with both the latest VTR
designs and the film systems that are still
sometimes in use.

This section discusses (1) special recording systems—including the digital VTR,
the longitudinal video recording system, the
magnetic bubble memory system, and the $\frac{1}{2}$-
inch VTR—and (2) film equipment and
operation.

The MBM System

There is some possibility that the development of recording systems may skip the digital VTR and go right
to some kind of **magnetic bubble memory (MBM)
system.** This system can store an incredible amount
of digital information on small chips (digital storage
devices). In contrast to the VTR and disc systems, the
MBM system has no moving parts and stores all its
information in rows and rows of chips. Random access
of any part of the stored information is an integral part
of the system. There is no tape wear, no clogging of
record and play heads, and no sync problems with
tape or disc drives, regardless of how often and how
much you jostle the video information around. A working MBM system would be an editor's dream.

The $\frac{1}{2}$-inch VTR

There are still some $\frac{1}{2}$-inch reel-to-reel VTRs in operation. These machines helped to revolutionize the independent video movement, because they were relatively
inexpensive and easy to operate. Unfortunately, they
cannot deliver a broadcast-quality picture, even with
the aid of time base correctors and other stabilizing or
image-enhancing equipment. But you still may find them

quite useful for reviewing "rushes" (program segments
taped for postproduction editing) and for many nonbroadcast applications (see 10.38). Besides, many
excellent and innovative productions never made it to
the "large format" and are available only on $\frac{1}{2}$-inch reel-
to-reel tapes.

FILM

Film used to be one of the major program sources in
television, including motion picture features, news,
documentaries, and commercials. Now, film in television is pretty much restricted to the playing of motion
picture features and occasional documentaries. Although many commercials are still produced on film,
they are immediately transferred to tape and distributed to the stations as videotapes.

Nevertheless, because film is still used in television production, you have to acquaint yourself with some
of its basic features and its basic television use.

Basic Features

The basic features include film format and sound track.
The film use concerns itself with the equipment nec-

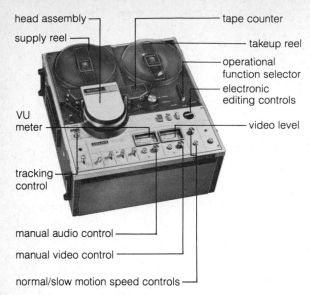

head assembly
supply reel
tape counter
takeup reel
operational function selector
electronic editing controls
VU meter
video level
tracking control
manual audio control
manual video control
normal/slow motion speed controls

a   b

10.38 **Sony AV 8650 ½-inch VTR** Controls for most helical scan VTRs include features such as forward, fast forward, record, and stop. Some of the more advanced models have separate controls for slow-motion and stop-motion, and stand-by (which starts rotating the video heads without moving the tape). The arrangement of the controls differs from model to model, but they fulfill identical functions.

10.39 **Film Formats** The film formats used in television are the 16mm film (a) and the 35mm film (b). The 35mm film is used only in networks and network-owned stations for the playback of feature films.

essary to project film or slides on television and some major operational aspects.

Film Format Like videotape, film is classified according to width: 8mm, Super-8(mm), 16mm, 35mm, and 70mm. Most television stations can play only the 16mm format, but networks and some "O and O" stations (owned and operated by one of the major networks) have facilities to play the high-quality 35mm theater prints (see 10.39).

Film Sound Film can be **"silent,"** which means there is no sound track on the film, or it can be **SOF** (sound

on film), whereby the film carries an audio track along with the pictures. All films used in television are SOF. But there are two principal types of sound on film: *optical sound* and *magnetic sound.*

Optical sound is re-created by shining a small light (the exciter lamp) through a **variable area track** (transparent spikes), which modulates (changes) light falling on a photoelectric cell. The resulting electrical signal is then amplified and perceived as sound (see 10.40).

The **magnetic sound track,** or **mag track**, consists of a narrow magnetic tape that runs down one side of the film (with a balance stripe running parallel on the other side of the film to maintain uniform film

Film Chain Also called film island, or telecine. Consists of one or two film projectors, a slide projector, a multiplexer, and a television film, or telecine, camera.

Multiplexer A system of mirrors or prisms that directs images from several projection sources (film, slides) into one stationary television film, or telecine, camera.

SOF Sound on film.

Telecine 1. Same as Film Chain, or film island. 2. The place from which the film islands operate. The word comes from *tele*vision and *cine*matography. Occasionally, the telecine is used for film storage and some minor film-editing jobs.

10.40 Optical Variable Area Sound Track The variable area sound track is an optical track whose light-transmitting areas differ, thus modulating (changing) the light of the exciter lamp. When received by the photoelectric cell, the light modulations are converted into electrical energy, the sound signal.

10.41 Magnetic Sound Track The magnetic sound track consists of a tiny magnetic tape that runs down one side of the film, often called "mag stripe." A second magnetic stripe runs parallel to the actual sound stripe on the opposite side of the film. This "balance stripe" is merely to compensate for the extra thickness so that the film runs evenly through the projector.

thickness). This magnetic stripe is an audiotape and performs all of its usual functions (see 10.41).

All television film projectors can accommodate either optical or magnetic sound. Some switch automatically from one to the other sound track. Before putting a film on the projector, check whether it has a magnetic or optical sound track. Then switch the projector either to optical or magnetic sound.

The Film Chain, or Film Island

In order to put a film on the air, you need to understand the film chain, or film island, and its components, and the basic factors of film operation.

The basic **film chain** or **film island** consists of at least one film projector, a slide projector, a multiplexer, and a television film camera, or, as it is frequently called, a telecine camera (from *tele*vision and *cine*matography). Occasionally the film island with its components is called the telecine system. Most film chains contain a second film projector. Let's take a brief look at each of these components: (1) the film projector, (2) the slide projector, (3) the multiplexer, and (4) the film camera. (See 10.42.)

Film Projector The television film projector is especially designed so that the (16mm) film speed of 24 frames per second corresponds to the 30 frames of the television picture. This synchronization is accomplished by the television film camera scanning the first film frame twice, the second three times, the third twice again, and so on. If a film projector is not synchronized with the television system, you will detect a slight flutter in the television picture and, sometimes, black shutter bars moving up and down the screen.

Most film projectors can accommodate large 20-

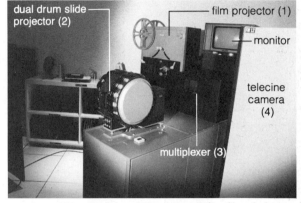

10.42 Film Chain or Film Island The film chain consists of (1) film projector, (2) slide projector, (3) multiplexer, and (4) the film, or telecine, camera.

inch (4,000-foot) reels (some even 5,000-foot reels) that allow a continuous projection of almost 2 hours of film programs, and tiny 50-foot reels. Although the film projectors have automatic film tension compensators, it is a good idea to use a *takeup reel* of the *same size as the supply reel*. This way, you maintain uniform film tension and drastically reduce the danger of film breakage. (See 10.43.)

Film projectors usually have a number of devices that facilitate operations:

1. The threading mechanism is usually kept as simple as possible so that, with some experience, you can thread the film within seconds.

2. The projectors can bring the film with its sound up to full speed within a fraction of a second. This "zero preroll" eliminates a preroll countdown.

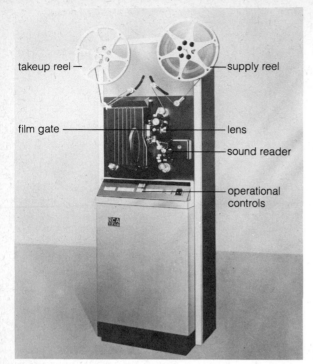

takeup reel —

supply reel

film gate —

lens

sound reader

operational controls

10.43   Television Film Projector The professional television film projector adjusts the 24-frames-per-second 16mm sound speed to the 30-frames-per-second electronic scanning of television. It can be remotely started and stopped, backed up in reverse, and stopped for still-frame projection without burning up the film. The largest reels can accommodate almost 2 hours of continuous film programming.

3.   All film projectors have a remote start-and-stop mechanism, which can be activated manually, or triggered by computer control. Most projectors have automatic cuing systems, whereby the film can be programmed in advance to stop and cue itself for the next segment in as many places as desired. This automatic cuing is accomplished by attaching small pieces of special tape to the film at the specific cuing points. The film projector senses these tapes and performs the necessary functions automatically.

4.   All television film projectors have a pickup device for both optical and magnetic sound. Some projectors can switch automatically from one type to the other.

5.   Most projectors can show a single film frame for extended periods without danger of burning the film.

6.   The projection lamp and the sound-exciter lamp

exchange themselves automatically if they happen to fail during the film projection.

As mentioned earlier, film islands usually have two film projectors to ensure maximum continuity of programming. As soon as the film of the first projector has run out, the second projector can be started and switched on the air.

Slide Projector   Transparency slide projectors have slides arranged on two vertically or horizontally arranged dual drums. The latter are called carousel drums. The more popular, vertically arranged dual drums have a slide capacity of 36 slides (18 each) (see 10.44). Dual-drum slide projectors permit reloading or changing slides while the machine is in operation. Most new drum slide projectors are designed for forward and reverse action. Some are equipped with a random selection device, through which you can punch up any slide without waiting for the drums to rotate one slide at a time until the desired slide finally appears in the gate. In case the projector lamp burns out, you can pull a large handle and put the spare lamp into operation.

To load a slide, simply stand *behind* the slide drums and hold the slide the way you want it to appear on the screen. Insert it *right side up* into the slide holder facing you. When you advance the slide drum so that the slide is near the projection lens, the slide will turn upside down automatically (see 10.45).

Slides are generally easier to use than studio cards. First, keeping them in order is much simpler than handling loose cards on various easels. Second, they can be changed on the air more cleanly and rapidly than studio cards. Third, the use of slides does not tie up a studio camera.

The disadvantage of using slides rather than studio cards is that the fixed television film camera cannot move on the slides.

Multiplexer   The **multiplexer** is a series of mirrors or prisms that direct the images from several projection sources, such as slides and film projectors, into a single fixed television film, or telecine, camera (see 10.46). Without the multiplexer, each film projector and each slide projector would need its own film camera. Film and slides are projected through **"ports"** (openings in the multiplexer) onto the multiplexer mirrors.

The Telecine, or Television Film, Camera   The **telecine,** or television film, camera is quite similar to a regular television camera. The three color pickup tubes are either Plumbicon or vidicon tubes. Most telecine cameras have automatic brightness and color correction features, which adjust to the various degrees of color temperature, saturation, contrast range, or general density of the films or slides projected.

Film Operation

The major factors in using film for television are (1) film quality check and storage, (2) film projection, and (3) film cuing and timing.

Film Quality Check and Storage Before putting a film on the projector, you should do a quality check. Such a check involves looking for *bad splices* (places where film broke during previous showings and was then glued together again), *torn sprocket holes,* scratches, and other serious injuries. It also includes a cursory look at *color consistency.* If you notice a marked change in color quality (from a warm, reddish overall hue to a cold, bluish hue, or from intensely saturated colors to washed-out colors, for example), warn the video engineer. Although the automatic color correction will compensate as much as possible for such changes, the video engineer may have to correct drastic color changes manually.

Lastly, check for *content.* Although television has become somewhat liberated as to what is considered proper for home viewing, some unsuitable material may, nevertheless, have escaped the scrutiny of the traffic department, which usually takes care of such matters. But *do not play censor.* Alert the program manager or the traffic department if you perceive a piece of film as too offensive for broadcasting.

Like videotape, store the film in a dry, cool, dust-free place. Place it in tightly closed cans in order to keep it from drying out; a very dry film becomes brittle and breaks easily in the projector. Label each film carefully with the title, category (feature, commercial), and house number.

Film Projection First of all, run the film through the film cleaner. When threading the film, follow the threading diagram that is usually supplied by the manufacturer. It is often attached to the projector. Here are a few items that deserve attention:

1. Before threading the film, make sure that the television film projector is on local control, rather than remote control. If you leave it on remote control, it may be accidentally started by someone from a control room, and you may get your fingers caught in the projector mechanism.

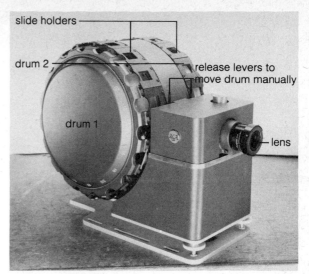

10.44 Slide Projector The dual-drum slide projector holds a total of 36 slides, which can be rapidly advanced or, with special additional equipment, randomly selected. In case the lamp burns out, you can pull the lamp assembly quickly into the spare-lamp position. The slide projector accepts regular 2 × 2 slides, even in the traditional paper mountings. However, because the cardboard tends to buckle under severe heat and thereby go out of focus, all slides used should be mounted in a more heat-resisting frame.

10.45 Loading a Slide With the RCA TP-7, the slide can be put into the projector right side up when put into one of the back holders. When the drum turns, the slide is automatically put upside down when reaching the gate.

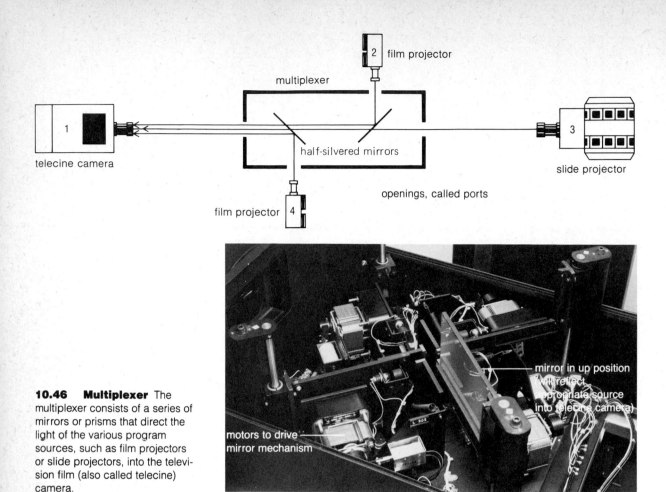

In the diagram:

- 2 film projector
- multiplexer
- telecine camera 1
- half-silvered mirrors
- 3 slide projector
- film projector 4
- openings, called ports

mirror in up position (will reflect appropriate source into telecine camera)

motors to drive mirror mechanism

10.46 Multiplexer The multiplexer consists of a series of mirrors or prisms that direct the light of the various program sources, such as film projectors or slide projectors, into the television film (also called telecine) camera.

2.   Be sure to thread the film *firmly* over the sound drum, and adhere to the prescribed loops. Otherwise the film will be out of lip-sync.

3.   Even if you are in a hurry, thread the film carefully. A careless threading job may result in severe film damage.

4.   Once you have threaded the film, start the projector and run the film for a little while to make sure that you have loaded the projector correctly. Back up the film to the cue you have designated.

5.   If the projector does not have an automatic switchover from optical to magnetic sound, make sure that the sound pickup device on the projector corresponds to the film sound track.

6.   Treat all film gently.

Film Cuing and Timing   With film, as with videotape, you need to employ some cuing and timing procedures in order to start and stop the film as programmed. We will briefly look at the SMPTE universal film leader, and end cue and timing.

Very much like the videotape leader we discussed earlier in this chapter, the **SMPTE universal film leader** shows numbers from 8 to 2 at equal 1-second intervals and a dial rotating around the leader numbers at each second (see 10.47). In fact, the television leader was borrowed from the SMPTE film leader. The film leader (which is commercially available and comes in large rolls) is spliced at the head of any film that needs cuing. You splice the leader at the film to be shown with the "picture start" frame and the highest number farthest away, and the lowest number (number 2) and the 2

10.47 SMPTE Universal Film Leader The SMPTE universal leader assists in the accurate cuing and picture alignment before the film is actually projected. The numbers, from 8 to 2, indicate 1-second intervals. The last two seconds of the leader are black in order to avoid showing numbers on the air if the film is punched up early. A clock-like dial at each number frame shows how close you are to the completion of each countdown second.

seconds of black closest to the beginning of the film to be cued.

If you use instantaneous starts, you do not need an SMPTE leader, except perhaps at the very beginning of a film reel in order to help the video engineer with the alignment. All you then do is put a short piece of black leader (opaque leader) between the films that are interrupted by another video source. You simply roll the black leader down to the first frame of the next film and start the projector directly on cue (eliminating the preroll altogether).

In a computer-assisted operation the master control computer tells the projectors when to start and stop. All you do is enter into the computer the running time of the film. Another highly accurate cuing system is the automatic start and stop of self-cuing projectors. In this case, you need to initiate the cuing by placing a small conductive cue tape directly onto the film. The projector senses these markers and reacts by rolling or stopping the film.

If you have neither of these automated devices, you need to time the film with a stopwatch. Just make sure that you *start* the watch with the *first frame of the film* (not when the leader numbers flash by). You then go by the stopwatch and call for a switch to the following video source as soon as the stopwatch indicates the end of the running time.

Sometimes you may still see or want to use the foolproof, though somewhat cumbersome, method of cue-marking a film. For cue-marking, you use a special cue marker, which looks like a small hole puncher. The cue marker perforates four frames of the film with small round or triangular holes. When punched at the very corner of the last frames, these cues appear as a brief white dot in the corner of the screen. When you see the dot, you must switch to the next video source. Projectionists in motion picture theaters still use a similar method when switching from reel to reel.

MAIN POINTS

1.   Special recording systems include (1) the digital VTR, which receives digital rather than analog information; (2) the LVR, which works like a multitrack audiotape recorder; and (3) the MBM, which can store a great amount of digital video and audio information on small but high-capacity chips.

2.   Film use in television is now generally restricted to the playing of motion picture features and the production and playback of occasional documentaries.

3.   Like videotape, film format is identified by width: 8mm, Super-8, 16mm, 35mm, and 70mm. Most television stations can handle only the 16mm format.

4.   The two principal types of sound on film are optical sound, created by modulating a light through a variable area on the side of the film, and magnetic sound, which is stored on a small audiotape that runs down one side of the film.

5.   The basic film chain or film island consists of at least one film projector, a slide projector, a multiplexer, and a television film or telecine camera.

6.   The major factors in film operation are: (1) quality check and storage; (2) film projection, whereby special care must be taken in threading the film; and (3) film cuing and timing.

FURTHER READING

Hodgdon, Dana H., and Stuart M. Kaminsky. *Basic Filmmaking*. New York: Arco Publishing, 1982.

White, Gordon. *Video Techniques*. Woburn, MA: Focal Press, 1982.

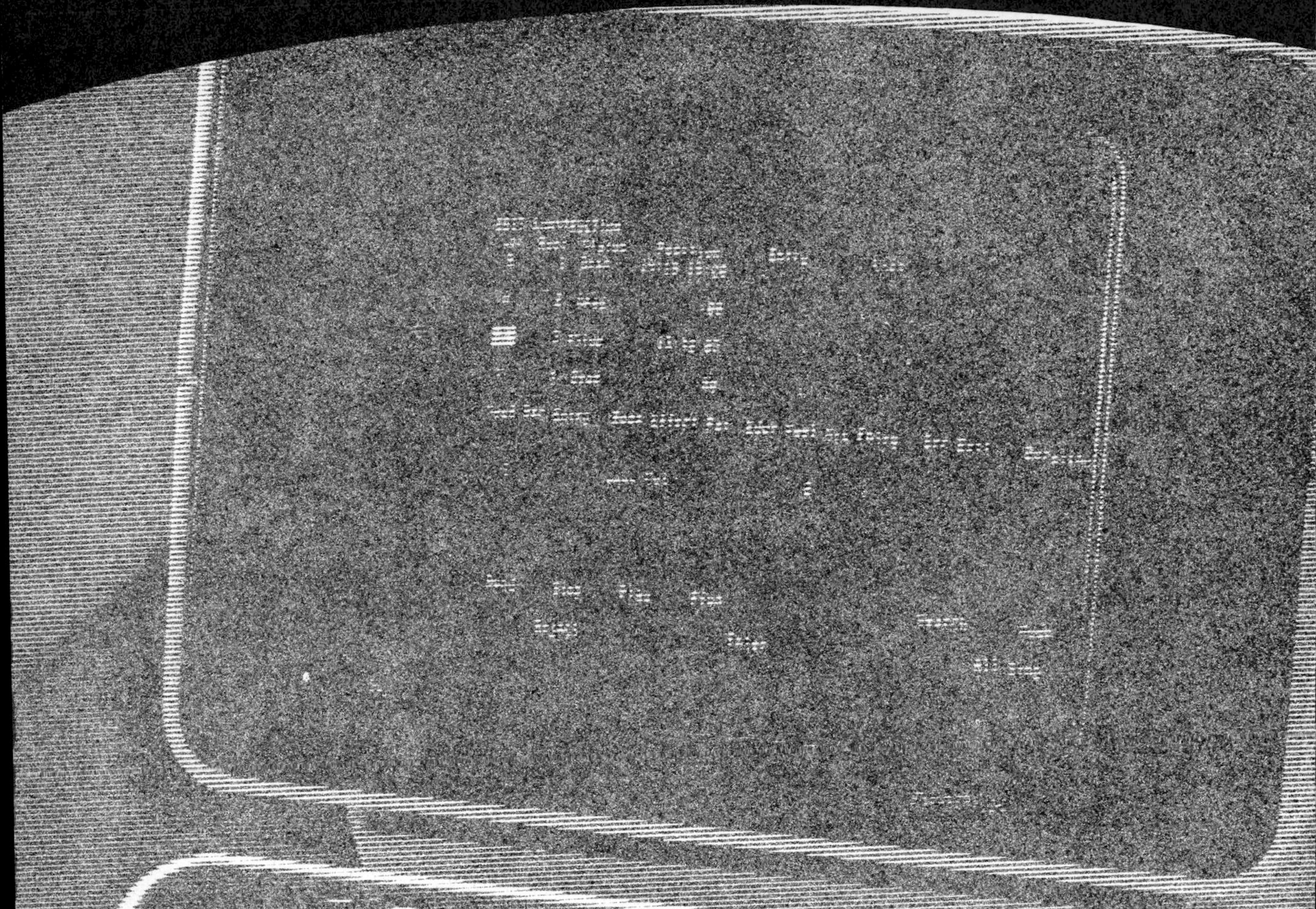

Postproduction Editing

In the last chapter, we talked about the various videotape recorders and recording processes. In this chapter, we will introduce the various aspects of postproduction editing.

Section One identifies:

1.   The major editing functions—to combine, trim, correct, and build.
2.   The principal editing modes—on-line and off-line, and assemble and insert.
3.   The address code systems—pulse count and SMPTE/EBU time code.
4.   The two basic editing systems—single-source and multiple-source systems.
5.   The editing process—the shooting phase, the review phase, the decision-making phase, and the operational phase.

Section Two describes:

1.   The basic transition devices, including the cut, dissolve, and wipe.
2.   The major editing principles: (1) continuity, (2) complexity, (3) context, and (4) ethics.
3.   Some of the more common computer terms that are primarily used in television operations.

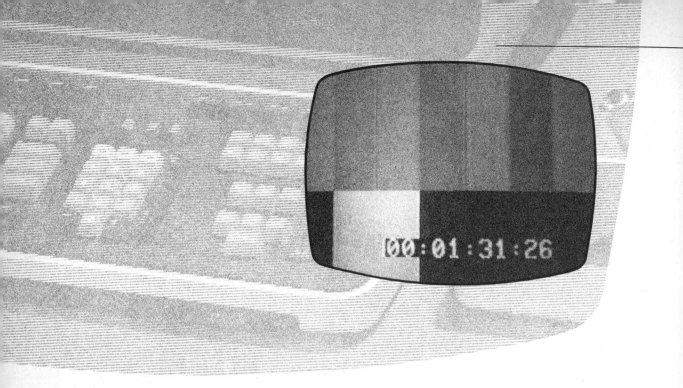

Television editing done after the production is known as **postproduction editing.** Its processes and principles differ from switching, which is editing done during production (see Chapter 12). Postproduction editing is also different from **hot editing,** a method occasionally employed in producing a completely edited tape *during* production. Hot editing means that you stop the videotape from time to time to correct mistakes, change the set or costumes, but then proceed by editing the next take directly onto the existing master tape. Most often, however, the various scenes are recorded individually for *postproduction* at a later time.

In this section, we will discuss (1) editing functions, (2) editing modes, (3) address code systems, (4) editing systems, and (5) editing process.

EDITING FUNCTIONS

The four basic editing functions are (1) to combine, (2) to trim, (3) to correct, and (4) to build.

Combine

The simplest editing is when you *combine* program portions by simply hooking the various videotaped pieces together in the proper sequence. The more care that was taken during the production, the less work you have to do in the postproduction stage. For example, most soap operas are shot in long, complete scenes or even longer sequences with a multicamera studio setup. The postproduction editing is often a matter of connecting the various sequences in the right order. There simply is not enough time for elaborate postproduction editing when you have to produce a one-hour play every day.

Trim

Many editing assignments involve *trimming* the available material to make the final videotape fit a given time slot or to eliminate all extraneous material. As an ENG editor, you will find that you often have to tell a complete story in an unreasonably short amount of time, and that you have to trim the

Postproduction editing means to edit *after* (post) the actual production. Depending on the time requirement or the magnitude of the project, postproduction editing may be done just minutes before air time (such as in news), or may take many times longer than the actual production (such as a complex documentary or dramatic production).

available material to its bare minimum. For example, the producer may give you only 20 seconds to tell the story of the downtown fire, although the ENG team had proudly returned with 10 minutes' worth of exciting footage. Paradoxically, when editing ENG footage, you will discover that while you have an abundance of similar footage, you may lack certain shots to tell the story in a coherent way. For example, when screening the fire footage, you may discover that there are many beautiful shots of flames shooting out of windows and fire fighters on ladders pouring water into the building, but that the stand-up reporter is woefully out of focus during his or her opening and closing remarks.

Correct

Much editing is done to *correct* mistakes, either by cutting out the bad portions of the scene or the bad takes, and/or by replacing them with good ones. This type of editing can be quite simple and merely involve cutting out a few seconds during which the talent made a mistake. But it can also become quite challenging, especially if the retakes do not quite fit

the rest of the recording. You may find, for example, that some of the corrected scenes differ noticeably from the others in color temperature, background sounds, or field of view (shot too close or too loose in relation to the rest of the footage). You are now faced with trying to correct the color temperature, background sounds, or field of view. As you can see, the simple editing has changed into rather complicated postproduction.

Build

The most difficult, but also the most satisfying, editing assignments are when you can *build* a show from a great many takes. In this case postproduction is no longer ancillary to production, but constitutes the major production phase. For example, when shooting *film style* during EFP, you use a single camera for all takes. As in film production, you repeat a brief scene, such as somebody getting out of a car, several times: once in a long shot, then from a different angle as a medium shot, and then perhaps two or three more times to get various close-ups. Then you shoot a similar sequence, except that the person is now getting into the car. The last part of the shooting day may include a long-shot, medium-shot, and close-up sequence of filling the car with gas. Once in postproduction, you have to pick the most effective shot and transition method and establish the desired story sequence. *All* the transitions are created in postproduction. Then the sound effects are added: traffic, car door opening and closing, gas pump, and so on. The show is literally built bit by bit.

EDITING MODES

The two principal editing modes are (1) on-line and off-line, and (2) assemble and insert.

On-Line and Off-Line Modes

On-line editing produces the final master copy that is *used on the air* or for dubbing off copies. Off-line editing produces a "workprint" (a term borrowed from film production), a preliminary and usually low-quality tape after which the higher quality master tape is modeled. The videotape you get through **off-line** editing is *not played on the air*. It may still show the time code window dub (the time code numbers being keyed over each frame), or it may

lack the complete audio mix. On-line editing is distinguished from off-line editing, therefore, not by the tape format or quality of the VTR, but rather by the intent, completeness, and quality of the editing. Thus, $\frac{3}{4}$-inch VCRs can be used for off-line and on-line editing. If you edit a $\frac{3}{4}$-inch tape with the intent of using all the editing information for producing another final (and usually larger format) master tape, your editing is *off-line*. However, if you edit the same material on $\frac{3}{4}$-inch tape with the intent of using it on the air as is, you have been engaged in on-line editing. In ENG, all editing is done on-line. The news tapes shot by the camera operators are immediately edited and broadcast directly from the $\frac{3}{4}$-inch cassette machines.

The major advantage of off-line editing is that you can take time for reviewing the unedited material and for making editing decisions without tying up expensive equipment. You may, for example, dub or bump down (dub onto a smaller tape format) all the original 1-inch videotapes to a $\frac{3}{4}$-inch or $\frac{1}{2}$-inch format, and review the tapes in a quiet corner in the station or at home. With the address code, you can identify the exact spot where you would like to make an edit and note these decisions on an editing shot list, or editing sheet (see 11.15). You can then proceed with the actual editing.

Too many times, people start editing without having properly thought about the editing sequence.

Address Also called birthmark. A specific location in a television recording, as specified by the time code.

Assemble Mode The adding of shots on videotape with their control tracks in a consecutive order.

Cutaway Shot A shot of an object or event that is peripherally connected with the overall event and that is neutral as to screen direction (usually straight-on shots). Used to intercut between two shots in which the screen direction is reversed.

Editing Log Also called editing shot sheet. A list compiled by the editor during paper-and-pencil editing. It includes the reel and scene numbers, exact addresses of in- and out-cues for each shot, the in- and out-sound cues, and prominent ambient sounds.

Electronic A-B Rolling 1. The editing of a master tape from two playback machines, one containing the A-roll and the other the B-roll. By routing the A and B playback machines through a switcher, a variety of transition effects can be achieved for the final master tape. 2. The projection of an SOF film on one film chain (A-roll), with the silent film projected from the other island (B-roll). The films can be mixed through the switcher.

Electronic Editing The joining of two shots on videotape without cutting the tape.

Frame 1. The smallest picture unit in film; a single picture. 2. A complete scanning cycle of the electron beam, which occurs every $\frac{1}{30}$ second. It represents the smallest complete television picture unit.

Insert Mode The inserting of shots in an already existing recording, without affecting the shots on either side, or the assembly of shots using a prelaid control track.

This is similar to starting to write a complicated paper without having first done an outline. Sometimes, by omitting the outline step, you may not only save time, but also preserve the freshness of thought and presentation. More often, however, you will run aground and get lost in a maze of detail. You will then have to go back, think about the story, do an outline, and start all over again. In the highly efficient business of television production, you cannot take such a chance. In all but the most routine editing of news tapes, you need to do an editing "outline," a list of the desired event sequences and the necessary transitions. We will discuss the specific ways of preparing for editing later in this chapter.

Figure 11.1 shows typical off-line and on-line editing modes for an electronic field production.

Assemble and Insert Modes

Two further edit modes are (1) assemble and (2) insert editing. One would think that when the editing task calls for assembling a series of shots or scenes, you use the assemble mode, and when you want to insert a shot somewhere or replace a scene with a more effective one, you switch to the insert mode. But this is not so. Most editing is done in the insert mode. Let's find out why.

When in the **assemble mode,** you can dub onto the tape in the *record VTR* (occasionally still called *master VTR*) shots selected from one or several *source VTRs* (occasionally still called **slave VTR**). Each of the segments that is dubbed from the source tape or tapes also transfers its *own control track.* (See 11.2.)

The record VTR is supposed to match the control tracks from one shot with the control tracks from the following shot so that the two control track segments achieve perfect continuity. Unfortunately, even the best of VTRs do not always succeed in this. As a result, some edits experience **sync roll** or momentarily tear.

When you are editing in the **insert mode,** you do not transfer the control track from the source videotape to the record videotape. Therefore, you must first "lay a control track" by recording black on the record, or master, videotape before using it for editing. The recording of black (and thereby laying a control track) happens in "real time," which means that you cannot speed up the process, but must wait 30 minutes for laying a 30-minute control track.

But here is what you gain: (1) All edits are equally roll-free and tear-free. In the insert mode, the control tracks of the individual source segments are not transferred to the record VTR, but replaced by the prelaid continuous control track on the master tape. This control track constitutes a *continuous* guide for the edit points and, therefore, makes the edits

---

Off-Line Helical scan editing system for producing videotape workprints. The workprint information is then fed into the on-line system for (automated) production of the release master tape.

On-Line A master editing system, usually using high-quality (1-inch or quadruplex) videotape recorders for high-band release master tapes.

Postproduction Any production activity that occurs after (post) the actual production. Usually refers either to editing of film or videotape or to postscoring and mixing sound for later addition to the picture portion.

Postproduction Editing The assembly of recorded material after the actual production.

Pulse-Count System A type of address code system used to identify exact locations on the videotape. It counts the control track pulses and translates this count into elapsed time and frame numbers.

Record VTR The videotape recorder that receives and assembles the various program segments as supplied by the source VTR(s).

Rough Cut The first tentative arrangement of shots and shot sequences in the approximate sequence and length.

Sound Bite Videotaped portions of an interview in which lip sync must remain intact.

Source VTR The videotape recorder that supplies the various program segments to be assembled by the record VTR.

Sync Roll Vertical rolling of a picture caused by switching from remote to studio, thereby momentarily losing synchronization; also noticeable on a bad videotape splice.

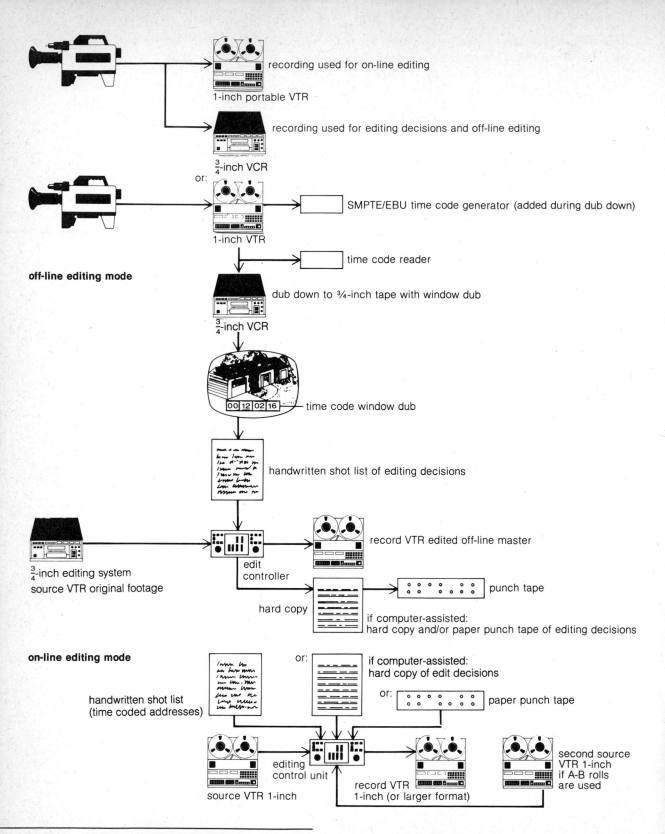

recording used for on-line editing

1-inch portable VTR

recording used for editing decisions and off-line editing

¾-inch VCR

or:

SMPTE/EBU time code generator (added during dub down)

1-inch VTR

off-line editing mode

time code reader

dub down to ¾-inch tape with window dub

¾-inch VCR

00 12 02 16 — time code window dub

handwritten shot list of editing decisions

¾-inch editing system
source VTR original footage

edit
controller

record VTR edited off-line master

hard copy

punch tape

if computer-assisted:
hard copy and/or paper punch tape of editing decisions

on-line editing mode

handwritten shot list
(time coded addresses)

or:

if computer-assisted:
hard copy of edit decisions

or:

paper punch tape

editing
control unit

source VTR 1-inch

record VTR
1-inch (or larger format)

second source
VTR 1-inch
if A-B rolls
are used

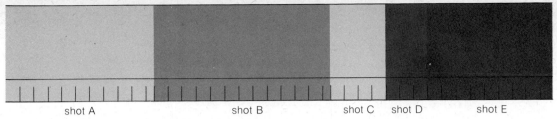

shot A   shot B   shot C   shot D   shot E

11.2   **Assemble Edit Mode** In the assemble mode, the control tracks from each segment are transferred to the master tape. Shot *A* is added to shot *B*, which again is added to shot *C*, and so forth.

more stable than by adding various control tracks (see 11.3). (2) You already have black on the tape, so you do not have to worry about recording black for the tape leaders, or whenever you want to leave some space for a commercial insert. (3) You can replace any scene in the tape with a new one of equal length and *insert* it without affecting the preceding or following edits.

ADDRESS CODE SYSTEMS

In order to identify and mark precisely each in- and out-cue and to have the VTR locate them with speed, accuracy, and especially reliability, *address code* systems have been developed. As we pointed out in the previous chapter, the slate identifies a particular

recorded segment on the videotape; the address code identifies an *individual frame*.

The two principal address code systems used are the *pulse-count system,* and the *SMPTE/EBU time code.*

Pulse-Count System

The **pulse-count system** simply counts the control track pulses and translates this count into elapsed time (hours, minutes, seconds) and frame numbers. Because there are thirty **frames** to a second, the seconds are advanced by one digit after twenty-nine frames (with the thirtieth frame making up the next second). (See 11.4.)

The advantage of the pulse-count system is that no special code has to be recorded onto the vid-

◀ **11.1**   **Off-Line and On-Line Editing Modes** For off- and on-line modes, the camera records the scene on a high-quality videotape recorder (in this case, a portable 1-inch VTR). The time code is supplied by a time code generator at the time of recording, or more frequently, later during dubbing. In order to obtain an off-line "master," the scene is simultaneously recorded on a $\frac{3}{4}$-inch VCR.

If the simultaneous recording is not feasible, the 1-inch "original master tape" can be dubbed down (dubbed to a smaller tape format)—in this case, a $\frac{3}{4}$-inch tape. While the master tape is being dubbed, a time code is added simultaneously to both tapes, with a window dub for the $\frac{3}{4}$-inch off-line copy (which shows the time code keyed into each frame). With this copy, a handwritten list of the editing decisions is prepared. From this list, an off-line $\frac{3}{4}$-inch videotape can be edited. If computer-assisted, the editing system on which the off-line tape is prepared can produce a **hard copy** of the editing decisions (simply a typed list of the handwritten shot list), or a punched paper tape, which includes all the editing decisions in binary form.

For the on-line editing, the original shot list or the hard copy can be used to program the on-line editor, or the punch tape can be fed into the on-line system. The source VTR with the original footage is then automatically edited to the final edited master tape.

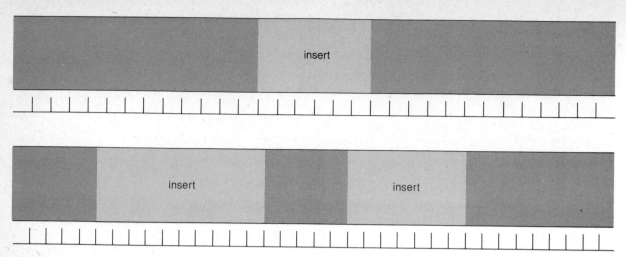

11.3 Insert Mode In the insert mode, the control track of the original segments is not transferred to the record VTR, but replaced by the prerecorded control track of the new master tape. The shots can be assembled in any order; some can be inserted in the middle of a tape without affecting the preceding or following recorded segments.

hrs   min   sec   frames

11.4 Time Display of Pulse-Count System The pulse-count system counts the control-track pulses and translates them into hours, minutes, seconds, and frames.

eotape either simultaneously with the program or afterward, because the control track is always part of the videotape recording. The disadvantage is that most pulse-count systems are not always frame-accurate. You may lose one or two frames when starting and stopping the VTR, or during fast or extremely slow shuttle speeds. This means that the edit may shift by a few frames from the designated edit point. In practice, this presents no great problem, as long as the editing is not dependent on frame-accuracy. Most ENG editing, which puts a premium on speed rather than frame-accuracy, uses the pulse-count system.

When more precise editing is required, as in synchronizing separate audio and video tracks, for example, the SMPTE/EBU time code is generally used. It provides not only frame-by-frame accuracy, but also common starting points for each separate tape.

The SMPTE/EBU Time Code System

Contrary to the control track pulses, which by themselves do not distinguish one frame from the other, the **SMPTE/EBU** (Society of Motion Picture and Television Engineers/European Broadcasting Union) **time code** (usually called phonetically the "Sempty time code") is an electronic signal that provides a specific **address** or "birthmark" for *each* electronic *frame*. The address is given, as with the pulse-count system, in elapsed time and frame number (see 11.5). To get the time code on the videotape, you need a *time code generator,* and to retrieve it, a *time code reader*. The time code generator "writes" (records) the time code on the cue track or a special address code track of the videotape. The time code reader displays the address as digital numbers (hours, minutes, seconds, frames) on the VTR or the edit control unit (see 11.5), and/or the reader keys the address directly in the pictures of the off-line workprint (see 11.6).

The larger VTRs have a built-in time code generator or plug-in provisions for it. Most portable VTRs and VCRs have jacks by which you can attach a time code generator. There are even some cameras that can generate a time code and feed it with the video signal to the VTR.

You need to attach the time code generator only if you plan to record the address code *simultaneously* with the program segments. Often, the time code is added in postproduction, *after* the program has already been put on the videotape.

The SMPTE/EBU time code is always used in complex postproduction work, such as editing and providing a variety of transitions and sound tracks for program segments that were shot "film style."

EDITING SYSTEMS

When VTR was first introduced, videotape was actually cut with a razor blade and **spliced** together similarly to audiotape or film. Today, editing is done with the aid of **electronic editing** systems that perform not only the actual **editing**—the joining of two or more videotaped segments—electronically, but many other crucial editing functions as well. The systems also facilitate the interfacing of the actual editing equipment with other production equipment, such as audiotape recorders, switchers, special effects units, time base correctors, and other signal-processing equipment.

Despite the dazzling variety of available electronic videotape editing equipment, there are only

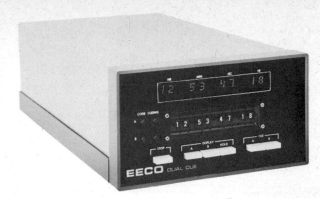

11.5   SMPTE/EBU Time Code Reader The SMPTE (Society of Motion Picture and Television Engineers)/EBU (European Broadcasting Union) time code identifies each television frame by hour, minute, second, and frame number. After twenty-nine frames, the seconds are advanced by one digit (there are thirty frames to a second). The time code is an electronic signal recorded on the address code track or the cue track.

11.6   SMPTE/EBU Time Code Screen Display The time code can be keyed directly over the image of the videotape for off-line editing. This way, each frame displays its time-code address.

two *basic systems:* (1) the single-source editing system, and (2) the multiple-source editing system.

The Single-Source Editing System

The single-source editing system consists of a single *source VTR* (sometimes called "slave" VTR), a *record VTR* (sometimes called "master"

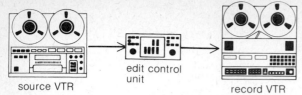

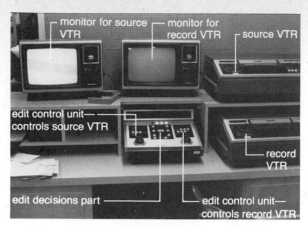

11.7 Single-Source Editing System In the single-source editing system, a single VTR supplies the material recorded when the actual event took place. The material is then selected and sent to the record VTR, which assembles the various pieces into a coherent sequence. One half of the edit control unit controls the source VTR, the other half the record VTR.

VTR), and an editing *control unit* or edit *controller* (see 11.8).

Source VTR   The source VTR supplies the material to be edited. Assuming for a moment that you are working with a $\frac{3}{4}$-inch VCR system, the source material may come from a single cassette that contains all the segments to be edited, or from several cassettes. Whatever it is, the material is played back on a single VTR.

Record VTR   The record VTR performs the actual edits. This means that it records the various segments as supplied by the source VTR and joins them at predetermined edit points. The "in" or "entrance" cue switches the record VTR from the playback to the record mode. The "out" or "exit" cue switches the record VTR back to the playback mode. Because you have only one source supplying video material, the transitions at the edit points are necessarily cuts only (see Section Two). Unlike film, where you can actually hold the individual frames and look at them, the television tape itself displays no image. In order to determine the precise edit in- and out-cues, you need auxiliary facilities. These are combined in the editing control unit.

Editing Control Unit   All editing control units must be able to perform at least these four basic functions: (1) selection of precise edit points (in- and out-cues), (2) control of VTR rolls and forward and reverse speeds, (3) control of play and record modes for assemble or insert edits, and (4) editing of audio and video tracks separately or together.

Most single-source editing control units can also perfom these additional tasks for you:

1.   Run a trial edit so that you can rehearse it before telling the editing control unit to perform the edit.

2.   Rewind the source VTR quickly so that you can review the completed edit.

3.   Back up automatically from the selected in-cue to the selected preroll. Usually, you will find a switch that gives you two or three preroll choices, such as a 2-second, 5-second, or 10-second preroll.

4.   *Trim* the edit point (moving the edit point forward or back by a few frames.

5.   Perform *split edits*. This means that you can edit video and audio separately without their affecting each other during the edit.

6.   Produce intelligible sounds at various speeds. However, you will have to put up with the "chipmunk" talk at higher than normal speeds, and the forced growls at lower than normal speeds, unless

11.8 Editing Control Unit The single-source editing control unit can locate the address of the intended segment of the source VTR and tell the record VTR where to put it.

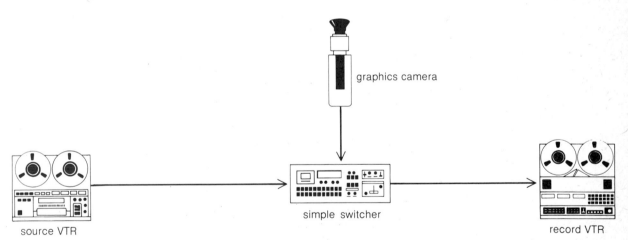

graphics camera

simple switcher

source VTR

record VTR

11.9 Extended Single-Source Editing System To add titles, the source VTR is sometimes fed into a simple switcher, as is a graphics camera (small television camera) or a character generator (device that generates letters electronically).

you have a sophisticated control unit with an audio time compressor/expander that maintains normal pitch at other than real-time speeds.

7.   Permit expansion of the system by interfacing more source VTRs and special effects equipment (see 11.9).

Most of the simpler single-source edit control units use the pulse-count system for an address code. These units are often called "back-space editors." More elaborate single-source control units can work with the pulse-count system as well as the SMPTE/EBU time code.

The Multiple-Source Editing System

The multiple-source editing system consists of *two or more* source VTRs (generally labeled with letters: *A, B,* and so forth), a computer-assisted control unit, and a record VTR. Most often, the multiple-source editing system is interfaced with a variety of production equipment, such as production switchers, multiple-track audiotape recorders, and special effects and signal-processing equipment (see 11.10). Most of the multiple-source editing systems use the SMPTE/EBU time code or give you a choice between the two address systems.

The key element of the multiple-source system is the elaborate editing control unit, which is capable of *storing* and *performing* many *different* editing functions automatically. Besides performing all the control functions of the single-source editing control unit, the multiple-source editing control unit can:

1.   Locate any frame on the videotapes of two or more source VTRs or record VTRs

2.   Preroll and run all source VTRs and the record VTR in sync, simultaneously or staggered

3.   Preview and perform a variety of transitions (cuts, dissolves, wipes, or special effects transitions) without having to interface a production switcher

4.   Advance automatically to the next in-cue

5.   Store up to a hundred editing decisions, which can be automatically recalled by the computer

6.   Shift any one of the edit points, whereby the computer adjusts all the other edit points accordingly

7.   Print a hard copy (print-out) of these editing decisions or produce a punched paper tape, which can be used for automatic on-line editing

8.   Interface various VTRs of different format. For example, you can use two 1-inch source VTRs and a 2-inch quad record VTR, or a $\frac{3}{4}$-inch VCR and a 1-inch VTR as sources

9.   Interface a variety of other production equipment

10.   Utilize additional space on the address track for the identification of videotape reels or scene numbers through the so-called "user bits"

One of the most important aspects of all control units is that they are *operator oriented*. This means that you do not have to learn complicated keyboard operations and special codes in order to perform simple editing maneuvers. Most single-source edit control units fulfill this requirement. However, when working with the more complex multiple-source edit control units, you have to learn a few computer codes and keyboard procedures. Constant efforts are being made to simplify operations so that the user can concentrate on the editing job at hand rather than learning how to use the editor. With some edit control units you can activate the various editing commands by touching the display screen with your finger.

Even if the machine is taking over a great many editing functions, you are still left with making the actual editing *decisions*. The most sophisticated editing control unit can only execute, not initiate, an editing command.

A-B Rolling   This videotape-editing technique is an adaptation of an established film-editing method. In film **A-B rolling,** you splice the first, third, and all subsequent odd-numbered shots together on one reel, constituting the A-roll, and all even-numbered shots on another reel, the B-roll. All shots are separated by black leader, which is spliced opposite the shots on the other reel. Both rolls are then printed together for the final composite print. Through A-B

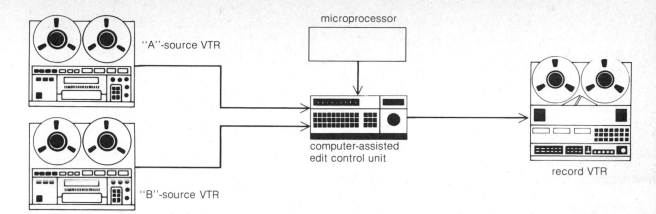

"A"-source VTR

microprocessor

computer-assisted
edit control unit

"B"-source VTR

record VTR

a

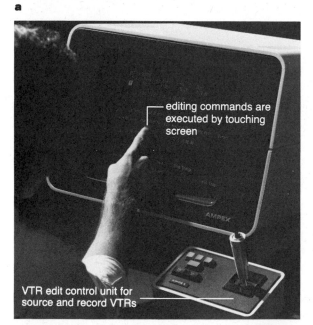

editing commands are
executed by touching
screen

VTR edit control unit for
source and record VTRs

b

c

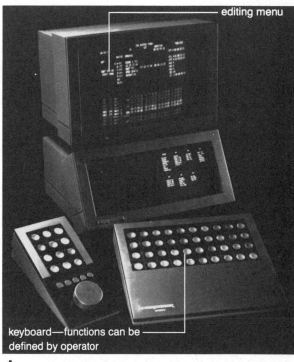

editing menu

keyboard—functions can be
defined by operator

d

11.10   Multiple-Source Editing System (a) The
multiple-source editing system can control two or more
source VTRs and locate the addresses of videotaped segments on both source VTRs for simultaneous editing on the
record VTR; (b) Ampex Ace Touch Screen; (c) CMX 3400
Multi-source Computerized Editing System; (d) CMX 3400
+ Multi-source Editing System responds to typed or spoken
word commands.

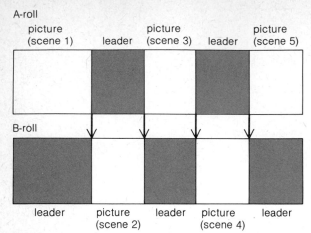

A-roll

picture (scene 1)　　leader　　picture (scene 3)　　leader　　picture (scene 5)

B-roll

leader　　picture (scene 2)　　leader　　picture (scene 4)　　leader

11.11　Film A-B Rolling In A-B rolling, roll A is composed of all odd-numbered shots, separated by leaders that correspond exactly to the even-numbered shots; roll B is composed of all even-numbered shots, separated by leaders that correspond exactly to the odd-numbered shots.

rolling, all splices are eliminated in the printing process (see 11.11).

Television A-B rolling is done in a similar way. Let us assume that you have to cover with an ENG camera the construction of a music center in your city. First you videotape the interview with the music director in one location and in one continuous take. This cassette (which contains the pictures and sound of the interview) constitutes the *A-roll*. In the interview, the music director makes frequent and direct references to particular sections of the partially completed building. After the interview, you videotape on a second cassette the various sections that the music director had pointed out. This cassette (with the scenes of the building sections and construction sounds) constitutes the *B-roll*. When combining the A-roll and B-roll in postproduction, you use the sound track of the A-roll (which contains the interview) as a guide and take from the B-roll those scenes that match the music director's references to specific locations of the A-roll (see 11.12).

In videotape editing, unlike film A-B rolling, you do not have to match the alternate shots with black.

The lengths of the B-roll inserts are usually determined by the sound track of the A-roll—in our example, the comments by the music director.

When doing the final editing, you put the A-roll on the source VTR *A*, and the B-roll on the source VTR *B*. Using the edit controller, you can then mark the in- and out-cues for both tapes (A-roll and B-roll) and edit them together on the record VTR. If you have only a single-source editor, you need first to record the A-roll (including all of the A-roll audio) and then insert-edit the desired B-roll portions (by continuing with the A-roll audio, or mixing it with portions of the B-roll background sounds). Obviously, this method is much more difficult and time consuming.

A-B-C Rolling This technique is similar to A-B rolling, except that three separate "rolls" (videotapes) are prepared. Let's assume that the music director you met earlier refers in his or her interview not only to the different sections of the music center under construction, but also to similar sections of a rival concert hall in a neighboring city. You can proceed with the A-B roll approach, but you videotape on the C-roll the sections of the rival concert hall that the music director had mentioned. Now you have the original interview and two additional video sources at your disposal. Again, the most efficient editing is done on a multiple-source editing system, which can control three source VTRs. Such a system offers you a variety of transitions and flexibility in previewing certain edits before performing them (see 11.13). For example, you may think that dissolves or wipes, rather than cuts, are best for comparing structures in the rival concert hall with similar sections of the concert hall under construction. But when you finally preview the dissolves, you find them much too disruptive, and quite incongruent to the A-roll audio. No harm done. You simply instruct the edit controller to give you quick wipes, or cuts.

Often, the B-rolls or C-rolls are used for additional audio, rather than video, information. You can also edit the three rolls on a single-source editing system by exchanging the A roll for the B or C rolls every time you need some portions from the latter two rolls. However, all the transitions are then restricted to cuts.

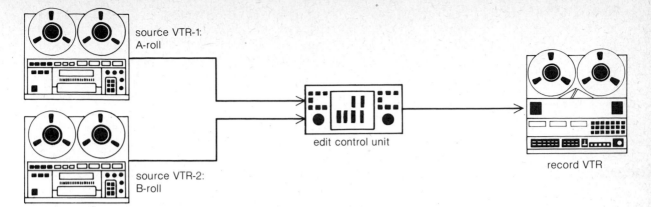

11.12   A-B Rolling in Videotape Editing The A-roll contains the primary footage (interview with sound track), and the B-roll the supplementary footage (shots of
locations as mentioned on the A-roll, with ambient sound). They are then edited onto
the record VTR.

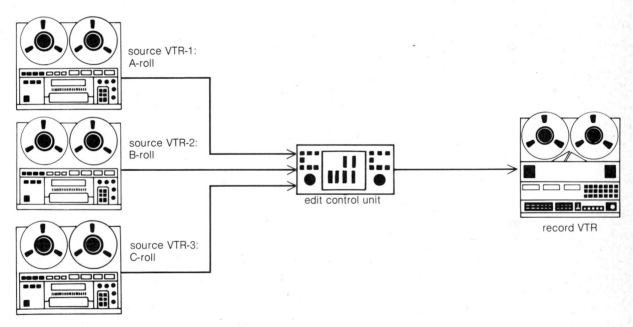

11.13   A-B-C Rolling In A-B-C rolling, three separate VTRs (with different, yet
related material) supply the videotaped source material for the final master tape.

The entire editing process happens in several steps, or phases: (1) the shooting phase, (2) the review phase, (3) the decision-making phase, and (4) the operational phase.

Shooting Phase

Much of the editing is already determined by the way the material is shot. Some directors or camera operators stop one shot or scene and begin the next without any pads (overlapping action), or without any consideration for continuity between the two. Others have the ability and foresight to visualize transitions between the shots or scenes and to provide images that "cut together" well in postproduction. Here are some suggestions:

1. As pointed out before, *do not stop* exactly *at the end* of a scene, but record a few more seconds before stopping the tape. For example, if the field reporter has just ended the introduction to a story, have him or her remain silent and in place for just a few seconds. This way, you will have some video pad in case the end of the actual report and the beginning of the following scene do not provide proper video or audio continuity. Often, the audio track needs manipulation. But then, you have to have something neutral to look at, even if it is only for a few frames. If you videotape a stand-up reporter in the field, have her or him remain silent and in place for a few seconds after the actual report.

2. Always get some cutaways at the end of videotaping. A **cutaway** is a brief shot that facilitates continuity between two shots, provides the necessary visual pad when editing according to sound bites, and, in more ambitious productions, helps to bridge jumps in time and/or location. The cutaway may or may not be part of the principal action, but it must somehow be related to the actual event. The most flexible cutaways are straight-on shots of people (looking or walking into the camera) or objects. For example, if you need to edit together two shots in which screen directions of a bicycle race are reversed

(the bicycles going from screen-left to screen-right in one shot, and the opposite way in the next), you can preserve the continuity and pretend that the bicycles travel in a single direction by intercutting a straight-on medium shot of two or three onlookers.[1] Reaction shots are always good cutaways. It is important to bring back a variety of cutaways (the editor may be tired of using a cutaway of reporters holding up small audio cassette recorders, or still photographers clicking away) and especially to make them long enough (at least 5 seconds). All too often, the editor is left with cutaways that are just a trifle too short to fit the transitional requirements (see 11.14).

3. When on an ENG assignment, try to get some shots that *identify* the *location* of the event. For example, after having covered the downtown fire, get a shot of the street signs of the nearest intersection, the traffic that has piled up in the street because of the fire, and some shots of the crowd. For good measure, get several wide shots of the event location. Now, you have cutaways that not only facilitate transitions, but also show the viewer exactly where the fire took place. Remember to record the ambient sound with the cutaways. The sound is often as important as the pictures for smooth transitions.

4. During ENG, **"slate"** (identify) the various takes verbally. This can be done by simply calling out the number of the take so that the hot on-camera mic transfers this instruction on the background sound track. Or, if you have a VTR-audio operator, the take number can be slated on the regular sound track via the external mic. After saying the take number, you should count backward from five or three to zero. This counting is similar to the beeper after the slate in studio productions. The counting helps to locate the take and to cue it up during the editing process.

5. When you are on an EFP assignment, or if there is time during ENG, be sure to *mark* each take on the *shot sheet* (see discussion in "Decision-Making Phase"). As pointed out before, accurate record keeping during a shoot will save you much time and frustration in postproduction. In ENG, the "shot

[1] Zettl, *Sight-Sound-Motion,* pp. 297–311.

sheeting" is done after you have returned to the station or the van during the playback and review of the tape.

Review Phase

In the review phase, you check the videotaped material for quality and suitability. If time allows, look at *all* the recorded material and check it against the shot sheet. You may find that part of a "bad" take is much better than that of a "good" take, and you may decide to use this portion in the final editing. On the other hand, if you are pressed for time, believe the entries in the shot sheet and concentrate on screening only the "circled" (good) takes. Go back to the bad takes only if you need additional material during editing.

If you expect to do extensive postproduction work (such as in EFP), make a dub (including the SMPTE/EBU "window" insert) for screening and paper-and-pencil editing (see the discussion in "Decision-Making Phase"). In this phase you may want to use the $\frac{1}{2}$-inch VCR format. These machines are just about as flexible as their larger format relatives, and their quality is good enough to detect major video and audio problems. Best of all, you can carry the machine rather easily to a quiet corner or any other place where you can work undisturbed.

Use the initial shot sheet for additional comments, or make notes about the various takes on a separate sheet. Be sure that you identify your comments by the scene and take number, as well as the specific address (pulse-count or time code system). Look for obvious video mistakes, such as out-of-focus shots, wobbly pictures caused by bad camera handling, or video breakup. Then *look behind* the principal action. Is the background appropriate? Too **busy,** or cluttered? Will the background yield some kind of continuity when the shots are edited together? How about the sound? Listen carefully not only to the foreground sounds, but also to the background sounds. Do you have too much ambience? Not enough? Note any obvious sound problems, such as trucks going by, somebody hitting the microphone or kicking the table, walkie-talkie chatter of the crew, or talent fluffs in a good take. Write down the address and nature of the sound problem.

a

b

c

11.14 Cutaways Screen directions can be perceived as continuous even though they are reversed (a, c) on the screen as long as they are connected by a neutral cutaway (b).

Decision-Making Phase

In the decision-making phase you select specific shots and decide on their sequence. Just how you go about making those decisions is far too large a subject to be discussed here. However, there are a few basic principles that may help you in this difficult job:

1. Be sure to know the *whole story* before starting the editing. If you do not know, ask the director or producer when doing a large production, or the producer, reporter, or camera operator when editing an ENG assignment. Although there are many editors who edit strictly on the basis of what shots go together and what shots do not, good editors base their decisions also, if not primarily, on the overall *communication purpose*.

2. When editing news stories, you rarely get a chance to learn enough of the total event to make optimal choices. Worse, you have to keep to a rigid time frame ("Be sure to keep this story to 20 seconds!") and work with limited footage ("Sorry, I just couldn't get close enough to get some good shots!"). Also, you have precious little time to get the job done ("Aren't you finished yet? We go on the air in 45 minutes!"). Very much like a reporter, ENG camera operator, or an emergency doctor, the ENG editor has to be able to work quickly, yet accurately, and without much chance for preparation. However, try to get as much information about the story before you start with the editing. Ask the reporter, the camera operator, or the producer to fill you in. After some practice, you will be able to "sense" the story contained on the tape, and edit it accordingly. The story is often more readily perceived by listening to the sound track than looking at the pictures.

3. When editing off-line, you usually have a little bit more time to contemplate editing decisions than during ENG operations. Assuming that you have gone through the review phase, you can now study the individual shots, decide on the shot sequence, and, finally, determine the exact in- and out-cues for each shot or shot sequence. You can go about this task in two ways: (1) Using the editor and the original shot list, do a **"rough-cut"** (a film term that means the first tentative arrangement of shots and shot sequences in their approximate sequence and

length). (2) Do **paper-and-pencil editing.** This means that you examine the various shots and log every editing decision on an **editing log,** or editing **shot sheet** (see 11.15). The important items to list are, of course, the reel and scene numbers, the exact address of the in- and out-cues for each shot, the sound in- and out-cues (in-cue: "In this crisis . . . ," out-cue: " . . . suggest these remedies."), prominent ambient sounds (restless audience), and any other information that facilitates the mechanical aspects of the editing process.

You can then use the editing log to produce an off-line tape. After translating the paper-and-pencil decisions into an actual edited tape, you may find that some shots are a little too long or short, or that you need a cutaway to improve continuity. If you match some B-roll video to an A-roll sound track, you may discover that the synchronization of video and audio is not always as precise as you wish it to be. Then you have to do some *trimming* (eliminating or adding some video) via the trim controls, or enter different in- and out-addresses.

Operational Phase

The operational phase can best be learned by doing. However, there are some operational procedures that will help you to do the actual editing job with confidence, speed, and accuracy—regardless of the model or type of edit control unit with which you may have to work.

1. If you share editing facilities, double-check on their availability. When interfacing additional equipment, such as a production switcher, audiotape recorder, or graphics generator, make sure that the additional equipment is properly scheduled and available. Make sure that you have proper patch cables and connectors.

2. Check the tapes that you intend to use for edit masters and see whether they have black recorded on them (and, therefore, a control track that is necessary for insert editing). If not, this will be the first thing you must do before getting started with actual editing. Many editors like to "lay the control track" with the same editing system actually used in order to minimize tracking problems during the editing.

Production Title: Production No.: Air Date:

Producer: Editor:

Reel	Scene	Take	Address	Length	Sound	Background Sound	Remarks
			in				
			out				
			in				
			out				
			in				
			out				
			in				
			out				
			in				
			out				
			in				
			out				
			in				
			out				
			in				
			out				
			in				
			out				
			in				
			out				

11.15 Editing Shot Sheet

3.   Set up both source and record VTRs. Check whether they are in the proper modes for the various functions. For example, the source VTR should be in the mix mode for audio, and the record VTR input selector switch should read "line" or "dub" (or whatever designation the VTR may have to indicate that it is ready to record) and be in the insert mode. Set the audio levels on the record machine. Set levels not by listening to the monitor speakers, but by watching the VU meters of the play and record VTRs. *Then* set the audio levels on the speakers of the source and record VTR monitors. Now you can mix sound by listening rather than just watching the VU meters.

4.   If you have a shot sheet, check briefly on the source VTR whether you have the right tape. Once again, play back the first few segments of the source tape. Listen carefully to the audio track. If you want to use a portion of an interview or speech, listen for longer pauses or natural breaks. These pauses prevent the audio of the next segment from following too closely. Whatever portions of an interview or speech you use intact—that is, with lip sync—are called **sound bites.** When using sound bites in a story, you cannot split or otherwise manipulate the audio and video tracks; they must be transferred intact.

5.   You can edit according to the shot list prepared during the off-line editing or "on the fly." When editing according to the shot list, your edit in- and out-points are determined by the address code display (pulse-count or time code). On-the-fly editing means that you select the successive edit points by simply running the source VTR until you come to a spot that fits onto the previously recorded segment. This spot represents the new in-cue. Such a method is preferred in ENG work, because it is much faster, though less accurate, than editing according to an address system.

6.   When doing the actual editing, run the source VTR to the first in-cue (by watching either the address code or the source monitor). You may do well to establish a routine for finding the proper edit points on the source VTR when editing on the fly. Many editors simply forward the source VTR at *normal speed,* watch for the proper edit point to approach, and then park the VTR at this point (putting into the

pause or search mode). If you miss the exact edit point by a few frames, simply use the joystick or dial to jog forward or back to the desired edit point. If, on the other hand, you are working with an address code, you can use accelerated speeds for your search, because you are searching for address code numbers, not specific pictures and sound.

7.   Assuming that you have already recorded a leader onto the record master tape (the tape in the record VTR), jog the record VTR to the first edit point (at exactly 0 seconds of the leader countdown) and put the record VTR in pause. Mark this point by entering a cue into the memory of the edit controller. The actual button for this has different names, depending on the equipment you are using. Now you can preview the edit, if you wish, or perform the edit. Usually a single button rewinds both the source and record VTRs to the preroll cue (usually 5 seconds), rolls the machines forward, performs or previews the edit (which means dubbing the selected source segment onto the record tape), and stops both VTRs a few seconds after the edit. If you did not designate an out-cue and control the stopping of the VTRs manually, let them run for a few seconds past the actual edit point so that you will have a pad for the next edit.

You now repeat this maneuver for the second edit: Forward the source VTR until you come to the in-cue, and park the source VTR. Back up the record VTR (assuming you have recorded beyond the next edit point) until you have located the exact in-cue for the next segment and park the record VTR by putting it in a freeze-frame mode. Mark the cue for both machines and perform the edit.

When working with more complex computer-assisted edit control units, you can enter on the keyboard or tell the computer any other way (like touching the display screen) the exact addresses of the in- and out-cues.

8.   Review the edit on the record VTR. If it is good, locate the in-cue for the next edit. Unless you are an experienced editor, you should *preview* the edit before performing it. In the preview mode, the record VTR simply picks up and displays the new segment from the edit point on, without actually recording it. If you want to shift the edit point forward or back by a few frames, you can "trim" the edit

with the trim control. This means that you do not have to jog the VTRs back and forth for a new edit point; you simply press the trim button a few times, causing the edit point to move a few frames forward (extend your segment) or back (make it slightly shorter). Trimming an edit is especially important when you need to shorten or lengthen audio pauses, or "clean up" the audio track from unwanted sounds (see point 10 in this section).

9.   When doing ENG editing, you edit for sound first (audio-only insert mode) and then match the track with the appropriate video (video-only insert mode). The sound track generally consists of the reporter's narration, SOT (sound-on-tape) bites (complete lip-sync portions of an interview, speech, or people's comments), and background sounds (usually on a separate track). When selecting the sound bites, you must transfer the video and audio of the original source tape (which shows a person talking) just as they are. However, once you have established who is doing the talking, you can split audio and video, and edit new visuals to the sound track of the talk or interview. This is often called "B-rolling." As you have properly anticipated, this method is quite similar to A-B rolling, except that you take all the audio and video information from a single roll—the original master tape on the source VTR—and then insert appropriate cutaways (see 11.16).

There has been a great reluctance in television production to show **"talking heads,"** which means people talking on close-ups without any supporting visual material. Do not overreact to this myth. As long as the heads talk well, there is no need for additional visual material—unless one person obviously refers to various locations or objects. Then you need a "B-roll" to explain the visual references. If they do not talk so well, you can always decide whether to use B-roll material or simply "tell it like it is."

10.   When you perform *split edits* (audio edits first and then video edits), make sure that you have "clean" audio at the edit in- and out-points. This means that you cannot end the audio of a segment edited onto the master tape with a "spillover"—an incomplete word, such as the "ne" of the word *nevertheless*. You should erase the "ne" on the recorded master tape

before proceeding to the next edit, whose sound bite starts with the *nevertheless*. Of course, starting an edit in mid-word (called upcutting), or worse, mid-sentence, is equally bad and must be corrected before going on to the next edit. This is just one more reason to let each video portion continue at least 2 seconds or so, in order to have enough video pad for the next edit.

11.   When finished with the editing, rewind the recorded master tape and play it uninterruptedly. You may discover some discrepancies between the audio and video tracks, or problems with continuity (see Section Two) that need correction. If you edit in the insert mode, you simply repeat one of the edits, wherever it may occur. If you have edited in the assemble mode, you must go back to the trouble spot and start all over again, regardless of whether the problem is in the audio or the video portion. You may have noticed that the laying of a control track (by recording black) is certainly a small price to pay for the editing flexibility and electronic stability you get in return.

12.   Unless your editing system is capable of producing a hard copy, punched paper tape, or a floppy disc on which all your recording decisions are faithfully recorded, you should make a protection copy of your edited tape. Of course, such a protection copy is not necessary when editing for daily newscasts. But if you are doing a documentary or feature, however short, make a copy.

MAIN POINTS

1.   Postproduction editing means to edit after the actual production. Postproduction may mean a simple hooking together of prerecorded program segments, or the actual building of a show.

2.   The four basic editing functions are (1) combining program segments by hooking together the various videotaped pieces in the proper sequence; (2) trimming to make the final videotape fit a given time slot or to eliminate extraneous material; (3) correcting mistakes by cutting out bad portions of a scene and replacing them with good ones; and (4)

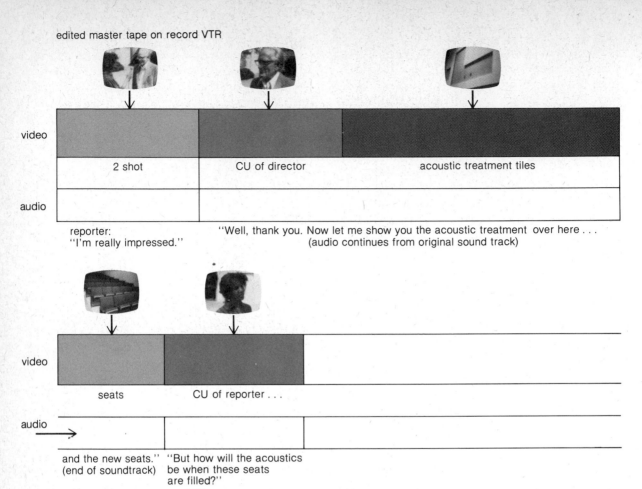

edited master tape on record VTR

video		
2 shot	CU of director	acoustic treatment tiles
audio		

reporter:
"I'm really impressed."

"Well, thank you. Now let me show you the acoustic treatment over here...
(audio continues from original sound track)

video		
seats	CU of reporter . . .	
audio		

and the new seats."
(end of soundtrack)

"But how will the acoustics
be when these seats
are filled?"

11.16 Matching Video to Audio When matching video to audio, you can take the original sound track that carries the comments of the concert hall director and do video-only edits to show what he is talking about. After the two-shot with the reporter and the director, we go to a close-up of the director with the second sound bite (the first one being the reporter's comment), but then we split audio and insert new video to illustrate on the video track what is being said on the audio track. Then we go back to the third sound bite—the reporter's question.

building a show from a number of prerecorded takes (shots).

3. The two principal editing modes are (1) on-line and off-line, and (2) assemble and insert. On-line editing produces the final master copy that is used on the air; off-line editing produces a preliminary copy, called workprint, which is not used on the air.

4. When editing in the assemble mode, each of the segments dubbed from the source tapes to the master tape transfers its own control track. However, the assembled control track on the master tape does not always achieve perfect continuity, causing an occasional breakup at the edit points. When editing in the insert mode, a control track must be "laid" (by recording black) first on the record, or master, tape. The source segments are then dubbed onto the record tape in any order, or inserted between existing scenes, without their original control tracks. The new continuous control track ensures stable edits.

5. The two types of address code systems are (1) the pulse-count system, and (2) the SMPTE/EBU time code. The pulse-count system counts the control track pulses and translates these into elapsed time and frame numbers. It is not as accurate as the SMPTE/EBU time code, which is recorded on a special videotape track.

6. There are two basic editing systems, the single-source system, and the multiple-source editing system. The single-source system consists of a single source VTR, which supplies the material to be edited; an edit control unit, which helps to select the precise edit point; and a record VTR, which performs the actual edits. A multiple-source VTR has two or more source VTRs.

7. Television A-B rolling means that there are two source VTRs: an A machine and a B machine. The material on the A roll can be combined with that on the B roll through special transitions.

8. The editing process consists of four phases: (1) the shooting phase; (2) the review phase; (3) the decision-making phase; and (4) the operational phase.

9. Many of the more obvious transitions from shot to shot are already considered in the shooting phase. In the review phase, the recorded material is checked for quality and suitability relative to the intended show. In the decision-making phase, the specific shots, their sequence, and the precise edit points are selected. These decisions are usually recorded on the editing shot sheet. In the operational phase, the actual edits are performed.

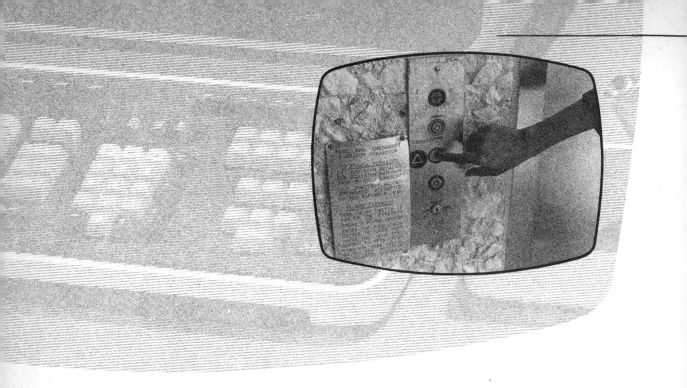

So far, we have been mostly concerned about the editing equipment and its technical potentials and requirements. In this section, we will concentrate on nontechnical or aesthetic factors and editing requirements: (1) basic transition devices, and (2) major aesthetic editing principles. Then, we will list some of the computer lingo that you will encounter most frequently in television production.

BASIC TRANSITION DEVICES

Whenever you put two shots together, you need a transition between them, a device that leads us to perceive the two shots as relating to each other in some specific way. There are four basic transition devices: (1) the cut, (2) the dissolve, (3) the fade, and (4) the wipe. All four have the same basic purpose: to provide an acceptable link from shot to shot. However, each one differs somewhat from the others in its function; that is, how we are to perceive the transition in a shot sequence.

The Cut

The **cut** is an instantaneous change from one image (shot) to another. It is the most common and least obtrusive transition device. The cut itself is not visible; all you see are the preceding and following shots. It resembles most closely the changing field of the human eye. Try to look from one object to another, one located some distance from the other. Notice that you do not look at things in between (as you would in a pan) but that your eyes jump from one place to the other, as in a cut.

The cut (like all other transition devices) is basically used for the clarification and intensification of an event. *Clarification* means that you show the viewer the event as clearly as possible. For example, in an interview show, the guest holds up the book he or she has written. In order to help the viewer see better, to identify the title of the book, you cut to a close-up.

Intensification means that you sharpen the impact of the screen event. In an extreme long shot, for example, a football tackle might look quite tame; when seen as a tight close-up, however, the action reveals its brute

Both types of editing—continuity and complexity editing—require a thorough knowledge of the aesthetic functions of the various transition devices. The choosing of effective shots is guided not only by aesthetic but also by ethical considerations.

force. Through cutting to the close-up, the action has been intensified.

The main reasons for using a cut are:

1.   To continue action. If the camera can no longer follow the action, you cut to another shot that *continues* the action.

2.   To reveal detail. As indicated above, if you want to see *more event detail* than the present shot reveals, you cut to a closer shot.

3.   To change place and time. A cut from an interior to the street indicates that the *locale* has now *shifted* to the street. In real-time television, a cut cannot reveal a change in time. But as soon as the event has been recorded on film or videotape, a cut can mean a jump *forward or backward in the event time,* or to another event that takes place in a different place at the same time (the "meanwhile-back-at-the-ranch" cut).

4.   To change impact. A cut to a tighter shot generally *intensifies* the screen event; a cut to a longer shot reduces the event impact.

5.   To establish an event rhythm. Through cutting, you can establish an *event rhythm*. Fast cutting generally gives the impression of excitement; slow cutting that of calm and tranquility (assuming the content of the screen material expresses the same feeling).

The Dissolve

The **dissolve,** or lap-dissolve, or simply "lap," is a gradual transition from shot to shot, whereby the two images temporarily overlap. Whereas the cut itself cannot be seen on the screen, the dissolve is a clearly visible transition. As such, it not merely constitutes a method of joining two shots together as unobtrusively as possible, but *represents a visual element* in its own right. You should, therefore, use the dissolve with greater discretion than the cut.

Basically, you use a dissolve (1) as a smooth bridge for action, (2) to indicate a change of locale or time, and (3) to indicate a strong relationship between two images.

For an interesting and *smooth transition* from a wide shot of a dancer to a close-up, for instance, simply dissolve from one camera to the other. The movements will temporarily blend into each other and indicate the strong association between the two shots. The action is not interrupted at all.

Where the mood or tempo of the presentation does not allow hard cuts, you can use dissolves to get from a long shot to a close-up or from a close-up to a long shot. A close-up of a soloist, for instance, can be dissolved into a long shot of the whole choir, which may be more appropriate than an instantaneous cut.

You can use a dissolve during continuous music. This is at least one way to change cameras in the middle of musical phrases when it would be awkward to cut.

You may prefer to indicate a *change of locale* by dissolving rather than cutting to the new set area. A *change of time* can also be suggested by a slow dissolve (long time lapse, slow dissolve; short time lapse, fast dissolve).

Matched dissolves are used for decorative effects or to indicate an especially *strong relationship* between two objects. For instance, a decorative use would be a sequence of two fashion models hiding behind sun umbrellas. Model one closes his or her sequence by hiding behind an umbrella; model two starts his or her sequence the same way. You can now match-dissolve from camera 1 to camera 2. Both cameras must frame the umbrellas approximately the same way before the dissolve. An example of an associative use is a close-up of a door in a very expensive dwelling match-dissolved to a close-up of a door in an old shack.

Depending on the overall rhythm of the event, you can use slow or fast dissolves. A very fast one functions almost like a cut and is, therefore, called a "soft cut."

Because dissolves are so readily available to you in television, you may be tempted to use them more often than necessary or even desirable. Do not overuse them; they create no rhythmic beat. Your presentation will lack precision and accent, and bore the viewer.

The Fade

In a **fade,** the picture either goes gradually to black (fade-out) or appears gradually on the screen from black (fade-in).

You use the fade to signal a definite beginning (fade-in) or end (fade-out) of a scene. Like the curtain in the theater, it defines the beginning and end of a portion of a screen event. As such, it is technically not a true transition.

Some experts use the term **cross-fade** for a quick fade to black followed immediately by a fade-in to the next image. Here the fade acts as a transition device, decisively separating the preceding and following images from each other. The cross-fade is also called a "dip to black" or a "kiss black."

In general, start each program by fading in the camera picture from black. The fade *from* black always indicates a beginning.

The fade *to* black suggests a complete separation of program elements. It usually indicates that one program element has come to an end. You should end every program by taking it to black. If you have to insert a commercial message in the program, you may want to go to black before the commercial, not so much to warn the viewer of the upcoming distraction as to tell him or her that this is a segment not directly connected with the material of the show.

Be careful not to go to black too often; the program continuity will be interrupted too many times by fades that all suggest final endings. The other extreme is the "never-go-to-black" craze. Some directors do not dare go to black for fear of giving the viewer a chance to switch to another channel. If a constant dribble of program material is the only way to keep a viewer glued to the set, the program content, rather than the presentation techniques, should be examined.

Complexity Editing The juxtaposition of shots that primarily, though not exclusively, help to intensify the screen event.

Continuity Editing The preserving of visual continuity from shot to shot.

Jump Cut 1. Cutting between shots that are identical in subject yet slightly different in screen location. Through the cut, the subject seems to jump from one screen location to another for no apparent reason. 2. Any abrupt transition between shots that violates the established continuity.

The Wipe

In a **wipe,** one picture seems to push the other off the screen. This is such an unabashed transition device that it must be classified as a special effect. A great variety of wipe configurations are available (see p. 376). Like the fade, the wipe generally signals the end of one scene and the beginning of another. Unlike the fade, it does not put a permanent stop to the show; it simply pushes on the next video sequence.

During a production, these transitions are easily accomplished through the switcher (see Chapter 12). In postproduction, any transition other than a simple cut can be achieved only through interfacing a switcher with the editing control unit, or with a sophisticated computer-controlled editing system that contains the various transitions in its software. We will discuss the various wipes and special effects transitions in Chapter 13.

MAJOR EDITING PRINCIPLES

The basic aim of editing is to tell a story with clarity and impact. Over the years of film and television production, we have established some basic editing principles and conventions that help us achieve this goal.

Most of your editing will be controlling the **continuity** of the edited event. This means that you have to preserve or establish some kind of visual and aural coherence from shot to shot and from scene to scene. Another challenge is that you often have to tell a complete story in an unreasonably short amount of time. In ENG, for example, usually the producer, not the material at hand, determines how long a story should be.

When editing EFP material, however, you will have a chance to go beyond mere continuity editing and to juxtapose shots, or audio and video, in ways that increase impact and meaning.

We will present some basic editing principles in four major groups: (1) continuity, (2) complexity, (3) context, and (4) ethics. You should realize that the list is far from exhaustive, and that editing principles are to be considered more as conventions than absolutes. They work well under most circumstances and are a basic part of the visual literacy of most television viewers and (one hopes) of television production personnel. However, depending on the event context and communication aim, some of the dos of editing may easily become the don'ts, and vice versa.

Continuity

In **continuity editing,** you should try to maintain or establish continuity in (1) subject identification, (2) subject location, (3) movement, (4) color, and (5) sound.

Subject Identification   The viewer should be able to recognize an object or subject from one shot to the next. Therefore, avoid editing between shots of *extreme changes in distance* or *angles* (see 11.17 and 11.18). If you cannot maintain a visual continuity for identification, bridge the gap by *telling* the viewer that the shot is, indeed, the same thing or person.

Despite what we have just said, trying to edit together shots that are *too similar* leads to even worse trouble: the **jump cut.** A jump cut occurs when you edit shots that are identical in subject yet slightly different in screen location. When edited together, the subject seems to jump from one screen location to another for no apparent reason. To avoid a jump cut, try to find a succeeding shot that shows the object from a different angle or field of view (see 11.19 and 11.20).

Subject Location   In order to establish some kind of orientation, we tend to expect a prominent object to maintain its relative screen position in subsequent shots. If, for example, you have two people talking to each other in an over-the-shoulder two-shot, the viewer expects the people to remain in their relative screen positions even during close-ups or reverse-angle shooting (see 11.21 and 11.22).

Most often, the maintaining of screen locations is decided in the shooting phase rather than in the post-production phase. You can avoid many frustrating hours in the editing room if you give some friendly advice to the camera operator on how to maintain proper subject location in subsequent shots.

When two people face each other while talking, you can draw an imaginary line, the **vector line,** between the two. When using a single camera for the reverse-angle shooting, you must shoot the reverse angle *from the same side of the vector line* (see 11.22). You cannot do one over-the-shoulder shot from the left side of the vector line (or, as it is sometimes called, "line of conversation" or "principal axis"), and the reverse angle from the right side. The same rule applies when shooting with multiple cameras. Both cameras must be kept on the same side of the vector line in order to keep the people from jumping into each other's screen position during a cut.

11.17 **Extreme Changes in Distance** When you cut from an extreme long shot to a close-up, we may not be able to recognize exactly whose close-up it is. You should zoom in somewhat, or cut to a medium shot, before cutting to the close-up.

 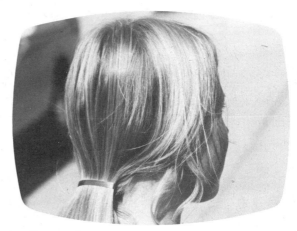

11.18 **Extreme Changes in Angles** A similar problem arises if you cut from extreme angles. It is difficult for the viewer to tell exactly whether or not the reverse angle shot is of the same person.

11.19 Jump Cut Sequences If the camera is not in the exact same position when repeating a take, or if the following shot is not sufficiently different in field or angle of view, the image seems to "jump" within the screen. Another common type of jump cut happens when a person is shown in successive shots, with each shot in an obviously different time and/or location.

a   c

11.20 Shot Sequences Avoiding Jump Cuts
A change in angle and/or field of view (tighter or farther away) causes a visual change sufficient to present separate, yet related, images, thus avoiding a jump cut. A cutaway (b) is sufficient to bridge a change in location and/or time, even if the images separated by the cutaway look fairly similar (a and c).

b

11.21 Maintaining Directions When moving from a medium shot to a close-up, note that the person needs to face in the same direction in subsequent shots and remain in approximately the same position on the screen.

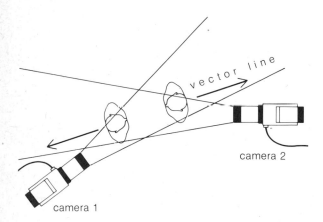

11.22 Maintaining Subject Location in Reverse-Angle Shooting When two people face each other, you can draw an imaginary line, a vector line, connecting them. For close-ups as well as over-the-shoulder shooting, keep both cameras on the same side of the vector line. Do not have one camera look at the scene from one side of it and the other camera from the other side. You should use the same focal-length setting on both cameras so that their relative positions to each other remain constant.

11.23 Shift of Screen Positions during Interview If the host sits in the middle, you will not be able to maintain screen positions on subsequent two-shots. A cut from a three-shot to a two-shot with the guest on screen-left puts the host on the right side of the screen. A subsequent two-shot with the guest at screen-right will switch the host to screen-left.

Even if you establish and observe a vector line, you may still violate the screen positions through improper placement of people. For example, if during an interview the host sits in the middle of two or more guests, you will not be able to maintain screen positions in subsequent two-shots (see 11.23).

As an editor, you may be able to render the jump less jarring by intercutting a close-up of either guest or host, provided that the camera operator brought back such essential cutaways. The best solution to the problem is, of course, to place the host to one side of the guests rather than in the middle (see 11.24). Such an arrangement is especially important if you shoot live-on-tape with multiple cameras.

Movement When editing, or cutting (with a switcher) on action, try to *continue* the action as much as pos-

sible from shot to shot. The following three paragraphs cover some of the major points to keep in mind.

When cutting on action (either by editing two shots together or switching from one camera to another), cut *during* the motion of the object or subject, not before or after it. For example, if you have a close-up of a person who is preparing to rise from a chair, cut to a wider shot just after he or she has started to rise but before he or she stands. Or, if you have the choice, you can let the person almost finish the action on the close-up (even if he or she goes out of the frame temporarily) before cutting to the wider shot. But do not wait until the subject has finished getting up before going to the wider shot.

If one shot contains a moving object, do not follow it up with a shot that shows the object stationary. Similarly, if you follow a moving object with a camera pan-

11.24 Maintaining Subject Location in Close-ups When shooting close-ups of two people conversing, bear in mind that the viewer expects them to remain in their relative screen positions. An abrupt position change would disturb the shot continuity. Also, we expect their eyes to meet in successive shots. Even if two people are widely separated, their eyes are supposed to meet in subsequent shots.

ning in one shot, do not cut to a stationary camera in the next. Equally jarring would be a cut from a stationary object to a moving one.

An object moving in a specific direction also forms a vector line. Do not cross this vector line with your camera or cameras on subsequent shots, or you will reverse the action (see 11.25). If you get footage in which the action has been shot from both sides of the vector line (resulting in a reversal of screen directions), you must separate the two shots by a cutaway or a head-on shot so that the reversed screen directions can be perceived as continuing.

Color Even if you are careful to white-balance the camera for each new location and lighting situation in ENG or EFP, you will find that the color temperatures do not always match. This is not too serious, as long as you assemble shots or scenes that differ in content

and/or location. For example, if you cut from a stand-up reporter in front of the city hall to the hearing chambers inside city hall, a change in color temperature is quite natural. However, suppose you are cutting from a medium two-shot to a close-up of a visiting celebrity. If her silk blouse, which looks reasonably white on the medium shot, turns blue on the close-up, you have problems with color continuity.

In ENG, such problems of color continuity are generally ignored. Just as with having the camera occasionally out of focus or shaking, we can ascribe the occasional mismatch of color temperature to the excitement and actuality of the event. But in EFP, or large studio productions, we have no such tolerance for color mismatch. In the studio, the color temperatures can be matched fairly well, even if you shoot film style over a period of several days. In EFP, however, matching colors is much more of a problem, especially

11.25   Proper Placement of Host for Maintaining Screen Positions By isolating the host at one side of the guests, you will have no trouble maintaining screen positions. Keep the close-up of the host on the left side of the screen, because we remember his screen-left position from the previous shot.

when shooting film style. The key problem is that you have relatively little control over the lighting. You may have to shoot part of a scene in bright sunlight, and the other part during an overcast day. Whereas color correction in postproduction is routine for film, it is a major, expensive undertaking for videotape. The more care that is taken to match colors during the production, the easier it is to maintain color continuity in postproduction.

Sound   When editing speech sounds, make sure that you preserve the general speech *rhythm.* The pauses between shots of a continuing conversation should be neither much shorter nor much longer than the ones in the unedited version. In an interview, the cut (edit or switcher-activated) occurs usually at the end of a question or answer. However, *reaction shots* are often smoother when they occur *during,* rather than at the

end of, phrases or sentences. But note that action is generally a stronger motivation for a cut than dialogue. If somebody moves during the conversation, you must show the move, even if the other person is still in the middle of a statement.

As you learned in Chapter 9, the continuity of background sounds, or **ambience,** is very important in maintaining continuity. This audio continuity is especially important if the background sounds are acting as environmental sounds—that is, giving clues to the environment in which the event takes place. But if a production is shot film style (often in different locations and stretching over several days or weeks), the ambience is anything but uniform. When building a scene through editing, you may have to use long shots that were shot one week, and close-ups that were shot two weeks later. If you now want to pretend a real-time sequence, you must make sure that the audio people

11.26 Reversal of Screen Directions Any motion generates a strong vector line. If you cut between cameras positioned on opposite sides of the motion, that is, across from each other on the vector line, you reverse the direction of the motion on the screen at each cut. Because such a reversal can become very confusing, you should keep all your cameras either on one or the other side of the vector line.

mix continuous (and credible) ambience with the dialogue in postproduction. Sometimes this requires adding a constant sound to the *entire sequence* in order to mask the problem of different, discontinuous sounds.

In music, try to *cut with the beat.* Cuts are like visualized bars; they determine the beat of the visual sequence and keep the action rhythmically tight. Cutting against the beat in music generally does not produce increased tension; rather it appears as sloppy editing. If the general rhythm of the music is casual or flowing, dissolves are usually more appropriate than hard cuts.

Complexity

Sometimes in your editing you are concerned not so much with the continuity of the event as its *intensification.* This means that through editing you reveal the *complexity* of the screen event. Thus, this type of editing is called **complexity editing,** in contrast to the continuity editing we just described. There are many ways of intensifying a screen event. You can edit to progressively closer shots, use carefully selected event details in several close-up series, increase the editing rhythm, or use high-intensity music or background sounds that go with or purposely against the visual structure.

Let's assume that you have to edit a downhill ski race for a sports show. If your intent is to give the viewer a general idea of the race, you show portions of the race in their natural sequence: the racer coming out of the starting gate; skiing down the upper, middle, and lower parts of the course; and finally coming through the finish. But if your communication aim is to give the viewer some idea of how difficult it is to race down an icy slope, you may want to depart from the natural sequence of events and show close-ups of skis trying to stay in contact with the snow, legs trying to absorb bumps, a face in utter concentration at the beginning of the race, a body being jerked out of the tuck position, and so forth. You are concerned not about event continuity, but about event complexity—that is, giving the viewer not simply a look *at* the event, but a closer look *into* it.

Context

In all types of editing, but especially editing news stories, you must preserve the true context in which the main event took place. Let's assume that the news footage of the speech by a local political candidate contains a funny close-up of an audience member sound asleep. But when you screen the rest of the footage, you discover that all other audience members were not only wide awake but quite stimulated by the candidate's remarks. Are you going to use the close-up? Of course not. The person asleep was in no way representative of the overall context in which the event—the speech—took place. The next day, you get news footage of the speech by the rival candidate. Most of the audience shots reveal a practically empty house. But, as the ENG camera operator assures you, he or she took a good number of close-ups of the few small groups of people present so that the hall would not look quite so empty. Can you use the close-ups? Yes, but only after you have established that the house was, indeed, practically empty.

You must be especially careful when using stock shots in editing. A **stock shot** is a shot that depicts a common occurrence—clouds, beach scenes, snow falling, traffic, crowds—that can be repeated in a variety of contexts because its qualities are typical. Some television stations either subscribe to a stock-shot library or maintain their own stock-shot collection. Here are two examples of using stock shots in editing. When editing the speech by the political candidate men-

tioned earlier, you find that you need a cutaway to maintain continuity during a change in screen directions. You have a stock shot of a news photographer. Can you use it? Yes, because a news photographer certainly fits into the actual event context. But should you use a stock shot of a crowded and lively audience instead of the embarrassingly empty rows of chairs? No, definitely not. After all, the empty hall, not a crowded audience, was the true context of the event.

Ethics

The willful distortion of an event through editing is not a case of bad aesthetic judgment, but a question of ethics. The most important principle for the editor, as for all other production people working with the presentation of nonfictional events, is to remain as true to the actual event as possible. For example, if you were to add applause simply because your favorite political candidate said something you happen to support, although in reality there was dead silence, you would definitely be acting in an unethical way. It would be equally wrong if you were to edit out all the statements that go against your convictions and leave only the ones with which you agree. If someone presents pro and con arguments, make sure to present the most representative of each. Do not edit out either all one side or all the other in order to meet the prescribed length of the segment.

Be especially careful when juxtaposing two shots that may generate by implication a third idea not contained in either of the two shots. To follow a politician's plea for increased armaments with the explosion of an atomic bomb may unfairly imply that this politician favors nuclear war. These types of **montage** are as powerful as they are dangerous. Be especially on the alert for montage effects between video and audio information. They may be more subtle than the video-only montages, but no less potent.

Do not engage in *staging* events in order to bring back exciting footage. For example, if a fire fighter has made a successful rescue, and all you got was the rescued person on a stretcher, do not ask the fire fighter to climb the ladder again to simulate the daring feat. Although reenactments of this sort have become routine for some ENG teams, stay away from them. There is enough drama in any event if you look close enough and shoot it effectively. You do not have to stage anything.

Finally, you are ultimately responsible to the viewers for your choices as an editor. Do not violate the trust they put in you. As you can see, there is a fine line between intensifying an event through careful editing and distorting an event through careless or unethical editing practices. The only safeguard the viewers have against irresponsible persuasion and manipulation is your responsibility as a professional communicator and your basic respect and love for your fellow human beings.

BASIC COMPUTER TERMINOLOGY

Although you may not want to become a computer expert, or even learn much about computers, you cannot avoid them entirely in television production. First, as you have learned, much television equipment is partially controlled by small computers. Second, the actual operation of some television equipment—especially editing equipment—is similar in many ways to that of simple microcomputers. Third, much of the computer lingo has invaded television production terminology. We will, therefore, briefly list here some of the computer terms that are used frequently in television production.

Analog Pertaining to representation by means of continuously variable physical quantities. For example, an analog signal fluctuates exactly like (analogous to) the original stimulus (physical quantity). The important aspect is that it is *continuously* variable and does not proceed in discrete steps (as in digital). You could think of a ramp as an analog representation and a staircase as a digital one.

Binary Digit A system that uses only two digits, 0 and 1. The binary digit, called *bit,* is the smallest amount of information a computer can hold and process. A charge is either present, represented by a 1, or absent, represented by a 0. The thousands of electronic circuits in a computer can handle such on-off switching with incredible speed.

Bit See Binary Digit.

Byte A series of bits—usually 8.

Computer A device that can receive, store, process, and display a set of instructions in a programmable way. All computers and microprocessors used in television are digital.

Cursor A special symbol (usually a rectangle) that indicates a certain position on the display screen.

Digital Pertaining to data in the form of digits. The original stimulus is translated into many *discrete* steps, represented by the binary digits 0 and 1. The computer rapidly manipulates many thousands of bits in a

sequence determined by the computer program. While the analog system may be represented by a ramp (continuous change), the digital system is more like a staircase (each step having a discrete value).

Disc A magnetic storage device, which is used for information storage additional to the computer's memory. The disc looks similar to a phonograph record. *Floppy discs,* made of relatively flexible material, are generally used for smaller computers. They have a more limited storage capacity than *hard discs.*

Disc Pack A disc pack consists of several hard discs mounted on a vertical shaft that spins the discs. Several "read/write" (playback and record) heads put the information on the disc and retrieve it. The disc pack can store a great amount of information and permits much faster access than magnetic tape. All digital still-store units use magnetic disc packs.

DOS Stands for Disc Operating System, which is a disc drive that can record, store, and play back digital information on a floppy disc. Most computer-assisted editing systems or digital framestore synchronizers use floppy discs for information storage.

DVE Stands for Digital Video Effect.

Firmware The basic instructions (program) that are built into the computer and that cannot be altered. It does not get lost when the computer is turned off. *See* ROM.

Floppy Disc See Disc.

Flowchart A block diagram in which certain symbols (diamonds, rectangles, arrows) represent the flow—the steps and their sequence—of an event. It is used by programmers to translate programs into computer logic.

Hardware The actual, physical equipment of a computer and its accessories.

Interface To connect various devices originally not part of a system in order to extend the system's capabilities.

K Stands for kilo, meaning 1,000. The computer's capacity is often expressed in K numbers.

LSI Stands for Large-Scale Integrated Circuits, generally used in microprocessors.

Memory Stores programs and data. *See* RAM and ROM.

Menu An index of the material stored.

Microcomputer A small computer that uses a microprocessor as its central processing unit (consisting of memory, control, and logic units).

Microprocessor A small-scale central processing unit, consisting of one or more large-scale integrated circuit chips (LSIs) that can perform input and output jobs but can also have a memory.

Modem A word made up of *mo*dulator and *demo*dulator. A modem modulates (changes) the computer signals so that they can be transmitted over special communication facilities (such as the ordinary telephone system) and demodulates these signals again (changes them back) so that the computer can accept them. With a modem, the computer can interact with other computers through regular telephones.

Page Information that occupies the total display screen area or a designated quantity of memory with a fixed address.

Printer A typewriter-like device that prints information stored in the computer at a rapid rate. The printed material is called *hard copy*. A typical word processor consists of a microcomputer with a display screen, at least one disc drive (DOS), and a printer.

Program A sequence of instructions encoded in a specific computer language to perform certain predetermined processes. The program is software.

RAM Stands for Random Access Memory, the main memory of the computer, which allows a single datum to be stored or retrieved without affecting the other data. Most microcomputers and microprocessors lose the information stored in RAM whenever the power is turned off. Important information is, therefore, frequently transferred from RAM to one of the auxiliary storage devices, such as the floppy disc, magnetic tape, or paper punch tape. Most computer-assisted editing systems have a hard-copy printer, which prints all the editing decisions.

Return A key on the computer keyboard that, when pressed, tells the computer that the instructions are finished. It usually activates a specific program routine.

Ripple To move or pass the lines one by one up or down the display screen.

ROM Stands for Read-Only Memory, the program that is built into the computer memory and cannot be altered. It does not disappear when the computer is turned off and is, therefore, called *firmware* (in contrast to the software RAM programs).

Scroll To move all the text upward on the display screen to make room for more at the bottom.

Software The programs that make the computer perform certain predetermined processes. These programs are generally part of RAM and get lost when the computer is turned off. Most software comes on floppy discs that can "boot" the computer (put the program into RAM via disc drive).

Storage Storing the input information either in RAM or in one of the auxiliary storage devices, for example, the disc or tape (such as an audio cassette).

Terminal A keyboard through which the computer can be given instructions. The terminal can be part of the computer or can be used from a remote location. Many terminals also contain a video display screen.

MAIN POINTS

1. There are four basic transition devices: (1) the cut, the instantaneous change from one shot to the other; (2) the dissolve, the temporary overlapping of two shots; (3) the fade, with the picture gradually appearing from black or going to black; and (4) the wipe, in which the second image fully or partially replaces the first one.

2. The four major editing principles are (1) continuity, (2) complexity, (3) context, and (4) ethics.

3. Continuity editing means to maintain or establish continuity in (1) subject identification, (2) subject location, (3) movement, (4) color, and (5) sound.

4. Complexity editing means that shots are assembled in order to intensify the event and show its complexity.

5. When working with nonfictional events, the most important editing principle is an ethical one: to remain as true to the actual event as possible.

FURTHER READING

Browne, Steven E. *The Videotape Post Production Primer.* Burbank, CA: Wilton Place Communications, 1982.

Shetter, Michael D. *Videotape Editing: Communication with Pictures and Sound.* Elk Grove Village, IL: Swiderski Electronics, 1982.

Zettl, Herbert. *Sight–Sound–Motion: Applied Media Aesthetics.* Belmont, CA: Wadsworth Publishing Co., 1976.

Switching or Instantaneous Editing

Instantaneous editing means switching from one video source to another, or combining two or more sources in some way, while the show or show segment is in progress. The technical device that makes instantaneous editing possible is the switcher.

Section One of this chapter describes the basic functions of the switcher and its layout and operation. It also examines some major features of large production switchers.

1.   The basic functions of a switcher are (1) to select an appropriate video source from several inputs; (2) perform basic transitions; and (3) create and/or access special effects.

2.   The basic switcher consists of a program bus, a preview bus, at least two mix buses, and a pair of fader bars that enable the mixing of two sources and fades.

3.   Large switchers have several mix/ effects banks (two buses make up a bank), and a variety of special effects equipment.

In Section Two we take a brief look at these additional features of large production switchers: (1) double reentry and cascading functions; (2) downstream keyer; (3) flip-flop controls; (4) quad-split controls; and (5) clip control.

Shifting from one video source to another or joining sources somehow while the show is going on is known as **switching** or **instantaneous editing.** This type of editing is done with a *video switcher.* We will now briefly describe (1) its basic functions and (2) its basic layout and operation.

BASIC FUNCTIONS

Video switchers can be relatively simple or extremely complex in their production function and electronic design. However, even the most complex, computer-assisted video-switching system performs the same basic functions as a simple production switcher. The complex ones can perform more visual tricks than the simple ones, and with greater reliability and electronic stability.

As you recall from Chapter 1, these are the *basic functions* of a production switcher: (1) select an appropriate video source from several inputs, (2) perform basic transitions between two video sources, and (3) create or access special effects. Most

switchers have further provisions for remote start and stop of videotape recorders, and for film and slide projectors. Some switchers automatically switch the program audio with the video. For example, when switching between two people telephoning each other, the switcher triggers the audio filter whenever you take the reaction shot (thereby giving the sound the characteristic "far" telephone quality while we listen in on the far end of the conversation), and switches back to the regular "close" audio whenever you take the "action" shot of the person talking. Program switchers that automatically switch all program audio with the video are called **audio-follow-video** switchers; they are primarily used in master control.

Production switcher refers to the switcher that is located in the studio control room or remote van. There are other types of switchers that simply assign certain pieces of equipment to specific locations or the equipment output to specific monitors. But these *assignment switchers,* or *routing switchers,* are quite different from the production switchers in design and function and will not be discussed here.

Unlike postproduction editing—in which you have, or must take, the time to deliberate exactly where and with what transition to combine two shots—*switching* demands *instantaneous* decisions. The aesthetic principles of switching are identical to those used in postproduction. However, the technology involved is quite different.

BASIC LAYOUT AND OPERATION

You learned in Chapter 1 that each video input on a switcher has its corresponding button. If you have only two cameras and all you want is to cut from one to the other, two buttons (one for camera 1 and the other for camera 2) are sufficient. However, because we are not content with merely cutting between two cameras for most production jobs, we need a slightly more complex switcher. Therefore, we need separate buttons for each camera, VTR, film island, other video source equipment, and remote inputs. All these buttons are arranged in rows, or **buses.**

Simple Switcher Layout

Let's look at a simple switcher that performs the most basic production functions: a cut, or "take," from one video source to another (camera 1 to camera 2, for example); a dissolve from one to the other; a fade from black and to black (signaling the beginning or end of a show or show segment); and a

superimposition, or **super** (one image overlapping the other, like stopping a dissolve in the middle). Also, because it is a good idea to see what pictures we get before punching them up on the air (sending the selected material—video signal—to the line-out, regardless of whether the signal actually goes on the air or to a VTR), we need some device that lets us preview the selected sources or effects (see 12.1).

As you can see in 12.1, there are four rows of buttons, or buses, as they are called. There is a **program bus;** two **mix buses** (mix bus A and mix bus B), called a *bank;* and a **preview bus.** Their arrangement varies greatly with different types of switchers. The preview bus, for example, may be right above the program bus. Each bus has buttons for cameras 1 and 2; film (representing the film island with any one of two film projectors or a slide projector); VTR for videotape; and remote, which is an auxiliary input for any additional video source needed, such as a second VTR or film island, or an actual remote feed. Then there is a black button, which puts the screen to black. The preview and program buses have an additional mix button. Let's find out what the individual buses and their buttons

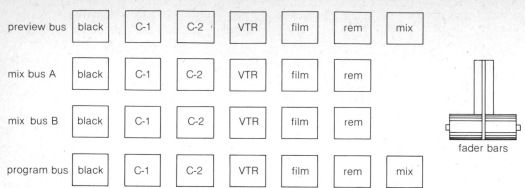

preview bus	black	C-1	C-2	VTR	film	rem	mix
mix bus A	black	C-1	C-2	VTR	film	rem	
mix bus B	black	C-1	C-2	VTR	film	rem	
program bus	black	C-1	C-2	VTR	film	rem	mix

fader bars

12.1   Basic Switcher This simple switcher has four buses: a program bus, two mix buses, and a preview bus. The pair of mix buses is called a "bank." Also, it has a pair of fader bars that can be pushed either individually or together into the mix bus A or B position. The program bus switches the inputs (cameras 1 and 2, VTR, film, remote) directly to the line-out. The mix buses go to the line-out, if the mix button on the program bus is punched up. The mix buses make possible the mixing of two inputs, as in a dissolve or super. Through the preview bus, any input can be previewed on a special monitor before being punched up on the air. The fader bars accomplish the mixing of two sources (dissolves, supers) and fades (from and to black).

can do. We will work from the bottom up, starting with the program bus.

Program Bus   The program bus represents in effect a selector switch for the line-out. It is a direct input-output link. It is, therefore, also called the "direct" bus. Whatever button you press sends its designated video input (such as camera 1 or VTR) to the line-out (see 12.2).

You can accomplish simple cuts among cameras 1 and 2, film, and VTR, and black with the pro-

gram bus only. For example, if you press the camera 1 button on the program bus, camera 1 goes on the air. If you now press the VTR button, the VTR's picture instantly replaces camera 1's image on the screen. In effect you have cut from camera 1 to the VTR. If you now press the black button, the screen goes to black instantly. To provide more transition possibilities than just simple cuts, such as dissolves and fades, and even such simple effects as a superimposition, we need two additional buses, the mix buses (at least in our switcher design).

Audio-Follow-Video   A switcher that automatically changes the accompanying audio along with the video source.

Bank   A pair of buses.

Bus, or Buss   A row of buttons on the switcher. A pair of buses is called a bank.

Fader Bars   A pair of levers on the switcher that can produce dissolves, fades, and wipes of different speeds, and superimpositions.

Mix Bus   Rows of buttons that permit the "mixing" of video sources, as in a dissolve and super. Major buses for on-the-air switching.

Mixing   Video: the combining of various shots via the switcher.

Preset Monitor   Also called PST monitor. Special preview monitor used by technical director for checking and adjusting special effects.

Preview Bus   Rows of buttons that can direct an input to the preview monitor at the same time another video source is on the air.

Program Bus   Also called direct bus. The bus on a switcher whose inputs are directly switched to the line-out.

Special Effects Controls   Also called SFX controls. Buttons on a switcher that regulate special effects. They include buttons for specific wipe patterns, the joystick positioner, and chroma key controls.

Switching   A change from one video source to another during a show, or show segment, with the aid of a switcher.

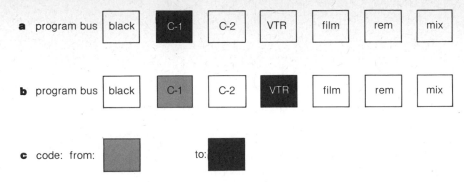

a program bus | black | C-1 | C-2 | VTR | film | rem | mix

b program bus | black | C-1 | C-2 | VTR | film | rem | mix

c code: from: ☐ to: ☐

12.2 Program Bus (a) Whatever is punched up on the program bus goes directly to the line-out. In this case, camera 1 is on the air. (b) If you now want to cut from camera 1 to the VTR input, you simply press the VTR button, and the VTR's picture goes to the line-out. (c) This code means going from one source to another source.

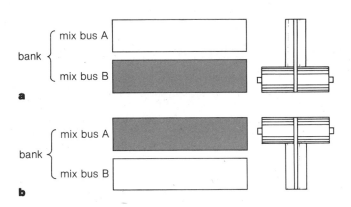

bank { mix bus A

mix bus B

a

bank { mix bus A

mix bus B

b

12.3 Fader Bar Positions (a) Fader bars in the "down" position activate mix bus B. (b) Fader bars in the "up" position activate mix bus A.

Mix Buses The mix A and mix B buses allow you to **mix** the images from two sources, such as the temporary mixing (overlapping) of camera 1 and camera 2 in a dissolve, or the total overlapping of the two cameras in a super. The **fader bars** gradually activate either bus A or bus B, depending on how far you move them toward the bus A position or the bus B position. The fader bars function as a pot (or fader) does on the audio board, except, of course, that the fader bars control the fading in or out of the picture, whereas the audio pot regulates the fading in and out, or mixing, of sound. The more they move into the "up" position, the more bus A

is faded in, and bus B faded out. When you move them down, bus B fades in, and bus A fades out (see 12.3).

Now, look at the switcher in 12.1 again. If you were now to press the camera 1 button on mix bus B, what would happen? Nothing. Why not? Because the mix buses have not yet been assigned to the line-out. This you do by pressing the *mix* button on the program bus. As you remember, everything that is punched up on the program bus goes directly to the line-out. This includes the mix buses. Once the mix buses are assigned, or "delegated," you can begin with the switching.

Preview Bus   The preview bus functions almost the same as a program bus, except that its line-out goes not on the air or to a recording device, but simply to a special monitor. If, for example, you press the camera 1 button on the preview bus, camera 1's picture appears on the *preview monitor,* regardless of what the line monitor shows. If you now press the VTR button, you preview the VTR leader. On the *preview monitor* (P/V monitor), the T.D. (technical director) and the director can check special effects, or compare the on-the-air image (which is displayed on the line monitor) and the upcoming image (which is displayed by the preview monitor) for continuity and other aesthetic factors. Obviously, the preview and line monitors should be close together.

The preview bus also allows you to check the *presetting* of the more complex effects (such as putting a title over a super) by routing the effects either to the preview monitor or, more often, to a special **preset monitor** (PST monitor). Because the preset monitor serves more a technical function (adjusting a special effect) than an aesthetic function (comparing the previous and following shots), it is usually placed closer to the T.D. than to the director.

Before we add some more buttons and buses to our simple switcher, let's do some basic switching exercises.

Basic Switcher Operation

Before doing any switching in the mix bus section, make sure that you have assigned the mix bus section to the line-out (by pressing the mix button on the program bus) and that you pay close attention to the position of the fader bars. If they are up, the A bus is active (on our switcher). If they are down, the B bus is delegated and, therefore, active.

Using our simple switcher in 12.1, how could you achieve a cut, dissolve, super, and fade?

Cut, or Take
As you remember, a cut is the instantaneous change from one image to another.

Let's work with the fader bars in the down, bus B, position. The director says, *Ready one.* This means that a cut to camera 1 is coming up, in this case a take from black to camera 1. You should be ready to press the camera 1 button on mix bus B. *Take*

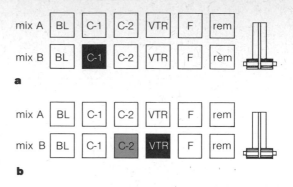

12.4   Cutting between Video Sources (a) With the B bus activated (both fader bars are down), the camera 1 button puts camera 1 on the air. (b) By pressing the VTR button, you accomplish a cut from camera 2 to the VTR.

one. You simply press the camera 1 button, bus B, and camera 1's picture appears on the line monitor. If camera 1 does not show up on the line monitor, you may have missed one or both of these important preswitching steps: (1) to press the mix button on the program bus, and (2) to have the faders in the bus B (down) position.

If you now want to cut to camera 2, simply press the camera 2 button on the same (mix B) bus. If you want to cut from camera 2 to VTR, simply press the VTR button (see 12.4).

You could accomplish the same switching on the program bus. However, transferring the switching to the mix buses extends the possibilities for dissolves and supers without activating additional buses.

Dissolve
For a dissolve from camera 1 to camera 2, press the camera 2 button on bus B while camera 1 is already punched up on bus A (and on the air, because the fader bars are still in the up position, activating bus A) (see 12.5). Now move both fader bars down to the B position. Depending on how fast you move the levers to the bus B position, your dissolve is either slow or fast. In any case, while you are moving the bars from A to B, you gradually fade out camera 1's picture on bus A, while simultaneously fading in camera 2's picture on bus B. Once the fader bars are in the B position, only camera 2's

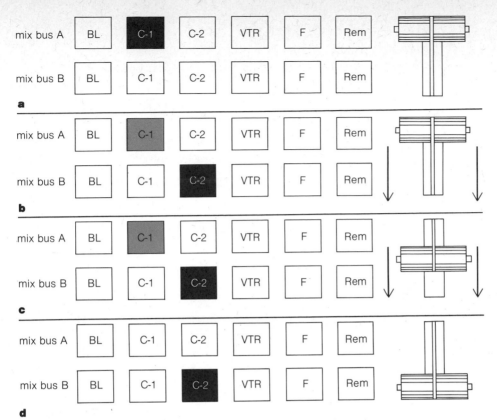

mix bus A	BL	C-1	C-2	VTR	F	Rem
mix bus B	BL	C-1	C-2	VTR	F	Rem

a

mix bus A	BL	C-1	C-2	VTR	F	Rem
mix bus B	BL	C-1	C-2	VTR	F	Rem

b

mix bus A	BL	C-1	C-2	VTR	F	Rem
mix bus B	BL	C-1	C-2	VTR	F	Rem

c

mix bus A	BL	C-1	C-2	VTR	F	Rem
mix bus B	BL	C-1	C-2	VTR	F	Rem

d

12.5   Dissolve (a) Camera 1 is on the air on bus A. (b) For a dissolve, you now punch up camera 2 on bus B. Nothing will happen as yet, because bus B is not activated (the fader bars are in the A bus position). (c) By pulling the fader bars down into the bus B position, you cause camera 1 gradually to fade out, as camera 2 fades in. In the middle position of the fader bars, both buses are activated; at this stage, the dissolve is identical to a superimposition. (d) With the fader bars all the way in the B bus position, bus A is deactivated (with camera 1 no longer visible on the screen) with only camera 2 remaining on the B bus. The dissolve has been completed. Be sure to move the fader bars all the way up or down; otherwise the tally lights for both cameras will stay on.

picture will be on the air. The dissolve is finished.

If you stop the dissolve halfway between the A and B buses, you have a superimposition.

Super   As we have just indicated, you can accomplish a superimposition by stopping a dissolve halfway between buses A and B (see 12.5c). Both buses will be activated, each delivering a picture with exactly one-half video (signal strength). If you want to favor the picture from the A bus (make the selected video source stronger), simply move the fader bars toward the A bus. Move it toward the B bus if you want to favor the B bus source.

Fade   You can fade in a picture on either bus by moving the fader bars from one mix bus, on which the black button has been punched up, to the other bus with the desired source punched up. Try to fade up on camera 2 from black. Assume that the fader bars are both in the bus B position. How would you

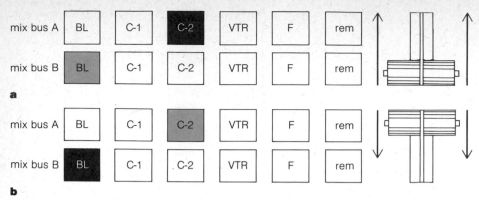

12.6 Fade in and Fade out (a) Fade in: Camera 2 on bus A is faded in from black on camera 1. In effect, you *dissolve* from bus B to bus A. (b) Fade out: You dissolve from bus A (with camera 2 on the air) to black on bus B.

do it? You can check your switching on 12.6a. Bus B is activated by both fader bars in the B position. The line monitor shows black, because the bus B black button is punched up. On the A bus, you punch up the camera 2 button. Now move both fader bars up to the A bus. Camera 2 gradually fades in from black. Going to black works in reverse. If you want to go from a video source to black, simply punch up the black button on the nonactivated bus and literally "dissolve" to black (see 12.6b).

Preview   Whenever you want to preview a source before switching to it, simply punch it up on the preview bus. If you want to preview a super, you need to transfer the on-the-air source (say camera 1) back to the program bus (thereby taking the mix buses off the line-out designation), preset your super on your mix buses, and punch the "mix" button on the preview bus. You will then see the super. Usually, a super is so easily accomplished that it does not need to be preset or previewed.

Larger Production Switchers

Because you have now become proficient in operating a simple switcher, we can go ahead and add a few buttons and buses to make the switcher more versatile. Specifically, we will cover in this section (1) effects buses, (2) multiple functions, and (3) additional switcher controls. In Section Two of the

chapter, we will elaborate more on double reentry and cascading functions, downstream keyer, and flip-flop controls.

Effects Buses   In order to extend the switcher to perform additional tricks, such as wipes, split-screen effects, title keys, and some of the more lively, video-gamelike effects you see during a newscast, we need even more buses and buttons.

As you recall from Chapter 11, a *wipe* is when one television picture seems to move off the screen, uncovering another. If the wipe stops before it is completed, you see two images side by side (or in the upper and lower half of the screen). This effect is called *split screen*. (We will discuss the various electronic effects more extensively in Chapter 13.) To preset a wipe, you need two additional buses: one bus for the inputs of the base picture (the picture about to be wiped off the screen) and one bus for the input of the video source that is doing the wiping, that is, replacing the base picture. A second pair of fader bars is now needed to perform the wipe and control its direction and speed.

In order to assign the **effects buses** from either the program or mix buses, and to route the effect to the preset and preview monitors, we need to equip these buses with an effects button. As you can see in 12.7, our simple switcher is beginning to look a little bit more complicated. You should realize, however, that these buses and buttons do not by

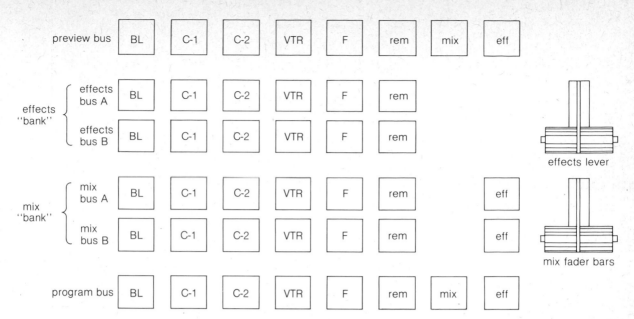

12.7 **Switcher with Special Effects Buses** The switcher has two effects buses and an effects lever. The program bus, mix, and preview buses each have an additional effects button, which assigns the effects buses to preview or the line-out.

themselves create the effect; it is rather the special effects generators, or SEGs, that perform this task (see Chapter 13). In smaller compact models, the SEG and other electronic equipment are built right into the switchers. In large production switchers, the special effects equipment is mounted in special racks.

Multiple-Functions Mix/Effects Buses

In order to keep the rows of buttons to a sensible minimum without curtailing the switcher's special effects capacity, the buses are usually made to perform multiple functions. Thus, we have no longer separate mix and effects buses, but pairs of mix/effects, or M/E buses, which you can use for either the mix (fades and dissolves) or effects (keys, wipes) functions. On many of the smaller yet highly flexible switchers, the program or direct bus can also be used as a mix bus, and the preview bus as a special effects bus (for keying). You can assign the different functions through delegation or mode controls (see 12.8).

Additional Controls

Even relatively unsophisticated production switchers have many more controls, which can be grouped roughly into these categories: (1) delegation controls, (2) special effects controls, and (3) color background controls.

1. *Delegation Controls.* **Delegation controls** determine the function of the buses. You have already successfully worked with these delegation or mode controls; the mix or effects button for the program bus is such a delegation control. When you press the mix button on the program bus in the simple switcher (as in 12.1), the mix buses are transferred to the line-out. When you press the mix button on the production switcher in which the mix and effects buses are interchangeable (see 12.9), the program bus and one of the effects buses become mix buses. On large production switchers, you can assign any one of the buses to a specific mix or effect function. The preview buses, too, can be assigned various roles. They may be used for special key effects or flip-flop cutting (see Section Two). This is all done

12.8   Switcher with M/E Buses (Central Dynamics VS-14) This switcher has four buses (from bottom to top): program bus (called direct bus), mix/effects bus B, mix/effects bus A, and the preview bus. The delegation buttons select the functions of the program bus: *direct* assigns the program bus the line-out function; *mix* changes the program bus into the principal mix bus; *effects* deactivates the mix bus and assigns buses A and B effects functions. The preview bus can be assigned a source selection function for the downstream keyer. There are also effects mode buttons and controls for wipe patterns, wipe positioner, color mattes, and key effects.

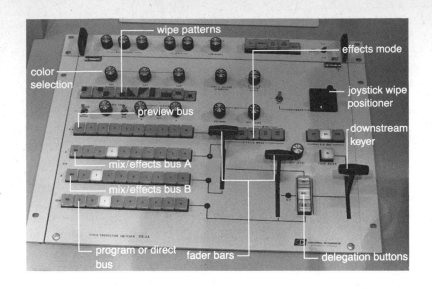

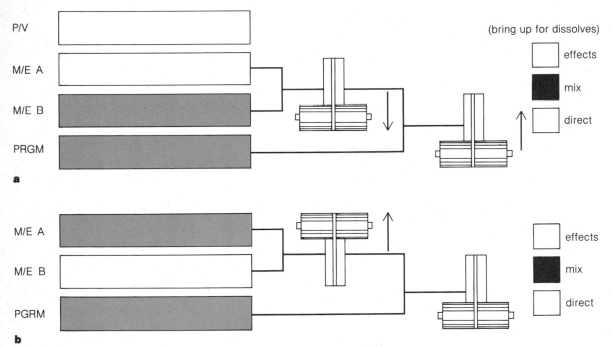

a

b

12.9   Mix Delegation of Program (Direct) Bus In order to delegate the program bus a mix function, you must press the *mix* button. The other mix bus is either the M/E bus A or B above the "program" bus, depending on the position of the effects levers. If they are in the "down" position, the M/E bus B is the second mix bus (the first being the reassigned program bus) (see *a*). If they are in the "up" position, the M/E bus A is the second mix bus (see *b*). You can now accomplish a dissolve by bringing the fader bars from the lower position (program/mix bus) to the upper position (second mix bus). If you now want to assign the program bus its direct line-out function again, you need to press the *direct* delegation button.

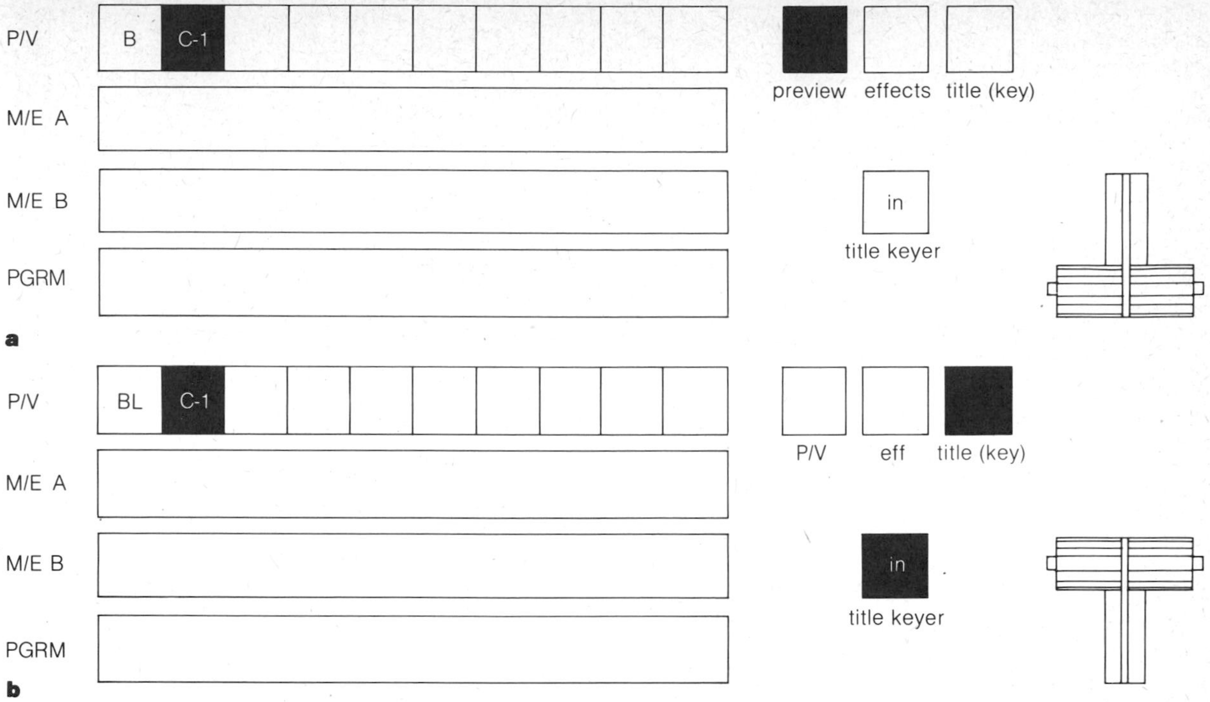

P/V [B | C-1 | | | | | | | | | |]   ■ preview □ effects □ title (key)

M/E A [   ]

M/E B [   ]   □ in
title keyer

PGRM [   ]

a

P/V [BL | C-1 | | | | | | | | | |]   □ P/V □ eff ■ title (key)

M/E A [   ]

M/E B [   ]   ■ in
title keyer

PGRM [   ]

b

12.10 Key Delegation of Preview Bus When the preview bus is assigned its preview functions, the preview delegation button must be pressed (see *a*). Camera 1 is now being previewed. When the preview bus is used as a key effects bus to supply the key source (camera 1), you must press the *title* delegation button and the title key *in* button, and bring the bars into the "up" position (see *b*).

to keep the switchers down to a (barely) manageable size (see 12.10).

2. *Special Effects Controls.* The most common **special effects controls** (sometimes called SFX controls) are the buttons for specific *wipe patterns* (see 12.11 and also Chapter 13). On large switchers, these controls can be extended to nearly 100 different patterns by dialing a number code into the switcher (see 12.11). You can also control the *direction* of the wipe (whether a horizontal wipe, for example, goes from left to right or right to left each time the fader bars are moved up or down). With the *joystick positioner* you can move any one of the patterns about the screen. There are also controls that give the wipes a soft or hard edge, and the letters different types of borders and shadows. The special effects section of most switchers includes the *chroma key* controls with which you can achieve a variety of picture inserts and backgrounds (see Chapter 13).

3. *Color Background Controls.* Most switchers have special color controls, with which you can provide special color backgrounds to your wipes and even give the letters of titles and other written information various colors or colored outlines. The controls consist of dials with which you can adjust the hue (the color itself), saturation (the color strength), and brightness (the relative darkness and lightness of the color; often called luminance on the switcher). (See 12.8.)

Very large production switchers have all these controls repeated for each pair of M/E buses (see

12.11 GVG (Grass Valley Group) Production Switches (a) This 1600 series has found wide acceptance in larger studios and production centers. (b) This relatively, simple, yet highly versatile switcher is used in smaller studios, remote trucks, and for postproduction.

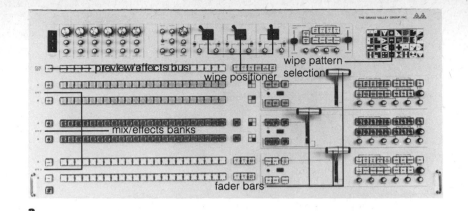

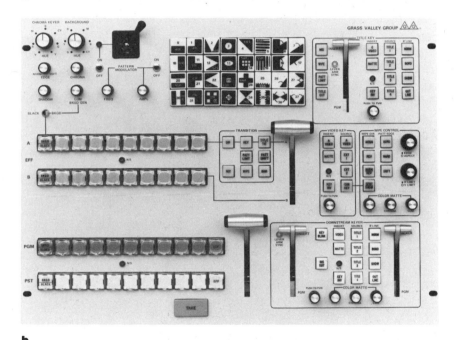

12.11) and a good number of additional magic buttons, which can make the screen image take on different shapes, color, and sizes. They can make the images move, flip, stretch, turn over, and do just about anything except pop out of the television screen (at least so far). We will mention some of these controls and effects in Section Two of this chapter and in Chapter 13.

Operation of Large Switcher

It takes switching experts quite some time to get to know all the potentials of a large switcher and to operate it efficiently. So, do not worry if you are a little confused when looking at, or even trying to operate, one of these technological marvels. Indeed, most switching has become so complex that we have to call on computers to assist us with memorizing the various special effects and even with executing them (see Section Two).

In general, all switchers, large or small, operate on the basic principles as outlined in the beginning of this chapter. Even on large switchers, the takes are accomplished by pressing buttons on one of the mix/effects buses, and the dissolves by presetting them on two buses and then moving the fader bars from one to the other bus. Effects are done in similar ways, except that they need to be selected first. You simply move the effects lever instead of the fader bars to activate the effects. Whenever you are asked to perform an effect live (without having the chance of trying it out first in several configurations before putting it on tape), *preset* the effect and check it in the preset or preview monitor before performing it. In any case, do not get too intimidated by the great number of colorful buttons on a large switcher. Do not confuse good switching with the ability to generate unusual effects. Good switching means that you can anticipate the director's signals for specific transitions or effects, and execute them with speed and reliability. You do not have to use all the buttons and levers on a switcher simply because they are there. Remember that a cut is still one of the cleanest and most efficient transition devices.

MAIN POINTS

1. Instantaneous editing means switching from one video source to another, or combining two or more sources, while the show, or show segment, is in progress.

2. The technical device that makes instantaneous editing possible is the video switcher—a panel equipped with rows of buttons, fader bars, and various effects controls.

3. All switchers, simple or complex, perform these basic functions: (1) select an appropriate video source from several inputs; (2) perform basic transitions between two video sources; and (3) create and/or access special effets.

4. Audio-follow-video switchers automatically switch the program audio with the video. Such switchers are primarily used in master control.

5. The switcher has a separate button for each input. There is a button for each camera, VTR, film island, or other video source, such as a remote input. The buttons are arranged in rows, called buses. Two identical buses make up a bank. The basic switcher has a program bus, a mix bank consisting of two identical mix buses, and a preview bus. A set of fader bars is necessary to achieve dissolves, fades, and supers.

6. The program bus is a direct input-output link and is, therefore, also called the direct bus. Whatever is punched up on the program bus goes directly to the line-out.

7. The mix bank (consisting of two identical buses) makes the mixing of two program sources possible, such as dissolves and superimpositions, and fade-ins and fade-outs.

8. The preview bus functions like the program bus, except that its line-out does not go on the air (or a VTR), but goes to a special preview monitor.

9. To perform special effects, such as wipes, split screens, or title keys, the switcher needs additional special effects buses, or a device that assigns the buses special effects functions. A mix bus that can also perform effects functions is called a M/E (mix/effects) bus.

10. Most switchers have at least these additional controls: (1) delegation controls that determine the function of the buses; (2) special effects controls with a variety of wipe patterns and a joystick positioner; and (3) background color, with which various colors can be generated for the background or letters of titles and other graphics.

11. Large switchers have several mix-effects banks and a great number of special effects control. They are usually computer-assisted.

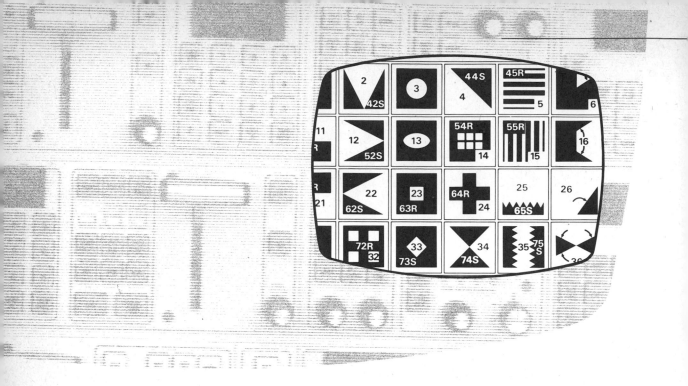

In this section, we will describe some additional features of large production switchers, and some specific switcher controls. They are (1) double reentry and cascading functions, (2) downstream keyer, (3) flip-flop controls, (4) quad-split controls, and (5) clip control. Finally, we will briefly mention the computer-assisted switchers, which can remember and automatically execute various effects and transitions sequences, and some aspects of switcher development.

SWITCHER FEATURES AND CONTROLS

Double Reentry and Cascading Functions

These mysterious terms simply mean that you can dissolve in and out of an effect rather than cutting to it, and that you can combine several effects. With a **double reentry switcher,** you can feed (reenter) an effect back into the mix bus twice as though it were a single video source. This way, you can dissolve into and out of the effect, or combine it with still another effect.

When you combine several effects, such as putting a title over a newscaster who has a picture insert over his or her right shoulder, you need to reenter the signal not just once or twice, but several times. We refer to these reentries as "cascading" from bank to bank, picking up additional effects at each bank (pair of buses). (See 12.12, 12.13.) For this reason, triple (or more) reentry switchers are called **cascading switchers.** In computer-assisted switchers, each M/E bank (pair of M/E buses) has a small microprocessor that remembers the effect programmed, thus making it possible for the T.D. to activate complicated cascading effects with a single button.

Downstream Keyer

The "downstream" in the **downstream keyer** refers to the manipulation of the signal *at the line-out* (downstream) stage. With a downstream keyer, you can insert (key) a title or other graphics over the signal as it leaves the switcher. This last-minute maneuver, which is totally independent of any of the controls on the buses, is done to keep as many of the M/E buses as possible available for the other switching and effects functions. (See 12.14.) Most switchers with a downstream keyer have a master fader (additional fader bars) with which you can fade to black the base picture together with the downstream key effect.

Large production switchers have several features that extend the mere selection function to the creation of special effects images. The computer-assisted switchers, for example, can become picture-generating production elements in their own right.

Flip-Flop Controls

Sometimes, in a fully scripted show or in an interview, you may have two cameras cover rather long but fast dialogue exchanges between two actors or performers. If the director decides to cover this conversation by cutting between the close-up of Ms. H. and Mr. L., for example, you can preset this **"flip-flop"** sequence on the switcher (assuming this option is part of the switcher), and then cut between the two cameras with the **cut bar** (a large button on the switcher, usually labeled *Take* and, therefore, also called the *take bar*). Most switchers use the preview bus and the program bus for this flip-flop function. This type of switching can also be accomplished through pressing the camera 1 button or camera 2 button on one of the mix buses, or even the program bus. However, the cut bar enables you to switch more quickly and more precisely on dialogue. All you do is press the same button whenever you want to switch from one person to the other.

Quad-Split Controls

Quad-split controls make it possible to divide the screen into four variable-sized quadrants and fill each one of them with a different image. This, of course, is a popular method of showing simultaneous actions in sports, the various kinds of sports a program will carry, or a glimpse of the show's highlights. To accomplish a quad-split, you need, first, four separate video inputs and a switcher that can perform the quad-split function. Just for good measure, most switchers offer a variety of border widths and border colors. There are, obviously, four separate controls necessary for the quad-split—each one to control its own quadrant (see Chapter 13).

Key Level Control, or Clip Control

With the **key level,** or **clip, control,** you can prevent the letters of a title from tearing during a key and have them appear sharp and clear. Technically, you adjust the luminance (brightness) of the key signal to seek out the brightest portion of your key source (the studio card or slide with the lettering on it) as cue for the transition between the cut-in (key) signal and the signal of the background picture. Operationally, you can preset the key effect and then watch in the preset or preview monitor whether or not the key letters are tearing or otherwise displaying fuzzy edges. You simply turn the key level control until the letters appear sharp. On switch-

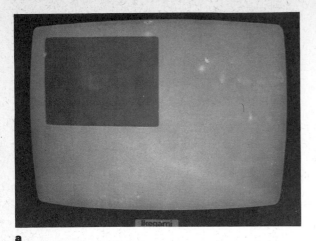

a

b

c

12.12   Cascading Function of Switcher In this
simple cascading effect, we start with an empty rectangle
(a), which provides the shadow effect for the white frame,
and the can (b). We then put still another effect: the
rose (c).

ers with downstream keyers, you can push down the
key level control button to display the key on the preset
monitor.

SWITCHER DEVELOPMENT

Computer-Assisted Switchers

Although switchers are getting more and more versatile, most operators are not expanding their abilities at
the same rate. To help you in the operation of the switcher,
the computer is once again called upon for assistance.
Computer-assisted switchers can be programmed to
remember and perform on call up to 100 different wipe
patterns and a variety of transitions (other than a cut)
at predetermined speeds. For example, you can preset

a dissolve to last from a fraction of a second to almost
10 seconds, and then have the switcher perform this
dissolve by pressing a button rather than moving the
fader bars up or down. Some switchers offer this option
in number of frames (remember, there are thirty frames
to a second), or in time units (seconds). Many times,
you need to set up a complete sequence of effects (as
for the various commercial and promotional announce-

Cascading Movement of signals
when the T.D. combines several
effects on a switcher and reenters the
signal several times. The signals
move from one bank to the next, picking up additional effects at each
bank.

Double Reentry A complex switcher
through which an effect can be fed
back into the mix section, or the mix
output into the effects section, for further effects manipulation.

Downstream Keyer Switcher control
that permits the T.D. to key a title or
other graphics over the signal at the
line-out, as the signal leaves the
switcher.

12.13　Cascading Effect In this single shot, we combine five different images through cascading from one effect to another.

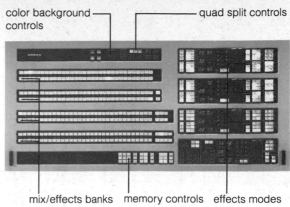

color background controls

quad split controls

mix/effects banks　memory controls　effects modes

12.15　Computer-Assisted Switcher The computer-assisted switchers still work on the A/B bus principle, but all mix and effects functions can be programmed. With a computer-assisted switcher, you can produce, store, and recall transition and special-effects sequences that would be impossible to do "live."

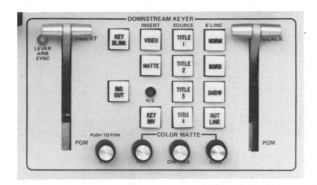

12.14　Downstream Keyer The downstream keyer is independent of the regular switching processes and keys the title over the switcher *output*—the line-out image.

ments during a newscast, for example). You can enter such sequences into the computer of the switcher and then recall the total sequence by simply pressing one button (see 12.15). Because each effect and transition can be identified by a number, you can keep a list of numbers and recall these numbers at a specific time in order to have the switcher perform a specific switching function. The transitions can also be programmed to occur at a specific rate.

Computer-assisted switchers are especially important when you do complicated postproduction work. In postproduction, the switcher is not used for instantaneous editing, but for special transitions and special effects. Because the switcher computer speaks digital language, it can be interfaced with other computer-assisted equipment, such as edit control units,

video-enhancing equipment, and especially audiotape recorders. All you really need to do is to program the various effects and transitions, rehearse them, and—if you like the sequence—activate it with the push of a button.

Master Control Switchers

Computer-assisted switching is especially important in master control. In fact, the computer is so important in master control operation that often the master control engineer assists the computer, rather than the other way around. The computer not only remembers and activates transition sequences, it also cues, rolls, and stops film projectors and VTRs, and calls up any num-

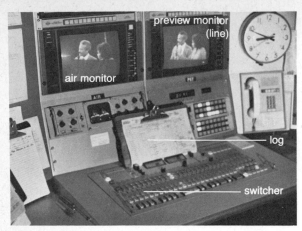

12.16 Master Control Switcher The master control switcher automatically activates all programmed transitions and effects, as well as other equipment (start and stop of VTRs and film projectors). It also constantly double-checks with the log.

ber of "slides" from the still-frame storer (see Chapter 13). (See 12.16.)

The development of switchers is going in basically two directions: to have the switcher perform more and more visual tricks, and to keep it simple enough so that the operator does not have to climb all over it to reach all the buttons, or take a variety of computer classes to use all its options. Efforts are being made to create smaller remote control units that activate certain programmed sequences, especially through voice data input. This means that all you need for the switching is to talk into a headset mic and *tell* the switcher (the machine, not the person operating it) what functions to perform. And, if all the black boxes work properly, you should be able to observe the transitions or effects on the monitors.

MAIN POINTS

1. The additional functions of large production switchers are (1) double reentry and cascading func-

tions, (2) downstream keyer, (3) flip-flop control, (4) quad-split controls, and (5) clip control.

2. With a double reentry switcher, an effect can be reentered twice into the mix bus, as though it were a single video source. Thus, a dissolve into or out of the effect is possible.

3. Cascading switchers permit the multiple reentry of an effect, whereby the effect picks up additional video elements each time it "cascades" from bank to bank.

4. The downstream keyer keys titles over the switcher output—the line-out image. It is independent of the other switching functions.

5. The flip-flop control permits the quick switching between two preset video sources via a single button, called cut bar or take bar.

6. Quad-split controls make it possible to divide the screen into four quadrants and fill each one with a different image.

7. The clip or key level control prevents the keyed image (such as letters) from tearing during the effect.

8. Most large switchers are computer-assisted. They can be programmed to remember and call up close to one hundred different wipe patterns and transitions at predetermined speeds.

9. Master control switchers are usually computer-operated. They not only switch from one program source to the next, but also preroll VTRs and film projectors, and call up any number of digital video effects or still-frame store images.

FURTHER READING

Paulson, C. Robert. *BM/E's ENG/EFP/EPP Handbook.* New York: Broadband Information Services, Inc., 1981.

Zettl, Herbert. *Sight–Sound–Motion: Applied Media Aesthetics.* Belmont, CA: Wadsworth Publishing Co., 1976.

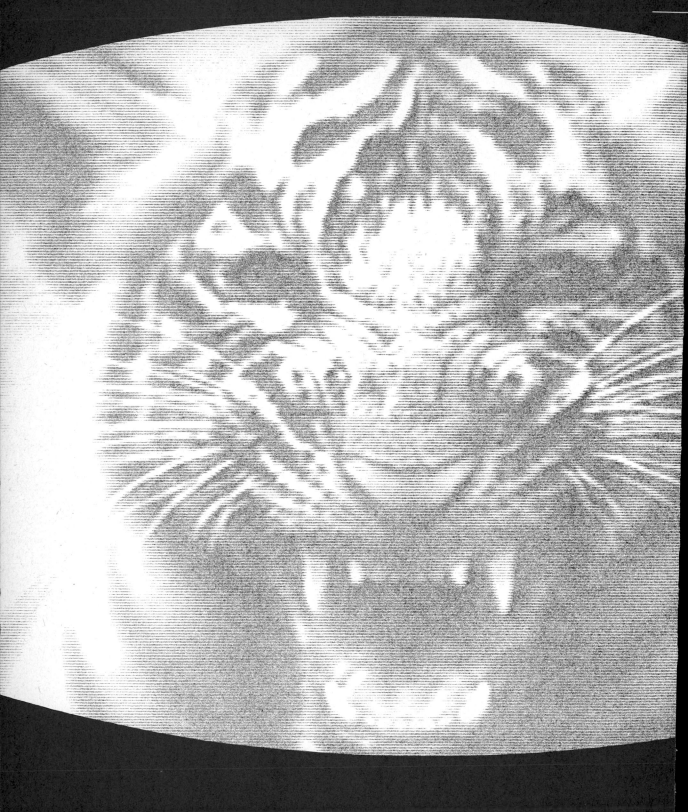

CHAPTER 13

Visual Effects

In Section One of this chapter, we are concerned with four major types of visual effects:

1.   Standard electronic effects, including superimposition, key, chroma key, and wipe. The popular key modes are (1) edge mode, (2) drop shadow, and (3) outline. Among wipes are the horizontal and vertical wipe, various wipe patterns, soft wipe, quad split, and spotlight effects.
2.   Digital video effects (DVE), which allow the creation of multi-images and the manipulation of the image size, shape, light and color, texture, and motion.
3.   Optical effects, including (1) rear projection, (2) gobos, (3) mirrors, (4) lens prisms, (5) star filter and diffusion filter, (6) defocus effect, and (7) the matte box effect.
4.   Mechanical effects, which simulate rain, snow, fog, wind, smoke, fire, lightning, and explosion.

Section Two describes (1) a workable digital video effects chart; (2) picture correction equipment, such as the time base corrector, framel-store synchronizer, and image enhancement devices; and (3) such nondigital effects as debeaming and video feedback.

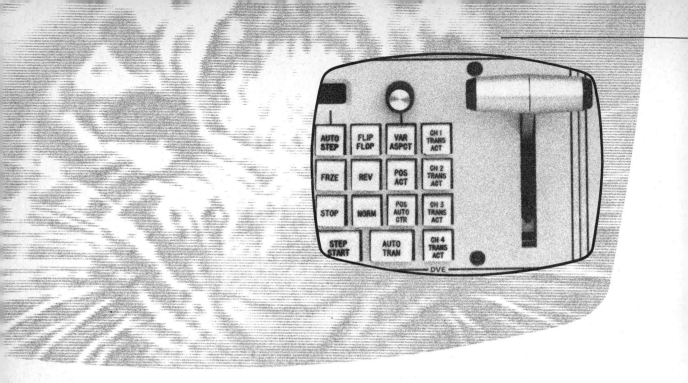

Although the various nonelectronic effects, such as rain, smoke, or fog, are used to simulate *reality,* many of the electronic effects seem to emphasize the *graphic* nature of the television screen. You are certainly familiar with the effect of putting a border resembling a picture frame around a freeze frame of a news event, and then having the event come to life, seemingly stepping out of the picture frame into the "real" space of the television screen. Another popular effect is the simulation of flipping picture book pages as a transition device between news stories. But sometimes an image is put through so many stretches, compressions, twists, splits, bounces, and color changes that it can, indeed, be called special.

The various electronic effects are so readily available that they may tempt the inexperienced television director to substitute effect for content. Do not fall into the trap of trying to camouflage insignificant content or badly shot or edited pictures with effects. As dazzling as the effects may be, they cannot replace the basic message. On the other hand, when judiciously used, many effects can enhance production to a considerable degree, and help greatly in the task of clarifying and intensifying the message.

Whenever you intend to use a visual effect, you should ask yourself: (1) Is the effect really necessary? (2) Does it help in the clarification and intensification of my message? (3) Can the effect be easily produced? (4) Is it reliable? If you can give a "yes" answer to all these questions, the effect is in. If there is a "no" or even a "maybe" to any one or several of them, the effect is out.

There are two further factors you might consider before setting up complicated effects. One is the relative *mobility* of modern television equipment. Now that the television camera and VTR are no longer studio-bound, certain effects that need complex machinery for simulation in the studio, like snow or fog, can be obtained simply by taking the camera outdoors during a snowstorm or on a foggy day. The other is the enormous communication power of television *audio.* In many instances, you can curtail or eliminate complicated video effects by combining good sound effects with a simple video presentation. The sound effect of pouring rain, for example, combined with a close-up of an actor dripping wet may very well preclude the use of a rain machine, which produces rainlike streaks on the

Combined with modern switchers, the electronic effects—generating equipment can produce a dazzling variety of special effects with ease and reliability. However, many of the complex electronic effects have become so common in television production that they have lost their "specialty" status; we will, therefore, call them simply *visual effects*.[1]

screen. To show a group of people sitting on the ocean beach, you do not need to set up a rear-screen projection of the ocean; a good sound effect of the surf over the close-up of the people basking in the sun will do the same job more easily. Or, better yet, take your camera and VTR to the beach, if you happen to have one available. On television, reaction is often more effective than action. For example, you can suggest an atomic bomb explosion by showing a close-up of an actor's face combined with the familiar sound of such an explosion. A keying-in of the mushroom cloud becomes superfluous

Nevertheless, a judicious use of visual effects presupposes that you know what effects are available to you.

In this section, we will discuss four types of visual effects: (1) standard electronic effects, (2) digital video effects, (3) optical effects, and (4) mechanical effects. There are two basic groups of electronic effects: (1) standard effects, and (2) digital video effects (DVEs). The standard electronic effects can be accomplished with the standard (analog) switcher and **special effects generator (SEG),** which is an

electronic device that makes special effects possible. The digital effects obviously need special digital effects equipment.

STANDARD ELECTRONIC EFFECTS

The standard electronic effects include (1) superimposition, (2) key, (3) chroma key, and (4) wipe.

Superimposition

A *superimposition,* or *"super"* for short, is a form of double exposure. The picture from one camera is electronically superimposed over the picture from another.

Occasionally, the super is still used for the *adding of titles* over a background picture or event, especially if the switching system does not permit title keying. When supering titles, one camera is

[1] See Gerald Millerson, *The Technique of Television Production* (London: Focal Press Limited, 1979), p. 368.

base picture
scanning

key source
scanning

13.1   Internal, or Normal, Key The internal, or normal, key simply cuts the letters into the base picture (by switching from the scanning of the base picture to that of the keyed letters) as they appear on the title card or slide. The key signal is also used to fill the base picture cutouts.

focused on the super card, which has white letters on a black background. The background picture can be supplied by either another camera (focused on a live event, such as a long shot of a sports stadium, or a studio card with a background scene) or any other video source (slide, film, or VTR). Because the black card does not reflect any light, or only an insignificant amount, it will remain invisible during the super.

More often, supers are used for creating the effects of *inner events*—thoughts, dreams, or processes of imagination. The traditional (and certainly overused) super of a dream sequence shows

a close-up of a sleeping person, with dream images supered over his or her face. Sometimes, we use supers to make an event more complex. For example, you may want to super a close-up over a long shot of the same dancer. If the effect is done properly, we are given a new insight into the dance. You are no longer photographing a dance, but helping to create it.

Key

Keying means electronically cutting out portions of a television picture and filling them in with another, or portions of another, image. The basic purpose of a **key** is to add titles to a base (background) picture, or to cut another picture (such as the image of a weather forecaster) into the base picture (the satellite weather map). The title card or slide for keying looks exactly like the super card or super slide; it has white letters on a black background. However, unlike a super, where the white letters are laid "on top" of the base (background) picture, in a key the letters are electronically cut into the base picture, with the black background of the title card becoming translucent, just as in a super.

During a key the scanning of the base picture proceeds undisturbed in all black areas of the key card, but is forced to yield (switch or cross over) to

Chroma Key   Special key effect that uses color (usually blue) for the background over which the keying occurs.

Digital Video Effects   Also called DVE. Visual effects produced by devices that change normal (analog) video signals into digital (numerical) information.

External Key   The cutout portion of the base picture is filled by the signal from an external source, such as a third camera (with the first camera providing the base picture, the second camera the key signal).

Gobo   A scenic foreground piece through which the camera can shoot, thus integrating the decorative foreground with the background action. In film, a gobo is an opaque shield that is used for partial blocking of a light.

Internal Key   The cutout portion of the base picture is filled with the signal that is doing the cutting.

Key   An electronic effect. Keying means the cutting in of an image (usually lettering) into a background image.

Matte Key   Keyed (electronically cut-in) title whose letters are filled with shades of gray or a specific color.

Polarity Reversal   The reversal of the grayscale; the white areas in the picture become black and the black areas white, as the film negative is to the print.

Rear Screen or R.P.   Translucent screen onto which images are projected from the rear and photographed from the front.

Soft Wipe   Wipe in which the demarcation line between the two images is softened so the images blend into each other.

Special Effects Generator, or SEG   An electronic image generator that produces a variety of special effects wipe patterns, such as circle wipes, diamond wipes, and key effects.

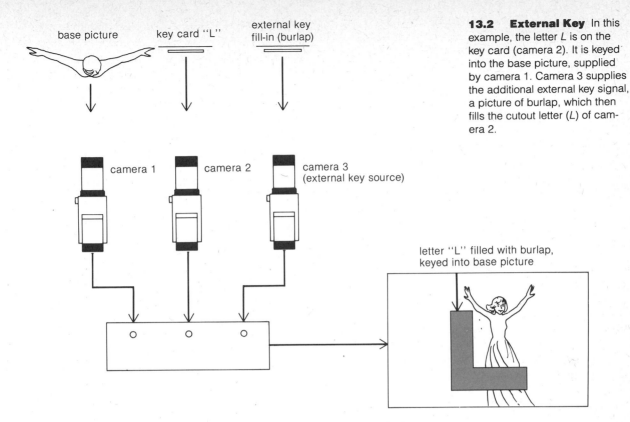

base picture   key card "L"   external key fill-in (burlap)

camera 1   camera 2   camera 3 (external key source)

letter "L" filled with burlap, keyed into base picture

13.2 External Key In this example, the letter *L* is on the key card (camera 2). It is keyed into the base picture, supplied by camera 1. Camera 3 supplies the additional external key signal, a picture of burlap, which then fills the cutout letter (*L*) of camera 2.

the scanning of the key source (the camera on the key card) whenever it hits the white letters.

You may become somewhat bewildered by reading and hearing about keys, mattes, and matte-keys—all seemingly meaning the same thing. It does not really matter what you call it, as long as you are consistent with your terminology, and as long as the other members of your team know what you mean. There are basically three types of keys: (1) internal key, (2) external key, and (3) matte key. Because chroma keying works on a different principle, we will treat it in a separate discussion.

Internal Key If the cutout portion of the base picture is filled with the signal that is doing the cutting, we speak of an **internal key,** or *normal key.* In order to achieve a clean key, in which the white letters are cut into the base picture without any tearing or breakup, the title card must be evenly lighted and the key level control adjusted so that the cross-

over (from the scanning line of the base picture to the scanning line of the key source—the white letters—and back) occurs exactly at the borders of the letters (see 13.1).

You can, of course, also key pictures of objects into the base picture, as long as they have enough contrast relative to the base picture so that their edges do not tear during the key.

External Key If the cutout portion of the base picture is filled by the signal from an external source, such as a third camera, we speak of an **external key.** For example, if you want the lettering to have some texture, you could put a third camera on a piece of burlap; the keyed letters then appear as though they were cut out of burlap. You could also fill the letters with an animated scene (see 13.2). There is ample opportunity for you to experiment with external keys. But again, do not get carried away by the technical wonders of external keying. If the effect contributes to the overall communica-

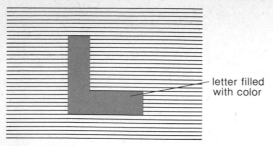

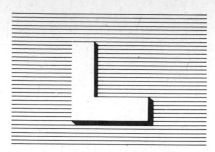

letter filled
with color

13.3   Matte Key In a matte key the cutout letters are
filled with shades of gray or with a certain color supplied by
the switcher.

**13.5   Matte Key in Shadow, or Drop-Shadow,
Mode** The shadow, or drop-shadow, matte key adds a
prominent shadow to the letter (attached shadow) as
though three-dimensional letters were illuminated by a
strong key light.

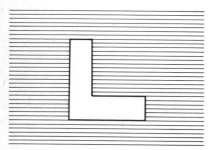

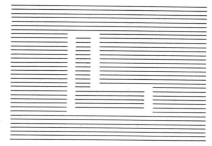

13.4   Matte Key in Edge Mode The edge matte key
puts a black border around the letters in order to make
them more readable than with the normal key.

13.6   Matte Key in Outline Mode The outline matte
key makes the letters appear in outline form. It shows the
contour of the letter only.

tion, use it. If it does not, discard it—however much
fun you may have had discovering the effect.

Matte Key   If the cutout portions are filled with
various grays or colors as generated by the switcher,
or embellished with contours and/or shadows, we
speak of a **matte key.** In a matte key, you fill the
keyed letters with shades of gray or a variety of colors
that are available through the switcher. You are also
engaged in matte keying when you select any one
of the more popular *key modes:* (1) the edge mode,
(2) the drop shadow mode, and (3) the outline mode
(see 13.3 through 13.6).

Only relatively sophisticated switchers allow you
to select among these matte key modes. This means
that you can electronically give each letter a distinctive outline, in addition to a specific color. The various modes are used whenever the letters are in

danger of getting lost in an especially busy (containing much detail) background. In the *edge* mode,
each letter has a thin, black-edge outline around
it (see 13.4). In the *shadow* mode, the letters obtain a black shadow contour, appearing three-
dimensional (see 13.5). In the *outline* mode, the
letters themselves appear in outline form, only their
contour remaining visible (see 13.6).

Chroma Key

Chroma key is a special effect that uses color
(chroma) and brightness (luminance) for keying.
Basically, the chroma key process uses a specific
color, usually blue, instead of black for the background over which the keying occurs. Like the black,
the blue becomes totally transparent during the key-

a

c

b

13.7 Chroma Key Effect For this chroma key effect, camera 1 focuses on a studio card showing a photo of a city skyline (a). Camera 2 focuses on a dancer in front of an evenly lighted blue background. The floor must also be rendered blue, either by painting it or, more commonly, by extending the blue backdrop (cloth) to the floor (b). When camera 2 is keyed over camera 1, the chroma key effect is completed; the dancer seems to be dancing in front of the city skyline (c).

ing and lets the picture of the second camera show through, without interfering with the foreground image. (See 13.7.) Blue is used because it is most opposite to the skin colors, thus reproducing them relatively undistorted during chroma keying. Actually any other color could be used for chroma keying.

As pointed out in Chapter 7, the chroma key area must be evenly painted (even saturation throughout the area) and especially evenly lighted. Any unevenness in lighting can interfere with the keying process.

Because anything in the foreground scene that approaches the blue chroma key background color becomes transparent during the keying, a newscaster, for example, should not wear blue in front of the chroma key set. A tie containing the same

blue as the background will let the keyed scene show through. Even some blue eyes become a problem during a close-up in chroma keying, although, fortunately, most blue eyes reflect or contain enough other colors to keep them from becoming transparent. However, the shadow areas on the outline of very dark-haired or dark-skinned performers may occasionally turn blue (or reflect the blue background), causing the contour to become indistinct, to "tear," or to assume its own color. Again, as mentioned in Chapter 7, you can counteract this nuisance to some extent by using yellow or light orange gels in the back lights. Because the yellow back light neutralizes the blue shadows, it sets off, and separates the performer quite distinctly from, the blue background during the chroma key process.

13.8 Chroma Key Background Matte in News In a background chroma key the background area behind the weathercaster is entirely filled with the keyed picture. The weathercaster seems to be right in the scene.

Until the development of digital video effects, the chroma key held a prominent position in television production. It was (and occasionally still is) used to matte live action into miniature sets or other background visuals for plays and musical and dance numbers. Here is an example. Let us assume that you would like to show a dancer performing on a rooftop with the city skyline as the background. Camera 1 focuses on a photograph of the city skyline; camera 2 focuses on a dancer who performs in front of an evenly lighted, well-saturated blue background (assuming you choose the color blue for your chroma keying). Through chroma keying, you now continuously cut the dancer's shape out of the base picture of the skyline and fill the cutout shape with the image of the dancer. The dancer now seems to be dancing on the rooftop (see 13.7 a–c).

Many news operations still work with chroma key effects, even if they have DVEs (digital video effects) at their disposal. Two of the more common chroma key effects in news are (1) the background key and (2) the TV screen simulation.

Background Key In order to use the background key effect in news, you must paint the background of the news set blue (or whatever color you may choose for chroma key) so that large background keys can be accommodated. The video source for the background scenes can be a camera focused on live action or on a studio card, a slide, film, or VTR (see 13.8).

Such effects are quite useful during EFP or during large remotes, especially if the talent is not able to stand directly in front of the desired background scene, such as the football stadium, city hall, or county hospital. When you are using such a chroma key effect during a sports remote, for example, the talent may even be in the studio, with the remote feed (long shot of the football stadium) serving as chroma key background. If you do the chroma keying on location, with the talent standing outdoors, watch out for the blue reflections from the sky. With blue as the chroma key color, the blue reflections may become translucent or cause the key contours to break up. To avoid such problems, switch to green

for the chroma key color and put the talent in front of a green cloth backdrop.

The basic idea for such a visual treatment makes sense: to associate the talent as much as possible with the story being told. However, there are serious aesthetic, rather than technical, problems with this kind of effect in news presentations:

1.   There is something strange about a newscaster who remains seated in the face of war, plane wrecks, or riots going on right behind him or her. If you plan to use this type of chroma key effect, have the newscaster stand, similar to a stand-up report on the scene.

2.   There is often a strange size relationship between the foreground figure (the newscaster) and the background figures. In many such chroma key effects, the people in the background appear much larger than the foreground figure (the newscaster)—a situation directly opposite to our actual visual experience. If you use such a background chroma key (in news or any other forms of presentation), try to

adhere to the normal principles of perspective (larger foreground than background figures). (See 13.9.)

3.   Because you have little control over the combined compositional effect between foreground and background, you run the risk of odd juxtapositions, such as a steel wrecking ball swinging right at the newscaster's shoulder, or the red light of a police car turning on the newscaster's head like a beacon.

Screen Simulation   Because of such perceptual problems, the background keying has been replaced by keying into the limited area over the newscaster's left or right shoulder. This area, which usually resembles a large television screen, is painted blue for the chroma keying (see 13.10). The technique is known as **screen simulation.** However, the problem with this setup is that you get only that part of the background image to show that happens to fall into the cutout area. In order to get the whole image (like a complete slide) onto the simulated screen, you can project the background image (slide) onto a monitor, then put a camera on the monitor and

key this camera's image into the simulated screen area (see 13.11).

With DVEs, you do not need any such cutout. All you do is position the effect wherever you want it to be. We will talk about such effects later in this chapter. Regardless of whether you use chroma key or DVE, the simulated screen requires extra production efforts and equipment. Therefore, many stations now use a real television monitor behind the newscaster for visual reinforcement. You can feed any desirable video to this monitor through the preview bus, if nothing else is available. The only problem is to keep as much light off the monitor as possible—no easy thing to do, especially because the set has to be in proximity to the (well-lighted) talent.

Wipe

In a wipe, a portion or all of one television picture is gradually replaced by another. Although, technically, the second picture is uncovered by the first moving away, perceptually it looks as though the second image pushes—wipes—the first image off the screen.

The two simplest wipes are the vertical and the horizontal. A *vertical wipe* gives the same effect as pulling a window shade down over the screen. Just as the window shade "wipes out" the picture you see through the window, the image from one camera is gradually replaced by the image from the other camera. The *horizontal wipe* works the same way, except that the picture is replaced sideways by the wipe image (see 13.12 and 13.13).

Wipe Patterns   The more complicated wipes can take on many different shapes. In a diamond wipe, one picture starts in the middle of the other picture and wipes it off the screen in the shape of a diamond. Or the wipe can start from the corner of one picture and shrink the other off the screen (diagonal or corner wipe). Box wipes and circle wipes are also frequently used. (See 13.14.)

Operationally, you can select the appropriate wipe configuration either by pressing a wipe button or by turning a rotor selector to the respective wipe position. The speed of the wipe is determined by how fast you move the *special effects levers,* which are like a second pair of fader levers, wired for a different function.

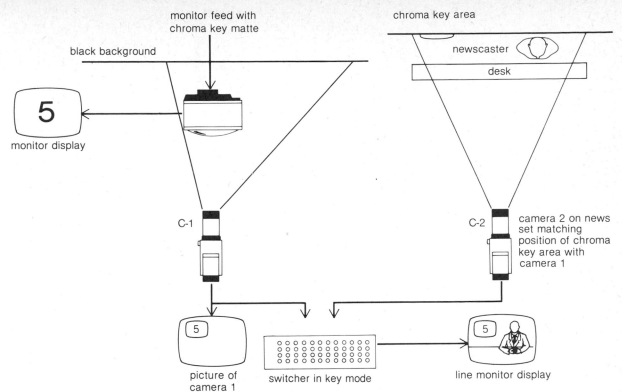

black background

monitor feed with chroma key matte

chroma key area

newscaster

desk

5

monitor display

C-1

C-2

camera 2 on news set matching position of chroma key area with camera 1

5

picture of camera 1

switcher in key mode

5

line monitor display

13.11   Full-Frame Picture in Simulated Screen Area In order to fill the simulated chroma key screen area in the news set with a complete image (number 5 in this case), you can feed a monitor with the matte information (5) and line up camera 1 on the monitor so that its position matches the chroma key area on camera 2. During matting, the whole matte information (the number 5) then appears behind the newscaster in the simulated screen area.

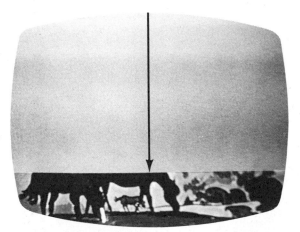

13.12   Vertical Wipe In a vertical wipe, one picture is gradually replaced from the bottom up or from the top down.

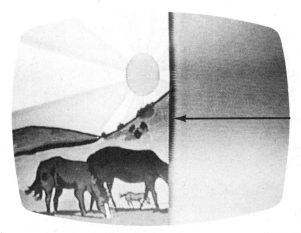

13.13   Horizontal Wipe In a horizontal wipe, one picture is gradually replaced from the side.

13.14　Wipe Patterns Wipes come in a variety of configurations. Large switchers often have almost 100 different wipe patterns. A group of push buttons on the switcher shows the various patterns available to you.

13.15　Soft Wipe In a soft wipe, the demarcation line between the two images is softened so that they blend into each other. The degree of softness can be adjusted with a rotary control on the switcher.

You can further influence the wipe pattern by feeding into it an additional signal from another source, such as the audio signal of the accompanying sound. If, for example, you modulate a circle wipe with an audio signal, the volume of the audio signal influences the size of the wipe (the circle shrinks and expands with the volume fluctuations of the sound). The frequency (the high and low pitch) of the audio signal influences the contour of the wipe. In our case, pitch fluctuations make the outline of the circle alternately smooth or uneven.

Soft Wipes Most switchers allow you to soften the edge between the two pictures of a wipe. Through a rotary button on the switcher, you can soften the edge just a little, or make it so soft that the two pictures practically blend into each other. You can use a **soft wipe** instead of a super in order to blend two related, yet separate images into a single picture (see 13.15).

Wipe Positions As pointed out in Chapter 12, any of the wipes can be stopped anyplace. All you have to do is stop moving the special effects levers. If the switcher has a *directional mode* switch for wipes, make sure it is set properly. In the normal mode, the vertical wipe moves from top to bottom. In the reversal mode, the wipe moves from the bottom to the top. In the normal/reverse mode, the wipe reverses itself every time you move the levers. If you use a box wipe or circle wipe, you have some latitude in changing its *shape*. For example, you can make an ellipse out of a circle or a rectangle out of a square. With the joystick, you can position the wipe pattern (such as a circle wipe) anywhere on the screen.

Split Screen If you stop a vertical, horizontal, or diagonal wipe in screen-center, you have a split-screen effect, or, simply, a split screen. Each half of the screen shows a different picture. To set up for an effective split screen with a horizontal wipe, one

a

c

b

13.16 Split Screen To set up for a horizontal split-screen effect, camera 1 frames the object designated to become the left half of the split screen in the left part of its viewfinder (a). Camera 2 frames the object designated for the right half in the right part of its viewfinder (b). In the completed split-screen image, the locations of subjects (a) and (b) are properly distributed (c).

camera must put its image (designated for the left half of the split screen) in the left side of its viewfinder, the other in the right side for the right part of the split screen. The unnecessary part of each picture is then wiped out by the other (split-screen) image. Always check such effects on the preview monitor. (See 13.16.)

A split-screen effect is frequently used to show an event from two *different viewpoints* on one screen. It is commonly done in a baseball game, where you show the batter and pitcher on one side of the split screen and a man leading off first base on the other. Or, you can show widely *separated events simultaneously,* such as two people located in different cities talking to each other almost face-to-face.

Quad-Split   A quad-split is a screen split four ways, with each quadrant usually showing a different picture. If you intend to use a different image for each quadrant, you must have four separate video inputs (see 13.17).

Through digital video effects, the quad-split can be further manipulated. We will cover these possibilities in the discussion on digital video effects later in this section.

Spotlight Effect   The **spotlight effect** looks like a soft-edged circle wipe, except that it lets the base picture show through (similar to a super). You can

13.17 **Quad-Split** Some switchers permit a quad-, or four-way, split. You can then fill each of the four screen areas with a different picture.

13.18 **Spotlight Effect** The spotlight effect looks like a soft-edge circle wipe, with the base picture showing through. It can be positioned anywhere in the picture to draw attention to a specific picture area. It is often used to identify a person in a crowd or a player on the field.

use it to draw attention to a specific portion of the screen as though you were shining a spotlight on it (see 13.18).

DIGITAL VIDEO EFFECTS (DVE)

Digital video effects are made possible by devices that change the normal (analog) video signal into digital (numerical) information. Just like digital audio, digital video lends itself readily to all sorts of manipulation. Although quite complicated technically, the *principle of DVE* is relatively simple. The DVE equipment can grab at any time any video frame from any video source (live camera, VTR, film, or slide), change it into digital information (numbers representing on-off pulses), manipulate it in a variety of ways, store it, and retrieve it on command. Think of the process of changing a color photograph into a mosaic of the same scene. Whereas the photograph—let's say of a face—shows you a *continuous* change of color, brightness, and shapes (analog), the mosaic presents a great number of *discrete* tiles, each one having a solid color and defined shape, and its own assigned number. If you want to change the shape of the nose in the "mosaic photo," you simply

take out some of the tiles, or add some here and there. Or, if you want a red nose and blue eyes, you can add some red tiles to the nose and some blue ones to the eyes. Obviously, this does not affect the black tiles of the hair. You can take out some of the tiles to make the whole picture smaller, or add some to make it larger. The DVE equipment eliminates, adds (by repeating available information), or shifts such picture "tiles" (digits) with incredible speed.

When finished with your new masterpiece, you probably could not remember all the patterns of the rearranged tiles unless you kept an accurate record of all the arrangements. The same is true of digital video effects. Once you have created the desired effect, you can put the steps for creating the effect into the pattern memory and give this "pattern" (the series of steps) a specific address. You can then keep a list of such address numbers and recall the effects at the appropriate time. Fast access to an effect or a series of effects is especially important when complex effects follow each other in rapid succession. Even the best T.D. with the most elaborate special effects switcher could not create all the effects contained in a simple opening and closing or the "bumpers" (the very brief, yet visually complex, program material separating the

13.19 Split-Screen Effects With digital video effects equipment, the screen can be split into many different sections, each one carrying the same image or at least one of four different images. Also, each one of the areas can be expanded or compressed.

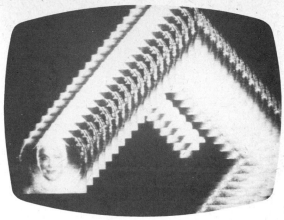

13.20 Echo Effect The echo effect looks as though one image were placed between two mirrors so that the images are repeated *ad infinitum*. The echo effect can be displayed as a static image, or shown as it multiplies. Also, the vanishing point (the point where the echo image seems to disappear at the horizon) can be moved up or down, so that we look at the image from above or below.

show from the commercial or public service announcements).

When digital video effects are interfaced with the standard (analog) effects of the switcher, the possibilities for visual effects are virtually endless. In order to make some sense out of the various digital effects potentials, we will divide them into these four areas: (1) creation and manipulation of multiimages, (2) manipulation of size and shape, (3) manipulation of light and texture, and (4) manipulation of motion.

Multiimage

The multiimage effects include the various possibilities of dividing the screen into various sections, or repeating a specific image on the screen. The former we call *split-screen* effects, the latter *echo effects*.

Split Screen With DVE equipment, you can split the screen not only into quadrants (quad-split), but into many more areas, each repeating the same image. In more elaborate systems, you can feed several separate images into the various screen areas, then select

any one of them and expand it through a wipe or a similar effect (see 13.19).

Echo Effect The **echo effect** is created when you repeat the same image as though it were placed between two opposite mirrors. Thus, it is also called the "mirror effect." It is especially effective for the manipulation of titles (see 13.20).

Size and Shape

An almost unlimited variety of effects are available to manipulate the size and the shape of an image. Some of the more prominent effects are (1) compression and expansion, (2) aspect ratio, (3) positioning and point of view, (4) perspective, (5) horizontal and vertical flip, and (6) auto key tracking.

Compression and Expansion Compression means that you can make a picture smaller—compress it—while keeping the entire picture intact. You can shrink the picture from its original full-screen size to a mere point on the screen (zero-size). Or, you can start with a zero-size image and expand it to full

13.21 **Compression** With digital compression, you can shrink a picture from its original full-screen size to a mere point on the screen. During the compression, you will not lose any picture elements—the picture is simply being compressed. When the process is reversed, it is called image expansion.

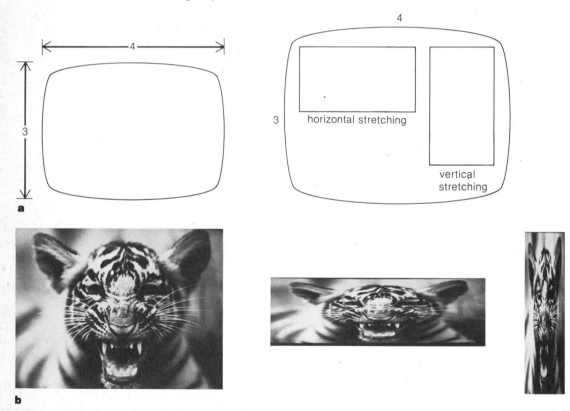

13.22 **Horizontally and Vertically Stretched Aspect Ratios** (a) With digital effects equipment, you can change the aspect ratio of television (three units high and four units wide) into horizontally or vertically stretched formats. (b) The image within the boxes can either be cropped or stretched and squeezed according to the new space.

frame. Some DVE equipment allows you to expand the picture beyond the frame (see 13.21).

Aspect Ratio   With DVE, you can even change the aspect ratio of an insert from the traditional 3×4 (three units high and four units wide—see Chapter 14) to a more horizontally stretched, or even vertically oriented, rectangle (see 13.22).

Positioning and Point of View   The compressed image can be positioned anywhere in the frame. For example, you can freeze the first frame of a news videotape, compress the image, and position it over the shoulder of the newscaster. You can then roll the VTR, letting the story come alive, and expand the image or wipe into it (see 13.23).

Perspective   You can distort the image in such a way that it looks three-dimensional. Although we can do this rather easily by distorting an actual object with the use of a wide-angle lens (or the zoom lens in the wide-angle lens position), before DVEs we had to draw titles so that they appeared three-dimensional. With DVEs, you can distort any letter or two-dimensional image and give it the illusion of the third dimension. You can even change the vanishing point (where all the parallel lines seem to converge on the horizon), thereby changing the point of view (looking at it from above or below, or straight on) and the illusion of depth (see 13.24).

Horizontal and Vertical Flip   With monochrome cameras, it is easy to flip a picture horizontally (like looking at it in a mirror), or vertically (putting it upside down). Most monochrome cameras have a control that reverses the horizontal and vertical "sweep" (the scanning) to create such a switch. The color camera does not allow such sweep reversals. However, once converted to digital form, the color image can be flipped vertically and horizontally, and in many more ways (see 13.25).

Auto Key Tracking   **Auto key tracking** refers to the automatic change of image size and position of the chroma key insert. For example, if you make the chroma key area larger (by enlarging the wipe pattern for example) or move it relative to the fore-

13.23   Positioning The compressed image can be positioned anywhere on the frame through a joystick positioner on the DVE unit. This technique is much more convenient to use in news presentations and has, therefore, largely replaced the chroma key matte of a simulated screen.

ground image, the compressed picture for the chroma key matte automatically moves and expands in order to fill the cutout area. This helps somewhat to maintain the perspective established in the previous shot.

Light and Texture

Because you are dealing with numbers representing certain individual, discrete picture elements—the "mosaic tiles"—you can manipulate not only the size and shape of an image, but also its light (brightness and color) and texture. Although it is easy enough to colorize a picture without digital equipment, digital colorizers are generally used for *correcting* color in postproduction.

Two of the more common effects that essentially influence our perception of texture are *posterization* and *mosaic.* One of the popular effects with monochrome equipment was **polarity reversal,** whereby all the light areas turned dark and the dark areas light—very much like in a film negative. The normal color camera chain cannot produce such an effect very easily. However, the polarity effect is certainly within the capability of most DVE units.

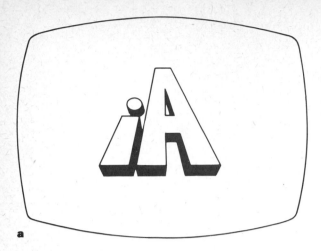

a

a

a

b

13.25   Horizontal and Vertical Flips With mono-chrome equipment, you can easily accomplish horizontal (a) and vertical (b) flips (reversal of the image) through electronic sweep (scanning) reversal. In order to perform such flips electronically with color images, you need DVE equipment; otherwise, you have to resort to a mirror.

b

c

13.24   Perspective Through digital effects manipulation, two-dimensional figures and letters can be made to look like they occupy three-dimensional space (a). With sophisticated DVE equipment, such as the Ampex ADO, the image can be distorted with the frame and made to appear floating in three-dimensional space (b and c).

The digital equipment simply exchanges the light "mosaic tiles" with the dark ones and vice versa, or one specific color with its complementary (opposite) color, thus producing a great variety of interesting color effects.

Posterization   This effect is also called **solarization.** For **posterization,** the DVE equipment is told to operate with perhaps only three (or four) types of mosaic tiles (picture elements): very bright ones, medium bright ones, and very dark ones. The subtle shading is purposely compressed into only a few prominent brightness values in order to achieve a flat, posterlike texture (see 13.26). You can achieve a similar effect through keying.

Mosaic   **Mosaic** is simply an exaggerated illustration of the digital process. The picture is divided into several discrete squares of equal size, yet of different brightness and color, in order to obtain a mosaiclike texture (see 13.27).

The posterization and mosaic effects change a realistic picture into a basically *graphic* image.

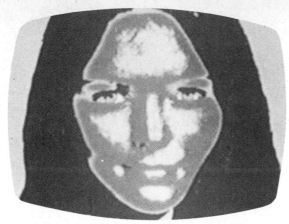

13.26 **Posterization** Posterization (or solarization) reduces the various brightness values to only a few (usually three or four) and gives the image a strangely flat, poster-like look.

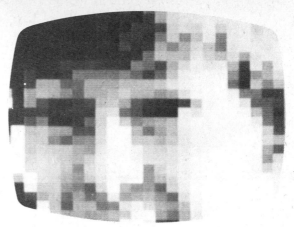

13.27 **Mosaic Effect** In the mosaic effect, an image is broken down into many equal-sized squares of limited brightness and color. The resulting screen image looks very much like a mosaic. Such an image is a greatly exaggerated graphic representation of a digitally constructed image.

Motion

There are so many possibilities to make the various effects move that we still have not developed a sensible and commonly used terminology. Do not be surprised when you stand in the control room during a production and hear the director using the sound language of cartoons (zoom, squeeze, bounce) when calling for certain animated effects. Some of the terms have been coined by DVE equipment manufacturers, others by imaginative production personnel. In this section, we will try to describe some of the most common effects. In Section Two, we will include a list of effects as developed by a DVE equipment manufacturer.

We perceive the major motion effects as (1) continual changes in picture size and position on a two-dimensional plane, (2) zooms, and (3) various kinds of rotation and bounces. Whereas some of these effects are used simply to get things moving on the screen, others are employed as extensions of the customary transitions.

Size and Position Changes These include the various forms of simulated *pans* and *tilts*. The pictures move left and right (pan) or up and down (tilt) at a predetermined rate and to a predetermined screen position. Also, when you use two video sources, you can create a **slide effect** from video A (first picture) to video B (second picture), which perceptually looks as though one sheet of paper were sliding off, revealing the other underneath. Technically, the second image pushes the other off the screen, which is one of the reasons why the slide effect is also called a *push-on* (see 13.28). The slide effect can also happen diagonally (see p. 397). **Snapshots** are multiple freeze frames that "update" (change) individually at various rates. This effect is similar to a ripple effect (see 13.29).[2]

Zoom Effects When you see a *continuous* expansion or compression, you perceive it as a *zoom*. You can start out with a tiny dot on the screen (zero-size) and "zoom" out to over eight times its size. Or, you can start out with the full-sized picture (which fills the complete screen) and "squeeze" it down to zero-size. Note that the *whole picture* expands or shrinks in this effect. With a regular zoom lens, you

[2]This terminology was developed by Vital Industries, Inc., for their SqueeZoom control system.

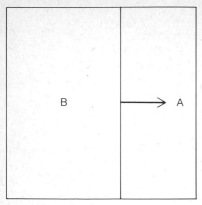

13.28   Slide Effect In a slide effect, the A-source video (the entire original picture) slides off to one side (or corner), revealing the B-source picture, which seems to lie underneath the A-picture. Although technically just the opposite, perceptually a wipe seems to push off the other image, and a slide seems to reveal the second image underneath.

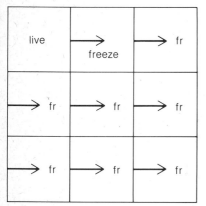

13.29   Snapshot Effect In a snapshot effect, the individual screen divisions show successively updated (new) freeze frames, according to the "live" video in one corner.

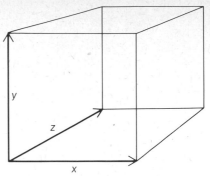

13.30   x-, y-, z-Coordinates The x-coordinate, or x-axis, indicates width; the y-axis, height; and the z-axis, picture depth.

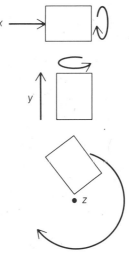

13.31   Rotation Effects The image can be revolved around the x-axis (flip or tumble), the y-axis (rotation, swing), or the z-axis (spin). These rotation effects can be combined with the compression, expansion, and position effects.

lose more and more of the peripheral areas of the picture, because its field of view shrinks progressively during a zoom-in. The reverse is true when we zoom out with a real zoom lens; we see more and more of the scene because the zoom lens changes to a progressively wider field of view.

This special effects zoom is often called "squeezezoom" because the manufacturer that first introduced this effect (Vital Industries, Inc.) gave the entire special effects unit the trademark "SqueeZoom." So, if you hear directors, producers, or T.D.s (technical directors) call for a "squeeze," they are talking about zooms, not oranges.

Many of the other effects combine these squeezezooms with position and size change of the image, and rotation.

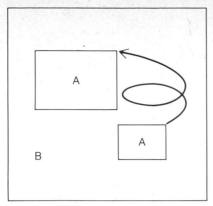

13.32 Fly Effect In the fly effect, the A-video zooms from zero to a certain image size, and at the same time it moves and spins into a specific screen position.

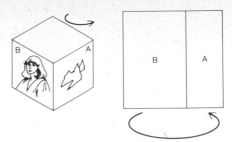

13.33 Cube Rotation In the so-called cube-spin, we perceive a rotating cube that has different pictures glued onto four of its sides.

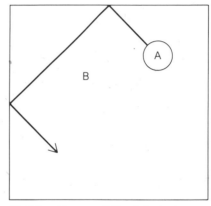

13.34 Bounce Effect In the bounce effect, the object seems to bounce from screen edge to screen edge, very much like the bouncing ball in a video game.

Rotation and Bounce Effects Some of the DVE units (such as the Ampex ADO unit) can rotate any image about all three axes: the x-axis, representing width; the y-axis, representing height; and the z-axis, representing depth (see 13.30 and 13.31).

Here we run into terminology problems. Common sense tells us that the rotation around the x-axis should be called flip or tumble (like flipping a coin); rotation around the y-axis should be revolve (like a revolving door); and rotation around the z-axis should be spin (like the spinning of a wheel). But special effects terminology works differently. The **y-axis rotation** is alternately called rotation, **flip,** or swing; the **x-axis rotation** is flip or tumble; and the **z-axis rotation** is tumble or spin. The best course is to agree on a terminology that works for you and your operation and then stick to it. Many production people are adopting the terminology introduced by Vital Industries (see Section Two of this chapter). Here are some of their more commonly used effects: "fly," which is a B-video insert expanding from zero to a certain size and position on the screen while rotating either on the x- or y-axis, or both (see 13.32).

Many special effects *transitions* use such axis rotation. The well-known **cube-flip** or "cube-spin" is a transition that looks as though various freeze frames were glued on a cube. When the cube is rotated, the B-video appears on one side of the cube, gradually replacing the A-video (see 13.33).

When no three-dimensional effect is used, the flips look as though book pages were being turned.

Bounce effects make the compressed B-video bounce from screen edge to screen edge on the A-video background. The B-video "bouncing ball" can change its shape or flip while bouncing (see 13.34).

As we have said repeatedly, such effects are designed to give an *abstract, graphic* look to the image—perhaps in order to seduce us into perceiving the images of people, when they finally appear and move about normally on the screen, as *real people* rather than mere TV pictures.

Optical effects include scenic devices prepared for the television camera, and attachments to, or manipulations of, the lens. Since the development of sophisticated electronic effects, the optical effects have lost their prominence in television production. Electronic effects are much easier to produce and far more reliable. However, some special effects are much more easily done with optical, rather than electronic, equipment. Also, some optical effects may come in handy, especially if you do not have access to elaborate electronic effects.

There are eight major optical effects: (1) rear projection, (2) television gobos, (3) mirrors, (4) lens prisms, (5) star filter, (6) diffusion filter, (7) defocus effect, and (8) matte box.

Rear Projection

Contrary to a regular slide projector, which projects a slide onto the front side of a screen, the rear screen projector throws a slide image, or a moving crawl, onto the *back* (13.35). The translucent screen, however, allows the camera to pick up the projection from the front. This way, scenic objects and performers can be integrated with the **R.P. (rear projection)** without interfering with the light throw of the projector.

The *rear screen* is a large (usually 10 × 12 feet, or roughly 3.20 × 4.00 meters) sheet of translucent, frosted plastic stretched by rubber bands onto a sturdy wooden or metal frame. The frame rides on four free-wheeling casters for easy positioning.

The rear screen projector has a high-powered lamp that throws a brilliant beam and, in conjunction with the projector lens, produces a brilliant, high-contrast image onto the screen.

Through a simple crawl attachment, the projector can transmit a moving image, such as a landscape or a street scene whizzing by, as seen out of a moving car, for example. Such moving background projections are often used in motion picture work where, when photographed with an actual scene in the foreground, they are called **process shots.**

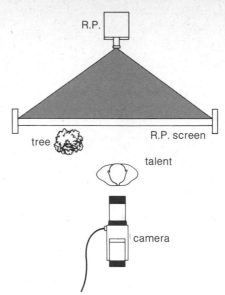

13.35   Rear Screen Projection The rear screen projector throws a bright image onto the back of a translucent screen. The image is then picked up by the camera from the front, usually in combination with other scenic pieces and/or performers.

Even without a projector, the rear screen lends itself to several interesting studio effects. If you place a cardboard cutout or a three-dimensional object between the screen and a strong light source, such as an ellipsoidal spot or a bare projection bulb, you can produce a great variety of shadow patterns on the screen. This technique is especially effective when integrated with a stylized set. (See 13.36.)

Rear screen projection is often integrated with other parts of the studio set. A few simple foreground pieces that match parts of the projected scene produce more realistic pictures than the R.P. alone could (see 13.37).

The use of a rear screen is, unfortunately, not without serious problems: (1) the setup takes up considerable studio space and time; (2) the lighting is difficult to do; (3) the number of performers (normally no more than two) and their action radius in front of the R.P. are severely limited; (4) the fairly noisy blower motors of the projector may be picked up by the studio microphone; and (5) the R.P. has

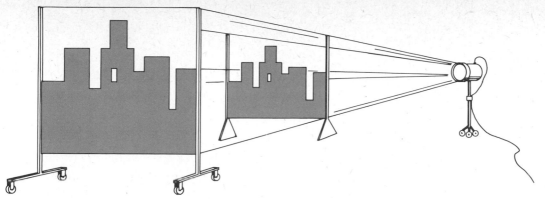

13.36 Rear Screen Use without Projector By placing a cardboard cutout, a sheet of Plexiglas or plastic painted with translucent paints, or even a three-dimensional object between a strong light source and the rear screen, you can achieve many interesting effects.

— drape hung in front of r.p. screen

13.37 Set Using Rear Screen Projection The rear screen projection is usually integrated with foreground set pieces in order to make the scene as realistic as possible.

— rear screen projection starts here

— 2-foot flat covering r.p. screen

fast falloff—meaning that the brightness of the projected image falls off as soon as the camera moves away from its central position and assumes an oblique angle.

Television Gobos

A television **gobo** is a cutout that acts as a decorative foreground frame for background action (see 13.38). Do not confuse the television gobo with the terminology used in film production. In film, a gobo is a large flag—the opaque shield that prevents undesirable light from spilling in certain set areas.

If you have chroma key equipment, such gobo effects are generally matted into the scene electronically. But if you want to dolly closer to the gobo to look through its opening, or arc past it, you need to use an actual gobo in the studio.

The traditional gobos consist of picture frames for a nostalgic scene, or cartoon settings (oversized keyholes, windows, doors, old model cars) through which we can observe the live action.

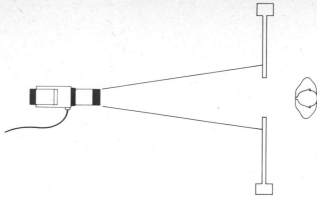

13.38 Television Gobo A television gobo is a cardboard cutout that acts as a special frame for a scene. Gobos are often used as decorative effects.

Mirrors

Mirrors are sometimes used to create unusual camera viewpoints. But they are a hazard in the studio, even if you are not superstitious, because they can reflect the lens of the camera that is shooting the scene. Any shots off a mirror reverse the image, and you cannot correct it unless you have horizontal sweep reversals in your camera or DVE system. Also, now that portable cameras have become so flexible, use of mirrors for unusual angle shots has become unnecessary.

In the absence of a portable camera or special lens attachments, however, you may find the mirror-periscope and multiimage mirrors helpful in achieving certain effects. (See 13.39 and 13.40.)

Lens Prisms

There are special rotating **lens prisms** that can be attached to the camera lens. The most common are the *image inverter prism* and the *multiple image prism.*

The image inverter prism rotates an image into any of several positions. The studio floor can become a wall or the ceiling, depending on the rotation degree of the prism. It is especially effective for putting the scene on a slight tilt. Through the disturbance of the horizon line, called **canting effect,** you can achieve a highly dynamic scene (see 13.41).

The multiple image prism produces strictly decorative effects similar to the DVE multiscreen image.

Star Filter

The **star filter** is a lens attachment that changes high-intensity light sources or reflections into star-like light beams. This method is often used to intensify the background for a singer or a musical group. The studio lights as caught by the wide-angle camera, or the glitter on the singer's dress as seen by the close-up camera, are all transferred into prominent starlike light rays crossing over the entire scene on the television screen. (See 2.15.)

Diffusion Filter

The **diffusion filter** gives the whole scene a soft, slightly out-of-focus look (see 2.16). Some diffusion filters soften only the edges of the picture, but leave the center clear and sharp. You can use the diffusion filter if you want to emphasize the gentle and soft character of a scene. If you do not have such a lens, you can achieve a similar effect by greasing the edges of a piece of glass with petroleum jelly and taping it over the lens. If you grease only the edges of the glass, leaving a clear area in the middle, you get the "soft look" around the edges, with the center remaining in clear focus. *Do not* grease the lens directly because it may well cause permanent damage to the expensive zoom lens. When shooting slides with a 35mm still camera, you can use the neutral density filter and grease it for the diffusion effect.

Try experimenting with various "filter media," such as plastic wrap, gauze, or nylons, which you

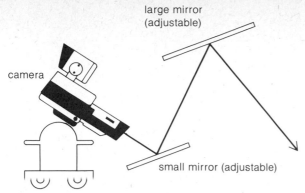

13.39 **Periscope** The mirror periscope, consisting of two adjustable mirrors hung in a movable frame, permits a variety of overhead shots of fairly static scenes. The mirror image is corrected by the second mirror.

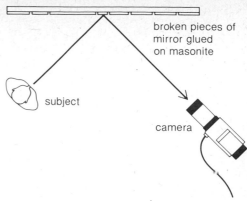

13.40 **Cubist Effect with Mirror** A cubistlike effect can be obtained by reflecting a scene or an object off a mirror mosaic. Simply break a mirror into several large pieces and glue them onto a sheet of plywood or masonite. When the camera shoots into this mirror mosaic at an angle (so that the camera cannot be seen in the reflection), the reflected scene takes on a startling, cubist effect.

can stretch over the lens. Whatever you do, try not to touch the lens itself with your fingers, tape, or the material you are using as a filter.

Defocus Effects

The defocus effect is one of the simplest, yet effective, optical effects. The camera operator simply racks out of focus and, on cue, back into focus again. This effect is used as a transitional device, or to indicate strong psychological disturbances or physiological imbalance.

Because going out of focus conceals the image almost as completely as going to black, it is possible to change your field of view or the objects in front of the camera during complete defocusing. For instance, you can go out of focus on a young girl seated at a table, change actors quickly, and rack back into focus on an old woman sitting in the same chair.

A slight defocusing can make the camera subjective; for instance, it may assume the function of the actor's eye to indicate progressively worsening eyesight. Also, you can suggest psychological disturbances by going out of focus on a close-up of the actor's face.

13.41 **Canting Effect through Prism Inverter** With a prism inverter, you can cant a shot. This effect can contribute to the intensification of a scene, making it dynamic and dramatic. When using an ENG/EFP camera, you can simply cant it a little on your shoulder for such an effect.

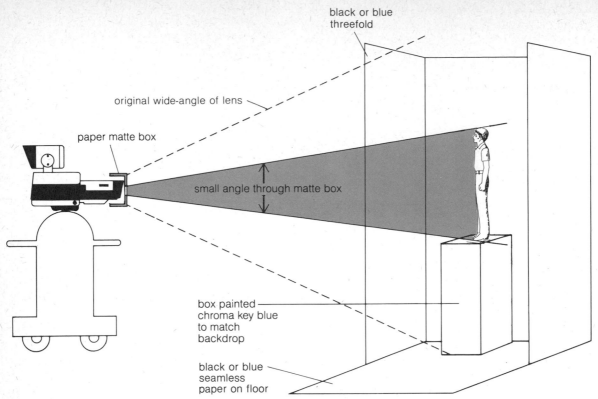

black or blue threefold

original wide-angle of lens

paper matte box

small angle through matte box

box painted
chroma key blue
to match
backdrop

black or blue
seamless
paper on floor

13.42   Matte Box With the aid of a matte box, you can isolate an object in an extreme long shot without overshooting the set. This technique is especially important if you want to reduce the size of an object or performer for chroma key matting.

Matte Box

Whereas in film a matte box has a variety of functions—shielding the lens from undesirable light, holding a filter or a matte slide, such as the well-known cutouts of a view through binoculars—the television matte box is simply a device to partially block the view of a wide-angle lens, or zoom lens position. The matte box physically reduces the field of view without changing the apparent distance from camera to object. If, for example, you want to matte (via chroma key) a tiny standing figure into a large, oversized room, you can have one camera focus on the room interior, the other on the chroma key set. This set consists of a large roll of (usually) blue cloth

or seamless paper that can be pulled down like a window shade from a batten near the lighting grid so that it even covers part of the floor. Have the person stand on the blue chroma key material, and photograph this scene from an extreme long-shot zoom position. The matte box prevents this camera from overshooting the chroma key set on this extreme long shot (see 13.42). Although there is a great variety of more or less complex matte boxes on the market, you can make an inexpensive but useful one yourself. Simply make a cardboard box that fits over the zoom lens (or a cylinder, if your zoom lens is round), cut a small opening (either rectangular or round) into the front part, and paint the inside black. Then tape the matte box over the lens. If you use a monochrome turret camera, you can make the matte box out of a small paper cup that fits over the lens.

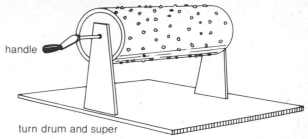

rough sandpaper
or black paper with white lines

handle

turn drum and super

13.43   Rain Drum A rain drum consists of a small drum (about ten inches [25 centimeters] in diameter), covered with rough black sandpaper or black paper with tiny white "glitches" painted on it. Turn the drum fairly fast (depending on how hard you want it to rain), take a slightly out-of-focus close-up of the rotating paper, and super the glitches over the scene. Make sure that you turn the drum so that the rain is coming down instead of going up.

MECHANICAL EFFECTS

Most mechanical effects are needed only in the presentation of television plays. Although small commercial stations may have little opportunity to do drama, colleges and universities are frequently involved in the production of plays.

The techniques for producing mechanical effects are not universally agreed upon. They offer an excellent opportunity for experimentation. Your main objectives must be (1) simplicity in construction and operation and (2) maximum reliability.

Remember that you can *suggest* many situations by showing an effect only partially and relying on the *audio track* to supply the rest of the information. Also, through chroma key matting, you can matte in many an effect from a prerecorded source, such as film or videotape.

Nevertheless, there are some special effects that are relatively easy to achieve mechanically, especially if the effect itself remains peripheral and authenticity is not a primary concern. Keep in mind that effects do not need to look realistic to the people in the studio; all that counts is how they appear on the television screen.

Rain   Soak the actors' clothes with water. Super the rain from a film loop or a rain drum (see 13.43). Try to avoid real water in the studio, because even a small amount can become a hazard to performers and equipment. Best yet, cover a portable camera with a plastic bag, wait for real rain, and shoot outside.

Snow   Spray snow out of commercial snow spray cans in front of the lens. Have the actors covered with plastic snow or soap flakes, or drop plastic snow from above.

Fog   Fog is always a problem. The widely used method of putting dry ice into hot water unfortu-

nately works only in silent scenes, because the bubbling noise it makes may become so loud as to drown out the dialogue. If you have to shoot fog indoors, rent one of the large, commercially available fog machines. If the fog does not have to move, simply use a diffusion filter.

Wind   Use two large electric fans. Drown out the fan noises with wind sound effects.

Smoke   Pour mineral oil on a hotplate. If the smell bothers the actors too much, super a stock shot of smoke over the scene. Do not let the oil get too hot, however. It may catch fire.

Fire   Do not use fire inside the studio. The risk is simply too great for the effect. Use sound effects of burning, and have flickering light effects in the background. A film loop with fire matted over the scene can also be very effective. For the fire reflections, staple some silk strips on a small batten and project the shadows with an ellipsoidal spot on the set (see 13.44), or reflect a strong spotlight off a vibrating plastic sheet.

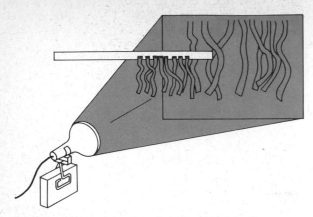

13.44 Fire Simulation To project flickering fire onto the set, move a batten with silk strips stapled on it in front of a strong spotlight. If you use an electric fan to activate the strips, you simply hold the batten close to the ground, with the strips being blown upward.

Lightning   Combine four to six photofloods or two photo flash units to a single switch. Lightning should always come from *behind* the set. Do not forget the audio effect of thunder. Obviously, the quicker the thunder succeeds the light flash, the closer we perceive the thunderstorm to be.

Explosions   As with fire, stay away from explosive devices, even if you have "experts" guarantee that nothing will happen. But you can *suggest* explosions. Take a close-up of a frightened face, increase the light intensity to such a degree that the features begin to wash out, and come in strongly with the explosion audio. Or, better yet, use some electronic effect on the face (or the whole scene) while the audio explosion rumbles on.

It should be pointed out again that one effect is rarely used in isolation. Effects, like any other production techniques, are *contextual*. They depend on the right blending of several visual and auditory elements, all within the context of the overall scene. The dialogue of the performers or actors is, of course, one of the prime means of reinforcing an effect, or making it believable in the first place.

MAIN POINTS

1.   Visual effects can be grouped into four large categories: (1) standard electronic effects, (2) digital video effects (DVE), (3) optical effects, and (4) mechanical effects.

2.   The four standard electronic effects are (1) superimposition, (2) key, (3) chroma key, and (4) wipe.

3.   A superimposition, or super, is a form of double exposure. The picture from one camera is electronically superimposed over the picture from the other.

4.   Keying means electronically cutting out portions of a television picture and filling them with another, or portions of another, image. The basic purpose of a key is to add titles to a base (background) picture.

5.   If the cutout portion of the base picture is filled with the signal that is doing the "cutting," we speak of an internal, or normal key.

6.   If the cutout portion of the base picture is filled by a signal from an external source, such as another camera picture, we speak of an external key.

7.   If the cutout portions are filled with various grays or colors generated by the switcher, we speak of a matte key.

8.   The standard matte key modes are (1) edge mode, (3) drop shadow mode, and (3) outline mode.

9.   Through chroma key we can cut an entire scene, such as a dancer performing, into a background picture (city skyline). One camera provides the base picture (photo of the skyline), while the other is focused on the dancer, moving in front of a plain, colored (usually blue) background. During the keying, the blue becomes translucent, letting the background picture show through without interfering with the foreground (dancer).

10.   In a wipe, a portion or a complete television picture is gradually replaced ("wiped off") by another. There are various wipe patterns that can be selected through push buttons on the switcher.

11.   Variations of the normal wipes are (1) the soft-wipe, whereby the outline of the keyed image blends

into the base picture; (2) the quad split, where the screen is split into four quadrants, each one displaying a different image; and (3) the spotlight effect, which emphasizes a certain section of the base picture with a light round circle, similar to an actual spotlight shining on the scene.

12.   The digital video effects (DVE) need equipment that changes the normal (analog) video signal into digital (on-off pulses) information. When interfaced with the standard (analog) effects, the possibilities for visual effects are virtually endless.

13.   Through digital video effects, we can create a variety of multi-images, such as the echo effect, and manipulate the size, shape, light and color, texture, and motion of the image. Some of the more common DVEs include compression and expansion of the image, positioning of the compressed image anywhere in the frame, posterization and mosaic effect (whereby the image looks like a solarized photo, or as if made up of many mosaic tiles), and zoom effects through continuous expansion and compression of the image (usually called squeezoom).

14.   Optical effects include (1) rear screen projection, (2) television gobos, (3) mirror effects, (4) lens prism effects, (5) star filter effects, (6) diffusion filter effects, (7) defocus effects, and (8) matte box effects.

15.   The mechanical effects are generally needed only in the presentation of television plays. The most common effects are rain, snow, fog, wind, smoke, fire, lightning, and explosions.

In this section, we will (1) include an effects chart by Vital Industries with symbols for 123 digital effects, (2) discuss some of the equipment and processes used for *picture correction,* and (3) briefly mention some additional nondigital electronic *visual effects* that are occasionally used.

EFFECTS CHART

Vital Industries, Inc., was one of the first DVE manufacturers to name and invent usable symbols for most of the video effects. Figure 13.45 shows their SqueeZoom effects chart.

PICTURE CORRECTION

The picture correction equipment and processes help to rid the television pictures of their occasional jitters and breakups; provide for roll-free switching among various nonsynchronous video sources, such as ENG or other remote feeds; improve colors, contours, and picture detail; and reduce video noise.

As you can see, some equipment and processes are primarily concerned with the *stabilization* of the image, others with *image enhancement.*

Image Stabilization

The two major image stabilization systems are (1) the time base corrector (TBC) and (2) the frame-store synchronizer.

Time Base Corrector (TBC)   You may recall that we briefly mentioned the functions of the time base corrector in Chapter 10. To remind you again, you use a time base corrector to free a television picture of jitters, occasional breakups and rolls, and some color distortions, caused by timing errors of the scanning process. Such errors are especially prevalent with $\frac{3}{4}$-inch or smaller format videotape recorders. The time base corrector continuously checks the "clocking" of the scanning and repeats scanning lines that may have been missed by the slightly out-of-sync scanning beam. Time base correctors are especially important when you play back videotapes that were recorded on VTRs other than your playback machine. The advantage of the *digital TBC* is that it can correct larger timing errors because it can

The various picture correction devices help to stabilize television images and enhance their quality. These picture correction devices are especially important when working with less than top-of-the-line equipment.

store more information than the regular TBC before reading it out at the correct scanning rate.

Frame-Store Synchronizer This is similar to a TBC, except that it has a memory large enough to store and read out *one complete video frame*. Its main application is to synchronize signals from a variety of video sources that are not **genlocked** (tied into the "house sync"—the synchronization system that keeps all electronic equipment within the station in step). With the **frame-store synchronizer,** for example, you can integrate the various ENG feeds (from live ENG cameras or portable VTRs) and even satellite feeds into the local news program without picture roll or breakup. If you happen to lose the signal from one of those remote sources in the middle of a feed, the frame-store synchronizer will remember the last picture sent (thanks to its whole-frame storage capacity) and faithfully display it as a freeze frame, until the signal is restored.

Also, because we now can grab, store, and retrieve a complete frame, we should now be able to modify the frame-store synchronizer so that we can manipulate in some way the frozen and digitized frame. This is exactly what is being done in DVE. All the sophisticated DVE units are based on the frame-store synchronizer. Before such modifications were made to the

frame-store synchronizer, some creative production people used to pull the plug on remote feeds (or feeds from a VTR) whenever they wanted a freeze frame. But this was the only special effect possible at that time. Today, the freeze frame is only one of many effects options.

Image Enhancement

Image enhancement is part of signal processing. It is used to maintain or improve picture quality when videotaping, dubbing, or broadcasting the original video signal. Not all the image enhancement equipment is digital, although there are constant efforts to make it so.

Let us now briefly mention the major image enhancement equipment.

Dropout Compensator We speak of **dropout** when portions of the video signal get lost because the videotape coating is uneven or there is some dirt on the tape. Dropout shows up as white glitches in monochrome television, or some colored specks in color television. The **dropout compensator** senses the missing signals portions and fills them in with information from the previous scanning line.

Image Enhancer   This electronic circuit makes the picture look sharper. Similar processes make the separation among various colors more distinct and enhance the contour of certain picture areas (such as images of objects and people). At the same time, it detects excessive video noise and eliminates it by substituting actual picture information.

Color Correctors   Digital color correctors are especially important for the telecine camera, because the color schemes can vary considerably within a film, and especially from film to film. Color correctors for videotape can select certain colors within a picture and change their hue, saturation, and brightness to a certain extent. Through color correction, you can, for example, adjust the color temperature of one shot to make it match the others. However, such color correction processes are quite time consuming. It is much better, therefore, to spend some extra time during the actual production (studio and especially EFP) to match the color temperatures of the various takes than to leave the color matching to postproduction.

Noise Reducers   Just as there are noise reducers for audio, there are also noise reduction devices for video. They are especially important when you videotape under low lighting conditions. A good digital noise reducer can detect a noise element in the picture and eliminate it by simply ignoring its number when reconverting into an analog (television scanning) signal.

Despite all the signal processing and image enhancement, the best guarantee for good picture quality is to put high-quality pictures on the videotape in the first place. Do not rely on postproduction to remedy production problems. Usually, you are so busy with the normal postproduction tasks, such as editing and audio sweetening, for example, that there is little time left for elaborate image enhancement maneuvers. However, image enhancement is essential if you want to broadcast directly from small-format videotape ($\frac{3}{4}$-inch and less), or if you want to dub up to a larger videotape format for duplication and distribution.

NONDIGITAL EFFECTS

Some nondigital effects have survived from the days of monochrome television. They are (1) debeaming, (2) video feedback, and (3) colorizing. All these effects can, of course, be done more efficiently and predictably with digital effects equipment. However, if you do not have access to DVE systems, you may want to experiment with these effects and apply them whenever appropriate.

Debeaming

Debeaming is the gradual reduction of the intensity of the scanning beam. The more debeaming you do with a monochrome television system, the fewer brightness variations you have and the more the image is reduced to stark black-and-white contrasts. The image seems at first to glow, as if it would emit its own light, and then to burn itself up until nothing is left but a nondistinct, light-gray screen. Through debeaming, the very structure of an object or person seems to be affected and changed (see 13.46).

Debeaming effects in color television can, of course, be even more dramatic. Some of the subtle colors that

Dropout   Loss of part of the video signal, which shows up on the screen as white or colored glitches. Caused by uneven videotape iron-oxide coating (bad tape quality or overuse) or dirt.

Frame-Store Synchronizer   Image stabilization and synchronization system that has a memory large enough to store and read out one complete video frame. Used to synchronize signals from a variety of video sources that are not genlocked.

Genlock   1. Locking the synchronization generators from two different origination sources, such as remote and studio. Allows switching from source to source without picture rolling. 2. Locking the house sync with the sync signal from another source (such as a videotape). The videotape can then be intermixed with live studio cameras, for example.

Scanning   The movement of the electron beam from left to right and from top to bottom on the television screen.

Video Feedback   The picture on the television set is photographed by a television camera and fed back into the same monitor, producing multiple images.

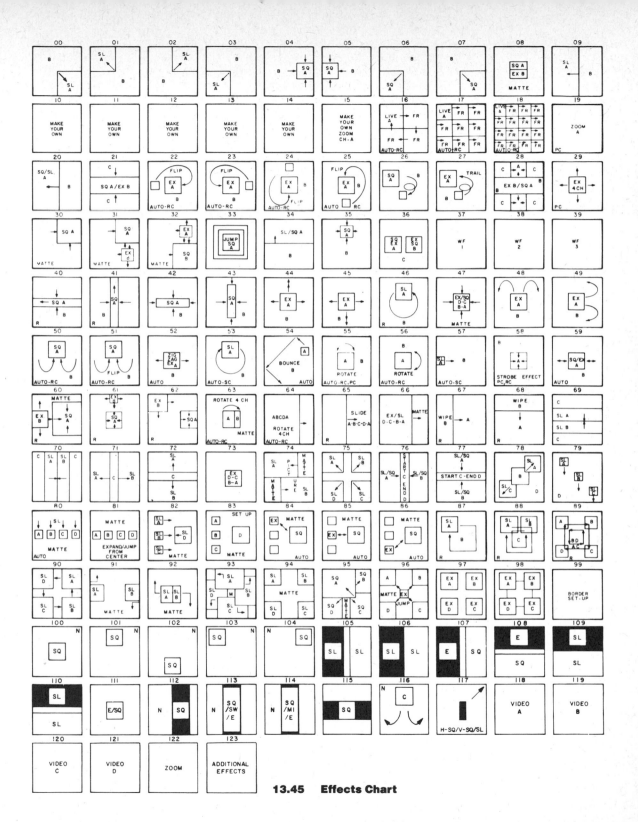

13.45   Effects Chart

13.46   Debeaming Effect Through debeaming, the graphic expressiveness of this woman's face is greatly intensified.

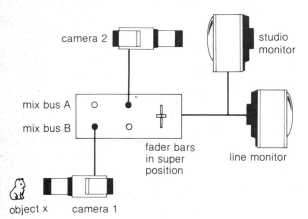

13.47   Video Feedback Principle The setup of video feedback is relatively simple. Camera 1 photographs object X and feeds it into the switcher on mix bus B. This picture is fed into the studio monitor. Camera 2 photographs the studio monitor, which now displays an image of object X. Camera 2 is fed into mix bus A. Cameras 1 and 2 are now superimposed and fed as a super into the line monitor, which now shows the multiple images of object X as multiplied by the closed feedback loop between cameras 1 and 2.

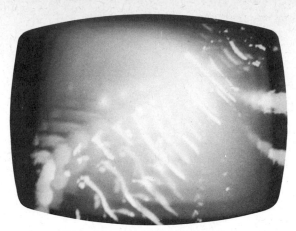

13.48   Video Feedback on Monitor You can also achieve video feedback without a switcher, simply by pointing the camera at the monitor that shows the camera's picture, and by feeding this monitor image back into the same monitor.

have blended harmoniously with the rest of the scene all of a sudden take on their own expressive life. They begin to dominate the scene first, and then consume it like a high-energy force. However, any indiscriminate use of such a powerful effect can just as easily and forcefully render the scene unbelievable, and thereby destroy, rather than intensify, your communication intent.

Video Feedback

When you photograph with a television camera an image off a studio monitor, and feed the photographed image back into the same monitor, the resulting image is mul-

tiplied very much as with two opposing mirrors. If you move the feedback camera slowly about the face of the monitor, you can get highly intense, glowing images that weave back and forth (see 13.47 and 13.48).

By canting (holding somewhat sideways) a portable monochrome camera, for example, and by including part of the feedback monitor frame (to have a video reference), you can get unpredictable and highly interesting patterns. If you now move the camera ever so slowly in front of the feedback monitor, you get an exciting variety of round, mandalalike feedback patterns.

Video feedback is the visual equivalent of sound reverberation (echo) effects.

Colorizing

With the aid of a special **colorizing** generator you can create any number of color patterns and supply a black-and-white image with a specific hue (color) or, in some cases, with two or three hues. Some colorizers shade all dark picture areas with one hue and all light ones with another. Needless to say, you can achieve highly unique color effects that would be difficult to get with a normal color camera. Some video artists prefer, therefore, to shoot their images in black and white for later colorizing. A more utilitarian application of the colorizer is to supply charts and graphs with various functional colors.

MAIN POINTS

1. An effects chart demonstrates graphically what the special effect will do.

2. Picture correction equipment and processes help to rid television pictures of jitters and breakups, provide roll-free switching among nonsynchronous video sources, improve colors and picture detail, and reduce video noise.

3. The two major image stabilization devices are the time base corrector (TBC) and the frame-store synchronizer.

4. Image enhancement equipment is used to maintain or improve picture quality when videotaping, dubbing, or broadcasting a video signal. The most common instruments are the dropout compensator, image enhancer, color corrector, and noise reducer.

5. Three nondigital effects have survived since the days of monochrome television: debeaming, video feedback, and colorizing.

6. Debeaming reduces the image's brightness variations and creates a solarizing effect. Video feedback is created by photographing with a television camera an image off the monitor, and feeding this image back into the same monitor. The resulting image looks like a digital echo effect. A colorizing generator can give color to a black-and-white image by assigning a special color to a specific grayscale value.

FURTHER READING

Millerson, Gerald. *The Technique of Television Production*. 10th ed. Woburn, MA: Focal Press, 1981.

Paulson, C. Robert. *BM/E's ENG/EFP/EPP Handbook*. New York: Broadband Information Services, Inc., 1981.

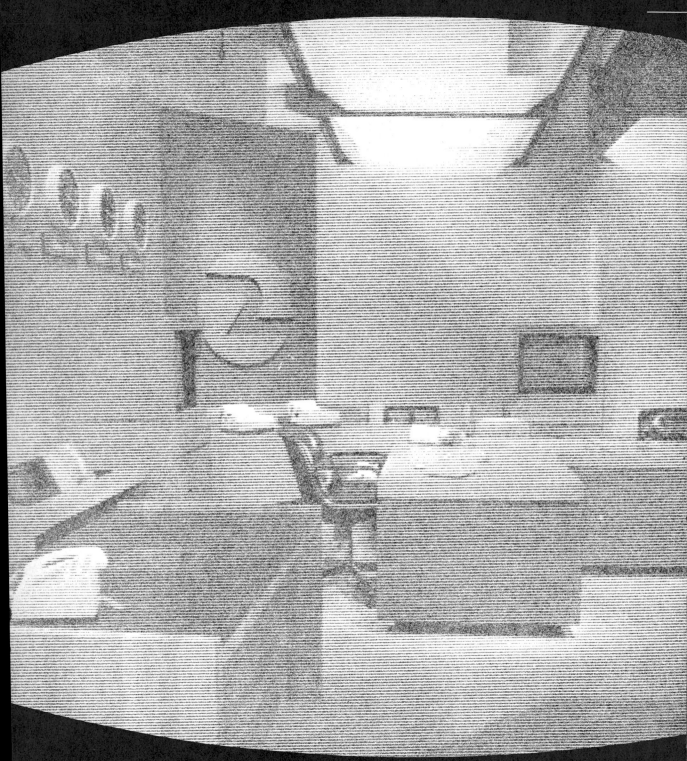

CHAPTER 14

Design

Design is an overall concept that should reflect a continuity of style in every design element seen on and off the screen.

In Section One of this chapter, we will stress these aspects of television graphics and scene design:

1. The specifications of television graphics: (1) aspect ratio, (2) scanning and essential areas, (3) readability, (4) color and color compatibility, (5) grayscale, and (6) style.

2. The major types of camera graphics: (1) the plain title card, (2) the key, or super, card, (3) the chroma key card, (4) the slide, (5) the mechanical crawl, and (6) maps and charts.

3. The operation of camera graphics, which means the effective handling of studio cards, maps, and charts that are placed on studio easels.

4. The three principal devices of generated graphics: (1) character generator (C.G.), (2) graphics generator, and (3) still store systems.

5. The types of scenery: (1) standard set units, (2) hanging units, and (3) platforms and set pieces.

6. Properties and set dressings.

Section Two looks at the important design concepts of balance, the preparation of television graphics, recurring set design problems, and several special elements of scenic design.

Design, or the lack of it, permeates everything the station shows on the air and off. It sets the style for a broadcast operation. The logo for CBS, for example, induces us to expect the same high quality from the network's programming (see 14.1).

But a handsome **logo** does not automatically carry its design qualities over to the programming or to the on-the-air graphics or scenery. What is important here is developing a design consciousness for *everything* you do; a well-executed logo is merely the symbol for such awareness, not its sole cause.

In Section One of this chapter, we will stress the major aspects of television graphics and scenery.

GRAPHICS

Television **graphics** includes all *two-dimensional* visuals specially prepared for the television camera, such as studio or title cards, illustrations, maps, or charts. Electronically generated titles, charts, or animations—even if appearing three-dimensional—are also part of television graphics.

The major purposes of television graphics are to give you *specific information,* such as the title of a show or the names of the actors, and to tell you something about the *nature of the event* (funny, tragic, hot news, futuristic, old-fashioned). Both functions are usually supported by appropriate sound.

Four major factors should be considered: (1) overall specifications, (2) types of camera graphics, (3) operation of camera graphics, and (4) generated graphics.

Specifications

Whenever you are preparing graphics for the television screen, you should pay close attention to (1) aspect ratio, (2) scanning and essential areas, (3) readability, (4) color and color compatibility, (5) grayscale, and (6) style.

Aspect Ratio   **Aspect ratio** means the relationship between height and width—the shape of the picture frame rectangle. The proportions of the television screen are 3:4; that is, anything that appears there is horizontally oriented within an area three units high and four units wide. All graphic information must,

Design is an overall concept that includes not only the lettering and layout on a studio card, or the plan for a set, but the logo of the station, its stationery, the office furniture, and the pictures in the hallways.

therefore, be contained within this aspect ratio. (See 14.2.) Within the television screen, however, the aspect ratio of pictures can be changed, as in a digital video matte.

Most artwork—studio cards or slides—is prepared in aspect ratio. Although our eyes can very readily adjust to some other aspect ratio, the television camera cannot. If you pull back far enough with the camera to include the entire out-of-aspect-ratio studio card, the information on it is likely to become so small that it is unreadable. (See 14.3.) Or, you can crop the card so that it fits the aspect ratio. But then you lose important information. (See 14.4.)

Slides can be used only if they are *horizontally* oriented. Vertical slides not only lose a portion of the information but also look bad on the screen. (See 14.5.)

Blackboards can present a special aspect-ratio problem. If, for example, the television teacher writes on the blackboard in his or her usual way, starting on the left side and moving across to the right side, you will not be able to fit the whole sentence into the shot unless you take a long shot of the entire board and reduce the legibility of the information

(see 14.6). One workable solution is to have the blackboard divided into several aspect-ratio fields. If the teacher stays within the borders, you can show the entire information in a close-up shot (see 14.7).

Occasionally in graphics, however, out-of-aspect ratio is not only usable but desirable. Take a chart with a steeply rising curve (see 14.8). A slow, tight tilt up the curve reveals the information more vividly than a long shot of the whole chart, or a shot of a chart drawn within the aspect ratio. The same is true, of course, for a horizontally oriented, out-of-aspect-ratio chart whose information gains in impact by a gradual revelation through a pan.

If you need to use graphic material that must be shown in its entirety, yet which is out of aspect ratio, mount it neatly on a large card that is in aspect ratio. You simply frame up on the large card, keeping the out-of-aspect-ratio information as nearly screen-center as possible.

Scanning and Essential Areas   Even when the graphic material is in aspect ratio, part of it still may not reach the home screen. Within the aspect ratio, there is a peripheral loss of picture area caused by the various electronic manipulations between cam-

14.1 The CBS Logo The logo of a station or network refeclts its design consciousness; it often sets its overall design style. (Courtesy of CBS)

14.3 Out-of-Aspect-Ratio Studio Card We usually call a graphic "out-of-aspect ratio" when it has an aspect ratio other than the 3 × 4 of the television screen. When an out-of-aspect-ratio studio card is shown in its entirety, the information usually becomes so small that it is no longer readable.

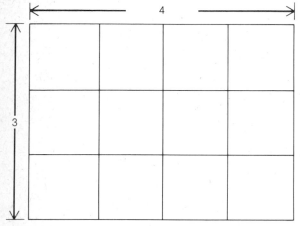

14.2 Television Aspect Ratio The television aspect ratio is three units high and four units wide. For HDTV (high definition television), it is three units high and five units wide.

era and home reception and the masking of the television screen. The picture you see in the camera viewfinder usually shows more picture area than the control-room monitor, and a good deal more than the home receiver. Each time you record a picture and play it back, you lose some of it. The amount lost depends on the transmission factors, the number of tape generations, and especially on the mask-

Aspect Ratio The proportions of the television screen, and therefore of all television pictures: three units high and four units wide.

Character Generator A special effects generator that electronically produces a series of letters and numbers directly on the television screen, or keyed into a background picture.

Color Compatibility Color signals that can be perceived as black-and-white pictures on monochrome television sets. Generally used to mean that the color scheme has enough brightness contrast for monochrome reproduction with a good grayscale contrast.

Crawl Graphics (usually credit copy) that move slowly up the screen; often mounted on a drum, or crawl. More exactly, an up-and-down movement of credits is called a roll, and a horizontal movement is called a crawl.

Digital Still Store System Also called electronic still store system, or ESS. An electronic device that can grab a single frame from any video source and store it in digital form on a disc.

Essential Area The section of the television picture, centered within the scanning area, that is seen by the home viewer, regardless of masking of the set or slight misalignment of the receiver. Sometimes called critical area.

Flat A piece of standing scenery used as a background or to simulate the walls of a room.

Graphics All two-dimensional visuals prepared for the television screen, such as title cards, charts, and graphs.

14.4 Information Loss of Studio Card with Vertical Aspect Ratio By moving the camera in closer so that the graphic fits the aspect ratio of the television screen, important information is lost in the cropping process.

14.5 TV Image of Vertically Oriented Slide Vertically oriented slides should not be used on television, because they lose their top and bottom information. Also, there are black spaces on the sides of the screen because the vertical slide does not fill the entire screen width.

ing and alignment (or rather misalignment) of the home receiver. The picture height and width may be simultaneously misadjusted on the receivers. In order to make sure that all the information on a card, for example, shows up on the home receiver, the camera must include in its shot the *scanning and essential areas* of the graphic.

The **scanning area** is framed by the camera and shown by the preview monitors in the station. It is the area actually scanned by the camera pickup tube.

The **essential area,** sometimes called critical area or safe title area, is centered within the scanning area. It is the portion seen by the home viewer, regardless of masking of the set, transmission loss, or slight misalignment of the receiver. Obviously,

Grayscale A scale indicating intermediate steps from TV black to TV white. Maximum range: ten grayscale steps; good: seven steps; poor: five steps.

Hand Props Objects, called properties, that are handled by the performer.

Key Card Also called super card. A studio card with white lettering on a black background, used for superimposition of a title, or for keying of a title over a background scene. For chroma keying, the white letters are on a chroma-key blue background.

Limbo Any set area used for shooting small commercial displays, card easels, and the like, having a plain, light background.

Props Properties: furniture and other objects used for set decorations and by actors or performers.

Roll Graphics (usually credit copy) that move slowly up the screen; often called crawl.

Scanning Area Picture area that is scanned by the camera pickup tube; more generally, the picture area actually reproduced by the camera and relayed to the studio monitors, which is further reduced by the masking of the home screen and general transmission loss.

Set Arrangement of scenery and properties to indicate the locale and/or mood of a show.

Threefold Three flats hinged together.

Twofold Two flats hinged together. Also called a book.

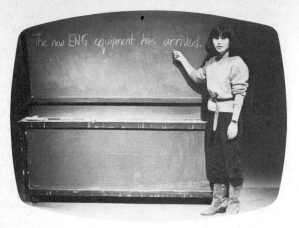
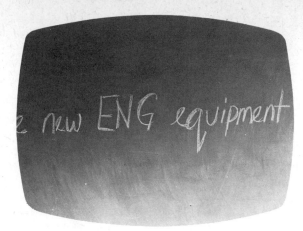

14.6 Aspect-Ratio Problem with Blackboard Writing Normal writing on the blackboard can present a serious aspect-ratio problem. The camera cannot show a close-up of a sentence that stretches over the width of the blackboard.

14.7 Aspect-Ratio Fields on Blackboard If the blackboard is divided into aspect-ratio fields, you can get a close-up of an entire sentence.

all essential information should be contained within the essential area (see 14.9).

The most popular studio card sizes are 11 × 14 inches (roughly 28 × 36cm), and 14 × 17 inches (roughly 36 × 43cm). In the metric system, 1 inch equals 2.54cm (centimeters, or $\frac{1}{100}$ of a meter).

The 11 × 14 card has a *scanning area* of 8 × $10\frac{2}{3}$ inches (roughly 20 × 27cm), centered within the card, and an *essential area,* centered within

the card (and the scanning area), of 6 × 8 inches (roughly 15 × 20cm). (See 14.10.)

The 14 × 17 card has a *scanning area* of 9 × 12 inches (or roughly 23 × 31cm), centered within the card, and an *essential area* of $7\frac{1}{8}$ × $9\frac{1}{2}$ inches (roughly 18 × 24cm). (See 14.11.)

Once you have settled on a standard size for your studio cards (the 11 × 14 size is the more economical), you can make a simple framing guide that

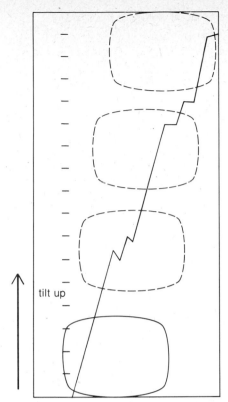

tilt up

14.8   Tilt on Vertically Oriented Chart Tilting up on a chart that reveals its information step by step vertically is often more dramatic than showing the information all at once.

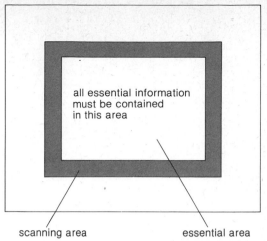

all essential information
must be contained
in this area

scanning area   essential area

14.9   Scanning and Essential Areas The scanning area is what the camera frames and the preview monitor shows. The essential area is what finally appears on the home television screen. All important information (such as titles and telephone numbers) must be contained within the essential area.

immediately shows the scanning and essential areas (see 14.12). You can mark the scanning area by using the slots as guides for thin pencil lines. These lines can serve as a framing guide for the camera operator. The cutout in the center reveals the essential area. Only what shows through the window appears on the television screen.

· The scanning area for the standard 35mm slide is defined by the customary slide mask. The essential area must be well within the visible slide area. Because a slide is so small, actual measurements become rather difficult and cumbersome to perform. But you can easily tell whether the information is contained within the essential area of a slide. If the letters of a title, for example, come close to the edges of the mask, the title extends beyond the

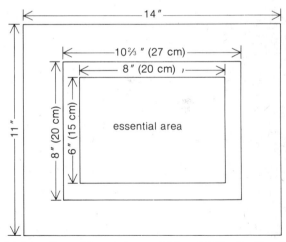

14″

10⅔″ (27 cm)

8″ (20 cm)

11″

8″ (20 cm)

6″ (15 cm)

essential area

14.10   Area Dimensions of 11 × 14 Studio Card
Overall size: 11 × 14 inches
Scanning area: 8 × 10⅔ inches
Essential area: 6 × 8 inches

The 11 × 14 card is popular because you can cut four cards from the standard 22 × 28 show card without any waste.

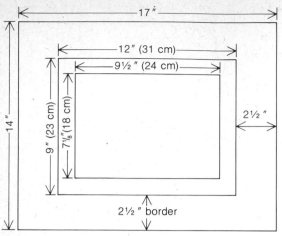

14.11 Area Dimensions of 14 × 17 Studio Card
Overall size: 14 × 17 inches
Scanning area: 9 × 12 inches (2½-inch border around scanning area)
Essential area: $7\frac{1}{8} \times 9\frac{1}{2}$ inches

14.13 Slide with Information beyond Essential Area Although we can read the information on this slide, the information goes beyond the essential area. When the slide is projected and televised, the beginning and ending letters of the middle line would be lost (see also 14.16).

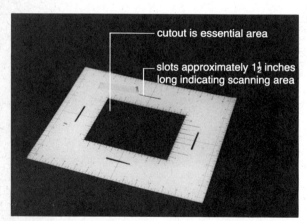

14.12 Framing Guide for Studio Cards To make a simple framing guide, take a standard studio card (in this case, an 11 × 14 card), and cut out the essential area (the 6 × 8-inch rectangle centered within the card). Then cut narrow slots 1 inch from the top and bottom edge of the essential area and $1\frac{1}{3}$ inches to either side of the essential area to mark the outside edges of the scanning area. Placing this guide on top of a studio card, you can mark the scanning areas by drawing a small pencil line through the slots. Through the cutout window, you can see whether the essential information is, indeed, within the essential area.

14.14 Slide with Information within Essential Area Keeping information within the essential area is especially important when using slides, because the television film camera cannot compensate for anything that lies outside this space.

14.15 Framing Guide for Prepared Slide You can make a framing guide for slides by cutting out the essential area of an underexposed (black) slide. The cutout should be 16 × 22mm. All essential information must show up in the cutout window. If the information is partially cut off by the black border, the slide is unusable.

essential area (see 14.13). If there is comfortable "breathing space" between the letters and the edges of the mask, the title lies within the essential area (see 14.14).

You may want to make a slide guide similar to the studio card guide. Simply take a severely underexposed 35mm slide, or put thin, opaque cardboard in a plastic slide holder, and cut out a window with the essential area dimensions ($\frac{5}{8} \times \frac{7}{8}$ inches, or 16 × 22mm). The aspect ratio of this cutout is not exactly 3 × 4, but close enough for our purposes (see 14.15).

You can now put this guide slide over the regular title slide. If you can read the title through the window of the guide slide, the title will read properly on the home television screen.

The surest way to test a slide is to project it on the preview monitor. If the letters come close to the edges of the preview monitor, the title extends beyond the essential area and will certainly be cut off on either side (see 14.16a and b).

Observing the essential area is even more important for slides than for studio cards, because the television film (telecine) camera cannot move on the slide to compensate for minor extensions (see 14.15).

a

b

14.16 Slide on Preview Monitor and Home Receiver (a) On the preview monitor, we can still read the whole title. Note, however, that the middle line goes to the edges of the preview monitor—a clear sign that the title is extending beyond the essential area. (b) When the slide is projected on the home receiver, the information that went beyond the essential area is lost (see 14.13).

Readability In television graphics, readability means that you should be able to read the words that appear on the television screen. As obvious as this statement is, it seems to have eluded many a graphic artist. Sometimes, we see titles explode onto and disappear from the screen so quickly that only people with superior perception abilities can actually read them. Or, the information is too numerous and small to be comprehended properly. Such read-

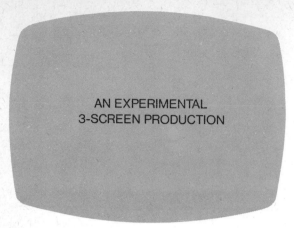

14.17 Plain Title Card The plain title card is prepared for the studio camera. It is shown as is and is not mixed with any other video source.

14.18 Illustrated Title This card reads well. The illustration and text are contrasting enough to show up well even under less than ideal reception conditions.

ability problems occur regularly when motion picture credits are shown on television. First, they generally extend beyond the essential area, and we can see only part of the title. Second, the smaller credit lines are usually impossible to read. The letters are much too tiny and crowded to show up properly on the television screen. Third, the letters themselves are not bold enough to show up well on the television screen, especially if they have a busy (highly detailed) background. What, then, makes for good readability? Here are some recommendations:

1. Keep all written information within the essential area.

2. Use relatively large letters with a bold, clean contour. The limited resolution of the television image does not reproduce thin-lined letters (letters with overly fine stems and serifs). Thin stems and serifs are especially susceptible to breakup when keyed. If you use a character generator (see p. 418), the various fonts (various styles of type) usually show up well on the television screen. However, even then they often need to be reinforced with a drop shadow or outline to achieve optimal readability.

3. Limit the amount of information. The less information that appears on the screen, the easier it is for the viewer to comprehend it. Some television experts suggest a maximum of seven lines or less per studio card.[1] It is more sensible to prepare a series of slides, each one displaying a small amount of information, than one slide with an overabundance.

4. Try not to letter over too busy a background. If you need to add lettering over a busy background—such as the scores and names of players over the live picture of a football stadium—make sure that the printing is simple and bold. If the background is relatively simple and plain, you can use some fancier lettering.

5. Watch the color and contrast relationship between the lettering and the background. Besides different hues, there should be a considerable brightness contrast between the letters and the background (see 14.17 through 14.20).

The same principles apply when you animate a title through special effects. In fact, if the title twists and tumbles about the screen, the letters must be

---

[1]Thomas D. Burrows and Donald N. Wood, *Television Production,* 2nd ed. (Dubuque, Iowa: William C. Brown, 1982), p. 211. See also Lewis B. O'Donnell, "Determination of Optimum Angles and Distances for Viewing Alphanumeric Characters and Geometric Patterns on a Television Receiver" (Ph.D. diss., Syracuse University, 1970).

14.19 Lack of Contrast This title does not read well. The brightness of the lettering and the background are much too similar for easy reading.

14.20 Good Contrast between Title and Background With more contrast between the lettering and the background, the title becomes more readable.

even more legible than if they were used for a straight title card.

Color and Color Compatibility

Because color is an important design element, you need to know something about its components and attributes, and how the television system reacts to them. This includes color compatibility, or the reproduction of color as shades of gray on the monochrome system.

As you learned in Chapter 2 (Section Two), color is determined by three factors: (1) hue, (2) saturation, and (3) brightness. *Hue* refers to the color itself—that is, whether it is blue, green, red, or yellow. *Saturation* (sometimes called *chroma*) indicates the color strength—a strong red or a pale blue, a washed-out green or a rich purple. *Brightness* (sometimes called *value* or *luminance*) indicates whether the color is dark or light.

If we had color reception exclusively, hue and saturation would be our primary concerns. In other words, you would be concerned primarily with the aesthetics of color—whether, for example, subtle greens and reds would harmonize (concern with hue), or whether you would like to have a stronger, more intense color instead of a pastel tone (concern with saturation). The lightness or darkness of the color (brightness) would, in this case, be relatively incidental.

The recognition and application of color harmony cannot be explained in a short paragraph. They need experience, practice, sensitivity, and taste. But there is one very general way of dealing with *color harmony* and *color balance* that may be of help to you. Rather than trying to say which colors go with what other colors, let us simply classify them in two main groups: (1) *high-energy* colors and (2) *low-energy* colors. The high-energy group includes basic, bright, highly saturated hues, such as red, yellow, orange, green, and a warm blue. The low-energy colors are more subtle hues with a low degree of saturation, such as the pastel colors, or the browns, dark greens, purples, and bluish grays.

To achieve balance, you can set a high-energy color against another high-energy color, so that they achieve equal graphic weight (such as yellow and red stripes), surround a high-energy color with a larger low-energy color area (such as a red dot on a dark gray ground), set off a small high-energy color area with a large low-energy color area (such as a subdued green area extending over most of the screen and a narrow red area filling the rest of it), or use two low-energy colors of similar graphic weight (such as a wide horizontal stripe of brown covering the bottom third of the screen, with a subdued blue covering the top two-thirds). One of the easiest ways to achieve balance is to use a low-energy

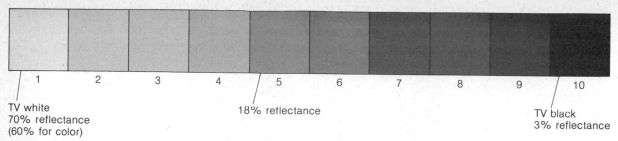

1   2   3   4   5   6   7   8   9   10

TV white
70% reflectance
(60% for color)

18% reflectance

TV black
3% reflectance

14.21   Ten-Step Grayscale   In the ten-step grayscale, the brightness range from the brightest point (TV white) to the darkest point (TV black) is divided into ten steps. Because it takes relatively little reflected light to produce a dark gray or even a medium gray on the television monitor (approximately the middle of the grayscale), step five on a ten-step grayscale, or step four on a seven-step grayscale, does not coincide with the middle of the light reflectance range (50 percent). In fact, a color with a reflectance of 50 percent is in the upper ranges of the grayscale, and actually registers as step two on the ten-step grayscale. A color that reproduces under normal circumstances in the middle ranges of a grayscale usually measures only about 18 percent reflectance. Because on the color receiver, white is actually a combination of red, green, and blue (additive mixing), TV white has only a 60 percent reflectance.

color background, with the foreground design in high-energy colors.[2]

Despite constant improvements being made in the camera pickup devices, highly saturated colors—such as the color *red*—still give the color camera trouble. As mentioned in Chapter 2, a highly saturated warm red is not handled very well by the Plumbicon pickup tube. Although it can reproduce the hue quite accurately, the whole electronic system seems to rebel against red, producing excessive noise and occasional "bleeding" (the color extending into other colors, just as in audio where one sound track bleeds into another). It may, therefore, be a good idea to stay away from saturated reds, especially in EFP, where you generally work with less than top-of-the-line equipment.

Another problem is the **moiré effect,** which shows up as color vibrations. This problem usually occurs when the camera looks at anything containing narrow, highly contrasting stripes, such as a thinly striped tie, striped dress, or herringbone jacket. When this pattern coincides in a certain way with the scan-

ning, various colors start to appear and later vibrate on the pattern. Although such *moiré* patterns may be an exciting special effect in a dance number, for example, they are disturbing on a straight title card or the dress of a newscaster, for example. Therefore, try to stay away from any contrasting texture, such as stripes or checkerboard patterns. They are visually jarring.

The monochrome (meaning "one color"—black and white) camera and receiver are insensitive to hue and largely insensitive to saturation. All they show you of a variety of colors is their relative *brightness*. Monochrome cameras and receivers are color blind; they translate every color they see into shades of gray. When you design graphics in color, do not just be concerned with the combination of hue and the degree of saturation, but pay special heed to whether or not the colors differ enough in brightness so that they show up as different grays on the monochrome receiver. This translation of color into grays is called **color compatibility.**

As long as there are monochrome receivers in use, you must consider the problem of color compatibility. To achieve a color design that has enough brightness contrast for good compatibility is not always an easy job. Even if you select colors that

[2]Herbert Zettl, *Sight-Sound-Motion* (Belmont, Calif.: Wadsworth Publishing Co., 1973), pp. 94–96.

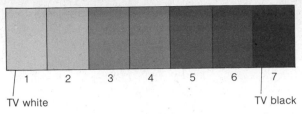

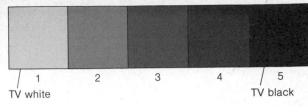

14.22 Seven-Step Grayscale Most good television systems reproduce only seven distinct steps of gray between TV white and TV black. The seven-step grayscale is, therefore, often preferred as the more realistic guide to color compatibility than the ten-step grayscale.

14.23 Five-Step Grayscale Many production people work on the assumption that most television receivers reproduce only five steps of gray, especially when reproducing a color show in black and white. They use the five-step grayscale as a standard for graphic art.

have various degrees of brightness, intense light levels may wash out all but the most extreme brightness contrasts. If a dark color (low degree of brightness) is illuminated by a large amount of light, it may show up a lighter gray on the monochrome receiver than a light color that is in a shadow area.

The surest way to determine whether you have enough brightness contrast in a color scene—that is, whether a color scheme is compatible—is to watch the scene on the monochrome monitor. If the picture looks sharp, if it has "snap," the colors are all right. If it looks washed out, lacking proper contrasts, the colors are not compatible. Often it is enough just to put a few color swatches in front of the camera under normal lighting conditions to see how they register on the grayscale. In fact, with a little experience you will find that just by squinting your eyes you can determine fairly well whether two colors have enough brightness contrast to ensure compatibility.

Experienced scenic and graphic artists often devise highly compatible color schemes without ever consciously checking relative brightness. A good painter usually juxtaposes colors that differ not only in hue but in brightness. You might want to look up some high-quality monochrome reproductions of famous paintings to see how "compatible" the color schemes are. (See Color Plates I and II.)

Grayscale The brightness of a color is usually measured by how much light it reflects. We have already talked about reflectance percentages in our discussion on lighting (Chapter 7). The television system

is not capable of reproducing pure white (100 percent reflectance) or pure **black** (0 percent reflectance); at best, it can reproduce an off-white (about 70 percent for monochrome television, and only about 60 percent for color), and an off-black (about 3 percent reflectance). We call these brightness extremes "TV white" and "TV black." If you now divide the brightness range between TV white and TV black into distinct steps, you have the television **grayscale.**

The most common number of brightness steps in a grayscale is ten (see 14.21). However, the system can reproduce all ten steps only under the most ideal conditions. A grayscale of seven steps is more realistic for monochrome television (see 14.22), and you may find that many color shows translate into only five (see 14.23). Just think if you had only five tubes of different grays to paint every conceivable scene on the television screen. This is the brightness limitation of most monochrome television.

In all areas of design for the color camera, a two-step brightness difference between two colors (such as the background color and the foreground color) when properly lighted is considered a minimum spread.

Style Style, like language, is a living thing. It changes according to the specific aesthetic demands of the people at a given location and time. To ignore it means to communicate less effectively. You learn style not from a book but primarily through being sensitive to your environment, by experiencing life with open eyes and ears, and especially an open heart. Some people not only sense the general style

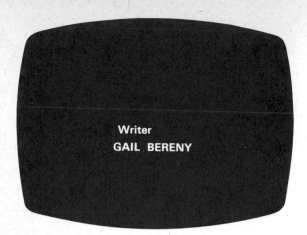

14.24 Key, or Super, Card A key, or super, card generally has white lettering on a black background. During the key or super operation, the black background drops out and lets the second video source show through.

that prevails at a given time, but manage to enhance it with a personal, distinctive mark.

Sometimes, it is the development of television equipment that influences presentation styles more than personal creativity or social need. As pointed out repeatedly in Chapter 13, the digital video effects equipment contributed not only to a new graphic awareness, but also to an abuse of the available graphic resources. Often, animated titles are generated simply because it is fun to see letters dance on the screen, rather than to express the nature of the show. Although flashy graphics in news may be tolerated because they express and intensify the urgency of the messages, they are out of place for shows that try to explore a quiet and deep relationship between two people in a television play. Whether or not you are style-setter, you should try to match the style of the artwork with the style of the entire show. But do not go overboard on style and identify your guest from China with Chinese lettering and your news story about the downtown fire with flaming letters. Do not abandon good taste for effect.

Types of Camera Graphics

Camera graphics includes all graphic material prepared for a television camera. The video image is created by the television camera (studio, ENG, or telecine camera) focused on the graphic material, such as a studio card or chart.

The major types of camera graphics include (1) the plain title card, (2) the key, or super, card, (3) the chroma key card, (4) the slide, (5) the mechanical crawl, and (6) maps and charts.

The Plain Title Card   The plain **title card** has simple information, such as the title of the show or the names of performers, writers, producer and director, printed on a plain colored (or gray) background. The plain title card is shot by the camera and displayed on the screen. It is generally not combined with any other video source (such as a live background scene or a chroma key background), but it may have some artwork drawn on the card in addition to the lettering (see 14.17).

Like all other camera graphics, the plain title card can be further enhanced and manipulated through electronic effects.

The Key, or Super, Card   The **key,** or **super, card** is usually a black card containing white lettering. During a super or key, the black background drops out, revealing the background scene over which the white letters appear (see 14.24). Because this title is combined with another video source, the background scene, the information given on the super card should be as terse as possible. Use simple, bold letters only, and try to restrict the amount of information. If the special effects on the switcher allow a matte key, you can then fill in the letters with various shades of gray or various colors.

If you want to identify a guest by keying a name over his or her picture on the screen, make sure that the super does not cut across the face (see 14.25). The viewer is interested in getting to know the guest on the screen as well as possible. Besides defeating this goal, covering someone's face with writing seems rather impolite. To avoid this problem, put the name of the guest, or any other super identification, as close to the lower edge of the essential area as possible. The camera operator will be able to frame the super in the lower part (lower third) of the viewfinder, thus placing identification on the guest's chest rather than his or her face (assuming you are on a medium shot).

CHARLES RILEY

CHARLES RILEY

a

b

14.25   Key Card with Name Identification If you super a name over a medium shot of a person, keep the lettering as close to the bottom edge of the essential area as possible (a). During the super, the name will then cut across the person's chest rather than his or her face (b).

The Chroma Key Card The **chroma key card** is much like the regular super card, except that the background for the white lettering is blue instead of black. Instead of supering the card or keying it in monochrome fashion (black will drop out) over the background scene, you key the lettering into the background scene through the *chroma key process.* Because blue drops out during the keying, only the letters remain. But chroma key cards also consist of various colored backgrounds with one or two words and a simple design placed in the upper right- or lefthand corner of the essential area. If slides are not available, such cards are used as background for news stories; matted into the news set, they provide an immediate visual identification of the story underway. More often, they are photographed and used as slides so that the change from one chroma key background to the next can be accomplished smoothly, without tying up a camera on the floor.

The Slide Slides are often more advantageous than studio cards because they do not tie up a studio camera and are not difficult to change on the air. As pointed out before, all pertinent information must be kept within the essential area, because the tele- cine camera cannot adjust for wider copy.

Because the lamps in television slide projectors are usually hot, and the alignment of the slides rel- ative to the multiplexer is quite critical, all slides should be mounted in one of the commercially available stiff plastic slide mounts. However, you can use the regular paper-mounted slides, if you do not leave them exposed to the hot projector lamp for too long. But with paper-mounted slides, you always run the risk of having the slide buckle under the heat and go out of focus.

The Mechanical Crawl The mechanical **crawl** con- sists of a large drum that can be turned either by hand or, more commonly, by an electric motor with adjustable speed. You can then letter the credits on a long piece of black paper and attach it to the crawl drum. When the drum is turning, the written infor- mation seems to roll up the screen in one contin- uous motion. This means that the drum must rotate away from the camera, not toward it.

The dimensions of the crawl differ widely, and there are no standard specifications. Its length depends on the amount of information, and its width on the width of the drum. But even with a crawl you have a scanning and essential area. Make sure, there- fore, that the credit line does not extend to the edges

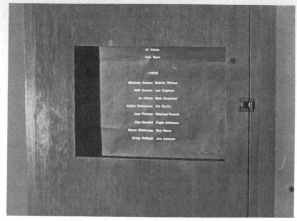

14.26 Crawl Drum and Crawl Opening, or "Window" The crawl is a strip of paper on which the long list of credits is lettered. As you rotate the drum in a direction away from the camera, the credit lines seem to move up the screen. The faster the drum rotates, the faster the lines appear.

of the crawl paper, but stays within the essential area of the crawl opening (approximately four-sevenths of the height and width of the opening). (See 14.26.)

Maps and Charts   Maps are an important visual aid for many television programs, especially newscasts. Usually, they are extremely simplified, showing only the detail that is most essential for the specific communication. For example, if you make a weather map of your area, you do not need to draw in the freeways. On the other hand, if you use the map to show the traffic patterns in the city, you need to show the major streets but not necessarily the location of parks and public buildings.

Commercially available maps are too detailed to be of much use in television. If you have to use an existing map, emphasize the major areas through bold outlines and distinctive colors. Make sure that all colors have enough brightness contrast for good black-and-white reception.

If large water areas are to be set off against land, as in a map of the San Francisco Bay Area, you have to decide whether to make the water darker or lighter than the land. The viewer may see the map in reversed polarity, which makes water areas look like land and land areas look like water. In general, making the land areas lighter ensures the correct orientation (see 14.27).

If you work in color, a fairly dark, saturated blue for the water and a light beige or green for the land will make the water lie under, rather than above, the land. Also, in monochrome reception, the water will appear dark and the land light.

We have already indicated that certain *charts* may be presented out of aspect ratio, if you intend to reveal the information gradually through a tilt or pan. In all other cases, try to contain the data in aspect ratio, so that the camera can take close-ups without losing important information.

Make sure that the charts are easy to read. Matter that gets lost in the transmission process is of no use to the home viewer. Maximum clarity—together with adherence to scanning and essential areas—should be your chief objective in preparing charts for television.

Many maps and charts can be displayed on the television screen directly through the use of graphics generators. However, they do not render the camera graphics obsolete. Maps and charts are often used with the performer who walks up to them and points out detail for the camera. Obviously this cannot be done with a generated graphic, unless you do some fancy matting.

Just make sure that in this case the graphic is large enough so that we can make out some of the detail even on a medium two-shot (the person and

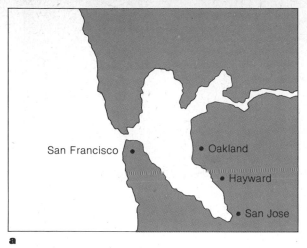
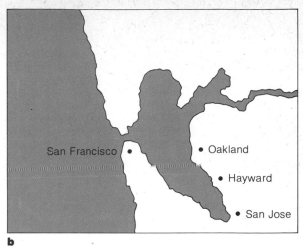

a   **b**

14.27   Polarity Reversal with Maps (a) When the water areas are lighter than the land areas, the water seems to be above the land. Therefore, the viewer may see the water and the land as exactly opposite to what they really are. (b) In order to make the land areas appear higher than the water, simply make them lighter in color (or brightness).

the map). Also, try to arrange the important detail in such a way that it can be easily framed by the camera and so that the close-up shot is within the 3 × 4 aspect ratio (see 14.7).

Operation of Camera Graphics

Studio cards are put on studio easels for easy camera pickup. You need at least two easels per studio so that you can cut from card to card. You can also change the cards on a single easel, either by flipping or pulling one after the other. Such "hot" flips or pulls, however, need practice so that they look smooth on the air. Although you should flip the cards as fast as you can, you should realize that a neat, slow flip looks better than a fast, sloppy one.

Always *bring the easel to the camera,* not the reverse. When placing the easel, make sure that it is square with the camera. Otherwise, the title looks as if it is running uphill or downhill on the screen. If the lettering runs uphill (high on the right), rotate the easel clockwise (see 14.28). If the lettering runs downhill (high on the left), rotate the easel counterclockwise (see 14.29).

When using charts, try to make them look attractive and place them so that the cameras *and* the performers can get to them easily. Fasten them securely to the easel so they do not fall off, even if someone bumps into them. Have a pointer ready; do not let the performers point to the chart with their fingers. If you have several on-camera charts on an easel, provide some mechanism for the talent to remove and put down the charts without having to stoop out of camera range.

When using title cards or charts in the field (during EFP or big remotes), beware of the ever-present wind. Use spring clamps or clothespins to fasten the studio cards to the easel, and sandbag the easel or tie it down with tent pegs. There are many tragicomic stories about easels being blown over and flying away just when the graphics camera was punched up on the air.

Try to avoid hot flips when in the field. If you have to do hot card flips, attach masking tape tabs on each card so that you can hold the rest of the cards while pulling the top card off the pile. As part of their standard equipment, big remote trucks usually have a character generator, which makes the whole graphics operation much less hazardous.

14.28 Copy Running Uphill (Keystoned) If the lettering is high on the right, or keystoned left, rotate the easel clockwise.

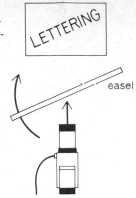

14.29 Copy Running Downhill (Keystoned) If the lettering is high on the left, or keystoned right, rotate the easel counterclockwise.

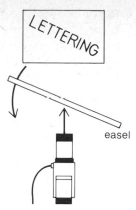

Generated Graphics

The advantage of electronically **generated graphics** is that they can be directly integrated into the television system. Generated graphics eliminate the often time-consuming intermediate steps of preparing a camera graphic and using a camera to change the graphic into appropriate video signals.

We will briefly discuss three devices: (1) character generator, (2) graphics generator, and (3) digital still store system.

Character Generator
The **character generator** looks and works like a typewriter, except that it writes letters and numbers on a television screen instead of paper. This titling device has all but replaced the conventional studio card titles, and has become an important production factor. For example, the person who operates the character generator often sits right next to the T.D. or director in the studio control room or the control room in a large remote truck in order to access on cue any one of the stored titles or produce new ones whenever necessary.

The more sophisticated character generators can produce letters of various sizes and fonts, and simple graphic displays such as sales curves or bars that show percentages. The letters as well as the background can be colorized with different hues and degrees of saturation.

All character generators are relatives of the computer word processor, except that their software is designed to generate a variety of graphics especially suited for the television screen. To prepare the titles or graphs, you enter the needed information on a computerlike keyboard. You can then either integrate the information directly into the program in progress, or store it for later use. When the information is stored in the computer memory (random access memory, or RAM), each title has a specific address (electronic page number) for easy and fast recall (see 14.30).

Most character generators have two output channels, one for preview and one for program. You use the preview channel for composing titles, and the program channel for integrating the titles with the major program material. The preview channel has a **cursor** (location indicator) that shows you where on the screen the word or sentence will appear. By moving the cursor into various positions, you can center the information, or move it anywhere on the screen. Various controls allow you to make certain words flash, to roll the whole copy up and down the screen, or to make it crawl sideways.

Although you have just learned that a crawl is copy moving up on the screen by means of a rotating drum, you must now modify this terminology somewhat when using a character generator. In this context a **crawl** means moving the lines *sideways* on the screen; an *up or down* movement is called a **roll**.

Graphics Generator With **graphics generators,** you can literally draw images on the screen. Thus, these systems are also called "video art" systems. Again, though the instruments are technically quite complicated, the operation of a graphics generator is relatively simple. Most models have few buttons or keys. You simply draw onto an electronic tablet, which looks like a sketch pad, with an electronic stylus, which again looks like a drawing pen, except that it has a wire coming out of its top. One monitor immediately reflects your artistic efforts, and the other offers a series of design options (such as color, thickness of line, styles of letters, or special effects) to improve your masterpiece. For example, if you prefer a different color from the one used, you simply touch the name of the new color as written out on the "menu" monitor, and your pen will draw in the new color. No messy inks or paints to worry about (see 14.31).

Other systems allow you to draw directly on the television screen. You can treat foreground images and background images separately, and even reposition them separately. Or you can select from a menu of standard symbols such as a cartoonlike person, stars, or dots, and animate them through a touch of the light pen. When finished, you can store your masterpiece in the computer memory (RAM) or on a disc, or integrate it live into the ongoing program video.

One word of caution is necessary concerning RAM, which is part of character and graphics generators as well as computer-assisted editing systems. This is a *temporary memory,* which forgets *everything* as soon as you turn off the electricity. If there is a power outage, or if someone accidentally unplugs the cord or turns off the power switch on the character or graphics generator, your art is lost and you have to start all over again—unless you transferred the RAM information onto a floppy disc earlier. If you preprogram a great amount of graphics, do not wait until you are finished to transfer. Periodically transfer your generated graphics (actually digital information) onto the floppy disc for safekeeping. Also, keep an entire electrical circuit (which may have several outlets) free for the computer-assisted equipment. This way, you will be sure that

14.30 Character Generator A character generator produces a variety of letters electronically. They can be stored and recalled at any time for a key or matte key. The lines can be moved right or left on the screen, rolled up or down, or crawled sideways.

nobody will overload this circuit and accidentally erase the computer memory.

Some graphics-generating systems have hardcopy printers, which can make a print-out of your art so that you can present it in a production meeting, or save it for posterity.

Digital Still Store System As a graphics *storage* system, rather than a graphics-generating system, the **digital still frame storage** devices play an important part in electronic graphics.

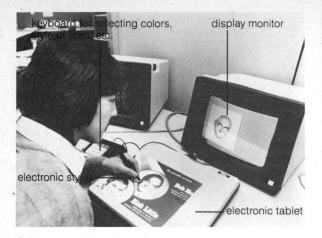

keyboard for selecting colors,
style of lines, etc.

display monitor

electronic stylus

electronic tablet

a

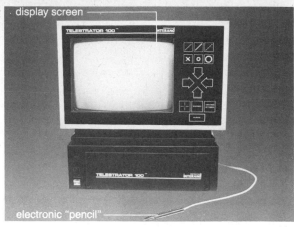

display screen

electronic "pencil"

b

14.31 Graphics Generator and Video Animation System (a) With an electronic stylus and tablet, a picture can be traced and transposed into a television image. The graphic art can then be computer-stored and accessed through the switcher at any time (Norpak IPS—2 Telidon Videotex System). (b) Through this Telestrator Video Animation System (Interand Corp.), you can draw and write letters and numbers in any size or shape to an existing television image. This system is often called an electronic blackboard.

The still store device—sometimes called ESS, or electronic still store system—can grab any frame from any video source (camera, videotape, film, slide) and store it in digital form on a disc. Some of the larger systems can store on their disc packs almost 80,000 stills, with immediate access to over 2,000 at any time (see 14.32). In effect, such a system is a large slide collection that allows you to access any one of the slides within about a tenth of a second. If the stills are taken from an actual sequence, you can play back the sequence in slow or fast motion, or real time (over a minute of real-time action).

Each still has its own address (house number) and can, therefore, be called up rather easily by the T.D., the master control operator, or the master control computer. This is how the name and vital statistics of a football or baseball player can be displayed on the television screen so readily and quickly. As with all computer discs, the still store disc packs must be kept meticulously clean. They are sensitive to dust and even smoke. On one of those days when everything goes wrong, the entire system can be put out of commission by a heavily smoking technician.

SCENERY

Television scenery consists of the *three-dimensional* aspects of design that are used in the studio. Its principal function is to create a specific environment—a faithful re-creation of a Victorian living room for a dramatic scene, a somewhat stylized workroom for a news show, a simple definition of space through pillars and sculptures for a modern dance number. Whatever the purpose, television scenery should allow for optimum camera movement and camera angles, microphone placement and boom movement, appropriate lighting, and maximum action by the performers and actors.

Because the television camera looks at a **set** both at close range and at a distance, scenery must be detailed enough to appear realistic yet plain enough to prevent cluttered, busy pictures. Also, because the camera, not the studio spectator, looks at the set, the scenery does not have to be continuous. One part of the set—for example, the main entrance of a house—may be in one corner of the studio, and another part—say the hallway—in another corner. The location of these portions depends entirely on the shooting sequence and on the director's camera placement.

Fortunately, the relative mobility of the television camera has made the building of elaborate sets largely unnecessary, at least in small station operation. If you need to shoot inside an elaborate Victorian parlor or outside at the drugstore corner, go there. Take the cameras to the location; do not try to bring the location into the studio.

Contrary to film, where the environment is an important dramatic agent, television's primary dramatic material or focus of attention is the human being. In general, the scenic environment, though important, remains secondary.

Nevertheless, all human actions take place in some sort of environment. The empty studio is rarely the most appropriate, or the most pleasing, one for human interaction. Even if you are seldom, if ever, called upon to design or construct elaborate scenery, you should nevertheless know the elements of this calling. The knowledge will aid you in managing the studio space, as well as screen space in general. The basic elements are (1) scene design, (2) types of scenery, and (3) properties and set dressings. How some of these elements are used and combined will be discussed in Section Two of this chapter.

14.32　Still Store System The still store system can grab a frame from any video source and store it in digital form on one of the discs of the disc pack. A large still store system can store almost 80,000 "electronic slides" (still frames) and let you access any one of them in less than a half second (usually only a tenth of a second).

Scene Design

Before you design a set, you must know what the show is all about. Talk to the director about his or her concept of the show, even if it is a simple interview. Arrive at a set by defining the necessary spatial environment for optimal communication rather than by inquiring what other stations are doing. For example, you may feel that the best way to inform viewers is not by having an authoritative newscaster read stories from a pulpitlike contraption, but instead by moving the cameras into the newsroom itself and out into the street where events are happening. If the interviewer is probing the guest's attitudes and feelings, you do not need a whole living room as a set. Two comfortable chairs in front of a plain back-

ground may make the scene complete. In any case, before deciding on a set, try to see the entire show in *screen images*. Try to imagine those you would like the viewers to see and work backward from there.

For example: "If in an interview I would like the viewer to see intimate close-ups throughout the show, what set do I need?"

"Two chairs."

Types of Scenery

If you are a member of the floor crew, or if you want to communicate intelligently with the scene designer, you should know the basic types of scenery and their primary functions. The construction of scenery for small stations is usually done by professional stage carpenters or similarly qualified personnel. In colleges, universities, and high schools, scenery is usually built by the theater department. The materials and techniques vary widely and depend almost entirely on the purpose of the show. Sometimes, the scenery must represent as real a setting as pos-

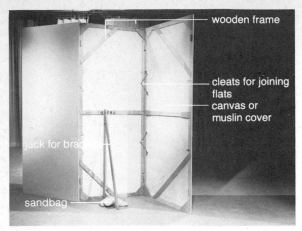

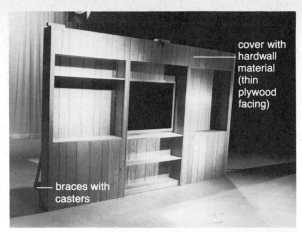

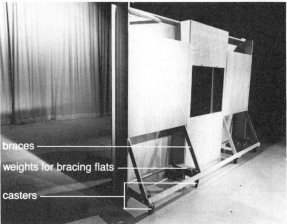

14.33 Softwall and Hardwall Scenery
The *softwall flat* consists of a wooden frame, a muslin or canvas cover, and some scenery "hardware," which are hinges and cleats with which the flats can be joined and braced.

The *hardwall flat* has a stronger wooden frame and is covered with hardwall material (plywood, Masonite, or other pressboard). It is usually bolted or C-clamped to the other scenic units.

sible; at other times, the set is purposely stylized, serving more of a decorative function. The most flexible scenery consists of neutral set units that can be decorated in a variety of ways.

We can divide scenery into four major groups: (1) standard set units, (2) hanging units, (3) platforms, and (4) set pieces.

Standard Set Units   Standard **set units** consist of softwall and hardwall *flats,* and a variety of *set modules*. Both are used to simulate interior or exterior walls.

Flats are background units, constructed of a lightweight wood frame and covered with muslin or canvas (softwall flats), or some kind of pressed fiberboard, Styrofoam board, or plywood (hardwall flats). The flats for standard set units have a uniform height, yet various widths. The height is usually 10 feet (approximately 3 meters), and 8 feet (approximately 2.50 meters) for small sets or studios with low ceilings. The widths range from 1 to 5 feet (30 centimeters to 1.50 meters). When two or three flats are hinged together, they are called **twofolds** or **threefolds.**

The *softwall flats* are easy to handle, assemble, and brace. However, because they are quite light and flimsy, they often shake when somebody closes a door or window on the set, or if somebody or some equipment brushes against them. They are ideal for rehearsal and for less demanding productions. Also, they can be easily stored, which is a big consideration when building standard set units.

The *hardwall flats* are much sturdier than soft-

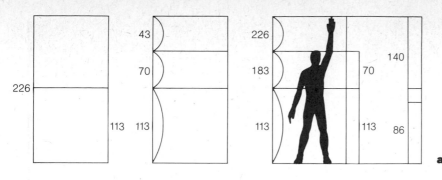

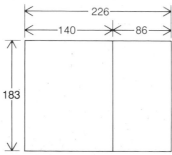

14.34 Le Corbusier Module (a) One famous module was designed by the Swiss-French architect Le Corbusier. His *Modulor* consists of a set of proportions that are modeled after the basic proportions of the human figure. All dimensions are in centimeters. You may want to try to use these dimensions for your scenery modules. (b) Sets constructed from modular units.

b

wall flats and preferred for most television productions. Hardwall units are generally built for a specific set and do not always conform to the standard set dimensions of the softwall scenery. The problem with hardwall scenery is that the flats are quite heavy and difficult to store. (In the interest of your, and the flat's, health, do not try to move hardwall scenery by yourself.) Also, hardwall flats sometimes reflect sound to such an extent that they interfere with good audio pickup. (See 14.33.)

Flats are supported by *jacks,* wooden braces that are hinged to the flats and are weighted down and held to the studio floor by sandbags or metal weights.

For small station operation, where you do not have the luxury of building new sets for every show, you may consider the use of set modules that can be used in a variety of configurations. A **set module** is a series of flats and three-dimensional set pieces whose dimensions match whether they are used vertically (right-side up) or horizontally (on their sides) (see 14.34). Many architects work with such

14.35   Muslin Cyc This muslin cyc runs on overhead tracks and can be moved like a draw curtain. It covers three sides of the studio and provides a smooth, neutral background for a variety of productions. Open-set designs, for example, depend on a good cyclorama (see Section Two of this chapter).

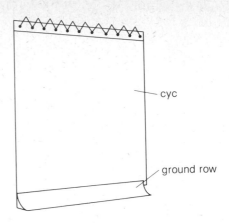

14.36   Ground Row A ground row is put along the bottom of a cyc to make the cyc blend into the studio floor.

modules, especially in large structures, where prefabrication is an essential building factor. The plastic, stick-together building blocks for children also have a modular design. A variety of set modules are commercially available (see 14.34b).

Hanging Units   Whereas flats stand on the studio floor, hanging units are supported from special tracks, the lighting grid, or lighting battens. They include (1) the cyc, (2) drops, and (3) drapes and curtains.

The most versatile hanging background is a *cyclorama,* or *cyc,* a continuous piece of muslin or canvas stretched along two, three, and sometimes even all four studio walls. Some cycs have a scrim (loosely woven material) stretched in front of them to break the light before it hits the cyc, producing a soft, uniform background (see 14.35). Most studios use a *ground row* to blend the bottom edge of the cyc into the studio floor (see 14.36). Some studios have *hardwall cycs,* which are not actually hanging units, but are built solidly onto the studio floor (see 14.37).

A **drop** is a wide roll of canvas with a background scene painted on it. It commonly serves styl-

ized settings, where the viewer is very much aware that the action is taking place in front of a drop. Some drops consist of large photomurals (which are commercially available) for more realistic background effects.

A **chroma key drop** is a wide roll of chroma key blue that can be pulled down and even stretched over part of the studio floor for chroma key matting.

You can make a simple and inexpensive drop by suspending a roll of *seamless paper* (9 feet wide and 36 feet long), which comes in a great variety of colors. You can use the seamless paper to make a **limbo** (plain) background, or you can paint on it or use it as a background for cookie projections. Hanging from a row of flats, seamless paper provides a continuous cyclike background. You simply roll it sideways and staple it at the top edge to the flats (see 14.38).

When choosing *drapes,* stay away from overly detailed patterns or fine stripes. Drapes are usually stapled to 1 × 3 battens and hung from the top of the flats. Most *curtains* should be translucent enough to let the back light come through without revealing scenic pieces that may be in back of the set.

Platforms The various types of platforms are elevation devices. The normal platforms are 6 or 12 inches high and can be stacked. Sometimes, the whole platform is called a **riser,** although technically a riser is only the elevation part of the platform without its (often removable) top. If you use a platform for interviews, for example, you may want to cover it entirely with carpet pieces. This cover will not only look good on camera, but also absorb the hollow sounds when somebody is moving about the platform.

Some of the 6-inch platforms have four casters so that they can be moved around. Such platforms are called **wagons.** You can mount a portion, or even a whole set, on a series of wagons and then move it rather easily in and out of the studio. Once in place, wagons should be secured with wooden wedges and/or sandbags so that they do not move unexpectedly (see 14.39).

Larger risers and hardwall scenery are often supported by a slotted steel frame, which works like a big erector set. You can cut the various slotted steel pieces to any length and bolt them together in any configuration. The advantages of slotted steel are that it is durable and relatively light, and it allows easy dismantling of scenic pieces.

Set Pieces Set pieces are an important scenic element. They consist of freestanding three-dimensional objects, such as pillars, **pylons** (which look like three-sided pillars), **sweeps** (curved pieces of scenery), folding screens, steps, and periaktoi (see 14.40). A **periaktos** is a large three-sided standing unit that looks like a large pylon. It moves and swivels on casters. Most periaktoi are painted differently on each of the three sides to allow quick scene changes. For example, if one of the sides of a periaktos is painted a warm yellow, and the other a chroma key blue, you can change the neutral yellow background to any scene by swiveling the periaktos (or series of periaktoi) to the chroma blue side while chroma keying a specific background scene.

Whenever you work with scenery, make sure that all the pieces are safely anchored and secured so that they do not tip over when bumped by performers or equipment. It is always better to over-

14.37   Hardwall Cyc A hardwall cyc usually takes up one or two sides of the studio. It is made out of hardwall material with an extremely smooth surface covering. The ground row is part of the cyc.

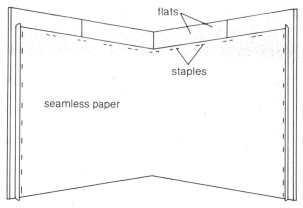

14.38   Seamless Paper Backdrop A seamless paper roll makes an excellent backdrop for a limited set area. You can use it as a plain backdrop, or paint it or texture it with cookie projections.

14.39 Platforms and Wagons Platforms are usually 6 inches or 12 inches high, although they can be made in any height, depending on the set requirements. They often have collapsible risers and a removable plywood top. Risers, which are part of a permanent set (such as a news or interview set), are generally covered with carpet.

Wagons are small platforms (typically 6 inches high), which roll on four casters.

brace than underbrace the set. As in all other aspects of television production, do not forsake safety for convenience or speed.

Properties and Set Dressings

Properties and set dressings are essential scenic elements. In television, they often do more to signify a particular environment than the background does.

There are three basic types of properties: (1) stage properties, or props, (2) set dressings, and (3) hand props.

Stage Props   Stage **props** include the common type of furniture and items constructed for a specific purpose, such as news desks, lecterns, or panel tables.

For the normal complement of shows, you need enough furniture to create settings for a modern living room, a study, an office, or a comfortable interview area. You can use real furniture. For the interview area, small, simple chairs are more useful than large, elaborate ones. It is often difficult to bring oversized chairs close enough together for intimate spacing of the two-shot. Try to get chairs and couches that are not too low; otherwise sitting and rising gracefully may become a problem.

Stage props for special shows, such as news desks and panel tables, are specially built to fit the overall design. But make sure that these props look stylish and that they work well. Because most sets of this kind are seen in their entirety only in the opening or closing shots, the properties used in them should be functional and look appropriate on the screen in a *close-up* as well as a long shot.

Set Dressings   Set dressings are a major factor in determining the *style* and character of the set. Although the flats may remain the same from one type of show to another, the dressing gives each set its distinguishing characteristic.

Set dressings include draperies, pictures, lamps and chandeliers, fireplaces, flower pots, indoor plants, candleholders, and sculptures. Secondhand stores provide an unlimited fund for these things. In case of emergency, you can always raid your own living quarters.

Hand Properties   Hand **properties** consist of all items that are actually *handled* by the performer or actor during the show. They include dishes, silverware, ashtrays, telephones, and typewriters. In television the hand props should be *realistic*. Use only

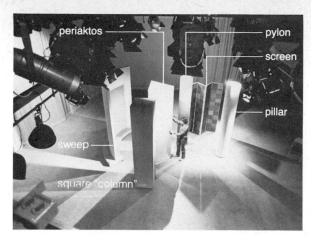

14.40   Set Pieces Set pieces are freestanding scenic elements that divide studio space, serve as backgrounds for limited set areas or foreground pieces, or signal the outer limits of a set.

and that they are actually available (this prop list is for the set on p. 439; see 14.59).

Most smaller stations have a collection of standard props: ashtrays, flower vases, rubber plants, tablecloths, tables, chairs, couch, and so forth. If you do an especially ambitious production, such as a period play, you can always call on the theater arts department of the local college, high school, or university, or rent them from a commercial company.

Set Props

Stuffed chair	Small bookshelf
Desk chair	Marble fireplace
Gold couch	Hallway mirror
Oak dresser	Victorian hat tree
Brown desk	Blue Persian rug
Small end table	

real objects for hand props. The papier-mâché chalice may look regal and impressive on stage; on the television screen it looks dishonest. Television is very much dependent on human action. These actions are *extended* through the hand props. If you want the actions to be sincere and genuine, the extension of such actions—the hand props—must be real as well. If you have to use food, make sure that it is fresh, and the dishes and silverware are meticulously clean. Liquor is generally replaced by water (for clear spirits), tea (for whiskey), or soda pop (for red wine). With all due respect for realism, such substitutions are perfectly legitimate.

The most important thing about hand props is to have them actually on the set for the performer to use. They represent a major production item and are anything but incidental.

Prop List   In order to procure the various props and ensure that they are all available at the time of camera rehearsal and the taping sessions, you need to prepare a *prop list*. Some production people divide the list into stage props, set dressings, and hand props. Others combine them into a single list. Whatever you do, double-check that all the props mentioned in the script are, indeed, written on the list

Set Dressings

Large lamp	Flower picture
Pewter cup	Posters and clippings
Glass sculpture	Rubber plant
Typewriter	Books (some must be suitable for close-ups—contemporary titles)
Telephone	
File box	Pillows for chairs
Coffee maker	Small kerosene heater inside fireplace
Clock	
Fireplace tools	

Hand Props

Lots of typewriter paper	Coffee cups (2)
Calendar	Coffee (instant)
Pens and pencils	Spoons
Beer can	Sugar container with sugar
Grocery bag with real groceries (normal 1-bag shopping items)	Jar of cream substitute
Comb.	

1.   Design is an overall concept that includes such things as the lettering on the studio cards, the station logo, the looks of the news set, and even the office furniture.

2.   The two major aspects of design are graphics and scenery.

3.   Television graphics include all two-dimensional visuals specifically prepared for the television camera, such as studio or title cards, special illustrations, maps and charts, and electronically generated titles, charts, or short animated graphic sequences.

4.   The specifications of graphics include (1) aspect ratio, (2) scanning and essential areas, (3) readability, (4) color and color compatibility, (5) grayscale, and (6) style.

5.   The television aspect ratio is 3 × 4, which means that the screen is three units high and four units wide (3 × 5 in high-definition television).

6.   The scanning area is what the camera frames and the preview monitor shows. The essential or safe title area is the portion seen by the home viewer, regardless of transmission loss or misalignment of the receiver.

7.   Good readability results when (1) the written information is within the essential area; (2) the letters are relatively large and of a clean contour; (3) the amount of information is limited; (4) the background is not too busy; and (5) there is good color and brightness contrast between the lettering and the background.

8.   Color balance can be most easily achieved by setting high-energy colors (highly saturated, bright hues) against a background of low-energy colors (more subtle hues with a lower degree of saturation).

9.   Most cameras that are less than top-of-the-line have some difficulty with highly saturated colors, especially saturated reds. The moiré effect is caused by thin, highly contrasting stripes.

10.   In order to make colors translate into effective monochrome (black-and-white) pictures, the major colors must have different brightness values.

11.   Most television systems reproduce at best ten separate steps of gray. These steps, ranging from TV white to TV black, make up the grayscale.

12.   In television design, the style of the artwork should match the style of the whole show.

13.   The major types of camera graphics include (1) the plain title card, (2) the key or super card, (3) the chroma key card, (4) the slide, (5) the mechanical crawl, and (6) maps and charts.

14.   Generated graphics means that titles and charts are electronically generated and displayed on the screen. They don't need a camera. The three principal devices for generated graphics are (1) the character generator (C.G.), (2) the graphics generator, and (3) the digital still store system.

15.   There are four general groups of scenery: (1) standard set units, that is, hardwall and softwall flats and set modules; (2) hanging units, such as the cyclorama and drops; (3) platforms; and (4) set pieces, such as pillars, screens, periaktoi.

16.   The three basic types of properties are (1) stage props, such as furniture, news desks, lecterns; (2) set dressings, such as pictures, draperies, lamps; and (3) hand props, which are items actually handled by the talent, such as dishes, telephones, typewriters.

In television design one needs an aesthetic sensibility, or an "eye," to see the stability or tension in a graphic. Just as important are a number of mechanical skills for preparing graphic materials or arranging a studio set.

In this section, we will briefly mention two important factors of pictorial balance—the tilted horizon line and graphic mass—and the major preparation steps of television graphics. Then we will describe some of the more common design problems and elements of scenic design.

BALANCE

Like any other graphic art, television graphics must exhibit both stability and tension. According to the nature of the show, the relative tension might be either low (communicating a calm feeling or stability) or high (excitement, agitation). The interrelationship of stability and tension in a nonanimated title (where nothing moves) is called **balance.** Balance depends on many visual factors, two of which seem especially pertinent to tel-

[3] For a more detailed discussion of balance, see Herbert Zettl, *Sight-Sound-Motion* (Belmont, Calif.: Wadsworth Publishing Co., 1973), pp. 150–171.

evision graphics.[3] One is the angle of the *horizon line* relative to the screen, and the other is the distribution of *graphic mass.*

Tilted Horizon Line

Whereas the lettering is generally kept parallel with the bottom or top edge of the television screen, the background may be tilted in various degrees so that its horizon line is out of whack. A tilted horizon expresses dynamism, excitement, increased energy, and tension. We are no longer standing on level ground (see 14.41 and 14.42). Equally, a level horizon line, one that is parallel with the bottom or top screen edge, suggests normalcy (see 14.43).

It is rather easy to generate excitement by using titles that are animated through special effects equipment. However, not all show themes and subjects are best expressed by animated letters that bounce and stretch and twist all over the screen. Before using animated special effects titles, always ask yourself whether or not the particular special animation or distortion effect is the best, and in your particular production situation the most efficient, way to reflect the nature of the show.

14.41 **Tilted Horizon Line** With a tilted horizon line, we assume a view different from everyday experience, thus increasing the visual energy of the scene and making it look and feel more dynamic.

14.42 **Tilted Horizon Line with Title** Though the lettering is usually kept parallel with the horizontal screen edges, and is therefore graphically stable, it does not render the background dynamism ineffective. On the contrary, the combination between foreground stability and background lability accentuates the general graphic energy of the title.

14.43 **Level Horizon Line** A horizon that is level, in this case parallel to the bottom and top edges of the screen, with the verticals perpendicular to the horizon, suggests normalcy; it makes us feel as though we were standing upright on level ground.

Graphic Mass

Balance depends also to a large degree on the distribution of **graphic mass** within the screen area. Graphic mass is any picture element that is perceived as occupying an area within the frame and as having relative weight.

A person standing in the middle of the screen is a graphic mass, as is a red dot or a title made up of successive letters. Because we have a tendency to organize our surroundings so that we can cope with them, you should cater to this predisposition by organizing letters or other visual elements into blocks. It is, after all, easier to perceive order and stability in related blocks of graphic material than in unrelated bits of graphic information that are scattered all over the screen area (see 14.44 and 14.45).

When balancing a title card, you translate all pictorial information (lettering and background images)

Balance Relative structural stability of picture elements (objects or events). Balance can be stable (little pictorial tension), neutral (some tension), or unstable (high pictorial tension). Refers to the interrelationship between stability and tension in a picture.

Floor Plan A plan of the studio floor, showing the walls, the main doors, and the location of the control room, with the lighting grid or batten pattern superimposed over the floor plan. More commonly, a diagram of scenery and properties in relation to the studio floor area.

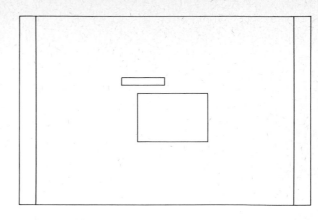

14.44 **Block Organization of Graphic Mass** By arranging the titles in blocks of graphic mass, you achieve a degree of balance appropriate for the information, and help the viewer comprehend related facts at one glance.

into blocks of graphic mass in order to achieve stable, neutral, or unstable stages of balance. In a stable balance, everything seems at rest (see 14.46). In a neutral balance, there is more tension within the screen (see 14.47). In an unstable balance, the graphic tension is purposely increased (see 14.48).

PREPARATION OF MAJOR GRAPHICS

Basic graphic arts techniques apply also to the preparation of television graphics. For graphics to come through as an intrinsic part of the television presentation, their assembling and manipulation before the cameras require skill, practice, and planning.

If you have an electronic character generator and graphics generator, the need for mechanical lettering and other camera graphics is drastically reduced. If, however, you do not enjoy such luxury, you may still have to rely on manual methods. Also, often you need to *draw* camera graphics, even if you have the electronic generators. On small remotes, or during EFP where titles need to be integrated on location, the normal studio card is still the simplest and least expensive titling device. We will, therefore, briefly look at the preparation of (1) studio cards, (2) slides, (3) crawls, and (4) maps and charts.

14.45 **Scattered Graphic Information** If the written material is not organized into distinct areas of graphic mass, the screen area looks unbalanced and the information is hard to grasp.

14.46 **Stable Balance** In a stable balance, everything in the picture seems at rest.

14.48 **Unstable Balance** In an unstable balance, the graphic tension is high. A tilted horizon line usually causes an unstable balance.

14.47 **Neutral Balance** In a neutral balance, there is tension within the frame, but the various elements neutralize the tension somewhat.

Studio Cards

Before starting with the lettering, make sure that the card has the proper outside dimensions and is cut straight and perfectly rectangular. A card whose bottom and top edges are not parallel can cause a great deal of frustration when used in the production.

Essential Area Each time you use a new card, check whether it is sturdy enough to stand securely on the easel, without danger of curling or folding up. Lay the framing guide over it and see whether the outside edges of the new card are cut straight. Then mark the scanning areas and essential areas.

If you have to work with studio cards of nonstandard dimensions (other than 11 × 14 inches or 14 × 17 inches), you need to know how to define the essential area. In this case, use the following procedure:

1. Draw both diagonals on the card (from corner to corner).
2. Measure the entire length of one of the diagonals.
3. Divide this length by 7 (see 14.49).
4. Mark off $\frac{2}{7}$ of the diagonal on either side from the midpoint (see 14.50).
5. Connect these points (see 14.51).
6. The area outlined is the *essential area* of the card.

Lettering Before starting with the actual lettering, do a rough *layout* of the titles and other visual information you want on the card. The layout shows you whether the title fits into the essential area, and whether the lettering "blocks" balance each other.

There are many *lettering methods*. Some people prefer *rub-on* or *glue-on letters*. Others use printing-

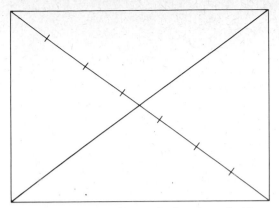

14.49 Drawing Diagonals In order to find the essential area, divide the diagonals of the studio card by 7. The metric system can help you in this endeavor, because you can measure the diagonals more accurately than with inches, and use the pocket calculator for the divisions.

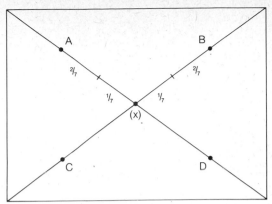

14.50 Marking Off Distance for Essential Area First, draw in the two diagonals (lightly). Then mark off $\frac{2}{7}$, starting from the midpoint (x) on each of the diagonals. The points A, B, C, and D indicate the corners of the essential area.

type devices that print the letters on strips. Usually, these machines have a variety of fonts available. *Striplettering* is convenient, because in case of a spelling mistake you simply replace a single strip instead of the whole studio card.

When rubbing or gluing on letters, pay attention to the proper spacing between letters. The various letters are not spaced according to an absolute scale (fractions of an inch), but by how we *perceive* the spacing.

The traditional **hotpress** is still an important lettering tool in many art departments. The reasons for its popularity are simplicity of operation, versatility, and quality results. Standard lead type is heated by the press (to about 250°F) and pressed upon a plastic film. The film is literally melted onto illustration board, clear **acetate cells,** or any other background material (see 14.52). A variety of colored *illustration board* is available. Make sure it has a matte surface to prevent glares.

Slides

Slides are prepared exactly like studio cards. The studio cards are then photographed. Because the scanning area for a slide is the area as approximately outlined by the standard mask, make sure that when photographing artwork, you line up the still camera near the outside edges of the studio card. This way you are

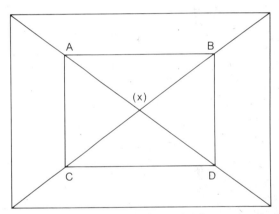

14.51 Drawing Essential Area Connecting the four points (A, B, C, D) defines the essential area of the studio card.

assured that the essential area of the slide is not too close to the slide mask (see 14.15).

A quick and simple system is to photograph the artwork with a Polaroid camera equipped with special 2 × 2 slide accessories.

If you prepare artwork for a normal super, or key, slide, print *black letters* on a *white card*. The photo-

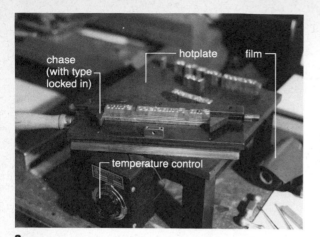

chase (with type locked in) — hotplate — film —

temperature control

a

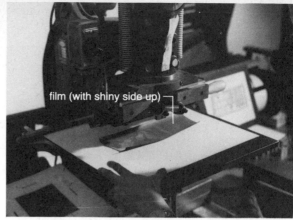

film (with shiny side up)

c

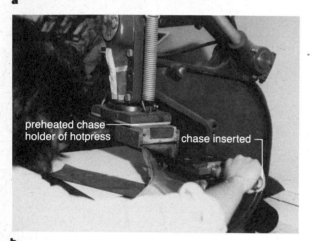

preheated chase holder of hotpress — chase inserted —

b

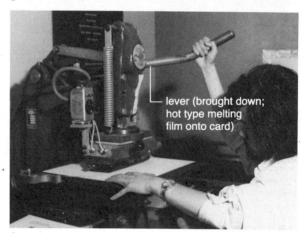

lever (brought down; hot type melting film onto card)

d

14.52 Kensole Hotpress (a) First, lock the type in mirror image into the chase and preheat the whole thing on a special hotplate to approximately 250°F. (b) Then insert the chase into the hotpress, whose head has also been preheated to the same temperature. (c) Line up the card underneath the chase and place the plastic film (which comes in a variety of colors) on it with the shiny side up. (d) Bring the lever down quickly and hold the hot type on the card very briefly. If you keep the lever down too long, the heated plastic will seep into the material and make the letters fuzzy-edged.

graphic process reverses the polarity of the artwork, and you can use the film negative with the black background and the white letters directly for the slide.

If you want to use a photograph, or a picture from a book, as a slide background, you can print the text on an acetate cell (clear plastic), put the cell on top of the background picture, and photograph both together. Make sure that the cell lies flat on the artwork and that it does not reflect any of the photo floods when you take a picture of the composite (background card and cell overlay). Watch for the proper balance between

foreground titles and background scene, and for proper brightness difference between the two. Most importantly, double-check to see whether the title lies within the essential area. Assuming you are using a regular studio card for the slide artwork, simply put the frame guide over the title card you are about to photograph.

Crawls

When preparing a crawl, first check the width of the crawl drum. A strip cannot be wider than the drum, or smaller than the crawl window (the opening in the crawl). When doing the layout, see to it that the longest credit line is shorter than the crawl window. You may find it convenient to take the dimensions of the window as the scanning area, and then figure the essential area from there. Measure the diagonal of the window and divide by 7. If you mark off $\frac{1}{7}$ on the diagonal, starting at one of the window corners, you have the approximate essential area (see 14.53).

Use lettering strips for the crawl. It is much easier to replace one strip than redo the whole crawl. Also, you can rearrange the strip quite easily in order to accommodate additional credit lines. Many printing machines produce black strips (with white letters on them for keying) that have white edges. These edges show up during the keying as thin, white, vibrating lines. Using a permanent marker felt pen, paint all white edges black.

Maps and Charts

The most important factor in preparing maps and charts is that they *show the essential information*. Maps and charts are used to supply information, not decorate the set. Emphasize the brightness difference in the color scheme so the chart and map can also be read well on black-and-white television sets. Outline in a contrasting color the various map areas so they can be read easily on the home receiver. Put all charts and maps in a place where cameras and talent can easily reach them, and fasten them securely to the easel so that they do not tip over. Watch for distracting shadows, especially when the talent and camera are near the map or chart.

One final word on graphics concerns *copyright.* Whenever you present printed material, including reproductions of famous paintings, professional photographs, illustrated books, and similar matter, you must obtain permission from the copyright holders.

SET DESIGN PROBLEMS

Some of the recurring design problems concern (1) set background unity and variety, (2) camera height, and (3) studio floor treatment.

Set Background

The set background is an important scenic element. It not only helps to *unify* a sequence of shots and place

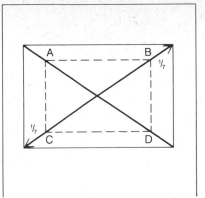

14.53   Essential Area in Mechanical Crawl To find the essential area in the window of a mechanical crawl, measure the diagonal of the window and divide it by 7. Then mark off $\frac{1}{7}$ of the diagonal, starting at each window corner. Points *A, B, C,* and *D* define the approximate essential area of the crawl.

the action in a single environment, but also provides necessary *variety.*

Unification of shots can be achieved through keeping the background in a *uniform color,* or by decorating it in such a way that the viewer can easily relate one portion of the set to another. Because in television we see mostly *environmental detail,* you must give viewers clues so that they can apply closure to the shot details and achieve, at least in their mind, a continuous environment. A uniform background color or design, or properties that point to a single environment, such as the typical furnishings of a kitchen—all help viewers relate the various shots to a specific location. The *variety* is achieved by breaking up large background areas into smaller, yet related areas. For instance, hanging pictures on a plain wall is a simple, effective method for background variety. However, make sure that such design elements are indeed in the view of most camera shots (see 14.54 and 14.56). As so often happens, pictures are hung the way we expect them to appear in a living room, for example, rather than in range of the camera shot (see 14.55).

Camera Height

Some camera operators adjust their cameras to the most comfortable working height, not necessarily to the most effective aesthetic point of view. Therefore, if you place persons in normal chairs on the studio floor, they are positioned lower than the average camera

14.54 Background for Long Shot This set designer provided proper background variety for the long shot only. The picture between the two people breaks up the center of the picture reasonably well and provides some visual interest for an otherwise dull shot.

14.55 Background Variety Missing in Close-up But on a close-up of the guest—the most frequent shot in the show—we have no background variety. The same is true in a close-up shot of the host.

working height; the camera looks down on them. This point of view carries subtle psychological implications of inferiority and also creates an unpleasant composition. You might do well, therefore, for any event where the performers are sitting most of the time, to place the chairs on a platform (anywhere from 6 to 12 inches high). Thus, the camera can remain at a comfortable operating height, shooting at the scene at eye level (see 14.57).

Studio Floor Treatment

One of the headaches of the scenic designer is the treatment of the studio floor. In long shots, it usually looks unattractive, as though the designer got tired of his or her idea before reaching the bottom of the picture.

The problems with decorating the studio floor are that the adornment must not interfere with camera and boom travel, and it must be easily removable once the show is over. The most popular floor treatments include (1) rugs and mats, (2) rubber tile, (3) glue-on strips, (4) paint, and (5) tanbark and sand.

Rugs and Mats Rugs are an excellent and realistic floor treatment. Unfortunately, they often get in the way of cameras and booms. When using a rug, tape its edges into place so that the camera can travel onto it

without bunching the rug under its dolly wheels or pedestal skirt. The same goes for grass mats. Secure them with green tape so they do not slip on the smooth studio floor. Usually, the rug is placed first so that the scenery and props can be put on portions of the rug, if necessary.

Rubber Tile Flexible rubber tile, which you can get in large (3 × 3 foot, or roughly 1 × 1 meter) squares of contrasting colors (usually off-white and off-black) make excellent floor patterns for dance sets, large halls, or hallways. You simply lay it on the studio floor in the desired pattern, and the natural adhesion keeps the tiles in place. Just for good measure, tape the outer edges to the studio floor so the camera travel does not move them about.

Glue-on Strips An excellent floor treatment technique is to use glue-on strips. These come in different patterns and have a removable backing like shelf paper. You can glue them securely onto the studio floor side by side, and remove them just as easily. Cameras and booms have no travel restrictions. Unfortunately, these glue-on patterns are quite expensive, and used only for especially important sets.

Paint Some set designers prefer to paint the studio floor with water soluble paint. However, most paints that stay on through rehearsals and the videotaping are

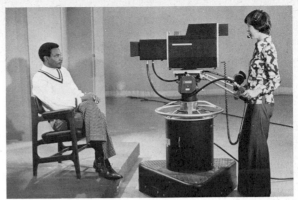

14.57 Compensating with Platform for Camera Height To avoid looking down at persons who are seated, place the chairs on a platform. The cameras can operate at a comfortable working height and yet shoot the scene from eye level.

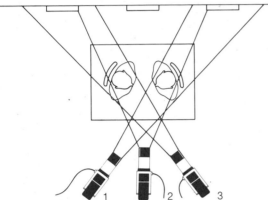

14.56 Proper Background for Close-up Now the picture is properly hung for background variety, although you would ordinarily not hang a picture in this position.

hard to remove and usually leave some residue on the studio floor.

Tanbark and Sand In order to simulate outdoor conditions, you can spread a layer of tanbark on the floor, and throw some small tree branches on top of it. Unfortunately, this floor does not allow the camera or the microphone boom to travel on it. The same is true when using sand. You can also use a combination of sand and tanbark for an increased realistic effect, especially if the script calls for a lot of action in the dirt. Again, if you have scenes that happen outdoors, try to shoot them outdoors with EFP equipment rather than going through the trouble of bringing the outdoors into the studio.

ELEMENTS OF SCENIC DESIGN

In this section, we will discuss (1) the floor plan, (2) the open set, and (3) scenery and postproduction.

The Floor Plan

All set design is drawn on the **floor plan,** which is literally a plan of the studio floor. It shows the floor area, the main studio doors, the location of the control room, and the studio walls. To have a specific orientation pattern according to which the sets can be placed, the lighting grid, or batten locations, are drawn on the floor area. In effect, the grid resembles the orientation squares of a city map. (See 14.58.)

The scale of the floor plan varies, but it is normally $\frac{1}{4}$ inch = 1 foot. You may want to consider using the metric scale for the floor plan. This is a much easier way to figure out proportions and fractions than the English system of measurement. One scale could be 1 centimeter = 1 meter. All scenery and set properties (furniture, lamps, and so forth) are then drawn to scale in the proper position relative to the studio walls and the lighting grid (see 14.59).

The floor plan is an important aid for all production and engineering personnel. It is essential for the floor

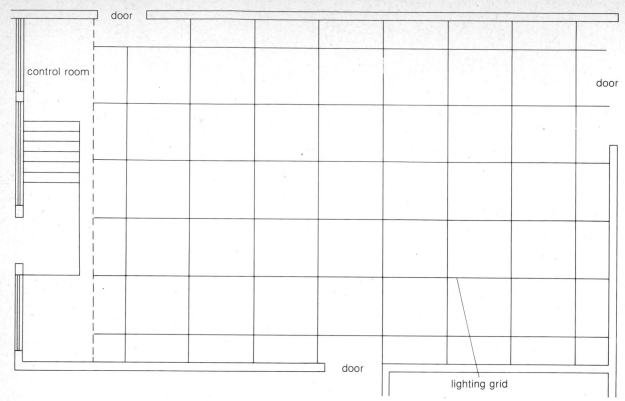

door

control room

door

door

lighting grid

14.58   Floor Plan Grid The floor plan shows the studio floor area, which is further defined by the lighting grid or the pattern of the lighting battens.

crew, who must set up the scenery and place the major set properties. The lighting technician needs it to plot the general lighting layout. The director uses it to visualize the show and block the major actions of performers, cameras, and microphone boom. The audio engineer can become familiar with specific microphone placement and other possible audio requirements. The performers use it to anticipate their movements and spot potential blocking problems.

Although you may not want to become a set designer, you should nevertheless learn how to draw a basic floor plan and translate it into an actual set, into movement of performers and cameras, and, finally, into television screen images.

When drawing a floor plan, watch for these potential problem areas:

1.   Most often, a floor plan shows scenery backing that is insufficient for the foreground piece—for example, a single 10-foot-wide flat as backing for a whole set of living room furniture. The tendency is to draw

furniture and other set pieces too small in proportion to the covering background flats. To indicate the prop furniture in the floor plan, you can use the templates architects use. You can then place the furniture first and draw the necessary background later.

2.   During the setup, you may notice that the available studio floor is always less than the floor plan indicates. Make sure, therefore, to limit the set design to the actual *available* floor space.

3.   Always place active furniture (used by the performers) at least 6 feet (roughly 2 meters) from the set wall, so that the back lights can be directed at the performance areas at not too steep an angle. Also, the director can use the space between wall and furniture for camera placement.

If you also use the floor plan for the lighting plot, simply add a transparent overlay to draw in the major light sources. If you design a set, or if you have to arrange a simple one without the aid of a floor plan,

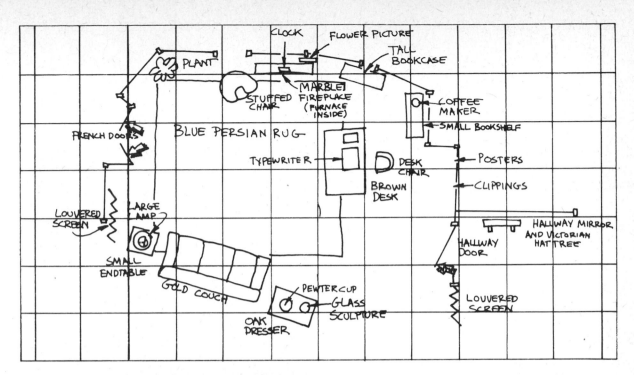

CLOCK
FLOWER PICTURE
TALL BOOKCASE
PLANT
COFFEE MAKER
STUFFED CHAIR
MARBLE FIREPLACE (FURNACE INSIDE)
BLUE PERSIAN RUG
SMALL BOOKSHELF
FRENCH DOORS
TYPEWRITER
DESK CHAIR
POSTERS
BROWN DESK
CLIPPINGS
LOUVERED SCREEN
LARGE AMP
HALLWAY MIRROR AND VICTORIAN HAT TREE
SMALL ENDTABLE
HALLWAY DOOR
GOLD COUCH
PEWTER CUP
LOUVERED SCREEN
OAK DRESSER
GLASS SCULPTURE

14.59 Completed Floor Plan The completed floor plan shows the exact location of the scenery and set properties, relative to the lighting grid or pattern of battens. The floor personnel use this plan as a guide for setting up the scenery and placing the major properties.

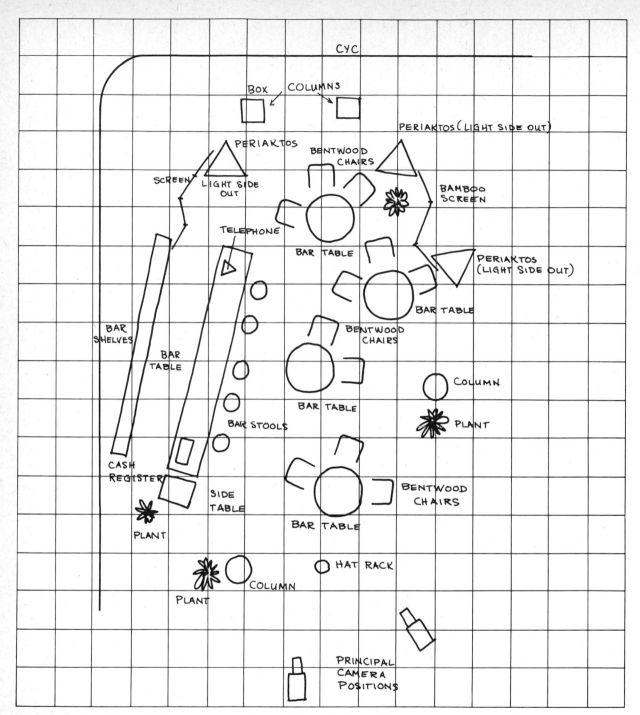

14.60   Open Set Floor Plan The open set is discontinuous. It does not have connecting walls as in an actual room or a closed set, which duplicates an actual room. Rather, the space is defined by a few major pieces of scenery and furniture.

14.61　Open Set and Set Detail In the open set the walls are incidental. Major emphasis is put on realistic set properties, such as chairs, tables, and realistic set dressing. (See 14.60 for floor plan.)

try to put it *where the lights are*. This means that you should place it in such a way that the back lights, key lights, and fill lights hang approximately in the right position. Sometimes a designer who is ignorant of television production will place a set in a corner of the studio where most of the lighting instruments have to be rehung to get proper illumination, when in another part of the studio the same set could have been lighted without moving a single instrument. As you can see once again, you cannot afford specializing in one television production activity by disregarding the other production aspects. Everything interrelates, and the more you know about the other production techniques and functions, the better your coordination of the various elements will be.

The Open Set

Contrary to the closed set, where the scenery is continuous and very much like the walls in an actual room, the **open set** is discontinuous. This means that you use only the most important parts of a room—perhaps the door, a sofa, a table with a lamp as a foreground piece, a few freestanding walls with pictures on them, and so forth (see 14.60). Because the camera rarely sees the whole room anyway, the viewer mentally fills in the missing parts of the room.

There are many advantages to the open-set method:

1.　The camera can look at the set and the action from many points of view without being restricted by closed walls.

2.　The performers or actors have great freedom of movement.

3.　The set is relatively easy to set up and strike (take down).

4.　The set is easy to light.

5.　The microphone boom can operate rather freely.

6.　The set is economical; it needs only a few flats and set pieces.

The open set can look extremely real, provided its individual portions are *realistically treated* (furniture, flats, pictures, lamps) and the director knows how to shoot *inductively,* that is, to suggest a continuous environment by showing only significant details. The uniform background for the open set may be the unlighted cyclorama, which appears not piecemeal, as holes in the set, but as a solid dark unit (see 14.61).

Scenery and Postproduction

When you videotape a show for postproduction and need to **strike** (disassemble) and reassemble a set or several sets between videotaping, make sure that you have an accurate record of what the set looked like. It is, of course, important to have everything look the same for all videotaping sessions. You will be amazed how quickly you forget just where the flower vase was, or how many books there were in the bookcase, or whether the trophy was on the right or left side of the mantelpiece. The videotape from the previous session may or may not show all the set locations. Therefore, you should take some pictures of the various sets in case you need them as location reference.

EFP presents a special problem for the designer. Although many interiors need no embellishment whatsoever, in many cases, you need to rehang some pictures, move some furniture around, or add some foreground pieces to give the room more depth. You must evaluate the environment not by what you see, but by what the *camera* is able to see. Again, protect yourself with photos so that you can duplicate the setting in subsequent taping sessions, and put back everything in its rightful place before leaving the premises.

One last word about design. In a successful design, all items interrelate and harmonize with one another—from the largest, such as the background scenery, to the smallest, such as the ashtray on the table. Good design displays a *continuity and unity of style.*

MAIN POINTS

1. Balance is the interrelationship between stability and tension in a nonanimated title. Balance can be stable, neutral, or unstable.

2. The relative stability of balance depends primarily on the angle of the horizon line relative to the screen and the distribution of graphic mass.

3. A tilted horizon line suggests dynamism and increased tension; a level horizon line reflects normalcy.

4. Graphic mass is any picture element perceived as occupying an area within the frame and as having relative weight. Titles should be arranged in blocks of graphic mass.

5. The most important aspects of graphics preparation are: (1) all essential information must be contained within the essential area; (2) the letters should be bold, have a clear contour, and contrast with the

background scene; and (3) maps and charts should show essential information only.

6. When designing a set, these recurring problems require special attention: (1) set background unity and variety, (2) camera height during the production, and (3) floor treatment.

7. A uniform (usually low-energy) background color or harmonizing colors ensure background unity, with some high-energy colored set pieces providing the necessary variety. When performers are put on a platform (as in an interview), the cameras can operate at a comfortable working height (with the pedestal raised so that the viewfinder is at the eye level of the camera operator) without looking down on the scene. Floors can be covered with special tiles and glue-on patterns without interfering with camera movement. Rugs are useful only if hot cameras do not have to move on and off them.

8. The major elements of scene design are: (1) the floor plan, which shows the scenery and stage properties in relation to the studio and to one another; (2) the open set, which has a discontinuous background; and (3) set requirements for postproduction.

9. A floor plan shows the exact location of the scenery and set properties relative to the lighting grid, which functions similar to the grids on a city map. The floor plan is essential for the director to prepare the preliminary blocking of talent, cameras, and microphone booms; for the lighting director to design the basic lighting setup; and for the floor crew to set up the scenery and place the major set properties.

10. When designing a lighting plot, the instruments and their principal beam directions are drawn on an overlay over the floor plan.

11. The open set is a discontinuous set—that is, the various areas of a room are not enclosed by a continuous wall (background flats). Highly realistic and strategically placed set pieces are the key to a successful open set.

12. When a show is shot for postproduction, during which the set has to be struck and set up again for each taping session, accurate photos of all details need to be taken. These photos will ensure consistency in the setup for the subsequent taping sessions.

FURTHER READING

Arnheim, Rudolf. *Art and Visual Perception.* Berkeley: University of California Press, 1974.

Dondis, Donis A. *A Primer of Visual Literacy.* Cambridge, MA: MIT Press, 1973.

Kepes, Gyorgy (Ed.). *Education of Vision,* and the other five volumes of the Vision and Values Series. New York: George Braziller, 1965–1966.

McKim, Robert H. *Experiences in Visual Thinking.* Monterey, CA: Brooks/Cole Publishing Co., 1972.

Zettl, Herbert. *Sight-Sound-Motion: Applied Media Aesthetics.* Belmont, CA: Wadsworth Publishing Co., 1976.

Also, see the various publications on magazine layout.

Television Talent

In this chapter we are concerned with television talent and the major ways of behaving in front of the camera, and with doing makeup and selecting what to wear.

Section One covers three principal areas: (1) performing techniques, (2) acting techniques, and (3) auditions.

1. Important aspects of technique for a performer are (1) the camera, (2) audio, and (3) timing. The performer and postproduction, floor manager's cues, and various prompting devices are also discussed as part of performing techniques.

2. Important aspects of acting techniques are (1) audience, (2) actions, (3) blocking, (4) speech and memorizing lines, (5) timing, and (6) the actor and postproduction and the actor's relationship to the director.

3. The various aspects of auditions are discussed with general guidelines for performing well under these circumstances.

Section Two outlines the techniques and principles of makeup and clothing and costuming. These major points are covered:

1. Reasons for makeup: to improve, correct, and change appearance.
2. Technical makeup requirements.
3. Makeup material.
4. Basic makeup techniques.
5. The line, color, texture, and detail for clothing and costumes to be worn on camera.

We can arbitrarily divide all television **talent** (which stands, not always too accurately, for all people performing in front of the television camera) into two large groups: (1) performers and (2) actors. The difference between them is fairly clear-cut. Television **performers** are engaged basically in nondramatic activities. They play themselves and do not assume roles of other characters; they sell their own personalities to the audience. Television **actors,** on the other hand, always portray someone else; they project a character's personality rather than their own.

In Section One we will cover the major aspects of the performing and acting techniques for television.

PERFORMING TECHNIQUES

The television performer speaks directly to the camera or communicates with other performers or the studio audience; he or she is also fully aware of the presence of the television audience at home. This latter audience, however, is not the large, anonymous, and heterogeneous television audience that modern sociologists study. For the television performer, the audience is a small, intimate group that has gathered in front of a television set.

If you are a performer, try imagining your audience as a family of three, seated in their favorite room, about 10 feet away from you. With this picture in mind, you have no reason to scream at the "millions of people out there in video land"; rather, the more successful approach is to talk quietly and intimately to the family who were kind enough to let you come into their home.

When you assume the role of a television performer, the camera becomes your audience. You must adapt your performance techniques to its characteristics and to other important production elements, such as audio and timing. In this section we will, therefore, discuss (1) the performer and the camera, (2) the performer and audio, (3) the performer and timing, (4) the performer and postproduction, (5) the floor manager's cues, and (6) prompting devices.

The people who appear on the television screen have varied communication objectives: some seek to entertain, educate, inform; others, to persuade, convince, sell. Nevertheless, the main goal of each of them is to communicate with the television audience as effectively as possible.

Performer and Camera

The camera is not a piece of dead machinery; it sees everything you do or do not do. It sees how you look, move, sit, and stand—in short, how you behave in a variety of situations. At times it looks at you much more closely and with greater scrutiny than a polite person would ever dare to do. It reveals the nervous twitch of your mouth when you are ill at ease and the expression of mild panic when you have forgotten a line. The camera does not look politely away when you scratch your ear. It faithfully reflects your behavior in all pleasant and unpleasant details. As a television performer, therefore, you must carefully control your actions without ever letting the audience know that you are conscious of doing so.

Camera Lens   Because the camera represents your audience, you must look directly into the lens whenever you intend to establish eye contact with your viewer. As a matter of fact, you must stare into the lens and keep eye contact much more than you would

with an actual person. The reason for this seemingly unnatural way of looking is that, when you appear on a close-up shot, the concentrated light and space of the television screen highly intensify your actions. If you glance away from the lens ever so slightly, you break the intensity of the communication between you and the viewer; you break, though temporarily, television's magic. Try to look into the lens as much as you can, but in as casual and relaxed a way as possible.

Camera Switching   If two or more cameras are used, you must know which one is on the air so that you can remain in direct contact with the audience. When the director changes cameras, you must follow the floor manager's cue (or the change of tally lights) quickly but smoothly. Do not jerk your head from one camera to the other. If you suddenly discover that you have been talking to the wrong one, look down as if to collect your thoughts and then casually glance into the "hot" camera and continue talking in that direction until you are again cued to the other camera. This method works especially well if you work from notes. You can always pretend to be looking at your notes, while, in reality, you are changing your view from the "wrong" to the "right" camera.

In general, it is useful to ask the director or floor manager if there will be many camera changes during the program, and approximately when the changes will happen. If the show is scripted, mark all camera changes in your script.

If the director has one camera on you in a medium-shot (MS) and the other camera in a close-up (CU) of the object you are demonstrating, it is best to keep looking at the medium-shot camera during the whole demonstration, even when the director switches to the close-up camera. This way you will never be caught looking the wrong way, because only the medium-shot camera is focused on you (see 15.1).

Close-up Techniques
The tighter the shot, the harder it is for the camera to follow fast movement. If a camera is on a close-up, you should restrict your motions severely and move with great care. Ask the director whether he or she plans close-ups and approximately when. In a song, for example, the director may want to shoot very closely to intensify an especially tender and intimate passage. Try to stand as still as possible; do not wiggle your head. The close-up itself is intensification enough. All you have to do is sing well.

When demonstrating small objects on a close-up, hold them steady. If they are arranged on a table, do not pick them up. You can either point to them or tilt them up a little to give the camera a better view. There is nothing more frustrating for camera operator and director than a performer who snatches the product off the table just when the camera has a good close-up of it. A quick look in the studio monitor will usually tell you how you should hold the object for maximum visibility on the screen. If two cameras are used, **"cheat"** (orient) the object somewhat toward the close-up camera. But do not turn it so much that it looks unnaturally distorted on the medium-shot camera.

Warning Cues
In most nondramatic shows—lectures, demonstrations, interviews—there is generally not enough time to work out a detailed blocking scheme. The director usually just walks you through some of the most important crossovers from one performing area to the other, and through a few major actions, such as especially complicated demonstrations. During the on-the-air performance, therefore, you must give the director and the studio crew visual and audible warning of your unrehearsed actions. When you want to get up, for instance, shift your weight first, and get your legs and arms into the right position before you actually stand up. This gives the camera operator as well as the microphone boom operator enough time to prepare for your move. If you pop up unexpectedly, the camera may stay in one position, focusing on the middle part of your body, and your head may hit the microphone, which the boom operator, not anticipating your sudden move, has solidly locked into position.

If you intend to move from one set area to another, you may use audio cues. For instance, you can warn the production crew by saying: "Let's go over to the children and ask them . . ." or, "If you

---

Actor A person who appears on camera in dramatic roles. The actor always portrays someone else.

Blocking Carefully worked out movement and actions by the talent, and movement of all mobile television equipment.

Cue Card A large, hand-lettered card that contains copy, usually held next to the camera lens by floor personnel.

Performer A person who appears on camera in nondramatic shows. The performer plays himself or herself, and does not assume someone else's character.

Talent Collective name for all performers and actors who appear regularly on television.

Teleprompter A mechanical prompting device that projects the moving copy over the lens, so that the talent can read it without losing eye contact with the viewer.

will follow me over to the lab area, you can actually see. . . ." Such cues sound quite natural to the home viewer, who is generally unaware of the number of fast reactions these seemingly unimportant remarks may trigger inside the television studio. You must be specific when you cue unrehearsed visual material. For example, you can alert the director of the upcoming slides by saying: "The first picture (or even slide) shows. . . ." This cuing device should not be used too often, however. If you can alert the director more subtly yet equally directly, do so.

Do not try to convey the obvious. The director, not the talent, runs the show. An alert director does not have to be told by the performer to bring the cameras a little closer to get a better view of a small object. This is especially annoying if the director has already obtained a good close-up through a zoom-in. Also, avoid walking toward the camera to demonstrate an object. Through the zoom lens, the camera can get to you much faster than you can get to the camera. Also, you may walk so close to the camera that it has to tilt up into the lights to keep your face in the shot, or so that the zoom lens can no longer be focused.

Performer and Audio

As a television performer, besides looking natural and relaxed, you must also be able to speak clearly and effectively; it rarely comes as a natural gift. Do not be misled into believing that a super bass and affected pronunciation are the two prime requisites for a good announcer or other performer. On the contrary: first, you need to have something important to say; second, you need to say it with conviction and sincerity; third, you must speak clearly so that everybody can understand you. So thorough training in television announcing is an important prerequisite for any performer.[1]

Microphone Techniques   In Chapter 8 we discussed the most basic microphone techniques. Here is a short summary of the main points about the

[1]Stuart W. Hyde, *Television and Radio Announcing,* 4th ed. (Boston: Houghton Mifflin Co., 1983).

performer always looking at medium-shot camera (C-1)

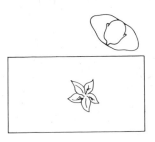

medium-shot camera on performer   CU camera on product

15.1   Eye Contact with Medium-Shot Camera
When one camera is used exclusively for close-ups of the product and the other for a medium-shot of the performer with the product (in this case, a plant), the performer should ignore the close-up camera and address the medium-shot camera only. This way, he or she will never be caught looking away from the viewer.

performer's handling of microphones or assisting the microphone operator.

Most often you work with a *lavaliere microphone.* Once it is properly fastened, you do not have to worry about it anymore. If you have to move from one set area to another on camera, make sure that the mic cord does not get tangled up in the set or set props. Gently pull the cable behind you to keep the tension off the mic itself.

When using a *hand microphone,* make sure that you have enough cable for your planned actions. Treat it gently. Speak across it, not into it. If you are interviewing somebody in noisy surroundings, such as in a downtown street, hold the microphone near you when you are talking, and then point it toward the person as he or she responds to your questions.

When working with a *boom microphone,* be aware of the boom movements without letting the audience know. Give the boom operator enough warning so that he or she can anticipate your movements. Move slowly enough that the boom can follow. Especially do not make fast turns, because they involve a great amount of boom movement. If you have to turn fast, try not to speak. Do not walk too close to the boom; the operator may not be able to retract it enough to keep you "on mic" (within good microphone pickup range).

Try not to move a *desk mic* once it has been placed by the audio engineer. Sometimes the microphone may be pointing away from you toward another performer, but this may have been done purposely to achieve better audio balance.

Audio Level   A good audio engineer will take your audio level before you go on the air. Many performers have the bad habit of mumbling or speaking softly while the level is being taken, and then, when they go on the air, blasting their opening remarks. If a level is taken, speak as loudly as you will actually do in your opening remarks. Thus the audio engineer will know where to turn the pot for an optimum level.

Opening Cue   At the beginning of a show, all microphones are dead until the director gives the cue for audio. You must, therefore, wait until you receive the opening cue from the floor manager or through the I.F.B. (interrupted feedback system) (see Chapter 9). If you speak beforehand, you will not be heard. Do not take your opening cue from the red tally lights on the cameras unless you are instructed to.

Performer and Timing

Television operates on split-second timing. Although the director is ultimately responsible for getting the show on and off on time, the performer has a great deal to do with successful timing.

Aside from careful pacing throughout the show, you must learn how much program material you can cover after you have received a three-minute, a two-minute, a one-minute, and a thirty-second cue. You must, for example, still look comfortable and relaxed although you may have to cram a lot of important program material into the last minute. On the other hand, you must be prepared to fill an extra thirty seconds without appearing to be grasping for words and things to do. This presence of mind, of course, needs practice and cannot be learned solely from a television handbook.

Performer and Postproduction

When you work on a show that presents a continuous event but is shot over a period of several days or even weeks for postproduction, make sure that you look exactly the same in all the videotaping sessions. Obviously, you must wear the same clothes. You must also wear the same jewelry, the same scarf, the same shirt, and the same tie from one taping session to the next. You cannot have your coat buttoned one time, and then unbuttoned the next. Makeup and hairdo, too, must be identical for all taping sessions. In order to have an easy and readily available reference, have Polaroid snapshots made of yourself from the front, sides, and back immediately after the first taping session.

Most importantly, you must maintain the same energy level throughout the taping sessions. For example, you cannot end one session full of energy, and then be very low key the next day when the videotaping resumes, especially when the edited version does not suggest any passage of time between the takes. On repeat takes, try to maintain identical energy levels.

Floor Manager's Cues

The floor manager, who is the link between the director and you, the performer, can communicate with you nonverbally even while you are on the air. He or she can tell you whether you are too slow or too fast in your delivery, how much time you have left, and whether you speak loudly enough or hold an object correctly for the close-up camera. We can group these visual cues into three types: (1) time cues, (2) directional cues, and (3) audio cues.

Although stations use slightly different cuing signals and procedures, they fall into one of these categories. If you are working with an unfamiliar production crew, ask the floor manager to go over the cues before you go on the air.

React to all cues immediately, even if you think one of them is not appropriate at that particular time. The director would not give the cue if it were not absolutely necessary. Truly professional performers are not the ones who never need any cues and can run the show alone; they are the ones who can react to all signals quickly and smoothly.

Do not look nervously for the floor manager if you think you should have received a cue; he or she will find you and draw your attention to the signal. When you receive a cue, do not acknowledge it in any way. The floor manager will know whether you noticed it or not.

The table of cues (see 15.2) indicates the standard time cues, directional cues, and audio cues that are used by most television stations with only minor variations.

Prompting Devices

Prompting devices have become an essential production tool for news. For some reason, the audience has come to expect the newscaster to talk directly to them rather than reading the news from a script, although we all know that the newscaster does not speak from memory. Prompting devices are also of great help to the performer who fears suddenly forgetting his or her lines or who has no time to memorize difficult copy for an on-camera announcement or commercial.

The prompting device must be totally reliable, and the performer must be able to read the prompting copy without appearing to lose eye contact with the viewer. Two devices have proved successful: (1) cue cards, and (2) the teleprompter.

Cue Cards   **Cue cards** are used for relatively short pieces of copy. There are many types, and the choice depends largely on what the performer is used to and what he or she likes to work with. Usually they are large poster cards on which the copy is hand-lettered with a heavy felt pen. The size of the cards and the lettering depends on how well the perform-

er can see and how far away the camera is. When cue cards are held properly, the floorperson holds the cards as close to the lens as possible, the hands do not cover any of the copy, and he or she follows the performer's lines (see 15.3).

As a performer, you must learn to glance at the cards without losing eye contact with the lens for more than a moment. Make sure the floorperson who is handling the cards has them in the correct order. If he or she forgets to change them at the appropriate moment, snap your fingers to attract the person's attention; in an emergency you may have to ad-lib until the system is functioning again. You should know the topic long before the show begins, and this study should enable you to carry on a sensible ad-lib at least for a short time.

Studio Teleprompter   The most effective prompting device is the **teleprompter.** It projects the magnified letters of the copy onto a glass plate placed directly in front of the camera lens. You can read the copy, which appears in front of the lens, and maintain eye contact with the viewer (the lens) at all times.

Most teleprompters work on the same principle. The copy, usually typed on a news typewriter with oversized letters, is placed in a special variable-speed crawl device. A simple vidicon camera reads the copy and relays it to monitors on all the active cameras (see 15.4). A mirror then projects the monitor screen with the moving copy onto the glass plate over the lens (see 15.5).

The advantage of using a television camera to "read" and monitors to display the copy is that all cameras show the same text perfectly synchronized. You have, therefore, the same copy displayed no matter what camera the director chooses to focus on you.

The roll of paper on which the copy is typed can hold continuous information for a full hour's newscast. The news script in front of you can serve as backup in case the prompting device fails. Also, you may want to glance down to the script to indicate story transitions.

When a teleprompter is used, the distance of the performer to the camera with the prompting device is no longer arbitrary. The camera must be

Time Cues

Cue		Meaning	Hand Signal
Stand By		Show about to start.	Extends arm above head and points with other hand to camera that will go on the air.
Cue		Show goes on the air.	Points to performer or live camera.
On Time		Go ahead as planned. (On the nose.)	Touches nose with forefinger.
Speed Up		Accelerate what you are doing. You are going too slowly.	Rotates hand clockwise with extended forefinger. Urgency of speedup is indicated by fast or slow rotation.
Stretch		Slow down. Too much time left. Fill until emergency is over.	Stretches imaginary rubber band between hands.
Wind Up		Finish up what you are doing. Come to an end.	Similar motion to speed up, but usually with extended arm above head. Sometimes expressed with raised fist, or with a good-bye wave, or by hands rolling over each other as if wrapping an imaginary package.
Cut		Stop speech or action immediately.	Pulls index finger in knifelike motion across throat.

Time Cues

Cue		Meaning	Hand Signal
5 (4, 3, 2, 1) Minute(s)		5 (4, 3, 2, 1) minute(s) left until end of show.	Holds up five (four, three, two, one) finger(s) or small card with number painted on it.
½ Minute		30 seconds left in show.	Forms a cross with two index fingers or extended hands. Or holds card with number.
15 Seconds		15 seconds left in show.	Shows fist (which can also mean wind up). Or holds card with number.
Roll VTR (and Countdown)		Projector is rolling. Film is coming up.	Holds extended left hand in front of face, moves right hand in cranking motion.
5–4–3–2–1 Take Film or VTR or 2–1 Take		Leader numbers as they flash by on the preview monitor, or VTR beeper countdown.	Extends five, four, three, two, one finger(s); or simply two, one finger(s); clenches fist or gives cut signal.

Directional Cues

Cue		Meaning	Hand Signal
Closer		Performer must come closer or bring object closer to camera.	Moves both hands toward self, palms in.
Back		Performer must step back or move object away from camera.	Uses both hands in pushing motion, palms out.

(continued)

Directional Cues (cont.)

Cue		Meaning	Hand Signal
Walk		Performer must move to next performing area.	Makes a walking motion with index and middle fingers in direction of movement.
Stop		Stop right here. Do not move any more.	Extends both hands in front of body, palms out.
O.K.		Very well done. Stay right there. Do what you are doing.	Forms an "O" with thumb and forefinger, other fingers extended, motioning toward talent.

Audio Cues

Cue		Meaning	Hand Signal
Speak Up		Performer is talking too softly for present conditions.	Cups both hands behind ears, or moves right hand upwards, palm up.
Tone Down		Performer is too loud or too enthusiastic for the occasion.	Moves both hands toward studio floor, palms down, or puts extended forefinger over mouth in shhh-like motion.
Closer to Mic		Performer is too far away from mic for good audio pickup.	Moves right hand toward face.
Keep Talking		Keep on talking until further cues.	Extends thumb and forefinger horizontally, moving them like the beak of a bird.

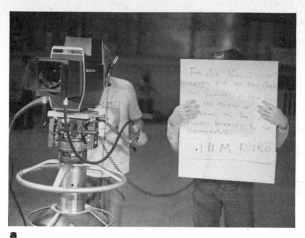

a

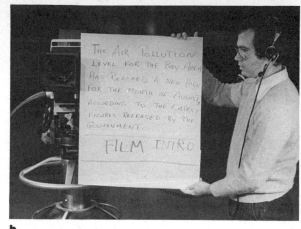

b

15.3   Handling Cue Cards (a) This is the wrong way to hold a cue card. First, the card is too far away from the lens, forcing the talent to lose eye contact with the viewer (the lens). Second, his hands cover up important parts of the copy. Third, he cannot follow the lines as read by the talent. He will not be able to change cards for smooth reading. (b) This is the correct way of holding a cue card. The card is as close to the lens as possible, the hands do not cover the copy, and the floor manager reads along with the talent, thereby facilitating smooth card changes.

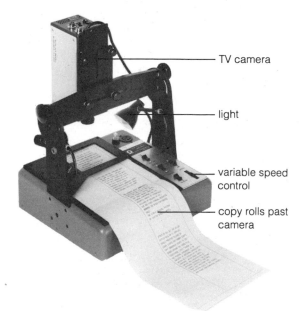

TV camera

light

variable speed control

copy rolls past camera

mirror projecting monitor image to glass plate

monitor displaying copy

copy as it appears to talent

15.4   Teleprompter Copy Reading Device A special crawl arrangement moves the copy at variable speeds past a simple stationary vidicon camera whose signal is then sent to the various teleprompter monitors, which display the copy.

15.5   Teleprompter Copy Display over Lens The monitor that displays the copy is mounted on the camera. A mirror projects the copy as it appears on the monitor screen onto a glass plate directly over the lens. You can read the copy without losing eye contact with the lens (the viewer). The advantage of this system is that a single copy can be displayed on two or more cameras simultaneously.

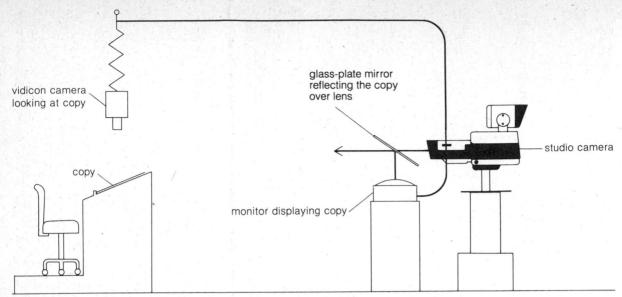

15.6   Simple News Prompting Device A simple prompting device consists of a small vidicon camera that looks directly down onto the copy. The vidicon camera's picture (the copy) is relayed directly into a monitor, which reflects its image via a glass-plate mirror over the camera lens. The copy is pushed up by the talent, who can control his or her own reading speed.

close enough for the performer to read the copy without squinting. But if the camera is too close, the home viewer can see the performer's eyes moving back and forth in an obvious reading motion. If you work with a new crew and director, make sure that the cameras are placed in such a way that both of these requirements are fulfilled.

More elaborate teleprompters use a character generator to reproduce the copy on the monitor screen. The advantage of this system is that the computer can be told just how long the copy should take, and it rolls the copy for the performer at exactly the right speed. Also, the letters are easy to read and do not depend on the quality of the typewriter ribbon or the vidicon camera. The disadvantage of the system is that the whole text must be typed into the character generator before it can be retrieved by the teleprompting system.

Some small stations have built their own prompting device for their news operation. It consists of a small vidicon camera that is mounted directly above the newscaster's desk, a monitor that is con-

nected to the vidicon camera, and a glass plate in front of the lens of the studio camera that is aimed at the newscaster. The news script, which lies on the desk in front of the newscaster, is picked up by the overhead vidicon camera and projected via the monitor onto the glass plate. The newscaster can control the speed with which the copy appears on the teleprompter monitor by simply pushing the script away from himself or herself. If you use this system, make sure that the text does not appear as a mirror image on the glass plate. You may have to reverse the scanning of the vidicon camera or reflect the monitor image by a mirror on the glass plate (see 15.6).

Field Teleprompter   Have you ever wondered how some correspondents can stand in the middle of a busy city street and report a well-written story without ever stumbling or searching for words? Well, some have the ability to do just that. Some of us, however, have to use some kind of prompting device even in the field. If the copy is brief, cue cards will do. But more and more ENG/EFP operations use a field teleprompter. The various models work on a similar principle. The copy is either hand-lettered or typed onto a paper roll, which is attached to the camera, either below or to the side of the lens. In some more elaborate models, the copy is back-lighted and projected onto a piece of clear plastic mounted in front of the camera lens. All prompters have a small electric motor that rolls the copy at varying speeds (see 15.7). The whole unit is very light and powered by the standard 12-volt battery pack or belt. Similar units can be used independently of the camera, and held by the floorperson or mounted on a tripod directly above or below the camera lens.

Regardless of the quality of the teleprompter, a good performer should always be familiar enough with the story or other copy to be able to talk about it intelligently in case the prompting device decides to go on strike.

copy typed on paper roll can be rolled with variable speed

glass plate projects copy over lens

15.7 Field Teleprompter Field teleprompters consist of simple rolls with typed or hand-lettered copy whose speed can be controlled by the floor manager. The copy is projected over the lens by a half-silvered mirror. Many times, the copy is simply placed on two rollers just below the camera lens, or hand-lettered on a series of cue cards.

ACTING TECHNIQUES

In contrast to the television performer, the television actor always assumes someone else's character and personality.

To become a good television actor, you must first learn the art of acting, a subject beyond the purpose of this chapter. This discussion will merely point out how to adapt your acting to the peculiarities of the television medium.

Many excellent actors consider television the most difficult medium in which to work. They always work within a studio full of confusing and impersonal technical gear; and yet they must appear on the screen as natural and lifelike as possible.

Many times "television" actors also work in motion pictures. The production techniques and the equipment used in film for television are identical to those of film for motion picture theaters, but film making for television is considerably faster. Film shot for the television screen requires acting techniques more closely related to live or videotaped television than to motion pictures.

It is difficult to set down rigid principles of tel-

evision acting techniques that are applicable in every situation. The particular role and even the director may require quite different forms of expression and technique from the actor. The television medium, however, dictates some basic behavior patterns that you must accept if you want to make it work for you instead of against you. Let's look briefly at some of these requirements, among them (1) audience, (2) actions, (3) blocking, (4) speech, (5) memorizing lines, (6) timing, (7) actor and postproduction, and (8) director-actor relationship.

Audience

When you act on television, you have no rapport with the audience—people you can see, or at least feel, and who applaud and elevate you to your best possible performance. In television, you are acting before constantly moving cameras that represent your assumed audience. Like the television performer, you must be camera-conscious, but you should never reveal your knowledge of the cameras' presence. The viewers (now the camera) do not remain in one position, as they would in the theater; they move around you, look at you at close range and from a distance, from below and from above; they may look at your eyes, your feet, your hands, your back, whatever the director selects for them to see. And at all times you must look completely convincing and natural; the character you are portraying must appear on the screen as a real, living, breathing human being. Keep in mind that you are playing to a camera lens, not to an audience; you need not (and should not) project your motions and emotions as you would when acting on stage. The television camera does the projecting—the communicating—for you. *Internalization,* as opposed to externalization, of your role is a key factor of your performance. You must attempt to *become* as much as possible the person you are portraying, rather than to *act out the character*. Thus, your reactions are as effective on television as your actions.

Actions

The television camera is restrictive in many ways. It looks at the set and at you mostly in close-ups. This means that your physical actions must be confined to the particular area the camera chooses to select, often unnaturally close to the other actors.

The television close-up also limits the extent of your gestures, concentrating on more intimate ways of emotional expression. A close-up of a clenched fist or a raised eyebrow may reflect your inner feelings and emotions more vividly than the broad movements necessary for the theater.

Blocking

You must be extremely exact in following rehearsed **blocking.** Sometimes inches become important, especially if the cameras are set up for special effects. The director may, for instance, want to use your arm as a frame for the background scene or position you for a complicated over-the-shoulder shot. The precise television lighting and the limited microphone radius (especially in small station production) are also factors that force you to adhere strictly to the initial blocking.

Once the show is on the air, you have an obligation to follow the rehearsed action carefully. This is not the time to innovate just because you have a sudden inspiration. If the director has not been warned of your change, the new blocking will always be worse than the previously rehearsed one. The camera has a limited field of view; if you want to be seen, you must stay within it.

Sometimes the director will place you in a position that looks entirely wrong to you, especially if you consider it in relation to the other actors. Do not try to correct this position on your own by arbitrarily moving away from the designated spot. A certain camera position and a special zoom-lens position may very well warrant unusual blocking to achieve a special effect.

The television cameras quite frequently photograph your stage business in a close-up. This means that you must remember all the rehearsed business details and execute them in exactly the same spot in which they were initially staged.

Speech

Compared to radio, the television boom microphone is generally a good distance away from you, so you must speak clearly. But speak naturally; projecting your voice in the theater tradition sounds artificial on television.

Memorizing Lines

As a television actor, you must be able to learn your lines quickly and accurately. If, as is the case in the soap operas, you have only one evening to learn an hour's role for the next day, you must indeed be a "quick study." You cannot ad lib during such performances simply because you have "lived" the role for so long. Most of your lines are important not only from a dramatic point of view but also because they serve as video and audio cues for the whole production team.

Even for a highly demanding role, you may have only a few weeks to prepare. A television actor should not rely on prompting devices; after all, you should live, not read, your role.

Timing

Just like the performer, the actor in television must have an acute sense of timing. Timing matters for pacing your performance, for building to a climax, for delivering a punch line, and also for staying within a tightly prescribed clock time. Even if you are videotaping a play scene by scene, you still need to observe carefully the stipulated running times for each take. You may have to stretch out a fast scene without making it appear to drag, or you may have to gain 10 seconds by speeding up a slow scene without destroying its solemn character. You must be flexible without stepping out of character.

Always respond immediately to the floor manager's cues. Do not stop in the middle of a scene simply because you disagreed with one. Play the scene to the end and then complain. Minor timing errors can often be corrected during the editing process.

Actor and Postproduction

Most of television acting is done piecemeal, which means that you are not able to perform a play from beginning to end the way you would do it in a theater. As already pointed out in the section on the performer and postproduction, you must make sure that your physical appearance remains the same throughout the production—unless the script calls for a change in appearance. But more importantly, you must maintain the same energy level between two segments that are later edited together into a continuous scene. You simply cannot be very "on" during the first part of the videotaping and then, a week later, when the scene is continued, project a low-energy mood. Television is a medium of continuity, and it is capable of projecting subtle nuances and levels of energy.

One of the most important things to watch when continuing with a scene whose first part may have been taped some days before is the *tempo* of your performance. If you moved slowly in the first part of the scene, do not race through the second part at top speed—unless the director wants such a change. Usually, it helps to watch the videotape of your previous performance so that you can continue the scene with the same energy level and tempo.

Director-Actor Relationship

As a television actor, you cannot afford to be temperamental. There are too many people who have to be coordinated by the director. Although the actor is important to the television show, so are other people—the floor crew, the engineer at the transmitter, the boom operator, and the video engineer.

Even though you may find little opportunity for acting in a small station operation, make an effort to learn as much about it as possible. An able actor is generally an effective television performer; a television director with acting training is generally better prepared for most directing assignments.

AUDITIONS

All auditions are equally important, whether you try out for a one-line off-camera uttering or the principal role in a dramatic series. Whenever you audition, you should try to give your best. This means that you should *prepare* yourself for the audition, even if you do not know beforehand what you may have to read. As a *performer,* wear something that fits the occasion and looks good on camera. Be properly groomed. Keep your energy up even if you have to wait half a day before you are called to utter your line.

If you get the script beforehand, study it carefully. For example, if you have to do a commercial on a particular brand of soft drink, get as familiar as possible with the product, the company that produces the product, and the advertising agency that is producing the commercials. Knowing about the product gives you a certain confidence that inevitably shows up in your delivery. Listen carefully to the instructions given to you before or during the audition. Remember that television is an intimate medium.

When instructed to demonstrate a product, practice before you are on camera to make sure you know how, for example, to open an easy-to-open package. Ask the floor crew to help you prepare a product for easy handling. Also, ask the director how close the camera will be, so that you can keep your actions within camera range.

As an *actor,* be sure to understand thoroughly the character you are to portray. Do not hesitate to ask the director or producer to explain the finer points of the character's emotional and physical behavior patterns. If these explanations run counter to your perceptions, do not argue. You are not auditioned on how well you can interpret a script, but how quickly and how well you perceive the director's or producer's image of a character and how close you can come to this image in your actions. This does not rule out creativity on your part. When auditions were held for the male lead in a television play about a lonely woman and a rather unscrupulous and crude man who wanted to take advantage of her, one of the actors added a little of his own interpretation of the character that eventually got him the part. While reading an intimate scene in which he was supposed to persuade the leading lady to make love to him, he manicured his fingernails with slightly rusty fingernail clippers. In fact, this aggravating fingernail clipping was later written into the scene.

Finally, when auditioning—as when participating in athletics or any competitive activity—be aware, but not afraid, of the competition.

MAIN POINTS

1.   Television talent means all persons who perform in front of the television camera. They are classified in two large groups: (1) television performers and (2) television actors.

2.   Television performers are basically engaged in nondramatic shows, such as newscasts, interviews, and game shows. They always portray themselves. Television actors always portray someone else; they project someone else's character.

3.   The television performer must adapt his or her performance techniques to the characteristics of the camera and other production elements: audio, timing, postproduction, the floor manager's cues, and prompting devices.

4.   Since the camera lens represents the audience, the performer must look into the lens if he or she intends to establish and maintain eye contact with the viewer. If cameras are switched, the performer must look over to the "hot" camera.

5.   During closeups, the performer's movements are severely restricted.

6.   One of the major requirements for a good television performer is clear and effective speech. Therefore, the performer must be thoroughly familiar with the basic announcing and microphone techniques.

7.   Timing is another important performance requirement. A good performer must be able to respond quickly, yet smoothly, to the floor manager's time and to any other cues.

8.   When a show is shot over several weeks, continuity has to be maintained. Performers must be careful to look the same from one taping session to the next, and to project the same energy level.

9.   Prompting devices have become essential in television production. The two most frequently used devices are (1) cue cards and (2) the teleprompter.

10.   Assuming that an actor already knows the art of acting, here are some additional areas of concern for the television actor: (1) the lack of an actual audience and the necessity to internalize one's role; (2) restricted gestures and movements because of the close-up; (3) exactness in following rehearsed blocking; (4) clear speech without projecting too much; (5) accurate timing; (6) maintaining continuity in physical appearance and energy level over a period of shooting sessions, or shifting drastically in mood and energy, if the show is shot out of sequence; and (7) keeping a good attitude toward a variety of directors.

11.   For an audition, the performer and actor should prepare as much as possible, dress properly for the occasion (role), sharpen the character through some prop or mannerism, and inquire about the floor manager's cues and respond to them immediately.

How a performer or actor looks in front of the camera may be less important than the substance of what he or she has to say or do. Nonetheless, your appearance on television is important because it can contribute to or distract from the actual presentation.

In this section, we will briefly discuss some peripheral, though important, aspects of performing and acting: (1) makeup techniques, and (2) clothing and costuming.

MAKEUP

All **makeup** is used for three basic reasons: to *improve* appearance, to *correct* appearance, and to *change* appearance.

Standard street makeup is used daily by many women to accentuate and improve their features. Minor skin blemishes are covered up, and the eyes and lips are emphasized.

Makeup can also be used to correct closely or widely spaced eyes, sagging flesh under the chin, a short or long nose, a slightly too prominent forehead, and many similar minor faults.

If a person is to portray a specific character in a play, a complete change of appearance may be necessary. Drastic changes of age, race, and character can be accomplished through the creative use of makeup techniques.

The different purposes for applying cosmetics require different techniques, of course. Improving someone's appearance calls for the least complicated procedure; to correct someone's appearance is slightly more complicated; and changing an actor's appearance may require involved and complex methods.

Most shows in small station operation require only makeup that improves the appearance of a performer. More complicated makeup work, such as making a young actor look eighty years old, is left to the professional makeup artist. You need not learn all about corrective and character makeup techniques, but you should have some idea of the basic (1) technical requirements, (2) materials, and (3) techniques of television makeup.

Technical Requirements

Like so many other production elements, makeup, too, must yield to some of the demands of the television camera. Some of these limitations are (1) color distortion, (2) color balance, and (3) close-ups.

Color Distortion As we pointed out earlier, the skin tones are the only color references the viewer has for color adjustment on a home receiver. Their accurate rendering is, therefore, of the utmost importance. Makeup plays a major role in this endeavor.

Generally, cool colors (hues with a blue tint) have a tendency to overemphasize their bluishness, especially in high color-temperature lighting. Warm colors (warm reds, oranges, browns, and tans) are preferred for television makeup. They usually provide more sparkle, especially when used on a dark-skinned face.

The basic foundation color should match the natural skin tones as closely as possible, regardless of whether the face is light (Caucasian or Asian) or dark (Chicano or Black). However, because the camera might emphasize dense shadow areas with a bluish or purple tint, especially on dark skin, warm rather than cool foundation colors are preferred. Be careful, however, that the skin color does not turn pink. As much as you should guard against too much blue in a dark face, you must watch for too much pink in a light face.

The natural reflectance of a dark face (especially of very dark-skinned Blacks) often produces unflattering highlights. These should be toned down by a proper pancake or a translucent powder; otherwise, the video engineer will have to compensate for the highlights through shading, making the dark picture areas unnaturally dense.

Color Balance Generally, the art director, scene designer, makeup artist, and costume designer should coordinate all the colors in production meetings. In small station operations, there should be little problem with such coordination because these functions may all be combined in one or two persons. At least you should be aware of this coordination principle and apply it whenever possible. Although colors can be adjusted by the video control operator, the adjustment of one hue often influences the others. Some attention to color balancing beforehand makes the technical "painting" job considerably easier.

In color television, the surrounding colors are sometimes reflected in the face and greatly exaggerated by the camera. Frequently, such reflections are inevitable, but you can keep them to a minimum by carefully watching the overall reflectance of the skin. It should have a normal sheen, neither too oily (high reflectance) nor too dull (low reflectance but no brilliance—the skin looks lifeless).

Close-ups Television makeup must be smooth and subtle enough so that the performer's or actor's face looks natural even in an extreme close-up. This is the direct opposite of theater makeup technique, in which features and colors are greatly exaggerated for the benefit of the spectator in the last row. A good television makeup remains largely invisible, even on a close-up. Therefore, a close-up of a person's face under *actual production lighting* conditions is the best criterion for judging the necessity for and quality of makeup. If the performer or actor looks good on camera without makeup, none is needed. If the performer needs makeup and the close-up of his or her finished face looks normal, the makeup is acceptable. If it looks artificial, the makeup must be redone.

Materials

A great variety of excellent television makeup materials are available. Most makeup artists in the theater arts departments of a college or university have up-to-date lists. In fact, most large drug stores can supply you with the basic materials for the average makeup for improving the performer's appearance.

Although women performers are generally experienced in cosmetic materials and techniques, men may, at least initially, need some advice.

The most basic makeup item is a **foundation** that covers minor skin blemishes and cuts down light reflections from an overly oily skin. Water-base cake makeup foundations are preferred over the more cumbersome grease-base foundations. The Max Factor CTV-1W through CTV-12W pancake series is probably all you need for most makeup jobs. The colors range from a warm light ivory color to a very dark tone for Blacks and other dark-skinned performers.

Women can use their own *lipsticks* or lip rouge, as long as the reds do not contain too much blue. For Black performers and actors especially, a warm red, such as coral, is more effective than a darker red that contains a great amount of blue.

Other materials, such as eyebrow pencil, mascara, and eye shadow, are generally part of every woman performer's makeup kit. Special materials, such as hair

---

Makeup Facial makeup: used to enhance, correct, or change facial features.

Pancake A makeup base, or foundation makeup, usually water-soluble and applied with a small sponge.

Pan Stick A foundation makeup with a grease base. Used to cover a beard shadow or prominent skin blemish.

pieces or even latex masks, are part of the professional makeup artist's inventory. They are of little use in the everyday small station operation.

Techniques

It is not always easy to persuade nonprofessional performers, especially men, to put on necessary makeup. You may do well to look at the guests on camera before deciding whether they need any. If they do, you must be tactful in suggesting its application. Try to appeal not to the performer's vanity but, rather, to his or her desire to contribute to a good performance. Explain the necessity for makeup in technical terms, such as color and light balance.

If you have a mirror available, seat the performer in front of it so that he or she can watch the entire makeup procedure. Adequate, even illumination is very important. If you have to work in the studio, have a small hand mirror ready.

Most women performers are glad to apply the more complicated makeup themselves—lipstick and mascara, for instance. Also, most regular television talent prefer to apply makeup themselves; they usually know what kind they need for a specific television show.

When using **pancake** base, simply apply it with a wet sponge evenly over the face and adjacent exposed skin areas. Make sure to get the base right up into the hairline, and have a towel ready to wipe off the excess. If close-ups of hands are shown, you must also apply pancake base to them and the arms. This is especially important for men performers who demonstrate small objects on camera. If an uneven suntan is exposed (especially when women performers wear bareback dresses or different kinds of bathing suits) all bare skin areas must be covered with base makeup. Bald-headed men need a generous amount of pancake foundation to tone down obvious light reflections and to cover up perspiration.

Be careful not to give male performers a baby-face complexion. It is sometimes even desirable to have a little beard area show. Frequently, a slight covering up of the beard with a beardstick is all that is needed. If additional makeup foundation is necessary, a **pan stick** foundation around the beard area should be applied first and set with some powder. A very light application of a yellow or orange greasepaint counteracts the blue of a heavy five-o'clock-shadow quite satisfactorily. There are professional beardcovers available, such as the Max Factor RCMA BC–2.

CLOTHING AND COSTUMING

In small station operation you are concerned mainly with **clothing** the performer rather than costuming the actor. The performer's clothes should be attractive and stylish but not too conspicuous or showy. Television viewers expect a performer to be well dressed but not overdressed. After all, he or she is a guest in the viewer's home, not a night club performer.

Clothing

Naturally, the type of clothing a performer wears depends largely on his or her personal taste. It also depends on the type of program or occasion and the particular setting. However, some types of clothing look better on television than others. Because the television camera may look at you from a distance and at close range, the lines and overall color scheme of your clothes are just as important as their texture and details.

Line Television has a tendency to put a few extra pounds on the performer. Clothing cut to a slim silhouette helps to combat this problem. Slim dresses and rather tight-fitting suits look more attractive than heavy, horizontally striped material, and baggy dresses and suits. The overall silhouette of your clothing should look pleasing from a variety of angles, and slim but comfortable on you.

Color The most important thing to consider about the colors you wear is that they harmonize with the set. If your set is lemon yellow, do not wear a lemon-yellow dress. Also, avoid wearing a chroma key blue, unless you want to become translucent during the chroma key matting; then even a blue tie may give you trouble.

Although you can wear black or a very dark color, or white or a very light color, as long as the material is not glossy and highly reflective, try to avoid wearing a combination of the two. If the set is very dark, try not to appear in a starched white shirt in front of it. If the set colors are extremely light, do not wear black. As desirable as a pleasant color contrast is, extreme brightness variations offer difficulties. Stark-white, glossy clothes can turn exposed skin areas dark on the television screen, or distort the more subtle colors. Black performers should try not to wear highly reflecting white or light yellow clothes. If you wear a dark suit, reduce the brightness contrast by wearing a pastel shirt. Pink, light green, tan, or gray all photograph well on color and monochrome television.

As always, if you are in doubt as to how well a certain color combination photographs, check it on camera under actual lighting conditions and in the set you are using.

Texture and Detail   Whereas line and color are especially important on long shots, texture and detail of clothing such as dresses, suits, and ties become important at close range. Textured material often looks better than plain, but do not use patterns that are too contrasting or too busy. Closely spaced geometric patterns such as herringbone weaves and checkered patterns cause a moiré effect, which looks like superimposed vibrating rainbow colors. Also, stripes in your clothing may extend beyond the fabric and bleed through surrounding sets and objects, an effect similar to color banding. Extremely fine detail in a pattern will either look too busy or appear smudgy.

The way to make your clothing more interesting on camera is not by choosing a detailed cloth texture, but by adding decorative accessories, such as scarves and jewelry. Although the style of the jewelry depends, of course, on the taste of the performer, in general, he or she should limit it to one or two distinctive pieces. The sparkle of rhinestones, which used to cause annoying glares on monochrome television, is an exciting visual accent on color television.

If a man and a woman, who are scheduled to appear on a panel show or an interview, were to ask you now what to wear for the occasion, what would you tell them?

Here is a possible answer. Both of them should wear something in which they feel comfortable, without looking wide and baggy. Both should stay away from blue, especially if chroma key matting is to be used behind them during the interview. If possible, they should find out the color of the set background and try to avoid similar colors in their outfits.

The woman might wear a slim suit, pantsuit, or dress, all with plain colors. Avoid black-and-white combinations, such as a black skirt and a highly reflecting white blouse or shirt. Also, avoid highly contrasting narrow stripes or checkered patterns. Wear as little jewelry as possible, unless you want to appear flashy.

The man might wear a slim suit, or slacks and plain coat. Wear a plain tie or one with a very subtle pattern. Do not wear a white shirt under a black or dark blue suit or coat. Avoid checkered or herringbone patterns.

Costumes

For small station operation, you do not need **costumes.** If you do a play or a commercial that involves actors, you can always borrow the necessary articles from a local costume rental firm or from the theater arts department of your local high school, college, or university. Theater arts departments usually have a well-stocked costume room from which you can draw most standard period costumes and uniforms.

If you use stock costumes on television, make sure that they look convincing even in a tight close-up. Sometimes the general construction and, especially, the detail of theater accessories are too coarse for the television camera. The color and pattern restrictions for clothing also apply for costumes. The total color design, the overall balance of colors among scenery, costumes, and makeup, is important in some television plays, particularly in musicals and variety shows where long shots often reveal the total scene, including actors, dancers, scenery, and props.

MAIN POINTS

1.   Makeup and clothing (or costuming) are important aspects of the talent's preparation for on-camera work.

2.   Makeup is used for three basic reasons: (1) to improve, (2) to correct, or (3) to change appearance.

3.   Makeup for television demands particular attention to color distortion by the camera, color balance, and close-up requirements.

4.   Warm colors look better than cool colors because the camera tends to emphasize the bluishness of cool colors. If makeup is used for special effects (changing appearance), the colors must harmonize with the color scheme of costumes and scenery.

5.   Makeup must be smooth and subtle to appear natural in the actual production lighting and even on extreme close-ups.

6.   The most basic makeup item is a foundation that covers minor blemishes. Water-based cake foundations, which come in a variety of skin tones, are generally used for television makeup.

7. The techniques of television makeup do not differ drastically from applying ordinary street makeup, especially if the makeup functions are to improve or correct appearance.

8. In clothing, these aspects must be considered: (1) line, whereby a slim cut is to be preferred; (2) color, which should harmonize, yet contrast with the dominant color of the set—a combination of black and white material should be avoided; and (3) texture and detail, which must not make the clothing appear too busy.

9. There is little use of costumes in small station operation. If stock costumes are used from existing collections (such as the college or local theater costume room), their construction and accessories must look convincing even in tight close-ups.

FURTHER READING

Dudek, Lee J. *Professional Broadcast Announcing.* Boston: Allyn and Bacon, Inc., 1982.

Egri, Lajos. *The Art of Dramatic Writing.* New York: Simon and Schuster, 1960.

Hyde, Stuart. *Television and Radio Announcing.* 4th ed. Boston: Houghton Mifflin Company, 1983.

Kehoe, Vincent, Jr. *The Technique of Film and Television Make-up.* Rev. ed. New York: Hastings House, 1976.

King, Nancy R. *The Movement Approach to Acting.* Englewood Cliffs, N.J.: Prentice-Hall, Inc., 1981.

Kirkman, Larry, James Hindman, and Elizabeth Monk Daley. *TV Acting: A Manual for Camera Performance.* New York: Hastings House, 1979.

Stanislavski, Konstantin. *An Actor Prepares.* New York: Theatre Arts Books, 1956.

Producing

This chapter describes the major aspects of producing. Because the range of activities a producer may encounter varies with the particular task, the emphasis here is on the principles of the production process.

Section One covers:

1.   Systems design for production, with four principal factors: (1) need assessment, (2) viewer involvement, (3) medium requirements, and (4) feedback and evaluation.

2.   Above-the-line production, which describes the basic functions of such personnel as producers, writers, and talent.

3.   Below-the-line production, which covers the technical facilities and functions of production engineers and other production personnel.

4.   Special production aspects, including (1) definition of program types, (2) copyright and clearances, (3) union affiliation, and (4) legal aspects.

5.   Production planning factors, such as need assessment, formulation of program idea, audience analysis, definition of process message, ideal broadcast time, explanation of the show as expressed in a treatment, and budget considerations.

6.   The actual production process, which considers such factors as how, where, when and by whom the production is to be done.

Section Two examines miscellaneous subjects of concern to a television producer: research tools, major parts of a program proposal, audience classifications and ratings, satellite transmission, and cable television.

As an originator of a mass communication process, you must bear responsibility toward the perceivers of the television program (the viewers) and toward the originating institution (the station, production company, or corporation for which you are working).

It is not always easy to serve both masters. In trying to fulfill your obligation to the public, you may propose a program series that is counter to the economic interests of the station. The program manager may tell you that he or she, the sales manager, and the general manager of the station are in agreement on the worth of your program idea of how a university campus operates and what college learning is all about; however, they all feel that such a series would probably attract only a highly specific audience, produce low ratings, and therefore hardly be an attractive package for time buyers who want to reach as large an audience as possible with their commercials. How about carrying such a series as **sustaining** (noncommercial) **programs,** as part of the station's public service? How about cable?

According to the program manager, there is a cable hookup in town that reaches the university and community college areas. He or she finally asks you to check with the public service director and to prepare a budget for the first three shows.

As you can see, you are already in the middle of rather delicate negotiations, the selling of your idea to people who look at the program series from highly divergent points of view and who apply different criteria for the relative success of the show. And all this work, before you have even had a chance to think much about the creative aspects of the production! Such is the lot of a producer.

Some people may get dismayed at the thought of having a show turned down because it does not seem financially feasible. But a skillful producer anticipates such problems, and approaches a show idea from a business as well as a creative point of view. There is nothing intrinsically wrong with combining art and money. The fact that novelists and painters get paid for their art does not cheapen their products. But if you sell an idea that has little or no

Producing means to see to it that a worthwhile idea gets to be a worthwhile television presentation. As a producer, you are in charge of this process. You are involved in managing a great number of people and in coordinating an even greater number of activities and other production details.

aesthetic or social value, for the sole purpose of improving the ratings and beating the competition, you are abusing the public and you are acting irresponsibly, even though you make money in the process.

Realizing that as a producer you must operate within the public's "interest, convenience, and necessity," how, then, can you develop an idea into an on-the-air television show? What are the techniques of television production?

Although each show idea has certain peculiar production requirements, there are nevertheless techniques, or at least approaches, that apply to television production in general. We will, therefore, attempt to acquaint you with a **systems design** that covers the major points of production. You should keep in mind, however, that some productions may require procedures that differ considerably from the standard. The systems approach as mentioned here should serve as a *guide* to problem solving, not a recipe.

Specifically, we will discuss (1) systems design for production, (2) above-the-line production, (3) below-the-line production, (4) special production aspects, (5) planning factors, and (6) the steps in the production process.

PRODUCTION SYSTEMS DESIGN

In television production, as in cooking, there is no single or correct way of getting things done. As a producer, you have to wear many hats, sometimes all at once. You may have to act as a psychologist and business person to persuade management to buy your idea, argue like a technical expert for a particular piece of equipment, or search like a sociologist for the needs and desires of a particular section of society. After some sweeping creative excursions, you will have to become quite pedantic and double-check on such items as whether there is enough coffee for the guests who will appear on your show.

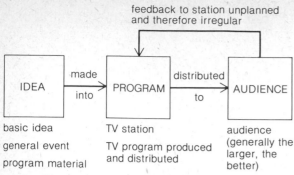

feedback to station unplanned and therefore irregular

IDEA →(made into)→ PROGRAM →(distributed to)→ AUDIENCE

basic idea
general event
program material

TV station
TV program produced and distributed

audience (generally the larger, the better)

16.1   Basic Television Communication System In the basic communication system the production process moves from the program idea to the program production. From there, it goes to the transmission of the program to a large audience. The feedback is unplanned and, therefore, irregular. (Werner J. Severin and James W. Tankard, *Communication Theories* [New York: Hastings House Publishers, 1976], pp. 28–42.)

Because production involves a great number of processes, each one interacting with the others, at least to some degree, we learn its function most profitably by considering it as a **system.** In the production system, as in any other, various elements and processes are linked together and interact with one another so as to achieve the desired product— in this case, the television audience experiencing the televised material in a specific way.

The system helps you to identify quickly, and fairly accurately and reliably, the major production elements each program requires, and the necessary interaction among them. Simply, the system assists you in determining which people you require, what they should do, and what equipment is necessary at what time in order to televise a show that fulfills a specific need of the audience, or that entices the audience to a specific reaction.

We will first describe the popular *content approach* to production and then the more effective *effect-to-cause* system.

Content Approach

Traditionally, we have approached television production from a content point of view. As a producer, you are often given program material from an outside source or assigned to work with outside content specialists. For example, you may be asked to work with a teacher who has been selected by the local school district to be the television teacher. Or you may be assigned to work with a local organization that wants you to make an exciting show out of their handing awards to their local heroes.

All too often in these situations, content dictates the production procedures. The local teacher assumes that he or she, as the content expert, ought to have some say in how the on-the-air lesson is to proceed, or the local service club assumes your station will bring cameras to their awards banquet to cover their procedures from beginning to end. Many producers agree to such an approach, not necessarily because it makes for exciting television, but because it gets the job done with a minimum of effort and friction between the client and the station. (See 16.1 and 16.2.) However, as widespread as this *content approach* may be, it has some serious flaws:

1.   The content (program material) is selected by someone who has little or no knowledge of how

Above-the-Line Production A budgetary division of production elements. It concerns mainly nontechnical personnel.

Below-the-Line Production A budgetary division of production elements. It concerns technical personnel and facilities.

Producer Creator and organizer of television shows; usually in charge of all financial matters.

Scale Basic minimum fees for television talent as prescribed by the talent union.

Systems Design A plan that shows the interrelationships of two or more systems. In television production, it shows the interrelation of all major production elements, as well as the flow (direction) of the production processes.

Treatment Brief description of a prospective television program.

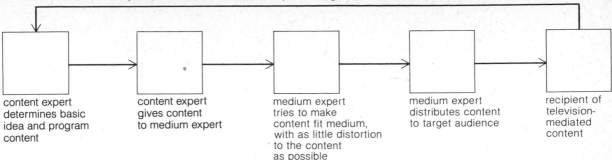

| content expert determines basic idea and program content | content expert gives content to medium expert | medium expert tries to make content fit medium, with as little distortion to the content as possible | medium expert distributes content to target audience | recipient of television-mediated content |

16.2   Content-to-Medium-to-Audience Process In this communication system the content is selected by someone who knows little about television. The content is then given to medium experts who try to make the content fit the requirements of the television medium. Routine production processes are usually employed. The program is then distributed to the target audience by the most convenient channel. If the recipients are students, they respond with planned feedback to the content expert, generally through examinations. (Severin and Tankard, *Communication Theories*, pp. 28–42.)

television works. Thus, the "content expert" selects his or her material simply by *what* should be communicated, not by *how* it may *appear* on the television screen, or how it will be *received* by a television audience.

2.   The so-called medium expert is handed the task of distributing the already selected material via television. In this way, the final criteria as to the television program's worthwhileness are generally stipulated by the content expert, not by the medium expert, or even the eventual receiver of the message. Thus, the medium expert has little influence on the content, which may or may not be suited to the television medium or the television audience.

3.   The separation of content expert and medium expert only fosters the development of mutual mistrust.

4.   Most seriously, the medium is considered a mere distribution device rather than a production element that has a great influence on the content as well as its reception by the television audience.

5.   The effect of the program is presupposed because of the content alone, not by how and how much the television viewer is affected.

Effect-to-Cause Approach

A more viable systems design seems to be one that focuses more on *viewer need* and, ultimately, on what he or she *experiences* during the program and his or her *response* afterward, rather than on content and how it can be molded into a television show. In effect, once you have ascertained a specific viewer need or desire, you work backward from viewer experience to what the medium requires in order to produce such an experience. Because the system starts with the viewer experience and works backward, we call it the **effect-to-cause approach** to production. (See 16.3.)

Need Assessment   Common sense tells us that we should ascertain the basic needs and desires of the television audience for specific programming, rather than superimposing programs on an unsuspecting public. The more goal-directed your communication is or the more specific your intended audience is, the more you ought to know about the overt and covert needs of the target audience.

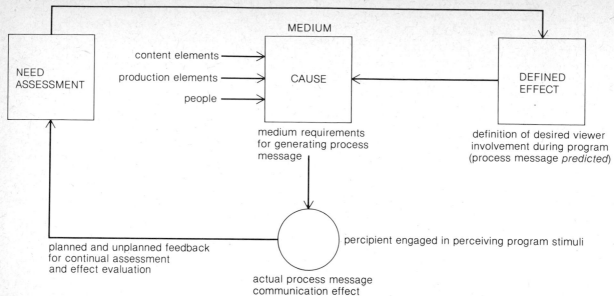

16.3   Effect-to-Cause System This production system starts not with content, but with the desired viewer experience—the process message *(defined effect)*. We then turn to the *medium* to find out what production elements are necessary to effect the desired viewer experience. These medium requirements include content elements, the customary production elements (such as lights, cameras, and audio), and the people necessary to get the production done. Thus, the medium *causes* the actual audience experience—the *effect*—to occur (through telecasting the program). The feedback offers a clue to how close the actual audience experience came to the defined (ideal) one. The closer they are, the more successful the communication has been.

It is relatively easy to find some of the overt needs of the audience. Simply ask them. But it is often difficult to find the more covert needs. For many centuries, the arts have catered to and even fulfilled many covert emotional and social needs of the public. Today, this responsibility has been largely relegated to the media (radio, television, film, and the press). But how can you do a need assessment? It is difficult enough to get some consensus on the overt needs; is it not asking too much of a producer to worry about possible covert needs? No, it is not. In fact, being concerned about overt and covert needs of the public is one of the producer's main responsibilities and sources for ideas.

Fortunately, you do not have to do all the need assessment by yourself. If your station does not have a need assessment expert, you may consider employing an independent research firm or, better yet, seeking the help of the mass communication, sociology, and psychology departments of the nearby university. After all, these departments know the latest developments in their field and usually have a number of expert faculty and students available to undertake such projects.

Viewer Involvement   Involvement describes the state of the viewer while watching a television program, and his or her response to the program afterward. Usually, the experience of the viewer relative to the program (the audiovisual stimuli) is extremely complex. Although we cannot make this perception process any less complex through programming, we can, to a certain degree, channel the viewer's experience and response. In its most obvious forms, a comedian can make us laugh with a funny joke; the close-up of a tender kiss of the reunited couple can make us experience human warmth and compassion, even love; a police officer approaching the gunman's trap can increase our anxiety; and an especially tragic news event or play can make us cry.

If the program is indeed geared to the viewer's overt and/or covert needs, the process of viewing the program is no longer a simple watching and listening but an involvement and, in its most ideal state, a *participation* in the audiovisual event. The viewer thus becomes a **percipient,** and we can define the perception process as an event (X) that—for the convenience of assigning it a place in the system—we put between the screen and the percipient (see 16.4). In other words, the real message of the communication lies in the interaction between the percipient and the audiovisual stimuli, not in an arbitrarily predetermined content that is distributed by television. This message we call the **process message.** It cannot exist independently of the viewer, or even before the actual process of perception.

Now, in order to arrive at this process message, we must give some direction to the viewer experience—or, more precisely, the percipient involvement. Taking a cue from instructional systems and programmed learning, we simply state a desired process message, an experience objective. Here are some examples:

1. *The process message* (perceived during the program) *should help the percipient to learn, and later apply, five simple steps of energy conservation.* In this objective we simply want the viewer (percipient) to *learn* five ways of energy conservation, which he or she might not have known before, and learn them well enough so that he or she can not only recount them but use them in his or her daily activities. (Obviously, they do not contain the recommendation for shutting off the television set; otherwise all subsequent process messages would not occur.) The process message contains action cues for overt activities, not unlike much advertising, which persuades the viewer to go and buy a specific product.

2. *The process message should make the percipient vicariously experience the beauty as well as the*

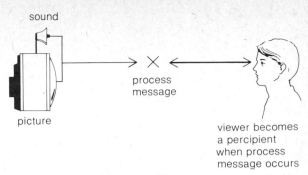

16.4   Process Message The process message is the interaction between the percipient (television viewer-listener) and the audiovisual stimuli of the television program (ordinarily called message).

immense physical power inherent in a football game. Here the objective is not to entertain the viewer with selected delayed football action but to give him or her a certain experience while he or she is perceiving the program. The ordinary televising of football games often fails to communicate the immense physical power of the sport, especially if the viewer has never actually played football. At the same time, the movements of the players, their reactions to one another in a play, and the structure of teamwork have an inherent beauty that, too, is often not clarified and intensified enough for the average viewer. But such a process message, which stresses the aesthetic values of football, could certainly contribute to emotional literacy, especially of those viewers who do not seek aesthetic stimuli in other programs, such as dance, drama, or music, or in other experiences, such as going to a concert or a dance recital.

3. *The process message should help the percipient to relax and escape for a while from the reality of the daily routine, laugh with the talent on the screen, and, hopefully, about himself or herself.* As you can see, a process message can also be stated in rather general terms. But even then, this process message contains an important clue: "laugh with the talent and about himself or herself." This means that the writer and director must develop characters with whom the percipient can identify, and/or situations

that contain highly personal, though universal, touches.

If you cannot state a show idea as a rather precise process message, you are not ready to think about the actual production requirements, such as equipment, talent, and so forth. However, once you feel comfortable with your process message or messages, you can move to one of the most important steps in the production process—deciding on the medium requirements.

Medium Requirements   As you have seen in previous chapters, because the medium demands certain production equipment and procedures, such as shot composition and sequence, lighting, and audio, you should now ask what it needs in order to meet the stated objective as fully as possible. When we talk about *medium,* we do not mean just the different pieces of production equipment, such as cameras, lights, and microphones, but also the people and agencies that work in television or are somehow connected with its operation.

Let's take objective 2 (power and aesthetics of a football game) and see what the medium might require so that the process message can be accomplished. We will simply jot down some of the major points that come to mind, without worrying at this time how they should be organized or how they may fit the systems design.

Here's the objective again: *The process message should make the percipient vicariously experience the beauty as well as the immense physical power inherent in a football game.*

1.   Who should be the percipients? Where and how should they perceive the program, and when? We are now approaching a precise audience definition. Housewives usually have a viewing pattern quite different from working women. Teenagers watch at different times from adults. Viewing customs on weekends are different from the rest of the week. Usually the program manager has a great deal to say about when the program will be aired, but you should have some idea of the preferred broadcast time. The type of audience generally dictates the ideal broadcast time.

2.   There are some key phrases in the objective: vicarious experience, physical power, and beauty. To give the percipient vicarious experience, you must *involve* her (or him) in the action, not just show something to look at. Involvement and power immediately suggest an extremely tight camera throughout the program. Close-ups and extreme close-ups not only intensify the physical force of the game but also bring the viewer into the fray. You may even want to try some subjective camera techniques, whereby the camera participates in the action.[1]

In this case, the equipment must be highly mobile—portable cameras and videotape units, for instance. Do you have them available? How many? If not, can you rent some? Or you may want to use some videotape slow motion or freeze frames. Again, when talking to the production manager, or engineering supervisor, you should have a pretty good idea of what you need and why. Postproduction will also undoubtedly take up a major portion of the production activities.

3.   Because you are building an event through several takes, with the action shot from various viewpoints, angles, and sometimes in slow motion (power and beauty elements), you will have to repeat a specific action over and over again. The shooting requirements make the coverage of a single game impractical, if not impossible. What you probably need is a football team that is willing to participate in this project. A high school or college team will probably be more willing than a professional team. In any case, they will be less expensive.

4.   The power factor suggests heavy use of audio. If you have the facilities for double-system sound (whereby you record the sound on audiotape, separately from the videotape), you can manipulate the sound track more easily in postproduction than when recording it single-system (all the sounds are recorded on the audio track of the videotape simultaneously with the pictures). In any case, you will probably want to emphasize the thumps, groans, and crashes to communicate the full impact of the

---

[1] Herbert Zettl, *Sight-Sound-Motion* (Belmont, Calif.: Wadsworth Publishing Co., 1973), pp. 230–233.

power aspect. This again demands that the mics be quite close to the action.

Because the production is not a mere *look at* a football game, but a *look into* a creative conception of the game, you can liberally add music or other related sounds for the intensification of the action.

5.   Unless the background music is especially written for the show and played by friends, you need clearance for the recording used. You also need written clearances from anyone who could object to your televising the team, such as the coach, the school official in charge of such activities (such as the athletic director or the dean), and any players who are interviewed or in some other way become featured talent on the program. These clearances are not necessary, of course, if you simply cover a regular game, because the game is then a public event. Don't ever rely on a verbal agreement. If you cannot get it in writing, look for another show.

6.   Beauty again. Perhaps you can intensify the event by manipulating the colors. Check with the video engineer about various special color effects. Perhaps you want to shoot part of the show in black-and-white and colorize it later.

7.   The heavy postproduction activities involved in this project need careful scheduling of editing equipment and time. You need an expert editor and, of course, an extremely sensitive director, whose major qualifications may not be an expert knowledge of football (though this would help) but should include a great sense of motion, composition, dynamic sequencing. The camera operators must have similar qualifications.

This coordination calls for preproduction meetings: with the director, camera operators, audio engineers, editor, floor manager, and production assistants. In fact, you may need to spend a great deal of time in such meetings. A thorough understanding of the process message by all members of the production team greatly facilitates the actual production later on. A second meeting should involve the players. The director should clue them in about the purpose of the show, and the process message.

8.   When can you get the players to meet? Where? Is the field reserved? What if it rains that day? Perhaps the rain will add to the power idea, and to beauty. You will need several shooting days. How many? How many production people do you need?

9.   What is it going to cost? Do you have a budget large enough to pay for the participants, the equipment used, and the materials needed (videotape and audiotape stock, and so forth)?

10.   The station wants to give the program wide publicity; it has already interested several local sports shops in buying program time. That brings up another thought. How many commercial inserts should you expect during the half-hour program time assigned to you by the programming department? Where in the show should these breaks occur? Check with the sales department. The editor can then edit the show with the commercial breaks in mind.

11.   The show requires special graphics. The art director should sit in during the first two briefing sessions.

12.   Do you need narration in certain places? Perhaps some rather poetic statements that express the power and beauty of the game? Or are the natural sounds and the music enough to clarify and intensify the event? If you decide on narration, you need a writer, unless you tackle the writing yourself. Also, the announcer has to be included in the postproduction schedule and the budget.

As you can see, the list goes on and on. The better your knowledge of the medium and the more you know about the specific requirements, the more detailed your list is and, most of all, the more prepared you are for the actual production. A good producer works out the problems *before* they arise. *Thorough preparation* is the key to an efficient and successful production.

What happened to content? It has become simply part of the medium requirements. If you go back over the previous list, you discover that "content" appears in several of the points. Thus, what is finally seen and heard and, we hope, perceived by the viewer is not just subject matter that has been predetermined independently of the medium and simply distributed thereby, but images that have been created as part of the medium requirement within the context of the basic process message.

Figure 16.5 shows the basic medium require-

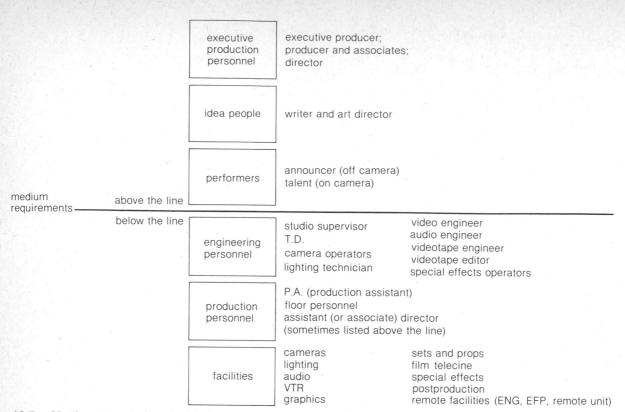

medium requirements	above the line	executive production personnel	executive producer; producer and associates; director
		idea people	writer and art director
		performers	announcer (off camera) talent (on camera)
	below the line	engineering personnel	studio supervisor T.D. camera operators lighting technician	video engineer audio engineer videotape engineer videotape editor special effects operators
		production personnel	P.A. (production assistant) floor personnel assistant (or associate) director (sometimes listed above the line)
		facilities	cameras lighting audio VTR graphics	sets and props film telecine special effects postproduction remote facilities (ENG, EFP, remote unit)

16.5 Medium Requirements Medium requirements include equipment and above- and below-the-line personnel. The medium requirements change with the process message.

ments as they occur in the average production (see also pp. 485–490).

Feedback and Evaluation

How do you know whether a show has been successful—whether the process message has indeed been perceived? This aspect of production is probably one of the most difficult to ascertain. When, as sometimes happens, viewers respond by telephone calls, postcards, and letters, record their comments as positive and negative responses. Try not to dismiss the negative responses. Analyze them and see what you can learn from them. But, equally, do not lose sight of the good responses because of several negative responses. Look at the various comments as objectively as possible.

Certain program formats include some stimu-lus for feedback; the talent may ask for the viewer's response, or the viewer may be obligated to respond—as when he or she is enrolled in a telecourse, for example. Ratings, of course, test viewer contact with the show, but not necessarily *impact*. Generally, however, a very popular show with a high rating must fulfill some kind of viewer need; otherwise the viewers would not watch it. Although the rating methods are usually contested when the ratings are low and praised when high and favorable, they are as good an indication of audience as is currently available. We will talk a little more about ratings in Section Two of this chapter.

Press reviews are sometimes biased and therefore not always reliable. Perhaps as a producer you may want to ask faculty and students of broadcasting to help in designing and administering a signif-

Personnel	Function
Executive Producer	In charge of one or several program series, has overall responsibility of complete series. Takes care of entire budget and handles station management, advertising agencies, financial supporters, salaries for principal actors.
Producer	In charge of individual production. Is responsible for all supervisory personnel working on it. Responsible for coordinating technical and nontechnical production elements. Often serves as writer, and sometimes as director of the show as well.
Assistant or Associate Producer	Assists the producer in all production matters. Often does the actual coordinating job, such as telephoning talent, confirming schedules, worrying about deadlines, and picking up the slides from the art department. Unfortunately, many secretaries are made to function as assistant or even full-fledged producers without the benefit of the authority and financial reward that ordinarily go with this responsibility.
Director	In charge of directing talent and technical facilities. Is responsible for transforming a script into video and audio images, and for creating the medium's part of the process message (the other part being the involvement of the percipient). Small stations combine the producing and directing functions in a *producer-director*.
Art Director	In charge of creative design aspects of show (set, display, graphics).
Talent	Performs and acts on television—live, on videotape, or on film. Large productions include dancers, singers, or extras in a play.
Writer	Writes television scripts. In small station operations, the writer's function is often assumed by the producer or the director.
Announcer	Reads narration but does not appear on camera. If on camera, the announcer moves up into the talent category.
Newscaster	Reports news. News operations usually have their own above-the-line personnel, which includes a news producer, assignment editor, writers, and reporters. But because most of them are regularly employed by a station, their salaries need not be considered in an above-the-line budget.

icant program evaluation test. In fact, you may want to evaluate the various steps of your system prior to the actual telecast so that you can *predict the process message* with some reliability.

Research organizations charge a considerable amount of money for testing a number of variables (like and dislike, recall of product name, character identification, and others) before the show is ever aired. In small television operations, you can hardly afford such "sneak previews." However, the precise formulation of a process message in relation to audience need should make the acceptance of your idea by the target audience less arbitrary.

ABOVE-THE-LINE PRODUCTION

As you can see from 16.5, medium requirements that deal with nontechnical elements—writers, producers, directors, talent, art directors, and others—

are diagrammed "above the line," whereas technical facilities—studio, cameras, scenery, graphic arts, and engineering personnel—are listed "below the line." This division comes from the custom of preparing two separate budgets, an above-the-line budget and a below-the-line budget. We will adopt this convenient grouping in our discussion of specific production elements.

The **above-the-line production** is accomplished mainly by nontechnical personnel. Above-the-line production elements consist of people and things an independent producer brings into the production facility: the talent, the director, sometimes the assistant director and production assistant, and the announcer. Table 16.6 shows the major above-the-line production workers with their principal functions, and the major facilities of a typical medium-sized television operation.

In large productions, the above-the-line personnel may also include script or dialogue editors

Personnel	Function
Engineering	
Studio or Remote Supervisor	Oversees all technical operations.
T.D.	Technical director; usually acts as crew chief and does the switching.
Camera Operators	Operate the cameras; often take care of the lighting.
Lighting Technician	In charge of lighting; usually in large production centers, or for large productions only.
Video Engineer	Shades cameras; often serves also as videotape operator on remotes.
Audio Engineer	In charge of all audio operations. Works audio board during the show.
Videotape Engineer	Runs videotape machines.
Videotape Editor	Edits videotapes and does other postproduction jobs, including audio sweetening. In some stations, the videotape editors belong to production staff rather than engineering. If an A.D. is assigned to the editing, he or she belongs above-the-line.
News Photographers	Almost always separate from camera operators. Operate exclusively ENG cameras.
Production	
(Some of these functions may be performed by engineering personnel. In small station operations, and especially in college and university operations, the engineering and production personnel functions often overlap considerably. For example, the simplified operation of the television camera certainly makes it possible for nonengineering personnel to function as camera operators. Certain labor union restrictions, however, may delimit the personnel functions quite explicitly.)	
P.A.	Production assistant. Assists the producer in all matters. During the production, takes notes of minor production problems during rehearsals. (Could also belong to the above-the-line personnel.)
Floor or Stage Manager	In charge of all floor activities. Directs talent on the floor, relays director's cues to studio talent, and supervises floor personnel.
Floorpersons (also called grips, stagehands, facilities persons)	Set up scenery and dress sets. Operate easel cards and graphics. Sometimes operate microphone booms and camera dollies. Assist camera operators in pulling cables. Usually act as properties, wardrobe, and makeup people, especially in small stations.
Associate or Assistant Director	Classified as below-the-line personnel in most television operations. Assists the director in all duties. Often supervises rehearsals and does the timing during the actual production. In difficult shows, gives the appropriate "ready" cues to cameras, audio, lighting, VTR, and so forth.
Graphic Artists	Prepare studio cards, slides, and other graphic material.
Character Generator or Electronic Graphics Operator	Programs character generator and operates it during the production.

(who edit the script for the specific show requirement), composers (for the original score), conductor and musicians (if there is live music during the production, or for postproduction dubbing), designers and art directors, a unit manager (in charge of day-to-day schedules and budgets), and production assistants. Of course, most small or medium-sized stations use their regular employees, who are on the station's payroll anyway. Only large networks or independent production companies regularly hire freelance above-the-line personnel.

BELOW-THE-LINE PRODUCTION

Below-the-line includes all the items that a production facility (network, independent studio, or independent production facility) is able to provide. Therefore, these items are almost always budgeted on a per-show basis. The **below-the-line production** has to do with coordinating the engineering and production personnel who operate equipment

Facilities	Producer's Involvement
	(Although most of these facilities are stipulated by the director of the specific show, you, as a producer, are nevertheless ultimately responsible for their use and cost):
Studio Use	Requests studio use and confirms studio schedules with production manager. Studio needs to be scheduled for rehearsal, setup, lighting, and actual production time.
Cameras	Checks with director on the agreed number of cameras. Establishes whether all the requested cameras are, indeed, needed.
Lighting	Checks with the T.D. or lighting person whether he or she has the proper information about the lighting needed. (Floor plan and lighting plot should be in the hands of the lighting person.)
Audio	Confirms with audio engineer special audio requests, such as guest to play a guitar number, or the exact instrumentation of a rock group.
VTR	Confirms with the videotape engineer the approximate length of the show, or various takes, and any special requests. This is simply a double-check on the director's request.
Telecine	Checks on availability and scheduling of film islands.
Graphics	Requests the necessary graphics, and sees to it that they are properly programmed and stored in the character generator, or promptly delivered to master control (slides) or the studio (charts, easel cards). This is an especially important job for the producer. A missing slide can seriously impair the whole production. Watches for unity in style.
Sets and Properties	Follows through on special set construction, and the purchase of special properties. Since some art directors may get carried away when sent on a shopping trip for properties, the producer should keep close watch over all purchases.
Makeup and Wardrobe	In large productions, confirms the availability of makeup rooms and personnel, and especially that the costumes are ready for use for the dress rehearsal.
Special Production Effects	Checks with engineering (studio supervisor) on all special effects that involve additional equipment and manpower, or unusual equipment use.
Postproduction	Checks on all postproduction schedules and facilities (VTR's editing facilities, video and audio dubbings, as well as personnel).
Remote Facilities	Checks on all aspects of EFP or other remote productions.

during the production and postproduction, as well as the necessary production equipment and facilities. Most often, the director of the show, the production manager, and the engineering supervisor (either studio supervisor or assistant chief engineer) determine exactly which technical facilities are necessary. However, as a producer, you cannot afford to leave all the below-the-line decisions to the director or the engineering personnel. Otherwise you may find yourself losing control not only of the production but especially of the below-the-line budget, for which, after all, you are responsible. A producer who is knowledgeable of all aspects of television production techniques (including the potentials and limitations of the major equipment, such as cameras, lights, VTRs, and audio equipment) can save considerable time, effort, and money without limiting the concept or production scope of the proposed show.

In EFP and all news operations, the producer must be thoroughly familiar with all technical requirements and possibilities. For example, as a news producer, you must be able to decide quickly on the equipment necessary for the event pickup and especially on the means of getting the story back into the studio (such as videotape, live microwave feeds, microwave links via helicopter or telephone, and so on—see Chapter 18 for more detail). An EFP assignment may require you to pass judgment on whether intercom links with the station are necessary, or whether to use studio-type or ENG equipment for the pickup.

Table 16.7 shows some of the major below-the-line production personnel and facilities.

Again, the below-the-line personnel are usually employed by the station. When you rent your facilities to an outside agency, however, the engineering and production personnel need to be included in the below-the-line budget.

Systems Design: Production Sequence

The above- and below-the-line production categories make it mandatory for you to organize the medium requirements into a specific *production sequence*. Sometimes, the process message requires that you start with the above-the-line items and then move to the below-the-line items. At other times, you must involve them both simultaneously. A careful analysis of the objective of the process message, however, generally suggests a production sequence. Obviously, you cannot order title slides if the writer has not yet finished the script and given you the title of the show. Nor can you argue with the director over the number of cameras before the sets have been designed and the action tentatively blocked by the director.

Make a list of sequence of events that you consider to be maximally efficient. Several of the operations occur at the same time, or run parallel with each other. Try to fit this sequence into your calendar and into the master production schedule of the station or production agency for which you work.

Besides helping you to determine the production sequence, the systems design aids you greatly in the production of a *program series*. You can, for example, state the objective of the process message and identify the medium requirements for each of the shows. You can then see which of the production activities overlap for the whole series. For example, you may find that the same set will do for the whole series, or that you can use certain graphics for more than one show. Or you may even be able to videotape two shows on the same day, one right after the other. You may also combine on-location work and shoot several sequences with the same crew.

Such a system is particularly beneficial if you produce a series of commercials, all treating the same product, or if you have to produce an instructional television series covering the same topic. (See 16.8.)

SPECIAL PRODUCTION ASPECTS

Besides the above- and below-the-line production processes, there are other important production aspects that you must consider. These are (1) definition of program types, (2) copyright and clearances, (3) union affiliation, and (4) legal aspects.

Program Types

All program types have been standardized by the FCC into eight categories: (1) Agricultural (A), (2) Entertainment (E), (3) News (N), (4) Public Affairs (PA), (5) Religious (R), (6) Instructional (I), (7) Sports (S), and (8) Other (O). The last (O) includes all programs not falling within the first seven. These program types are not to overlap one another.

Furthermore, there are subcategories, which may overlap with any of the preceding types. They are (1) Editorials (EDIT), (2) Political (POL), and (3) Educational Institution (ED). Some stations add their own combinations, such as Editorials/Political, or Political/Educational Institution, in order to accommodate programs that do not exactly fit the above FCC program types. In any case, the educational institution category (ED) includes all programs prepared by, on behalf of, or in cooperation with educational institutions.

Copyright and Clearances

If you use copyrighted material on your show, you must procure proper clearances. Usually, the name of the copyright holder and the year of the copyright are printed right after the © copyright symbol. Some photographs, reproductions of famous paintings, and prints are often copyrighted, as are, of course, books, periodicals, short stories, plays, and musical scores. Check with the station's attorney about special copyright clauses and public domain.

SHOW/SCENE SUBJECT	DATE/TIME	LOCATION	FACILITIES	TALENT/PERSONNEL
energy conservation shows 1 + 2 Openings + closings	Aug. 8 11:30 - 4:30	Solar heating plant	normal EFP as per FAX of 7/2	Janet + Bill – EFP crew as scheduled DIRECTOR: JOHN H.
energy # 2, 3, 4 Sections on Solar panel demonstrations	Aug. 10 8:30 - 2:30	Solar heating plant	normal EFP as per FAX of 7/2	Janet + Bill – EFP Crew as Scheduled DIRECTOR: JOHN H.
energy # 1, 3 installation of Solar heating panels	Aug. 11 8:30 - 4:30	Terra Linda Housing Project	normal EFP as per FAX of 7/2	NO TALENT (V.O. in post) EFP crew as scheduled DIRECTOR: MARGE P.

16.8   Multiple Production System In this system, the major production elements—date/time, location, facilities, and talent/personnel—are listed so that you can plug in the shows or scenes that overlap in certain production aspects. As you can see, in our show, "Energy Conservation," we do the openings and closings for shows 1 and 2 on the same day (Aug. 8). Two days later, the same talent, director, and crew go back to the same location to do the scenes from shows 2, 3, and 4 that deal with the demonstrations of a variety of solar panels. By now, the crew is accustomed to the location and to the director, so the brief scenes should take even less time than allocated. The scenes that show the installation of solar panels are shot at a different location with a different director in charge. No talent is needed because these brief scenes will be the B-roll with voice-over from a solar energy expert. More time is allotted because the crew is dependent on the workers installing the panels.

   With such a systems approach, it is easy to make changes, and to add scenes or take them out according to production need.

You will need clearances for the use of recorded music, as well as the performance of written music, on the air. All published music is subject to performance royalties, with three major organizations holding most of the music copyrights: (1) ASCAP—the American Society of Composers, Authors and Publishers; (2) BMI—Broadcast Music, Incorporated; and (3) SESAC—The Society of European Stage Authors and Composers. If the licensing society is not indicated on the label of the recording, for example, check the large music catalogs of any one of these societies. Larger stations have standing contracts with these societies; all you have to do then is to report the music used on the air.

Union Affiliation

Most directors, writers, and talent belong to a guild or union, as do almost all below-the-line personnel. As a producer, you must be alert to the various union regulations in your production area. Most unions not only stipulate salaries and minimum fees, but also specific working conditions, such as overtime, turnaround time (stipulated hours of rest between workdays), rest periods, who can legally run a studio camera and who cannot, and so forth.

If you use nonunion personnel in a unionized station, or if you plan to air a show that has been prepared outside the station with nonunion talent, check with the respective unions for proper clearance.

There are two basic types of unions: those for *nontechnical* personnel, and those for all *technical* personnel.

Nontechnical Unions   These include mainly unions for performers, writers, and directors.

AFTRA   *American Federation for Television and Radio Artists.* This is the major union for television talent. Directors sometimes belong to AFTRA, especially when they double as announcers and on-the-air talent. AFTRA prescribes basic minimum fees, called **scale,** which differ from area to area. Most well-known talent (such as prominent actors and local news anchorpersons) are paid well above scale.

DGA   *Directors' Guild of America, Inc.* A union for television and motion picture directors and associate directors. Sometimes, floor managers and production assistants of large stations and networks belong to the "guild."

WGA   *Writers' Guild of America, Inc.* A union for writers of television and film scripts.

SAG   *Screen Actors Guild.* Important organization, especially when film is involved in television production. However, also includes some actors for videotaped commercials.

SEG   *Screen Extras Guild.* A union for extras participating in major film productions or filmed television series.

AFM   *American Federation of Musicians.* Important only if live orchestras are used in the production.

Technical Unions   These include all television engineers and occasionally a variety of production personnel, such as microphone boom operators, ENG camera operators, and floor personnel.

IBEW   *International Brotherhood of Electrical Workers.* This union includes studio, master control, and maintenance engineers and technicians. It may also include ENG camera operators and floor personnel.

NABET   *National Brotherhood of Broadcast Employees and Technicians.* Another strong engineering union that may also include floor personnel and nonengineering production people (boom operators, dolly operators).

IATSE   *International Alliance of Theatrical Stage Employees and Motion Picture Machine Operators.* It includes film camera people and ENG camera operators. There is still some confusion about how to classify ENG camera operators. Many of them switched from operating 16mm film cameras to ENG cameras and stayed with their old (IATSE) union affiliation. Others were classified engineers and, therefore, affiliated with pure engineering unions.

Be especially careful when you ask studio guests to do anything but answer questions during an interview. If they give a short demonstration of their talents, they may be classified as performers and automatically become subject to AFTRA fees. Also, do not request the floor crew to do anything that is not directly connected with their regular line of duty, or they, too, may collect talent fees. Camera operators usually have a contract clause that assures them a substantial penalty fee if they are willfully shown by another camera on the television screen.

Legal Aspects

Before you accept a script or go into rehearsal, make sure that the material is well suited for television presentation. Sometimes a script that reads well may become quite objectionable when presented in a certain manner. Be guided by good taste and respect for the viewing public, not just by laws. There is a fine line between using an expletive simply to "liven up an otherwise dull interview" and using it as an essential part of characterization by one of the actors.

Check with the station attorney or legal counsel about up-to-date rulings on **libel** (written defamation), **slander** (oral defamation), the right of privacy (not the same in all states), **Canon 35** (courtroom television), obscenity laws, **Section 315** of the Communications Act (affording candidates for public office equal opportunities), and similar matters.

PRODUCTION PLANNING

Because each television production is unique, it has very specific production requirements. Therefore, the clearest way to give you an idea of the entire production process is to list a series of steps and add some of the major factors and questions you ought to consider along with them. The steps you will follow in a real situation may not always match the ones outlined here, either in number or sequence, but the basic patterns of activity remain. The factors indicated here follow the effect-to-cause systems design, as mentioned previously.

1. **Need Assessment:** Is the program idea truly in the public interest? If the idea were developed into a television show, what, if anything, would the viewer gain by it? Remember that relaxation and entertainment, just plain fun, are indeed important program objectives. Check with the assessment person, the program director, the public service director, or anyone else whose judgment you trust, about defined needs. Most of all, stay attuned to life around you. Keep up with the news; observe how people live, what they say, how they feel. Talk to community leaders. Exchange ideas with communication experts, such as mass communication educators, sociologists, philosophers, and artists. Sensitive artists are usually very much aware of the prevailing social climate and of future needs.

2. **Formulation of Program Idea:** Before stating a program objective, try to arrive at a general program idea. Narrow it down to manageable proportions. Do not try to solve all the world's problems in 27:30 minutes. If you have decided on a worthwhile issue, do some research on it. Try to get all the information you can so that you can present a balanced point of view.

Once you have a general idea about the program, it is time to do some brainstorming. This old, yet effective, technique has helped to produce some excellent program ideas. The key to successful brainstorming is to accept initially *all* ideas without subjecting them to any value judgment. It usually works better with two or more people, because one person's ideas might trigger further ideas in the other people. Write down all of the ideas, no matter how wild they may seem at first glance. Only when finished with the brainstorming session should you exercise some judgment and try to sort out the more workable ideas. Print them on cards for further reference.

3. **Audience:** What specific type of audience would you like to reach? Teenagers? Senior citizens? Families? Housewives? Working men and women? Gen-

eral works on mass communication research, and sociological studies, as well as rating services, usually have a fairly good definition of audience types and their demographic (sex, age, income, and so on) and ecological (metropolitan area, rural area, and so on) parameters. If the issue is important enough, fight for the right of minority audiences (audiences that have special interests, in contrast to mass audience; not an audience defined by ethnic criteria) to receive the information, despite the likelihood that the ratings will be low. Although in a commercial station one of your major objectives is to make money, you also have a responsibility as a public servant.

4. **Stating Objective for Process Message:** What would you like the viewer to get out of your program? What do you want him or her to experience, to feel, to think, during the show? After the show? What specifically will the percipient gain by your program? Often, the determination of the ideal audience and the process message go hand in hand.

5. **Channel:** Once you have formulated the process message, decide which channel might be the most effective way for reaching the audience. For example, if you want to address a highly specific audience, such as the voters of a particular section of a city or county, open-air broadcasting might not be the most effective channel to choose. You may find that a particular cable company, which has many TV households wired in your target area, is the more effective channel. Using open-air channels simply because they are available does not necessarily guarantee effective television communication. When producing for corporate television, neither the open- nor the closed-circuit channels may be the best way of program distribution. In this case the "bicycling" (distributing by mail from place to place) of videotape cassettes may reach the target audience most effectively (the employees can watch the tape individually on their own time).

The channel you use for your program should have little influence on production quality. Regardless of whether you produce a network spectacular, a show on shopping hints for a small cable company, or a pep talk by the vice president of a large corporation, you should strive for the highest production quality possible under the circumstances.

6. **Time:** In general, the type of audience determines a specific telecasting time, such as morning, noon, late afternoon, early evening, late evening, weekend. What time would be ideal for your purposes? What are your extreme time limits? What compromises are you prepared to make?

When using cable for your program distribution, you may think of repeated showings at different times. Early morning hours and late evenings have become popular times, especially if you want to avoid colliding head-on with network programs.

7. **Specific Program Ideas:** Now it is time to gather ideas for your program or series of programs. There are many ways of doing this, but whatever method you choose should have some system to it. If, for example, your proposed series has a magazine format, with each of the programs containing several segments, you may want to assign a particular person to each of the sections and have each person prepare idea lists for these segments. Let's assume you are doing a program series on the elderly and you have three or four people assisting you. You can now assign one of them to create a card file of names of possible celebrity guests who are advanced in years, and who could talk about their present activities and problems. Another of your assistants might take over the cooking segment of the show and list on cards either elderly people who are outstanding gourmet cooks, or simply recipes that can be easily prepared by a single person with a minimum of kitchen facilities. A third person may list the social, legal, and health services available for the elderly. It is then up to you, the producer, to look through this material and combine the cards for the various programs.

8. **Treatment:** A **treatment** is a brief explanation of what your proposed program or program series is all about (see Section Two). Most programs are initially proposed to the program manager or executive producer as a treatment. Some of the more elaborate treatments have some storyboardlike illustrations. The treatment should not only say *what* the proposed show is all about, but it should also

reflect in its writing the *style of the show*. Hence, the style of a treatment for a situation comedy series should differ from one dealing with an investigative report on a cover-up of a crime.

9. **Tentative Budget:** With the treatment, you should submit a tentative budget, although you do not as yet know all the above-the-line and below-the-line requirements (see 16.9). If the show is produced in your station, the above-the-line cost will probably be absorbed by the station (directors, announcers, art director, and so forth are all employed by the station on a regular salary). The estimate for the below-the-line budget must be based on the *approximate* facilities you think you need. Check with the engineering supervisor on the current rates. Again, it may be that your station requires a budget only for moneys that are *actually paid out,* such as the construction of a new set by an outside agency, union scale for freelance talent, copyright release fees, and others. Larger stations, however, require a budget for both above-the-line and below-the-line expenditures, regardless of whether the cost is, at least partially, absorbed by the salaries of regularly employed personnel.

10. **Presentation:** Now you are ready to prepare and present your program proposal. Although proposals vary greatly in format and length, they must contain at least the treatment and a tentative budget. (We list the major points of a proposal in Section Two.) Usually, such proposals are given to the executive producer of the station, or directly to the program manager. If you deal with a network, you need to go through an agent. For program proposals that concern educational or public service issues you should contact the public service director of the station. Documentaries are usually under the jurisdiction of the news department.

If your initial contact at the station feels that there is some merit in your proposal, he or she will hand it on to higher management; in small stations, to the general manager and the comptroller or business manager. Be realistic in your initial budget, but do not make it too small. It is psychologically, as well as financially, more appropriate to agree to a budget cut than to have to ask for more money later on.

If your show is to be sponsored (either by a single client or through participating spots), the sales manager will, of course, participate in the initial decision-making process. Often the presumed "salability" of your program idea is a decisive factor in the preliminary negotiations. The sales manager would like to know how the show is going to turn out before you have even started producing it. As pointed out before, the networks usually pretest pilot programs as to public appeal.

If a single client becomes the sponsor of your show, you will have to include his representative in at least the preliminary production meetings. The client is usually very much interested in your budget.

PRODUCTION PROCESS

As soon as you have the go-ahead for your project, you need to start the *actual* production process. This process includes many steps that sometimes progress in a logical and comfortable sequence, sometimes overlap, and sometimes seem to be almost totally out of control. Keep this in mind when we list these principal production steps: (1) mode, (2) above-the-line considerations, (3) initial production conference, (4) script conference and below-the-line considerations, (5) scheduling, (6) facilities request, (7) final budget, (8) log information, (9) publicity and promotion, (10) rehearsals and performance, and (11) feedback and evaluation.

Note that in each step, you should have some evaluation of your progress. This implies that you know at each given moment where you are and where you should be. These continual checks are one of the earmarks of a good system.

1. *Mode:* Now is the time to think about how and where the program can best be produced—in the studio, as EFP, as a big remote, or as a combination of all three. As you have seen from our previous discussions of equipment, studio and field productions have very dissimilar below-the-line production requirements (facilities and operating personnel). Again, use a systems approach if you do a series. Do not just consider one show at a

SHOW: _____

VTR DATES: _____

AIR DATES: _____

TECHNICAL EQUIPMENT AND SERVICES--PRODUCTION	Rate per hour	Hours	Estimate	Actual Cost
Cameras				
Audio				
Lighting				
VTR				
Slo-mo				
Telecine				
Telco (Telephone Co. for remotes only)				
Electronic Support				
Videotape Stock				
SUBTOTAL:				

TECHNICAL EQUIPMENT AND SERVICES--POST-PRODUCTION				
VTR Editing				
Dubbing				
Electronic Support				
Videotape Stock				
SUBTOTAL:				

NON-TECHNICAL EQUIPMENT AND SERVICES				
Sets and Properties				
Graphics				
Make-up				
Wardrobe				
SUBTOTAL:				

PERSONNEL				
Technical Supervisor				
Technical Director				
Engineers (Audio, video, cameras, boom, VTR, maintenance)				
Floor Manager				
Floor Crew				
VTR Editor				
SUBTOTAL:				

	Estimate	Actual Cost
Technical Equipment and Services--Production SUBTOTAL:		
Technical Equipment and Services--Postproduction SUBTOTAL:		
Non-technical Equipment and Services SUBTOTAL:		
Personnel SUBTOTAL:		
TOTAL:		

SHOW: _____

VTR DATES: _____

AIR DATES: _____

SERVICE	ESTIMATE	ACTUAL COST
Producer		
Director		
Associate Director		
Associate Producer		
Writer		
Production Assistant		
Secretary		
Casting Director		
Costume Designer		
Art Director/Scenic Designer		
Music (Orchestra Leader)		
SUBTOTAL:		
Cast		
Contingency		
TOTAL:		

DATE: _____   AUTHORIZED BY: _____

16.9   Sample Budget Note that in small and medium-sized stations the producer, director, associate producer and director, writer, secretary, and art director are part of the regularly employed production staff. As salaried personnel, they do not require special above-the-line budget considerations. The services of casting director, costume designer, and orchestra leader are required for large-scale productions only. (Budget adapted from ABC program estimates. Courtesy of ABC Television.)

time, but see the whole series as an interrelated production effort.

Most shows demand a particular production mode. For example, if you do a documentary on the conditions of the various residence hotels in your city, you would certainly not want to re-create the hotel rooms in the studio, but would go to the location with your EFP equipment. On the other hand, if you do a magazine-type show on the elderly, you may very well stage the major part of the production in the studio, and shoot only a minimum portion of each program on location. Remember that the studio affords optimal control, but that EFP offers a great variety of scenery and locations at little additional cost. Also, the postproduction for EFP usually takes much more time than for studio shows, especially if you need to do extensive post audio dubbing and color corrections.

2. *Above-the-Line Considerations:* Once you have picked the production mode, you need to select a *director* in whom you have confidence and who is sufficiently sensitive to the program topic that he or she can work toward the process message. In small stations, you probably will have to direct as well as write the script for the show.

In larger production centers, you may have the luxury of hiring a *writer,* who must know the medium and also show some interest in the project. Make sure that this specialist understands the program objective and, especially, the proposed process message. If he or she disagrees with the process message or the whole idea of the program and does not come up with a better one, do not use him or her. The script such a writer produces may be technically quite efficient but will probably lack inspiration and enthusiasm. Agree on a fee before delivery of the script; some writers charge amounts that can swallow up your whole budget.

You still may need to hire *talent.* For most simple shows—interviews, panel discussions, documentaries, or in-depth reports—you have the talent in mind when you conceive the program format. However, if you have to cast the talent, consult a casting agency and/or the director of the show. It should be the director, not you, who makes the final

talent selection, assuming the talent falls within the allocated budget. Your budget should remain flexible as to categories. Try to establish some money reserves in a contingency fund.

The assistant producer, if you have one, is most likely assigned to you permanently and needs no special consideration. The art director, too, works within the station and is readily available for consultation.

3. *Initial Production Conference:* Before the below-the-line considerations, call the initial production conference, which, ideally, should be attended by the producer, assistant producer, director, writer, art director, talent (if already specified), production manager, and engineering supervisor. Sometimes, in small operations, the program manager sits in on the initial meeting. In any case, you may want to invite him or her. In this meeting you present the process message objective and let the writer discuss the basic show treatment. Set up an agenda and stick to it. Listen carefully to all suggestions, but do not let the conference deteriorate into an anecdote session. Have your assistant (P.A.) write down all major suggestions. If the program is relatively simple, many below-the-line items are discussed in this initial meeting.

These are the specific assignments that should be made at the production conference: (1) To writer: complete script with deadline. (2) To art director: tentative floor plan (set design) with deadline. (3) To director: list of complete technical facilities with deadline, and list of talent (if not decided already). (4) To production manager: schedule rehearsal and air times, studio facilities, floor crews, and postproduction facilities. (5) To engineering supervisor: assignment of T.D. and studio or EFP crews. (6) To all: precise budget figures for all necessary expenditures. From now on, the various key production people establish their own lines of communication and contact one another in order to fulfill the assignment within the specified time. Obviously, the art director must get together with the writer and the director in order to work out a suitable set, and the director must consult the production manager about specific technical requirements, such as number of cameras, type of audio equipment, preproduction work (pretaping or filming of certain show elements), or postproduction (editing, dubbing).

Many of the production activities occur from now on simultaneously, or in an order most convenient to the parties involved. However, you must keep track of all such activities. Because deadlines are essential for efficient teamwork, make sure that they are adhered to.

List the telephone numbers (home and work) and address of each key production member. Give this list to all key production members so that they can all communicate with one another.

4. *Script Conference and Below-the-Line Considerations:* As soon as the writer has finished the script, call another production conference. Ideally, it should include the same people who attended the first one. But now you are involved primarily in below-the-line matters. These persons are especially important to this meeting: writer with *completed* script (the script still being open for minor changes), director, art director with tentative floor plan, T.D. with a good idea of technical facilities needed, production manager, floor manager, and talent. Previous to this conference you should have received the completed script and talked over the medium requirements with the director.

In case the process message requires an unusually precise and thorough understanding of all production members (as in the football show mentioned earlier in this chapter), you should schedule subsequent meetings with the entire production personnel (camera operators, audio engineers, videotape editors, floor personnel) so that the director can communicate the specific production concepts and medium requirements. Such meetings are not a waste of time. The more the entire production staff understands the total concept of the show, the less work you will have during actual production.

In this script conference, or shortly thereafter, you should work out two important production details: scheduling and facilities request.

5. *Scheduling:* Check with the production manager (who, in turn, is in touch with the engineering supervisor) about studio availability for rehearsal and taping sessions (or live on-the-air presentation). Check with the director about rehearsal schedules. Make sure that time schedules are distributed to all production and engineering personnel. If a schedule change becomes necessary, let everybody connected with the production know immediately, including any production people who work outside the station. Double-check all schedule items. Have your assistant call the people about the schedule and send them a reminder by mail. Then call again.

6. *Facilities (FAX) Request:* The person who fills out the final facilities **(FAX)** request form varies from station to station. In small station operations, it is often the producer. The facilities request usually contains information concerning date and time of rehearsal or taping sessions, or on-the-air performances; title of production, names of producer and director (and sometimes talent); and all technical facilities, such as cameras, microphones, lights, sets, graphics, costumes, makeup, VTRs, and special production needs. It also lists the studio and control room needed and, if you work closed-circuit, the distribution facility (see 16.10). The facilities request, like the script, is an essential communications device. Be as accurate as you possibly can when preparing it. Later changes only invite costly errors.

The facilities request should generally have the floor plan and lighting plot attached. Make sure that the graphics (slides, crawl) are ordered well in advance unless you use a character generator. The art department has many other things to do, and generally adheres strictly to deadlines.

If you need to prepare special effects titles and bumpers, be sure to schedule and request the facilities and people for these "preproduction" jobs. Do not get so wrapped up in the "big" production that you forget the seemingly minor detail. In television production, *everything* is important.

Because several key departments must receive the same information, carbon copies are necessary. Usually, they are different colors, each of which is assigned permanently to a specific department; for example, the yellow copy may go to engineering, the blue to the art department, the pink to the originator of the facilities request, and so on. The

A performer who works for scale (minimum union rate) is sometimes hard to find. Every station has a rate card for its below-the-line production costs, such as studio rentals for a minimum number of hours, daily rates (which then are somewhat less than the hourly rate), and the equipment and production personnel supplied. You may be requested to prepare separate below-the-line budgets for studio work and EFP. If you are away from home base, be sure to include in the budget transportation, housing, and meals. If you have to ship equipment, you need to insure it.

8. *Log Information:* As a producer, you have the responsibility to give the traffic department, which prepares the log, all the necessary information, such as rehearsal dates and times (if they involve equipment), commercial inserts, if any, and major facilities used. Generally, a copy of the facilities request goes directly to traffic. But double-check, nevertheless, on whether they have all the vital information. If the log is made up by computer, you can easily check at any one of the keyboard terminals as to whether the complete information has reached traffic, and, ultimately, the computer.

9. *Publicity and Promotion:* The best show is worthless if nobody knows about it. While the preproduction activities are in full swing, meet with the publicity and promotions departments (usually combined in one department, especially in smaller stations).

The function of these departments is to minimize the gap between the potential and the actual television audience. In other words, it is the job of publicity and promotion to inform all set owners of upcoming shows and to stimulate them to tune to those programs. The higher the number of television households tuned to your program, in relation to the total number of television households in your station's reach, the higher the rating figure (see Section Two). Although the quality and success of your show are not necessarily expressed by high ratings, it is still desirable to reach as many viewers in your target audience as possible. Be sure, therefore, to inform your publicity and promotion people of exact data concerning your show. Give them some infor-

16.10 FAX (Facilities) Request Form The facilities request form is an essential communication device. It informs various departments of when and where specific facilities are needed.

departments that generally get copies of the facilities request are (1) production, (2) engineering, (3) VTR editing, (4) traffic, and (5) art.

If you have a computer facility, the facilities request could become part of the computer program.

7. *Final Budget:* The facilities request gives you the exact data you need for the below-the-line budget. You are now ready to prepare the final budget for the show. The sample includes above-the-line production expenses, although, as pointed out before, they are frequently absorbed by salaries to station personnel. In order to prevent any misunderstanding on how much a specific service or item costs, no actual figures are supplied here (see 16.9). Check with the union headquarters about their minimum fees (most services in larger cities are above scale).

mation about the show, such as the show's "angle" or celebrities who will appear on your show, so that they can use the information in their press releases.

10. *Rehearsals and Performance:* If you have done your job right, you can now let the director of the show take over. He or she will conduct the necessary rehearsals and direct the final videotape or on-the-air performance. Try to stay out of the director's way as much as possible. If you have suggestions concerning the show, take notes or dictate your comments to the P.A. during the rehearsal and then discuss them with the director (and talent and crew if necessary) during the break. During the actual performance, do not interfere at all—unless you see a big mistake that obviously escaped the director's attention, or if something totally unexpected happens that needs your immediate attention.

Make a special effort to receive your guests properly and try to keep them calm and relaxed until show time. It does not befit you or the station to have VIPs left wandering around the hallways, trying to find the right studio.

11. *Feedback and Evaluation:* The rehearsals (if any) give you the opportunity to evaluate the initial show concept and make changes when necessary. Also, listen to the suggestions of other people, without becoming dependent upon them. If the show solicits feedback ("please call such-and-such a number"), see to it that the feedback facilities are indeed working. There is nothing more annoying to the viewer than to find that his well-intentioned efforts to communicate with the station are ignored. Keep accurate records of all feedback received. Remember to write thank-you notes to the people who have made special contributions to the program.

Complete all required reports (such as music clearances and AFTRA forms) unless the director takes care of such matters. Pay all bills promptly.

Each time you have aired a show, file a cassette copy ($\frac{3}{4}$-inch or $\frac{1}{2}$-inch) for archival purposes. In case some viewer or organization challenges the show, or portions of the show, you have an accurate record of what was done and said on the air. Often, the news department uses such archives as a "morgue," a source for people and places that have, all of a sudden, become newsworthy again. Label each cas-

sette carefully and enter the code used in your archives book for easy recovery. File the script for each show in your archives book so that you have a quick reference to the show content.

As we said in the beginning, producing means coordinating many people, activities, and things. Triple-check everything. Do not leave anything to chance. Yet, even the most skillful producer will not be able to come up with a successful program if there is no important idea to start with. If you really care about helping people to live better and happier lives, if you are indeed sensitive to your surroundings, then you will find significant program ideas in abundance.

MAIN POINTS

1.   Producing means to see to it that a worthwhile idea gets to be a worthwhile television show. The producer manages a great number of people and coordinates an even greater number of activities and production detail.

2.   Efficient television productions use a systems approach that helps to identify the major production elements each program requires, and the necessary interaction among them.

3.   The basic television system moves from idea to the production, and finally to the distribution of the program to the audience.

4.   The most appropriate system, called the effect-to-cause system, starts with the idea, then defines the desired audience effect, and moves from there backward to what the medium requires in order to achieve such an effect.

5.   The above-the-line production elements include nontechnical personnel, such as producer, director, talent, writers, and the expenditures connected with their work.

6.   The below-the-line production consists of coordinating the engineering personnel, additional staff production people, as well as the necessary production equipment, personnel, schedules and budgets.

7. Special production aspects to be considered are (1) program types as defined by the FCC, (2) copyright and clearances, (3) union affiliation of above- and below-the-line personnel, and (4) legal aspects.

8. Effective production planning usually follows the steps of the production system. Using the effect-to-cause system, the basic planning steps are (1) need assessment, (2) formulation of the program idea, (3) analysis of the target audience, (4) stating the process message objective, (5) picking the appropriate channel, (6) determining the ideal broadcast time, (7) collecting ideas and material for the shows, (8) writing a program treatment, (9) tentative budget, and (10) putting all the information in an attractive presentation package.

9. The actual production process includes these basic considerations: (1) mode (studio production, EFP, big remote), (2) above-the-line personnel and budget, (3) initial production conference with the key above-the-line personnel during which the process message is explained, (4) script conference and below-the-line considerations—an analysis of the completed script and the floor plan will suggest the necessary technical facilities, (5) scheduling, (6) facilities request, (7) final budget, (8) log information, (9) publicity and promotion, (10) rehearsals and videotaping or broadcast; and (11) feedback and evaluation of production.

10. Each of the steps of the production process requires its own evaluation criteria so that problems can be detected and eliminated before the completion of the entire production.

In this section, we will discuss (1) some research tools for the producer, (2) the major points of a proposal, (3) audience classifications and ratings, and, briefly, (4) major aspects of satellite transmission and cable.

RESOURCES

As a producer, you must become somewhat of a scrounger and researcher. On occasion, you may have to procure a skeleton for your medical show, a model of a communication satellite for your show on electronic communication, or a wedding dress of the 1800s for your history series. Or, you may have only a half hour to get accurate information about a former mayor of your city who is about to celebrate his or her ninetieth birthday.

Every good producer has a few reference books and a few contacts in the community that can supply the needed information quickly and reliably. The following list contains only a few of the basic reference works with which you should start your producer's library.

Obviously, the list is not complete, and you will surely want to augment it with a few more pertinent titles.

1. *Telephone Directories.* There is a great deal of information contained in a telephone book. Get the directories of your city and the outlying areas. Also, try to get the telephone directories of the larger institutions with which you have frequent contact, such as the city hall, the police department, the fire department, other city or county agencies, major federal offices, city and county school offices, colleges and universities, and museums.

2. *Airline Schedules.* Try to keep your airline directory as up-to-date as possible. It might be a good idea to have a contact person in a travel agency.

3. *Transportation.* You need the numbers of one or two taxi companies, and the schedules of the bus and train stations. Keep in mind that taxis can be used to transport *things* (such as the skeleton for your medical program) as well as people.

4. *Reference Books.* Your reference library should have an up-to-date dictionary; a set of *Who's Who in America* and the regional volumes; a good, up-to-date dictionary of international biography; an up-to-date encyclopedia, which presents subjects in a clear and

A good producer must have quick access to a great variety of information and know how to interpret audience behavior through ratings figures. He or she must also know how to present an idea for production and the various ways of getting the show distributed to specific audiences.

concise manner (for example, you may find the simple, yet concise, *World Book Encyclopedia* more helpful than the detailed *Encyclopædia Britannica*); and a comprehensive, up-to-date atlas. Get on the mailing list of the Government Printing Office so you know what is available. Your station probably has its own broadcasting references (including FCC and legal aspects of broadcasting), but you should, nevertheless, keep a current copy of the *Broadcasting Yearbook* handy.

5. *Library.* Establish good relations with the reference section of your public and university libraries. An efficient and friendly librarian can, and is usually happy to, dig up all sorts of information with amazing speed. Most large libraries offer computer search services. They can access on-line (with the computer responding immediately) any type of information from over 200 data bases.

6. *Other Resources.* Your local Chamber of Commerce usually has a list of the various community organizations and businesses. It may come in handy to have a list of the major foundations and their criteria for grants. If you are doing a series on a special subject (medical practice, energy conservation, housing developments, and so forth), you will have to get some major reference works in that area.

PROGRAM PROPOSAL

As mentioned before, there is no standard format for a program or program series proposal. However, every proposal should include this minimum information: (1) show or program series title; (2) show treatment; (3) target audience; (4) ideal broadcast time; and (5) tentative budget. If you propose a program series, you should attach a sample script of one of the shows.

1. *Program Title.* Keep it short, but memorable. Perhaps it is the lack of screen space that forces television to work with shorter titles than movies. For example, the movie title *Alice Doesn't Live Here Any More* was changed to *Alice* on television.

2. *Show Treatment.* Keep it brief and concise. All it should do is give a busy executive an idea of what the show is about. Do not include specific production information, such as type of lighting or camera angles. Save this information for the script (see 16.11).

3. *Target Audience.* Simply indicate which people you would like to have watch the show: the elderly, preschoolers, housewives and househusbands, or general audience (everybody who has access to a tel-

evision set). The target audience should have been an important factor in the formulation of the process message.

4. *Ideal Broadcast Time.* State the day of the week and the time you would like to see the program on the air. The broadcast time is defined by the viewing habits of the target audience. Be prepared to make compromises. However, you may get a better exposure by distributing the program through other means, such as cable.

5. *Tentative Budget.* Before preparing the tentative budget, make sure that you have accurate figures for production costs and union wages.

Be as *neat as possible* in whatever you present. If you have a lot of erasures in your treatment, or worse, spelling mistakes, you run the risk of getting your proposal rejected outright. Producers are especially sensitive to first impressions, and the greatest show on earth may be dismissed perfunctorily because it is written up on college binder paper rather than neatly typed and bound in a folder. It is not just the idea that counts in television production, but also the form and style in which it is presented.

Once accepted by the initial contact person, the proposal is usually handed over to the executive producer or program manager of the station. If the program falls into the public service category, the public service director decides its fate.

AUDIENCE AND RATINGS

As a producer, you will probably hear much about the various aspects of specific television audiences and, above all, about ratings, which are an indication of how much of an audience you reached with the show. Ratings are especially important for commercial stations, because the cost for commercial time sold by the station is primarily determined by audience size. Although you do not have to be an expert in audience analysis and ratings to be an effective producer, you should at least know some of the basic concepts and terminology.

Audience Classification

Broadcast audiences, like audiences for all mass media, are usually classified by demographic and ecological characteristics. The standard **demographic factors** include sex, age, education, ethnic background, and income or economic status. The **ecological factors** pertain to the area in which the audience is located: metropolitan, urban, suburban, or rural. Of course, when determining the process message or when conducting a communication effects study, you have to refine the audience categories and include profession, working hours, buying habits, and even personality and persuasibility variables.[2] However, many producers simply take a neighbor as model and gear their communication to that particular person and his or her habits.

Ratings

An audience **rating** is the percentage of television households with their set tuned to a station in a given population (total number of television households). You get this percentage by dividing the number of house-

[2]See Alexis S. Tan, *Mass Communication Theories and Research* (Columbus, Ohio: Grid Publishing, 1981), pp. 167–190.

Downlink Receiving earth station for satellite signals.

Fiber-Optic Cable Thin, transparent fibers of glass or plastic used to transfer light from one point to another. When used in broadcast signal transmission, the electrical video and audio signals are transduced into light impulses at the transmitting end, and back to electrical signals at the receiving end. Advantages include immunity to electrical interference, thinness and light weight, and large two-way channel capacity.

Rating Percentage of television households with their set tuned to a station in relation to total number of television households.

Share Percentage of television households tuned to a station in relation to all other stations in that area.

Transponder Receiver and transmitter in satellite.

Uplink Earth station transmitter used to broadcast television signals from the earth to a satellite.

The play concerns a mountain climber who wants to commit suicide. His troubles were quite ordinary: getting laid off from an executive position after having been with the same company for sixteen years; drinking a little too much; and family fights that got more and more vicious. So he escapes to a little mountain village, leaving wife, one spoiled daughter, the BMW, and the suburban mansion behind. His method of suicide, however, is somewhat extraordinary: attempting to climb solo the 3,000 foot high, almost vertical, "killer wall" of Pyramid Peak. Killer wall has been successfully climbed only twice before by teams of highly experienced climbers. Many attempts have resulted in tragedy. He would simply be another casualty.

He begins to climb. First carelessly, joyfully uninhibited. But gradually it turns into yet another struggle for him: he against the wall, against the mountain. A rescue team is on its way because they fear he had climbing partners who had fallen to their deaths. (After all, a solo attempt on killer wall would be suicidal.) He is only three hundred feet below the summit when his fatigue turns into numbing exhaustion. Now it is time to give in. Instead, he rigs a self-belay. He is fighting for his life. He is now only 100 feet below the summit—and slips. His ice ax pops out of the ice, his crampons break loose. But he is jerked to a halt by the rope of his self-belay. The rescuers move in— and he cries for help.

The story is told through a series of flashbacks, revealing his thoughts while climbing and the gradual change from giving up to having a new will to live.

16.11   Show Treatment (Entitled "Killer Wall")

holds tuned to your station by the total number of television households:

$$\frac{\text{Number of TV households tuned in}}{\text{Total number of TV households}} = \text{Rating figure}$$

As you can see, the rating figure does not say whether the household whose set is turned on has any people watching, or if so, how many; nor does it give any indication of the impact of the program on the viewer.

A **share** is the percentage of television households tuned to your station in relation to all the other stations in your area. Here is how you arrive at a share:

$$\frac{\text{TV households tuned to "X" station}}{\text{TV households tuned to other stations}} = \text{Share}$$

The various rating services, with A. C. Nielsen and The Arbitron Company being the two most prominent, query carefully selected representative *samples* either by a meter attached to the television sets of the TV households in the sample (Nielsen) or through a diary (Arbitron).[3]

SATELLITE TRANSMISSIONS

Satellites play a great part in broadcast communication. Television and radio stations, as well as cable companies and private enterprises, use satellites for video and audio signal transmission. Once the satellite is properly positioned in a *geosynchronous* orbit (it moves 22,300 miles above and synchronous with the earth, remaining in the same position relative to the earth), the signal transmission is relatively simple. The television signals are sent to the satellite through an **uplink** (earth station transmitter), received and amplified somewhat by the satellite, and rebroadcast by the satellite's own transmitter back to one or several receiving earth stations, called **downlinks.** The receiver-transmitter unit in the satellite is called a **transponder,** a combination of *trans*mitter and res*ponder* (receiver). Because the satellite transmission is not directional,

[3] See Roger D. Wimmer and Joseph R. Dominick, *Mass Media Research* (Belmont, Calif.: Wadsworth Publishing Co., 1983), pp. 271–295.

simple receiving stations can be set up in many widely scattered parts of the world, making satellite links economically feasible (see 16.12). In fact, three strategically placed satellites can cover the whole earth.

CABLE

Cable television is a distribution device for broadcast signals via coaxial or fiber-optic cable. The signal is distributed and continuously amplified from the **head end,** along a **trunk,** to many **feeder lines,** from which the various homes are connected through **drop lines** (see 16.13).

Cable television, however, has developed into much more than a distribution device of hard-to-receive broadcast signals. It frequently uses satellites to feed its head ends with its own network programming. Many cable companies have large production facilities that rival those of local stations in technology and production. With the advent of fiber-optic cables, each wired household has the capacity of receiving and feeding back through up to 200 channels or more, and feeding digital audio and video information from the home to the cable company offices.

A **fiber-optic cable** consists of many thin, flexible strands of glass that transport light from one end to the other. To transport the video and audio television signals, the electrical signals are changed (transduced) into pulses of light at the input stage, and then changed back into electrical signals at the output stage.

Fiber-optic systems have many significant advantages: immunity to electrical interference, thinness and light weight, and a large two-way channel capacity.

MAIN POINTS

1. A television producer needs ready access to resources, such as telephone directories; airline schedules; information on taxis, buses and trains; and basic reference books.

2. Although there is no standard format for a program proposal, or a program series proposal, these items must be included: (1) show or program series title, (2) show treatment, (3) target audience, (4) ideal broadcast time, and (5) tentative budget.

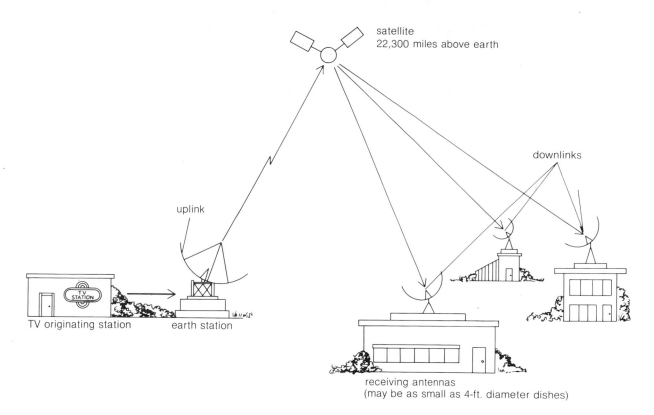

satellite
22,300 miles above earth

downlinks

uplink

TV originating station

earth station

receiving antennas
(may be as small as 4-ft. diameter dishes)

16.12   Satellite Uplink and Downlinks The originating television station
sends its signal to the earth station (uplink), which beams the signal to the satellite.
The satellite receives the signal, amplifies it, and transmits it back down to earth.
There the signal can be received by a number of rather small receiving antennas
(downlinks), amplified again, and distributed to the home receivers.

3.   An audience rating is the percentage of television
households with their set tuned to a station in a given
population (TV households tuned in on a station divided
by the total number of households in that area). A share
is the percentage of television households tuned to a
specific station in relation to all other stations in that
area.

4.   Television and radio stations, as well as cable
companies and private enterprises, use satellites for
video and audio transmission. The television signals
are sent to the satellite through an uplink (earth station
transmitter), amplified and rebroadcast by the satellite's own transmitter (called transponder—a combination of transmitter and responder) back to one or
several earth receiving stations, called downlinks.

5.   Cable television is a distribution device for broadcast signals via coaxial or fiber optics cable. The signal
is distributed and continuously amplified from the head
end, along the trunk, to many feeder lines, to which the
various homes are connected through drop lines.

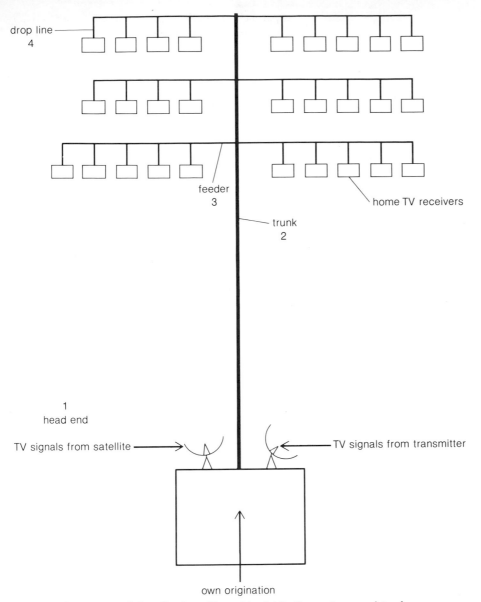

drop line
4

feeder
3

home TV receivers

trunk
2

1
head end

TV signals from satellite ⟶

⟵ TV signals from transmitter

own origination

16.13   Cable Television System The cable distribution system consists of (1) the head end, where the signals are collected or originated; (2) the trunk, through which the signals are sent and to which the feeders are connected; (3) the feeders, which bring the signal to various sections of a city (street, blocks); and (4) drop lines, which connect the feeders to the individual homes.

FURTHER READING

Baldwin, Huntley. *Creating Effective TV Commercials*. Chicago, IL: Crain, 1982.

Baldwin, Thomas F., and D. Stevens McVoy. *Cable Communication*. Englewood Cliffs, NJ: Prentice-Hall, Inc., 1983.

Becker, Samuel L. *Discovering Mass Communication*. Glenview, IL: Scott, Foresman, 1983.

Bittner, John R. *Broadcast Regulation*. Englewood Cliffs N.J: Prentice Hall, Inc., 1982.

Eastman, Susan Tyler, Sydney W. Head, and Lewis Klein. *Broadcast Programming*. Belmont, CA: Wadsworth Publishing Co., 1981.

Fourie, H. P. *Communication by Objectives*. 2nd ed. Johannesburg: McGraw-Hill Book Co., Inc., 1982.

Strong, William S. *The Copyright Book: A Practical Guide*. Cambridge, MA: The MIT Press, 1981.

Tan, Alexis S. *Mass Communication Theories and Research*. Columbus, Ohio: Grid Publishing, 1981.

Taylor, John P. *What Broadcasters Should Know About Satellites*. New York: Television/Radio Age, 1981.

Wimmer, Roger D., and Joseph R. Dominick. *Mass Media Research*. Belmont, CA: Wadsworth Publishing Co., 1983.

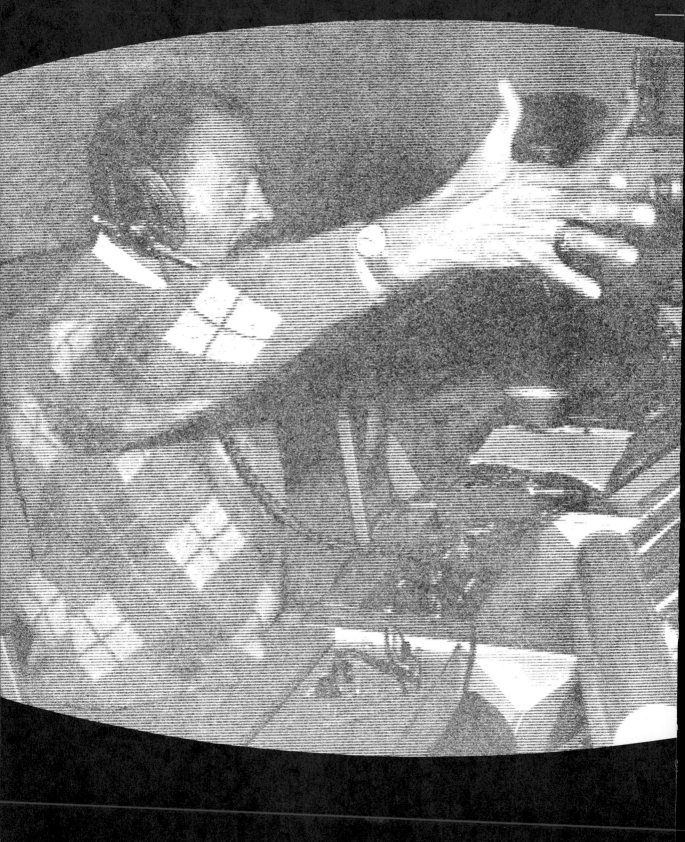

Directing

A good television director must fulfill a great number of roles: those of an artist, psychologist, technical expert, coordinator. Moreover, these roles must be fulfilled with reliability, style, and especially consistency.

Section One of this chapter will discuss:

1.   The major aspects of control room directing: (1) coordination, (2) terminology, (3) timing, (4) rehearsal methods, and (5) on-the-air performance.

2.   The major aspects of film-style directing: (1) script analysis, (2) visualization and sequencing, (3) technical coordination, (4) timing, (5) directing talent, (6) rehearsal and taping, and (7) directing for EFP.

In Section Two we will look at: (1) visualization and sequencing (picturization), (2) the various script formats (fully scripted show, semiscripted show, show format, and fact sheet), and (3) the major aspects of script preparation.

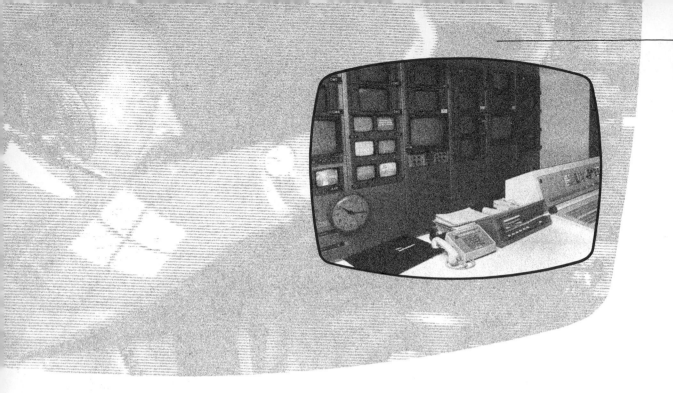

This section describes (1) the director's roles, (2) control room directing methods, and (3) film-style directing methods.

DIRECTOR'S ROLES

A television director, like a producer, must have many talents. He or she is expected to be a distinctive artist, a psychologist who can encourage people to give their best, and a technician who can solve problems on which the engineers have given up. Above all, a director is expected to coordinate and keep track of many production details within rigidly prescribed time frames. A good television director fulfills all these roles reliably and with a personal style.

The Director as Artist

As a director, you must be able to translate a script or an actual event (such as an interview, parade, or tennis match) into *effective television pictures and sound*. You must decide on the people (talent and crew) and the production elements that will give you these television picture and sound images. The coordination of the various production elements requires as much, and often even more, creative effort as the initial idea and visualization stages.

The Director as Psychologist

The television director must deal with a variety of people who approach television production from many different perspectives: producers who worry about budgets, technical people who are primarily interested in the technical quality of pictures and sound, performers who are sometimes temperamental, designers who have strong ideas about what a set should look like, or the mother of a child actor who may feel that your close-ups of her daughter are not tight enough.

Not only do you have to get everybody to perform at a consistently high level, you have to get them to *work as a team*. Although there is no formula for directing a team of such diverse individuals, there are some factors that facilitate the human relations aspect of your job:

The development of new equipment has had a profound influence on television directing. A director must now be able to work in two distinct ways: (1) as a control room director who continuously coordinates all production elements from the beginning to the end of the show, and (2) as a director who breaks down an event into short videotaped segments for extensive postproduction. This latter technique is called "film-style," because motion pictures are shot in a similar discontinuous manner.

1. Be well prepared and know what you want to accomplish. You cannot possibly get people to work for a common goal if you do not know what the goal is.

2. Know the functions of each team member.

3. Be specific about what you want the talent to do. Do not be indecisive with your instructions or intimidated by a celebrity. The more professional your talent is, the more readily he or she will follow your direction.

4. Project a secure attitude. Be firm, but not harsh, when giving instructions.

5. Do not ridicule somebody for making mistakes. Point out the problems and suggest ways of solving them.

6. Treat your colleagues with respect and compassion.

The Director as Technical Expert

In order to give effective instructions to a technical crew, you must know the limitations as well as the potentials of the equipment being operated. In this respect, a television director is like a conductor of a symphony orchestra. The conductor may not be able to play all the instruments of the orchestra, but he or she certainly knows the sounds the various instruments can generate and how they ought to be played to produce good sounds. The preceding chapters in this book were designed to give you this technical production background.

The Director as Coordinator

As a television director, you must coordinate many different production elements and processes. This goes beyond directing in the traditional sense, which generally means blocking talent and helping them achieve peak performances. Especially when directing nondramatic shows, you must spend most of your efforts on cuing members of the production team (engineers and nontechnical production personnel) to initiate certain video and audio functions, such as getting appropriate camera shots, rolling VTRs, riding audio levels, switching among cameras and special video effects, retrieving electronically generated graphics, switching to remote feeds, and so on. Even so, you still need to pay attention to the performers, who sometimes, and quite rightly so, feel that they play second fiddle to the television machine. You also need to do this coordinating within a rigid time frame in which every second has a price tag attached. Such coordinating needs practice, and you should not expect to be a competent director immediately after reading this chapter.

DIRECTING METHODS

As we pointed out earlier, there are two principal methods of television directing: (1) **control room directing,** which generally involves the simultaneous coordination of two or more cameras, the switcher, audio, and other production elements; and (2) **film-style directing,** which means directing a number of separate takes for postproduction.

In *control room directing,* you need to be concerned not only with the visualization of each shot, but also with the proper sequencing (also called picturization) of the various shots. It includes the directing of live shows; live-on-tape productions (shows that are produced as if they were live, but which are routed to a videotape recorder rather than the transmitter for delayed broadcast); and longer, usually multicamera, show segments that are later assembled, but not otherwise altered, in relatively simple postproduction. Control room directing always involves the use of a switcher, even if a single camera is used for some of the scenes.

When directing *film-style,* you are primarily concerned with the visualization of a single shot; the sequencing is done exclusively in postproduction. Generally, a single camera is used for film-style productions. Even if several cameras are used to cover a scene, they are not connected to a switcher; rather, each camera acts as an iso camera feeding its signal into its own VTR. No switcher is used in film-style productions.

We will now briefly describe the major aspects of control room and film-style directing. Many of the control room directing techniques also apply to film-style directing. We will, therefore, include many *general* aspects of television directing in the discussion of control room directing.

CONTROL ROOM DIRECTING

The major aspects of control room directing are (1) coordination, (2) terminology, (3) timing, (4) rehearsal, and (5) on-the-air performance.

Coordination

Control room directing usually involves coordinating many technical operations as well as the actions of the talent. This coordination is done from a central command station: the control room (see p. 23). In the beginning, the coordination of the various production elements—cameras, audio, slides, videotape, remote feeds, and the clock—provides the greatest challenge. Managing this complex production machinery is, indeed, no easy job. During a

---

Back-Timing The process of figuring additional clock times by subtracting running times from the clock time at which the program ends.

Camera Rehearsal A full rehearsal with cameras and other pieces of production equipment. Similar to the dress rehearsal in theater.

Clock Time Also called schedule time. The time at which a program starts and ends.

Control Room Directing Simultaneous coordination of two or more cameras, the switcher, audio, and other production elements.

Dress Dress rehearsal. Same as camera rehearsal. Final rehearsal with all facilities operating. The dress rehearsal is often videotaped.

Dry Run A rehearsal without equipment during which the basic actions of the talent are worked out. Also called blocking rehearsal.

Film-Style Directing Directing separate takes for postproduction, not necessarily in the show sequence.

Front-Timing The process of figuring out clock times by adding given running times to the clock time at which the program starts.

Objective Time Also called clock time. The time we measure by the clock.

simple two-camera show, for example, you (1) talk and listen to studio engineers and production crew: camera operators, microphone boom operator, floor manager, floorpersons; (2) converse with the people in the control room, telecine, and VTR room: T.D., audio engineer, light board operator, telecine operator, videotape operator, character generator operator, and master control engineers; (3) watch at least six monitors all the time: two camera preview, telecine, VTR, general preview, and line; (4) watch the time: the control-room clock for the schedule (or log) times, and the stopwatch for the running times of the individual show segments and inserts; (5) listen to the program audio (usually one of the most difficult tasks for the beginning director); and (6) follow the script.

Once you have mastered control of the machine to some extent, your most difficult jobs are translating a show idea or script into medium requirements and dealing with people, those in front of the camera (talent) and those behind it (production crew and engineers).

Terminology

Like any other human activity in which many people work together for a common task, television directing demands a precise and specific language. This jargon, which must be understood by all members of the team, is generally called the director's *terminology*. By the time you learn television directing, you will probably have mastered most of the production jargon in general and perhaps even the greater part of the director's specific language. But because the latter is such an essential factor for the successful functioning of the production team, you may want to review some of the most common director's signals (see 17.1 through 17.6). If you want to use this section as a general review, simply cover up the column that shows the director's signals and try to call out the necessary commands by looking at the picture or the action.

The director's terminology is subject to habit and change. In some stations directors may use a term that differs somewhat from yours or one listed here, although this list is fairly standard throughout the industry. Whatever language you use, it must be understood by everyone concerned. It also should be precise and clear. There is little time during a show to do much explaining; the shorter and less ambiguous the signals are, the better the communication is. In 17.1 through 17.6, we list the director's terminology in these groups: (1) visualization, (2) sequencing, or picturization, (3) special effects, (4) audio, (5) VTR and film chain cues, and (6) floor direction.

Timing

Correct, split-second timing is essential in all television operations. Every second of a day's telecast is preplanned and logged. All television stations work on similarly tight program schedules. For them time is money, and they hire salespersons to sell time.

Running Time The duration of a show or show segment. Also called program length.

Run-Through Rehearsal.

Sequencing Same as picturization. The control and structuring of a shot sequence.

Subjective Time The duration we feel. Also called psychological time.

Take 1. Signal for a cut from one video source to another. 2. Any one of similar repeated shots taken during videotaping and filming. Sometimes *take* is used synonymously with *shot*. A "good take" is the successful completion of a shot, a show segment, or the videotaping of the whole show. A "bad take" means an unsuccessful recording; another "take" is required.

Walk-Through An orientation session with the production crew (technical walk-through) and talent (talent walk-through), by actually walking through the set and explaining the key actions to both parties.

Walk-Through Camera Rehearsal A combination of walk-through and camera rehearsal in order to save time. Usually conducted by the director from the studio floor, with all technical production positions manned and operational.

From:	Action	To:	Director's Cue

Headroom, or tilt up.

Center it, or pan left.

Pan left.

Pan right.

Tilt up.

Tilt down.

Action		**Director's Cue**
From:	**To:**	

From	To	Director's Cue
		Pedestal up, or crane up.
		Pedestal down, or crane down.
		Dolly in.
		Dolly out.
		Zoom in, or tighter.
		Zoom out, or looser.

(continued)

	Action		Director's Cue
From:		**To:**	

Truck right.

Arc left.

17.2 Sequencing or Picturization Cues

Action	Director's Cue
Cut from camera 1 to camera 2.	*Ready two—take two.*
Dissolve from camera 3 to camera 1.	*Ready one for dissolve—dissolve.*
Horizontal wipe from camera 1 to camera 3.	*Ready three for horizontal wipe* (over 1)—*wipe.*
	Or: *Ready effects number x* (the number being specified by the switcher program)—*wipe effects.*
Fade in camera 1 from black.	*Ready fade-in one—fade-in one.* Or: *Ready up on one—up on one.*
Fade out camera 2 to black.	*Ready black—go to black.*
Short fade to black between cameras 1 and 2.	*Ready cross-fade to two—cross-fade.*
Cut between camera 1 and film on F-2.	*Ready F-two* (assuming the film is coming from film chain 2)—*take F-two.* (Sometimes you simply call the camera number as it appears on the switcher. If, for example, the telecine camera of film island no. 1 is labeled 6, you say: *Ready six—take six.*)
Cut between VTR and slide.	*Ready slide—take slide.* Or: *ready slide on F-two—take F-two* (assuming the slide is on F-2).
Cut between slide and slide.	*Ready change slide on F-two—change slide.*
Going to black or taking out super before new slide comes up.	*Ready slide on F-two—slide out, change slide, up on slide.*
Dissolve between camera 3 and VTR (assuming that VTR is already rolling and locked in).	*Ready VTR two for dissolve—dissolve.*

Action	Director's Cue
Super camera 1 over 2.	*Ready super one over two—super.*
To return to camera 2.	*Ready to lose super—lose super.* Or: *Ready to take out one—take out one.*
To go to camera 1 from the super.	*Ready to go through to one—through to one.*
Super slide over base picture on camera 1..	*Ready super slide* (over 1)—*super.* Or: *Ready super F-two* (assuming that the slide appears on F-2)—*super.*
Key studio card title on camera 1 over base picture on camera 2.	*Ready key one over two—key.*
Fill keyed-out title from studio card on camera 1 with yellow hue over base picture on camera 2.	*Ready matte-key one, yellow, over two—matte-key.*
To have title from character generator appear in drop-shadow outline over base picture on camera 1.	*Ready C.G.* (for character generator) *drop shadow over one—key C.G.* (Sometimes, the director may use the name of the character generator manufacturer, such as Chyron Thus, you would say: *Ready Chyron over one—key Chyron.* Because the character generator information is almost always keyed, the "key" is usually omitted in the ready cue.) Or: *Ready effects, drop shadow—take effects.* Some directors simply call for an insert, which refers to the downstream keyer. Usually, the lettering mode (drop shadow or outline) is already programmed into the character generator. So you just say: *Ready insert seven—take insert.*
To have background scene from slide (F-1) appear behind newscaster on camera 2.	*Ready matte* (or *chroma,* or *chroma matte*) *one over two—matte.* Or: *Ready F-one effects over two—effects.*
To have a wipe pattern appear over a picture, such as a scene on camera 2 replace a scene on camera 1 through a circle wipe.	*Ready circle wipe two over one—wipe.*
	(Any other wipe is called for in the same way, except that the specific wipe pattern is substituted for the circle wipe.)
	(If you need a soft wipe, whereby the edges of the wipe pattern are purposely soft and indistinct, simply call for *Ready soft-wipe* instead of *Ready wipe.*)
To have an insert (B video) grow in size in a zoomlike motion, replacing the base picture (A video).	*Ready squeeze out—squeeze.* Or: *Ready effect sixteen—squeeze out.*
To achieve the reverse squeeze (B video getting smaller).	*Ready squeeze in—squeeze.*
To achieve a great many transitions through wipes.	*Ready wipe effect twenty-one—wipe.*

Many of the more complicated effects are preset and stored in the computer program. The retrieval goes by numbers. All you do to activate a whole effects sequence is call for the number: *Ready effects eighty-seven—take effects.* If everything goes right, and if the number of the effect actually matches the one under which it is stored in the computer, the effect sequence should proceed without further ado.

17.4 Audio Cues

Action	Director's Cue
To activate microphone in the studio.	*Ready to cue talent* (or something more specific, like "Mary")—*cue her.* (The audio engineer will automatically open her mic.) Or: *Ready to cue Mary—open mic, cue her.*
To start music.	*Ready music—music.*
To bring music under for announcer.	*Ready to fade music under—music under, cue announcer.*
To take music out.	*Ready music out—music out.* Or: *Fade music out.*
To close the microphone in the studio (announcer's mic) and to switch over to the sound on film or videotape.	*Ready SOF* (or SOT, sound on tape) *close mic, track up.* Or: *Ready SOF* (SOT)—*SOF* (SOT).
To roll audiotape.	*Ready audiotape—roll audiotape.* (Do not just say: Roll tape, because the T.D. may start the VTR.)
To fade one sound source under and out while simultaneously fading another in (similar to a dissolve).	*Ready cross-fade from* (source) *to* (other source)—*cross-fade.*
To go from one sound source to another without interruption (usually two pieces of music).	*Ready segue from* (source) *to* (other source)—*segue.*
To increase the volume of the program speaker for the director.	*Monitor up, please.*
To play sound effect from cartridge machine.	*Ready sound effect no. X on audio cart.* Or: *Ready cart no. X—sound effect.*
To put slate information on videotape (either open floor manager's mic or talkback patched to VTR).	*Ready to read slate—read slate.*

The Standard Rate and Data Book tells how much a station's time is worth in dollars and cents.

Timing is important to television in another sense as well. It produces the pace of a show. In a well-paced show, the viewer perceives the progression and the speed to be appropriate with the theme and the mood of the content or the story.

We will first take up the control of the clock time, the **physical** or **objective time** as listed in the log. Then we will briefly discuss the time we feel, **psychological** or **subjective time,** and how we relate it to program matter.

Objective Time   When you look at the log (see p. 26), you will see that it lists two types of time: (1) the time when a program, or program segment, such as a commercial, begins and ends, and (2) how long a program, or program segment, runs.

The start-stop time is called **clock time** or **schedule time.** The time specifying how long a program runs is called **running time** or **length.** Except for the very end of the broadcast day, the end time of one program always marks the beginning time for the next. The running time may be as short as 10 seconds for a commercial announcement, or as long as 2 or 3 hours for a television special or a film.

Clock Time   All clocks in all television stations are synchronized with one another, as far as the minute and second hands are concerned. Only the hour hands show local time. *Clock time,* therefore, is the single most important element of synchronizing programs within a station and among stations. If, for example, your log shows that the network news program comes in at 6:30:00 P.M., your local programming must end exactly at 6:30:00 P.M. Master control will then switch from your local news program, which may have started at 5:30:00 P.M., to network at 6:30:00 P.M. The network will come in on this time, regardless of whether you are ready for it or not, that is, whether you have ended your local news program a little earlier or whether your local newscaster is still in the process of saying good-bye to the audience.

Action	Director's Cue
To start videotape for recording of a program.	*Ready to roll VTR one—roll VTR one.* (Now you have to wait for the "in-record" confirmation by the VTR operator.)
To "slate" the program after the VTR is in the record mode. The slate is on camera 2, the opening scene on camera 1. We are assuming that the alignment signal and reference level audio tone are already on the tape.	*Ready two, ready to read slate—take two, read slate.*
Putting the opening beeper on the audio track and fading in on camera 1. (Do not forget to start your stopwatch as soon as camera 1 fades in.)	*Ready black. Ready beeper—black, beeper. Five—four—three—two—one—up on one.* (See countdown illustration.)
To stop the videotape on a freeze frame.	*Ready freeze—freeze.*
To roll videotape out of a freeze frame mode.	*Ready to roll VTR three—roll VTR three.*
To roll a videotape for slow motion effect.	*Ready VTR four slo-mo—roll VTR four. Or: Ready VTR four slo-mo—slo-mo four.*
To roll a VTR as a program insert, while you are on camera 2; sound is on tape. Assuming a 5-sec. roll.	*Ready to roll VTR three, SOT—roll VTR three, five—four—three—two—one, take VTR three, SOT.*
	If you do not use a countdown because of instant start, simply say: *Ready VTR three, take VTR three.* (Start your stopwatch for timing the VTR insert.)
To return from film or VTR to camera and live announcer on camera 2. (Stop your watch and reset it for the next insert.)	*Ten seconds to two, five seconds to two. Ready two, ready cue announcer—cue announcer, take two.*
To cut to VTR commercial (SOT) from a tape cassette or cartridge. (Usually, the switchers are labeled CART, regardless of whether the VTR is from a cassette machine or a cartridge.)	*Ready to take cart—take cart.* (Usually the VTR carts have instant start, so no prerolls are necessary. Some directors call them "video carts" to distinguish them from audio carts.)
Roll cue Countdown	*Ready to roll film, F-two, SOF—roll film, four—three—two—one, take F-two, SOF.* (Assuming you still work with a countdown. Otherwise: *Ready film, SOF, F-two—take F-two.* The T.D. rolls and takes the film at the same time.) Start your stopwatch as soon as the film appears in the F-2 monitor.

Running Time   Obviously, you must control the *running time* of your newscast (60:00 min.) so that your program finishes at the exact time the network comes in. You may have several commercial inserts within a feature film. If you take too long getting in and out of the commercials at the scheduled breaks, you will run long with the last part of the film and miss the start-time of the next program. Or, if you control the running time of a commercial, you may have to cut it short by 2 or 3 seconds. Considering that each second of a commercial can cost the sponsor $1,000, or much more for network spots, this seemingly slight timing error can become quite expensive.

Timing Techniques   In order to control objective time (the clock, or schedule, time, and the running time, or length), you must keep an eye on at least two instruments: the *control-room clock* and your *stopwatch*.

The *control-room clock* helps you meet the schedule times—the end times of programs, which represent the beginning times of other programs. In a computer-controlled operation, these schedule times are fed into the computer. The computer then prerolls films and VTRs so that they come on the air exactly at the specified clock time, or switches from one program source to another at the exact clock time as shown in the log. If a schedule change

Action		Director's Cue
From: **To:**		**Director's Cue**

Move talent to camera left.

Move talent to camera right.

Have talent turn toward camera, face camera, or turn in.

Have the woman turn to her left.

Turn the object clockwise (counterclockwise).

To floor manager to flip from one studio card to another.

Ready change card—change card. Or simply: *Card.*

To microphone boom operator to raise boom so that microphone will no longer appear in the camera shot.

Boom up, or *mic up.*

To stop the entire action.

Cut.

Audio	Video	Your Actions
Newscaster finishes preceding story and intros VTR story.	Newscaster	Watch for the word in the script you marked for a roll cue (assuming you use a 2-start).
Speaks cue word.		*Roll VTR-four. Two—one—take VTR-four.*
Newscaster reads the copy over the silent VTR off camera.	The VTR appears on the line monitor.	Start your stopwatch. You read along with the newscaster in your script. Now *do not* take your VTR timing from the newscaster's narration. The newscaster may be off with his or her timing and finish the narration after the film has already ended. Look at your *stopwatch.* Give warning cues. *Ten seconds to one* (assuming that camera 1 will be coming back on the newscaster). *Five seconds to one. Ready one. Take one.*
The newscaster should have reached the end of the voice-over narration.	The newscaster is on the line monitor.	

becomes necessary, traffic (or anyone responsible for the change) feeds the new information to the computer, which then automatically adjusts the schedule times of all programs ahead of the change. If you do not end a locally produced program on time, the computer overrides you and switches to the network according to the schedule time as logged. So, you had better be ready.

The *stopwatch* helps you measure the length of show segments, the running time of videotape inserts, such as a news story or commercial. Do not use your stopwatch to time entire shows, unless they are videotaped for later playback. Except for the highly accurate digital ones, stopwatches may be off as much as 2 seconds in a 30-minute program. Worse yet, if you go by the running time as shown on your stopwatch for timing a local program, you may not be able to meet the next program source at the scheduled time.

When videotaping a program segment, you can use the stopwatch for the overall timing because the time code gives you a highly accurate timing of the overall show anyway. If you have VTR inserts within the show you are videotaping, you need to use *two stopwatches:* one for measuring the overall time of the show, the other for the running times of the inserts.

Remember to *start your stopwatch* at the beginning of each program insert and to stop it and reset it at the end. Inexperienced directors are apt to forget to start their watches at the beginning of a film or VTR insert.

Because accurate timing of program inserts is especially important during newscasts, we will briefly describe some of the more common timing procedures.

Timing News Inserts   All news inserts are timed with a regular or digital stopwatch. When running silent or voice-over videotape inserts, you must rely entirely on your stopwatch for the end-cue; with SOT (sound on tape) inserts, you have an additional word end-cue. (See 17.7.)

Cut back to the newscaster exactly at the end of the VTR insert; otherwise the line monitor shows black (one of the reasons to record black at the end of each videotape), or worse, the snow that appears when there is no video signal.

As soon as you are back on the newscaster, *reset* your stopwatch for the forthcoming VTR insert.

If the newscaster is too early with his or her narration, simply stay with the VTR insert until your stopwatch indicates the end time of the insert. Some directors go by the narration and cut out of the insert as soon as the newscaster has finished the voice-over narration. If you do this only once or twice, you do not affect your overall timing too much. However, if you cut out early too often, your overall timing of the newscast will certainly be off (you will run short), and you may have to stretch with filler material at the end of the newscast.

When running an SOT insert, you must time the insert with a stopwatch as you would a silent VTR insert. However, in this case, you have an additional end-cue—the last few words on the sound track of the videotape insert. Your actual out-cue is no longer the stopwatch time, but the *word end-cue*. Your script may have the following information.

Video		Audio
VTR 0:20	SOT	Ends: " . . . looking forward to it."

After the 10-second cue (or 5-second cue, if this is one of your procedures), you *listen* carefully for the end-cue: " . . . looking forward to it." After "it" you cut to the next video source, even if your stopwatch is a second or two over or under the end time of 20 seconds. But you need the stopwatch time, nevertheless; otherwise, you would have to listen carefully throughout the VTR insert for the end-cue (see also 17.23).

Although the computer that controls master control operations does all the figuring of start and end times of programs and program inserts, you still need to know how to use **back timing** and **front timing** to meet the scheduled program times as displayed by the log.

Back-Timing One of the most common time controls involves cues to the talent, so that he or she can end the program, such as a newscast, on the scheduled time. In a 30-minute program, the talent normally expects a 5-minute cue, and subsequent cues with 3 minutes, 2 minutes, 1 minute, 30 seconds, and 15 seconds remaining in the show. In order to figure out such time cues quickly, you simply *back-time* from the scheduled end time, or (which is the same thing) the start time of the new program segment. For example, if your log shows that your live "What's Your Opinion?" panel discussion show is followed by a Salvation Army PSA (Public Service Announcement) at 4:29:30, at what clock times do you have to give the talent the standard time cues? You simply start with the end time, 4:29:30, and *subtract* the various time segments. For example, your 15-second cue should come at $4:29:30 - 0:00:15 = 4:29:15$.

Here is how you proceed with back-timing this particular program:

4:24:30	5	Back-time to here
4:26:30	3	
4:27:30	2	
4:28:30	1	
4:29:00	30 sec.	
4:29:15	15 sec.	
4:29:30	black →	Start here

If you record a program in the live-on-tape mode (directed and produced like a live show, but put on videotape instead of on the air) and time the VTR with a stopwatch, you need to back-time from the *running time* of the program for the end-cues.

Let's assume that your show has a running time of 28:30 minutes. The time cues to the talent would have to come at the following stopwatch times (assuming you use a regular stopwatch):

23:30	5-min. cue
25:30	3-min. cue
26:30	2-min. cue
27:30	1-min. cue
28:00	30-sec. cue
28:15	15-sec. cue
28:30	black

Digital stopwatches can be made to run forward or in reverse. When you are videotaping a program, you will probably want the watch to run in reverse, showing you at any point in the show the *remaining* running time. Because the watch in the reverse shows the time left till the end of the program anyway, no back-timing is necessary.

SCHEDULE (or CLOCK) TIME	SEGMENT TITLE	RUNNING TIME (or LENGTH)
5:00:20	OPENING	
5:00:35	FEATURE FILM	
5:11:03	TRAFFIC SAFETY PSA	
5:11:13	SOAP COMMERCIAL	
5:11:33	FEATURE FILM	
5:23:51	SALVATION ARMY PSA	
etc.		

a

SCHEDULE TIME	SEGMENT TITLE	RUNNING TIME
5:00:20	OPENING	00:15
5:00:35	FEATURE FILM	10:28
5:11:03	TRAFFIC SAFETY PSA	00:10
5:11:13	SOAP COMMERCIAL	00:20
5:11:33	FEATURE FILM	12:18
5:23:51	SALVATION ARMY PSA	

b

17.8 Figuring Running Times (a) Schedule times and (b) running times. To figure the running times, you take the last clock time and subtract the one immediately preceding it. In this example, you subtract 5:11:33 from 5:23:51, which gives you the running time of 12:18 for the last feature film segment. You then continue on to the next segment.

Although the log usually shows both schedule times and running times, the script or program format may, for example, give you only start and end clock times for each program segment. In order to figure running times from clock times, you must, once again, back-time. As an example, we will take a feature film that is interrupted by commercials and PSAs. Because the end-cues for the films are determined by running time (stopwatch times) only (end-cue marks are no longer used), you must figure out the running time for each program segment from the clock times as indicated on the program format (see 17.8a).

What is the running time for each segment? Again, you start at the last clock time given and work backward. How long is the last feature film segment as shown on the format? 5:23:51 − 5:11:33 = 12:18 minutes. Try now to figure out all the remaining running times, before checking your results (see 17.8b).

When subtracting time, you may find it convenient to take a minute from the minute column and convert it into seconds, especially when you have to subtract a high number of seconds from a small number. Similarly, you can take an hour from the hour column and convert it into minutes.

$$\begin{array}{rr} 5:15:22 \rightarrow & 5:14:82 \\ -\ \ 14:27 \rightarrow & -\ \ 14:27 \\ \hline & 5:00:55 \end{array}$$

$$\begin{array}{rr} 5:02:43 \rightarrow & 4:62:43 \\ -\ \ 55:30 \rightarrow & -\ \ 55:30 \\ \hline & 4:07:13 \end{array}$$

Front-Timing   In order to keep a show on time (such as a live newscast with many recorded inserts), you need to know more than the starting and end times of the program and the running times of the various inserts. You also need to know *when* (clock time) the inserts are to be run; otherwise, you will not be able to figure whether you are a little ahead or behind with the total show.

In order to figure out the additional clock times for each break or insert, simply *add* the running times to the initial clock time as shown in the log or the program format. Try to figure out the additional clock times for the program rundown (see 17.9a). At what clock time, for example, does the PSA come up? Look at 17.9b to see how schedule (clock) times should appear on the log, or program rundown sheet. If you figured correctly, you will have to hit the PSA slide at exactly 6:34:40.

When front-timing, as when back-timing, remember to compute time on a sixty scale rather than a hundred scale.

$$
\begin{array}{r}
6:33:\ 42 \\
+\quad 0:\ 58 \\
\hline
6:33:100 \rightarrow 6:34:40
\end{array}
$$

Simply compute the seconds, minutes, and hours individually, and then convert them to the sixty scale.

$$
\begin{array}{r}
4:\ 39:\ 47 \\
45:\ 29 \\
+\quad 18:\ 30 \\
\hline
4:102:106 \rightarrow 4:103:46 \rightarrow 5:43:46
\end{array}
$$

Production Time   Now that you have learned the various timing techniques for timing programs and inserts, you must acquaint yourself with another form of time control—the production schedule.

The production schedule tells you when you should be doing what. Here is an example of a production schedule for a simple studio production:

8:30– 9:00 A.M. Tech meeting
9:00–12:00 P.M. Setup and lighting
12:00–12:30 P.M. Meal
12:30– 1:00 P.M. Prod meeting: Host and guests

1:00– 1:30 P.M. Run-through with cameras
1:30– 2:00 P.M. Notes and reset
2:00– 2:30 P.M. Tape
2:30– 3:00 P.M. Spill
3:00– 3:30 P.M. Strike

As you can see from this production schedule, a production day is divided into *blocks of time* during which certain activities are to take place.

8:30–9:00 A.M. *Tech meeting*. You start the day with a technical meeting during which you discuss with the crew what the show is all about and what is required. This is the time to acquaint the technical personnel with the process message—in our case, a discussion of the advantages and disadvantages of nuclear power by three scientists. The lighting director should know that two of the three guests are women—one blond, the other Asian with black hair. The third scientist is a Black male. (You need more back light for the Black guest than for the other two.) There is a model of a nuclear reactor that needs to be positioned and lighted in a separate set area. You may also explain what camera shots you want to get and if you have any special audio requirements. The technical director may advise you of some of the existing or potential technical problems.

9:00–12:00 P.M. *Setup and lighting*. This should be sufficient time to set up a routine set and to do an especially good job on lighting. Although as a director you are not directly involved in this production phase, you should, nevertheless, keep an eye on the setup and the lighting. For example, the model of the nuclear reactor may be just a little too far away from the set, and the lighting director may have forgotten where you want the blond scientist to sit. Check whether there is more back light for the Black scientist than for the other guests. Are the mic cords out of camera range? One of the scientists will get up and walk to the nuclear reactor model to point out certain features. Does she have enough mic cord to get from her seat to the model?

12:00–12:30 P.M. *Meal*. Everybody is expected back at 12:30 sharp, not 12:32 or 12:35. This means that everybody has to be able to leave the studio at exactly 12:00, *even if there are still some technical details*

SCHEDULE TIME	SEGMENT TITLE	RUNNING TIME
6:29:30	NEWS PROMO	0:10
	OIL CO. COMMERCIAL	0:20
	NEWS LV	2:17
	NEWS VTR (SOT)	1:05
	NEWS LV	0:20
	NEWS VTR (VO)	0:58
	SAFETY PSA SLIDE	0:10

a

SCHEDULE TIME	SEGMENT TITLE	RUNNING TIME
6:29:30	NEWS PROMO	0:10
6:29:40	OIL CO. COMMERCIAL	0:20
6:30:00	NEWS LV	2:17
6:32:17	NEWS VTR (SOT)	1:05
6:33:22	NEWS LV	0:20
6:33:42	NEWS VTR (VO)	0:58
6:34:40	SAFETY PSA SLIDE	0:10

b

left undone. Minor technical problems can be solved during your production meeting.

12:30–1:00 P.M. *Prod meeting: Host and guests.* When the host and the guests come to this meeting, they have already been introduced to one another by the producer and gone through makeup. Now is the time to acquaint everybody with the opening and closing, and with the handling of the nuclear reactor model. The A.D. and the floor manager must attend this meeting. Ideally, the T.D. should also participate in this meeting. The P.A. takes notes. Check with the guests as to the correct spelling of their names and their titles, and check whether the key slides or character generator program agree. If titles are to be added later, circulate a sheet among crew and talent to confirm the correct spelling of their names. Have them initial the sheet if their names are correctly spelled. Double-check with the floor manager whether there is a pointer for the scientist who explains the nuclear reactor. The P.A. should write down all production items that still need attention.

1:00–1:30 P.M. *Run-through with cameras.* You now explain to the camera operators the opening and closing shots, and the shots of the reactor model. Then you go through the opening and the close with all facilities (theme music, credits, and name keys). This is also a good opportunity to practice the guest's crossover from the set to the reactor area and her pointing out certain features of the model. Watch for unwanted shadows and listen to unwanted noises during these actions. Dictate to the P.A. any production problems you may discover during this rehearsal.

1:30–2:00 P.M. *Notes and reset.* You now gather the key production people—producer, A.D., T.D., L.D. (lighting director), floor manager, host, and the guests if necessary. Ask the P.A. to read the notes one by one, just in the order as written down. Direct the production team to take care of the various problems. At the same time, the rest of the crew should get the cameras into opening positions, reset the slides or the character generator, load the VTR with tape, and make minor adjustments to the lighting.

2:00–2:30 P.M. Tape. You should be in the control room and roll the tape at exactly 2:00 P.M., not 2:05 or 2:10. If all goes well, the half-hour show should be **"in the can,"** or finished, by 2:30.

2:30–3:00 P.M. Spill. This is a period of grace, because we all know that television involves a complicated, temperamental machine, and many people. For example, you may have to redo the opening or close because the computer of the character generator decided to flip to another "page" or because the host stumbled on the Asian name of one of the nuclear scientists. Or you may have to stop the tape because the scientist got her mic cord tangled on her way to the reactor model.

3:00–3:30 P.M. Strike. This is the time for you to thank the talent and crew, talk with the producer about the show you just taped and/or upcoming productions, and keep at least one eye on the strike. If you have a good floor manager, do not interfere with the strike. Trust your crew to take down the set, get the expensive model of the nuclear reactor out of the studio in one piece, and have the studio clean for the next production.

One of the most important aspects of a production schedule is *sticking to the time* allotted for each segment. You must learn to get things done within the scheduled time block, and more importantly, to jump to the next activity *at the precise time as shown on the schedule,* regardless of whether you are done with your previous chores. Do not use up the time of a scheduled segment with a previously scheduled activity. A good director terminates an especially difficult blocking rehearsal in midpoint in order to meet the scheduled "notes and reset" period. Inexperienced directors often spend a great amount of time on a relatively minor detail of the show, and usually go on the air without having rehearsed the

rest of the show. The production schedule is designed to prevent such discrepancies.

Here is an example of a production schedule of a 1-hour soap opera. The setup and lighting have been accomplished during the preceding night.

6:00– 8:00 A.M.	Dry block—Rehearsal hall
8:00– 8:30 A.M.	Tech meeting
8:30–10:00 A.M.	Camera blocking
10:00–10:15 A.M.	Reset
10:15–11:15 A.M.	Run-through
11:15–12:15 P.M.	Meal
12:15–12:45 P.M.	Notes and reset
12:45– 1:45 P.M.	Dress rehearsal
1:45– 2:30 P.M.	Notes and reset
2:30– 3:30 P.M.	Tape
3:30– 4:30 P.M.	Spill

Note that there is only a 1-hour rehearsal for a 1-hour, rather complicated show, but that there is more time given for "notes." This means that the *discussion* of production problems plays a major role in good television directing. We will take up this point again in the discussion of rehearsals.

Subjective Time The control of subjective, or psychological, time, the time we feel, is much more subtle and difficult than the control of objective time. Unfortunately, there is no mechanical timing device to tell you whether an actor races through his or her lines too fast, or whether a whole scene is paced too slowly, and therefore drags for the viewer. In determining subjective time, you must rely on your subjective judgment and on your sensitivity to the relation of one movement to another or one rhythm to another. Although two persons move with the same speed, one may seem to move much more slowly than the other. What makes the movements of the one person appear faster or slower?[1]

Watch how rush-hour traffic reflects nervous energy and impatience while actually the vehicles move considerably more slowly than when traveling on an open freeway. Good comedians and musi-

[1]Herbert Zettl, *Sight-Sound-Motion* (Belmont, Calif.: Wadsworth Publishing Co., 1973), pp. 275–276.

cians are said to have a "good sense of timing." This means that they have excellent control of their subjective time.

Try to pick three or four recordings of the same piece of music, such as Beethoven's Fifth Symphony, as interpreted by different conductors. Most likely, you will find that some play the same piece of music much faster than others, depending on their overall concept of the piece and, of course, their personal temperament and style.

When dealing with subjective time, we have many ways of expressing its relative duration. You hear of speed, tempo, pace, hurrying, dragging, and other similar expressions. In order to simplify the subjective time control, you may want to use only two basic concepts: *pace* and *rhythm*. The **pace** of a show or a show segment is how fast or how slow the segment or the entire show feels. **Show rhythm** has to do with the pacing of each show segment in relation to the next, and to the whole show.

There are many ways of increasing or decreasing the pace of a scene, a segment, or an overall show. One is to *speed up* the action or the delivery of the dialogue, very much like picking up the tempo of a musical number. Another is to *increase* the *intensity,* the relative excitement, of a scene. Usually, this is done by introducing or sharpening some *conflict,* such as raising the voices of people arguing, having one car almost go out of control while being pursued by another, or having the lead mountain climber slip at an especially tricky point. A third possibility is to *increase* the **density** of the event, by simply having more things happening within a specific section of running time. For slowing down a scene, you do just the opposite. Whatever you change, you must always perceive your pacing in relation to the other parts of the show and to the whole show itself. Fast, after all, is fast only if we are able to relate the movement to something slower.

Rehearsal

Ideally, you should be able to rehearse everything that goes on videotape or on the air. Unfortunately, in practice this is hardly the case. Because the scheduled rehearsal times always seem insufficient, the prerehearsal preparations, just discussed, become extremely important. To make optimal use of the available time during the scheduled rehearsals, you might try the following methods: (1) script reading, (2) dry run, or blocking rehearsal, (3) walk-through, (4) camera rehearsal, and (5) walk-through camera rehearsal combination.

Script Reading   Under ideal conditions every major production would begin with a script-reading session. Even for a relatively simple show, you should meet at least once with the talent, the producer, the P.A. (production assistant), and the key production personnel (associate director, T.D., floor manager) to discuss and read the script. Bring the floor plan along. In this session, which normally doubles as a production meeting, explain these points: (1) process message objective, including the purpose of the show and its intended audience; (2) major actions of the performers, the number and use of special hand props, and major crossovers; and (3) the performer's relationship to guests. In an interview, for example, discuss with the host the key questions, what he or she should know about the guest, and the general tone expected. Usually such talent preparation is done by the producer. Try to get a rough timing on the show by clocking the major scenes and show segments as they are read.

The script-reading sessions are, of course, particularly important if you are rehearsing a television drama. Indeed, the more thorough the script reading is, the easier the subsequent rehearsals are. In such sessions, you should discuss at length the process message objective, the structure of the play (theme, plot, environment), and the substance of each character. An extremely detailed analysis of the characters is probably the most important aspect of the dramatic script-reading session. The actor or actress who really understands his or her character, role, and relation to the whole event has mastered the major part of his or her screen performance. More than any other, the television actor or actress must understand a character so well that he or she is no longer "acting out," but living, the role. Such internalization can be facilitated through extensive script-reading sessions.

After this kind of session, the actors tend to block themselves (under the director's careful guidance, of course) and to move and "act" naturally. There is no need for you to explain each move. Once the actors understand their roles with head and heart, their actions are motivated.

Dry Run or Blocking Rehearsal **Dry runs** or **blocking rehearsals** are required only for complex shows, such as dramas, daytime serials, videotaped comedy series, and scenes from variety specials. After the script-reading session, you call for the *dry run,* during which the basic actions of the talent are worked out. By that time, you must have a very good idea of where the cameras should be in relation to the set, and the actors in relation to the cameras. The dry run presupposes a detailed floor plan and a thorough preparation by the director. It also presupposes that the actors have internalized (understood with head and heart) their characters and roles. Tell them approximately where the action is supposed to take place (the approximate location in the imagined set area; the actual set is rarely available at this point), and let them block themselves. Follow their actions with the director's viewfinder. Watch their actions as *screen images,* not from the point of view of a live audience. Adjust their blocking and your imagined camera positions so that you have a reasonable assurance that you will achieve the visualized screen image in the actual camera rehearsal. Be ready to give *precise directions* to the actor who is asking what to do next. A good actor, rather than always knowing what to do without the director's help, asks what he or she should do, and then does it with precision and conviction.

Generally, try to observe these points in a dry run:

1. Hold the dry run in the studio or a rehearsal hall. In an emergency, any room will do. Use tables, chairs, chalk marks on the floor for sets and furniture.

2. Work on the blocking problems. Use a viewfinder. Have the P.A. take notes of the major blocking maneuvers.

3. Keep the camera and microphone movements in mind when blocking the actors. Some directors

walk right into the spot where the active camera will be and watch the proceedings from the camera's point of view.

4. Call out all major cues, if it will help.

5. Go through the scenes in the order in which they are to be taped. If you do the show live, or live-on-tape, try to go through the whole script at least once.

6. Time each segment and the overall show. Allow time for long camera movements, music bridges, announcer's intro and close, the closing credits, and so forth.

7. Reconfirm the dates for the upcoming rehearsals.

Walk-Through The **walk-through** is an orientation session that helps the production crew and performers understand the necessary medium and performance requirements quickly and easily. You can have both a *technical* and a *talent walk-through* or, if you are pressed for time, a combination of the two. The walk-throughs as well as camera rehearsals occur shortly before the actual on-the-air performance or taping session.

Technical Walk-Through Once the set is in place, gather the production crew (A.D., floor manager, floor personnel, T.D., lighting director, camera operators, audio engineer, boom operator) and explain to them the process message objective and your basic concept of the show. Then walk with them through the set and explain these key factors: (1) basic blocking and actions of talent, (2) camera locations and traffic, (3) special shots and framings, (4) mic placements and boom location, (5) basic cuing, (6) scene changes and prop changes, if any, (7) major lighting effects, and (8) easel positions.

The technical walk-through is especially important on *remote telecasts,* where the crew must often work during the setup under the guidance of the floor manager rather than the director, who is isolated in the remote truck.

Talent Walk-Through While the production people go about their tasks, take the performers or actors on a short excursion through the set and explain once again their major actions, positions, and cross-ings. Always try to block talent in such a way that the talent, rather than the cameras, does most of the moving. Tell them where the cameras will be in relation to their actions. Here are some of the more important aspects of the talent walk-through:

1. Point out to each performer or actor his or her major positions and walks.

2. Explain briefly where and how they should work with specific props. For example, tell the actor that the coffee urn will be here, and how he or she should walk with the coffee cup to the couch: in front of the table, not behind it. Explain your blocking to the talent from a camera point of view.

3. Once again explain the major visualization and sequencing, or picturization, aspects.

4. Have the performers or actors go through their opening lines and then have them skip to the individual cue lines.

5. Give everyone enough time for makeup and dressing before the camera rehearsal.

During this talent walk-through, try to stay out of the production people's way as much as possible. Finish your walk-through rehearsal early enough so that everybody can take a break before camera rehearsal.

Camera Rehearsal In small station operations, **camera rehearsal** and final dress rehearsal, or **dress,** are almost always the same. Frequently, the camera rehearsal time is cut short by technical problems, such as minor or major lighting adjustments and camera adjustments. One attribute you must have as a television director is patience. You may get nervous when you see most of the technical crew working frantically on the key camera five minutes before air time. There is nothing you can do, however, except realize that you are working with (1) a highly skilled group of technicians who know just as well as you do how much depends on a successful performance, and (2) a highly complicated machine which, like all other machines, sometimes works and sometimes breaks down.

The two basic methods of conducting a camera rehearsal for a live or live-on-tape production are the stop-start method and the uninterrupted run-through. A stop-start rehearsal is usually conducted from the control room, but it can also be done, at least partially, from the studio floor. An uninterrupted run-through rehearsal is always conducted from the control room.

With the stop-start method you interrupt the camera rehearsal whenever you find something wrong; then you go back to a logical spot in the script and start again, hoping that the mistake is not repeated. This is a thorough, but time-consuming, method.

The uninterrupted run-through rarely remains uninterrupted. However, you should call for a **cut** (stop all action) only when a grave mistake has been made, one that cannot be corrected at a later time. All minor mistakes and fumbles are corrected *after* the run-through. Dictate to the P.A. all items that need to be corrected. These notes are then read during rehearsal breaks. Because most plays are videotaped, your uninterrupted run-through will be interrupted at each scene or segment as marked in the script. Because camera rehearsals are generally videotaped for protection and for additional material in the postproduction editing process, you need the scene breaks to stop and start the videotape and to slate each scene. If you plan to do the entire show live, or videotape the show in one uninterrupted take, you should go through as long a segment as possible in the uninterrupted run-through. A long stretch without any interruptions not only gives you an overview of the general development and build of the play, but also helps the performers or actors enormously in their pacing. The uninterrupted run-through is one of the few opportunities for you to get a feeling of the overall rhythm of the show.

Walk-Through Camera Rehearsal Combination
Necessary as the previously mentioned rehearsal procedures seem, they are rarely possible in small station operations. First, most directing chores in a small station are of a nondramatic nature, demanding less rehearsal effort than for dramatic shows. Second, because of time and space limitations, you are lucky to get rehearsal time equal to or slightly more than the running time of the entire show. Forty or even thirty minutes rehearsal time for a half-hour

17.10   Camera Positions Because the normal camera setup is from left to right—with camera 1 on the farthest left side of the action and the highest-number camera on the farthest right side—camera 1 should give you a view from slightly left, and camera 3 from slightly right. In this illustration, the cameras are obviously crossed. It will simplify your directing chores if you keep them in the basic left-to-right position.

show is not uncommon. Most often, you have to jump from a cursory script reading to a camera rehearsal immediately preceding the on-the-air performance or taping session.

In these situations, you have to resort to a **walk-through camera rehearsal** combination. Because you cannot rehearse the entire show, you simply pick the most important parts and rehearse them as well as possible. Usually these are the *transitions* rather than the parts between the transitions.

Here are some of the major points for conducting a walk-through camera rehearsal:

1.   Do this type of rehearsal from the *studio floor*. If you try to conduct it from the control room, you will waste valuable time explaining shots and blocking through the intercommunication system, even if you happen to have a first-rate floor manager.

2.   Get all production people into their respective positions—all camera operators at their cameras (with the cameras uncapped and ready to go), the microphone boom ready to follow the sound source, the floor manager ready for cuing, the T.D. and audio engineer ready for action in the control room.

3.   Walk the talent through all the major parts of the show. Rehearse only the critical transitions and

shots. For example, if the performer has to demonstrate a small object, show him or her how to hold the object and the camera operator how to frame it.

4.   Call your shots over the "hot" boom (or any other) microphone into the control room and have the T.D. switch the particular camera on line, so that everybody can see the image on the line monitor from the studio floor.

5.   As soon as the talent knows how to go on from there, skip to the end of his or her segment and have the talent introduce the following segment.

6.   Rehearse all major walks and crossovers on camera. Look through the camera's viewfinder to check the framing (especially of the camera that is getting ready for the next shot; the on-the-air camera is punched up already on the studio monitor).

7.   Give all cues for music, sound effects, lighting, videotape rolls, slating procedures, and so forth to the T.D. via the open studio mic, but do not have them executed (except for the music, which can be reset rather easily).

8.   Have the floor manager cue the talent and mark the crucial spots with chalk or masking tape on the studio floor.

a   b

17.11   Zoom Lens Position The relative size of objects can sometimes give you a clue as to the focal length of the zoom lens setting. Camera 1 (a) is zoomed in quite tightly, whereas camera 2 is on a wide-angle zoom position. Camera 2 (b) can, therefore, be dollied or trucked while on the air; camera 1 cannot.

If everything goes fairly well, you are ready to go to the control room. Avoid getting hung up on some minor detail while on the floor. Always view the problems in the context of the overall show. For example, do not fret over a picture that seems to hang slightly high while neglecting to rehearse the most important crossovers with the talent. In the control room, contact the cameras by number and find out whether the operators can communicate with you. Then from the control room rehearse once more the most important parts of the show—the opening, the closing, major talent actions, and camera movements.

Once you are in the control room, the only way you can see the action on the floor is through the camera preview monitors. Most control-room windows are either blocked with monitors or scenery or, as in most modern control rooms, nonexistent. You should, therefore, develop the ability to determine camera positions and zoom lens positions from how the pictures appear on the monitors. (See 17.10 and 17.11.)

Try to rehearse the opening and closing of a show from the script for yourself, prior to camera rehearsal. Sit in a quiet corner with the script and, using a stopwatch (for practice), start calling out the

opening shots: *Ready to roll VTR two, roll it,* and so on, or *Fade-in two, ready to key effects,* and so on. By the time you enter the control room, you will practically have memorized the opening and closing of the show and will be able, therefore, to pay full attention to the monitors and audio.

As much as you may be pressed for time, try to remain cool and courteous to everybody. Also, this is not the time to make drastic changes. Although there are probably some other ways in which the show might be directed, and even improved, the camera rehearsal is not the time to try them out. Be sure to finish the rehearsal early enough to allow time to reset the rehearsed production elements and *to give crew and talent a short rest* before the actual on-the-air performance or taping session. Do not rehearse right up to air time.

On-the-Air Performance

Directing the on-the-air performance, or the final taping session, is, of course, the most important part of your job as a director. After all, the viewers do not sit in on the script conferences or your rehearsals; all they see and hear is what you finally put on the air.

Stand-by Procedures   Here are some of the most important stand-by procedures immediately preceding the on-the-air telecast:

1.   Call on the intercom every member of the production team who needs to react to your cues—camera operators, boom operator, floor manager and other floor personnel, videotape operator, lightboard operator, audio engineer, and character generator operator.

2.   Check with the floor manager and make sure that everyone is in the studio and ready for action.

3.   Announce the time remaining until the on-the-air telecast (or taping) and ask whether the floor manager is ready with the slate (for videotape identification). Precious time can be lost in television studios simply because the slate is not ready or properly labeled. Indicate which camera will take the slate, choosing one that is not involved in the opening shot. To avoid such troubles, most stations use a character generator for slating.

4.   Alert everyone to the first cues.

5.   Tell the floor manager who gets the first cue.

6.   Check with the videotape engineer as to whether he or she is ready to roll the tape, and with the camera operators and audio engineer about their opening actions.

7.   Line up the slate on one camera and the opening shot on the other.

8.   Check on the opening slide, VTR insert, or character generator display.

The Show   Assuming you videotape in the live-on-tape fashion, you must first go through the usual videotape rolling procedures (see p. 511). Once the videotape is properly rolling and slated, you can begin with the actual recording. You are now *on the air*. Imagine the following opening sequence:

Up on (or *fade-in*) *one. Music. Fade music. Cue announcer. Ready to key effects over one. Key effects* (opening titles from the character generator). *Change effects. Key out* (or *lose key*). *Music out. Slowly.*

Ready two on Lynn (the performer). *Ready to cue Lynn. Cue Lynn, take two. One, get a close-up*

of the book (Lynn is holding). *Ready one, take one. Two, stay on Lynn. Ready two, take two. One on the easel. Zoom out a little. Good. Ready one, take one. Two on the easel. Good. Ready two for a dissolve. Dissolve to two. Ready to roll VTR-four. Roll it. Two—one—take VTR-four* (assuming a fast 2-second start).

By now you are well into the show. Remember to watch the time carefully. After the 5-minute cue (if any), you must prepare for the closing. Are the closing credits ready? Again, watch the time.

Thirty seconds. Wind her up. Wind her up (or give her a wrap-up). *Fifteen* (seconds). *Ready effects* (credits). *Two zoom out. Ready music. Cut her. Music. Good. Music under, cue announcer. Two, keep zooming. Ready to roll effects. Roll them. Ready to key one over two. Key. Key out. Fade to black. Music out. Hold. Stop VTR. OK, all clear.*

Good job, everyone.

Unfortunately, not every show goes as smoothly as that. You can contribute to a smooth performance, however, by paying attention to these important on-the-air directing procedures:

1.   Give all signals clearly and precisely. Appear relaxed but alert.

2.   Cue talent before you come up on him or her with the camera. By the time he or she starts to speak, you will have faded in the picture.

3.   Indicate talent by name. Do not tell the floor manager to cue just "him" or "her," especially when there are several anticipating "hims" or "hers" in the studio.

4.   Do not give a ready cue too far in advance, or the person may have forgotten it by the time your take cue finally arrives.

5.   Do not pause between the **take** and the number of the camera. Do not say: *Take*———(pause)———*two*. Some T.D.s may punch up the camera before you say the number.

6.   Keep in mind the number of the camera already on the air, and do not call for a take or dissolve to that camera.

7.   Do not ready one camera and then call for a take of another. In other words, do not say: *Ready*

one, take two. If you change your mind, nullify the ready cue and then give another.

8.   Talk to the cameras by number, not by the name of the camera operator. What would you do if both camera operators were named Mary?

9.   Call the camera first before you give instructions. For example: *Camera 2, give me a close-up of the display. Camera 3, cover shot. Camera 1, dolly in.*

10.   After you have put one camera on the air, immediately tell the other camera what to do next. Do not wait till the last second; for example, say *Take two. One, stay on this medium shot. Three, on the easel.* If you reposition a camera, give the operator time to reset the zoom lens; otherwise, the camera will not stay in focus during subsequent zooming.

11.   If you make a mistake, correct it as well as you can and go on with the show. Do not meditate on how you could have avoided it while you are neglecting the rest of the show. Pay full attention to what is going on. If recording live-on-tape, stop the tape only when absolutely necessary. Too many false starts can take the energy out of even the most seasoned performer and production crew.

12.   Spot-check the videotape after each take to make sure that the take is technically acceptable. Then go on to the next one. It is always easier to repeat a take, one right after the other, than to go back at the end of a strenuous taping session.

13.   If you use the stop-start method or, especially, the film-style approach to videotaping, you may want to play back each take before going on to the next one. If you do not like the take, tell the crew how to change the take before taping it again.

14.   If there is a technical problem that you have to solve from the control room, tell the floor manager about it on the intercom, or use the S.A. system to inform the whole floor about the slight delay. This way the talent knows that there is a technical delay and, what's more, that the delay was not caused by them.

15.   During the show, speak only when necessary. If you talk too much, people will stop listening and may miss important instructions.

In film-style directing, you do not intend to record on tape a finished product that needs little or no postproduction for broadcast; rather, your aim is to produce effective videotape segments that can be shaped into a continuous program through postproduction. Film style directing is often used when *production control* is paramount, or when you need more *mobility and flexibility* in EFP than a big remote unit can afford.

Realizing that many aspects of the preparation for control room directing and its major techniques can be easily adapted to film-style directing, you should take note of the special requirements of film-style directing in regards to these activities: (1) script analysis, (2) visualization and sequencing, (3) technical coordination, (4) timing, (5) directing talent, (6) rehearsal and taping, (7) directing for EFP, and (8) postshow duties.

Script Analysis

When you prepare a script for film-style directing, you look for small segments that can be covered in single takes. The criteria for these segments are based almost exclusively on *production efficiency* rather than story development (see Section Two for examples). Some television directors who developed their craft in the control room still find it difficult to disregard organic connections between shots and to "butcher" a script in favor of production efficiency. What they fail to realize, however, is that film-style directing does not culminate in a finished or nearly finished production, but merely supplies basic material (however important) for the postproduction people (editing, special effects, and sound).

Visualization and Sequencing

When directing film-style, you are concerned much more with **visualization** than with **sequencing** (or **picturization**), because all the sequencing will be done in postproduction. This means that you are concerned much more with what the camera sees in each take than with the transitions from shot to shot, or the continuity of a series of shots.

In film-style directing, you concentrate on the point of view of a *single camera* for each take. For example, if the script calls for a long shot in order to establish the scene and then for a series of close-ups, you can work exclusively on the long shot, then move to the close-ups. Or, if more convenient, you can videotape the close-ups first, and then do all the long shots later. As in film making, you will find yourself repeating an action several times in order to get various fields of view (long shots, medium shots, close-ups) or angles. Pay close attention to every detail so that the action is, indeed, *identical* when repeated. If, for example, a mother kisses her departing daughter on the left cheek in the medium shot, do not let her switch to the right cheek during subsequent takes, or during the close-ups of the same scene. Such gross directing mistakes can obviously not be "fixed" in postproduction. In order to minimize such problems, some directors use several cameras to shoot a single action simultaneously from various points of view. But note that there is no switcher involved and that each camera feeds its video signal to its own VTR. The producer can tell you whether the expense of additional equipment and personnel is worth the time saved. Some producers and directors recommend the two-camera approach as the most efficient method of film-style production.

Although visualizing shots is of primary importance in film-style directing, you should not neglect, or worse disregard, sequencing (picturization). In fact, visualization is often influenced by how it will connect with the previous and following shots—the sequencing of shots. You have probably noticed that the example of the kissing scene was actually more a continuity than a visualization problem. The mother's kiss might look equally impressive when planted on the right or left cheek of her daughter. But when seen as a long shot to close-up sequence, the switching from left to right becomes a problem.

As a director, you are responsible for providing the editor with usable cutaways. Do not leave the cutaways to the camera operator; tell him or her what to shoot. Cutaways are not merely a safety device;

in film-style directing, they constitute an essential production element.

Technical Coordination

As we have said, in film-style directing, you videotape one shot at a time. Therefore, your coordinating job is much less demanding than in control room directing. You can concentrate on each shot, and you do not need to worry about the various other production elements, such as the switcher, graphics, or special effects. Even if there are different technical requirements from shot to shot, you have time to concentrate on each one separately. For example, in EFP you might shoot with natural light when recording the various long shots, and apply special lighting techniques only during close-ups. Generally, there is no need to worry about a title slide, special effects transition, or background music; all this will be done in postproduction.

Timing

In film-style directing, you obviously do not have to worry about the log and getting a program on and off the air on time. Both time modes, objective and subjective, are determined more in postproduction than in the videotaping of the various segments. However, the individual shots must reflect the pace and rhythm of the overall show. For example, if you have everybody speak at a very slow rate, you make it very hard for the editor to have the show move at a brisk overall pace. Some directors ask for a stopwatch time for each take, so they have a rough idea how "fast" or "slow" each take was.

Your most important concern about timing is to get the job done as scheduled. Although it may be an accepted practice in film directing to extend the shooting schedule whenever necessary, you do not enjoy this privilege in television. You are bound by the overall production time as much as the control room director.

Directing Talent

Because in film-style directing your coordinating job is much less involved than in control room directing, you can devote more time to the talent. You have the opportunity before each take to tell the performers or actors what you want them to do. Just make sure you know what you want the talent to do before directing them to do it.

Rehearsal and Taping

Film-style directing has its own rehearsal technique. Basically, you rehearse each take immediately prior to videotaping it. You walk the talent through the take, explaining what they should do and not do. In the meantime, the crew has had a chance to watch you and get a general idea of what you have in mind. You are always in close and direct communication with the camera operator. During the rehearsal, you can watch the camera shot in the monitor (assuming the camera output is fed into a monitor) or look through the camera's viewfinder and make the necessary adjustments just before the actual taping. Once satisfied with the talent performance and the technical operation (microphone placement, lighting, point of view, and mobility of camera), you can proceed with the videotaping of the scene. If something goes wrong (such as the noise of an airplane interrupting your Civil War scene), do a retake. But be careful not to wear out talent and crew. When you feel that you have a good take, play it back to see whether it is, indeed, acceptable for postproduction. Make sure that you have a good monitor available for the playbacks of your videotaped segments, especially when doing EFP. The immediate playback is, after all, one of the advantages of videotape over film.

Because you are usually shooting out of sequence, you as the director have to provide the necessary continuity for the performers and actors. Outline for talent and crew what happens before and after the taping of the scene so they have a point of reference for their actions.

Make sure you follow your *production schedule*. Especially in EFP, there is a tendency to spend much too much time on the first few takes because you have the better part of the day still ahead of you. But then, all of a sudden, you find yourself running out of time and are forced to rush through the remaining takes at breakneck speed. Such procedures are not conducive to quality productions.

Directing for EFP

Most directing for EFP is done film-style. Unless you do a big remote (see Chapter 18), you rehearse and videotape one take at a time. Some EFP operations employ a small switcher so they can cut from camera to camera while in the field. But even then, the action is cut into short, usually out-of-order sequences. The following list presents some guidelines for directing for EFP. We assume that a single camera and the film-style production approach are used.

1. Be meticulous in script preparation. There is simply no time for you to do extensive script analysis in the field. Nonetheless, even after the most careful script preparation, you may be forced to change certain camera shots and blocking procedures. Try to be as firm and quick in your decisions as possible. Be open-minded to suggestions from the production crew and talent, but do not be indecisive. Once you have made the change, stick to it. If some blocking or camera movement gives you special problems, solve them right then and there. Do not assume that you "can take care of it" in postproduction. Even the most skillful editor cannot perform miracles. The better the raw material, the easier it is for an editor to shape it into a good show.

2. Know the locale and the environment in which the production takes place. If the regular production survey does not give you enough time to get to know the place well, go back to it *before* the actual production. Although technical operations are not your immediate concern, you should still check on the availability of power (wall outlets), lighting requirements, and acoustics (large hall, small room, or traffic noise coming from a nearby freeway).

3. Ask the producer whether he or she has secured accommodations and/or parking for talent and crew. If you are doing outdoor shooting, are the most basic conveniences available for talent and crew?

4. Be sure to have a good monitor available in the field so you can preview camera shots and postview the videotaped segments. Play back each take before moving on to the next one. This way, you can repeat the take without having to rehearse it again. If you work ENG-style, with the camera feeding directly

into a portable VTR, walk with the camera operator and point out what shots you have in mind. Look through the camera viewfinder to check special compositions.

5.   Watch out for too much camera movement. Because the ENG/EFP camera is so portable, there is the temptation to have it move in each shot. But an excessively moving camera is a sure sign of an amateur crew and director. The primary motion is usually supplied by objects and people moving in front of the camera.[2] Put the camera on a tripod whenever possible. This not only keeps the camera steady, but also prevents unmotivated camera movement.

6.   Once again, be aware of shot continuity, even if you shoot out of sequence. Videotape a generous number of cutaways during each production session. Do not wait until the very end of the production to do the cutaways. Especially when shooting outdoors, the weather and light may have changed so drastically that you cannot use the cutaways for the earlier scenes.

7.   Be sure to *slate* each take and have it recorded on the shot sheet. Properly identified shots save an incredible amount of time in postproduction.

Postshow Duties

After the show, give thanks to crew and talent. If something went wrong, do not storm into the studio blaming everyone but yourself. Wait until you can think objectively about the situation. Then do not just criticize but, instead, make suggestions on how to avoid similar mistakes in the future.

Do not forget the necessary production reports, music lists, and union contracts (if you act as producer-director). File a marked script for future reference.

POSTPRODUCTION ACTIVITIES

If a show is assembled in the postproduction editing process, the director is generally still in charge of the editing decisions. In practice, however, rela-

[2]Zettl, *Sight-Sound-Motion,* pp. 285–288.

tively simple editing tasks are generally handled by the videotape editor, with a minimum of supervision (or, as editors like to call it, "interference") by the director. Nevertheless, it is a good idea for you as a director to work with the editor until the completion of the postproduction. Actually, there is little difference from a directing point of view whether you tell the T.D. to take 2, or tell the editor to edit this shot to that. In any case, try to work *with*, not against, him or her. An experienced editor can help you greatly in the sequencing process. But do not be afraid to assert yourself, especially if you feel strongly about a certain editing decision, especially if you are the *producer*-director.

During the actual editing process, you can either do the off-line editing yourself, or do a paper and pencil edit or a rough cut and then hand it over to the editor (see Chapter 11). When editing, your major concern is no longer the visualization, but the *sequencing or picturization.* You experience first-hand how valuable your awareness of continuity and your cutaways are in the postproduction process.

You should also supervise the audio sweetening, especially if you have extensive audio postproduction as well.

When finished, check the entire tape for serious technical and aesthetic discrepancies. Even a good editor might not see a jump cut until the final screening of the tape. When everything looks right, have a protection copy made of the edited tape.

GENERAL COMMENTS

As a television director, you have to bear responsibility toward your *audience,* the great many individuals whose lives you will inevitably touch, however temporarily; to your *station,* whose members have put their trust in you to use their efforts for a successful communication of their ideas and messages; toward your *production team,* whose performance is directly dependent upon your skill; and finally toward *yourself.* Like any other artist, you must always try to do your best possible job, no matter how trivial it may seem at the time. After all, the mark of the professional is *consistency,* to come up consistently with a high-quality product, regardless of the scope of the task.

Directing, finally, means to guide with sureness, understanding, and compassion; to guide and coordinate a great number of people and events into a coherent whole, into video and audio images that ultimately affect the percipient in a positive way.

MAIN POINTS

1. A television director must be an artist who can translate a script or an event into effective television pictures and sound, a psychologist who can work with people of different temperaments and skills, a technical expert who knows the potentials and limitations of the equipment, and a coordinator who can keep track of a multitude of production elements.

2. The two principal methods of television directing are (1) control room directing, which generally involves the simultaneous coordination of two or more cameras, the switcher, audio, and other production elements; and (2) film-style directing, which involves directing separate, often nonsequential, takes for postproduction.

3. The major aspects of control room directing are (1) coordination of technical operations and talent; (2) the use of a precise terminology, involving mainly cues to talent, engineering and production crews; (3) the control of objective (clock) time and subjective time (the pace of a show or show segment); (4) the various methods of rehearsal, including script reading, dry run or blocking rehearsal, walk-through, camera or dress rehearsal, and walk-through camera rehearsal combination; and (5) the on-the-air performance.

4. The major aspects of film-style directing are (1) script analysis, during which the small script segments that can be covered in single takes are isolated; (2) visualization of each single take; (3) consideration of shot sequence in the visualization process, including the videotaping of cutaways; (4) directing talent; and (5) the rehearsal, which consists of a run-through of the segment prior to each take (videotaping).

5. A director must strictly observe the production schedule, which lists the time allotted for each directing activity, such as dry run, camera rehearsal, and taping.

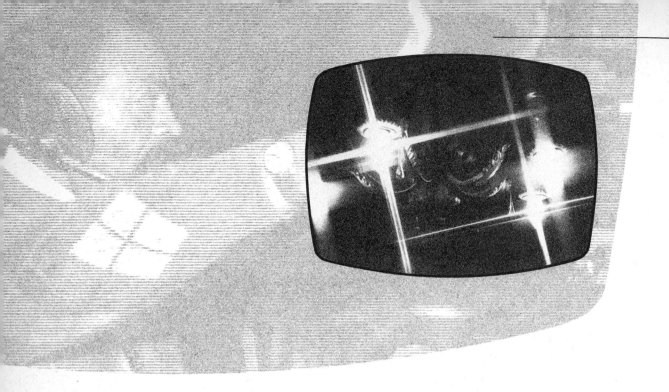

The preparation aspect of directing becomes especially crucial if you need to analyze and organize a script for live (or live-on-tape) or film-style productions. We will, therefore, briefly discuss these preparation factors: (1) visualization and sequencing (picturization), (2) script formats, and (3) script preparation.

VISUALIZATION AND SEQUENCING (PICTURIZATION)

As a director, you should be able to convert a scene mentally into television images—video and audio images that appear on the screen and from the loudspeaker. Directing starts with *visualizing* the *key images* and deciding where the people and things should be placed relative to the camera, and the camera relative to the event (people and things). Then, you must consider the *sequencing,* or *picturization,* of the event portions. By this process you determine how and where the people have to move, and how many cameras you need in order to achieve the event sequence with all the necessary transitions.

As indicated in the previous chapter, the director, as well as the producer, should start with the process message, the experience the percipient is supposed to undergo during or after the program, and work *backward* to what the medium needs in order to precipitate such an experience (see Chapter 16).

Medium Functions

Before you can adequately determine the medium requirements and the directing approach or style, you should think about the *principal functions* of the medium—whether you want to use the medium primarily to observe an event, take a closer or more intimate look at an event, or create a new event with the medium.

The Medium Looks At   When using the medium (principally the cameras and microphones) to *look at* an event, you are trying to report an event to the viewer as accurately as possible. Because the camera is innately selective (it does not have peripheral vision nor can it sense the total environment), you have to make certain decisions about what to include or what to leave out when covering an event. These decisions should be guided by the event itself—by what the event really is, rather than by what you think it ought to be. You are basically a reporter, not a dramatist.

Like any other production activity, television directing requires careful preparation. Even if you are called upon to direct an unrehearsed live event, such as a tennis match or a downtown parade, you can prepare for the assignment by defining the process message, visualizing the key shots, and then deciding on the type and location of equipment.

The Medium Looks Into When the medium *looks into* the event, it scrutinizes from an extremely close point of view. Consequently, it reveals aspects of the event we ordinarily would not, or could not, see. Let's take modern dance, for example. If you *look at* the event, you simply record the dancers' movements as well as possible. The camera observes the dance as someone who is watching it in the theater (see 17.12). But if you use the camera to *look into* the dance, you select and intensify essential parts (see 17.13). Perhaps we will never see the dance exactly the way we see it in the rehearsal hall or on stage. But we will see portions of arms, bodies, hands, and feet, revealing the basic movements and the basic structure of the dance and intensifying the essential rhythm. In sports we would no longer watch how somebody takes the high hurdles, for the purpose of studying the athlete's technique, but we would instead fasten on the skill, the grace, and the beauty of the motion. Or, perhaps, we could use the camera in such a way that the screen event reveals the incredible physical and psychological strain of such a race.

Note, however, that we are still using the actual event as the prime material for the video experience. We do not go beyond the event but simply into it. We are probing its essence.

The Medium Creates When we create a video event, we use the external event, such as the dance or the hurdler, simply as raw material for our electronic manipulations. The event as *created* by the medium exists nowhere except on the screen. The *screen* event is the *primary* experience. For example, in the modern dance you would use the dancers as space manipulators to define screen space, or simply as energy sources for your electronic manipulations. If you use keying or matting, a dancer moving by may become an abstract pattern in motion, which, nevertheless, is caused by the energy of the dancer (see 17.14).

Because you are concerned mainly with the electronic manipulation of the screen image, you could do away with the camera and create a number of effects through digital effects equipment.

In reality, these distinctions are not always as clear-cut as they might appear in this discussion. The three medium functions frequently overlap to some extent. However, a clear understanding of each function will certainly help you in your basic approach to the subject matter and in your formulation of the process message objective. If you want just to report an event, such as the planting of new trees along the neighborhood street, you look at it from a rather detached point of view. If you want to show the importance of these trees for

17.12   The Medium Looks At When *looking at* an event, the camera merely reports it as faithfully as possible. The camera takes on an objective point of view.

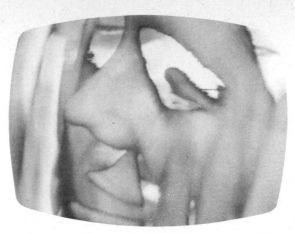

17.14   The Medium Creates When the medium creates, it takes the outer event simply as raw material for the electronic manipulation. The actual event can exist only as a screen event.

17.13   The Medium Looks Into When *looking into* an event, the camera scrutinizes it from a variety of points of view. The camera looks at the event at close range. The camera's viewpoint becomes *introspective*.

beautifying the neighborhood and for helping to make people happier by their presence, you should move the camera into the event and capture the reactions of people looking at the trees, touching the trees, and putting their hands into the soil while planting the trees. If you want to demonstrate the symbolic importance of the trees as bearers of new life and hope, and as elements that counteract decay, you may want to create an appropriate experience with the camera based on the energy of the tree-planting event, such as leaf patterns, the movement of groping hands keyed into the fresh branches, and so on.

It is quite likely that your process message objective allows any one of the three medium approaches within a single program. Your coverage of the original event should, then, be handled in such a way that you have all three options open in the postproduction process.

Fact Sheet   Also called rundown sheet. Lists the items to be shown on camera and the key ideas that should be expressed verbally by the performer. Serves often as a guide to a show format.

Medium Requirements

What and how much equipment do you need? How should it function? These questions can be answered quickly and accurately only after a great deal of experience. In general, try to get by with as *little* equipment as possible. If you can do a show with two cameras,

```
INTERVIEW

DATE:    March

PLACE:   Studio 2

TIME:    4:00-5:00 p.m.

MODE:    VTR record

LENGTH:  10:00min.



     VIDEO

CU of host.                HOST--INTRODUCES SHOW.
Host faces camera.

2-shot of host and guest.  HOST--INTRODUCES GUEST.

Host turns to guest.       HOST--ASKS FIRST QUESTION.
CU guest.
                           GUEST-ANSWERS.
_____

INTERVIEW:                 INTERVIEW WITH GREAT EMPHASIS ON
Favor guest with CU's      WHAT GUEST HAS TO SAY.
and XCU's.

_____

CLOSING:

2-shot of host and guest.  HOST--MAKES CLOSING REMARKS.
Host faces camera and
closes show.
```

do not request three. Otherwise, you might feel obliged to use the third camera, not because you need it but because it is there. Such redundancy is not only costly but often an obstacle to the sequencing process of the beginning director. You might, for example, be enticed to cut frequently among the three cameras instead of staying on the one camera that delivers the most expressive picture.

Here is an example. You have to videotape a two-person interview (host and guest). The process message objective states that the percipient should gain a deeper insight into the thinking and feeling and general behavior of the guest. The script indicates only the opening and the closing by the host, and leaves the visualization and sequencing basically up to you, the director (see 17.15). What would you do?

How do you preconceive this interview? How do you see it and hear it? The process message and the admittedly vague script suggest that the *key visualization* should be a *close-up* of the guest's face. The viewer should not only see the guest but be able, at least to some extent, to look into his or her personality.

With all due respect to the host, he or she simply is not important in this interview. Therefore, you do not need to show the host at all, except for the opening and closing of the show.

When figuring out the medium requirements, we can decide on two obvious production items right away. Because the participants do not move about, we can use lavaliere mics for the audio pickup. The lighting should be normal; that is, we should have enough light on the guest's face so that his or her features are clearly visible and the colors as undistorted as possible. How about cameras? Three or two? You really do not need three, and if you perceive the show sequence within the context of the process message, you may not even

17.16 Visualization and Sequencing of One-Camera Interview

Video	**Staging**	**Visualization and sequencing, or picturization**	**Audio**
Opening CU of host. Host faces camera.	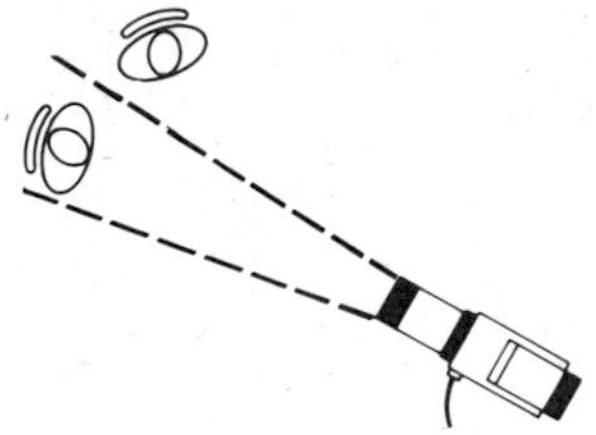	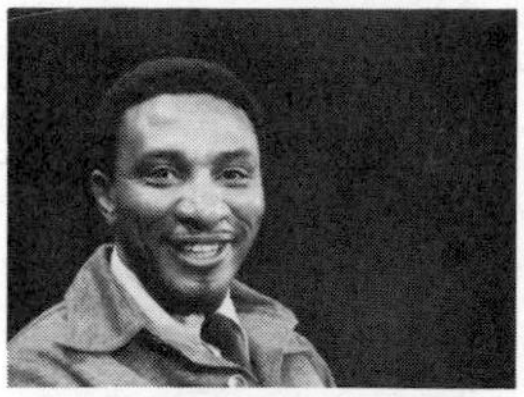	Introduces show.
Zoom back to 2-shot.	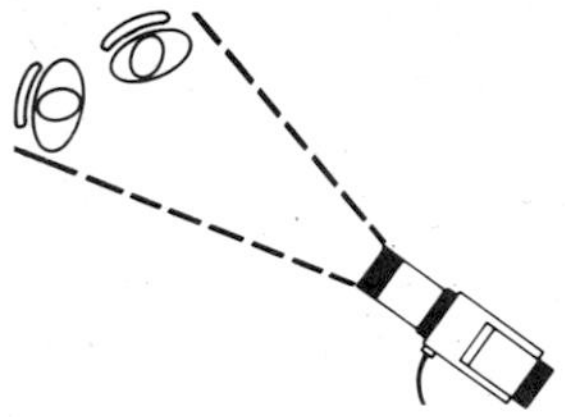	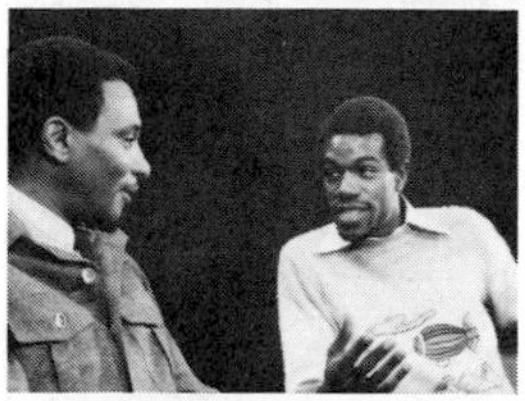	Introduces guest.
Host turns to guest. Zoom in to CU of guest.	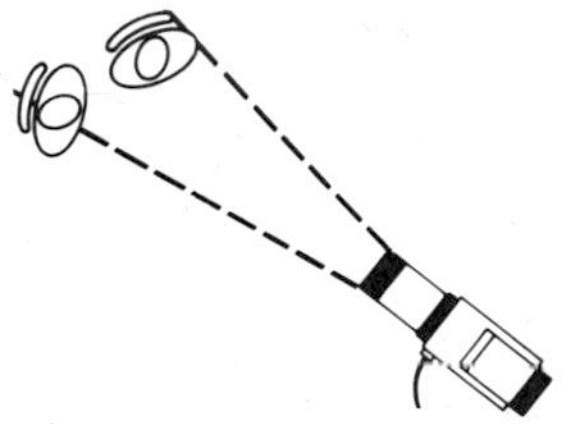	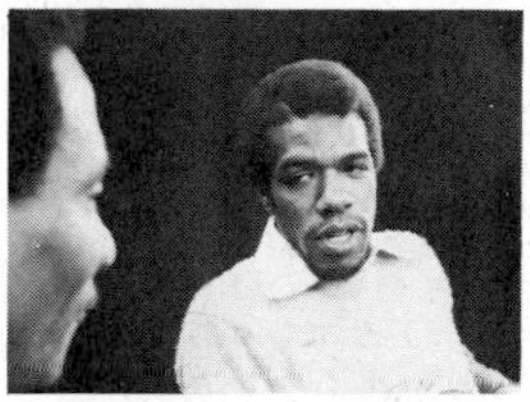	Asks first question.
During interview stay on guest. Vary between MS and XCU.	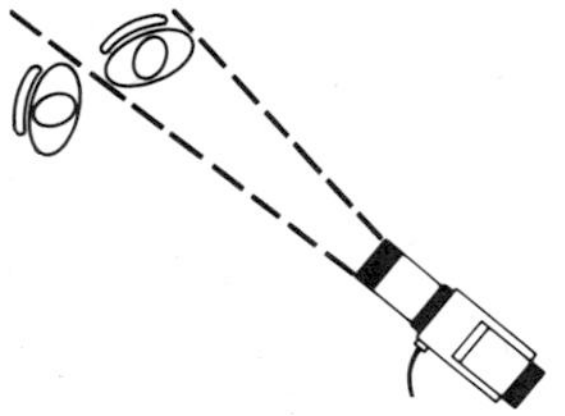	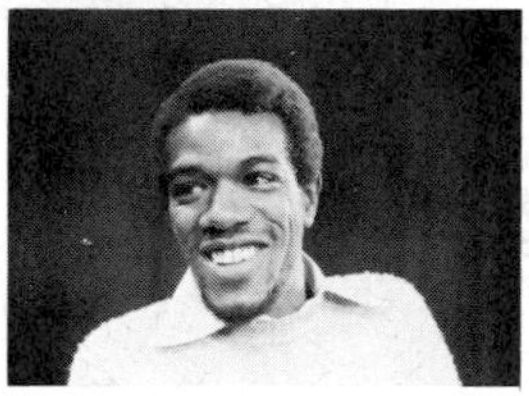	Continues questions and answers.

(continued)

need two. Your justification for one camera is that you will stay on the guest's face throughout the interview, sometimes viewing it at very close range, and sometimes from a little farther back. Figure 17.16 shows a possible visualization and sequencing approach to this interview with only one camera.

As you can see in this exercise, the director first reveals the basic relationship of host and guest. They are obviously sitting next to each other. Then the director concentrates on the guest, the object of the process message.

The way the interview is staged (set up for the camera), the camera does not have to move at all. The host turns into the camera for the opening and closing, but he or she faces the guest for the rest of the interview. The camera zooms in on the guest and stays there.

If you want the host to play a more active role vis-

Video	Staging	Visualization and sequencing, or picturization	Audio
Closing Zoom back to 2-shot. Host faces camera.			Wraps up interview.
			Closes show.

ually, you can maintain the same setup but have the camera zoom back to a two-shot from time to time, or even arc right, in order to get more of a full-face shot of the host than is possible from the original camera position.

Visualization and Sequencing Aids

When visualizing a script or even a nonscripted show segment, you are greatly aided by the *storyboard* and the *floor plan*. By learning to "read" the storyboard and the floor plan, you will be able to spot possible production problems before they actually occur, decide on major equipment and its use, and anticipate the major directing tasks in regard to talent and crew.

Storyboard   The **storyboard** is usually drawn on special storyboard paper, which has areas representing the television screen and audio and other information (see 17.17).

The storyboard contains key visualization points and audio information (see 17.18). Most commercials are carefully storyboarded before they ever go into production. Many directors use small thumbnail sketches of key visualization points. Such visualizations are not drawn on storyboard paper, but usually sketched into the script. (See 17.28, a fully-scripted drama, for an example of this.)

A good storyboard offers immediate clues to certain production requirements, such as general location, camera position, approximate focal length of the lens, method of audio pickup, degree of postproduction, actions of the talent, set design, and hand props.

Floor plan   When looking at a floor plan, you need to visualize some of the key shots, and then derive camera positions from these visualizations. It is important that you visualize the foreground as well as the background of the shots, because the camera sees both. A prop list can give some clues to potential production problems. Figure 17.19 shows a rough floor plan for a brief interview. The customary prop list is attached.

Take a look at the floor plan and try to visualize some of your key shots, such as a CU of the guest, an opening two-shot, with the host introducing the guest, an occasional reaction shot of the host.

The way the chairs are placed, a two-shot would be difficult to achieve.

If the camera shoots from straight on, the chairs

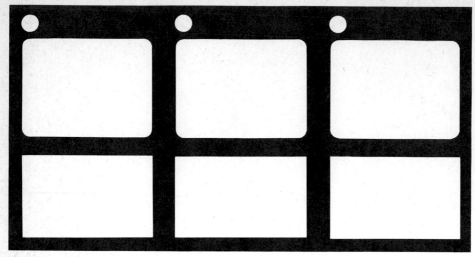

17.17   Storyboard Paper

are much too far apart. At best, the two people would seem glued to the edges of the screen, putting undue emphasis on the painting in the middle. Also, you would overshoot the set on both ends (see 17.20a).

If you shoot from the extreme left, you get an over-the-shoulder shot from the host to the guest. Assuming you pull the camera way back in order to get a narrow-angle zoom lens position (reducing the space between the two people), you again overshoot the set and do not see the host straight on (see 17.20b).

If you cross-shoot with the other camera, you can get a reverse-angle shot of the host, but again you overshoot. Also, you have the rubber plant growing out of the host's head (see 17.20c).

What other problems do we have with the setup as indicated on the floor plan? Let's go down the prop list. Two *plain, off-white* hardwall panels are hardly the most interesting background. The surface is too plain, and its off-white color is too bright for the foreground scene, rendering the skin tones of the two persons unusually dark. If a performer happens to be black, the contrast problem with the white background is even more extreme. You cannot correct the problem by selective lighting. See how close the chairs are to the background flats? Any key light and fill light will inevitably strike the background too. Also there is not enough room between the chairs and the flats for adequate

backlighting, unless you want to tolerate a top light shining straight down on the people. The acoustics may also prove to be less than desirable, because the microphones are very close to the hardwall flats.

The *large upholstered chairs* are definitely not the right chairs for an interview. They look too pompous and would engulf their occupants in upholstery. Moreover, the chairs cannot be placed close enough to each other for adequate camera shots.

The *rubber plant* is in the way, from whatever angle you might shoot; at least it does not make much sense if part of it is seen behind the host only.

Because most of the shooting must be done from extreme angles (assuming you have to go ahead with this setup), the *painting* is utterly useless. If you want to break up some of the plain background with a picture, you must hang it in such a way that you have it in the *actual shot* of one of the cameras (which means that it would have to hang in a spot where there are presently no flats to support it). You may even wonder about the compatibility of Monet's subtle impressionistic colors when viewed in black-and-white television. As pleasant as this painting may look in color, in black-and-white it may look like nothing but a few indistinct gray blobs.

Lastly, because the chairs are not on a platform, the cameras have to look *down* on the performers, unless

VO: I DRINK MILK

BECAUSE I ASK A LOT OF MY BODY.

(POUR EFFECT)

AND THE THINGS I GET FROM MILK
ARE THE THINGS MY BODY NEEDS.

(POUR EFFECT)

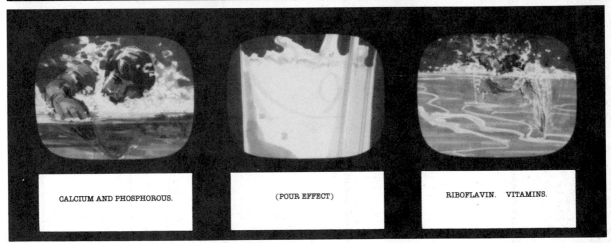

CALCIUM AND PHOSPHOROUS.

(POUR EFFECT)

RIBOFLAVIN.   VITAMINS.

17.18   Storyboard of Milk Commercial Courtesy of
McCann-Erickson, Inc. and California Milk Advisory Board

(continued)

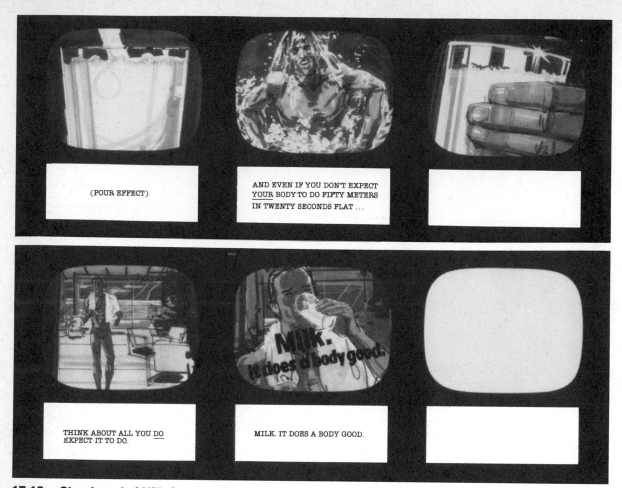

17.18   Storyboard of Milk Commercial (cont.)

The following text captions appear within the storyboard panels:

(POUR EFFECT)

AND EVEN IF YOU DON'T EXPECT YOUR BODY TO DO FIFTY METERS IN TWENTY SECONDS FLAT ...

THINK ABOUT ALL YOU <u>DO</u> EXPECT IT TO DO.

MILK. IT DOES A BODY GOOD.

the camera operators pedestal all the way down and work the whole interview from a very awkward position.

Now, let's suggest some possible solutions to these problems:

1.   Enlarge the background. Use flats of a different color and texture (such as medium-dark wood panel pattern). Perhaps break up the background with a few narrow flats or large pylons.

2.   If you hang pictures on the flats to break up plain surfaces, hang them in places where they will be seen in the most frequent camera shots.

3.   Put the whole set on a platform.

4.   Use smaller and simpler chairs and place them closer together.

5.   Get rid of the rubber plant. Although rubber plants in a set look great to the naked eye, they become a compositional obstacle when the camera is on.

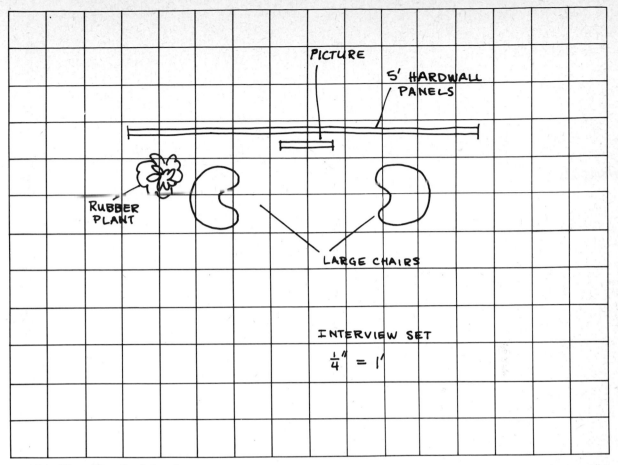

17.19 Floor Plan for Interview

6. Move the chairs out, away from the background flats.

Figure 17.21 shows how the suggested corrections might be integrated in a new floor plan.

What other ways could you suggest to solve these problems? As you can see, even a cursory study of the floor plan can tell you a great deal about potential production problems. The more complicated the show becomes, the more time and effort you should give to the basic preproduction analysis of the floor plan.

SCRIPT FORMATS

There are four basic types of script formats: (1) the fully scripted show, (2) the semiscripted show, (3) the show format, and (4) the fact or rundown sheet.

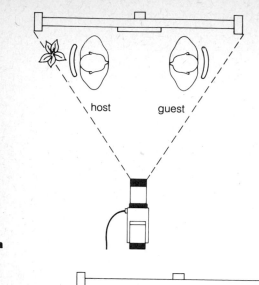

a

host   guest

Prop List

Set	2 hardwall panels (plain, off-white)
Set props	2 chairs (large upholstered)
	1 rubber plant
	1 Monet painting (Notre Dame)
Hand props	none
Cameras	2 RCA TK47
Microphones	2 lavalieres
Lighting	normal

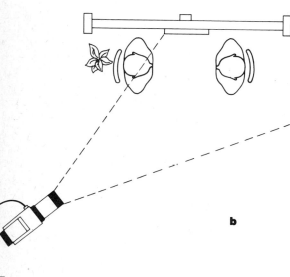

b

17.20   Two-Shot in Interview Set A straight-on two-shot places the two people too far apart, causing you to overshoot the set (a). An over-the-shoulder shot from the host's point of view (POV) results in overshooting the set (b). An over-the-shoulder shot from the guest's POV overshoots the set again, causing problems with the rubber plant (c).

The Fully Scripted Show

A complete script includes every word that is to be spoken during a show, as well as detailed audio and video instructions. Dramatic shows, comedy skits, news shows, and most major commercials are **fully scripted.** There are advantages and disadvantages in directing this sort of show. The advantages are that you can visualize and sequence the complete show before going into rehearsal. You have definite cue lines, and you know where the camera goes at what time and what shot it gets. The disadvantage is that you are tied down to following the script very carefully. Also, if the actor or performer forgets to give you the exact text and begins to ad-lib, your shooting procedure may be seriously affected.

 Newscasts are usually fully scripted. Figure 17.22 shows an excerpt from a typical one.[3] The large typeface is quite popular—the talent and the director can read the large type more easily than the normal pica typeface.

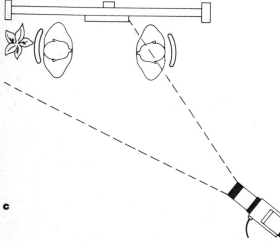

c

[3]Figures 17.22 and 17.28 are *marked* scripts. See the section "Live or Live-on-Tape Production" on page 547 for an explanation of script marking.

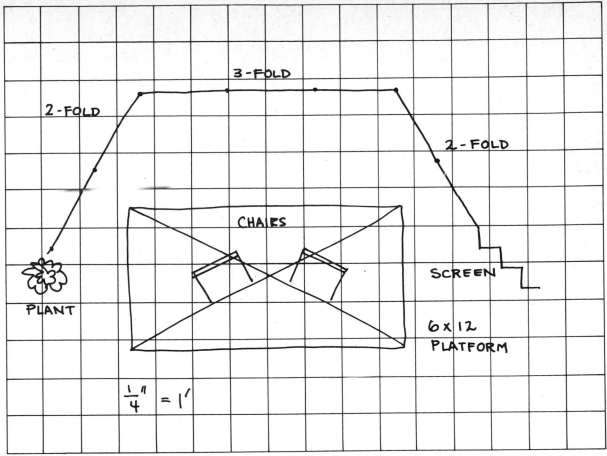

17.21 Floor Plan for Improved Interview Set This interview set has adequate background cover in back and on the sides. The smaller chairs are on a platform, so the camera can shoot from eye level. The chairs are also far enough away from the background so that the back lights can function without becoming top lights.

Some news scripts use white paper for all straight on-camera news copy, and yellow (or any other agreed-upon color) paper for all tape insert copy. This way the newscasters and you, the director, know by the color of the paper whether straight copy or a VTR is coming up. This type of color coding is especially helpful when you have to pull some copy in order to keep the show on time.

Documentaries or *documentary-type* shows, too, are frequently fully scripted. The major camera shots and the major actions of the performers are listed in the video column, and every spoken word and sound effect is listed in the audio column. Figure 17.23 shows an example of a fully scripted documentary-type show.

As you can see in this script sample, the video and audio instructions are separated. This script format is widely used for nondramatic shows. The video column is on the left side of the page, and the audio column on the right. Note that in the audio column all instructions for audio control are usually written in uppercase letters, whereas the spoken lines are upper and lower case.

Dramatic shows have a script format all their own (see 17.24). The exact camera shots are generally left

Panel 1:

CHEMICAL DUMP

NOON   12-14

Special effects: box wipe over newscaster's shoulder with digital still store slide #146 and name key "San Francisco" in box. Newscaster (Dwight) is on camera 1.

BOX
DS 146
KEY SF

ROLL
VT 4

VO

① SAN FRANCISCO FIRE INVESTIGATORS ARE NOW SAYING THE TWO INCIDENTS OF CHEMICAL DUMPING IN THE CITY ARE NOT RELATED.

Videotape recorder 4 is started on a 2-second preroll. Newscaster (Dwight) narrates over videotape (VOT = voice over tape) for 30 seconds.

THE FIRST CHEMICAL DRUMS WERE DISCOVERED YESTER-DAY MORNING IN THE BACK OF A DUMP TRUCK. POLICE AND FIRE UNITS ESCORTED THE TRUCK TO A DUMP IN BRISBANE WHERE THE CHEMICALS

Panel 2:

CHEMICAL DUMP

3-3-3

Camera 2 is on the air, showing the newscaster.

DWIGHT

② LATER IN THE DAY, FIREMEN WERE CALLED TO INVESTIGATE

ROLL VT3
VO : 15
DS - 147

AN ABANDONED DRUM OF CHEMICALS. IT TURNED OUT TO BE PHOSPHOROUS TRI-CHLORIDE... A CHEMICAL USED IN THE METAL INDUSTRY. FIRE INVESTIGATORS SAY SOMEONE APPARENTLY WANTED TO GET RID OF IT, BECAUSE OF ITS HIGHLY TOXIC

Videotape is prerolled. Videotape recorder 3 is on a 2-second roll and put on the air after the word "chemicals." Digital still store slide #147 is keyed over scene. The newscaster narrates over the videotape for 15 seconds.

After the word "properties" camera 1 is put on the air, showing the newscaster (Dwight).

PROPERTIES. ①

Panel 3:

CHEMICAL DUMP

2-2

Videotape is still playing with newscaster narrating over tape.

VTR/VO
DWIGHT

CAUGHT FIRE... MORNING RUSH HOUR TRAFFIC WAS TIED UP BECAUSE THE BAYSHORE WAS CLOSED OFF TO KEEP DRIVERS FROM GETTING IN CONTACT WITH THE FUMES.

FIRE INSPECTORS SAY THEY WERE UNABLE TO TELL WHAT THE CHEMICAL WAS BECAUSE IT WAS COMPLETELY CONSUMED IN THE

At the 30:00 second mark, sound on tape (SOT) will come in for 7 seconds. The SOT end cue is given. Camera 2 is on the newscaster.

SOT :07   FIRE. ②

END "DON'T KNOW FOR SURE"

Panel 4:

CHEMICAL DUMP

4-4-4-4

The newscaster is on camera 1, narrating this last part directly into the camera (camera 1 has a looser shot of Dwight). Man camera 2 so that the box wipe can be accommodated.

DWIGHT

① THEY SAY THE DUMPING WAS AN ISOLATED, BUT THOUGHTLESS INCIDENT.

BOX SQUEEZE
OUT BUMPER
SFX 12
VT-1

(THEME)
(COMMERCIAL)

The "bumper" material appears in a box wipe over the newscaster's shoulder and is enlarged to full screen size through a squeeze zoom. The material in the box is the special effects #12. After the "bumper," the commercial is rolled on videotape recorder 1. During the bumper "squeeze," the news theme is played.

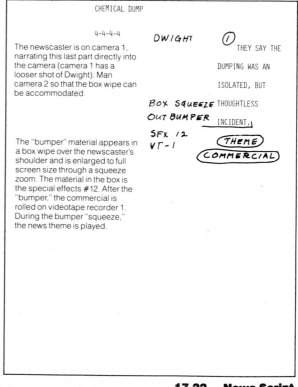

17.22   **News Script**

Up on effects: TITLE
  Wipe to:
VTR SOT
  (showing animated
  cardio-vascular system
  of body)
	(THIRD SEGMENT)
	
	IN CUE: "HIGH BLOOD PRESSURE IS MAINLY A DISEASE
	OF THE CARDIO-VASCULAR SYSTEM OF THE BODY...."

	OUT CUE: "...MILDER ONES ARE HEADACHES, ESPECIALLY AT THE BACK OF THE NECK... DIZZINESS...AND DROWSINESS."
Glenda on Cam	Of course, having these symptoms doesn't necessarily mean you have high blood pressure. But, if you haven't seen a doctor in a long time, you might check. By the time you get mild symptoms, the disease may be fairly well advanced.

Squeeze-zoom out and key
  Super "Strokes...7,000"
 	
Also key "GENERAL
  POPULATION - 1 in 1,000"
  "BLACK POPULATION -
  2 TO 3 IN 1,000"
	And, further down the road there are more
	severe complications, such as stroke, from which
	over seven-thousand people died in Los Angeles
	County in 1970.
	
	The rate of death for black people from strokes
	is up to three times as high as that of the general
	population, which adds another kind of meaning to
	that old phrase: "different strokes for different
	folks."

VTR SOT	IN CUE: "OTHER COMPLICATIONS ARE THE INCREASED PROBABILITY OF ATHEROSCLEROSIS..." OUT CUE: "...THROUGH THE NARROWED BLOOD VESSELS TO THE HEART AND/OR LUNGS."

MARY-ALICE SHOWS UP, FINALLY. WE SEE HER FROM SUSAN'S PERSPECTIVE
MAKING HER WAY THROUGH THE CROWDED COCKTAIL ROOM OF THE CHARLEY
BROWN BAR. SHE FINALLY REACHES SUSAN'S TABLE AND DROPS INTO THE
EMPTY CHAIR LIKE SOMEONE WHO HAS MANAGED TO GRAB THE ONLY REMAIN-
ING SEAT ON THE SUBWAY DURING RUSH HOUR.

                    MARY-ALICE:
Sorry, I'm late. But I couldn't get off work any sooner.

                      SUSAN:
Work? I thought the teachers' strike is still on. (BREAKS OUT IN
A SHORT LAUGH, FULL-BODIED AND COMING FROM THE BELLY, AS ONE WOULD
EXPECT FROM A PROFESSIONAL SINGER.)
By God, what are you all dressed up for? Sit down relax.

                    MARY-ALICE:
Yes, it is still on. But I have another—well, how are you?

                      SUSAN:
Another job? What job? What would you like to drink? Still on
daiquiries? (TRIES TO GET THE ATTENTION OF THE COCKTAIL WAITRESS
WHO IS BUSY WITH THE ADJOINING TABLE. BOTH SUSAN AND MARY-ALICE
WATCH THE GIRL IN ANTICIPATION. SUSAN FINALLY SUCCEEDS IN GETTING
THE WAITRESS'S ATTENTION.)

                      SUSAN:
Miss!

                     WAITRESS:
Yes. What can I get you?

MARY-ALICE:

(NOT WAITING FOR SUSAN TO ORDER THE DRINK FOR HER)

Bring me a good daiquiri.

(THE WAITRESS TURNS TO SUSAN.)

SUSAN:

And another Dubonnet on the rocks for me.

(THE WAITRESS LEAVES. SUSAN TURNS TO MARY-ALICE.)

Well, now tell me about the new job.

MARY-ALICE:

Well, the teachers' strike is not all that good. We don't get
any money from the union. This is OK for the teachers whose hus-
bands have good jobs. But for the ones who live alone...

SUSAN:

Isn't Robert helping out?

MARY-ALICE:

Bob? No. On the contrary. He is still expecting gourmet food,
exclusive French wines, you know.

SUSAN:

You call him "Bob" now? He didn't like that.

MARY-ALICE:

I don't know how to tell him that I don't have any money and that
we have to change our life style. At least as long as the strike
is on. Well, a change would be good anyhow. I don't know.

SUSAN:

Do you still love him?

to the director. But the actor's internal and external actions are generally spelled out, as are the dialogue (upper and lower case) and additional audio material (upper case only).

The Semiscripted Show

A show is **semiscripted** when the dialogue is indicated but not completely written out. In general, the opening and closing remarks are fully scripted, but the bulk of the dialogue or commentary is only alluded to, such as: DR. HYDE TALKS ABOUT NEW EDUCATIONAL IDEAS; DR. WOLFRAM REPLIES.

This type of script is almost always used for interviews, programs of an educational nature, variety programs, and other program types in which a great amount of ad-lib commentary or discussion occurs.

The important part of semiscripting a show is indicating specific cue lines that tell the director when to roll a videotape or when to break the cameras to another set area. (See 17.25.)

The Show Format

The **show format** lists only the order of particular show segments, such as "interview from Washington," "commercial no. 1," "book review," and so forth. It also lists the major set areas in which the action takes place, or other points of origination, and major clock and running times for the segments. (See 17.26.)

A show format is frequently used in shows that have established performance routines, such as a daily morning show or a variety show. Most panel discussion shows or daily interview shows with one established host and several guests are directed from a show format.

The Fact, or Rundown, Sheet

A **fact** or **rundown sheet** lists the items that are to be shown on camera and indicates roughly what should be said. No special video and audio instructions are given. The fact sheet is usually supplied by the advertising agency that likes to have a particular performer ad-lib its commercials (see 17.27).

Generally the director rewrites the fact sheet into a show format so that he or she and the talent know what they are supposed to do. Directing solely from a fact sheet is not recommended. Ad-libbing by both director and talent rarely works out satisfactorily. Their efforts will necessarily remain uncoordinated.

SCRIPT PREPARATION

To explain all the intricacies of analyzing and interpreting nondramatic and dramatic scripts would go far beyond the scope of this handbook. We have already pointed out the importance of translating a script into medium requirements through proper visualization and sequencing, or picturization, processes.

Script Analysis

Live or Live-on-Tape Production   Let us emphasize some of the major points once more:

1.   Read the video and audio columns to get an overall idea of what the show is about and how complex the production will be.

2.   Try to "lock in" on a key shot, key action, or some key technical maneuver. For example, you may lock in on the part in a script where the lead guitar player has a particularly beautiful solo. How do you see him or her? How do you want this passage to appear on the screen? Then you can work backward from the selected shot to the actions that precede it and forward to the ones that follow it. In a dramatic script, this locking in may occur at the very opening scene, at the closing scene, or at any particularly striking scene somewhere in the middle.

3.   In the context of the process message objective, translate the script into specific video and audio images, and, of course, the necessary production equipment and procedures.

Analyzing a dramatic script is, of course, quite a bit more complicated than translating the video and audio instructions of a nondramatic script into the director's production requirements. A good dramatic script operates on many conscious and unconscious levels, all of which need to be interpreted and made explicit. Above all, you should be able to define the **theme** of the play (the basic idea; what the story is all about), the **plot** (how the story moves forward and develops), the **characters** (how one person differs from the others), and the **environment** (where the action takes place). In general, television drama emphasizes theme and character rather than plot, inner rather than outer environment.

After the locking-in has occurred, go back to the beginning of the script and look for *organic units of action or development* that you could videotape one at a time. For example, if you have people come to a party and the hosts argue about the coffee in the kitchen, some of the more obvious segments would be the greeting of the visiting couple at the door, the introduction of the couple to the rest of the guests in the living room, and the argument in the kitchen. You would videotape each of these three segments separately, preferably in that order.

Film-Style Production   As pointed out in Section One, your major criterion for **script analysis** in film-style production is production efficiency, not organic segments. When preparing a script for film-style directing, you need to have a thorough understanding of the program content, but the number and sequence of takes are now governed by a systems approach (see p. 481). Using our example of the couple arriving for the party, you may want to start taping with all the scenes that take place in the kitchen, because the studio and the kitchen set are available only at that particular time. Then you may want to do all the outside scenes in front of the house: the saying hello and good-bye, and the departing of the guests. You may have to do the introductions of the couple and other living room scenes toward the end of the production, because this is the only time when you can get the entire cast (necessary for the indoor party) together.

Perhaps you want to analyze a script for film-style shooting by using the production system on page 481. You may need more categories of production elements than listed there, but at least this provides some guidelines for the analysis.

After analyzing the script (for either mode of production), you should mark it accordingly for on-the-air presentation or videotaping.

Script Marking

Proper **script marking** is essential for all control room directing, because you need to coordinate many people and machines within a continuous time frame. In film-style directing, you have much more time to communicate your intentions to the talent and members of the production crew. You do not have to clutter your script with large symbols. Rather, you can write more extensive notes on how you want each take to look. Script marking is, therefore, less crucial.

Live or Live-on-Tape Production   Because the many monitors in the control room command your close attention, you should free yourself from the script as much as possible. One way is to mark the major cues on the script in your own way. Although there are standard marking symbols, you will probably develop some special ones that work best for you. Whatever symbols you use, keep these points in mind:

1.   Your marking symbols should be clear and unambiguous.

2.   Once you have arrived at a workable system, stick to it. Standardize your symbols as much as possible.

3.   Do not overmark your script. Too many confusing symbols are worse than none at all.

4.   Place your cues before the desired action.

5.   If the shots or camera actions are clearly written in the video column, or the audio cues in the audio column, simply underline or circle the printed information. This keeps the script looking clean. But if the printed instructions are hard to read, do not hesitate to repeat them with your own symbols (see 17.28).

Before you mark a script, you should have the process message, the key visualization points, and the major sequencing, or picturization, processes in your head. In most cases this means that you need a floor plan prior to script marking, unless the show occurs in a standard set, such as for the daily newscast. If the show requires rehearsals, do preliminary script marking *in pencil* so you can make quick changes without creating a messy or illegible script. Once you are ready for the dress rehearsal, however, you should have marked the script in bold letters so you can read your markings even in the relatively dim light of the control room. Have the A.D. and the floor manager copy your markings for their own scripts.

Figures 17.22 and 17.28 are examples of marking a variety of script formats.

Film-Style Directing   The marking of the script for film-style directing consists of a careful breakdown and indication of the various takes, their location (living room, kitchen, front door), and principal visualization (camera point of view, field of view). You then number the takes in the proposed production sequence. Thus, you

VIDEO	AUDIO
	GLENDA:
Two-shot of Glenda and Mario	But more important are the reasons that involve health. Medical science has linked obesity to a number of harmful diseases, including diabetes, strokes, heart attacks, hardening of the arteries, cancer of the uterus, and high blood pressure.
	MARIO:
	Because of this high rate of health hazards the insurance companies put a different kind of pressure on fat people: high insurance rates. Isn't that true, Dr. Ryan?
	DR. RYAN:
Cut to CU of Dr. Ryan	(SAYS THAT THIS IS QUITE TRUE AND THAT INSURANCE COMPANIES DO NOT GENERALLY INSURE MARKEDLY OVERWEIGHT PEOPLE AT NORMAL INSURANCE RATES.)

MARIO:

Cut to CU
of Mario

And what about employers? How do they feel about fat people? Here are four people who can tell us about their experiences.

LYNN:

Cut to CU
of Lynn

(SAYS THAT SHE FOUND MANY MEDIUM SIZED OR SMALL COMPANIES HAVE A WEIGHT LIMIT FOR EMPLOYEES AND CAN THEREFORE NOT HIRE HER.)

JUDY:

Cut to CU
of Judy

(AGREES WITH LYNN AND SAYS THAT THERE IS NO QUESTION THAT THERE IS A GREAT AMOUNT OF DISCRIMINATION IN JOBS FOR FAT PEOPLE. ELABORATES.)

Etc.

WHAT'S YOUR OPINION?

SHOW FORMAT   INDIVIDUAL SCRIPT ATTACHED

VTR DATE: 2/3   FAX NO: 2-437

AIR DATE: 2/17   VTR HOUSE NO: POL-2143

DIRECTOR: Millar   TOTAL TIME: 28:30

O P E N

VIDEO

OPENING TEASER/ VTR

EFFECTS

AUDIO

SOT

    ANNOUNCER: The Television
Center of San Francisco State
University presents, What's Your
Opinion... A contemporary view
of higher education in Cali-
fornia.

KEY C.G. TOPIC TITLE   Today's topic is:

——————————————— COMMERCIAL ———————————————

OPENING STUDIO SHOT   BOB INTRODUCES GUESTS

KEY C.G. NAMES OF GUESTS

CU'S OF GUESTS   GUESTS DISCUSS TOPIC

----------------------- COMMERCIAL -----------------------

C L O S E

ADDRESS C.G. KEY

ANNOUNCER: To obtain a copy of
today's program, please write to
BCA Department, San Francisco
State University, San Francisco,
California, 94132. Be sure to
tune in next week when we

KEY NEW TITLE (C.G.)

present: FOREIGN STUDENTS—
BURDEN OR BENEFIT?

THEME MUSIC UP AND OUT

```
JENNER ALBUM COMMERCIAL          DATE:        TIME:
PROPS: Jenner Album
       Jenner Poster with Band Background
       Jenner Album Display
NOTE:  Play  Cut 1, Side 2, of Jenner Album
       as background during commercial.
1.  New Choban recording of songs by Jenner.
2.  Best yet.  Great variety.
3.  New arrangements.  Excellent band backing her up.
4.  Songs that touch everybody.  Sung with passion.
5.  Excellent recording.  Technically perfect, true
    Barsotti quality.  Wide frequency range does full
    justice to her voice.  Available in stereo or
    four-channel.
6.  Special introductory offer.  Expires Oct. 20.
    Hurry.  Ask for the new Barsotti recording of Jenner.
    At Tower Records.
```

end up with a list of takes that refers to the original script by page number. Here is an example:

Location	Take no.	Script page no.
kitchen	1	28
	2	17
	3	42
front door	4	5
	5	7
	6	162
	7	165

In the script itself, you are free to use any markings you prefer. Usually, it helps to work from small story-board sketches drawn next to the dialogue lines. This way, you can quickly recall what you had in mind when preparing the script.

Much more important than script marking is keeping an accurate record of each take. Be sure to slate each take and record it on the shot sheet. Circle the good takes on the shot sheet, or indicate whether the take was good (acceptable) or no good (unacceptable). Such seemingly minor details save much time and frustration during postproduction.

MARY-ALICE SHOWS UP, FINALLY. WE SEE HER FROM SUSAN'S PERSPECTIVE

MAKING HER WAY THROUGH THE CROWDED COCKTAIL ROOM OF THE CHARLEY

BROWN BAR. SHE FINALLY REACHES SUSAN'S TABLE AND DROPS INTO THE

EMPTY CHAIR LIKE SOMEONE WHO HAS MANAGED TO GRAB THE ONLY REMAIN-

ING SEAT ON THE SUBWAY DURING RUSH HOUR.

                        MARY-ALICE:

Sorry, I'm late. But I couldn't get off work any sooner.

                        SUSAN:

Work? I thought the teachers' strike is still on. (BREAKS OUT IN

A SHORT LAUGH, FULL-BODIED AND COMING FROM THE BELLY, AS ONE WOULD

EXPECT FROM A PROFESSIONAL SINGER.)

By God, what are you all dressed up for? Sit down, relax.

                        MARY-ALICE:

Yes, it is still on. But I have another—well, how are you?

                        SUSAN:

Another job? What job? What would you like to drink? Still on

daiquiries? (TRIES TO GET THE ATTENTION OF THE COCKTAIL WAITRESS

WHO IS BUSY WITH THE ADJOINING TABLE. BOTH SUSAN AND MARY-ALICE

WATCH THE GIRL IN ANTICIPATION. SUSAN FINALLY SUCCEEDS IN GETTING

THE WAITRESS'S ATTENTION.)

                        SUSAN:

Miss!

                        WAITRESS:

Yes. What can I get you?

17.28 Marking Dramatic Script Dramatic scripts generally have no audio or video instructions written in. This way the writer does not dictate the director's specific visualization and picturization processes. You should, therefore, write the key video instructions into the script yourself. Sometimes it is quite helpful to use small thumbnail sketches to indicate key visualization or blocking maneuvers.

MARY-ALICE:

(NOT WAITING FOR SUSAN TO ORDER THE DRINK FOR HER)

Bring me a good daiquiri.   *90   MA*   ③

(THE WAITRESS TURNS TO SUSAN.)

SUSAN:

And another Dubonnet on the rocks for me.   *91   S + Waitress*   ①

(THE WAITRESS LEAVES. SUSAN TURNS TO MARY-ALICE.)

Well, now tell me about the new job.   *100   CU MA*   ③

MARY-ALICE:

Well, the teachers' strike is not all that good. We don't get

any money from the union. This is OK for the teachers whose hus-

bands have good jobs. But for the ones who live alone...

SUSAN:

Isn't Robert helping out?

MARY-ALICE:

Bob? No. On the contrary. He is still expecting gourmet food,

exclusive French wines, you know.   *101   CU S*   ①

SUSAN:

You call him "Bob" now? He didn't like that.   *102   CU MA*   ③

MARY-ALICE:

I don't know how to tell him that I don't have any money and that

we have to change our life style. At least as long as the strike

is on. Well, a change would be good anyhow. I don't know.   *103*

                                                        XCU S   ①

SUSAN:

Do you still love him?   *104*

                                                XCU MA   ③

```
SHOT LIST
CAMERA ①

BAR SCENE

SHOT #

85      XS       SUSAN
87      CU        S
89      CU  S  ZOOM
            BACK TO INCLUDE
               WAITRESS

91      S AND WAITRESS
101     CU   S
103     X CU   S
```

17.29   Shot Sheet For complicated, fully scripted shows, the camera operators work from a shot sheet. Each camera has its own shot sheet, which lists every shot a camera has to get. For example, the shot sheet for camera 2 of the scene as marked by the director (see 17.28) lists 13 shots. As soon as camera 2 is free from the previous shot (after the tally lights have gone off), the camera operator can look at the shot sheet and frame up on the next shot without specific instructions from the director. The shot sheet usually contains the minimum amount of information to remind the operator of the rehearsed shot sequence and type of framing. Some cameras come equipped with a shot-sheet holder directly below the viewfinder.

MAIN POINTS

1.   Directing starts with visualizing the key images, which means interpreting the individual shots as television images. These visualized images must then be seen in proper sequence, a process called sequencing, or picturization. Proper visualization and sequencing will determine to a large extent what equipment is required and how the talent and equipment should be blocked.

2.   The specific approach to directing is often clarified by emphasizing one of the three basic medium functions: (1) the medium looks at—to give the audience as objective a view of the event as possible; (2) the medium looks into—to scrutinize the event from an extremely close point of view; and (3) the medium creates—to use the external event simply as raw material for the electronic manipulations, which then become the new screen event.

3.   A clear idea of process message, visualization, and sequencing will aid in determining the medium requirements. The less equipment, the easier the director's coordination job will be.

4.   The two main visualization and sequencing aids are (1) the storyboard and (2) the floor plan. The storyboard is a series of sketches of key visualization points with accompanying audio information. A floor plan is a diagram of the scenery relative to the studio walls or the cyclorama, and the location of set pieces and set properties. Some floor plans also contain the major locations of cameras and microphone booms.

5.   There are four basic types of script formats: (1) the fully scripted show, (2) the semiscripted show, (3) the show format, and (4) the fact or rundown sheet.

6.   Script preparation involves two main activities: (1) script analysis, which includes scene and shot breakdowns when prepared for postproduction, and (2) script marking.

FURTHER READING

Blum, Richard A. *Television Writing: From Concept to Contract*. New York: Hastings House, 1980.

Dean, Alexander, and Lawrence Carra. *Fundamentals of Play Directing*. 3rd ed. New York: Holt, Rinehart and Winston, 1974.

Garvey, Daniel, and William L. Rivers. *Broadcast Writing*. New York: Longman, 1982.

Gradus, Ben. *Directing the Television Commercial*. New York: Hastings House, 1981.

Hilliard, Robert L. *Writing for Television and Radio*. 4th ed. Belmont, CA: Wadsworth Publishing Co., 1984.

Hodge, Francis. *Play Directing*. 2nd ed. Englewood Cliffs, NJ: Prentice-Hall, Inc., 1982.

Remotes

Television remotes can be done by one person with a single ENG camera—VTR unit, but they can also involve tons of equipment and many engineering and production people. In this chapter, we will examine the production features of three kinds of remotes: (1) ENG, electronic news gathering; (2) EFP, electronic field production; and (3) big remotes. Although we have mentioned ENG and EFP throughout this book, we will discuss them again with big remotes in the light of specific remote production requirements.

In Section One, we will take up:

1. The major production features, communication systems, signal transmission, and ethics of ENG.
2. The important preproduction, production, and postproduction aspects of EFP.
3. The preproduction surveys, production, and postproduction procedures of big remotes.

In Section Two, we will describe:

1. The more typical setups of sports remotes, specifically of baseball, football, soccer, basketball, tennis, boxing and wrestling, and swimming.
2. How to read location sketches and interpret them into production requirements.

ELECTRONIC NEWS GATHERING, OR ENG

ENG is the most flexible of remote operations. As pointed out in Chapter 2, one person can handle a complete ENG assignment, as long as the signal can be videotaped with the portable VTR. But even if the signal has to be relayed back to the station or transmitter, ENG requires only a fraction of the equipment and people of a big remote. The major disadvantage of ENG is that the pictures and sound thus produced are generally of lower quality than when using studio equipment. This is of little consequence in news, where we generally deal with brief, one-time news stories. However, ENG equipment and production methods are often considered not good enough for productions that require top picture and sound quality.

We will now take up (1) the major production features of ENG, (2) communication systems, (3) signal transmission, and (4) ethics.

Production Features

The major production features of ENG are the *readiness* with which you can respond to an event, the *mobility* possible in the coverage of an event, and the *flexibility* of the ENG equipment systems.

Readiness Because ENG equipment is so compact and self-contained, you can get to an event and videotape or broadcast it faster than with any other type of television equipment. One of the important operational differences between ENG and EFP or big remotes is that in ENG you *do not need preproduction surveys.* ENG systems are specifically designed for *immediate* response to a breaking story.

Mobility ENG equipment can go wherever you can go. It can operate in a car, an elevator, a helicopter, or a small kitchen. You do not need an expensive studio pedestal to get smooth dolly or trucking shots; riding in a shopping cart with the ENG camera can often accomplish the same thing. Low-angle shots

When a television show is done outside the studio, we call it a *remote telecast*, or simply, a remote. During a remote, the program can either be telecast live or videotaped for broadcasting at a later time or for postproduction.

(with the camera looking up at the object from below eye level) are as easy to accomplish as high-angle shots (from above eye level) with the ENG camera; simply lie on the floor and point the camera up for the low-angle shots, or climb a ladder and point the camera down for the high-angle shots.

Flexibility With ENG equipment, you can either videotape an event or transmit it live, and you can use the ENG camera and VTR as a single independent unit or as part of a multicamera setup (see Chapter 2 for the various systems generally used). This systems flexibility makes it possible to use ENG cameras in ENG, EFP, big remotes, and even studio productions.

Communication Systems

ENG has such a high degree of readiness not only because of the mobile and self-contained camera/ VTR unit, but also because of elaborate communication devices. Most ENG cars are equipped with receivers, called scanners, that continuously monitor the frequencies used by the police and fire departments, a paging system, two-way radios, and sometimes even mobile telephones (see Chapter 8). The scanners lock in on a certain frequency as soon as they detect a signal and let you hear the conversation on that frequency.

These communication systems also make it possible for the news department of your station to get in touch with you while you are on the way to, or back from, an assignment, and give you a chance to respond immediately to police and fire calls. Sometimes, the news departments use special codes to communicate with their "cruising" field reporters in order to prevent the competition from getting clues to a breaking story.

Signal Transmission

When you have to do live ENG, your usual car or station wagon no longer suffices. You need to be accompanied by a news van or production vehicle,

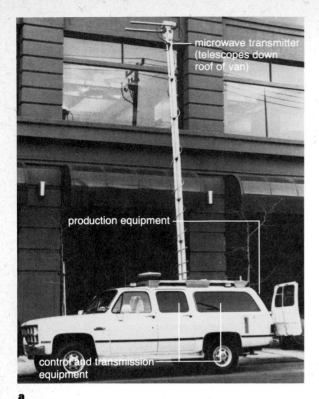

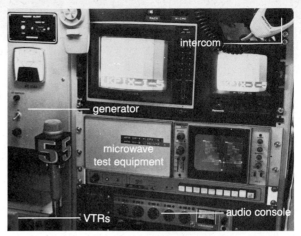

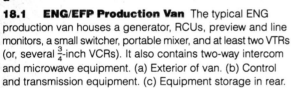

18.1   ENG/EFP Production Van The typical ENG
production van houses a generator, RCUs, preview and line
monitors, a small switcher, portable mixer, and at least two VTRs
(or, several ¾-inch VCRs). It also contains two-way intercom
and microwave equipment. (a) Exterior of van. (b) Control
and transmission equipment. (c) Equipment storage in rear.

whose main function is to supply power (if necessary) and relay the audio and video signals back to
the station and ultimately to the transmitter for the
live telecast. (See 18.1.)

This type of signal transport usually needs two
major links: (1) from the camera (and microphone)
to the ENG vehicle, and (2) from the vehicle to the
station.

Camera-to-Vehicle Transmission   If you need to
maintain optimal camera mobility during a live
pickup, you cannot use a camera cable but must

Big Remote A production outside
the studio to televise live and/or record live-on-tape a large scheduled
event that has not been staged specifically for television. Examples include
sporting events, parades, political
gatherings, or special hearings.

Instant Replay Repeating for the
viewer, often in slow motion, a key
play or other important event, immediately after its live occurrence.

Microwave Relay A transmission
method from the remote location to
the transmitter involving the use of
several microwave units.

Multiplexing A method of transmitting video and audio signals on the
same carrier wave.

Remote A television production
done outside the studio.

18.2   Portable Microwave on ENG Camera (Ikegami HL-79E) When cable runs become too difficult or cumbersome for the operation of the camera, a small microwave transmitter can be attached to the camera. It is powered by the camera power supply (usually the camera battery).

18.3   Tripod-Mounted Microwave System Tripod-mounted microwave transmitters can relay the camera signal to the production van over considerable distance. However, the transmitter must be in line of sight with the receiver at the production van. This unit has a transmission range of over 20 miles.

microwave the signal back to the production vehicle (see 18.2).

Small portable battery-powered transmitters can be mounted on the camera or carried in a backpack. These low-powered systems can transmit on several frequencies, which is called frequency agility, thereby minimizing the possibility of interference by other stations covering the same event. More powerful microwave transmitters are mounted on a tripod that can be placed close to your camera action radius. Thus, you can work a considerable distance away from the production vehicle while using only a relatively short cable run from camera to microwave transmitter (see 18.3).

The main problem with camera-to-van microwave links is interference, especially if there are several different television crews covering the same event. Even if you use a system with relatively great frequency agility, your competition may be similarly agile and overpower you with a stronger signal.

Vehicle-to-Station Transmission The longer, and usually much more complex, signal link is from the production van to the station. (Although sometimes the signal is sent directly to the transmitter, we will call the end point of this last link before the actual

broadcast the "station.") You can send the signals from the production van directly to the station only if you have a clear, unobstructed line of sight (see 18.4).

In order to get past normal obstacles, such as buildings or hills, most production vans have their microwave antennas mounted on telescoping masts (see 18.1).

More often, however, several microwave links (minilinks) are necessary for the proper microwave transport. In metropolitan areas the various television stations have permanent **microwave relays** installed in strategic locations so that the production vans can send their signals back from practically any point of their coverage area. If these permanent installations do not suffice, helicopters are used as microwave relay stations (see 18.5).

For big remotes the microwave links are usually supplied by the telephone company.

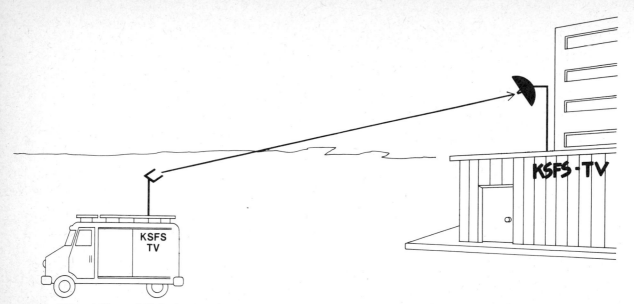

18.4 Direct Line of Sight between Remote Van and Station You can microwave the signal from the remote van back to the station only if there is a clear, unobstructed line of sight.

Ethics

Whenever engaged in ENG, you must realize that you are intruding on an event, and that the people involved are usually under more than normal stress. Although your first responsibility is to get the story, you must also make every effort not to add to the stress or suffering of the people involved. Also, keep a low profile to minimize the chances of somebody performing for you simply to gain attention, or worse, of people staging a media event. For this reason many stations have opted not to put their station logos on ENG vehicles and cameras. Only the microphones usually identify the station or network.

ELECTRONIC FIELD PRODUCTION, OR EFP

Electronic field production, or EFP, uses ENG as well as studio techniques. From ENG it borrows its mobility and flexibility; from the studio it borrows its production care and quality control. But as pointed out in Chapter 1, the studio still affords the highest degree of production control. EFP takes place in the field, and you have to adapt to the field conditions. When working in the field, you must make compromises, even when the conditions may prove exceptionally good. Most often, you work under less than ideal conditions. When you are shooting outdoors, the weather is a major liability. When you are shooting indoors, space limitations are generally the principal handicap. Good lighting and audio are always hard to achieve in EFP, regardless of whether you are outdoors or indoors.

Let us take a brief look at the important points of preproduction, production, and postproduction.

Preproduction

Unlike ENG, which has little or no preparation time for covering a breaking story, electronic field productions must be carefully *prepared*. The major points of these preparations are (1) technical and produc-

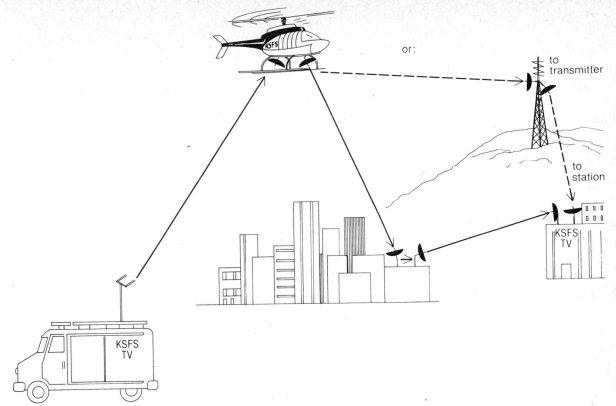

18.5 Minimicrowave Links from Production Van to Station If there is no clear line of sight between the production van and the station, the microwave signal must be transported in steps, called "links," from the van to the helicopter, from the helicopter to a permanently installed microwave link in the city, or to the transmitter, and from there to the station.

tion surveys, (2) production systems, (3) equipment, and (4) communication systems.

Surveys EFP needs careful on-site surveys of technical and production requirements. These surveys, which are identical to those of big remotes, are necessary to bring the specific requirements of the location into accord with those of the process message. We will describe the specific survey items in the section on big remotes.

Production Systems There are several types of EFP systems, some of which overlap with ENG and some with big remotes. Most programs produced in the

field are recorded on videotape for postproduction. However, this is not always the case. For example, we could also utilize EFP for a simple live pickup at the local airport, using two or three ENG cameras, a small switcher, and a moderate lighting setup.

Figures 18.6 through 18.8 show the three basic systems used in EFP. You may notice that these systems closely resemble the various recording modes as discussed in Chapter 10 (see 10.1 through 10.4). But the EFP systems include the possibility for audio and video transmission to the station for live broadcast.

Which system you choose depends on the medium requirements as determined by the process

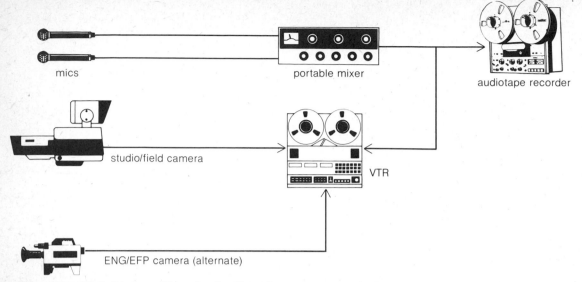

mics

portable mixer

audiotape recorder

studio/field camera

VTR

ENG/EFP camera (alternate)

18.6 Film-Style System When shooting film-style, you may use a single high-quality camera (or, sometimes, a top-of-the-line ENG/EFP camera) for the videotaping of short scenes. To meet the particular audio requirements of the assignment, you may choose several mics to be controlled through a portable mixer. The audio signals are then fed to the VTR and a portable audiotape recorder.

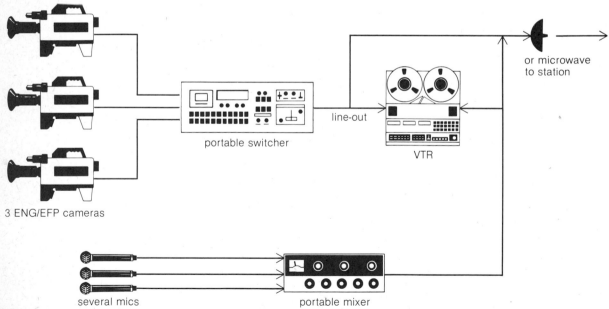

or microwave to station

portable switcher

line-out

VTR

3 ENG/EFP cameras

several mics

portable mixer

18.7 Multicamera and Switcher System In the multicamera and switcher system, two or more ENG/EFP cameras are connected to a portable switcher. The line-out program material is then either videotape recorded or microwaved back to the station. The audio signals from the various mics are sent to the portable mixer and from there either to the VTR and/or to the microwave transmitter.

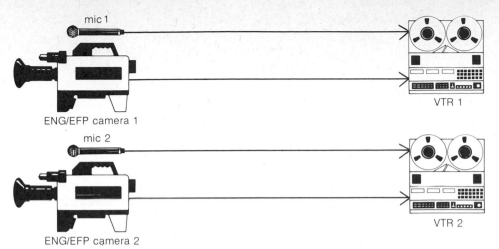

18.8 Iso Camera System When isolated cameras are used, each of the two or more cameras feeds its output to its own VTR. The audio is also recorded separately for each of the iso cameras. The program is then assembled in postproduction.

message—what it is you want to accomplish with the proposed program—and by the location.

Equipment Generally, higher quality equipment is used for EFP than for ENG. The cameras are the top ENG models or convertible cameras. Some film-style productions even use a high-quality studio camera. One-inch VTRs are generally used; $\frac{3}{4}$-inch cassette machines serve as backup and produce a review copy. High-quality microphones are used for the voice pickup and the recording of environmental sounds. When several mics are needed, a portable mixer does some of the premixing. When the audio pickup is critical, multiple-track recorders are pressed into service. In that case, the various sound sources are isolated as much as possible and recorded on separate tracks for further manipulation in postproduction. Even for simple electronic field productions, high-quality lighting instruments with various directional and color controls are a must.

Communication Systems In film-style EFP, you can get away without elaborate intercom systems, because the director, talent, and crew talk over and rehearse each shot before videotaping it. But as soon as you use multiple cameras for simultaneous shooting, you need an intercom system to coordinate the production efforts among production and technical personnel (see Chapter 9, Section Two). Unless you do a live pickup, you need no communication link other than a regular telephone between the production location and the station.

Production

Throughout this book, we have referred to the special requirements of EFP. We will now list a few points that deserve special attention.

1. Work as efficiently as you can and stick to the production schedule as much as possible. There will always be unforeseen production problems. But evaluate these problems in the context of the overall production. Do not spend an undue amount of time on relatively minor production problems at the beginning of the shooting day and then ignore much larger problems when time is running out at the end of the day.

2. When taping historical stories, make sure that everything in your shot matches the period depicted. Especially when outdoors, pay close attention to pic-

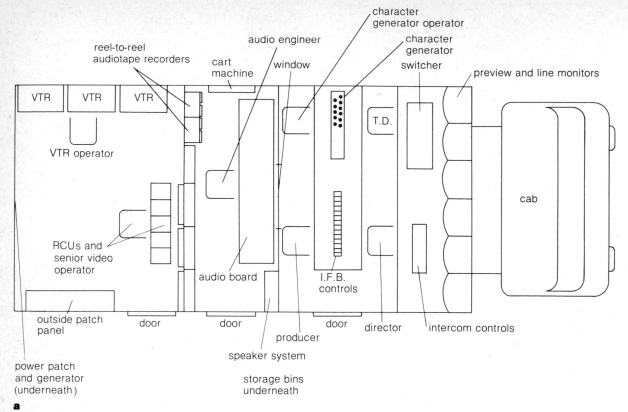

18.9 **Remote Truck** (a) The remote truck represents a complete control center. It contains preview monitors, line and off-the-air monitors, CCUs, a complex switcher, audio control equipment, and videotape facilities. The larger remote units also contain character generators for titles. For especially complex remotes, a second remote truck contains the equipment for instant-replay operations. (b) Program control section (switcher and preview monitors). (c) Audio control section. (d) VTR section. (e) Remote truck storage bins.

ture and sound backgrounds. In the heat of taping a rather difficult Civil War scene, it is easy to over-look the airplane passing over the mountain range at the horizon, or to miss the distant car horns.

3. Slate all takes, including cutaways, and log them carefully so that you can easily locate them again in postproduction. Record location sound and room noise for each new location.

4. Even if you are pressed for time, allow time for meals and rest periods. Be sensitive to the mood and needs of the production team.

5. When you are finished videotaping, put every-thing back the way it was. Double-check that you

have all the equipment before leaving the location. Some producers or directors make up a checklist and have the P.A. run down the list before leaving or changing locations.

Postproduction

The most common postproduction problems when working with material shot in the field are matching the color temperatures of the various takes and get-ting clean audio. Again, you need to look at the problems within the context of your total produc-tion resources—available time, money, equipment, and personnel. Do not get too frustrated if you can-

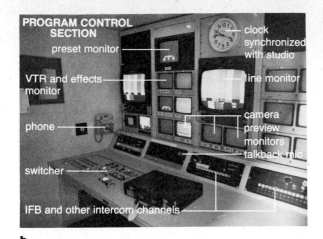

PROGRAM CONTROL SECTION

preset monitor

clock synchronized with studio

VTR and effects monitor

line monitor

phone

camera preview monitors

talkback mic

switcher

IFB and other intercom channels

b

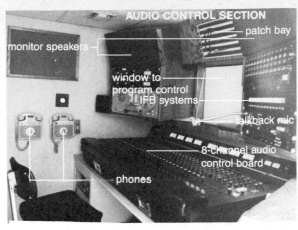

AUDIO CONTROL SECTION

patch bay

monitor speakers

window to program control IFB systems

talkback mic

8-channel audio control board

phones

c

VTR SECTION

3 1-inch VTRs also used for instant playback

d

air conditioner

Bay Area Mobiletape

storage

storage bins

power connection

e

not eliminate all the problems in postproduction. After all, the field simply does not afford you the same production controls as the studio.

BIG REMOTES

A **big remote** is done to televise live (or record live-on-tape) a large, scheduled event that has not been staged specifically for television, such as important sports happenings, parades, political gatherings, or special hearings.

All big remotes use high-quality cameras in key positions, ENG/EFP cameras for greater mobility, and an extensive audio setup. The cameras and the various audio elements are coordinated from a mobile control center, the **remote truck.** Compared to the ENG or EFP production vehicles, the remote truck is much larger; it houses a greater quantity of equipment and more elaborate equipment.

The remote truck represents a compact studio control room on wheels. It contains (1) a program control center with preview and line monitors, a switcher with special effects, a character generator, and various intercom systems (P. L., P. A., and elaborate I.F.B. systems); (2) an audio control center; (3) a VTR center with several high-quality VTRs that can handle regular recordings, do instant replay, and play in slow-motion and freeze-frame modes; and (4) a technical center with camera controls, patchbays, generator, and microwave transmitter (see 18.9 a–e).

Because the telecast happens away from the studio, some of the *medium requirements* and therefore *production procedures* are different from the usual studio productions. We will, therefore, discuss these production aspects: (1) preproduction: remote survey, (2) production: equipment setup and operation, (3) postproduction: some editing considerations and postshow duties.

Preproduction: The Remote Survey

If you have to cover a scheduled event, such as a parade, a political gathering, or a sports event, thorough preparation is essential to the success of the remote. The major part of this preparation involves the **remote survey.**

As the name implies, a remote survey is an investigation of the premises and the circumstances carried out in advance of the telecast. It should provide you with answers to some key questions as to the *nature of the event* and the *technical facilities* necessary to televise it.

Contact   Your first concern is to talk to somebody who knows about the event. This person, called the **contact person,** or simply **contact,** may be the public relations officer of an institution, or some other person in a supervisory capacity. On the phone, find out how much the contact person knows about the event to be covered, and whether or not he or she can refer you to other people who might answer some of your questions. In any case, get the full name, position, address, business phone, and home phone of the contact. Then make an appointment for the actual remote survey. Ideally, the time of day of the survey should be the same as the scheduled remote telecast, because the location of the sun is extremely important for outdoor remotes.

Survey Party   The survey itself is concerned with production and technical problems. The *remote survey party* includes, therefore, people from production and engineering. The minimum party usually consists of the producer, the director, and the T.D. of the remote. Additional supervisory personnel from production and engineering, such as the production manager and the engineering supervi-

sor, may join the survey party, especially if the remote is to cover an important event.

In general, the production requirements are first determined; engineering then tries to make the planned production procedures technically possible. Depending on the complexity of the telecast, extensive compromises must often be made by production people as well as engineers.

As a director, you can make such compromises only if you know what the particular technical setup and pickup problems are and what changes in the production procedures will help to overcome them. You should, therefore, familiarize yourself with the production problems as well as the engineering problems of television remotes. Although many of the production and engineering survey questions overlap, we will, for better clarification, consider them separately.

Production Survey   The following table (18.10) lists the key questions you should ask during the production survey.

Engineering Survey   In the *engineering survey* (see 18.11), you list only those points that have a direct influence on production procedures and, ultimately, on your portion of the remote survey. Technical points that have already been mentioned in the production survey, such as cameras and microphones, need not be indicated again. Although most of these points concern the engineering department, as producer-director you should be thoroughly familiar with them so that you can, if necessary, gently remind the engineers of their particular survey duties.

Like a floor plan, a good sketch of the location in which the remote is to take place can help you in preparing for the production and in anticipating major production problems. (See 18.19, 18.20, and 18.21.)

Production

There is no clear-cut formula for setting up equipment for a remote telecast. As with a studio production, the number of cameras, the type and number of microphones, the lighting, and so forth depend

Survey Item	Key Questions
Contact	Who is your principal contact? Title, address, business phone, home phone. Who is your alternate contact? Title, address, business phone, home phone.
Place	Where is the exact location of the telecast? Street address, telephone number.
Time	When is your remote telecast? Date, time.
Nature of Event	What is the exact nature of the event? Where does the action take place? What type of action do you expect? Your contact person should be able to supply the necessary information.
Cameras (stationary)	How many cameras do you need? Try to use as few as possible. Where do you need the cameras? Never place your cameras on opposite sides of the action. In general, the closer together they are, the easier and less confusing the cutting will be. Shoot with the sun, never against it. Keep it behind or to the side of the cameras for the entire telecast. The press boxes of larger stadiums are generally located on the shadow side of the stadium. Always survey the remote location during the exact time of the scheduled telecast—from 2:00 to 4:00 P.M., for instance—so that you can observe the exact location of the sun and the prevailing lighting conditions. If it is not a sunny day, try to determine the position of the sun as closely as possible. Are there any large objects blocking the camera view, such as trees, telephone poles, or billboards? Will you have the same field of view during the actual time of the telecast? A stadium crowd, for instance, may block the camera's field of view, although at the time of the survey the view was unobstructed. Can you avoid large billboards in the background of shots, especially when the advertising competes with your sponsor's product? Do you need special camera platforms? How high? Where? Can the platforms be erected at this particular point? Can you use the remote truck as a platform? If competing stations are also covering the event, have you obtained exclusive rights for your camera positions? Where do you want iso cameras positioned?
Cameras (mobile)	Do you need to move certain cameras? What kind of floor do you have? Can the camera be moved on a field dolly, or do you need remote dollies (usually with large, inflatable rubber tires)? Will the dolly with camera fit through narrow hallways and doors? Can you use ENG/EFP cameras? What is their action radius? Can you connect them to a remote truck by cable (less chance of signal interference or signal loss), or do you have to get the signal back to the remote truck by microwave? For most events, the camera should be as unobtrusive as possible. Indeed, there is some concern that it and other television gear might act as a catalyst in touchy situations, such as riots and demonstrations. An unobtrusive camera location somewhat removed from the center of action might be preferred to a portable camera that is moved up close to the event.
Lighting	For the remote originating indoors, you almost always need additional lighting. If you need additional lighting, what kind and where? Again, the particular event may make certain lighting procedures difficult, if not impossible. For example, if you put cameras in an orchestra hall, the musicians usually complain about "too much glare and heat" from the additional lighting required. Or, if you cover a committee hearing, the members are usually less than delighted to be in this kind of spotlight. They like to look good but are often hesitant to accept the technical requirements of good television. Can the lighting instruments be hung conveniently, or do you need light stands? Do you need to make special arrangements for back lights? Will the lights be high enough so that they are out of camera range? Do you have to shoot against windows? If so, can they be covered or filtered to block out undesirable daylight?

(continued)

Survey Item	Key Questions
Audio	Proper sound pickup is usually a major problem on remotes. Either the microphones are too far away from the sound source, or the ambient noise is too great. What type of audio pickup do you need? Where do you need it? What is the exact action radius as far as audio is concerned? Can the microphones be seen? Can they be used by the sound source? Generally, remote telecasts tolerate the microphone to be seen in the shot. What type of microphone do you need? Can you get by with lavalieres? Try to use them as much as possible, even outdoors. Besides ensuring good audio pickup, the lavaliere usually allows the person wearing it to feel less conscious of having to speak "for the microphone" than if he or she is confronted with a hand mic close to the face. Where do the microphones have to be? How many do you need? Do you need wireless microphones? Otherwise, how long must the mic cables be? Do you need special audio arrangements, such as audio foldback, or a speaker system that carries the program audio to the location? Can you tie into the "house" public address system, or do you need long-distance mics for special sound pickups over a great distance? Where do you want the mics to be located?
Intercommunications	The importance of a reliable intercommunication system for remotes cannot be stressed enough. It is not uncommon for the members of the production team to be widely scattered over the whole production area and physically isolated. The only contact they have with one another and the director is the intercom system. What type of intercom system do you need? Do you have to string special lines or can the floor crew plug their earphones into the cameras? If you need separate lines, where do they have to go? Determine how many I.F. B. channels and/or stations you need and where they should go. Remote trucks should be able to supply at least three separate I.F. B. channels. Some elaborate systems have as many as eight separate channels. If the director has to coordinate different people at the production site from the remote truck, he or she needs a P.A. (Public Address) talkback system. Because the floor manager cannot be in several locations at once, the talkback system permits the director immediate contact with the people in the performance area. Do you have an outside telephone available in the remote truck? (The engineers usually hook up a telephone so they can communicate with the station and the transmitter.)
Miscellaneous Production Items	Where do you need easels for title cards (or other title devices)? Do you need a special clock? Where? Do you need line monitors, especially for the announcer? How many? Where should they be located? Will the announcers need a preview monitor to follow special iso playbacks? Do you need a special chroma key background? Where should it be hung so that it can be properly lighted and covered by one of the field cameras? If your program is videotaped, the floor manager needs a VTR slate. Is one slate enough? Sometimes you may want several in order to be able to slate a program from any one of the cameras used. How much videotape do you need? Has the condition of the tape been checked before the remote?
Permits and Clearances	Have you (or the producer, if you do not act as producer-director) secured clearances for the telecast from the police and fire departments? Do you have clearances from the originators of the event? In writing? Do you have parking permits for the remote truck and other station vehicles? Do you have passes for all engineering and production personnel, especially when the event requires admittance fees or has some kind of admission restrictions? Do you have proper liability insurance, if necessary? Check with the legal department of your station.
Special Production Aids	Does everybody involved in the telecast have a rundown sheet of the approximate order of the events? These sheets are essential for the director, floor manager, and announcer, and extremely helpful to the camera operators, audio engineer, and additional floor personnel. Does the director have a "spotter"—somebody who knows the event intimately and who can spot and identify the major action and people involved? In sports, spotters are essential.

Survey Item	Key Questions

Power	Assuming you do not work from a battery pack or your own generator, is enough electricity available at the remote site? Where? You will need at least 80–125 amperes for the average remote operation, depending on the equipment used.
	
	  Has your contact person access to the power outlets? If not, who has? Make sure that he or she is available at the times of the remote setup and the actual production.
	
	  Do you need special extensions for the power cable?

Location of Remote Truck and Equipment	Where should the remote truck be located? Its proximity to the available power is very important if you do not have a generator for power. Are you then close enough to the event location? Keep in mind that there is a maximum length for camera cables beyond which you will experience video loss (usually beyond 2,000 feet or roughly 700 meters). Does the truck block normal traffic? Does it interfere with the event itself? Make sure that parking is reserved for the truck. Do you need special RCUs for portable cameras? Do you need special receiving stations for wireless video and/or audio equipment? Where are they located?
VTR	If the program is recorded, do you have the necessary VTR equipment in the truck? Do you need additional VTRs for instant replay? If you have to feed the signal back to the station to be videotaped, are the remote signal transmission devices (microwave link and telephone wire if the audio is sent separately) working properly? Are the phone lines ordered? Do you have enough tape to cover the full event? Have you made provisions for switching reels without losing part of the event (switching over to a second VTR)? Are your iso cameras properly patched into separate VTRs?
Signal Transmission	If the event has to be fed back to the station for videotape recording or directly to the transmitter for live broadcasting, do you have a good microwave location? You can send the video signal (or the multiplexed video and audio signals) only if you have a clear, unobstructed line of sight from the point of origin to the transmitter. Otherwise you need microwave minilinks, or the larger relays, a service generally supplied by the telephone company. Have you made arrangements for this with the telephone company? Or can you send the video signal via cable? Sometimes you can use existing cable systems for signal transmission. Watch for possible sources of video and audio signal interference, such as nearby x-ray machines, radar, or any other high-frequency electronic equipment. Double-check on the special requirements for feeding the satellite uplink.
Routing of Cables	How many camera cables do you need? Where do they have to go? How many audio cables do you need? Where do they have to go? How many intercom lines do you need? Where do they have to go? How many A.C. (power) lines do you need? Where do they have to go? Route the cables in the shortest possible distance from remote truck to pickup point, but do not block important hallways, doors, walkways, and so on. Try to route cables above doorways and doors. Tape all loose cables to the floor so that the danger of someone's tripping is at least minimized. Put a floor mat over the cables at the key traffic points. If you have to cover a great span with free-hanging cables, relieve the tension by tying them on a strong rope stretched over the same distance. Be careful not to run mic cables parallel to power cables.

Lighting	Are there enough A.C. outlets for all lighting instruments? Are the outlets fused for the lamps? Do not overload ordinary household outlets.
	
	  Do you have enough extension cords and distribution boxes (or simple multiple wall plugs) to accommodate all lighting instruments?
	
	  Remember the A.C. line for the announcer's monitor and the electric clock.

Telephone Lines	Do you have access to telephone lines for communication to the station and transmitter? For the audio feeds? Make prior arrangements with the phone company.

entirely on the event to be covered or, rather, the process message as defined in the preproduction meetings.

Employing a great number of cameras, microphones, and other types of technical equipment does not necessarily guarantee a better telecast than when using less equipment. In fact, one or two ENG/EFP camera and VTR units are sometimes much more flexible and effective than a cumbersome remote truck with the fanciest of video, audio, recording, and switching gear. However, for such standard big remote operations as the coverage of major sports events, the remote truck gives you the necessary production flexibility and control. As an elaborate control center on wheels, the remote truck makes possible productions of high technical quality.

Although in general the setup in a remote does not differ significantly from the setup and use of the cameras in studio productions, the instant-replay procedures deserve special mention because they are used almost exclusively in remote operations.

Instant Replay

Instant replay means that a key play or other important event is repeated for the viewer, often in slow motion. Instant-replay operations usually use isolated, or "iso," cameras and VTRs that have fast shuttle speeds and slow-motion capability, or instant replay video disc recorders. In large productions, the instant-replay operation uses its own switcher. We will now consider the role of each of these components.

Isolated Camera

When watching an instant replay of a key action, you may notice that the replay either duplicates exactly the sequence you have just seen or, more frequently, shows the action from a slightly different angle. In the first case, the picture sequence of the regular game coverage—that is, the line output—has been recorded and played back; in the second case, the pickup of a separate camera, which was not involved in the general coverage, has been recorded and played back. This separate camera is the isolated, or iso, camera. Its principal function is to follow key plays and other key action for instant replay. Iso cameras are also used in a variety of studio and remote productions to get visual sequences that can later be used in postproduction

editing. For example, when videotaping an orchestra performance with a multicamera setup, you may have an iso camera on the conductor at all times. This way, you are covered with a logical cutaway during postproduction. In large productions, two or more iso cameras are used. Sometimes, all cameras are used in iso positions, with each camera's output being recorded by a separate VTR. When playing back the VTRs in sync during postproduction, you can treat the VTRs like live cameras and mix and remix the various images as much as you want.

Instant-Replay Recording

The output of the iso camera is usually recorded and played back on a 1-inch VTR. The VTR used for instant replay should have a fast shuttle speed, so you can locate the specific replay scene quickly, and a variable playback speed (from zero speed—freeze frame—to several times normal speed). This way, you can park the VTR in the freeze-frame mode, punch it up on the air for instant replay, and let the still picture come alive by simply putting the VTR in a slow motion or regular motion forward mode. A slow motion control unit (see Chapter 10, p. 277) makes this operation smooth and easy to handle.

Some remote trucks still use the large video disc system. The advantage of the video disc is that the retrieval time of the playback scene is extremely fast. The disadvantages are that the unit is rather bulky and that it can record only about 40 seconds.

Instant-Replay Switcher

In large sports remotes, a separate switcher is used for the instant replay operation. The small switcher is usually located right next to the large production switcher in the remote truck, enabling the T.D. to feed the instant replay VTR, or VTRs, with either the iso camera picture or the line-out picture of the regular coverage.

Special Effects

During the replay, DVEs (digital video effects) are often used to explain a particular play. You may have seen the screen divided into several "squeezed" boxes or corner wipes, each displaying a different aspect of the play.

The whole instant-replay operation is normally guided by the producer or the associate director because the director is much too occupied with the regular coverage to worry about the various replays and special effects. Also, the producer, who is free to follow the game, can become adept at spotting key plays and deciding which ones to have replayed; hence, he or she can pay full attention to the replay procedures.

Let us now briefly discuss some of the major production procedures of remote telecasts for (1) the director, (2) the floor manager, and (3) the talent.

Director's Procedures

Here are some of the major production items you should consider during the remote setup, the on-the-air telecast, and directly after the telecast.

Setup   The setup includes all activities before the actual telecast of the remote event. Thorough set-up planning is especially important for sports remotes (see 18.12 through 18.18).

1.   As soon as the remote truck is in position, conduct a *thorough* technical and talent walk-through. Tell the technical staff where you want the cameras located, where they should move, what lighting you want, where the major action is to take place, what audio you need, where the announcer is going to be, what intercom system you need where, and so forth. Explain the major visualization points to the camera operators. Explain to everybody the process message objective.

2.   Be as decisive and precise as possible. Do not change your mind a hundred times before deciding on what you really want. There is simply no time for such deliberations on a remote.

3.   Work through the floor manager and T.D. as much as possible. Do not try to direct everything yourself.

4.   Pay special attention to the intercom system. During the telecast, you will have no chance to run in and out of the remote truck to the actual site of the event; all your instructions will come via remote control from the truck. Make sure that the floor manager thoroughly understands the whole proceedings. He or she holds one of the most important production positions during a remote.

5.   Usually, you as a director have no control over the event itself; you merely try to observe it as faithfully as possible. If an announcer is involved for narration and explanation of the event, walk through the event site with him or her and explain as best you can what is going to happen. Double-check on the announcer's rundown sheet and the specific information concerning the event.

6.   Check the telephone line to the transmitter or station.

7.   Check with the videotape operator on the length of the tape. Will it be sufficient to cover the whole event, or at least part of it, before a new tape is needed? If you have only one VTR in the truck, when is the best time for a reel change?

8.   Walk through the site again and try to visualize the event from the cameras' positions. Are they in the optimal shooting position? Do you have all of them on only one side of the principal vector so that you will not reverse the action on the screen when cutting from one camera to the other? If you are outdoors, is any one of the cameras shooting into the sun? Where will the sun be at the end of the telecast? Do you need special covers in case of rain or snow? Try to get the cameras as close to the action as possible in order to avoid overly narrow-angle zoom lens positions.

9.   Remember that you are a *guest* while covering a remote event. Try to work as quickly and as unobtrusively as possible. Do not make a big spectacle of your production.

On-the-Air Telecast   Once you are on the air and the event is unfolding, you cannot stop it because you have missed a major point. Try to keep on top of the event as well as possible. If you have a good spotter, you will be able to anticipate certain happenings and therefore be ready for them with the cameras. Here are some general points to remember:

1.   Speak loudly and clearly. Usually the site is noisy and the camera operators and the floor crew may not hear you. Yell if you have to, but do not get frantic.

2.   Listen to the floor manager. He or she may be able to spot special events and report them to you as they occur.

3. Watch the monitors carefully. Often the off-cameras will show you especially interesting shots. But do not be tempted by cute, yet meaningless or even event-distorting, shots. If, for example, the great majority of an audience listens attentively to the speaker, do not single out the one person who is sound asleep, as colorful a shot as this may be. Report the event as truthfully as you possibly can. If the event is dull, show it. If it is exciting, show it. Do not use production tricks to distort it to fit your previous expectations.

4. Listen to the audio. Often, this will give you clues as to the development of the event.

5. If things go wrong, keep calm. If a spectator blocks the camera, cut to another camera, instead of screaming at the camera operator.

6. Exercise propriety and good taste in what you show to the audience. Avoid capitalizing on accidents (especially during sports events) or situations that are potentially embarrassing to the person in front of the camera, even if such situations might appear hilarious to you.

After the Show The remote is not finished until all equipment is struck and the remote site restored to its original state. Here are some points that are especially important for the director:

1. If something went wrong, do not storm out of the remote truck accusing everybody, except yourself, of making mistakes. Cool off first.

2. Thank everyone for his or her efforts. Nobody ever *wants* a remote to look bad. Thank especially the contact person and others responsible for making the event and the remote telecast possible. Leave as good an impression of you and your team as possible with the persons responsible. Remember that you are representing your station and, in a way, the whole of the "media" when you are on remote location.

3. If you do not have a producer, complete all the necessary production forms.

4. Thank the police for their cooperation in reserving parking spaces for the remote vehicles, controlling the spectators, and so forth. Remember that you will need them again for your next remote telecast.

5. See to it that the floor manager returns all the production equipment to the station.

Floor Manager's Procedures

As a floor manager (also called stage manager), you have, next to the director, the major responsibility for the success of a remote telecast. Because you are close to the scene, you have often more overview of the event than the director, who is isolated in the remote truck. Here are some of the major points you should consider:

1. Familiarize yourself with the event ahead of time. Find out where it is taking place, what its major development is, and where the cameras and microphones are relative to the remote truck. Make a sketch of the major event developments and the equipment setup (see Section Two).

2. Triple-check all intercom systems. Find out whether you can hear the instructions from the remote truck, and whether you can be heard there. Check whether the intercom is working properly for the other floor personnel. Check all I.F.B. channels.

3. Try to control the traffic of onlookers around the major equipment and action areas. Be polite, but firm. Try to work around the crews from other stations. Be especially aware of reporters from other media. It would not be the first time that a news photographer just happened to stand right in front of the key camera while snapping his or her pictures. Try to appeal to their sense of responsibility. Tell them that you, too, have a job to do in trying to inform the public.

4. Have your slate ready if the telecast is to be videotaped.

5. Check on all cables and make sure they are properly secured so that potential hazards are minimized.

6. Try to contact a member of the police assigned to the remote. Clue him or her in on its major aspects. The police are generally cooperative and especially helpful in controlling spectator traffic.

7. Help the camera operators in spotting key event detail and in moving their cameras.

8. Give all cues immediately and precisely. Make sure the talent sees the cues. (Most of the time, announcers are hooked up to the I.F.B. via small earphones, so that the director can cue them directly without the floor manager as an intermediary.)

9. Have several 3 × 5 cards handy so you can write cues and pass them to the talent.

10. Have the necessary title cards ready and in order. You will need a large clip to fasten the cards to the easel during a windy day. While doing hot flips of title cards, hold the cards behind the one you are pulling so that they do not all come flying off the easel.

11. After the telecast, pick up all the production equipment for which you are directly responsible— easels, platforms, sandbags, slates, and earphones. Double-check whether you have forgotten anything before you leave the remote site.

Talent Procedures

The general talent procedures, as discussed in Chapter 15, also apply for remote operations. However, here are some points that are especially pertinent for remote telecasts:

1. Familiarize yourself thoroughly with the event and your specific assignment. Know the process message objective and try to do your part to effect it.

2. Check out your microphone and your communication system. If you work with an I.F.B. system, check it out with the director or the T.D.

3. Check whether your monitor is working. Have the T.D. punch up a camera on the line-out.

4. Check with the director on the show format and fact sheet.

5. If you have the help of a contact person or a spotter, discuss with him or her the major aspects of the event and the communication system between the spotter and yourself, once you are on the air.

How is the spotter going to tell you what is going on while the microphone is hot?

6. While on the air, tell the audience what they cannot see for themselves. Do not tell them the obvious. For example, if you see the celebrity stepping out of the airplane and shaking hands with the people who came to meet him or her, do not say, "The celebrity is shaking hands with some people," but tell who is shaking hands with whom. If a football player lies on the field and cannot get up, do not tell the audience that apparently the player got hurt; they can see that for themselves. But tell them who the player is and what might have caused what type of injury. Also, follow up this announcement with more detailed information on the injury and how the player is doing.

7. Do not get so involved in the event that you lose your objectivity. On the other hand, do not remain so detached that you appear to have no feelings whatsoever.

8. If you make a mistake in identifying someone or something, admit it and correct it as soon as possible.

9. Do not identify parts of the event solely by color. There are still many viewers who watch the telecast in black-and-white. For instance, do not refer to the boxer just as the one in the red trunks, but also as the one on the left side of the screen.

10. As much as possible, let the event itself do the talking.

Postproduction

If you have done a remote pickup for postproduction editing, try to match in the final edited tape version the relative energy and general feeling of the original event. This is true especially when the process message objective implies a *reflection* of the event rather than a reconstruction of it. Do not try to energize the screen event by fast cuts and montage effects. Simply edit for continuity. Try to avoid jump cuts and reversals of screen directions. If you have provided the editor with enough cutaways, he or she can bridge a reversal of screen directions without too much effort or loss of continuity (see

Chapter 11). Usually the audio provides the necessary continuity, even if the visuals may not always cut together as smoothly as you might desire.

As a producer or a director, or a combination thereof, your major postshow duty is to write thank-you letters. Do not neglect this task, as anticlimactic as it may seem after a successful production. If you had little cooperation, try to find the source of the trouble and gently suggest ways of improving cooperation. Do not get angry. It is more likely than not that you will have to work with the same people in future telecasts.

Again, check on the release forms and file them for future reference. If you have time, hold a postproduction meeting with the production people and the talent, and talk about the good points and the not-so-good points of the remote. Listen to the suggestions of the crew and try to apply them during your next remote.

MAIN POINTS

1. A television show done outside the studio is called a remote telecast, or a remote.

2. The three types of remotes are (1) ENG (electronic news gathering), (2) EFP (electronic field production), and (3) big remotes.

3. ENG is the most flexible of remote operations. It offers speed in responding to an event, maximum mobility while on location, and flexibility in transmitting the event live or recording it on portable videotape.

4. When doing live ENG, the various forms of signal transmission (from camera to production van, from the production van to the station, and from the station to the remote van) become a major production item.

5. The major disadvantages of ENG are that (1) the production quality is lower than that of a studio production and lower even than that of an EFP or a big remote; and (2) switching among multiple cameras is not possible.

6. When engaged in ENG, the remote crew should keep as low a profile as possible in order to minimize the media intrusion into the event.

7. Contrary to ENG, which has little or no preparation time for covering a breaking story, EFP must be carefully prepared. In this respect it is similar to big remotes. However, the on-site operations of EFP are much more flexible than those of the big remote.

8. The three basic EFP systems are (1) film-style, using a single camera for each shot; (2) multicamera and switcher system, where two or more cameras feed into a switcher, enabling instantaneous editing for the various scenes; and (3) the iso camera system, whereby each of two of more simultaneously shooting cameras feeds its signal into its own videotape recorder.

9. A big remote is done to televise live, or live-on-tape, a large, scheduled event that has not been staged specifically for television. Examples include sporting events, parades, political gatherings, or special hearings.

10. All big remotes use high-quality cameras in key positions, and ENG/EFP cameras for more mobile coverage. Big remotes usually require extensive audio setups.

11. Big remotes are coordinated from the remote truck. It contains (1) a program control center with preview and line monitors, switcher, character generator, and a variety of intercom systems; (2) an audio control center, including a large audio console, cart machines and reel-to-reel audiotape recorders; (3) a VTR center with several high-quality VTRs that can be used for recording, instant replay, play in slow-motion and freeze-frame modes; and (4) a technical center with power supply (generator), camera controls, patch bays, and a microwave transmitter.

12. Big remotes require extensive production and engineering surveys as part of the preproduction activities.

13. In sports remotes, instant replay is one of the more complicated production procedures. Instant replays are handled by a producer or associate director.

14. If postproduction is involved after a big remote, care must be taken that the edited event reflects as accurately as possible the energy of the original event.

No two big remotes are exactly the same. There are always special circumstances that require adjustments and compromises. Because of the complexity and specific production challenges, big remotes are an ideal way to learn television production. Once you have done a few big remotes, you will be pleased to find that the studio is, after all, an ideal place for doing television production and that ENG, EFP, and big remote equipment and procedures will never render the studio obsolete.

In this section, we will describe typical setups for sports remotes, explain how to "read" location sketches, and give examples of indoor and outdoor remote setups.

SPORTS REMOTES

Many big remotes are devoted to the coverage of sports events. The number of cameras used and their function depend almost entirely on who is doing the remote. Networks use a great amount of equipment and personnel for the average sports remote. For especially important games, such as the Super Bowl, twenty-four or more cameras and countless mics may be used and controlled from dual remote units—one truck devoted to the regular pickup, and the other to instant replays and special effects. However, local stations, if engaged in a sports pickup at all, must get by with far less equipment. Often, a local station supplies the key production and engineering personnel (producer, director, associate director, P.A., floor manager, T.D., audio) but hires a remote service that includes a large remote truck, all equipment, and extra personnel. Figures 18.12 through 18.18 illustrate the minimum video and audio pickup

requirements for (1) baseball, (2) football, (3) soccer, (4) basketball, (5) tennis, (6) boxing or wrestling, and (7) swimming. Sometimes, small ENG/EFP cameras are used in place of the larger high-quality studio/field cameras, or are added to the minimal setups described here.

LOCATION SKETCHES

As we pointed out in the discussion on remote surveys in Section One, the success of a remote depends to a large degree on the thoroughness of your preparation. However, there are times when you cannot attend the all-important location surveys. In this case, you need a **location sketch.**

Reading Location Sketches

If the remote is to take place indoors, the location sketch should indicate the general dimensions of the room or hallway and the location of windows, doors, furniture, and the principal action (place where people are seated, or where they will be walking). It would help if the sketch

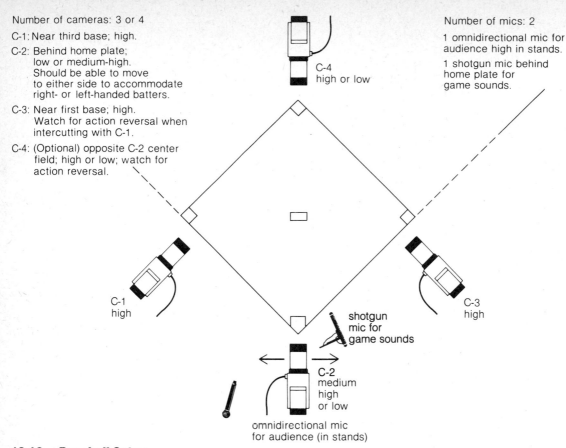

Number of cameras: 3 or 4

C-1: Near third base; high.

C-2: Behind home plate; low or medium-high. Should be able to move to either side to accommodate right- or left-handed batters.

C-3: Near first base; high. Watch for action reversal when intercutting with C-1.

C-4: (Optional) opposite C-2 center field; high or low; watch for action reversal.

C-4 high or low

Number of mics: 2

1 omnidirectional mic for audience high in stands.

1 shotgun mic behind home plate for game sounds.

C-1 high

C-3 high

shotgun mic for game sounds

C-2 medium high or low

omnidirectional mic for audience (in stands)

18.12   Baseball Setup

also contained such details as household outlets, actual width of especially narrow hallways and doors, direction the doors open, especially narrow stairs, prominent thresholds, rugs, and other items that may present some problems for the movement of cameras on tripods or dollies.

The sketch of an outdoor remote should indicate the buildings, the remote truck, the major power source, steps, steep inclines, fences, the location of the sun during the remote, and the quality of floor or ground (smooth enough for a camera to move or too rough).

Here are two examples of how to "read" an indoor (see 18.19 and 18.20) and outdoor (see 18.21) location sketch. Both sketches contain major camera and audio setups.

Indoor Remote: Public Hearing

The occasion is an important public hearing in the city hall (see 18.19). What can you tell from this sketch? How much preparation can you do? What key questions does the sketch generate?

Limiting the questions to the setup within this hearing room, what are the camera, lighting, audio, and intercom requirements? Let's take these problems one by one.

Cameras   How many cameras do you need and where should they be located? You should be able to see all three supervisors on an LS and get CUs of each. You should be able to see the witnesses and counselors

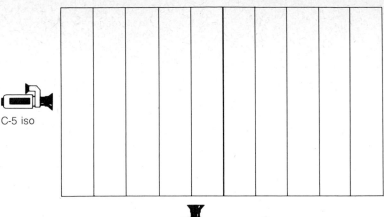

Number of cameras: 4 or 5

C-1, 2, 3:
High in the stands, near the 20-50-20 yard lines (press box, shadow side).

C-4: Portable or on special dolly in field.

C-5: (Optional) iso camera behind goal (portable ENG/EFP, or big camera).

Number of mics: 2

1 omnidirectional mic for audience (in stands).

1 shotgun or parabolic (mobile) on field.

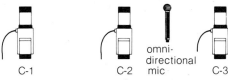

mobile camera ← → C-4   portable shotgun mic

omnidirectional mic

C-1   C-2   C-3

18.13   Football Setup

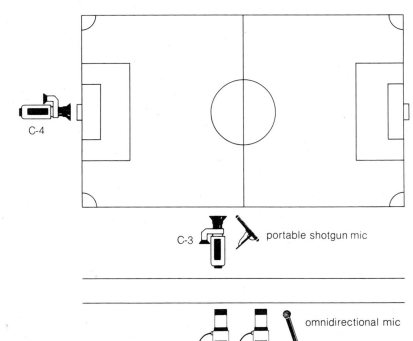

C-4

C-3   portable shotgun mic

omnidirectional mic

18.14   Soccer Setup   C-1   C-2

Number of cameras: 3 or 4

C-1: Left of center line (high).

C-2: Right of center line (high).

C-3: Mobile on field.

C-4: (Optional) behind goal.
May be used as iso camera.

All three cameras are in shadow side of field.

Number of mics: 2

1 omnidirectional mic in stands for audience.

1 shotgun or parabolic mic on field (portable).

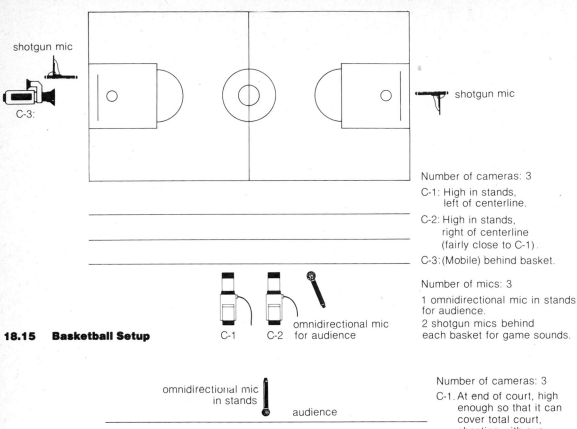

officials and benches

shotgun mic

C-3:

shotgun mic

Number of cameras: 3

C-1: High in stands,
left of centerline.

C-2: High in stands,
right of centerline
(fairly close to C-1).

C-3: (Mobile) behind basket.

Number of mics: 3

1 omnidirectional mic in stands
for audience.
2 shotgun mics behind
each basket for game sounds.

18.15   Basketball Setup

C-1   C-2   omnidirectional mic
for audience

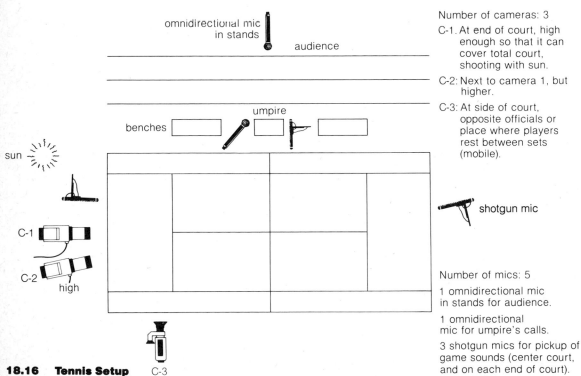

omnidirectional mic
in stands

audience

Number of cameras: 3

C-1. At end of court, high
enough so that it can
cover total court,
shooting with sun.

C-2: Next to camera 1, but
higher.

C-3: At side of court,
opposite officials or
place where players
rest between sets
(mobile).

benches   umpire

sun

shotgun mic

C-1

C-2
high

Number of mics: 5

1 omnidirectional mic
in stands for audience.

1 omnidirectional
mic for umpire's calls.

3 shotgun mics for pickup of
game sounds (center court,
and on each end of court).

18.16   Tennis Setup   C-3

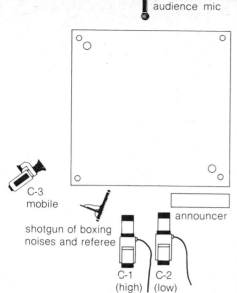

omnidirectional
audience mic

C-3
mobile

shotgun of boxing
noises and referee

C-1
(high)

C-2
(low)

announcer

Number of cameras: 2 or 3

C-1: High enough so that it
can overlook the
entire ring.

C-2: About 10 feet to the
side of camera 1. Low,
slightly above ropes.

C-3: Optional. ENG/EFP
mobile camera carried
on floor, looking
through the ropes.

Number of mics: 2

1 omnidirectional
mic for audience.

1 shotgun mic for
boxing sounds and referee.

18.17   Boxing and Wrestling Setup

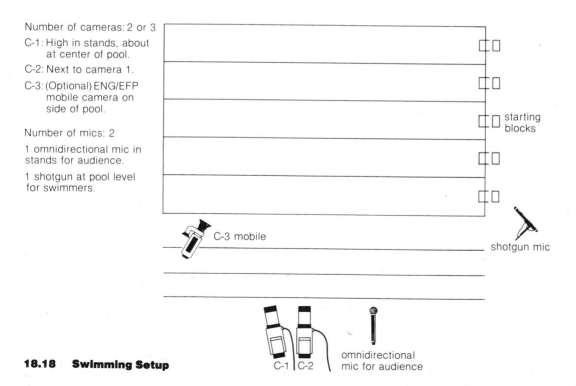

Number of cameras: 2 or 3

C-1: High in stands, about
at center of pool.

C-2: Next to camera 1.

C-3: (Optional) ENG/EFP
mobile camera on
side of pool.

Number of mics: 2

1 omnidirectional mic in
stands for audience.

1 shotgun at pool level
for swimmers.

starting
blocks

C-3 mobile

shotgun mic

18.18   Swimming Setup

C-1 | C-2

omnidirectional
mic for audience

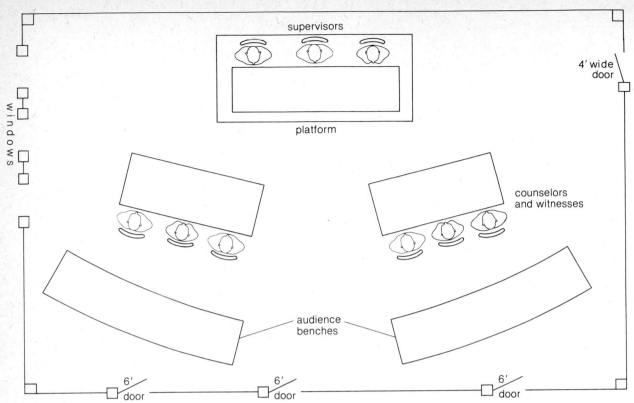

18.19 Location Sketch of City Hall Hearing Room This sketch contains most of the essential information for preparing a remote coverage of the hearings. Although not in scale, it shows the relationship of the principal action areas. It would be helpful to know the height of the supervisors' platform and the nature of the floor (hardwood, tile, or carpet).

in CUs and LSs. You should also see some of the audience reaction and the workings of the press. This means one camera looking at the supervisors and one at the witnesses, the counselors, and the audience.

Actually, two cameras will do. Where should they be placed? Look again at 18.19. Because the supervisors will talk with the witnesses and counselors rather than with the audience and the press, they will look most frequently in the direction of the witness table. Similarly, the witnesses and the counselors will look at the supervisors' bench. This direction (from witness to supervisor) represents the line of conversation, the *principal vector* that you should not cross with the cameras. If you place cameras on both sides of it, your

screen directions would be reversed when you switch from one camera to the other. The supervisors and the witnesses would no longer seem to talk to each other in subsequent close-ups, but away from each other. To shoot the faces from as straight on as possible, the cameras should be placed on the right side rather than the left side of the vector. Fortunately, there is a side door through which the cameras can enter and all the cables can be routed without blocking the main access doors in the rear of the chamber. Also, fortunately, the supervisors' bench is high enough so that one of the cameras can shoot over the witnesses without the need for a special platform. The other camera (which covers the witnesses and the audience) has a clear view of

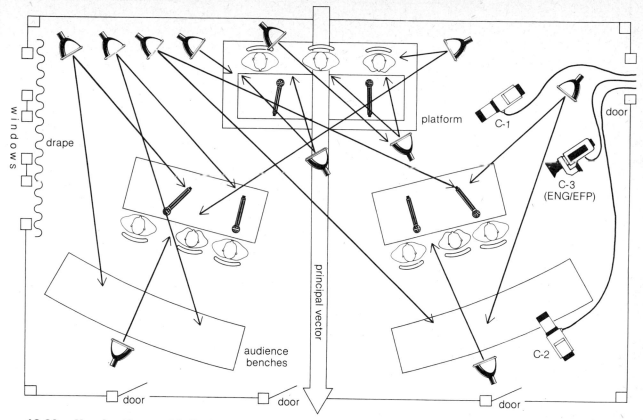

18.20   Hearing Room with Facilities Note that the optional camera 3 could very well be a mobile ENG/EFP camera. As a mobile camera, it can work along the wall, opposite the draped window.

the witness table (see 18.20). By zooming in and out, you can get tight close-ups, or cover the whole bench in a long shot. The normal 10:1 zoom range should do, without the necessity for range extenders (at least according to the sketch). If you want a third camera for additional shots and protection, it should be located next to camera 2, facing the witness table and the audience. Why there? In this location (see 18.20), camera 3 can get reaction shots from the audience and the press, and relieve camera 2 for close-ups or long shots of the witness table. In an emergency, if camera 1 should fail, camera 2 can still truck left and get a reasonably good shot of the supervisors' bench. Try, therefore, to get three cameras for this remote, although, as we said

before, you could manage with two. The third camera could very well be an ENG/EFP camera, stationed next to camera 2. From there, you could walk along the wall toward the audience and turn around to get shots of the supervisors.

Because this hearing is of statewide importance and will be picked up by other stations and cable companies, you need to use high-quality cameras whenever possible.

Lighting   The A.D. informs you that, in spite of the large window, the lighting is quite dim inside the chamber. The hearing is scheduled for 10:00 A.M. The large window presents a definite lighting problem. Although it does not provide sufficient light for the room, its glare tends to silhouette the persons who are sitting between the camera and the window. The sketch does not include any draperies. Try, therefore, to arrange to have the window covered with something before the telecast.

Now you need additional lighting. How high is the chamber ceiling? Quite high, according to the A.D. You can, therefore, tell the T.D. or lighting director to get some back lights which may also serve as audience lights, into the corners of the room behind the supervisors' bench. You also need some lights for the witnesses and some lights for the supervisors' bench. Exactly where the lights should be can be judged more accurately once the lighting director (or camera operator) sees the chamber. In any case, the lights should not blind the people, nor should the cables block access doors or aisles. Try to get by with as few instruments (floodlights) as possible. Are the wall outlets sufficiently fused for the lighting instruments? Do you know where the fuse box is located? Make sure that the additional lighting is tolerated by the supervisors and that they and the witnesses are prepared for it. Usually, when people know what to expect, they accept the temporary inconvenience more readily (see 18.20). Have the room completely lighted *before* the people arrive. You may want to have the lights dimmed by about 50 percent when the people enter, and then slowly bring them up to 100 percent intensity.

Audio   Because the chamber is already equipped with a P.A. system, tie into the existing mics. If the system is not operational, desk mics are the most logical answer. Set up a dual redundancy system for extra protection. Make sure that the mic cables do not interfere with camera movement. String the cables behind the cameras, not in front of them (see 18.20).

Intercommunications   Because there is no cuing involved (no cues are given to the supervisors, for example), the floor personnel (one person for each camera) can eliminate additional cables by plugging their earphones into the cameras. Remember the slate, if the proceedings are to be videotaped.

Special Considerations   The camera that needs most protection by the floor manager is camera 1, because it is closest to an access door. Perhaps you can have this area closed off with ropes that can be struck quickly in case of an emergency. Do not lock this right door unless you have checked with the fire marshal and received his or her OK. By the way, do you have *written*

clearances from the Board of Supervisors and the counselors? Again, try to make the additional lighting as inconspicuous as possible. The counselors, the witnesses, or the audience may occasionally stand up. Can you still shoot around them? If the doors are kept closed during the hearing, you can always move camera 1 in front of the middle door for an unobstructed shot of the bench.

As you can see, at least at this point, the remote of the public hearing does not seem to present too many unusual problems. With the preparation as just demonstrated, you should have little trouble with the actual production, barring unforeseen technical problems.

More complicated remote productions need more intricate and thorough survey and preparation procedures than in the preceding example. But basically the *process* remains the same. As in any other production, the more time and effort you spend on preparation, the easier the actual production will be.

Outdoor Location: Dance

This remote is intended for a "live-on-tape" multi-camera pickup with a minimum of postproduction. Again, the quality requirements are high, because the dance company intends to send copies of the tape to various foundations. As you can see, the location sketch shows the action area as well as the major facilities (see 18.21).

Let us take a closer look at the location sketch and see whether it gives all the essential information.

Remote Truck   The remote truck is parked in an ideal spot. It is close to a power source (A/V Center) and the camera positions (minimizing cable runs). Also, it is in a rather protected spot, away from traffic.

Cameras   The cameras are in good shooting positions. All point away from the sun and should be able to cover the total dance area. Camera 2 is high enough (lens height is approximately 9 feet) to get good views of the dance from above; camera 1 is lower, yet still high enough to get good long shots if necessary. The sketch should contain the height and width of the steps. Can the tripod fit on one of the steps, or do you need a special box to support the front leg of the tripod? Because these are steps leading to a bookstore, you can assume that the steps are fairly narrow. Camera 3 is the ENG/EFP camera. This is the right choice. It is low and highly mobile; it can get occasional close-ups or move with the dancers. Its main shooting positions

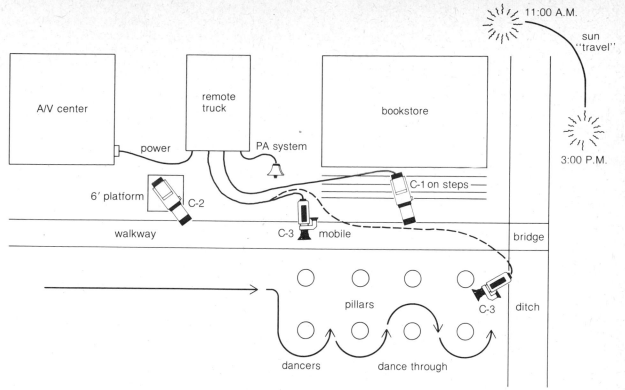

18.21 Outdoor Location Sketch: Dance Note that camera 3 (mobile
ENG/EFP on long cable) can work along the walkway and also alongside the ditch.

are the walkway and along the ditch. You need to make
sure that it has enough cable and two cable pullers to
facilitate mobility. You need to be careful not to have
camera 3 step into the view of camera 1 or 2. All cameras are close enough to the action so that normal
zoom lenses (10× or 15×) can be used.

Lighting Because the videotaping is scheduled for
11:30 A.M.–2:30 P.M., you should have sufficient light
throughout the videotaping. The sun is mostly in back
of the cameras, so there is no danger of getting the
sun into shots. Just make sure that camera 3 does not
get carried away, shooting from the back of the "stage"
toward the buildings and perhaps into the sun.

Audio Because the dancers dance to prerecorded
music, all you need is a good P.A. system. Instead of
the single P.A. speaker, you might set up two or three
speakers closer to the action. This allows you to keep

the volume down, while ensuring that the dancers can
hear the music throughout the action area, even if the
wind is blowing.

Intercommunications There are no special intercom
problems. You can assume that the floor manager has
his or her own intercom setup. If not, he or she can still
tie into one of the stationary cameras without much
difficulty. A floorperson (perhaps one of the camera 3
cable pullers) can take care of the slate.

Special Considerations You should be concerned about
pedestrian traffic along the walkway. Find out how people can get to the bookstore and the A/V Center without
having to walk in front of the cameras. You may need
to contact both the bookstore and the A/V Center to
put up notices about the telecast and the rerouting of
traffic. Make sure you contact the campus police about
the telecast and have them do the necessary pedes-

trian traffic control. If both facilities (bookstore and A/V Center) are to remain open during the telecast, the cables must be properly routed so that nobody trips over them.

Check on where the dancers can change or wait during the inevitable taping delays. Do not count on a sunny, warm day. Perhaps they can establish their temporary dressing rooms in the A/V Center. Ask the choreographer to have coats or blankets ready for the dancers. Although this may not be the television director's main concern, it shows that you know your business and, ultimately, keeps the dancers warm. Finally, keep an eye on the weather forecast.

Again, it should be pointed out that the preceding considerations represent the *minimal* preparation for a remote of this kind. Once you have gone through these, or similar, preparatory steps, compare your notes with the technical supervisor and/or T.D. of the remote.

MAIN POINTS

1. Many big remotes are devoted to the coverage of sports events. Networks typically use a great amount of equipment and personnel for the coverage of sports events, but good coverage is also possible with less equipment.

2. There are standard setups for most sports events, which can be embellished with more cameras and audio equipment.

3. Location sketches are a valuable preproduction aid for big remotes. For an indoor remote, they may show the general dimensions of a room or hallway; the location of windows, doors, furniture; and the principal action areas. Outdoor location sketches may show buildings, location of the remote truck, location of the power source, steep inclines or steps, the quality of the floor (smooth enough for dollying or not), and the location and/or direction of the main event.

4. A good location sketch can aid the director in deciding on major camera locations, focal lengths of zoom lenses, lighting and audio setups, and intercommunication systems.

FURTHER READING

Fuller, Barry J., Steve Kanaba, and Janyce Brisch-Kanaba. *Single Camera Video Production*. Englewood Cliffs, NJ: Prentice-Hall, Inc., 1982.

McQuillan, Lon B. *The Video Production Guide*. Santa Fe, NM: Video-Info Publications, 1983.

You are now in command of one of the most powerful means of communication and persuasion. Use it wisely and responsibly. Treat your audience with respect and compassion. Whatever role you play in the production process—pulling cables or directing a network show—you influence many people. Because they cannot communicate back to you very readily, they must—and do—trust your professional skills and judgment. Do not betray that trust.

Above-the-Line Production   A budgetary division of production elements. It concerns mainly nontechnical personnel.

A-B Rolling   A-B rolling in video production means that various shots on the A-roll and B-roll are edited together in postproduction. Preparation of a film for printing. All odd-numbered shots are put on one reel (A-roll), with black leader replacing the even shots. The even-numbered shots, with black leader replacing the odd shots, make up the B-roll. Both rolls are then printed together onto one film, thus eliminating splices.

AC   Alternating Current; electrical energy as supplied by normal wall outlets.

Acetate   Cellulose acetate, usually called cell: a transparent plastic sheet used in preparation of graphic material.

Actor   A person who appears on camera in dramatic roles. The actor always portrays someone else.

Additive Primary Colors   Red, blue, and green. Ordinary white light (sunlight) can be separated into the three primary light colors. When these three colored lights are combined in various proportions, all other colors can be reproduced.

Address   Also called birthmark. A specific location in a television recording, as specified by the time code.

Ad Lib   Speech or action that has not been scripted or specially rehearsed.

AFTRA   American Federation of Television and Radio Artists. A broadcasting talent union.

AGC   Automatic Gain Control. Regulates the volume of the audio or video levels automatically, without using pots.

Ambience   Background sounds.

Analog Sound Recording   Audio recording system in which the electrical sound signal fluctuates exactly like the original sound stimulus over its entire range.

Aperture   Diaphragm opening of a lens; usually measured in f-stops.

Arc   To move the camera in a slightly curved dolly or truck.

Aspect Ratio   The proportions of the television screen and therefore of all television pictures: three units high and four units wide. For HDTV: three by five.

Assemble Mode   The adding of shots on videotape in a consecutive order.

Audio   The sound portion of television and its production. Technically, the electronic reproduction of audible sound.

Audio-Follow-Video   A switcher that automatically changes the accompanying audio along with the video source.

Audio Synchronizer   Instrument that divides the audiotape into imaginary frames, corresponding with those of the videotape, to synchronize audio and video in videotape postproduction.

Audiotape Recorder (ATR)   See Reel-to-Reel.

Audio Track   The area of the videotape used for recording audio information.

Auto Key Tracking   Automatic change of image size and position of the chroma key insert.

Back Focus   The distance between zoom lens and camera pickup tube at which the picture is in focus at the extreme wide-angle zoom position. In monochrome cameras, the back focus can be adjusted by moving the pickup tube through the camera focus control.

Background Light   Also called set light. Illumination of the set pieces and backdrops.

Back Light   Illumination from behind the subject and opposite the camera.

Back-Timing   The process of figuring additional clock times by subtracting running times from the clock time at which the program ends.

Balance   1. Audio: a proper mixing of various sounds. 2. Video: relative structural stability of picture elements (objects or events). Balance can be stable (little pictorial tension), neutral (some tension), or unstable (high pictorial tension). Refers to the interrelationship between stability and tension in a picture.

Banding   Distortion of a videotaped picture caused by quad videotape recorders. Shows up as wide, differently colored bands horizontally dividing the picture.

Barn Doors   Metal flaps in front of lighting instruments that control the spread of the light beam.

Barrel Distortion   Effect, caused by wide-angle lens, that makes all vertical lines appear to be somewhat curved.

Base   See Baselight.

Baselight   Even, nondirectional (diffused) light necessary for the camera to operate optimally. Customary baselight levels for studio cameras are: for standard three-tube Plumbicon cameras, 150–250 ft-c (foot-candles); for one-tube color cameras, 75–200 ft-c; for vidicon tube cameras, 150–300 ft-c; for monochrome I-O cameras, 75–100 ft-c.

Base Station   Also called camera processing unit or CPU. Equipment, separate from the camera head, that is used with digitally controlled cameras to process signals coming from and going to the camera.

Batten   A horizontal metal pipe that supports lighting instruments in a studio.

Beam Splitter   Optical device within a color camera that splits the white light into the three primary colors: red, green, and blue.

Beeper   A series of eight low-frequency audio beeps, exactly one second apart, put at the beginning of each take for videotape cuing.

Below-the-Line Production   A budgetary division of production elements. Concerns technical personnel and facilities.

Bias Light   A small light that illuminates the front surface of the pickup tube to boost the video signal without undue increase in noise. Especially useful when the camera operates at low light levels.

Big Remote   A production outside the studio to televise live and/or record live-on-tape a large scheduled event that has not been staged specifically for television. Examples include sporting events, parades, political gatherings, or special hearings.

Black   Darkest part of the grayscale, with a reflectance of approximately 3 percent; called TV black. "To black" means to fade the television picture to black.

Blocking   Carefully worked out movement and actions by the talent, and movement of all mobile television equipment.

Blocking Rehearsal   See Dry Run.

Body Mount   Frame support worn by ENG camera operator to balance and distribute camera's weight.

Boom   Same as Crane.

Brightness   Attribute of color that determines how dark or light a color appears on the monochrome television screen, or how much light the color reflects.

Broad   A floodlight with a broadside, panlike reflector.

Bus (or Buss)   A row of buttons on the switcher. A common central circuit that receives from several sources or feeds to several separate destinations. A pair of buses is called a bank. See Mix Bus.

Bust Shot   Framing of a person from the upper torso to the top of the head.

Busy Picture   The picture, as it appears on the television screen, is too cluttered.

Cable Television   1. Distribution device for broadcast signals via coaxial or fiber-optic cable. 2. Production facility for programs distributed via cable.

Calibrate   To preset a camera to remain in focus throughout the zoom.

Cameo Lighting   Foreground figures are lighted with highly directional light, with the background remaining dark.

Camera   The general name for the camera head, which consists of the lens (or lenses), the main camera with the pickup tube(s) and the internal optical system, electronic accessories, and the viewfinder.

Camera Chain The television camera (head) and associated electronic equipment. For conventional cameras, this equipment includes the camera control unit, sync generator, and the power supply. In digitally controlled cameras, the equipment consists of the base station, or camera processing unit, and the remote control unit.

Camera Control Unit Also called CCU. Equipment, separate from the camera head, that contains various video controls, including registration, color balance, contrast, and brightness. With the CCU, the video operator adjusts the camera picture during the show.

Camera Graphics All graphic material prepared for a television camera. The video image is created by the television camera focused on the graphic material, such as a studio card or chart.

Camera Head The actual television camera, which is at the head of a chain of essential electronic accessories. In some ENG/EFP cameras, the camera head contains all the elements of the camera chain.

Camera Left and Right Directions given from the camera's point of view; opposite of "stage left" and "stage right," which are directions given from the actor's point of view (facing the audience or camera).

Camera Light Small spotlight, also called eye light or inky-dinky, mounted on the front of the camera; used as an additional fill light. (Frequently confused with Tally Light).

Camera Rehearsal A full rehearsal with cameras and other pieces of production equipment. Similar to the dress rehearsal in theater.

Camera Sled Camera mount, consisting of a high hat on a low-angle dolly, used for low-angle dramatic shots.

Cam Head A special camera mounting head that permits extremely smooth tilts and pans.

Canting Effect Visual effect in which the scene is put on a slight tilt through disturbance of the horizon line.

Cap 1. Lens cap; a rubber or metal cap placed in front of the lens to protect it from light or dust. 2. Electronic device that eliminates the picture from the camera pickup tube.

Cardioid The heart-shaped (cardioid) pickup pattern of a unidirectional microphone.

Cart See Cartridge.

Cartridge, or Tape Cartridge Also called cart for short. An audiotape recording or playback device that uses tape cartridges. A cartridge is a plastic case containing an endless tape loop that rewinds as it is played back.

Cascading Movement of signals when the T.D. combines several effects on a switcher and reenters the signal several times. The signals move from one bank to the next, picking up additional effects at each bank.

Cassette A video- or audiotape recording or playback device that uses tape cassettes. A cassette is a plastic case containing two reels, a supply reel and a takeup reel.

C-Clamp A metal clamp with which lighting instruments are attached to the lighting battens.

CCU See Camera Control Unit.

Cell See Acetate.

Character The person who appears in a play. Usually defined by clarifying and intensifying specific physiological traits (the way the person looks, moves, runs, behaves, dresses) and psychological traits (the way the person thinks, feels, plots, schemes, loves).

Character Generator A special effects generator that electronically produces a series of letters and numbers directly on the television screen or keyed into a background picture.

Charge-Coupled Device (CCD) Also called chip. The imaging device used in some color cameras instead of a camera pickup tube. Within the device, image sensing elements translate the optical image into a video signal. It has the advantage of small size but does not produce pictures equal in quality to those produced with pickup tubes.

Cheat To angle the performer or object toward a particular camera; not directly noticeable to the audience.

Chroma Key Special key effect that uses color (usually blue) for the background over which the keying occurs.

Chroma Key Card A studio card similar to a regular key card, except that the background for the white lettering is blue instead of black.

Chroma Key Drop A well-saturated blue canvas drop that can be pulled down from the lighting grid to the studio floor, or even over part of it, as a background for chroma key matting.

Chrominance Channel The color (chroma) channels within the color camera. A separate chrominance channel is responsible for each of the three primary color signals.

Clip To compress the white and/or black picture information, or prevent the video signal from interfering with the sync signals.

Clip Lights Small internal reflector bulbs that are clipped to pieces of scenery or furniture via a gator clip.

Clipper A knob on the switcher that selects the whitest portion of the video source, clipping out the darker shades.

The clipper produces high-contrasting blacks and whites for keying and matting.

Clock Time Also called schedule time. The time at which a program starts and ends.

Close-up Object or any part of it seen at close range and framed tightly. The close-up can be extreme (extreme or big close-up) or rather loose (medium close-up).

Closure Short for psychological closure. Mentally filling in spaces of an incomplete picture.

Clothing Regular clothes worn on camera, rather than a costume.

Color Bars A color standard used by the television industry for the alignment of cameras and videotape recordings.

Color Compatibility Color signals that can be perceived as black-and-white pictures on monochrome television sets. Generally used to mean that the color scheme has enough brightness contrast for monochrome reproduction with a good grayscale contrast.

Colorizing The creation of color patterns or color areas through a color generator (without a color camera).

Color Temperature Relative reddishness or bluishness of light, as measured in degrees Kelvin. The norm for indoor TV lighting is 3,200°K, for outdoors 5,600°K.

Comet-Tailing Occurs when the camera pickup tube is unable to process extremely bright highlights that are reflected off polished surfaces or bright lights in a very dark scene. The effect looks like red or blue flames tailing the bright object.

Complexity Editing The juxtaposition of shots that primarily, though not exclusively, help to intensify the screen event.

Condenser Microphone A microphone whose diaphragm consists of a condenser plate that vibrates with the sound pressure against another fixed condenser plate, called the backplate.

Contact A person, usually a public relations officer, who knows about an event and can assist the production team during a remote telecast.

Continuity Editing The preserving of visual continuity from shot to shot.

Contrast The difference between the brightest and the darkest spots in the picture (often measured by reflected light in foot-candles), expressed in a ratio. The maximum contrast ratio for color cameras is 30:1.

Control Room A room adjacent to the studio in which the director, the technical director, the audio engineer, and sometimes the lighting technician perform their various production functions.

Control Room Directing Simultaneous coordination of two or more cameras, the switcher, audio, and other production elements.

Control Track The area of the videotape used for recording the synchronization information (sync spikes), which is essential for videotape editing.

Convertible Camera A camera adaptable for studio or field—that is, either a studio camera that can be stripped down to be portable or an ENG/EFP camera that can accept certain accessories to become a studio camera.

Cookie (A short form of *cucalorus,* Greek for breaking up light, also spelled *kukaloris.*) Any cutout pattern that, when placed in front of a spotlight, produces a shadow pattern. The cookie, usually made from a thin, cutout metal sheet, is inserted into a pattern projector.

Costume Special clothes worn by an actor or actress to depict a certain character or period.

Crab Sideways motion of the camera crane dolly base.

Cradle Head Cradle-shaped camera mounting head. Permits smooth up-and-down tilts and horizontal pans.

Crane 1. Camera dolly that resembles an actual crane in both appearance and operation. The crane can lift the camera from close to the studio floor to over ten feet above it. 2. To move the boom of the camera crane up or down. Also called boom.

Crawl Graphics (usually credit copy) that move slowly up the screen; often mounted on a drum, or crawl. An up-and-down movement of credits is called a roll, and a horizontal movement is called a crawl.

Cross-Fade 1. Audio: a transition method whereby the preceding sound is faded out and the following sound faded in simultaneously. The sounds overlap temporarily. 2. Video: a transition method whereby the preceding picture is faded to black and the following picture is faded in from black.

Cross-Keying Key-lighting from both sides of the camera. The key lights from one side act as fill for the key lights from the other side.

Cube Flip Also called cube-spin. A visual effect in which various freeze frames appear to be glued on a cube.

Cue Signal to start, pace, or stop any type of production activity or talent action.

Cue Card A large, hand-lettered card that contains copy, usually held next to the camera lens by floor personnel.

Cue Track The area of the videotape used for such audio information as in-house identification or the SMPTE address code. Can also be used for a second audio track.

Cut 1. The instantaneous change from one shot (image) to another. 2. Director's signal to interrupt action (used during rehearsal).

Cutaway Shot A shot of an object or event that is peripherally connected with the overall event and that is neutral as to screen direction (usually straight-on shots). Used to intercut between two shots in which the screen direction is reversed.

Cut Bar A button or small metal bar that activates the mix buses alternately. The effect is cutting between two preset shots.

Cyc Cyclorama; a U-shaped continuous piece of canvas for backing of scenery and action.

DC Direct Current.

Debeaming The gradual reduction of scanning beam intensity. The picture becomes a high-contrast picture, with detail in the white and black areas no longer visible, gradually deteriorating into a nondistinct, light-gray screen.

Delegation Controls Buttons on a switcher that determine the function of the buses.

Demographic Factors Audience research factors concerned with such items as age, sex, marital status, and income.

Density 1. The number of events happening within a certain time unit. Visual density can be expressed as a multiple superimposition or key, or successively as a series of quick, montagelike cuts. Audio density may be a chord consisting of many notes or a rapid series of many notes, or the simultaneous playing of several audio tracks. 2. The degree of complexity in the vertical (depth) development of an event.

Depth of Field The area in which all objects, located at different distances from the camera, appear in focus. Depth of field is dependent upon focal length of the lens, *f*-stop, and distance between object and camera.

Depth Staging Arrangement of objects on the television screen so that foreground, middleground, and background are clearly defined.

Diaphragm 1. Audio: the vibrating element inside a microphone that moves with the air pressure from the sound. 2. Video: adjustable lens-opening mechanism that controls the amount of light passing through a lens.

Dichroic Mirror A mirrorlike color filter that singles out, from the white light, the red light (red dichroic filter) and the blue light (blue dichroic filter), with the green light left over.

Diffused Light Light that illuminates a relatively large area with an indistinct light beam. Diffused light, created by floodlights, produces soft shadows.

Diffusion Filter Lens attachment that gives the scene a soft, slightly out-of-focus look.

Digitally Controlled Camera A camera that uses microprocessors primarily to automate the alignment of the camera and ensure optimal performance under a variety of production conditions.

Digital Sound Recording Audio recording system that translates original sound stimuli into many computer-type, on-off pulses. Compared to analog sound recording, this system has a better signal-to-noise ratio.

Digital Still Store System Also called electronic still store system, or ESS. An electronic device that can grab a single frame from any video source and store it in digital form on a disk.

Digital Video Effects Also called DVE. Visual effects produced by devices that change normal (analog) video signals into digital (numerical) information.

Digital VTR A videotape recorder that receives digital, rather than analog, information. The signals can be more easily manipulated for video enhancement and special effects.

Dimmer A device that controls the intensity of the light by throttling the electric current flowing to the lamp.

Directional Light Light that illuminates a relatively small area with a distinct light beam. Directional light, produced by spotlights, creates harsh, clearly defined shadows.

Dissolve A gradual transition from shot to shot, in which the two images temporarily overlap. Also called lap-dissolve, or lap.

Distortion 1. Optical: near objects look large, far objects look comparatively small; achieved with wide-angle lenses. 2. Audio: unnatural alteration or deterioration of sound.

Dolly 1. Camera support that enables the camera to move in all directions. 2. To move the camera toward (dolly in) or away from (dolly out or back) the object.

Double Headset A telephone headset (earphones) that carries program sound in one earphone and the P.L. information in the other. Also called split intercom.

Double-Muff Headset Special earphones used when working close to a high-volume sound source, such as a rock band, to keep out environmental sounds.

Double Reentry A complex switcher through which an effect can be fed back into the mix section, or the mix output into the effects section, for further effects manipulation.

Double System The simultaneous recording of pictures and sound on two separate recording devices: the pictures on film or videotape and the sound on audiotape recorder.

Downlink The antenna (dish) that receives the signals coming from the satellite.

Downstream Keyer Switcher control that permits the T.D. to key a title or other graphics over the signal at the line-out, as the signal leaves the switcher.

Drag Degree of friction needed in the camera mounting to allow smooth panning and tilting.

Dress 1. What people wear on camera. 2. Dress Rehearsal: final rehearsal with all facilities operating. The dress rehearsal is often videotaped. 3. Set Dressing: set properties.

Drop Large, painted piece of canvas used for scenery backing.

Drop Lines Section of cable television distribution system that connects individual homes.

Dropout Loss of part of the video signal, which shows up on the screen as white glitches. Caused by uneven videotape iron-oxide coating (bad tape quality or overuse) or dirt.

Dropout Compensator An electronic device that detects dropout (partial loss of the video signal) and substitutes for missing information the information from the preceding scanning line. Usually part of the more sophisticated videotape recorders.

Dry Run A rehearsal without equipment during which the basic actions of the talent are worked out. Also called blocking rehearsal.

Dual-Redundancy The use of two identical microphones for the pickup of a sound source, whereby only one of them is turned on at any given time. A safety device that permits switching over to the second microphone in case the active one becomes defective.

Dub The duplication of an electronic recording. Dubs can be made from tape to tape, or from record to tape. The dub is always one generation away from the recording used for dubbing.

Dubbing Down The dubbing (transfer) of picture and sound information from a larger videotape format to a smaller one.

Dubbing Up The dubbing (transfer) of picture and sound information from a smaller videotape format to a larger one.

Dynamic Microphone A microphone whose sound-pickup device consists of a diaphragm that is attached to a movable coil. As the diaphragm vibrates with the air pressure from the sound, the coil moves within a magnetic field, generating an electric current.

Echo Effect Visual effect in which the same image is repeated as though it were placed between two opposite mirrors.

Ecological Factors Audience research factors concerned with where the members of the audience live, such as city, suburb, country, and so forth.

Editing The selection and assembly of shots in a logical sequence.

Editing Log Also called editing shot sheet. A list compiled by the editor during paper-and-pencil editing. It includes the reel and scene numbers, exact addresses of in- and out-cues for each shot, the in- and out-sound cues, and prominent ambient sounds.

Effects Bus Rows of buttons that can generate a number of electronic effects, such as keys, wipes, and mattes.

Effect-to-Cause Approach A production approach, or a system, that starts with the definition of the viewer experience and works backward to the production elements the medium requires in order to produce such a viewer experience.

EFP Electronic Field Production. Television production activity outside the studio usually shot for postproduction (not live).

EIAJ Abbreviation for Electronic Industries Association of Japan. Established the EIAJ Type No. 1 Standard for $\frac{1}{2}$-inch helical scan videotape recorders. In general, the standard assures that any monochrome tape recorded on one such recorder can be played back on any other monochrome or color recorder, and any color tape can be played back on any other color VTR, provided that they meet the EIAJ Type 1 Standard.

Electron Gun Produces the electron (scanning) beam.

Electronic A-B Rolling 1. The editing of a master tape from two playback machines, one containing the A-roll and the other the B-roll. By routing the A and B playback machines through a switcher, a variety of transition effects can be achieved for the final master tape. 2. The projection of an SOF film on one film chain (A-roll), with the silent film projected from the other island (B-roll). The films can be mixed through the switcher.

Electronic Editing The joining of two shots on videotape without cutting the tape.

Ellipsoidal Spotlight Spotlight producing a very defined beam, which can be shaped further by metal shutters.

ENG Electronic News Gathering. The use of portable cameras, videotape recorders, lights, and sound equipment for the production of daily news stories and short documentaries. ENG is usually done for immediate postproduction, but the pictures and sound can also be transmitted live from the field.

ENG/EFP Cameras Electronic news gathering or electronic field production cameras. Replacing the film camera for news reporting, these television cameras are portable, self-contained, and largely automated.

Environment   Where the action of a television drama takes place. In general, television drama emphasizes inner rather than outer environment.

Equalization   1. Audio: controlling the audio signal by emphasizing certain frequencies and eliminating others. Equalization can be accomplished through an equalizer manually or automatically. 2. Video: controlling the video signal by emphasizing certain frequencies and eliminating others.

Essential Area   The section of the television picture, centered within the scanning area, that is seen by the home viewer, regardless of masking of the set or slight misalignment of the receiver. Sometimes called critical area.

External Key   The cutout portion of the base picture is filled by the signal from an external source, such as a third camera (with the first camera providing the base picture, the second camera the key signal).

External Optical System   The television lens and certain attachments to it.

Fact Sheet   Also called rundown sheet. Lists the items to be shown on camera and the key ideas that should be expressed verbally by the performer. Serves often as a guide to a show format.

Fade   The gradual appearance of a picture from black (fade-in) or disappearance to black (fade-out).

Fader, or Slide-Fader   A sound-volume control that works by means of a button sliding vertically or horizontally along a specific scale. Similar to pot.

Fader Bars   A pair of levers on the switcher that can produce dissolves, fades, and wipes of different speeds, and superimpositions.

Falloff   The speed (degree) with which a light picture portion turns into shadow areas. Fast falloff means that the light areas turn abruptly into shadow areas. Slow falloff indicates a very gradual change from light to dark.

Fast Lens   A lens that permits a relatively great amount of light to pass through (low *f*-stop number). Can be used in low lighting conditions.

FAX   Facilities request form.

Feed   Signal transmission from one program source to another, such as a network feed or a remote feed.

Feedback   Audio: piercing squeal from the loudspeaker, caused by the accidental reentry of the loudspeaker sound into the microphone and subsequent overamplification of sound. 2. Video: wild streaks and flashes on the monitor screen caused by reentry of a video signal into the switcher and subsequent overamplification. 3. Communication: reaction of the receiver of a communication back to the communication source.

Feeder Lines   Section of cable television distribution system that brings the signal to various parts of a city.

Fiber-Optic Cable   Thin, transparent fibers of glass or plastic used to transfer light from one point to another. When used in broadcast signal transmission, the electrical video and audio signals are transduced into light impulses at the transmitting end, and back to electrical signals at the receiving end. Advantages include immunity to electrical interference, thinness and light weight, and large two-way channel capacity.

Field   One-half a complete scanning cycle, with two fields necessary for one television picture frame. There are 60 fields per second, or 30 frames per second.

Field of View   The portion of a scene visible through a particular lens; its vista.

Fill Light   Additional light on the opposite side of the camera from the key light to illuminate shadow areas and thereby reduce falloff. Usually accomplished by floodlights.

Film Chain   Also called film island, or telecine. Consists of one or two film projectors, a slide projector, a multiplexer, and a television film, or telecine, camera.

Film-Style Directing   Directing separate takes for postproduction, not necessarily in show sequence.

Fishpole   A suspension device for a microphone; the microphone is attached to a pole and held over the scene for brief periods.

Flag   A thin, rectangular sheet of metal or plastic used to block light from falling on specific areas.

Flare   Dark, or colored, flashes caused by signal overload through extreme light reflections off polished objects or very bright lights.

Flat   1. Even, not contrasting; usually refers to lighting. Flat lighting is highly diffused lighting with soft shadows. 2. A piece of standing scenery used as a background or to simulate the walls of a room.

Flat Response   Measure of a microphone's ability to hear equally well over the entire frequency range.

Flip   Reversal of the video image. Accomplished on monochrome equipment with electronic sweep reversal and on color with DVE equipment.

Flip-Flop Control   Switcher mechanism that gives the T. D. the option of cutting between two cameras with a single button, called the cut bar.

Floodlight   Lighting instrument that produces diffused light.

Floor Plan   A plan of the studio floor, showing the walls, the main doors, and the location of the control room, with the lighting grid or batten pattern superimposed over the floor plan. More commonly, a diagram of scenery and properties in relation to the studio floor plan.

Fluid Head   Most popular mounting head for light-weight ENG/EFP cameras. Because its moving parts operate in a heavy fluid, it allows very smooth pans and tilts.

Focal Length   The distance from the optical center of the lens to the front surface of the camera pickup tube with the lens set at infinity. Focal lengths are measured in millimeters or inches. Short-focal-length lenses have a wide angle of view (wide vista); long-focal-length (tele-photo) lenses have a narrow angle of view (closeup). In a variable-focal-length lens (zoom lens) the focal length can be changed continuously from wide angle to narrow angle and vice versa. A fixed-focal-length lens has a single designated focal length only.

Focus   A picture is in focus when it appears sharp and clear on the screen (technically, the point where the light rays refracted by the lens converge).

Focus Control Unit   Control that activates the focus mechanism in a zoom lens.

Follow Focus   Controlling the focus of the lens so that the image of an object is continuously kept sharp and clear, regardless of whether camera and/or object move.

Follow Spot   A large, high-powered spotlight that can reduce its light beam from a rather large circle to a small "spot." Used primarily to follow a specific action on stage.

Foot-Candle   The unit of measurement of illumination, or the amount of light that falls on an object.

Format   Type of television script indicating the major programming steps; generally contains a fully scripted show opening and closing.

Foundation   A makeup base, upon which further makeup is applied, such as rouge or eye shadow.

Frame   1. The smallest picture unit in film, a single picture. 2. A complete scanning cycle of the electron beam, which occurs every $\frac{1}{30}$ second. It represents the smallest complete television picture unit.

Frame-Store Synchronizer   Image stabilization and synchronization system that has a memory large enough to store and read out one complete video frame. Used to synchronize signals from a variety of video sources that are not genlocked.

Freeze Frame   Arrested motion, which is perceived as a still shot.

Frequency Response   Measure of the range of frequencies a microphone can hear and reproduce.

Fresnel Spotlight   One of the most common spotlights, named after the inventor of its lens, which has steplike concentric rings.

Friction Head   Camera mounting head that counter-balances the camera weight by a strong spring. Good only for relatively light cameras.

Front Focus   The proper relationship of the front elements of the zoom lens to ensure focus during the entire zoom range. Front focus is set at the extreme closeup position with the zoom focus control. Color cameras have a front-focus adjustment only because the pickup tubes cannot be moved.

Front-Timing   The process of figuring out clock times by adding given running times to the clock time at which the program starts.

***f*-stop**   The calibration on the lens indicating the aperture, or diaphragm opening (and therefore the amount of light transmitted through the lens). The larger the *f*-stop number, the smaller the aperture; the smaller the *f*-stop number, the larger the aperture.

Full Track   An audiotape recorder, or recording, that uses the full width of the tape for recording an audio signal.

Fully Scripted   Used to describe a show for which the dialogue is completely written out and detailed video and audio instructions are given.

Gaffer Grip   A strong clamp used to attach small lighting instruments to pieces of scenery, furniture, doors, and other set pieces. Sometimes called gator clip.

Gain   Level of signal amplification for video and audio signal. "Riding gain" is used in audio, meaning to keep the sound volume at a proper level.

Gator Clip   Same as Gaffer Grip.

Gel   Generic name for color filter put in front of spotlights or floodlights to give the light beam a specific hue. "Gel" comes from "gelatin," the filter material used before the invention of much more heat- and moisture-resistant plastics.

Generated Graphics   Graphic material that is electronically generated and used directly on the air or stored for later retrieval.

Generating Element   The major part of a microphone. It converts sound waves into electrical energy.

Generation   The number of dubs away from the master tape. A first-generation dub is struck directly from the master tape. A second-generation tape is a dub of the first-generation dub (two steps away from the master tape), and so forth. The greater the number of nondigital generations, the greater the quality loss.

Genlock   1. Locking the synchronization generators from two different origination sources, such as remote and studio. Allows switching from source to source without picture rolling. 2. Locking the house sync with the sync signal from another source (such as a videotape). The videotape can then be intermixed with live studio cameras, for example.

Giraffe Also called tripod boom. A medium-sized microphone boom that can be operated by one person.

Gobo A scenic foreground piece through which the camera can shoot, thus integrating the decorative foreground with the background action. In film, a gobo is an opaque shield that is used for partial blocking of a light.

Graphic Mass Any picture element that is perceived as occupying an area within the frame and as relatively heavy or light.

Graphics All two-dimensional visuals prepared for the television screen, such as title cards, charts, and graphs. (See Generated Graphics.)

Graphics Generator Also called video art system. Device that allows designers to "draw" images directly on the screen electronically.

Grayscale A scale indicating intermediate steps from TV black to TV white. Maximum range: ten grayscale steps; good: seven steps; poor: five steps.

Half-Track An audiotape recorder, or recording, that uses one-half the width of the tape for an audio signal on one pass, and the other half on the reverse pass.

Halo Dark or colored flare around a very bright light source or a highly reflecting object. Same as flare.

Hand Props Objects, called properties, that are handled by the performer.

Hard Copy A computer printout showing in typewritten form all editing decisions of the completed helical scan workprint or the master tape. (Soft-copy information appears only on the computer screen.)

Head Assembly 1. Audio head assembly: a small electromagnet that (a) erases the signal from the tape (erase head); (b) puts the signals on the audiotape (recording head); and (c) reads (induces) them off the tape (playback head). 2. Video head assembly: a small electromagnet that puts electric signals on the videotape or reads (induces) the signals off the tape. Video heads are usually in motion.

Head End Section of cable television distribution system where signals are collected or originated.

Headroom The space left between the top of the head and the upper screen edge.

Helical Scan, or Helical VTR A videotape recording of a videotape recorder in which the video signal is put on tape in a slanted, diagonal way (contrary to transverse scanning, which goes across the tape). Since the tape wraps around the head drum in a spirallike configuration, it is called helical (from helix, spiral). Also called slant-track.

High-Band Refers to the frequency of the video information. High-band videotape recorders operate on a high-frequency range (10 megacycles), which provides operationally higher quality pictures with less video noise and better resolution than low-band recordings. Most high-quality color machines are high-band.

High Definition Television (HDTV) The use of special cameras and recording equipment for the production of high-quality pictures. The pictures have a higher resolution (show smaller detail more clearly) than regular television pictures.

High Hat Cylinder-shaped camera mount that can be bolted to scenery or a dolly to permit panning and tilting of the camera without tripod or pedestal.

High Key High-intensity overall illumination. Background is generally light.

High-Z High impedance.

HMI Light HMI stands for Halogen-Metal-Iodide lamp. An extremely efficient, high-intensity light that burns at 5,600°K—the outdoor illumination norm. It needs an additional piece of equipment, a ballast, to operate properly.

Horizontal Plane Lines parallel to the horizon in a picture. Should be kept level unless a special effect is intended.

Hot 1. A current or signal-carrying wire. 2. Instruments that are turned on, such as a hot camera or a hot microphone.

Hot Editing Method of assembling shots when producing a completely edited tape during production. The editor stops the videotape from time to time to correct mistakes or to change the set or costumes and proceeds by editing the next take directly onto the existing master tape.

Hot Spot Undesirable concentration of light in one spot; especially noticeable in the middle of a rear screen projection.

House Number The in-house system of identification; each piece of recorded program must be identified by a certain code number. This is called the house number, since the numbers differ from station to station (house to house).

Hue One of the three basic color attributes, hue is the color itself—red, green, blue, yellow, and so on.

IBEW International Brotherhood of Electrical Workers. Union for studio and master control engineers; may include floor personnel.

I.F.B. Interrupted feedback system. A small earpiece worn by the on-the-air talent that carries program sound or the instructions from director or producer.

Image Orthicon, or I/O   A specific type of pickup tube used in some monochrome cameras.

Impedance   A type of resistance to the signal flow. Important especially in matching high- or low-impedance microphones with high- or low-impedance recorders. Also, a high impedance mic works properly only with a relatively short cable (a longer cable has too much resistance), whereas a low-impedance mic can take up to several hundred feet of cable. Impedance is also expressed in high-Z or low-Z.

Impedance Transformers   Device allowing a high-impedance mic to feed a low-impedance recorder, or vice versa.

Incandescent Light   The light produced by the hot tungsten filament of ordinary glass-globe light bulbs (in contrast to fluorescent light).

Incident Light   Light that strikes the object directly from its source. Incident light reading is the measure of light (in foot-candles) from the object to the light source. The foot-candle meter is pointed directly into the light source or the camera.

Input Overload Distortion   A distortion caused by a microphone when subjected to an exceptionally high-volume sound. Condenser microphones are especially prone to this kind of distortion.

Insert Mode   The inserting of shots in an already existing recording, without affecting the shots on either side.

Instantaneous Editing   Same as Switching.

Instant Replay   Repeating for the viewer, often in slow motion, a key play or other important event, immediately after its live occurrence.

Intercom   Abbreviation for intercommunication system for all production and engineering personnel involved in the production of a show. The most widely used system has telephone headsets to facilitate voice communication on several wired or wireless channels.

Internal Key   The cutout portion of the base picture is filled with the signal that is doing the cutting.

Internal Optical System   The series of mirrors and filters or prisms and filters inside a color camera that processes the three primary light colors.

In-the-Can   Finished television recording, either on film or videotape; the show is now "preserved" and can be rebroadcast at any time.

Inverse Square Law   The intensity of light falls off as $\frac{1}{distance^2}$ from the source. Valid only for light sources that radiate light uniformly in all directions, but not for light whose beam is partially columnated (focused), such as from a Fresnel or ellipsoidal spot.

Ips   An abbreviation for inches-per-second, indicating tape speed.

Iris   Same as lens diaphragm. Adjustable lens-opening mechanism.

Isolated Camera   Also called iso camera. A camera used for instant replay action or for postproduction videotapes.

Jack   A socket or phone-plug receptacle (female).

Jogging   Frame-by-frame advancement of videotape with a VTR.

Joystick Positioner   Switcher control that allows the I.D. to move wipe patterns about the screen.

Jump Cut   1. Cutting between shots that are identical in subject yet slightly different in screen location. Through the cut, the subject seems to jump from one screen location to another for no apparent reason. 2. Any abrupt transition between shots that violates the established continuity.

Kelvin Degrees   The standard scale for measuring color temperature, or the relative reddishness or bluishness contained in white light.

Key   1. Key light: principal source of illumination. 2. Lighting: high- or low-key lighting. 3. An electronic effect. Keying means the cutting in of an image (usually lettering) into a background image.

Key Card   Also called super card. A studio card with white lettering on a black background, used for superimposition of a title, or for keying of a title over a background scene. For chroma keying, the white letters are on a chroma-key blue background.

Key Level Control   Also called clip control. Regulator on switcher that prevents title letters from tearing during a key.

Kicker   Kicker light, usually directional light coming from the side and back of the subject.

Knee Shot   Framing of a person from the knees up.

Lag   Smear that follows a moving object or motion of the camera across a stationary object. It occurs especially with color cameras and monochrome vidicon cameras under low light levels.

Lavaliere   An extremely small microphone that can be clipped onto a jacket, a tie, a blouse, or other piece of clothing. A larger model is suspended from a neck cord and worn in front of the chest. Also called neck or chest mic.

Leader Numbers   Numerals used for the accurate cuing of the videotape and film during playback. The numbers from 10 to 3 flash at 1-second intervals and are synchronized with short audio beeps.

Lens Optical lens, essential for projecting an optical (light) image of the scene onto the film or the front surface of the camera pickup tube or tubes; lenses come in various fixed focal lengths or in a variable focal length (zoom lenses), and with various maximum apertures (lens openings).

Lens Format A somewhat loose term for the grouping of lenses that have focal lengths appropriate to a particular size of camera pickup tube. Hence, we have lenses that fit the 1-inch, $\frac{2}{3}$-inch, and the $\frac{1}{2}$-inch pickup tube formats.

Lens Prism A prism that, when attached to the camera lens, will produce special effects, such as the tilting of the horizon line, or the creation of multiple images.

Lens Turret Round plate in front of a camera holding up to five lenses, each of which can be rotated into shooting position.

Level 1. Audio: sound volume. 2. Video: signal strength (amplitude) measured in volts.

Libel Written defamation.

Light Angle The vertical angle of the suspended lighting instrument. A 45-degree angle is considered normal.

Lighting Triangle Same as Photographic Principle: the triangular arrangement of key, back, and fill lights. Also called triangle lighting.

Light Level Light intensity measured in foot-candles.

Light Plot A plan, similar to a floor plan, that shows the type, size (wattage), and location of the lighting instruments relative to the scene to be illuminated and the general direction of the beams.

Light Ratio The relative intensities of key, back, and fill. A 1:1 ratio between key and back lights means that both light sources burn with equal intensities. A 1:$\frac{1}{2}$ ratio between key and fill lights means that the fill light burns with half the intensity of the key light. Because light ratios depend on many production variables, they cannot be fixed. A key:back:fill ratio of 1:1:$\frac{1}{2}$ is often used for normal triangle lighting.

Limbo Any set area used for shooting small commercial displays, card easels, and the like, having a plain, light background.

Line Monitor Also called master monitor. The monitor that shows only the line-out pictures, the pictures that go on the air or on videotape.

Line-out The line that carries the final video or audio output.

Lip-Sync Synchronization of sound and lip movement.

Location Sketch A rough, hand-drawn map of the locale of a remote telecast. For an indoor remote the sketch shows the dimensions of the room and the location of furniture and windows. For an outdoor remote the sketch indicates the buildings and the location of the remote truck, power source, and the sun during the time of the telecast.

Location Survey Written assessment, usually in the form of a checklist, of the production requirements for a remote.

Lockup Time The time required by a videotape recorder for the picture and sound to stabilize once the tape has been started.

Log The major operational document. Issued daily, the log carries such information as program source or origin, scheduled program time, program duration, video and audio information, code identification (house number, for example), the title of the program, the program type, and additional special information.

Logo A visual symbol that identifies a specific organization such as a television station or network.

Longitudinal Video Recording (LVR) System A video recorder that records multiple parallel tracks longitudinally along a tape. More than 200 video heads stacked on top of each other produce video tracks on a $\frac{1}{4}$-inch tape.

Long Shot Object seen from far away or framed very loosely. The extreme long shot shows the object from a great distance.

Low-Angle Dolly Dolly used with high hat to make a camera mount for particularly low shots.

Low-Band Refers to the frequency of the video information. Low-band recorders operate in a relatively low-frequency range, which suffices for monochrome pictures but introduces excessive video noise in color.

Low Key Low-intensity overall, yet selective illumination. Background is generally dark.

Luminance Channel A separate channel within color cameras that deals with brightness variations and allows color cameras to produce a signal receivable on a black-and-white television. The luminance signal may be taken out of the green channel or electronically combined from the three chrominance signals.

Macro Position Position on zoom lens that allows it to be focused at very close distances from the object. Used for closeups of small objects.

Magnetic Bubble Memory (MBM) A video recording system that stores large amounts of digital information on small chips. It allows ready access to any part of the information and eliminates problems of tape wear, clogging of heads, or sync errors.

Magnetic Sound Track A narrow magnetic tape that runs down one side of the film. It operates exactly like a normal audiotape. Sometimes a second stripe runs along the opposite side of the film in order to achieve the same thickness for both film edges.

Mag Track   See Magnetic Sound Track.

Makeup   1. Facial makeup: used to enhance, correct, or change facial features. 2. Film makeup: combining several films on one big reel.

Master Control   Nerve center for all telecasts. Controls the program input, storage, and retrieval for on-the-air telecasts. Also oversees technical quality of all program material.

Master Monitor   Same as line monitor. Shows only the line-out pictures, those that go on the air or videotape.

Master VTR   A videotape recorder that supplies the original program material for dubbing by the "slave" VTR(s). Same as Record VTR.

Matte Key   Keyed (electronically cut-in) title whose letters are filled with shades of gray or a specific color.

Medium Shot   Object seen from a medium distance. Covers any framing between long shot and close-up.

Microphone   Also called mic. A small, portable assembly for the pickup and conversion of sound into electrical energy.

Microprocessors   Small digital computers used in color cameras to set up and maintain a camera's optimal performance under a variety of production conditions.

Microwave Relay   A transmission method from the remote location to the transmitter involving the use of several microwave units.

Minimum Object Distance   Point at which the camera is about as close as it can get and still focus on the object.

Mix Bus (or Buss)   1. A mixing channel for audio signals. The mix bus combines sounds from several sources to produce a mixed sound signal. 2. Rows of buttons that permit the mixing of video sources, as in a dissolve and super. Major buses for on-the-air switching.

Mix-Down   Final combination of sound tracks on a single or stereo track.

Mixing   1. Audio: the combining of two or more sounds in specific proportions (volume variations) as determined by the event (show) context. 2. Video: the combining of various shots via the switcher.

Mix-Minus   Type of multiple audio feed missing the part that is being recorded, such as an orchestra feed with the solo instrument being recorded.

mm   Millimeter, one-thousandth of a meter. 25.4 mm = 1 inch.

Moiré Effect   Color vibrations that occur when narrow, contrasting stripes of a design interfere with the scanning lines of the television system.

Monitor   1. Audio: speaker that carries the program sound independent of the line-out. 2. Video: high-quality television receiver used in the television studio and control rooms. Cannot receive broadcast signals.

Monochrome   One color. In television it refers to a camera or monitor that reacts only to various degrees of brightness and produces a black-and-white picture.

Montage   The juxtaposition of two often seemingly unrelated shots in order to generate a third overall idea, which may not be contained in either of the two.

Mosaic   Visual effect in which an image is broken down into many equal-sized squares of limited brightness and color.

Multiple-Microphone Interference   The canceling out of certain sound frequencies when two identical microphones close together are used for the same sound source.

Multiplexer   A system of mirrors or prisms that directs images from several projection sources (film, slides) into one stationary television film, or telecine, camera.

Multiplexing   1. A method of transmitting video and audio signals on the same carrier wave. 2. The transmitting of separate color signals on the same channel without mixing. 3. The transmitting of two separate audio signals on the same carrier wave for stereo broadcasts.

NAB   National Association of Broadcasters.

NABET   National Association of Broadcast Employees and Technicians. Union for studio and master control engineers; may include floor personnel.

Narrow-Angle Lens   Same as long-focal-length lens. Gives a narrow vista of a scene.

Natural Cutoff Lines   Imaginary lines formed by a photographed person's eyes, mouth, chin, waist, hemline, or knees. These lines should not coincide with the screen edge.

Neutral Density Filter (ND)   A filter that reduces the incoming light without distorting the color of the scene.

Noise   1. Audio: unwanted sounds that interfere with the intentional sounds; or unwanted hisses or hums inevitably generated by the electronics of the audio equipment. 2. Video: electronic interference that shows up as "snow."

Nonsymmetrical Division   Framing a picture so that distinct vertical objects are off to one side, rather than in the center, or so that the horizon is at the one-third or two-thirds mark, rather than in the middle.

Normal Lens   A lens with a focal length that will

approximate the spatial relationships of normal vision when used with a particular film or pickup tube format.

Noseroom The space left in front of a person looking toward the edge of the screen. Also called leadroom.

Objective Time Also called clock time. The time we measure by the clock.

Off-Line Editing process for producing videotape workprints (not intended for air use). The workprint information is then fed into the on-line system for (automated) production of the release master tape.

Omnidirectional A type of pickup pattern in which the microphone can pick up sounds equally well from all directions.

On-Line A master editing system, using high-quality videotape recorders for high-band release master tapes.

Open Set A set constructed of noncontinuous scenery, with large open spaces between the main groupings.

Operating Light Level Amount of light needed by the camera to produce a video signal. Most color cameras need from 100 to 250 foot-candles of illumination for optimal performance.

Optical Sound Track Variations of black and white patterns, photographed on the film and converted into electrical impulses by an exciter lamp and a photoelectric cell.

Oscilloscope Electronic measuring device showing certain electronic patterns on a small screen.

Over-the-Shoulder Shot Camera looks over a person's shoulder (shoulder and back of head included in shot) at another person.

P.A. Public Address loudspeaker system. Same as studio talkback.

Pace Perceived duration of the show or show segment. Part of subjective time.

Pan Horizontal turning of the camera.

Pancake A makeup base, or foundation makeup, usually water-soluble and applied with a small sponge.

Pan Stick A foundation makeup with a grease base. Used to cover a beard shadow or prominent skin blemish.

Pantograph Expandable hanging device for lighting instruments.

Paper and Pencil Editing The process of examining various shots and logging every editing decision on an editing log or editing shot sheet.

Patchboard Also called patchbay. A device that connects various inputs with specific outputs.

Pattern Projector An ellipsoidal spotlight with a cookie (cucalorus) insert, which projects the cookie's pattern as shadow.

Peak Program Meter Also called PPM. Meter in audio console to measure loudness. Especially sensitive to volume peaks, it indicates overmodulation.

Pedestal 1. Heavy camera dolly that permits a raising and lowering of the camera while on the air. 2. To move the camera up and down via studio pedestal. 3. The black level of a television picture. Can be adjusted against a standard on the oscilloscope.

Perambulator Boom Also called big boom. Special mount for a studio microphone. An extension device, or boom, is mounted on a dolly, called a perambulator, that permits rapid relocation anywhere in the studio.

Percipient The television viewer in the act of perceiving television audio and video stimuli (a television program). Implies a certain degree of involvement in watching a television program.

Performer A person who appears on camera in nondramatic shows. The performer plays himself or herself and does not assume someone else's character.

Periaktos A triangular piece of scenery that can be turned on a swivel base.

Perspective 1. Sound perspective: far sound must go with far picture, close sound with close picture. 2. All lines converging in one point.

Photographic Lighting Principle The triangular arrangement of key, back, and fill lights, with the back light opposite the camera and directly behind the object, and the key and fill lights on opposite sides of the camera and to the front and side of the object. Also called triangle lighting.

Pickup Sound reception by a microphone.

Pickup Pattern The territory around the microphone within which the microphone can hear well, that is, has optimal sound pickup.

Pickup Tube, or Camera Tube The main camera tube that converts light energy into electrical energy, the video signal.

Picturization Same as Sequencing.

Pixel Small silicon sensing devices arranged in a mosaiclike pattern for the light-sensitive imaging area of a CCD (Charge-Coupled Device) holding an electric charge.

P.L. Abbreviation for Private Line, or Phone Line. Major intercommunication device in television production.

Playback The playing back on a monitor or television receiver of videotape-recorded material through a videotape recorder (in the playback mode).

Plot   How the story develops from one event to the next.

Polarity Reversal   The reversal of the grayscale; the white areas in the picture become black and the black areas white, as the film negative is to the print.

Polar Pattern   The two-dimensional representation of a microphone pickup pattern.

Pop Filter   A bulblike attachment (either permanent or detachable) to the front of the microphone that filters out sudden air blasts, such as plosive consonants (*p*'s, *t*'s, *k*'s) delivered directly into the mic.

Ports   1. Slots in the microphone that help to achieve a specific pickup pattern and frequency response. 2. Holes in a multiplexer for various video sources.

Posterization   Also called solarization. Visual effect that reduces the various brightness values to only a few (usually three or four) and gives the image a flat, posterlike look.

Postproduction   Any production activity that occurs after the production. Usually refers either to editing of film or videotape or to postscoring and mixing sound for later addition to the picture portion.

Postproduction Editing   The assembly of recorded material after the actual production.

Pot   Abbreviation for potentiometer, a sound-volume control.

Preamp   Abbreviation for preamplifier. Weak electrical signals produced by a microphone or camera pickup tube must be strengthened by a preamplifier before they can be further processed (manipulated) and amplified to normal signal strength.

Preroll   To start a videotape and let it roll for a few seconds before it is put in the playback or record mode in order to give the electronic system time to stabilize.

Preset Board   A program device into which several lighting setups (scenes) can be stored, and from which they can be retrieved, when needed.

Preset Monitor   Also called PST monitor. Special preview monitor used by technical director for checking and adjusting special effects.

Pressure Zone Microphone (PZM)   Microphone mounted on a reflecting surface to build up a pressure zone at which all the sound waves reach the microphone at the same time. Ideal for group discussions and audience reaction.

Preview Bus   Rows of buttons that can direct an input to the preview monitor at the same time another video source is on the air.

Preview Monitor   1. Any monitor that shows a video source, except for the line (master) and off-the-air monitors. 2. A monitor that shows the director the picture he or she intends to use as the next shot.

Prism Block   Compact internal optical system of prisms and filters that separate white light into the three primary colors.

Process Message   The interaction between the percipient and the audiovisual stimuli of the television program.

Process Shot   Photographing foreground objects against a usually moving background projection.

Producer   Creator and organizer of television shows; usually in charge of all financial matters.

Production Switcher   Switcher located in the studio control room or remote van.

Program Bus   Also called direct bus. The bus on a switcher whose inputs are directly switched to the line-out.

Program Speaker   Also called audio monitor. A loudspeaker in the control room that carries the program sound. Its volume can be controlled without affecting the actual line-out program feed.

Props   Properties: furniture and other objects used for set decorations and by actors or performers.

Pulse-Count System   A type of address code system used to identify exact location on the videotape. It counts the control track pulses and translates this count into elapsed time and frame numbers.

Pylon   Triangular set piece, similar to a pillar.

Quad   Abbreviation for quadruplex videotape recorders.

Quadruplex   A scanning system of videotape recorders that uses four rotating heads for recording and playing back of video information. All quadruplex, or quad, recorders use 2-inch-wide videotape.

Quad-Split   Switcher mechanism that makes it possible to divide the screen into four variable-sized quadrants and fill each one with a different image.

Quarter-Track   An audiotape recorder, or recording, that uses one-fourth of the width of the tape for recording an audio signal. Generally used by stereo recorders. The first and third tracks are taken up by the first pass of the tape through the recording heads, the second and fourth tracks by the second pass, when the tape has been reversed (that is, the full takeup reel becomes the supply reel for the second recording).

Quartz Light   A high-intensity light whose lamp consists of a quartz or silica housing (instead of the customary glass) and a tungsten-halogen filament. Produces a very bright light of stable color temperature (3,200°K).

Racking   1. Rotating the lens turret of the monochrome camera in order to change lenses. 2. Moving the monochrome camera tube closer to or farther away from the stationary lens by means of the focus knob on the camera.

Radio Frequency   Usually called RF; broadcast frequency, which is divided into various channels. In an RF distribution, the video and audio signals are superimposed on the radio frequency carrier wave.

Range Extender   An optical attachment to the zoom lens that will extend its narrow-angle focal length.

Rating   Percentage of television households with their set tuned to a station, in relation to total number of tele-. vision households.

Rear Screen, or R.P.   Translucent screen onto which images are projected from the rear and photographed from the front.

Record VTR   The videotape recorder that receives and assembles the various program segments as supplied by the source VTR(s).

Reel-to-Reel   A tape recorder that transports the tape past the heads from one reel, the supply reel, to the other reel, the takeup reel. Used in contrast to cassettes or cartridge recorders.

Reflected Light   Light that is bounced off the illuminated object. Reflected light reading is done with a light meter (most of them are calibrated for reflected light) that is held close to the illuminated object.

Registration   Adjusting the scanning of the three color tubes so that their images overlap (register) perfectly.

Relay Lens   Part of the internal optical system of a camera that helps to transport (relay) the separated colored light into a pickup tube.

Remote   A television production done outside the studio.

Remote Control Unit (RCU)   Part of the camera chain with which the video operator achieves optimal pictures during remote production.

Remote Survey   An inspection of the remote location by key production and engineering persons so that they can plan for the setup and use of production equipment.

Remote Truck   The vehicle that carries production equipment such as CCUs, switcher, monitors, audio control console, intercom systems, and VTRs, and which serves as production control center.

Resolution   The characteristic of a camera that determines the sharpness of the picture received. The lower a camera's resolution, the less fine picture detail it can show. Resolution is influenced by the pickup tube, lens, internal optical system, and the television set. It may be improved by digital image enhancers.

Reverberation   Audio echo; adding echo to sound via an acoustical echo chamber or electronic sound delay;

generally used to liven sounds recorded in an acoustically dull studio.

RF   Abbreviation for Radio Frequency, necessary for all broadcast signals, as well as some closed-circuit distribution.

Ribbon Microphone   A microphone whose sound-pickup device consists of a ribbon that vibrates with the sound pressures within a magnetic field. Also called velocity mic.

Riser   1. Small platform. 2. The vertical frame that supports the horizontal top of the platform.

Roll   1. Graphics (usually credit copy) that move slowly up the screen, often called crawl. 2. Command to roll tape or film.

Rough Cut   The first tentative arrangement of shots and shot sequences in the approximate sequence and length.

R.P.   Rear screen Projection; also abbreviated as B.P. (Back Projection).

Rundown Sheet   Same as Fact Sheet.

Running Time   The duration of a show or show segment. Also called program length.

Runout Signal   The recording of a few seconds of black at the end of each videotape recording in order to keep the screen in black for the video changeover.

Run-through   Rehearsal.

S.A.   Studio Address system. See Studio Talkback.

Saturation   The color attribute that describes a color's richness or strength.

Scale   Basic minimum fees for television talent as prescribed by the talent union.

Scanning   The movement of the electron beam from left to right and from top to bottom on the television screen.

Scanning Area   Picture area that is scanned by the camera pickup tube; more generally, the picture area actually reproduced by the camera and relayed to the studio monitors, which is further reduced by the masking of the home screen and general transmission loss.

Schedule Time   See Clock Time.

Scoop   A scooplike television floodlight.

Screen Simulation   Type of chroma keying in which the chroma key area is confined to a simulated television screen behind the newscaster.

Scrim   A spun-glass material that is put in front of a lighting instrument as an additional light diffuser.

Script Marking   A director's written symbols on a script to indicate major cues.

Section 315 Section of the Communications Act that affords candidates for public office equal opportunity to appear on television. All candidates must, for example, be charged equal fees.

SEG See Special Effects Generator.

Selective Focus Emphasizing an object in a shallow depth of field through focus, while keeping its foreground and background out of focus.

Semiscripted Used to describe a show for which the dialogue is indicated but not completely written out. The opening and closing of the show are usually fully scripted, with the middle only semiscripted.

Sequencing Same as Picturization. The control and structuring of a shot sequence.

Servo Stabilizer Mechanism in special camera mounts, such as the Steadicam, to absorb wobbles and jitters.

Servo Zoom Control Zoom control that activates motor-driven mechanisms.

Set Arrangement of scenery and properties to indicate the locale and/or mood of a show.

Set Light See Background Light.

Set Module Piece of scenery of standard dimension that allows a great variety of interchange and configuration.

Shading Adjusting picture contrast; controlling color and black-and-white levels.

Share Percentage of television households tuned to a station in relation to all other stations in that area.

Shot Box Box containing various controls for presetting zoom speed and field of view; usually mounted on the camera panning bar.

Shotgun Microphone A highly directional microphone with a shotgunlike barrel for picking up sounds over a great distance.

Shot Sheet List of every shot a particular camera has to get. It is attached to the camera to help the camera operator remember a shot sequence.

Show Format Lists the order of the various show segments according to appearance.

Show Rhythm Indicates how well the parts of the show relate to each other sequentially, how well the show flows.

Side Light Usually directional light coming from the side of the object. Acts as additional fill light and provides contour.

Signal-to-Noise Ratio The relation of the strength of the desired signal to the accompanying electronic interference, the noise. A high signal-to-noise ratio is desirable (strong video or audio signal or weak noise).

Signature A specific video and/or audio symbol characteristic of one particular show.

Silent Film Film without a sound track, or film run silent.

Skew A distortion of videotape caused by variations in tape tension which affect the length of the video tracks. Shows up as a hooklike curve at the top of the screen or a curve swinging back and forth. It can be corrected by adjusting the skew control.

Slander Oral defamation.

Slant Track Same as Helical Scan.

Slate 1. To identify, verbally or visually, each videotaped take. 2. A little blackboard, or whiteboard, upon which essential production information is written, such as title of the show, date, and scene and take numbers. It is recorded at the beginning of each videotaped take.

Slave VTR A videotape recorder that records a program copy off the master recorder. Same as Record VTR.

Slide Effect A visual effect in which the original picture slides off to one corner, revealing a second picture that seems to lie beneath the first.

Slow Lens A lens that permits a relatively small amount of light to pass through (high f-stop number). Can be used only in well-lighted areas.

Slow Motion A scene in which the objects appear to be moving more slowly than normal. In film, slow motion is achieved through high-speed photography and normal playback. In television, slow motion is achieved by a multiple scanning of each television frame.

Small Format Refers to the small size of the camera pickup tube (usually $\frac{2}{3}$-inch) or, more frequently, to the narrow width of the videotape: $\frac{1}{4}$-inch, $\frac{1}{2}$-inch, $\frac{3}{4}$-inch, and even 1-inch (although 1-inch is often regarded as large-format tape). Small-format equipment (cameras and videotape recorders) is actually very small in size and highly portable.

SMPTE Society of Motion Picture and Television Engineers.

SMPTE/EBU Time Code An electronic signal recorded on the cue or address track of the videotape or on an audio track of a multitrack audiotape through a time code generator, providing a time address (birthmark) for each frame in hours, minutes, seconds, and frame numbers of elapsed tape.

Snapshot A visual effect in which the individual screen divisions show successively updated freeze frames.

Snow Electronic picture interference; looks like snow on the television screen.

SOF Sound On Film.

Softlight A television floodlight that produces extremely diffused light. It has a panlike reflector and a light-diffusing material over its opening.

Soft Wipe Wipe in which the demarcation line between the two images is softened so the images blend into each other.

Solarization Same as Posterization.

SOT Sound On Tape. The videotape is played back with pictures and sound.

Sound Bite Videotaped portions of an interview in which lip-sync must remain intact.

Source VTR The videotape recorder that supplies the various program segments to be assembled by the record VTR.

Special Effects Controls Also called SFX controls. Buttons on a switcher that regulate special effects. They include buttons for specific wipe patterns, the joystick positioner, DVE, and chroma key controls.

Special Effects Generator, or SEG An electronic image generator that produces a variety of special effects wipe patterns, such as circle wipes, diamond wipes, and key effects.

Splice The spot where two shots are actually joined, or the act of joining two shots. Generally used only when the material (such as film or videotape) is physically cut and glued (spliced) together again.

Spotlight A light instrument that produces directional, relatively undiffused light.

Spotlight Effect Visual effect that looks like a soft-edge circle wipe with the base picture showing through. Used to draw attention to a specific picture area.

Stability The degree to which a camera (or camera chain) maintains its initial electronic setup.

Stand-by 1. A warning cue for any kind of action in television production. 2. A button on a videotape recorder that activates the rotation of the video heads or head drum independently of the actual tape motion. In the stand-by position, the video heads can come up to speed before the videotape is actually started.

Star Filter A filterlike lens attachment that changes high-intensity light sources into starlike light images.

Station Break Interruption of a show to give station identification (usually on the half-hour or hour) and present nonprogram material (commercials, public service announcements).

Steadicam Special body mount worn by a field camera operator. Built-in stabilizers hold the camera steady while the operator moves.

Stock Shot A shot of a common occurrence—clouds, storm, traffic, crowds—that can be repeated in a variety of contexts because its qualities are typical. There are stock-shot libraries from which any number of such shots can be obtained.

Stop-Motion A slow-motion effect in which one frame jumps to the next, showing the object in a different position.

Storyboard A series of sketches of the key visualization points of an event, accompanied by corresponding audio information.

Strike To remove certain objects; to remove scenery and equipment from the studio floor after the show.

Striped Filter Extremely narrow, vertical stripes of red, green, and blue filters attached to the front surface of the pickup tube of a single-gun camera. They divide the incoming white light into the three light primaries without the aid of dichroic mirrors or prism beam splitters.

Strip Light Also called cyc light. Several self-contained lamps arranged in a strip; used mostly for illumination of the cyclorama.

Studio Camera Heavy, high-quality camera that cannot be maneuvered properly without the aid of a pedestal or some other type of camera mount.

Studio Monitor A monitor (television set) located in the studio carrying assigned video sources, usually the video of the line monitor.

Studio Talkback A public address loudspeaker system from the control room to the studio. Also called S.A. (Studio Address) or P.A. (Public Address) system.

Subjective Time The duration we feel. Also called psychological time.

Subtractive Primary Colors Magenta (bluish red), cyan (greenish blue), and yellow. When mixed, they act as filters, subtracting certain colors.

Super Short for superimposition, the simultaneous showing of two full pictures on the same screen.

Supply Reel Reel that holds film or tape, which it feeds to the takeup reel.

Sustaining Program Program that is not commercially supported.

Sweep 1. Electronic scanning. 2. Curved piece of scenery, similar to a large pillar cut in half.

Sweep Reversal Electronic scanning reversal; results in a mirror image (horizontal sweep reversal) or in an upside-down image (vertical sweep reversal). Used in monochrome cameras only.

Switcher 1. Engineer or production person who does the video switching (usually the technical director). 2. A panel with rows of buttons that allows the selection and assembly of various video sources through a variety of transition devices, and the creation of electronic special effects.

Switching   A change from one video source to another during a show, or show segment, with the aid of a switcher.

Sync   Electronic pulses that synchronize the scanning in the origination source (live cameras, videotape) and the reproduction source (monitor or television receiver).

Sync Generator   Part of the camera chain; produces electronic synchronization pulses.

Sync Roll   Vertical rolling of a picture caused by switching from remote to studio, thereby momentarily losing synchronization; also noticeable on a bad videotape splice.

System   The interrelationship of various elements and processes whereby each element is dependent on all others.

System Microphone   Microphone consisting of a base upon which several heads can be attached.

Systems Design   A plan that shows the interrelation of two or more systems. In television production, it shows the interrelation of all major production elements, as well as the flow (direction) of the production processes.

Take   1. Signal for a cut from one video source to another. 2. Any one of similar repeated shots taken during videotaping and filming. Sometimes *take* is used synonymously with *shot*. A good take is the successful completion of a shot, a show segment, or the videotaping of the whole show. A bad take is an unsuccessful recording; another take is required.

Takeup Reel   Reel that takes up film or tape from the supply reel. Must be the same size as the supply reel in order to maintain proper tension.

Taking Lens   Also called on-the-air lens. Refers to the lens on turret cameras that is actually relaying the scene to the camera pickup tube.

Talent   Collective name for all performers and actors who appear regularly on television.

Tally Light   Red light on camera and inside the camera viewfinder, indicating when the camera is on the air.

Tape   Plastic ribbon, approximately $\frac{1}{1000}$-inch thick, varying in width from $\frac{1}{8}$-inch to 2 inches and coated with iron oxide (dull side). It is used to record magnetic impulses from video or audio sources.

Tape Cartridge   See Cartridge.

Target   Light-sensitive front surface of the camera pickup tube, which is scanned by an electron beam.

Telecine   1. Same as Film Chain, or Film Island. 2. The place from which the film islands operate. The word comes

from *tele*vision and *cine*matography. Occasionally, the telecine is used for film storage and some minor film-editing jobs.

Telephoto Lens   Same as long-focal-length lens. Gives a closeup view of an event relatively far away from the camera.

Teleprompter   A mechanical prompting device that projects the moving copy over the lens, so that it can be read by the talent without losing eye contact with the viewer.

Test Tone   A tone generated by the audio console to indicate a zero VU volume level. The zero VU test tone is recorded along with the color bars to give a standard for the recording level.

Theme   What the story is all about; its essential idea.

Threefold   Three flats hinged together.

Tilt   To point the camera up and down.

Time Base Corrector (TBC)   An electronic accessory to a videotape recorder that helps to make playbacks or transfers electronically stable. It keeps slightly differing scanning cycles in step.

Time Compressor   Instrument that allows a recorded videotape to be replayed faster or slower without altering the original pitch of the audio.

Time Cues   Cues to the talent about time remaining in the show.

Title   Studio title card or slide, or an electronically generated title.

Tongue   To move the boom with the camera from left to right or from right to left.

Tracking   1. An electronic adjustment of the video heads so that in the playback phase they match the recording phase of the tape. It prevents picture breakup and misalignment especially in tapes that have been recorded on a machine other than the one used for playback. 2. Another name for Truck (lateral camera movement).

Transponder   A satellite's own receiver and transmitter.

Transverse Scanning   The direction of the video signal scanning in quadruplex recorders. Transverse scanning puts the signal across (transverse) the videotape rather than in a helical (diagonal) or lengthwise pattern.

Treatment   Brief description of a prospective television program.

Tripod   A three-legged camera mount, usually connected with a dolly for easy maneuverability.

Truck   To move the camera laterally by means of a mobile camera mount.

Trunk   Section of cable television distribution system

through which signals are sent and to which the feeders are connected.

Tungsten-Halogen The kind of lamp filament used in quartz lights. The tungsten is the filament itself; the halogen is a gaslike substance surrounding the filament.

Turret Lens A lens that is mounted on the turret of a monochrome camera. Usually in contrast to a zoom lens.

Twofold Two flats hinged together. Also called a book.

Two-Shot Framing of two people. A three-shot frames three.

Unidirectional A type of pickup pattern in which the microphone can pick up sounds better from the front than from the sides or back.

Uplink Earth station transmitter used to send television signals from the earth to a satellite.

Variable Area Track An optical sound track on film. It modulates the light of the exciter lamp through various shapes of translucent areas so that, when received by the photoelectric cell, the light variations produce identical variations in the electric current (audio signal).

Variable-Focal-Length Lens Zoom lens.

Vector Line A dominant direction established by two people facing each other or through a prominent movement in a specific direction.

Vertical Key Light Position The relative distance of the key light from the studio floor, specifically with respect to whether it is above or below the eye level of the performer. Not to be confused with high- and low-key lighting, which refers to the relative brightness and contrast of the overall scene.

Vertical Sweep The vertical scanning.

Video 1. Picture portion of a telecast. 2. Nonbroadcast production activities and the use of inexpensive equipment for a variety of purposes. Usually the equipment includes a portable camera, a microphone, a videotape recorder or video cassette recorder, and a monitor.

Video Cassette A plastic container in which a videotape moves from supply to takeup reel, recording and playing back short program segments through a video cassette recorder. Similar in construction and function to the audio cassette recorder.

Video Disc A phonograph recordlike disc that can store video (picture) information of short event segments. Needs a special playback device.

Video Disc Recorder A recording device that records and plays back video signals on a disc that looks like a phonograph record.

Video Feedback The picture on the television set is photographed by a television camera and fed back into the same monitor, producing multiple images.

Video Leader Generally called academy leader. Visual and auditory material that precedes any color videotape recording. The SMPTE prescribes for the standard video-portion blank tape for threading; 10 sec. of color bars; 15 sec. of slate information; 8 sec. of numbers or black; 2 sec. of black ahead of the program information.

Videotape A plastic, iron-oxide-coated tape of various widths (from $\frac{1}{4}$-inch to 2-inch) for recording of video and audio signals, as well as additional technical code information.

Videotape Recorder Also called VTR. Electronic recording device that records and stores on videotape video and audio signals for later playback or postproduction editing.

Video Track The area of the videotape used for recording the video information.

Viewfinder Generally means electronic viewfinder (in contrast to the optical viewfinder in a film or still camera); a small television set that displays the picture as generated by the camera.

Visualization Mentally converting a scene into a number of key television images. Images do not need to be sequenced at that time.

Volume The relative intensity of the sound; its relative loudness.

VTR Videotape recorder or recording.

VU Meter A Volume-Unit meter; measures volume units, the relative loudness of amplified sound.

Boldface page numbers indicate where a subject is fully discussed.